Career Information
in
Counseling and Teaching

Career Information in Counseling and Teaching

Third Edition

Lee E. Isaacson
Purdue University

Allyn and Bacon, Inc. Boston, London, Sydney, Toronto

To Ardis

Library of Congress Cataloging in Publication Data
Isaacson, Lee E
  Career information in counseling and teaching.
  Includes bibliographical references and index.
  1. Student Counselors, Training of. 2. Vo-
  cational guidance—Study and teaching. I. Title.
LB1731.18 1977   371.4′25′07   76–57687
ISBN 0–205–05785–3

Contents

Appendices 521

Preface

Recent developments have made significant impact on the relationship between individuals and work in our society. Several of these have become increasingly important since the second edition of this book was published in 1971. This revision is an attempt to stay abreast of relationships that are now changing and to anticipate relationships whose appearance in the near future seems likely.

For example, the proposition that American school systems adopt the concepts of career education was made in 1971. During the intervening years, these ideas have attracted increasing numbers of supporters, both inside and outside our educational structure. Undoubtedly, this influence will continue to spread. Greater emphasis on equal employment opportunities for women (in fact, for all prospective workers), has provided new legislation and a massive change in the employment practices across this country. National attention has been focused on the need to conserve energy and to develop new resources of power to operate our factories, warm our homes, transport our people. Our concern for conservation of all resources has been alerted much sooner than the doleful predictions of the Club of Rome would have suggested. The changing birthrate in our country, and in other industrialized nations, suggests change in allocations of our work force, at a time when evolving responsibilities toward developing nations around the world may produce new demands for sharing the products of our efforts. And the list goes on.

This book is intended for those who participate, or expect to participate, in the career development process of both youth and adults. Career development is viewed as a continuing, lifelong process in which the individual often is assisted by many people. During childhood and adolescence, the team of professional assistants includes the counselor, the teacher, the media specialist, and a cadre of supporting personnel, both professional and para-professional. Beyond the educational setting, counselors in rehabilitation agencies, community organizations, or other agencies are working cooperatively with psychologists, social workers, administrators, clergymen, and psychiatrists. Each person may play a significant role, though not always a major one, in the career development process for a particular individual. Coordination and teamwork ordinarily produce more effective involvement in the process.

Although major changes have been made throughout the book, this edition retains the general structure of the two previous editions. The first part of the book provides a new chapter setting a philosophic position and relating career information to career education but retains the chapter describing the major theories of career development. Part II considers the relationships between worker and the job—the various characteristics that must be brought to the job, and the ways in which the job imposes restrictions and demands on the worker. In Part III, we look at ways in which the world of work can be organized, including several new classification schemes. Part IV includes a discussion of the various preparatory routes followed to qualify for various jobs. Part V discusses career materials and how they are organized and managed, with special attention to computerization and other new approaches. The final part considers the use of career information in the various stages of career development, relating these materials directly to career education concepts in the schools and beyond.

Career information, like the individuals who use it, is dynamic, constantly changing, exploring new options, and discarding old ways. Consequently, it is impossible to present the reader with a compendium of all the practical applications currently in use. An effort has been made to include enough of these practical applications to illustrate the underlying principles that have much more durability. The book is the result of an effort to provide both breadth and depth in sufficient scope to familiarize the reader with the field, without ignoring important aspects or weighing one down with excessive detail. The reader must accept the reality that maintaining currency in techniques, procedures, and materials, is as lifelong in nature as the career development process itself.

The author gratefully acknowledges a debt to an array of individuals who helped make this revision possible. They include a group of colleagues whose professional dedication has been both supportive and challenging; professional friends and former teachers whose search for understanding has provided a worthy model; students whose questions deserved better answers; fellow authors whose work has influenced this effort both directly and indirectly; and above all, a wife with great patience, encouragement, and willingness to help. A special note of thanks goes to Charlotte Brown, whose skill in decoding the author's scrawl resulted in many typed pages of manuscript.

Lee E. Isaacson
Purdue University

PART

I

Career Information and Career Education

1

Gaining a Perspective of Work and Career

Throughout existence, humanity has engaged in purposeful activity. A recent Special Task Force states:

> It is both humbling and true that scientists are unable, in the final analysis, to distinguish all the characteristics of humans from those of other animals. But many social scientists will agree that among those activities most peculiar to humans, work probably defines man with the greatest certainty. To the archaeologist digging under the equatorial sun for remains of the earliest man, the nearby presence of primitive tools is his surest sign that the skull fragment he finds is that of a human ancestor, and not that of an ape.[1]

Earliest prehistoric man maintained himself and his family by hunting and fishing. Anthropologists have shown how this simple, essentially nomadic life was replaced, as cultures became less primitive, by a system of division of labor, with some men primarily occupied as hunters, others as fishermen, herdsmen, and traders. As social structures became more sophisticated, the occupations of farmers and craftsmen evolved. During the early period of this transition, the individual family involvement in specialization of task was a limited, part-time, almost incidental activity, perhaps growing out of individual interest or group recognition of an unusual skill. Nevertheless, the trend toward focusing effort on a specific group of tasks had started, and at that point the concept of career was born.

WORK AND SOCIETY

From prehistoric times, work has been a crucial factor in social organization. Greek and Roman civilizations each had a complex occupational structure. Many of the turning points in history have been reached as a result of the changing relationship between man and work. The early medieval guilds of craftsmen were created for occupational purposes, but the guilds exerted a social force that further weakened the semislavery of the feudal period. The Hanseatic League and similar groups of free cities organized, at least in part, to promote trade. The medieval university developed essentially to provide educational preparation for certain professional fields. The Protestant Reformation laid the foundation for a new view of man, and the period of discovery and exploration provided a vision of new opportunities. The Industrial Revolution accelerated occupational specialization and provided the means of transforming resources into new forms of wealth. The opening of vast geographic areas in the western hemisphere for settlement and development substantiated the idea that almost any man could, if he wished, acquire some of the ingredients of independence and self-actualization—a homestead, a business, a mine, a factory, a profession, or a job. Winters has contrasted the influence of the Protestant work ethic and the frontier myth on the American work ethic, concluding that the early industrial labor union movement's opposition to "labor as merchandise to be bought and sold" had significant historical impact.[2]

Recent decades have produced tremendous expansion in the number and nature of jobs. New relationships between man and machine, employer and employee, society and citizen have evolved and in the dynamic structure of today's world will continue through endless mutations and modifications.

The closing of geographic frontiers and the application of automation to many jobs have led some people to believe that we stand at the threshold of a new era in the relationship between people and work in a society in which a relatively few workers can produce the goods and services needed to support all the others. Such projections raise tremendous implications and questions for society. For example, Hoffman and Rollin have considered the implication of Toffler's *Future Shock*.[3] They point out that Toffler's emphasis on rapidity of change, as demonstrated in such factors as population growth, production, the number of scientists, use of energy, application of speed, increased innovation, social mobility, and the information explosion, foretells both the stress on individuals and society and the need to develop effective coping strategies. The recent study sponsored by the Club of Rome investigating the global interrelationships of accelerating industrialization, rapid population growth, widespread malnutrition, depletion of nonrenewable resources, and a deteriorating environment similarly underscores the societal challenges that will modify the relationship between man and work.[4]

An old adage points out that the more things change, the more they remain the same. Undoubtedly, there are powerful forces in present-day society that will change the relationship between individuals and work; so it has been for many decades. Although no one can completely foretell the future, some easily identifiable forces will have obvious impact in the years ahead. The Civil Rights legislation of the 1960's has opened many occupational opportunities for minority members; closely related to this is the increasing number of women entering employment, often in fields traditionally thought to be "men's work." Changing life styles with greater emphasis on conservation, personal freedom, the search for self-actualization and decreased emphasis on materialism also have produced impacts that will become even more obvious as time passes. Availability or accessibility of crucial resources can have tremendous impact on the world of work and society, as pointed out by the Club of Rome report.

Gaymer has suggested that counselors will have increasing impact on the lives that students will live after they leave school.[5] She feels that students need to develop the following understandings before they leave school:

1. That future working lives will differ radically from the present and the past.
2. That they will change their jobs more often.
3. That they will relocate more often.
4. That they will change type of work more often.
5. That they will require "up-dating" and will trade in education for newer models to remain employable.
6. That they will have to be more competitive.

She proposes that career planning will be a way of life by which the individual finds and maintains a place in life.

DEFINITION OF WORK AND CAREER

Because society and work are interdependent, we identify work as good and as an activity that sustains society now and enhances its likelihood of future maintenance. Quey has defined work as purposeful mental and physical human activity that deliberately points beyond the present by creating economic products or values to be consumed in the future.[6] The previously mentioned Report of a Special Task Force includes the following excellent statement concerning the definition of work:

We measure that which we can measure, and this often means that a rich and complex phenomenon is reduced to one dimension, which then becomes prominent and eclipses the other dimensions. This is particularly true of "work," which is often defined as "paid employment." The definition conforms with one readily measurable aspect of work but utterly ignores its profound personal and social aspects and often leads to a distorted view of society.

Using housework as an example, we can see the absurdity of defining work as "paid employment." A housewife, according to this definition, does not work. But if a husband must replace her services —with a housekeeper, cook, baby-sitter—these replacements become workers and the husband has added to the Gross National Product the many thousands of dollars the replacements are paid. It is, therefore, an inconsistency of our definition of work that leads us to say that a woman who cares for her own children is not working, but if she takes a job looking after the children of others, she is working.

Viewing work in terms of pay alone has also produced a synonymity of "pay" and "worth," so that higher-paid individuals are thought by many to have greater personal worth than those receiving less pay. At the bottom of this scale, a person without pay becomes "worthless." The confusion of pay with worth is a result of historical events and traditions apparently rooted in the distinction between "noble" and "ignoble" tasks.[7] History might have been otherwise and garbage men, for example, in recognition of their contribution to health, might have been accorded monetary rewards similar to those received by physicians. Certainly, it takes little reflection to conclude that, except in crude economic terms, no one is worth nothing, nor is anyone worth a hundred times more than another merely because he is paid a hundred times as much.

We can come closer to a multi-dimensional definition of work if we define it as "an activity that produces something of value for other people." This definition broadens the scope of what we call work and places it within a social context. It also implies that there is a purpose to work. We know that the housewife is *really* working, whether she is paid or not; she is being productive for other people. Substituting the children a woman cares for does not change the nature of her work, only the "others" for whom she is productive. And voluntary tasks are certainly work, although they are not remunerated. Some people at various stages in their lives may be productive only for themselves, a possible definition of leisure.[8]

Far broader than the usual definition, this meaning of work permits the inclusion of many activities that formerly were not always encompassed. Surely, the status of the housewife, for example, is clarified; but not all problems are as neatly solved. Nevertheless, this broader definition is likely to gain widespread recognition and acceptance since it reflects a trend toward liberalization of what may be properly placed under the rubric of work.

Terkel, in his introduction to *Working,* has succinctly summarized this broader view:

> Perhaps it is time the "work ethic" was redefined and its idea reclaimed from the banal men who invoke it. In a world of cybernetics, of an almost runaway technology, things are increasingly making things. It is for our species, it would seem, to go on to other human matters. Freud put it one way. Ralph Helstein puts it another. He is president emeritus of the United Packinghouse Workers of America. "Learning is work. Caring for children is work. Community action is work. Once we accept the concept of work as meaningful—not just as the source of a buck—you don't have to worry about finding enough jobs. There's no excuse for mules any more. Society does not need them. There's no question about our ability to feed and clothe and house everybody. The problem is going to come in finding enough ways for man to keep occupied, so he's in touch with reality." Our imaginations have obviously not yet been challenged.[9]

As modern society has increased in complexity, the opportunity for an individual to be clearly identified throughout a productive life with a single, specific aspect of work has sharply declined. Later, this chapter describes the trend toward occupational change and the greater likelihood of individuals returning to school or training programs for retraining or re-cycling as preparation for the performance of a new set of tasks—a new job. The term "career" has come to be used in a broad sense to describe an individual's lifelong work pattern—the way in which the individual expresses self and relates to society through work. Super has defined career as the sequence of occupations, jobs, and positions occupied during the course of a person's working life.[10] An even broader definition has been proposed by Norris, Zeran, Hatch, and Engelkes who suggest that "career" is "the totality of meaningful experiences of an individual which typically includes some combination of vocational and avocational involvement. The rewards of such activity may be in the activity itself or in the final product."[11]

Shartle has defined *position* as a group of tasks performed by one person; a *job* as a group of similar positions in a single plant, business establishment, educational institution, or other organization; and an *occupation* as a group of similar jobs found in several establishments.[12]

FUNCTION OF WORK

Work is seldom, if ever, only a means by which an individual sustains life. Work has many other functions of equal or sometimes greater importance to both society and the individual. It is the one way in which the indi-

It is work which gives flavor to life.

AMIEL

To youth I have but three words of counsel—work, work, work.

BISMARCK

All work, even cotton-spinning, is noble; work is alone noble. . . . A life of ease is not for any man, nor for any god.

CARLYLE

There is no substitute for hard work.

EDISON

I look on that man as happy, who, when there is question of success, looks into his work for a reply.

EMERSON

Work is love made visible. And if you cannot work with love but only with distaste, it is better that you should leave your work and sit at the gate of the temple and take alms of those who work with joy.

GIBRAN

Every child should be taught that useful work is worship and that intelligent labor is the highest form of prayer.

INGERSOLL

Never is there either work without reward, nor reward without work being expended.

LIVY

Though a little one, the master-word [work] looms large in meaning. It is the open sesame to every portal, the great equalizer in the world, the true philosopher's stone which transmutes all the base metal of humanity into gold.

OSLER

Hard work is the best investment a man can make.

SCHWAB

vidual relates to society. Work provides the person, and often the family as well, with status, recognition, affiliation, and similar psychological and sociological products essential for participation in a complex society.

The Report of a Special Task Force responds as follows:

Why is man a worker? First of all, of course, man works to sustain physical life—to provide food, clothing, and shelter. But clearly work is central to our lives for other reasons as well. According to Freud, work provides us with a sense of reality; to Elton Mayo, work is a bind to community; to Marx, its function is primarily economic. Theologians are interested in work's moral dimensions; sociologists see it as a determinant of status, and some contemporary critics say that it is simply the best way of filling up a lot of time. To the ancient Greeks, who had slaves to do it, work was a curse. The Hebrews saw work as punishment. The early Christians found work for profit offensive, but by the time of St. Thomas Aquinas, work was being praised as a natural right and a duty—a source of grace along with learning and contemplation. During the Reformation, work became the only way of serving God. Luther pronounced that conscientious performance of one's labor was man's highest duty. Later interpretations of Calvinistic doctrine gave religious sanction to worldly wealth and achievement. This belief, when wedded to Social Darwinism and *laissez-faire* liberalism, became the foundation for what we call the Protestant ethic. Marx, however, took the concept of work and put it in an even more central position of life: freed from capitalistic exploitation, work would become a joy as workers improved the material environment around them.

Clearly work responds to something profound and basic in human nature. Therefore, much depends on how we define work, what we conceive work to be, what we want work to be, and whether we successfully uncover its meaning and purpose. Our conception (and misconception) of ourselves, the wisdom with which public policy is formulated on a range of issues, and the rationality with which private and public resources are allocated are influenced greatly by the degree to which we penetrate the complex nature of work.

Because work, as this report illustrates, plays a pervasive and powerful role in the psychological, social, and economic aspects of our lives, it has been called a basic or central institution. As such, it influences, and is influenced by, other basic institutions—family, community (particularly as a political entity), and schools—as well as peripheral institutions. Work, then, provides one institutional perspective—but a broad one—from which to view these interrelationships that affect ourselves and our society.

.   .   .

The economic purposes of work are obvious and require little comment. Work is the means by which we provide the goods and services needed and desired by ourselves and our society. Through the economic rewards of work, we obtain immediate gratification of transient wants, physical assets for enduring satisfactions, and liquid assets for deferrable gratifications. For most of the history of mankind, and for a large part of humanity today, the economic meaning of work is paramount.

Work also serves a number of other social purposes. The work-place has always been a place to meet people, converse, and form friendships. In traditional societies, where children are wont to follow in their parents' footsteps, the assumption of responsibility by the children for one task and then another prepares them for their economic and social roles as adults. Finally, the type of work performed has always conferred a social status on the worker and the worker's family. In industrial America, the father's occupation has been the major determinant of status, which in turn has determined the family's class standing, where they lived, where the children went to school, and with whom the family associated—in short, the life style and life chances of all the family members. (The emerging new role of women in our society may cause class standing to be co-determined by the husband's *and* wife's occupations.)[13]

The Report further describes the contribution of work to the development of self-esteem through the sense of mastery acquired in dealing with objects of work, and through reinforcement of the idea that the worker is engaging in activities that produce something valued by others. This definition recognizes one of the psychological pressures experienced by the unemployed, that is, not to have a job is not to have something that is valued by one's fellow human beings.

If we assume the position that work is one of the central components of life activities for most adults, it is easy to assume that the satisfaction derived from work is an important determinant in the total satisfaction incurred by the individual. This is, obviously, a nebulous concept that does not permit precise measurement. One approach to determining job satisfaction has been to ask workers, "What type of work would you try to get into if you could start all over again?" One might logically infer that workers who choose the same occupation see greater likelihood of satisfaction in their present occupation than in any other field that they deem available. Occupations that are chosen most frequently are those in which incumbents appear to have the greatest degree of control and also the feeling that what they do is recognized as important by others. Table 1, presented in the previously mentioned Report, reveals the percentages of various occupational groups who would choose the same occupational field again.[14]

The Report also reviews a recent study showing that workers, when asked to rank order the aspects of work they considered most important, listed the following: interesting work, enough help and equipment to get the job done, good pay, opportunity to develop special abilities, job security, and seeing the results of one's work. The workers said that the most oppressive features of work were: constant supervision and coercion, lack of variety, monotony, meaningless tasks, and isolation. From these data, the Report concludes that "an increasing number of workers want more autonomy in tackling their tasks, greater opportunity for increasing their skills, rewards that are directly connected to the intrinsic aspects of work, and greater participation in the design of work and the formulation of their tasks."

TABLE 1. *Percentages in Occupational Groups Who Would Choose Similar Work Again*

PROFESSIONAL AND LOWER WHITE-COLLAR OCCUPATIONS	%	WORKING-CLASS	%
Urban university professors	93	Skilled printers	52
Mathematicians	91	Paper workers	42
Physicists	89	Skilled autoworkers	41
Biologists	89	Skilled steelworkers	41
Chemists	86	Textile workers	31
Firm lawyers	83	Blue collar workers, cross section	24
Journalists (Washington corr.)	82	Unskilled steelworkers	21
Church university professors	77	Unskilled autoworkers	16
Solo lawyers	75		
White collar workers, cross section	43		

From: Report of a Special Task Force to the Secretary of Health, Education and Welfare, *Work in America*, p. 16 (from Robert Kahn, "The Work Module," 1972).

In summary, this section has attempted to sketch the deep and continuing relationship between individuals and work in our society. This relationship not only impounds large portions of the individual's time, but it also impinges on all aspects of life and the life of the family.

THE NEED FOR CAREER PLANNING

In the previous pages, we briefly considered the importance of work in the lives of individuals. We have seen how work provides both physical and psychological sustenance, affiliations with society, as well as status within the group, and also sets the life style of the individual and the family. Therefore, any activity of such major importance must inevitably concern most people contemplating the assumption of work roles. It thus seems logical to expect elementary and secondary students to begin to express interest in their future relationship with work and to plan with varying degrees of effectiveness for their entrance into the world of work.

In accepting a developmental approach to guidance, we expect such a program to focus on the decisions or adjustments most commonly met at each developmental level, or about to be encountered at the next level. On this basis, we may reasonably conclude that high school and college students who will soon leave school will show primary concern for areas related to their post-school life, such as vocational problems and further education.

Many research studies have demonstrated the validity of this assumption. Froehlich, for example, found that the problems brought to a free community counseling center were about 29 per cent educational problems, about 60 per cent vocational problems, and about 11 per cent personal problems.[15]

Remmers and Shimberg reported that 40 to 50 per cent of their group of 15,000 teenagers checked items that revealed a concern for the future.[16] They found that nearly 50 per cent of the ninth-graders in their sample were already worried about how they should earn a living after high school.

Similar reports in studies by Mooney and by Laycock show extensive concern by youth about their educational and vocational future.[17, 18]

More recent studies confirm that the youth of today face the same quandries as the youth of three decades ago. Flanagan reports that his study revealed quite unrealistic and unstable career choices being made by high school students in 1960.[19] For example, he found that only 13 per cent of 11th grade boys indicating a particular choice from a list of 36 occupations in 1960 reported the same choice in 1966. Half of the 11th grade boys in both 1960 and 1970 indicated plans to graduate from a four-year college, although probably not more than half of these would likely be able to complete such plans. He concluded that if secondary school education is to be relevant to the needs of students, it is essential that the students be assisted in selecting careers at an earlier time.

Prediger, Roth, and Noeth report a national study, sampling 8th, 9th, and 11th graders in 33 states in the spring of 1973.[20] Seventy-eight per cent of the 11th graders in the sample reported a need for more help in making career plans, as compared with 30 per cent who desired help with personal problems. Results for 8th graders were similar: 73 per cent were concerned about help with career plans and 39 per cent wanted help with personal problems. They report that 20 per cent of the 11th graders exhibited very low level involvement in career planning, and another 50 per cent barely approach a minimum desirable level. Much misinformation was found—53 per cent of the 11th graders believed that one-third of all job openings required a college degree, 41 per cent of the 8th graders believed that few women work outside the home after marriage, and 61 per cent of the 11th graders believed that most persons remain in the same job throughout their adult lives.

Biggers reports that he found high school seniors as limited in their ability to use information in vocational decision-making as they were in the 4th grade.[21] The increased age and school experience did not appear to improve the students' use of occupational information. Biggers concluded that more attention must be given to helping students use such materials in the career choice process.

The recently developed emphasis on Career Education also underlines the recognition of need by youth for more extensive assistance in career planning and development activities. This need exists also in adults who for various reasons are involved in career change and readjustment. The process is complex and requires much time and effort. The individual must learn a great deal about self—abilities, interests, motivations, values —and about the surrounding world. In all of this, the individual needs accurate, usable information about the world of work.

EXPLORING THE CONCEPT
OF CAREER EDUCATION

Career education is a concept whose time of fruition appears to be the last quarter of this century. American education is now clearly moving toward the development and implementation of this idea, which brings the freshness of tomorrow to a notion that has lain fallow for many decades. Although the proposal of career education was directed toward the American elementary and secondary school, its fundamental idea is relevant to all ages and conditions of mankind, both school age and beyond. Its growth and application is obviously school-centered, however, and its ramifications involve almost every agency and organization in our social structure dealing with children and adults.[22]

Classic statements of educational philosophy and purpose have long recognized the responsibility of American education to prepare its clientele for useful and worthy lives. For example, in 1918 the seven cardinal principles proposed by a famous study commission included the following objectives for secondary education: health, command of the fundamental processes, worthy home membership, vocation, citizenship, worthy use of leisure time, and ethical character.[23] Twenty years later, *The Purpose of Education in American Democracy* suggested these purposes or objectives of education: self-realization, human relationships, economic efficiency, and civic responsibility.[24]

American educators and patrons of schools have generally accepted these statements or have developed similar propositions for their local situation. Indeed, it would be difficult, even if one so wished, to mount an effective attack on such creeds. They have served and doubtless will continue to serve as respected statements of goals. When concern and criticism have developed, they usually have been the result of imperfect intermediate objectives or programmatic implementation; occasionally, the breadth of generalization has created difficulty.

The historical review of American education in the sixties and early seventies is beyond the scope of this volume. Many emerging thrusts of that period have produced an impact on the schools. For example, the application of industrially developed procedures such as Systems Analysis and PPBS (Planned, Programmatic, Budget Systems) by government agencies has demonstrated the possible usefulness of such approaches in the educational domain. Expanding emphasis on accountability, a continuing search for increased effectiveness, a wider recognition and acceptance of the pluralistic nature of our society, and a greater desire to use our natural and human resources wisely have all been motivating factors in the press to restate educational purposes.

In the early 1970's, Marland, as Assistant Secretary of Education and later as Commissioner of Education, provided the impetus that focused the attention of both the U.S. Office of Education and the nation's school systems on the idea of Career Education.[25] Typical of his viewpoint is this statement:

> All education is career education, or should be. And all our efforts as educators must be bent on preparing students either to become properly, usefully employed immediately upon graduation from high school or to go on to further formal education. Anything else is dangerous nonsense. I propose that a universal goal of American education, starting now, be this: that every young person completing our school program at grade 12 be ready to enter higher education or to enter useful and rewarding employment.[26]

At the same time, Marland proposed action by the U.S. Office of Education to implement this idea, including: planning major improvements in the vocational education program to place emphasis in occupational areas that reflect national shortages and high future needs; providing more flexible options for high school graduates to continue on to higher education or to enter the world of work; improving vocational education by including people from business, industry, and organized labor who are knowledgeable about career opportunities of the future; and building a broader professional leadership that is committed to a career education system.

At about the same time, a task force of the American Vocational Association released a report that described Career Education as a people-oriented concept needed by all people and intended for all.[27] This report proposed that Career Education had the responsibility for helping individuals to develop:

1. Favorable attitudes toward personal, psychological, social, and economic significance of work.
2. An appreciation for the worth of all types and levels of work.
3. Decision-making skills necessary for choosing career options and changing career directions.
4. Capability of making considered choices of career goals, based on the development of the self in relation to a range of career options.
5. Capability of charting a course for realization of self-established career goals in keeping with individual desires, needs, and opportunities.
6. Knowledge, skill, attitudes necessary for entry and success in a career.

Similarly, Ryan has proposed five major goals of Career Education, including the following:[28]

1. To develop self-understanding and the ability to make rational decisions.
2. To develop interpersonal and human relationship skills.
3. To develop citizenship skills.
4. To develop understanding of careers and career development and to develop producer and consumer skills.
5. To foster internalization of work-oriented attitudes and values.

All of these factors imply that every individual must have a wide knowledge of careers and the world of work as a basis for understanding and appreciating the relationship between work and the individual; and further, that the individual must be able to plan wisely for the future if he or she is to obtain from work those satisfactions and attainments that our society attaches to successful careers.

Few people would deny that our technological society offers little place or reward for either the uneducated or the unskilled worker. With the skill and knowledge to put a man on the moon already demonstrated, many people contend that it should be no more difficult to eliminate ignorance and poverty in our society. The National Advisory Council on Vocational Education states that the fulfillment of individual potential is this nation's historic mandate.[29] This group proposes that to implement this edict, the following steps must be taken:

1. Recognize that employment is an integral part of education. Every school must become involved in employment placement activities.
2. Part-time employment should become a part of the curriculum. Provision should be made to maintain school responsibility for the drop-out until graduation from school or graduation age is reached.
3. Priority should be given to programs for the disadvantaged without separating the disadvantaged from the educational mainstream.
4. Encourage parents and students to participate in the development of vocational programs.
5. Establish residential schools for those who need them most.

Statements such as the foregoing emphasize a changing role for American education, a role in which the school uses career education to tie the educational system and the community together so that each serves the other in an on-going relationship.[30] Accomplishing this task presupposes that educational experiences are geared toward developing economic independence and an appreciation for the dignity of work.[31] Such an educational system would include successive decision points at which students would be prepared to decide to pursue a job, seek further education, or develop some combination of both. Implicit in such proposals is the mirror image for post-secondary years of life—that life includes decision points at which the individual is prepared to decide to continue in a job (or seek a new one), to return to the educational system for further preparation, or to combine the two activities in some way.

This view of education changes the existing structure in two major ways. First, it expands the school to include all of the community and its economic activity. No longer would learning activities be confined to a building or campus designated as "the school"; this location would be only one of many learning centers. Second, the time span encompassed by education is no longer restricted to a few childhood and adolescent years, terminating with a "rites of passage" ceremony labeled as commencement. Education, instead, would be available on a lifelong basis with the individual returning at appropriate points, either on a full-time or part-time basis, for retraining or up-dating.

Four models of career education are beginning to emerge. These are usually labeled as school-based, experienced-based, home- and community-based, and residential-based models.[32] Each term implies the general focus or thrust of the model. Although each model appears to be a separate plan serving a distinct clientele, there is an obvious underlying relationship and continuity from one model to another. The residential model remains somewhat vague, but its intent is to serve those whose environment does not permit access to the benefits of one of the other models, whether because of geographic isolation, cultural deprivation, or other reasons. In the experience of the typical individual, contact with two or more models might be expected to occur.

An analysis of published materials related to Career Education has led Herr to conclude that the concept includes the following: [33]

1. An effort to diminish the separateness of academic and vocational education.
2. An area of concern that has some operational implications for every educational level or grade from kindergarten through graduate school.
3. A process of insuring that every person exiting from the formal educational structure has job employability skills of some type.
4. A direct response to the importance of facilitating individual choice-making so that occupational preparation and the acquisition of basic academic skills can be coordinated with developing individual preference.
5. A way of increasing the relevance or meaningfulness of education for greater numbers of students than is currently true.
6. A design to make education an open system so that school leavers, school dropouts, and adults can reaffiliate with school when their personal circumstances or job requirements make this feasible.
7. A structure whose desired outcomes necessitate cooperation among all elements of education as well as among the school, industry, and community.
8. An enterprise requiring new technologies and materials of education (i.e. individualized programming, simulations).
9. A form of education for all students.

CAREER EDUCATION AS ON-GOING CAREER GUIDANCE

The essence of career education can be distilled in the concept that an individual, once school-leaving age has been reached, is always prepared for either of two options—namely, leaving the formal learning setting and entering the world of work with skills, knowledge, and attitudes that make him/her immediately and appropriately employable, or remaining in the learning environment where higher level skills, knowledge, and attitudes will be acquired to permit entry into work at a later time and at a higher level. Implicit in this concept is the continuous intertwining of education and work as the means by which career actualization is attained. The old idea of "completing" one's education and then going to work is replaced by the notion that the worker may revert to the learning center for retooling, upgrading, or self-improvement and then return to work many times.

The individual progresses through five steps as follows:

AWARENESS→ EXPLORATION→ DECISION MAKING→ PREPARATION→ EMPLOYMENT

Awareness is the stage at which the individual begins to realize that many different career paths are available, offering him/her differing opportunities and imposing different demands. Self-awareness also is an aspect of this step—the individual begins to identify similarities and differences in abilities, interests, motivations, and goals between self and others.

Exploration is the stage in which the individual becomes more knowledgeable and understanding of the common and unique characteristics of occupations and of people. For most individuals, this process continues to some extent throughout life, although the degree of conscious involvement will vary.

Decision Making is the stage at which the individual applies the information accumulated about "jobs" to the information about "self" and begins to formulate tentative "dreams" for the future. These ideas gradually come into focus sufficiently to provide the base for tentative planning.

Preparation is the stage at which the individual begins to act on those tentative plans by choosing subjects, school programs, or other experiences that are observed to be related to performance in the tentatively chosen field. Skills, knowledge, and attitudes are developed until the individual reaches the entry level for that choice. At this point, he/she elects to seek employment or to continue to a higher level of preparation.

Employment is the actual entrance into the world of work.

These steps are not discrete, self-contained entities. Rather, each shades into the next step. At any point in this process, the individual may remain for an indeterminate period, may move on to the next stage, or may revert to an earlier step in a spiraling application of a systems approach. As indicated, once the individual "goes to work," advancement in a career may come from the acquisition of greater skills either on the job or by returning to school, or by a combination of both. The worker also may become *aware* of other opportunities in the chosen field or in an unrelated field; *exploration* may lead to a *decision* to pursue that area, thus necessitating *preparation* as a prelude to *entrance* there.

SCOPE AND DEFINITION
OF CAREER INFORMATION

An essential ingredient in each stage is accurate, usable information about the world of work and the relationship of individuals to it. Those who assist individuals in the various stages of career development, whether in the classroom, the counseling office, or in other settings, must not only understand the work environment and how people relate to it, but more important, must also be able to help the student, or counselee, or client, to translate that knowledge and understanding into concepts that are personally meaningful.

The awareness stage of Career Education is often thought to comprise the early years of school in which developing individuals widen their understanding of the world around them, including the world of work. It would be difficult to argue against this position except to contend that the stage is not restricted to the younger years exclusively, but rather extends onward from that period. The traditional educational model would start with the child and the family circle, gradually expanding the frame of reference to include neighborhood, community, state, region, nation, and world. Similarly, one might expect understanding of the world of work to expand from a superficial knowledge of what "Daddy and Mother do" to "neighborhood helpers," and on to a broadening and deepening awareness of the general structure of the occupational world.

Insight develops as an expansion of the knowledge and understanding that the person already has conceptualized. Career information only has meaning and use to individuals if it relates to where they are and where they want to go in their thinking. In other words, career information must have relevance and must be understandable. Generally, the individual is forming impressions and fitting together various ideas and thoughts to form a bigger picture that is broad in scope but probably lacking in detail. The information needed must fit this kind of situation; it should sketch out the major points, show the important relationships and the unique, identifying factors, and provide indications of where more facts can be obtained. Although used for comparable purposes, materials useful for a third-grader, a high school junior, a widow re-entering the labor market, or a physically handicapped worker must clearly vary according to the individual being served.

Most individuals in the middle school years and immediately following will be at least partially involved in the exploratory stage. Obviously, as indicated, individuals at later points in life may return to this stage of career development because of factors that change their work pattern. Using the "big picture"—the general view that the individual holds of the world around him/her, and the general values and goals considered important, he/she begins to look at some of the more specific details in that picture to clarify ways in which one can satisfyingly relate to that world. Broad generalities are only minimally useful at this point; the individual now needs detailed and specific career information at a level and in the quantity appropriate for his or her development.

As the person moves into the decision-making stage, the need for information becomes even greater. Now involved in attempting to weigh and balance the perceptions of the world of work against perceptions of self, now and in the forseeable future, the individual needs detailed, understandable, appropriate information on both sides of this equation, and often help in translating the data into a frame of reference. "Choosing" a vocation necessitates understanding by the helper (teacher, counselor, psychologist, social worker, or other) of the ways in which such choices are made. This helping process requires exploration of theories of vocational choice and development, the general structure of the world of work, ways in which personal and societal goals are satisfied by work, and how the decision-making process operates. Rational choices can be exercised only if the person making choices understands the options available.[34]

As choices are made, tentative and highly subject to change though they may be, the individual now must assess the extent to which the skills, knowledge, and other characteristics required for satisfactory performance in the "chosen field" already exist or must be acquired or developed. Those deficiencies—the difference between where one is and where one wants to be—constitute the base for the preparatory program to be sought. Again, information becomes crucial to pursuing this goal. Identifying appropriate training or educational programs, or the means to informal acquisition of skill in those areas without formalized programs, gaining admission or access to the needed preparation, and successfully completing the program are all aspects of this phase and involve constant use of career information.

"Entering" a vocation requires information about the induction process: how does the individual make the transition from preparation to application of skill? Are there "rites of passage" or other initiation procedures? Are there groups, agencies, or individuals who perform essential functions in accomplishing the transfer? Are there placement options or other decisions to be made? Do all entry positions offer equal opportunity for "success" or other satisfactions that motivate the individual? If not, then how can the individual maximize opportunities to gain those goals of greatest personal value?

In addition to these broad informational demands, the counselor has other considerations if he/she is to meet the above requirements effectively. Usually he/she must make available a wide range of materials to counselees as they progress through the various phases. This necessitates collecting a variety of publications, evaluating them for potential use, often abstracting information from them, and filing them in some system to assure easy access. The counselor also needs information regarding effective use of career information with individuals as well as with groups of counselees.

Career information can be defined as "valid and usable materials about the world of work that are appropriate for assisting the individual seeking vocational guidance." This includes: materials that describe the world of work, including its structure and organization; the demands that work imposes on the individual, and the rewards and benefits it bestows; how and where one prepares to enter the field; and the educational, personal, and experience requirements one must meet to enter, remain, or advance in the job.

Three terms relate to the topic we are considering: "occupational information," "educational information," and "social information." Each term refers to a special aspect of our topic, and collectively they make up the area covered by the broader term "career information." Occupational information is used ordinarily to refer to material directly concerned with duties, requirements for entrance, supply and demand, and sources of additional information about positions, jobs, and occupations. Educational information refers to materials about all types of existing or potential educational and training opportunities, including nature and purpose of the program, requirements for admission and retention, costs, special features, facilities and staff, and similar items. Social information refers to materials that help the individual understand the human and physical environment that surrounds him/her and the ways in which individuals relate to one another and to the existing or anticipated environment. One could, no doubt, contend successfully that there are certain aspects of educational and social information that are not directly related to an individual's career. For the most part, however, the educational preparation a person seeks has a relationship to present or expected role in society—career. Similarly, success in that career is intimately related to how well one can interact with others and with the world around him or her, and how effectively one can interact with those surrounding factors. In dealing with a client, a counselor may momentarily be primarily concerned with a circumscribed problem, such as training opportunities or interpersonal relationships, but he/she will soon relate this to the broader, over-all development of the individual. The terms "occupational," "educational," and "social" information will be used in this volume when we are focusing on that specific topic. When we are concerned with the whole field, we will use the term "career information."

Whether one approaches the development and execution of career plans from the point of view of career education, general and traditional education, vocational education, vocational guidance, or social services, certain concepts are basic to all approaches. One of these concepts is the general recognition of the developmental or process aspect of guidance. If the heart of the process is decision-making, then guidance is needed at all life stages involving decisions. This begins to appear in the elementary school years, when every child makes certain decisions and adjustments, and probably builds toward a peak during the secondary school years and the few years immediately following high school. These are the years when most individuals find themselves facing frequent decisions not only with immediate implications, but also with long-range effects on their lives. With increased education, maturity, and experience, individuals can be expected to become increasingly self-directive as they enter adulthood, and the need for guidance services decreases, although it probably never entirely disappears.[35] Guidance services are, then, most needed during the years of adolescence and early adulthood. For this reason, one can expect their greatest prevalence in the secondary and post-secondary school. One also presumes that access to help in decision-making would be available to all individuals as they encounter situations in which the need for such help is felt. Gysbers and Moore have proposed a reconceptualization of guidance from an ancillary, crisis-oriented, process-centered activity to a comprehensive developmental conception based on personal and societal needs organized programmatically around person-centered goals and activities designed to meet those needs.[36] Similarly, Blocher and Miller have defined vocational guidance as follows: [37]

> Vocational guidance is a broad social function concerned with applying scientific knowledge and human understanding toward the development of social processes and individual learning experiences. Its purpose is to promote the maximum realization of human potential for social contribution and self-fulfillment through work. Vocational guidance seeks to contribute to the organization of a society which provides opportunities for all its members to meet material and psychological needs in socially constructive ways. Vocational guidance is intended to help individuals relate themselves to work within the framework of a life style that is personally satisfying, socially constructive, and economically productive. Since each individual interacts with his particular social, cultural, and physical environment in a unique way, vocational guidance recognizes that work will not have the same meaning, nor even the same centrality for human beings with differing needs, perceptions and characteristics. The concerns, processes, and functions of vocational guidance are defined by the range of human needs and social problems in the society, and by the state of development of supporting sciences and disciplines.

It is logical to expect the school to provide assistance in career planning to its students since it has prolonged contact with almost all youths during the period when most of them inevitably become concerned about this matter. At the same time, one must recognize the existence of many other social and governmental agencies with a similar responsibility. These agencies may either provide assistance in career planning to a special segment of the community, or provide a particular service to a broader group. Some of these agencies, such as state employment services and rehabilitation agencies, have concern and responsibility for performing services related to career planning for both youth and adults in the community. There may be differences in the clientele served, the particular services supplied, and the setting used. Nevertheless, the commonalities among the counselors serving these various groups in these various settings are tremendous and they furnish a basic point of departure for our consideration of career information. The counselor, in or out of school, is involved in all phases of vocational guidance.

FUNCTION OF THE PROFESSIONAL
IN CAREER PLANNING

The process of career planning and development extends across a considerable span of time and space and inevitably involves many people who have contact with and influence on the individual. Sometimes the contacts are sequential; for example, the influence of elementary and secondary teachers as the individual moves through the typical educational program. At any given point in a person's life span, there will be many others who are directly or indirectly involved in the career development process as first experienced at that point. Some of these people are deliberately and obviously involved, whereas others, whose impact may be equally great, are more indirectly or tangentially related to the process.

The school counselor and the teacher are examples of two people whose simultaneous impact occurs in almost every person's life. One can demonstrate such team relationships in settings outside the school; for example, in the mental hospital, the physician, clinician, counselor, social worker, educational therapist, and work supervisor all deal with the patient and his/her future that lies beyond the hospital gate after discharge. Each can work independently with the individual, concerned only for the specific area in which he/she has major responsibility. It is reasonable to assume, however, that the future welfare of the patient may be better served if those involved in recovery recognize and understand the roles and functions of the others and if an effort is made to prevent gaps or duplication by coordinating efforts. As an illustration of this team relationship that makes up the career planning process, let us consider briefly the teacher and the counselor.

Both the teacher and the counselor are important members of the guidance team in every school. Each makes a unique contribution to the career planning process that supplements the work of the other. Neither can effectively replace the other, nor can either do both aspects of the task that needs to be done if students are to be given the maximum assistance in planning for their futures. The failure of either to perform his/her function adequately will result in career planning built on a weaker foundation and therefore more likely to be inadequate.

All members of the educational team are concerned with working toward the goals of the school. Each, however, has a special approach and a special area of responsibility. The teacher has basic responsibility for the instructional phase of the school program. The major contact with students is in the instructional situation—the classroom. This classroom contact gives certain immediately identifiable advantages; for example, more direct contact with each student than any other member of the school staff; he/she sees the student almost every day and is in a position to observe changes and developments on the part of the student and to provide stimuli and suggestions when the student is at the most receptive point. He/she inevitably has many informal contacts with the student, before, during, and after class. In most student contacts, the teacher sees the student within the framework of the student's peer group—classmates and friends.

Since the teacher's basic assignment is instruction, he/she must give major attention to this responsibility. If a free period, specifically scheduled for classroom preparation, is used instead to counsel with a student who is seeking help, then the teacher helps one student, but at the same time does a disservice by making classwork less effective. Obviously, there are times when the teacher can schedule counseling sessions without interfering with his/her basic responsibility, and he/she should take advantage of these times as often as possible.

Further, the teacher's instructional responsibility requires setting and maintaining academic standards in classes. This forces him/her into an evaluative or judgmental role—he/she must assign grades. Students and teachers do not always evaluate educational progress identically; in fact, neither can be totally objective. Grading can interfere with the development of a counseling relationship between student and teacher; some students will decide, since the teacher's assigned grade doesn't match their own estimate, that the teacher doesn't really understand them. Others will be reluctant to talk freely and openly to the teacher because they will feel that such confidences might some time be used against them.

Because of common interest in the subject area or for other reasons, the teacher will build a bond or relationship with a few students that is stronger than can be built by any other staff member. With this group, for which he/she serves as a sort of "anchor person," the teacher can serve a unique guidance function. He/she can probably fill the counseling role with these students even more effectively than the school counselor.

However, the teacher has a larger responsibility in career planning than serving only the group of students who are attracted by this special relationship. The school years, especially in the junior and senior high schools, are developmental and exploratory periods for career planning. Students, almost unanimously, are seeking knowledge and insight that will later help them reach firm vocational commitments. The classroom teacher has both an opportunity and a responsibility to assist in this aspect of student maturation and development. The more the teacher understands the process of vocational choice and the world of work in general, the more he/she can assist students or others who come to him/her to develop healthy attitudes toward work, to see the broad perspective of work, to understand the vocational areas related to one's subject field, and to acquire the understanding that will lead to wise career choices.

The counselor, on the other hand, can focus primary concern on the goal of maximizing individual development. He/she works toward this goal in many ways, some of which have been briefly discussed. In order to have the time to carry on the special tasks that make up this role, the counselor must be freed from instructional responsibility and the grading that goes with it. This allows him/her to see students in a situation that does not require a judgmental relationship with them. The advantages are obvious—he/she is more accessible and the student may feel freer to talk about personal problems and concerns.[38]

The counselor's special training should have direct application to career planning. He/she should be able to use effectively the individual inventory system of the guidance program—even adding to it as students seek answers to specific questions about their aptitudes and interests. He/she should have at his/her command, through the information service, a wider knowledge of the resources available in order to provide the information that the student needs at any specific time to develop career plans. Training in counseling should make him/her more proficient than any other staff member in helping students integrate the understanding of self and of the world of work that is the crux of vocational counseling.[39, 40]

Career education suggests that career guidance and career development are the continuing responsibility of all school personnel, stretching over the entire educational life of the individual. This idea of shared involvement, encompassing both instructional activities as well as counseling relationships, is a far different concept from the practice followed in many schools. If teachers are to infuse career education concepts into regular classroom activities, some major curricular revisions become necessary. If the counselor is to share career guidance activities with the teachers and other staff, some remodeling of counselor role is required. The teacher must continually seek ways of relating classroom experiences to future planning, and the counselor must build consultative skills. One particularly encouraging aspect in the growth of the career education movement has been the emphasis on using all community resources to help young people learn about the world of work. As this idea gains wider acceptance, the teacher and counselor can include employees, union representatives, government officials, and an array of workers in planning and developing appropriate experiences. Local work settings also can be used for a variety of involvements ranging from observation in the awareness stage to tryout participation in the preparation phase. These experiential opportunities based on closer cooperation between school and community can only increase the effectiveness of career planning by the students.

In the same way, the other teams in other agencies must recognize the team relationship and strive toward closer cooperation. In dealing with school-age youths, it is important to recognize that not all team members are necessarily within the structure of the school. With some youths, in fact, the team members with major influence may be outside the school in the neighborhood youth center or other social agency. The team that deals with most adults will ordinarily be outside the school—in the social agency, the employment service, the rehabilitation center, the community counseling center or similar locations. Perhaps, with the increasing likelihood of continuing education and frequent need for retraining to meet changing career needs, a school or educational representative also may be a member of this team that focuses mainly on adults making changes and adjustments in order to re-enter the world of work.

NOTES

1. Report of a Special Task Force to the Secretary of Health, Education and Welfare, *Work in America*, (Cambridge, Mass.: The MIT Press, 1973), p. 1.
2. R. A. Winters, "Another View of the American Work Ethic," *Vocational Guidance Quarterly*, vol. 21, no. 1 (September, 1972), pp. 31–34.
3. S. D. Hoffman and S. A. Rollin, "Implications of *Future Shock* for Vocational Guidance," *Vocational Guidance Quarterly*, vol. 21, no. 2 (December, 1972), pp. 92–96.
4. D. H. Meadows, D. L. Meadows, J. Randers, and W. W. Behrens III, *The Limits To Growth* (Washington: Potomac Associates, 1972).
5. R. Gaymer, "Career Counseling—Teaching the Art of Career Planning," *Vocational Guidance Quarterly*, vol. 21, no. 1 (September, 1972), pp. 18–24.
6. R. L. Quey, "Toward a Definition of Work," *Personnel and Guidance Journal*, vol. 47, no. 3 (November, 1968), pp. 223–227; and "Structure of Work as Purposeful Activity," *Vocational Guidance Quarterly*, vol. 19, no. 4 (June, 1971), pp. 258–265.
7. T. Veblen, *The Theory of the Leisure Class*, (New York: Modern Library, 1934).
8. Report of a Special Task Force to the Secretary of Health, Education and Welfare. *op. cit.*, pp. 2–3.
9. S. Terkel, *Working—People Talk About What They Do All Day and How They Feel About What They Do*, (New York: Pantheon Books, 1974), pp. XXII–XXIII.
10. D. E. Super, "Vocational Development Theory: Persons, Positions, and Processes," in *Perspectives on Vocational Development*, ed. J. M. Whiteley and A. Resnikoff, (Washington: American Personnel and Guidance Association, 1972), p. 15.
11. W. Norris, F. R. Zeran, R. N. Hatch, and J. R. Engelkes, *The Information Service in Guidance*, 3rd edition, (Chicago: Rand, McNally and Company, 1972), p. 31.
12. C. L. Shartle, *Occupational Information—Its Development and Application*, 3rd edition, (Englewood Cliffs, N.J.: Prentice-Hall, Inc., 1959), p. 23.
13. Report of a Special Task Force to the Secretary of Health, Education and Welfare. *op. cit.*, pp. 1–4.
14. ———, p. 16, from Robert Kahn, "The Work Module," 1972.
15. C. P. Froehlich, "Factors Related to the Effectiveness of Counseling," (unpublished Doctoral thesis, School of Education, The George Washington University, 1948).

16. H. H. Remmers and B. Shimberg, *Manual for SRA Youth Inventory*, (Chicago: Science Research Associates, Inc., 1949).

17. R. L. Mooney, "Surveying High School Students' Problems by Means of a Problem Check List," *Educational Research Bulletin*, vol. 21 (March, 1942), pp. 57–69.

18. S. R. Laycock, "Helping Adolescents Solve Their Problems," *The Education Digest*, (November, 1942), p. 32.

19. J. C. Flanagan, "Some Pertinent Findings of Project TALENT," *Vocational Guidance Quarterly*, vol. 22, no. 2 (December, 1973), pp. 92–96.

20. D. J. Prediger, J. D. Roth, and R. J. Noeth, "Career Development of Youth: A Nationwide Study," *Personnel and Guidance Journal*, vol. 53, no. 2 (October, 1974), pp. 97–104.

21. J. L. Biggers, "The Use of Information in Vocational Decision-Making," *Vocational Guidance Quarterly*, vol. 19, no. 3 (March, 1971), pp. 171–176.

22. U.S. Office of Education, *Career Education*. (Washington: U.S. Government Printing Office, 1971).

23. Commission on the Reorganization of Secondary Education, *Cardinal Principles of Secondary Education*. (U.S. Office of Education, Bulletin 35, Washington, 1918).

24. Educational Policies Commission, *The Purpose of Education in American Democracy*. (Washington: National Educational Association, 1938).

25. S. P. Marland, Jr. "Marland on Career Education," *American Education*, vol. 7, no. 1 (1971), pp. 25–28.

26. S. P. Marland, Jr. "Career Education Now," *Vocational Guidance Quarterly*, vol. 20, no. 3 (March, 1972), pp. 188–192.

27. American Vocational Association Task Force, "Task Force Report on Career Education," *American Vocational Journal*, vol. 47, no. 1 (Jan., 1972), p. 12.

28. T. A. Ryan, "A Systems Approach to Career Education," *Vocational Guidance Quarterly*, vol. 22, no. 3 (March, 1974), pp. 172–179.

29. National Advisory Council on Vocational Education, "Career Preparation for Everyone," *Vocational Guidance Quarterly*, vol. 20, no. 3 (March, 1972), pp. 183–187.

30. K. B. Hoyt and others, *Career Education: What It Is and How To Do It*, (Salt Lake City, Utah: Olympus Publishing Co., 1972).

31. I. M. Hefzallah and W. P. Maloney, "Public Perspectives on Career Education," *Vocational Guidance Quarterly*, vol. 22, no. 3 (March, 1974), pp. 195–199.

32. E. L. Herr (ed.), *Vocational Guidance and Human Development*, (Boston: Houghton Mifflin Co., 1974), pp. 48–53.

33. E. L. Herr (ed.), *Review and Synthesis of Foundations for Career Education*. (Washington: Government Printing Office, 1972).

34. T. M. Rauner, "Occupational Information and Occupational Choice," *Personnel and Guidance Journal*, vol. 41, no. 4 (December, 1962), pp. 311–317.

35. D. E. Super, "A Developmental Approach to Vocational Guidance: Recent Theory and Results," *Vocational Guidance Quarterly*, vol. 13, no. 1 (Autumn, 1964), pp. 1–10.

36. N. C. Gysbers and E. J. Moore (eds.), Career Guidance, *Counseling and Placement Elements of an Illustrative Program Guide*. (Columbia, Mo.: University of Missouri, 1974).

37. D. H. Blocher, and C. H. Miller in *Vocational Guidance in the 1970's,* edited by H. Borow, (Boston: Houghton Mifflin Co., for National Vocational Guidance Association, 1970).

38. R. P. Overs, "A Sociological Analysis of Vocational Counseling: The General Pattern," *Vocational Guidance Quarterly,* vol. 12, no. 3 (Spring, 1964), pp. 159–162; and "A Sociological Analysis of Vocational Counseling: The Physician's Role as a Model," *Vocational Guidance Quarterly,* vol. 12, no. 4 (Summer, 1964), pp. 237–245.

39. W. G. Hill, "The State of the Field," *Vocational Guidance Quarterly,* vol. 11, no. 3 (Spring, 1963), pp. 151–157.

40. J. Samler, "Commentary," *Vocational Guidance Quarterly,* vol. 11, no. 3 (Spring, 1963), pp. 157–161.

2

Theories of Career Development

In western democratic societies, individuals have considerable freedom of choice relative to "life work" or career. This was not always the case; nor is it universally true today. In medieval days, serfdom and slavery controlled the lives of most; even those with rank and power were relatively restricted in choices available to them. The extension of democratic ideals, with concomitant increases in freedom, has influenced the relationship between people and the work they do. Recent trends, such as concern for the alleviation of poverty, extension of rights to minority and alienated groups, and the greater emphasis on the individual as a person, suggest the likelihood of an expansion of this influence. Career education concepts, for example, recognize that choice and decision relative to career are lifelong.

Early childhood and adolescence are periods of physical, mental, and emotional growth and development. During these years, individuals develop the body, intellect, and personality they will use for the rest of their lives. Major choices and decisions are often made for them by significant adults; nevertheless, the experiences encountered during this period will have persistent influence on later choices and decisions made by the individual.[1]

The subsequent period of late adolescence and early maturity are often tumultuous and fraught with crucial problems and decisions. Many of the concerns encountered at this time are inconsequential; some have an influencing impact over weeks or months; and a few are so fundamental that they produce lasting effects on the individual. Some of these situations are met with an immediate spontaneous reaction or choice. Others are resolved only after careful study and contemplation. Later evaluation of the response can range from "total error" to "bull's eye." Most members of the helping professions contend that the likelihood of a wise and satisfying decision is enhanced when the individual has had sufficient opportunity for advance preparation before involvement in decision-making.

Recognition of the changing nature of both individuals and jobs supports the career education view of an intermittent, if not continual, relationship between education and work. It is no longer true that an individual makes a commitment to a job that is binding for all time. Teachers and school counselors have an obvious influence and involvement in the choices and decisions made by students during childhood and adolescence. Counselors in non-school agencies, employment offices, rehabilitation centers, and elsewhere are also instrumental in career planning and readjustment. Each of these professionals must have some understanding of the factors that influence the individual in the process of career development. The way in which assistance is provided will be influenced by the way in which the helper views the process.

BUILDING A FRAME OF REFERENCE

Every profession, as well as many skilled crafts, requires a thorough grounding in pertinent knowledge—both developed and theoretical. For example, the physician must have not only an understanding of biology, chemistry, and physics, but also a complete grasp of anatomy, kinetics, optics, and enzymology. Similarly, the automobile mechanic must know basic physics and also the theories related to the internal combustion engine, aerodynamics, hydraulics, and structures. Whether dealing with the complexities of the human body or the modern automobile, one must have a theoretical basis on which understanding and insight can be developed. To understand either a malfunctioning liver or steering mechanism it is necessary to know first how these units operate in normal situations, how they interact with related parts, how the behavior of each part can be influenced and modified, what factors or events can produce malfunction, and how to identify needed basic information in the presenting situation. From this basic theoretical position, either specialist can then analyze the pertinent data, evaluate appropriate alternatives, and anticipate likely results accruing from each choice.

This analogy can be extended to the helping professions. For example, if one is to teach effectively, it is first essential to know how learning takes place. As numerous college instructors have demonstrated, simply knowing one's subject matter does not automatically mean that one's students will learn. If the instructor is to teach, attention must be given to the class—what the students are like, what backgrounds they have, what interests them, what they want to accomplish, what motivates them, and how they learn; then the subject is approached according to these data.

Counselors in training and prospective teachers, possibly beginners in almost every field, are inclined to overlook the significance of this fundamental principle—that one can perform effectively in a professional position only when one has mastered the knowledge and theory on which that profession is based. The beginner is often so concerned with building skill or competency—how to do something—that it is easy to overlook the more essential factor—why that something is done. The "why" is based on the theoretical or factual background that serves as the frame of reference with which the professional approaches each student, client, or patient. Without that frame of reference, one operates only as a technician even though one's skill may be superb.

Shertzer and Stone have identified four functions of theories appropriate to our discussion.[2] They first point out that theory summarizes and generalizes a body of information; secondly, that theory facilitates understanding and explanation of complex phenomena. Both of these functions are implicit in the illustration above. Further, theory serves a predictive function by helping one to estimate what will happen under certain conditions. Finally, theory stimulates further research and fact finding. All of these functions are necessary for the professional practitioner—teacher, counselor, or otherwise.

Unlike the physical and biological sciences, in which centuries of study and research have contributed to a vast reservoir of knowledge and theory, the behavioral sciences are still very much in a developmental stage. As might be expected, there have been and will be an increasing effort made to gain a greater understanding of how careers are built. The professional literature of the past two decades includes many articles and books that deal with career choice and development. Our lack of psychological and sociological sophistication has prevented the development of a definitive statement describing the process of career development. Several writers have prepared statements reflecting insight into segments of the process or suggesting an approach to a broader aspect of the process. Many of these writings can properly be thought of as "position papers" presented for discussion and criticism by colleagues.[3] We have often gone beyond that point and prematurely labeled them as theories. Although most of the writers would hesitate to suggest that they have proposed anything as broadly-based and well-developed as a theory, the label has, nevertheless, stuck. Carkhuff, Alexik, and Anderson have pointed out that most of the various positions to be considered in the remainder of this chapter have certain theoretical short-comings.[4]

The reader may be inclined to wonder if attention to "position papers" can be justified. Why not wait until research presents us with a complete and usable theory of career development? The question deserves an answer, and Osipow has presented an excellent response.[5] He points out that counselors and teachers daily face clients and students, that they work in the "here and now" with actual situations. Actions must be taken, decisions must be made, and plans must be developed. Unless the professional limits himself/herself to sympathetic listening and good wishes, some basis must be found for action. Thus, even incomplete theory is far better than none at all. Further, Osipow states that theory precedes and accompanies empirical knowledge and orients it while it is developing, thus gradually separating "folklore" from theory.

In this chapter, we will present a brief summary of the more widely accepted views of career development. Some views are solidly based on extensive research; others are primarily empirically based. The goal is to give the reader sufficient understanding to provide him/her with a theoretical base that at least partially answers the "why" for every subsequent chapter. The reader need not develop a thorough and comprehensive understanding of each writer's position. Such an understanding properly belongs in advanced classes and seminars, for which this book is not intended.

The reader who desires more detail about the theoretical positions included in this chapter has several options available. A scholarly and analytic review can be found in Osipow's writing.[6] Recent statements by the theorists describing the current status of research related to their viewpoints can be found in the APGA publication edited by Whiteley and Resnikoff.[7] Another excellent analysis of the writing of major theorists can also be found in the book by Pietrofesa and Splete.[8] The serious reader will want to have direct contact with the original statements of at least some of the theorists; it is hoped that the footnotes in this chapter will help the reader select among those items for further exploration.

For the most part, the statements that we will consider here tend to emphasize either a psychological need approach or a self-concept and developmental viewpoint. The writings of Hoppock, Holland, and Roe tend to follow the first approach; those of the Ginzberg group, Super, and Tiedeman tend to stress ideas related to self-concept and developmental theories.

Psychological need is often discussed from the approach proposed by Maslow.[9] He suggested that each individual has certain psychological needs that can be arranged in hierarchical order from basic or "lower-order" to "higher-order." These needs are considered to be:

1. The physiological needs
2. The safety needs
3. The need for belonging and love
4. The need for importance, respect, and self-esteem
5. The need for information
6. The need for understanding

7. The need for beauty
8. The need for self-actualization

The self-concept theorists, on the other hand, consider the primary factors in human behavior to be the perception the individual holds of self and the desire to maintain and enhance a favorable self-concept. Thus, the person engages in activities that support a positive view of self and attempts to avoid activities that do not lend themselves to this positive self regard.

In the following pages, we will review, one by one, the views held by these six theorists; then we will attempt to integrate these positions into a general statement.

HOPPOCK'S COMPOSITE THEORY

Hoppock has proposed the following series of ten postulates, which make up the body of this theory. A more extensive discussion of this viewpoint can be found in Hoppock's writing.[10]

1. Occupations are chosen to meet needs. Every individual has many needs. Some of them are essentially physical, such as the need for food, rest, and shelter. Other needs can be more properly described as psychological in nature, such as the need to maintain contact with others, to be held in esteem and respected by others, to feel secure against real or anticipated threats, and to feel a sense of success or accomplishment. Each individual will face all of the physical needs and certainly most of the psychological needs; the impact of these needs will vary widely, however. The gourmand, for example, emphasizes and capitalizes on the need for bodily nourishment, whereas the ascetic individual not only disregards this need but also tends to de-emphasize and minimize it. Most of us find ourselves somewhere between these two extremes.

Similarly, some individuals have a strong psychological need for contact with other people. They like social activities or other experiences that permit them to be near or with many other people and to converse with them. Other individuals prefer a more isolated life. They are happier when they are by themselves with only occasional social interchange, and then preferably with people singly or in small groups.

Hoppock proposes that the reaction by the individual to these physical and psychological needs influences the selection of an occupation.

2. The occupation that we choose is the one that we believe will best meet the needs that most concern us. The individual who feels strongly the need for security will show interest in occupations that tend to meet this need. He/she will seek employment in which tenure and regularity of income are important characteristics and will avoid employment opportunities that lack these, even though the alternative might offer the opportunity of greater return. Similarly, the person who feels strongly the need for status or the respect of others will seek the position that seems most likely to meet this need.

Each person has many needs that, as a composite, influence behavior. Few people are controlled by a single need, or a very few needs, to the point that career choice is based on this alone. Rather, an entire array of needs produces forces that bear on the individual, some stronger than others. The person will be influenced in choice of occupation by all of these needs, probably in proportion to the importance of each need.

3. Needs may be intellectually perceived, or they may be only vaguely felt as attractions that draw us in certain directions. In either case, they may influence choices. The extent to which the individual perceives why he/she is attracted by certain occupations or repelled by others, depends, at least in part, on the amount of self-understanding or insight. He/she may clearly recognize the motivating factors that cause this reaction; on the other hand, he/she may only realize that the activity is pleasant and attractive without understanding what is propelling him/her in that direction. In the latter case, the individual is seeking to satisfy a need that is not understood at an intellectual or verbal level, but that nonetheless influences behavior and causes him/her to seek a satisfying outlet.

4. Career development begins when we first become aware that an occupation can help to meet our needs. As an individual's life experiences develop, one finds that certain types of behavior are gratifying or pleasing and that others, on the contrary, are distasteful and unpleasant. One tends to seek experiences of this first type and to avoid the latter ones. As he/she becomes aware of a variety of occupations or work situations, he/she gradually comes to realize that certain of these provide satisfying experiences and that others offer displeasing and frustrating experiences. As one becomes aware of these differences in terms of likes and dislikes, he/she is attracted to certain jobs and away from others. At this point, according to Hoppock, occupational choice actually starts. Since experiences have an impact on the individual almost from birth onward, one has a broad framework of personal characteristics or felt needs long before reaching the point maturationally when he/she will be seriously concerned with making a vocational selection.

This viewpoint emphasizes the developmental aspect of career planning. Early attitudes and concepts of various occupations may exert influence later when the individual turns more seriously to considering how to spend his/her life. As one proceeds through experiences in and out of school, one acquires knowledge of various occupations either directly through contact with them or indirectly and vicariously through reading, television, movies and other means of communication. This knowledge (sometimes misinformation and misconceptions) is used in developing general impressions and attitudes that gradually influence the ultimate choice.

5. Career development progresses and occupational choice improves as we become better able to anticipate how well a prospective occupation will meet our needs. Our capacity thus to anticipate depends upon our knowledge of ourselves, our knowledge of occupations, and our ability to think clearly. If the range of existing occupations were narrow and the entering qualifications for each field were low, one might reasonably proceed on a trial and error basis of experimenting with each occupation until he/she finds a field that is satisfying and rewarding. This is an approach not unlike that often used in purchasing a pair of shoes. Having a general impression of the type, size, and quality of shoe that we are seeking, we often "try on" several pairs that the salesperson shows us until we select one that generally "best fits" the several variables such as comfort, style, and durability that we feel are important in our decision.

Since the range of occupations is very wide and since many require extremely long and complex training programs before entrance, the "tryout" method is usually not appropriate. One will then more likely do better knowing thoroughly personal characteristics—needs—and also the nature and characteristics of occupations generally, so that these two vast areas of knowledge can be integrated in the process of making a choice.

6. Information about ourselves affects occupational choice by helping us to recognize what we want, and what we have to offer in exchange. Hoppock here emphasizes that application of the adage "know thyself" is essential in making an appropriate occupational choice. As the individual develops insight into desires, ambitions, goals, and values or philosophy of life, he/she understands better "what one wants out of life." As self-understanding of these factors is paralleled by insight into abilities, interests, aptitudes, personality characteristics, and similar strengths and weaknesses, one can then match these personal attributes against a contemplated occupation and thus decide more accurately the possibilities of successfully competing within that occupation in acquiring the emoluments that are important.

7. Information about occupations affects occupational choice by helping us to discover the occupations that may meet our needs, what these occupations offer us, and what they will demand of us. Satisfying vocational choices are more likely to occur as the individual successfully tests knowledge of assets and liabilities against knowledge of occupations and their characteristics. Even though an individual has complete insight into personal traits, this is of no value in making vocational plans unless a knowledge of occupations is available so that the two bodies of information can be compared, matched, and integrated.

Lack of knowledge about a wide range of occupations obviously has an effect on the vocational choice of the individual, since one cannot choose something of which one is totally ignorant. Similarly, basing a choice on limited knowledge can result in dissatisfaction and failure. Many unhappy workers have found that the superficial mental image of their chosen field is at variance with reality. For example, many counselors have encountered boys who indicate an interest in engineering because they feel that they would be happier in outside work and who do not realize that most successful engineers soon find themselves largely, if not entirely, confined to inside desk work.

One cannot evaluate fully an occupation and what it can offer the individual without a complete understanding of the occupation. Likewise, two or more occupations cannot be compared fairly unless each is thoroughly understood.

8. Job satisfaction depends upon the extent to which the job that we hold meets the needs that we feel it should meet. The degree of satisfaction is determined by the ratio between what we have and what we want. If a job meets the psychological and physical needs that are most important to the individual, he/she likes or is satisfied with the job. On the other hand, if the individual's job leaves certain needs unsatisfied, he/she feels discontented and frustrated and usually indicates a dislike for the work. Since the extent and intensity of needs vary from one individual to another, the amount of job satisfaction that accrues to the individual cannot be measured in objective, tangible units, but instead must be thought of in terms of a proportion or ratio that compares what the worker wants from the job with what is actually derived from it.

This postulate implies that the worker whose job provides those things desired—self-respect, status, opportunity to move ahead, or whatever —has job satisfaction. In other words, the ratio between what he/she wants and what is derived is favorable to the job. As long as that ratio is maintained, the worker will cling to the job without thought of looking elsewhere. When the ratio is in the other direction, where what is wanted compared to what is obtained is unfavorable to the job, he/she will look about for other job possibilities where the ratio appears more favorable. As soon as he/she finds another job that offers a more desirable balance, he/she will abandon the old job for the newer one.

It is important to emphasize that what the worker derives from a job is far more than just the cash in a pay envelope. It includes how he/she looks at self, how others in the peer group look at his/her job, the importance of the work performed, and numberless other abstract variables that range from the simple to the complex. Occasionally something as elementary as a uniform that identifies the worker with fellow workers, or an assigned title, produces a favorable ratio between the two factors and results in job satisfaction.

9. Satisfaction can result from a job which meets our needs today, or from a job which promises to meet them in the future, or from a job that we think will help us to get the job we want. Both sociologists and psychologists have described the tendency, common in our culture, to work toward long-range goals or objectives that can be met only with the investment of long periods of effort and waiting. The term "delayed gratification" is often applied to this willingness to postpone until the indefinite future the meeting of certain needs that are important to the individual.

Even though certain needs felt by the individual, especially many of the physical needs, must be at least partially satisfied on a short-term basis, for many needs the ultimate satisfaction becomes a long-range goal. For many workers, the indication that this goal can be attained in the foreseeable future provides sufficient incentive or reward for work in the present. For example, many individuals who feel intensely the need to hold a position of importance in an organization will accept the lowest position in the company as a starting place for their careers if they see the possibility of eventual promotion and advancement to a position that holds the status they desire so strongly. As long as such satisfaction appears to be reasonably attainable, many workers will forgo immediate satisfaction of needs in the hope of finally gaining greater satisfaction. When the goal appears to be unattainable or too far distant, the worker will grow discontented and unhappy and probably will turn to a job that offers either immediate satisfaction of the needs or satisfaction within a shorter period.[11] This newer position is often described as having greater opportunity.

10. Occupational choice is always subject to change when we believe that a change will better meet our needs. As indicated above, the amount of satisfaction felt by the worker is a ratio between what the job offers in need satisfaction and what is wanted. If either of these factors changes, the ratio is obviously changed. If the job offers the worker less satisfaction for any reason, the favorable balance may be upset to the point at which the worker will change jobs if he/she sees another position that offers greater likelihood of meeting needs. Similarly, since each individual is constantly changing, it is possible that the needs or wants felt by the individual will change as he/she encounters new experiences. When needs change, the balance between the two factors may be disrupted to the point at which the worker seeks a new position that will better meet the new needs. For example, an individual may find that a job that requires constant and extensive travel is highly satisfying; but after marriage and the establishment of a family, he may find the long absences from home so displeasing that he seeks a different position that will permit him to be home more of the time.

HOLLAND'S THEORY OF VOCATIONAL CHOICE

Holland's theory has been discussed in numerous articles and monographs to which the reader should turn for more detail than can be included here.[12] Holland assumes that a person expresses personality through the choice of a vocation, and that the devices we usually describe as interest inventories are really personality inventories. Further, he assumes that each person holds stereotypical views of various vocations. These stereotypes have psychological and sociological relevance for the individual and many of them have demonstrable validity. Holland says that members of a vocation have similar personalities and therefore they will respond to many situations and problems in similar ways. Thus they will create what he labels as a characteristic interpersonal environment. Finally, he assumes that vocational satisfaction, stability, and achievement depend on the extent to which the individual's personality and work environment are compatible.

Proceeding from these assumptions, Holland states that we can classify individuals into a limited number of personality types, and that work situations or environments can similarly be classified into a few categories. Personality types include realistic, investigative, artistic, social, enterprising, and conventional. We will consider each category briefly.

The *realistic* person deals with environment in an objective, concrete, and physically manipulative manner. He/she avoids goals and tasks that demand subjectivity, intellectual or artistic expressions, or social abilities. He/she is described as masculine, unsociable, emotionally stable, materialistic. He/she prefers agricultural, technical, skilled trade, and engineering vocations. He/she likes activities that involve motor skills, things, and structure, such as athletics, scouting, crafts, shop work, etc. He/she avoids supervisory and leadership roles, social situations in which one would be the center of attention, and intellectual or verbal tasks that require abstract thinking. He/she has a single outlook, more mathematical than verbal ability, and the operation of machines, tools, and vehicles increases the sense of well-being and power. The parents of the realistic type tend to be poorly educated, often foreign born. The tendency toward self-abasement is consistent with the lower socio-economic status of the home.

The *investigative* person deals with environment by the use of intelligence, manipulating ideas, words, and symbols. He/she prefers scientific vocations, theoretical tasks, reading, collecting, algebra, foreign languages, and such creative activities as art, music, and sculpture. He/she avoids social situations and sees self as unsociable, masculine, persistent, scholarly, and introverted. He/she achieves primarily in academic and scientific areas and usually does poorly as a leader. He/she has a complex outlook and scores high in both verbal and mathematical aptitudes. The investigative person is more scholarly, original, independent, and self-confident, but less practical, emotionally stable, and conventional than the realistic person.

The *artistic* person deals with environment by creating art forms and products. He/she relies on subjective impressions and fantasies in seeking solutions to problems. He/she prefers musical, artistic, literary, and dramatic vocations, and activities that are creative in nature. He/she dislikes masculine activities and roles such as auto repair and athletics. He/she sees self as unsociable, feminine, submissive, introspective, sensitive, impulsive, and flexible. He/she is usually more original than the members of any other group and has higher verbal than mathematical aptitude.

The *social* person handles environment by using skills in handling and dealing with others. He/she is typified by social skills and need for social interaction. He/she prefers educational, therapeutic, and religious vocations, and such activities as church, government, community services, music, reading, dramatics, etc. He/she sees self as sociable, nurturant, cheerful, conservative, responsible, achieving, and self-accepting. He/she has a positive self image and considers self to be a leader, good speaker, popular, and aggressive. He/she tends to have high verbal and low mathematical aptitude. He/she has much concern for human welfare and for helping dependent individuals.

The *enterprising* person copes with environment by choices expressing adventurous, dominant, enthusiastic, and impulsive qualities. Characterized as persuasive, verbal, extroverted, self-accepting, self-confident, aggressive, and exhibitionistic, he/she prefers sales, supervisory, and leadership vocations and activities that satisfy a need for dominance, verbal expression, recognition, and power. He/she likes athletics, dramatics, public speaking, interviewing. He/she dislikes confining, manual, non-social activities. He/she sees self as dominant, sociable, cheerful, adventurous, impulsive, and emotionally stable. He/she asserts self by struggling for power, developing athletic abilities, acquiring possessions, and exploiting others. He/she differs from the conventional person by being more sociable, aggressive, dominant, original, and adventurous, and less responsible, dependent, and conservative.

The *conventional* person deals with the environment by choosing goals and activities that carry social approval. The approach to problems is stereotyped, correct, and unoriginal. He/she creates a good impression by being neat, sociable, conservative. He/she prefers clerical and computational tasks, identifies with business, and puts a high value on economic matters. He/she sees self as masculine, shrewd, dominant, controlled, rigid, and stable, and has more mathematical than verbal aptitude. He/she reduces stress by social conformity and by ingratiating self with others. He/she differs from the social person by possessing greater self-control, and by being more hard-headed and less dominant and nurturant.

According to Holland, a person can be typed into one of these categories by expressed or demonstrated vocational or educational interests, by employment, or by scores obtained on such instruments as the Kuder Preference Record, the Strong Vocational Interest Blank, or the Self Directed Search. The last, an instrument developed by Holland, consists of occupational titles and activities that can be divided equally among the six type areas. An individual can be expected to demonstrate a primary pattern (highest score) and secondary directions (other high scores). Consistency between primary and secondary areas usually indicates stability, whereas inconsistency usually produces change from one category to another. A consistent pattern not only relates to the individual's vocational direction but also may suggest the level of vocational aspiration or achievement.

Holland proposes that the six personality types are related to personal needs as described by Murray.[13] In other words, the various types are indicative of the needs felt by the individual. Murray was concerned not only with personal needs, but also with environmental presses. Holland accounts for these environmental factors by developing a set of environmental models that he defines as the situation or atmosphere created by the people who dominate a given environment. His environmental models are built on the assumption that their dominant features are created by individuals who control the situation. The environmental conditions of the models reflect the personality attributes of those in control. Each category will be briefly described below.

The *realistic* environment involves concrete, physical tasks requiring mechanical skill, persistence, and physical movement. Only minimal interpersonal skills are needed. Typical realistic settings include a filling station, a machine shop, a farm, construction work, or a barber shop.

The *investigative* environment requires the use of abstract and creative abilities rather than personal perceptiveness. Satisfactory performance demands imagination and intelligence; achievement usually requires a considerable time span. Problems encountered may vary in level of difficulty but they will usually be solved by the application of intellectual skills and tools. The work is with ideas and things rather than with people. Typical settings include a research laboratory, a diagnostic case conference, a library, work groups of scientists, mathematicians, and research engineers.

The *artistic* environment demands the creative and interpretive use of artistic forms. One must be able to draw on knowledge, intuition, and emotional life in solving typical problems. Information is judged against personal, subjective criteria. The work usually requires intense involvement for prolonged periods. Typical settings include a play rehearsal, a concert hall, a dance studio, a study, a library, or an art or music studio.

The *social* environment demands ability to interpret and modify human behavior and an interest in caring for and dealing with others. The work requires frequent and prolonged personal relationships. The work hazards are primarily emotional. Typical work situations include school and college classrooms, counseling offices, mental hospitals, churches, educational offices, and recreational centers.

The *enterprising* environment requires verbal skill in directing or persuading other people. The work requires directing, controlling, or planning activities of others, and an interest in others at a more superficial level than the social environment. Typical settings include a car lot, a real-estate office, a political rally, and an advertising agency.

The *conventional* environment involves systematic, concrete, routine processing of verbal and mathematical information. The tasks frequently call for repetitive, short-cycle operations according to an established procedure. Minimal skill in interpersonal relations is required since the work is mostly with things and materials. Typical settings include a bank, an accounting firm, a post office, a file room, and a business office.

Holland suggests that each model environment is sought by the individual whose personality type is similar to those controlling the environment. It is assumed that he/she will be comfortable and happy in a compatible environment and uneasy in an environment that consists of different

personality types. A congruent person-environment match presumably results in a more stable vocational choice, a higher vocational achievement,
higher academic achievement, better maintenance of personal stability, and
greater satisfaction.

Individuals are rarely pure prototypes of one of the six personality
types. In other words, many people express a predominant or primary
similarity to one of the patterns, supplemented by lesser similarity to another of the groups. Some groups are more compatible, or consistent, with
each other than other combinations might be. For example, a high correlation between social and enterprising is thought to be consistent and reflects
a sociable, dependent type of person; on the other hand, a low relationship
between these two areas appears to be inconsistent.

Further research by Holland has revealed that the interrelationships
among the six occupational classes can be demonstrated by arranging the
six classes in a hexagonal pattern. This idea is illustrated in Figure 2–1. If
connecting lines are drawn from each point to each of the others and inter-
correlations are then placed on each connecting line, one finds that the

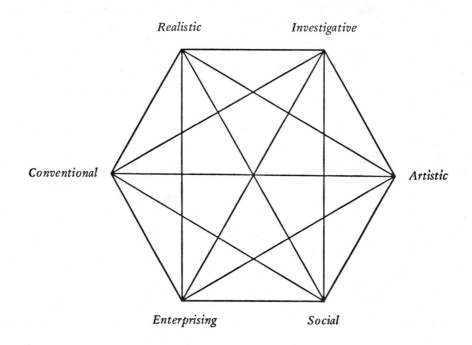

FIGURE 2–1.

Holland's Hexagonal Model

highest correlations tend to be on the shortest lines. Thus, the hexagonal pattern places those classes most closely related in nearest proximity and those least related at opposite points. Although Holland reports different indices of correlation for men and women, the basic relationships appear to hold for both sexes.

Holland also has undertaken the development of an occupational classification system related to the model environment construct. Still in a preliminary stage, this approach may lead to the development of instruments that may help individuals in the exploration stage of career choice.

One measure of the significance of a hypothetical or theoretical position is the extent to which it lends itself to further research. Holland's theory has stimulated numerous research studies that are regularly reported in various professional journals. For example, between 1971 and 1975, about two dozen articles appeared in *The Journal of Vocational Behavior* and *The Journal of Counseling Psychology* reporting studies of various aspects of Holland's theory. Typical of these articles are:

> H. M. Hughes, Jr., "Vocational Choice, Level, and Consistency: an Investigation of Holland's Theory on an Employed Sample." *Journal of Vocational Behavior*, vol. 2, no. 4 (October, 1972), pp. 377–88.
>
> D. W. Lacey, "Holland's Vocational Models: A Study of Work Groups and Need Satisfaction." *Journal of Vocational Behavior*, vol. 1, no. 2 (April, 1971), pp. 105–22.
>
> D. L. Lee and B. Hedahl, "Holland's Personality Types Applied to the SVIB Basic Interest Scales." *Journal of Vocational Behavior*, vol. 3, no. 1 (January, 1973), pp. 61–68.
>
> R. F. Morrison and S. J. Arnold, "A Suggested Revision in the Classification of Nonprofessional Occupations in Holland's Theory." *Journal of Counseling Psychology*, vol. 21, no. 6 (November, 1974), pp. 485–88.
>
> J. M. Morrow, Jr., "A Test of Holland's Theory of Vocational Choice." *Journal of Counseling Psychology*, vol. 18, no. 5 (September, 1971), pp. 422–25.
>
> M. C. Viernstein, "The Extension of Holland's Occupational Classification to all Occupations in the Dictionary of Occupational Titles." *Journal of Vocational Behavior*, vol. 2, no. 1 (April, 1972), pp. 107–22.

ROE'S THEORY OF CAREER CHOICE

Anne Roe has studied extensively the personality characteristics of scientists.[14] She became convinced that there were real differences between the life and physical scientists and the social scientists in the way in which they deal with people. Furthermore, she concluded that the differences that she observed grew out of early childhood experiences. She published a statement describing her theory of the influence of early childhood experiences in 1957.[15] This statement was revised and modified in a monograph appearing in 1964.[16]

A brief summary of Roe's revised theoretical position can be obtained from the following quotation from the monograph that she prepared with Siegelman:

Proposition 1: Genetic inheritance sets limits to the potential development of all characteristics, but specificity of the genetic control and the extent and nature of the limitations are different for different characteristics.

It is probable that the genetic element is more specific and stronger in what we call intellectual abilities and temperament than it is in such other variables as interests and attitudes.

Proposition 2: The degrees and avenues of development of inherited characteristics are affected not only by experience unique to the individual, but also by all aspects of the general cultural background and the socioeconomic position of the family.

Proposition 3: The pattern of development of interests, attitudes, and other personality variables with relatively little or non-specific genetic control is primarily determined by individual experiences through which involuntary attention becomes channeled in particular directions.

The important word here is involuntary. The elements in any situation to which one gives automatic or effortless attention are keys to the dynamics of behavior. This proposition is clearly related to hypotheses concerning the relations between personality and perception.

a. These directions are determined in the first place by the patterning of early satisfactions and frustrations.
   This patterning is affected by the relative strengths of various needs and the forms and relative degrees of satisfaction which they receive. The two latter aspects are environmental variables.
b. The modes and degrees of need satisfaction determine which needs will become the strongest motivators. The nature of the motivation may be quite unconscious.

   Possible variations are:

1. Needs satisfied routinely as they appear do not become unconscious motivators.
2. Needs, for which even minimum satisfaction is rarely achieved, will, if higher order (as used by Maslow, 1954), become expunged or will, if lower order, prevent the appearance of higher order needs and will become dominant and restricting motivators.
3. Needs, the satisfaction of which is delayed but eventually accomplished, will become (unconscious) motivators, depending largely upon the degree of satisfaction felt. Behavior that has received irregular reinforce-

ment is notably difficult to extinguish. (C. B. Ferster and B. F. Skinner, 1957).

The degree of satisfaction felt will depend, among other things, upon the strength of the basic need in the given individual, the length of time elapsing between arousal and satisfaction, and the values ascribed to the satisfaction of this need in the immediate environment.

Proposition 4: The eventual pattern of psychic energies, in terms of attention directedness, is the major determinant of interests.

Proposition 5: The intensity of these needs and of their satisfaction (perhaps particularly as they have remained unconscious) and their organization are the major determinants of the degree of motivation that reaches expression in accomplishment.

Roe has proposed that the emotional climate in the home—the relationship between parent and child—is of three types. It can be one of emotional concentration on the child, or avoidance of the child, or acceptance of the child. These types of emotional climate are thought to have a circular relationship, with each type shading into the others. Each type is also thought to have two subdivisions that shade into each other and into the adjacent sub-category of the other types. The relationship among these types and subdivisions is demonstrated by the figure that Roe first proposed in her 1957 article.

Emotional concentration on the child includes subdivisions in which the parents are overprotecting and overdemanding. The overprotecting parents encourage dependency in the child and limit exploratory behavior. Parents are indulgent, allow special privileges, and show affection. They limit the child's friendships, protect him/her from other children. They intrude into the child's life and expect to be told everything that he/she thinks or experiences. The overdemanding parents set high standards for their child and enforce conformity to the standard. They expect the child to be constructively busy and they select friends for the child in accordance with the standards they set. They tell him/her what he/she is to think and feel.

The avoidance type of climate has two extremes, ranging from rejection to neglect. Parents who are emotionally rejecting of their child are more extreme in behavior than the demanding parent. Their attitude toward the child is one of coldness, hostility, derogation, and ridicule. They may leave him/her alone and also prevent contact with other children. They establish rules to protect themselves from intrusions by the child into their lives. The neglecting parents do not express hostility or ridicule, they simply ignore the child. They provide a minimum of physical care and no affection. They leave him/her to shift for oneself but make no effort to avoid the child.

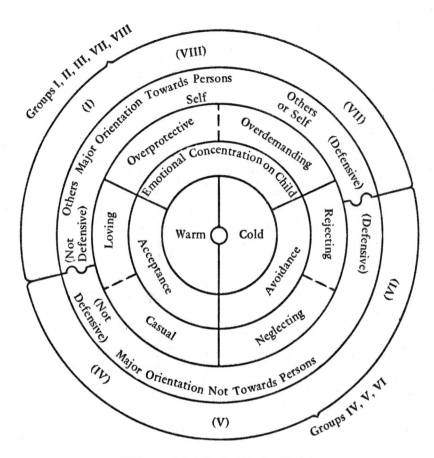

FIGURE 2–2. Roe's Circular Model

The acceptance category includes the subdivisions of casual accept-ance and loving acceptance of the child. The casually accepting parents pay some attention to the child and are mildly affectionate. They accept the child as part of the general situation, and are responsive if not occupied with other matters. They are easygoing, make few rules or little effort to train the child, and do not enforce rules or training efforts. The loving, accepting parents give the child warmth and affection. They help with things that are important without being monopolistic. They tend to reason rather than punish. They give praise when warranted and try to help with problems. They invite his/her friends to the home, encourage independ-ence and allow the child to take chances in growing up.

Roe suggests that these six subdivisions produce two types of be-havior. The approximate categories of loving, overprotective, and over-demanding produce a major orientation toward persons. The areas of casual, neglecting, and rejecting result in a major orientation away from persons. Both of these range from defensive to non-defensive. Person-oriented occupational areas include those of service, business contact, organizations, general culture, and the arts and entertainment. Occupations that are not person-oriented are in the categories of technology, outdoors, and science. Thus, an individual whose family provided an accepting or protective environment is likely to seek an occupation working with others in service or business contact or similar work situation, whereas the individual whose background was casual or neglecting is more likely to move toward technical or scientific occupations.

Roe's proposal has generated considerable research, only a small part of which has shown support for her position. Several problems, no doubt, contribute to the lack of research support. First, an accurate evaluation would necessitate a long-term study following the individual through childhood, adolescence, and well into maturity. Second, many of Roe's proposals are generalizations and thus are vague and ambiguous. Third, parental behavior is inconsistent, not only between parents, but even within a specific parent. Fourth, many influences beside the home environment bear on the child.

GINZBERG AND ASSOCIATES' THEORY

One of the earliest theories of vocational choice appeared in 1951 as the result of a team effort to study the developmental events that influence vocational choice.[17] The study on which Ginzberg, Ginsburg, Axelrad, and Herma based their proposed theory focused on a group of boys ages 11 to 23 who were attending either a university-related school or the university, and on two other supplementary groups. The major group came from higher socio-economic backgrounds and were mostly college-bound. One other group was essentially made up of sons of white fathers employed in unskilled and semi-skilled occupations. The second sample was a small group of college sophomore and senior women who were socially privileged and intelligent. The total sample used in the study was quite small and cannot be considered representative of the general population.

The group concluded that four variables bear on vocational choice— a reality factor, the educational process, emotional factors, and personal values. The reality factor, they said, includes the person's response to environmental pressures that lead to making vocational decisions. The quality and quantity of education available to the individual either limits or opens the range of choices one can make. Emotional factors include the personality aspects that bear on vocational choice. Personal values influence the nature of choices made by the individual.

Like their colleague, Super, the group was obviously influenced by the life-stages concept of Buehler.[18] They pictured the vocational choice process as covering three principal periods, which they called fantasy, tentative, and realistic periods. The fantasy period, they said, is an early childhood period preceding any serious vocational consideration. The time is exemplified by arbitrary choices that lack any rational or realistic base but that often reflect idealized choices drawn from influences within the child's environment.

The tentative period begins when the child begins to recognize that there are certain activities that he/she likes or has an interest in. He/she next finds that he/she performs some activities more ably than other activities and that he/she excels in some of these compared with other children, and more value is attached to some activities than to others. Finally, he/she begins to fit together ideas of interest, ability, and value as more attention is given to a career choice. He/she thus moves on to the third phase of vocational choice, the realistic period.

The realistic period comprises several stages, including exploration, crystallization, and specification. The exploration stage covers the period in which the individual is actively involved in implementing tentative choices. Chronologically, he/she is usually at the entry job or college level and tends to evaluate vocationally related experiences in a realistic manner. As a result of the interaction of experiences and evaluation of them, he/she gradually fixes on a fairly clear vocational pattern during the crystallization period. He/she reaches the specification period when a pattern has clearly focused on a particular position or occupation.

The whole process from fantasy to specification covers from ten to fifteen years and consists of a series of compromises between wishes and opportunities. The process is irreversible and consists of clear-cut periods that vary considerably from person to person. The fantasy period may extend up to age 10 or 12. The realistic period is usually entered by age 17 or 18, and crystallization occurs for most individuals in the period from 19 to 21. The researchers point out that some individuals appear to enter this stage, and later developments then may upset or change what appeared to be fairly solid choices. Some others never progress beyond the crystallization point. Many factors—biological, psychological, or environmental—affect the individual's progress.

The group concluded that boys from lower socio-economic level families followed the same general pattern as did those from more favored homes. The principal difference detected between the two groups was a striking increase in passivity among the lower income boys. They expressed interest and concern in future occupations during earlier years but were decidedly less inclined to assume an active role in bringing their hopes into actuality. The group also concluded that there were definite differences in choice patterns between men and women. They found three groups within the small sample of college women they studied. One group was career-oriented, one was marriage-oriented, and the third group hoped to combine both. Even the career-oriented women appeared to be less fixed on specific vocational goals than the boys. The researchers concluded that the possibility of marriage and its effect on a woman's career has a heavy impact on the career planning of all women.

Ginzberg recently restated the major points in the group's proposal, in light of the research that has developed since the original statement.[19] Three major components of the earlier position have been modified somewhat. These include the ideas (1) that the occupational decision-making process extends from pre-puberty to the early twenties, (2) that many of the decisions have an aspect of irreversibility, and (3) that the choice process always ends in compromise.

The group now sees the decision-making process as parallel to the individual's working life. Recognition is now given to the satisfactions that the individual derives from early career choices. If these are not adequate for the individual, the likelihood of a new choice is increased. The probability of the individual's responding by making a decision to move toward other opportunities depends, in part, on the amount of flexibility—that is, freedom from family responsibilities, indebtedness or other restrictions—and on the pressure or opportunity encountered in the present work situation.

The irreversibility factor now appears to be less influential because it is possible to delay final, firm decisions over several years and so keep one's options open for a prolonged period. Similarly, there has been an increase in what can be thought of as new opportunities for training previously considered unattainable. An example of this is acquisition of educational benefits through military service or company programs that allow the individual to pursue preparation beyond the level previously thought to be the terminal level.

Finally, they suggest that the substitution of *optimization* for *compromise* may be more relevant to most circumstances. The word optimization implies a dynamic, continuing kind of adjustment and readjustment, with the worker continually attempting to coordinate changing desires with changing circumstances in a way that appears to be most likely productive of favorable results.

SUPER'S THEORY OF VOCATIONAL DEVELOPMENT

Probably no one has written as extensively about vocational development as has Super.[20] His earlier theoretical statements were written in response to the theory proposed by Ginzberg and associates. Super has fitted together the aspects of developmental psychology with self-concept theory. In his 1953 *American Psychologist* article, he originally suggested ten propositions; these were later reorganized into a new list of eleven propositions and appeared in *Vocational Development: A Framework for Research*, (pp. 89–96). These were again revised and appeared as twelve propositions

in *Scientific Careers and Vocational Development Theory,* (pp. 118–20).
That list of twelve propositions will be used here as the basis for our consideration of Super's theory.° For purposes of our discussion, we will
group related propositions together in the same combinations suggested by
Super.

Proposition 1: Vocational development is an ongoing, continuous, generally irreversible process.

Proposition 2: Vocational development is an orderly, patterned, and predictable process.

Proposition 3: Vocational development is a dynamic process.

These three statements describe Super's view of the vocational development process. Like Ginzberg and his associates, Super has drawn
heavily from the life-stages concepts proposed by Buehler.[21] He identifies
these life stages as growth, exploration, establishment, maintenance, and
decline.

The *growth* stage consists of a period when primary emphasis is on
physical and psychological growth, ordinarily reaching into the adolescent
period to perhaps 14 or 15 years of age. During this growth stage the individual forms attitudes and behavior mechanisms that will be important
components of the self-concept for much of life. Simultaneously, experiences provide a background of knowledge of the environment generally,
including the world of work, which ultimately will be used in tentative
choices and in final selections.

The *exploratory* stage begins with the individual's awareness that an
occupation will be an aspect of life. During the early or fantasy phase of
the exploratory stage, the expressed choices are frequently unrealistic and
often closely related to the play life of the individual.[22] Examples are seen
in young children's choices of such careers as cowboys, soldiers, and astro-
nauts. These choices are nebulous and temporary, and usually have little,
if any, long-term significance for the individual. Some adolescents, and
even adults, have not advanced beyond the fantasy stage; their understanding of self or of the world of work is not sufficiently developed to make
effective choice possible. The person may be responding in terms of "if I
could do anything in the world" and ignoring or refusing to accept the inevitability of compromise. In the tentative phase of the *exploratory* stage,
the individual has narrowed choice to a few possibilities. Because of uncertainty about ability, availability of training, or access to employment
opportunity, the list may contain choices that will later disappear. The

° Reprinted by permission of the publisher from D. E. Super and P. B. Bachrach,
Scientific Careers and Vocational Development Theory. (New York: Teachers College
Press, 1957).

realistic phase of this stage, still preceding actual entrance into work, narrows the list to occupations that the individual feels are attainable and that provide the opportunities thought to be most important. This stage usually extends to the middle twenties.

The *establishment* stage, as the name implies, relates to the early encounters within the work experience. During the establishment stage, the individual, at first often by trial and error, attempts to ascertain if the vocational choices and decisions made during the exploratory period have validity. Some of this period is simply try-out. The individual may accept a job with a definite assumption that he/she will change positions or occupations if this one does not fit. As one gains experience and proficiency, the individual becomes stabilized; that is, he/she brings into self-concept aspects of this occupation and adjusts the position by investing self in the work. He/she accepts the occupation as one offering the best chance to obtain satisfactions that are personally important. This period is thought to extend to the middle forties.

During the *maintenance* stage, the individual attempts to continue or enhance the occupational situation. Since both the occupation and the individual's self-concept have some aspect of fluidity, the maintenance stage involves a continual process of adjustment. Essentially the person is concerned with continuing the satisfying parts of the work situation and revising or changing unpleasant and annoying aspects. Usually the maintenance period is believed to extend approximately to age 65.

The *decline* stage includes the pre-retirement period during which the individual's emphasis in work is focused on keeping the job and meeting the required standards of output. The worker is now more concerned with retaining the position than with enhancement. The period terminates with the individual's withdrawal from the world of work.

Super views vocational development as consisting of an interaction between the individual—behavior, attitudes, ambitions, and values—and the social factors that surround him/her. This dynamic interaction produces a series of compromises as the individual matches what he/she would like against the realities and attempts to identify what is attainable.

Proposition 4: Self-concepts begin to form prior to adolescence, become clearer in adolescence, and are translated into occupational terms in adolescence.

Proposition 5: Reality factors (the reality of personal characteristics and the reality of society) play an increasingly important part in occupational choice with increasing age, from early adolescence to adulthood.

Proposition 6: Identification with a parent or parent substitute is related to the development of adequate roles, their consistent and harmonious interrelationship, and their interpretation in terms of vocational plans and eventualities.

Personality theorists have long contended that early childhood, during which most children are intensely exposed to the values and interrelationships of the immediate family, has continuing influence on the individual's later life. During these years, the basic shape of the self-concept is formed, and the early testing of it occurs within the usually comfortable climate of family and elementary classroom.

As indicated above, during the pre-teen years most individuals increasingly see the continuing relationship between work and the adults who make up their immediate world. Since in American culture one's position in the world of work is important, this relationship becomes a major influence on self-concept.[23] During the educational period, one's anticipated occupation or role plays a part in the development of one's self-concept.[24] Each person attempts to maintain or enhance a favorable self-concept; thus, he/she is led toward activities that will permit keeping or improving the image that he/she would like to have of self. As the inner drive toward this ideal self-concept pushes the individual strongly, he/she encounters restricting factors that may come from personal limitations or from the surrounding environment. These factors interfere with attaining the ideal self-concept and result in the individual's compromising or accepting less than the ideal.[25] It is developmentally logical for him/her, in turn, to begin to view self in terms of some possible future relationship with work. As an individual matures, experiences provide a basis for evaluating both strengths and weaknesses and the "real world" as it is encountered. As problems are faced, one learns to cope with these varied experiences and to find satisfying solutions.

The individual can be helped in this maturational process in two ways: (1) by assisting to develop abilities and interests, and (2) by assisting to acquire an understanding of self and strengths and weaknesses so that satisfying choices can be made. Both of these aspects emphasize the school's role and guidance program in assisting the individual maximize development as a person. The teacher, with frequent classroom contacts, can best observe latent or under-developed abilities and then challenge the individual to push toward higher, but nonetheless attainable, goals. The counselor may also discover undeveloped potential through data obtained from tests or other sources.

If the school provides adequate opportunity for youth to develop, it has built into its program frequent opportunities for reality testing. Both teacher and counselor can help each youth find more of these testing areas.

An adult role model apparently is of significant importance as the adolescent begins to take on the attributes of adulthood. This adult, who may or may not be a family member, serves as a model for many relationships, including one with work. It appears likely that the difficulties encountered by many ghetto adolescents in adjusting to the world of work (often labeled "establishment") may be due in part to the lack of adult role models who have developed satisfactory work adjustments.

Proposition 7: The direction and rate of the vertical movement of an individual from one occupational level to another are related to his intelligence, parental socio-economic level, status needs, values, interests, skill in interpersonal relationships, and the supply and demand conditions in the economy.

Proposition 8: The occupational field which the individual enters is related to his interests, values, and needs, the identifications he makes with parental or substitute role models, the community resources he uses, the level and quality of his educational background, and the occupational structure, trends, and attitudes of his community.

Since choice of an occupational field precedes any advancement in that field, let us consider *Proposition 8* before we discuss *Proposition 7*. An individual can only choose among alternatives of which he/she is aware. The extent of familiarity with many options is largely a product of interests and resources, the adult role models considered important, and the local environment in which he/she is developing. If local opportunity is constricted by either economic limitations or attitudinal factors, then the impact on the individual is likely also to be narrowing. The socio-economic level of the adult role models makes a significant contribution since the early contact with the world of work is largely brought about through parents, family, and friends.[26] Hearing parents and their friends discuss experiences at work; observing the impact of occupational success, failure, or frustration; and obtaining or losing chances at education, travel, or other experience because of family circumstances greatly influence the individual's later work history.[27]

We can reasonably suggest that the relationship between economic supply and demand and opportunity for vocational advancement is similar to the relationship between genetic inheritance and later physical development. An active, expanding economy offers frequent opportunity for vocational advancement in many areas; whereas an inactive, lethargic, or declining economy limits opportunity and may hold many individuals in lower level positions longer than their ability, experience, and motivations would otherwise suggest.

The individual's mental ability is an important contributor to academic success, which, in turn, will open or close many doors to and within occupations. The ability to deal effectively with others is crucially important in most work situations.[28] "Being in the right place at the right time" or "getting the breaks" is important, since the individual must first have an opportunity to demonstrate competency before acquiring either stability or advancement in a job.

We often think that anyone can attain any goal, in true Horatio Alger tradition, if only one tries hard enough. In actuality, however, factors over which we often have no control set limits that can be surpassed or extended only by Herculean effort, if at all.

Proposition 9: Although each occupation requires a characteristic pattern of abilities, interests, and personality traits, the tolerances are wide enough to allow both some variety of individuals in each occupation and some diversity of occupations for each individual.

Many years of research have clearly established the concept of individual differences as far as abilities, interests, and personality are concerned. The range of personal characteristics varies widely both within and between individuals. Within each person are traits or abilities so pronounced that often they are used to caricature the individual. At the same time, there are other areas in which the person is relatively weak or inept.

The range of abilities, personality characteristics, and other traits is so wide that every person has the requisites for success in many occupations. Research in the field of rehabilitation has demonstrated that even the severely handicapped individual has a choice of many occupations in which the person can perform satisfactorily. For the person without serious physical or emotional impairment, the gamut of possibilities is wide indeed.

Few occupations require special abilities, skills, or traits in excessive quantity. Just as most athletic activities involve only certain muscles or muscle groups, so, too, most jobs require only a few specific characteristics. A person, then, can perform successfully in any occupation for which he/she has the qualifying characteristics. The lack of a certain skill, or its presence in minute quantities, excludes a person from an occupation only if the occupation requires that skill in larger quantities.

For each ability or trait required in the performance of a particular occupation one might expect to find a modal quantity that best fits the nature of the work. On either side of this amount is a band or range of this characteristic that will meet satisfactorily the demands of the work. To illustrate, picture an extremely simple task that requires, hypothetically, only a single characteristic. In studying this task, we might ascertain the quantity of this trait that would best meet the requirements of the job. We would expect that a person could perform satisfactorily even though he/she possessed somewhat less or more of the trait as long as it surpassed the minimum requirement. Obviously, the range for different traits will vary in each occupation, and the range in a given trait will vary among occupations.

To illustrate this point further, let us imagine three different workers with variable amounts of three different characteristics. Worker A has a high amount of the first trait, an average amount of the second trait, and a low amount of the third trait; Worker B has a low amount of the first trait, an average amount of the second trait, and a high amount of the third one; Worker C has an average amount of all three traits. Let us further assume that the minimums held by Workers A and C exceed the minimum threshold required to perform a job that demands only these three characteristics, and that their maximums are not so great as to impede their performance. Each worker, although different from the other two, therefore can perform the job successfully.

Since the patterns of characteristics required in various occupations will rarely be unique, one can expect to find considerable overlap from one job to another. Thus there will be some occupations in which a particular distribution of assets can result in satisfactory performance, just as there will be some patterns of ability that can result in satisfactory performance in a given occupation.

Proposition 10: Work satisfactions depend upon the extent to which the individual can find adequate outlets in his job for his abilities, interests, values, and personality traits.

Proposition 11: The degree of satisfaction the individual attains from his work is related to the degree to which he has been able to implement his self-concept in his work.

The individual who finds pleasure and satisfaction in work does so because the position held permits use of characteristics and values in a way that is important. In other words, the experiences encountered in work are compatible with the mental image held of self—they give sufficient opportunity to be the kind of person he/she pictures self to be.

If the work performed does not provide the possibility to be the type of person he/she pictures self to be, discontent develops. This dissatisfaction will usually cause him/her to look for a work situation where the possibility to play the role sought seems brighter.

The relationship of the work situation to the individual's role must be thought of in the broad sense. The professions and higher managerial positions probably provide the greatest opportunities, as viewed by most, for the intrinsic satisfactions that come from work itself. Many individuals gain great satisfaction from work that to some appears boring and monotonous. Other workers find satisfaction in jobs that they, too, may consider routine and unchallenging but that provide them the chance to be the kind of persons they want to be, to do the things they want to do, and to think of themselves as they wish.

Proposition 12: Work and occupation provide a focus for personality organization for most men and many women, although for some persons this focus is peripheral, incidental, or even nonexistent, and other foci such as social activities and the home are central.

Recent changes in the relationship of women to the world of work and the now generally accepted view (mentioned in Chapter 1) of considering homemaking as an occupation make necessary some revision in this proposition if it is to have relevance today. Essentially, the major point here is that for many people, regardless of the nature of the job they fill, the work they do is an expression of their personalities. For other individuals, both men and women, the work in which they engage is simply a means to an end and they seek opportunities for self-expression in places other than their work.

The extensive writing that Super and his colleagues have placed in the professional literature is based solidly on research. Much of Super's research has been longitudinal in nature and focused on a group of ninth grade boys who were first studied in 1951. This group has been regularly followed since that time in a study planned for a twenty-year period. In addition to these studies, many other writers have built hypotheses on Super's theory, many of which are reviewed by Osipow.[29]

TIEDEMAN AND O'HARA'S THEORY OF CAREER DEVELOPMENT

As indicated earlier, the proposal of a theoretical position by one individual influences another to react, question, modify, and counter-propose. In such manner are the writings of Tiedeman and of Tiedeman and O'Hara related to the work of Super and also to Ginzberg and his associates.[30,31,32] Tiedeman and O'Hara have drawn certain concepts from both sources and then proceeded to modify or develop further the earlier proposal.

Tiedeman and O'Hara suggest that career development is a process of organizing an identification with work through the interaction of the individual's personality with society. They consider personality development as a process in which the individual is involved in both differentiation and integration. Differentiation focuses on the ways in which the individual uniquely expresses individuality—in other words, how he/she shows self as different from all other individuals. Integration refers to the ways in which the individual adjusts self to others so that he/she is an acceptable part of society.

Tiedeman and O'Hara suggest that one key aspect of their proposal is an emphasis on the relationship between personality and career as it is developed in the process of making career choices. Like Super, they see career development as spanning most of the individual's lifetime. The vocational aspects of a person's life, if they are not to dominate and control his/her total actions, must be fitted into a larger life pattern. Tiedeman and O'Hara use the term "ego identity" to refer to the personal meanings, values, and relationships on which the individual builds broader integration with society. The ego identity is formed through the interaction of three factors: the individual's biological constitution, psychological make-up, and the society or sub-culture in which he/she exists.

Tiedeman sees decision as crucial in vocational development. The decisions made by the individual regarding school, work, daily activities, and similar facets of total life form and structure vocational development. Each decision includes two periods or aspects; each of these periods has substages, as indicated in the following outline:

  I. The Period of Anticipation
   A. Exploration
   B. Crystallization
   C. Choice
   D. Specification
  II. The Period of Implementation and Adjustment
   A. Induction
   B. Transition
   C. Maintenance

During the exploration stage, the person considers a number of alternatives or possible goals. Within the range of the alternatives is the context of choice. He/she attempts to consider self in relation to the possible choices that are seen. He/she enters the stage of crystallization as the choices become clearer, better understood, and evaluated. As a person chooses a particular goal, this goal influences his/her behavioral system. The greater the certainty with which the choice is made, the greater the impact on behavior. The final stage of the anticipatory period occurs after the choice has been made and before the individual moves to implement the choice. During this specification stage, he/she elaborates and perfects the image anticipated as a result of this choice.

The period of implementation begins as the person moves to act on the choice made. At this stage of induction, the individual is involved in fitting goal and field into the broader framework of the group or of society. As he/she gains confidence, the interaction between person and group expands, and he/she undertakes an effort to incorporate group goals into personal goal and field. If successful, a modification and an accommodation of group and individual goals is the result. The person then enters the maintenance stage, in which he/she tries to continue this satisfying equilibrium.

Tiedeman and O'Hara see the movement from one stage to another as a reversible process so that the person may move in either direction at any given moment. Both advance and retreat occur in the decision-making process. Advancement usually predominates, so the person moves ultimately from indecision to choice to action.

Vocational development is thus seen as the summation of a complex series of decisions made by the individual over a considerable span of time with each previous decision having an impact on later choices. Not all decisions occur longitudinally or sequentially. Thus, at any given moment the person may be at several different stages of choice on related aspects of life. The crystallization and resulting action on one of these aspects has an impact on all of the other aspects that are in process as well as an impact on subsequent decisions. In the same way, the experiences the person encounters as a result of a decision will affect other decisions. The implied role of the counselor is to be a catalyst in freeing the person to make decisions and act on them in relation to choices already made and those still possible.

OTHER THEORIES

The reader who wishes to pursue vocational choice theory will find many helpful articles in the professional literature in addition to those discussed in this chapter. An early article by Bordin focuses attention on vocational choice.[33] More recently, he and his colleagues have proposed a theory of vocational development built on a psychoanalytic orientation.[34] The work of Beilen is helpful in understanding the developmental approach discussed in part with Super's postulates.[35]

Recently, Miller proposed that a learning-theory approach to vocational decisions could contribute to a better understanding of the choice process as well as provide a basis for further theory development.[36] Woody also has proposed the application of behavior therapy, a technique based on learning theory, to problems of vocational choice.[37]

Krumboltz recently described his view of how people move into the occupations they choose.[38] He identifies four influential factors, including: (a) genetic endowment, (b) environmental conditions and events, (c) learning experiences, and (d) task approach skill—in other words the effectiveness of the individual in learning new skills and behaviors. Further, he believes an individual is more likely to express a liking for an activity in which the person has received positive reinforcement or encouragement and is less likely to prefer activities in which no reinforcement was received or in which punishment was encountered.

AN ECLECTIC VIEW

The various positions or "theories" we have considered approach the topic from several different frames of reference; some are based on specific personality theories, others almost totally ignore personality formation, some are concerned with human development throughout lifetime, and others focus on a specific period. There are, of course, many other fundamental differences among them. Osipow has provided an excellent and detailed evaluation of each theory, and the reader who desires more information about each "theory" will find his discussion helpful.[39] If the reader is seeking a briefer critical comparison, the article by Carkhuff, Alexik, and Anderson will be useful.[40]

Since the positions have been developed from differing bases, there is considerable risk in any attempt to mix them together. Nevertheless, there are some generalizations on which several writers appear to agree. These points are useful for us here since they provide the foundation for understanding the topic of career information and how it can be used in helping the individual in the career development process.

The following tentative generalizations are suggested as reflecting the consensus of most of the writers considered earlier in this chapter:

1. The career development process is an ongoing, lifelong aspect of human existence.
2. Since the process is essentially developmental in nature, it is generally predictable but also can be modified by changing circumstances even to the point of being reversible as the individual attempts to optimize the benefits and satisfactions derived from the worker–job relationship.
3. Individuals have differing patterns of ability, interests, and personality as a result of the interaction of genetic inheritance and environmental factors. These characteristics are influenced by parental attitudes and behaviors, by the impact of other role models, and by the experiences that make up the life of the individual.
4. Occupations also have differing patterns of characteristics required or expected of successful workers. In most situations, some accommodation of variation is possible with a "band concept" identifying the tolerable limits for most successful participants.
5. The extent to which a person develops and applies his/her unique pattern of individual characteristics depends on attitudes, motivations, and values. These can be approached either from the basis of psychological need or the development of self-concept. They impinge on the individual's perception of reality (now) and possible reality (future) and probably determine the extent to which the individual responds to existing opportunity.
6. The individual learns about jobs and their relationship to the individual specifically and to society generally from many sources, including the family, peer groups, community, school, media, and the planned and unplanned experiences of everyday life. The attitudes toward and knowledge of work developed in the growth, exploration, and crystallization periods of childhood and adolescence will have lasting influence on the worker–job relationship of the adult years.
7. The optimization that the individual seeks in the worker–job relationship is the product of the interaction between the individual (including abilities, interests, personality, values, etc.) and the realities of his/her situation (including economic conditions, opportunity, and chance factors of either positive or negative value). The ability and desire of the individual to capitalize on these interactions influence the level of optimization.

8. The degree of satisfaction experienced by the worker (either the extent to which the individual's self-concept is implemented or psychological needs are met) is largely determined by the extent to which the potential for optimization is apparent to the individual and is viewed as agreeable and acceptable.

RELATION OF CAREER THEORIES
TO CAREER PLANNING

The theories discussed here let the reader develop a frame of reference by which one can understand the factors that affect the individual involved in the process of career development.

Since most students in schools, as well as out-of-school youth in the adolescent years, are embroiled in this process, it has special importance to teachers and counselors. Most theories emphasize that career development is a long-range, gradual process involving the acquisition of self-understanding and of knowledge of the world of work.[41]

Recognition that the process requires time, study, and adjustment may be helpful in overcoming the impression occasionally met that this is an event, rather than a process, that can be condensed into an afternoon with a counselor or interested teacher.

Probably more important than pushing a boy or girl toward an early, and possibly precipitous, choice is the recognition that there occur in the life of each youth certain crucial points involving key decisions that will later have great influence.[42] Helping to identify these important points in sufficient time so that careful planning by student, school, and parent can be accomplished is one of the significant responsibilities of teachers, counselors, and others who work with youth.[43]

Although the professional literature is replete with theoretical writings, it is important for the counselor and the teacher to approach the literature with some caution. As indicated in the beginning of this chapter, there is now no theory of career development sufficiently refined and substantiated to stand without question. Each theory reviewed in this chapter is still in an embryonic stage, and considerable gestation is necessary before any generalized acceptance is likely to occur. Many factors, including large areas of psychology and sociology that remain inadequately researched, contribute to this state of uncertainty.

NOTES

1. A. Roe, "Early Determinants of Vocational Choice," *Journal of Counseling Psychology,* vol. 4, no. 3 (Fall, 1957), pp. 212–217; D. K. Switzer, A. E. Grigg, J. S. Miller, and R. K. Young, "Early Experiences and Occupational Choice:

A Test of Roe's Hypothesis," *Journal of Counseling Psychology*, vol. 9, no. 1 (Spring, 1962), pp. 45–48; and A. C. Utton, "Recalled Parent-Child Relations as Determinants of Vocational Choice," *Journal of Counseling Psychology*, vol. 9, no. 1 (Spring, 1962), pp. 49–53.

2. B. E. Shertzer and S. C. Stone, *Fundamentals of Counseling*, 2nd edition (Boston: Houghton Mifflin Company, 1974), pp. 236–237.

3. V. H. Hewer, "What Do Theories of Vocational Choice Mean to a Counselor?" *Journal of Counseling Psychology*, vol. 10, no. 2 (Summer, 1963), pp. 118–125.

4. R. R. Carkhuff, M. Alexik, and S. Anderson, "Do We Have a Theory of Vocational Choice?" *Personnel and Guidance Journal*, vol. 46, no. 4 (December, 1967), pp. 335–345.

5. S. H. Osipow, *Theories of Career Development*, 2nd edition (New York: Appleton-Century-Crofts, 1973), pp. 4–9.

6. *Ibid.*

7. J. M. Whiteley and A. Resnikoff (eds.) *Perspectives on Vocational Development* (Washington, D.C.: American Personnel and Guidance Association, 1972).

8. J. J. Pietrofesa and H. Splete, *Career Development: Theory and Research* (New York: Grune and Stratton, 1975).

9. A. H. Maslow, *Motivation and Personality* (New York: Harper and Row, Publishers, 1954).

10. R. Hoppock, *Occupational Information*, 4th edition (New York: McGraw-Hill Book Company, 1976), pp. 90–100.

11. V. A. Kohout and J. W. M. Rothney, "A Longitudinal Study of the Consistency of Vocational Preferences," *American Educational Research Journal*, vol. 1, no. 1 (January, 1964), pp. 10–21.

12. J. L. Holland, "A Theory of Vocational Choice," *Journal of Counseling Psychology*, vol. 6, no. 1 (Spring, 1959), pp. 35–45; "A Theory of Vocational Choice, Part I: Vocational Images and Choice," *Vocational Guidance Quarterly*, vol. 11, no. 4 (Summer, 1963), pp. 232–239; "A Theory of Vocational Choice, Part II: Self Descriptions and Vocational Preferences; Part III: Coping Behavior, Competences and Vocational Preferences," *Vocational Guidance Quarterly*, vol. 12, no. 1 (Autumn, 1963), pp. 17–24; "A Theory of Vocational Choice, Part IV: Vocational Daydreams," *Vocational Guidance Quarterly*, vol. 12, no. 2 (Winter, 1963), pp. 93–97; *The Psychology of Vocational Choice* (Waltham, Mass.: Blaisdell Publishing Company, 1966); "A Psychological Classification Scheme for Vocations and Major Fields," *Journal of Counseling Psychology*, vol. 13, no. 3 (Fall, 1966), pp. 278–288; *Making Vocational Choices: A Theory of Careers* (Englewood Cliffs, N.J.: Prentice-Hall, Inc., 1973); and J. L. Holland and R. C. Nichols, "Explorations of a Theory of Vocational Choice: III, A Longitudinal Study of Change in Major Fields of Study," *Personnel and Guidance Journal*, vol. 43, no. 3 (November, 1964), pp. 235–242; J. L. Holland and S. W. Lutz, "The Predictive Value of a Student's Choice of Vocation," *Personnel and Guidance Journal*, vol. 46, no. 5 (January, 1968), pp. 428–436; J. L. Holland, "The Present Status of a Theory of Vocational Choice," *Perspectives on Vocational Development*, eds., J. M. Whiteley and A. Resnikoff (Washington: American Personnel and Guidance Association, 1972), pp. 35–59.

13. H. A. Murray, *Explorations in Personality* (New York: Oxford Press, 1938).
14. A. Roe, "Analysis of Group Rorschachs of Biologists," *Journal of Projective Techniques*, vol. 13, no. 1 (March, 1949), pp. 25–43; "Psychological Examinations of Eminent Biologists," *Journal of Consulting Psychology*, vol. 13, no. 4 (August, 1949), pp. 225–246; "Analysis of Group Rorschachs of Physical Scientists," *Journal of Projective Techniques*, vol. 14, no. 4 (December, 1950), pp. 385–398; "A Psychological Study of Eminent Biologists," *Psychological Monographs*, vol. 65, no. 14; "A Psychological Study of Eminent Physical Scientists," *Genetic Psychology Monograph*, no. 43 (1951), pp. 121–239; "A Study of Imagery in Research Scientists," *Journal of Personality*, vol. 19, no. 4 (December, 1951), pp. 459–470; "Psychological Tests of Research Scientists," *Journal of Consulting Psychology*, vol. 15, no. 6 (December, 1951), pp. 492–495; "Analysis of Group Rorschachs of Psychologists and Anthropologists," *Journal of Projective Techniques*, vol. 16, no. 2 (June, 1952), pp. 212–224; "Group Rorschachs of University Faculties," *Journal of Consulting Psychology*, vol. 16, no. 1 (February, 1952), pp. 18–22; "A Psychological Study of Eminent Psychologists and Anthropologists and a Comparison With Biological and Physical Scientists," *Psychological Monographs*, vol. 67, no. 2 (1953).
15. A. Roe, "Early Determinants of Vocational Choice," *Journal of Counseling Psychology*, vol. 4, no. 3 (Fall, 1957), pp. 212–217.
16. A. Roe and M. Siegelman, *The Origin of Interests.* APGA Inquiry Studies No. 1. (Washington, D.C.: American Personnel and Guidance Association, 1964), pp. 5–6.
17. E. Ginzberg, S. W. Ginsburg, S. Axelrad, and J. L. Herma, *Occupational Choice: An Approach to a General Theory* (New York: Columbia University Press, 1951).
18. C. Buehler, *Der Menschliche Lebenslauf als Psychologisches Problem* (Leipzig: Hirzel, 1933).
19. E. Ginzberg, "Toward a Theory of Occupational Choice: A Restatement," *Vocational Guidance Quarterly*, vol. 20, no. 3 (March, 1972), pp. 169–176.
20. D. E. Super, "Vocational Adjustment: Implementing a Self-Concept," *Occupations*, vol. 30, no. 1 (September, 1951), pp. 1–5; "A Theory of Vocational Development," *American Psychologist*, vol. 8, no. 5 (May, 1953), pp. 185–90; "Career Patterns as a Basis for Vocational Counseling," *Journal of Counseling Psychology*, vol. 1, no. 1 (Spring, 1954), pp. 12–20; "Personality Integration Through Vocational Counseling," *Journal of Counseling Psychology*, vol. 2, no. 3 (Fall, 1955), pp. 217–226; with others, *Vocational Development: A Framework for Research* (New York: Teachers College Press, Columbia University, 1957); *The Psychology of Careers* (New York: Harper and Row, 1957); with P. B. Bachrach, *Scientific Careers and Vocational Development Theory* (New York: Teachers College Press, Columbia University, 1957); "The Critical Ninth Grade: Vocational Choice or Vocational Exploration," *Personnel and Guidance Journal*, vol. 39, no. 2 (October, 1960), pp. 106–109; "Some Unresolved Issues in Vocational Development Research," *Personnel and Guidance Journal*, vol. 40, no. 1 (September, 1961), pp. 11–14; "Consistency and Wisdom of Vocational Preference as Indices of Vocational Maturity in the Ninth Grade," *Journal of Educational Psychology*, vol. 52, no. 1 (February, 1961), pp. 35–43; with others, *Career Development: Self-Concept*

Theory. (New York: CEEB Research Monograph No. 4, 1963); "A Developmental Approach to Vocational Guidance," *Vocational Guidance Quarterly,* vol. 13, no. 1 (September, 1964), pp. 1–10; "Goal Specificity in the Vocational Counseling of Future College Students," *Personnel and Guidance Journal,* vol. 43, no. 2 (October, 1964), pp. 127–134.

21. Buehler, *op. cit.*
22. Donald E. Super and others, *Vocational Development: A Framework for Research* (New York: Teachers College Press, Columbia University, 1957).
23. Robert P. O'Hara and David V. Tiedeman, "Vocational Self-Concept in Adolescence," *Journal of Counseling Psychology,* vol. 6, no. 4 (Winter, 1959), pp. 292–301.
24. F. L. Field, C. D. Kehas, and D. V. Tiedeman, "The Self-Concept in Career Development: A Construct in Transition," *Personnel and Guidance Journal,* vol. 41, no. 9 (May, 1963), pp. 767–771.
25. Donald E. Super and others, *Career Development: Self-Concept Theory* (New York: College Entrance Examination Board, 1963).
26. D. Hagen, "Careers and Family Atmospheres: An Empirical Test of Roe's Theory," *Journal of Counseling Psychology,* vol. 7, no. 4 (Winter, 1960), pp. 251–256.
27. R. J. Smith, C. E. Ramsey, and G. Castillo, "Parental Authority and Job Choice: Sex Differences in Three Cultures," *American Journal of Sociology,* vol. 69, no. 2 (September, 1963), pp. 143–149.
28. Lawrence Lipsett, "Social Factors in Vocational Development," *Personnel and Guidance Journal,* vol. 40, no. 5 (January, 1962), pp. 432–437.
29. Osipow, *op. cit.*
30. R. P. O'Hara and D. V. Tiedeman, "Vocational Self-Concept in Adolescence," *Journal of Counseling Psychology,* vol. 6, no. 4 (Winter, 1959), pp. 292–301.
31. D. V. Tiedeman, "Decision and Vocational Development: A Paradigm and Its Implications," *Personnel and Guidance Journal,* vol. 40, no. 1 (September, 1961), pp. 15–20.
32. D. V. Tiedeman and R. P. O'Hara, *Career Development: Choice and Adjustment* (New York: College Entrance Examination Board, 1963).
33. E. S. Bordin, "A Theory of Vocational Interests as Dynamic Phenomena," *Educational and Psychological Measurement,* vol. 3, no. 1 (Spring, 1943), pp. 49–65.
34. E. S. Bordin, B. Nachmann, and S. J. Segal, "An Articulated Framework for Vocational Development," *Journal of Counseling Psychology,* vol. 10, no. 2 (Summer, 1963), pp. 107–117.
35. Harry Beilin, "The Application of General Developmental Principles to the Vocational Area," *Journal of Counseling Psychology,* vol. 2, no. 1 (Spring, 1955), pp. 53–57.
36. A. W. Miller, Jr., "Learning Theory and Vocational Decisions," *Personnel and Guidance Journal,* vol. 47, no. 1 (September, 1968), pp. 18–23.
37. R. H. Woody, "Vocational Counseling With Behavioral Techniques," *Vocational Guidance Quarterly,* vol. 17, no. 2 (December, 1968), pp. 97–103.
38. J. D. Krumboltz, Presidential Address—Division 17, American Psychological Association Convention, Chicago, September, 1975.
39. Osipow, *op. cit.*
40. Carkhuff, Alexik, and Anderson, *op. cit.*

41. T. L. Hilton, "Career Decision-Making," *Journal of Counseling Psychology,* vol. 9, no. 4 (Winter, 1962), pp. 291–298.
42. P. Glick, Jr., "Anticipated Occupational Frustration," *Vocational Guidance Quarterly,* vol. 11, no. 2 (Winter, 1963), pp. 91–95.
43. Lloyd Meadow, "Toward a Theory of Vocational Choice," *Journal of Counseling Psychology,* vol. 2, no. 2 (Summer, 1955), pp. 108–112.

PART I   Supplementary Learning Experiences

The following activities are proposed as ways in which the reader can easily test, explore, or apply the concepts and insights presented in Part I. The list is not intended to be exhaustive or comprehensive, but merely suggestive.

1. Drawing on your own developmental experiences, propose *your* theory of career development.
2. Interview at least two or three older workers and develop a career history for each. Relate each history to a theory of career development.
3. Interview two or three youngsters from each level—elementary, junior high, senior high school—to identify their career plans and the rationale they have used in planning.
4. Interview two or three school principals on each level to determine the efforts made by each school to assist its students in career development.
5. Interview two or three teachers at each level to determine what helps they feel their school provides for career development.
6. Interview two or three school counselors to identify their viewpoint of career counseling.
7. Interview two or three parents of children at each level to identify the career development help they want the school to provide for their children.

PART

II

Factors Influencing Workers and Their Careers

3

Psychological and Physical Factors

Acceptance of the idea of individual differences among people is now so widespread that it is no longer necessary to build a case for it. Such differences are created and emphasized through the interaction of the biological inheritance, the specific environment that surrounds the individual, and the unique characteristics of the person. The differences are both psychological and physical.

The theories of career development, which we considered in the previous chapter, are all based on the principle of individual differences. Roe and Hoppock, for example, emphasize the influence of psychological need in vocational choice. Super's postulates clearly specify the relevance of individual differences. Tiedeman stresses the unique interaction between personality and the surrounding environment. This acceptance of the concept of individual differences carries with it the assumption that such differences are identifiable and measurable. Thus we find that undergirding each of the theories of career development is the trait and factor theory. Each theory that we considered goes beyond the basic idea that people are different by focusing on how the individual expresses and exploits these differences.

In this chapter, we will consider some of the interrelationships between the worker and the job. We are proceeding from the assumption that the individual has a unique pattern of abilities, interests, and other personality components, and that each occupation similarly has a characteristic pattern of traits that it requires of the worker. The spectrum of personal characteristics of the individual is broad enough for the typical person to meet the patterns required in a wide variety of jobs. Conversely, the pattern demanded by a specific job has sufficient flexibility and tolerance to accommodate a wide variety of prospective job holders.

This set of premises runs a double danger of misinterpretation. If erroneously taken in the broadest possible context, one would be forced to say that each individual has the personal characteristics that make possible success in any job and that the pattern required by every job is a universal one found in all people. The indefensibility of such a position is obvious when one contemplates the possibility of a color-blind paint mixer, or an accountant without numerical aptitude. At the other extreme, one could be forced to postulate that each individual is so unique that there exists only one job, or more precisely one position, that can be filled successfully and that each position is so demanding that only one individual can perform in it successfully. If such specificity were widespread, our complex society soon would be totally immobilized by the impossible task of matching individuals and positions.

A much more realistic viewpoint is one that assumes that most human characteristics, as well as job requirements, spread out over a normal distribution. A few individuals and some jobs do have such unique characteristics that only a few possible matches exist at any given time (some of the artistic positions, for example, such as Metropolitan Opera soloist). Other characteristics are so universal and the tasks so elemental that one might conclude that practically every person meets at least the minimum requirements for the jobs. Most people and most occupations fall somewhere between these two extremes; we must, therefore, conclude that some considerations must be given to balancing human characteristics against occupational demands, if success and satisfaction are to be maximized for the individual and productivity and effectiveness assured for the occupation.

Psychologists tell us that much remains to be learned about the human personality and its components. At best, we have incomplete theories and crude instruments that provide some information, although often sketchy and vague. In some sectors, research has already resulted in the development of instruments and techniques that provide valid and reliable information.[1] The professional psychologist, however, is always aware that even when he/she uses the broadest possible range of instruments, in the most exact manner, under ideal circumstances, he/she can hope, at best, for only a partial picture of the individual. Other behavioral scientists face almost identical problems when they attempt to study the world of work. Occupations, like people, are dynamic and frequently changing.

The concept of vocational counseling as the business of "putting square pegs in square holes" implies ascertaining the characteristics of the individual and matching these against the known characteristics demanded by occupations. Although the concept probably contains a germ of truth, it oversimplifies reality. Both the pegs and the holes have many dimensions, some of which can be measured only approximately or not at all.

Vocational counselors find themselves in the same dilemma that many other professional people encounter. They are dependent on other professions for the tools, techniques, and knowledge that they must use in the practice of their art. Until these are adequately developed, their work remains inexact and restricted. On the other hand, the increasing complexity of society, with its greater concern for all individuals and its greater dependence on the effective use of all human resources, requires the counselor to use the skill and knowledge presently available.

The counselor and the teacher who wish to use career information effectively, either in the counseling room or the classroom, must focus constantly on the multi-dimensionality of both individual and job and on the interrelationship of the two.

This chapter will look at the psychological and physical requirements that the occupation imposes on the worker and at the hiring requirements imposed by the employer. In other words, we are addressing the question "What kind of psychological characteristics and how much of each must a worker have to perform successfully this particular task?" We are not here concerned with "What are workers who perform this task like?" To some extent the responses to the two questions may be expected to overlap, but the approach to each is from opposite sides of the equation.

Hewer has pointed out that one criticism of the trait and factor theory is the belief that it is not possible to describe all dimensions of personality.[2] This criticism is equally valid when applied to the dimensions of work. Each position, like each person, is so tremendously complex that we do not yet have either an adequate taxonomy or precise measurement instruments capable of classifying each position. Nevertheless, it is possible to perceive some of the broader relationships between man and work, and our discussion will focus on these.

One of the basic resources for anyone involved in assisting others in the career development process is the *Dictionary of Occupational Titles*.[3] It serves a wide variety of purposes, provides a tremendous quantity of information, and is invaluable as a tool for counselors and others. In the *Dictionary*, occupations are assigned a code number based on the occupation's relationship to other occupations and on the extent to which the worker is involved in the treatment of data, people, or things in the task he/she performs. The first half of this classification system is called the "Occupational Group Arrangement" and the second part is called the "Worker Traits Arrangement." These arrangements will be considered in more detail in Chapter 6. Within the "Worker Traits Arrangement" consideration is given to the qualification factors with which we are here concerned.

The material included in this section of the *Dictionary* has been developed primarily by the use of job analysis, in which the worker is studied in his/her work situation by a skilled and trained observer. Reports by many job analysts observing workers who are presumably assigned to do the same job in a wide variety of settings are compiled, and from these a general statement based on the commonalities is synthesized. Such information is extremely valuable in providing a general picture of the occupation as it exists most commonly. One must, however, keep in mind that this is a general picture and not a specific picture. To say that American men are, on the average, 68 inches tall does not rule out the fact that many are shorter than 54 inches, or taller than 80. At the same time, the existence of such deviation does not minimize the value of measures of central tendency and the statements that can be based on them.

Early attention to these various worker characteristics was shown by the publication in 1955 of a now out-of-print volume entitled *Estimates of Worker Trait Requirements for 4,000 Jobs.*[4] This early volume provided a summary of the estimated psychological and physical requirements of a group of representative occupations. This pioneer work has now been expanded to cover all coded occupations in the *Dictionary.* It has been incorporated into the *Dictionary* itself under the heading of "Qualifications Profile" as part of the "Worker Traits Arrangement" in Volume II.

The major portion of this chapter will focus on those items included in the "Qualifications Profile" as illustrative of information available about psychological and physical requirements of jobs. The items in the "Qualifications Profile" include:

Training Time
Aptitudes
Interests
Temperaments
Physical Demands

Aptitudes, interests, and temperament are commonly considered to be psychological factors. We will consider each of these attributes briefly, focusing on what these characteristics are and on how they relate to work. As we examine each characteristic, we will briefly mention tests frequently used to measure each trait. Detailed study of measurement instruments properly belongs elsewhere, since our purpose is only to identify examples of tests associated with each area. Each factor can also be estimated with techniques other than formal assessment devices. Since the best resource for this approach is the Worker Traits Arrangement in the *Dictionary,* we also will consider non-test assessment when we study the *Dictionary* in Chapter 6. Some extensive research projects have collected valuable data in these areas, so we will examine representative samples of these.

Training time, which refers to the special educational preparation required of the worker, will be examined, as will items that are essentially physical in nature, such as Physical Capacities and Demands and also Working Conditions. The final section of the chapter will consider Hiring Requirements—demands made by the employer of the worker that may exceed the requirements actually needed to perform the job satisfactorily.

APTITUDES

As used in the *Dictionary*, aptitudes are defined as specific capacities and abilities required of an individual in order to learn or adequately perform a task or job duty.[5, 6, 7, 8] Much research has been completed and numerous articles and books published dealing with the subject of aptitudes. Any attempt to provide a complete bibliography in this area would require a volume in itself. *Aptitudes and Aptitude Testing* by Bingham[9] is an early classic in this field. More recent volumes would include Super and Crites' *Appraising Vocational Fitness through Psychological Means,*[10] Goldman's *Using Tests in Counseling,*[11] and Cronbach's *Essentials of Psychological Testing.*[12]

Super points out that the term "aptitude" often is used in a confusing manner by coupling the term with an occupation and thus speaking of "aptitude for teaching." Such usage implies a broad general characteristic related to the specific occupation. Recent research results indicate that "aptitude" is more properly used to refer to a specific psychological factor that contributes in varying degree to success in various occupations. It is a capacity or potential that has stability, unity, and independence. Different authors report varying numbers of aptitudes, partly explained by input factors such as the types of psychological measurements included, statistical treatment factors, and subjective factors such as grouping and classifying results.

The *Dictionary* includes aptitude material based on several years' experience by the Employment Service in using the *General Aptitude Test Battery* to measure aptitudes found important in job success. Some of the material reported is based on actual test norm data for specific occupations; most of the data listed, however, are estimates of needed aptitudes based on job analysis information.

Eleven aptitudes are included: G—Intelligence; V—Verbal; N—Numerical; S—Spatial; P—Form Perception; Q—Clerical Perception; K—Motor Coordination; F—Finger Dexterity; M—Manual Dexterity; E—Eye-Hand-Foot Coordination; C—Color Discrimination. Definitions of each aptitude will be quoted below.

Five levels are used to indicate the extent of each aptitude required, except for Intelligence, for which the lowest two levels are combined. The aptitude levels are indicative of that proportion of the working population possessing the aptitude to a degree necessary for satisfactory job performance. The following scale is used:

1. The top 10 percent of the population. This segment of the population possesses an extremely high degree of the aptitude.
2. The highest third exclusive of the top 10 percent of the population. This segment of the population possesses an above average or high degree of the aptitude.

3. The middle third of the population. This segment of the population possesses a medium degree of the aptitude, ranging from slightly below to slightly above average.
4. The lowest third exclusive of the bottom 10 percent of the population. This segment of the population possesses a below average or low degree of the aptitude.
5. The lowest 10 percent of the population. This segment of the population possesses a negligible degree of the aptitude.

The digit indicates how much of each aptitude the job requires for satisfactory or average performance. The average requirements, rather than maximum or minimum, are used in the *Dictionary*. Each worker trait qualifications profile includes an indication of the amount of each aptitude required for average performance in the jobs within that broad area.

The following illustrative situations are drawn from Appendix B of *Estimates* to provide a definition of each of the 11 aptitudes and an occupational example of several of the levels for each aptitude.[13]

APTITUDE G—INTELLIGENCE

General learning ability. The ability to "catch on" or understand instructions and underlying principles. Ability to reason and make judgments. Closely related to doing well in school.

Level 1

Underwriter (insurance): Decides whether applicants for insurance are justifiable risks. Brings into play a knowledge of insurance, finance, and economics. Must be able to read a medical report and understand it. Must be informed on occupations and their hazards. Must have the ability to work with actuarial formulae. Must have the capacity to study and relate all phases of an insurance problem and come to a decision beneficial to the needs of the applicant and to the interests of the company.

Level 2

Draftsman, Topographical (profess. & kin.): Drafts topographical maps using surveying notes, topographical photographs, and other maps. Computational, geographical, and geological knowledges are involved, as well as drafting principles. Transferring the various types of information from original sources and planning the map according to the purpose for which intended requires the ability to interpret a variety of technical data.

Level 3

Mail Sorter (clerical): Separates mail into pigeon holes of mail rack according to state, address, name of person, organization, or other scheme. Recognizing and identifying types of mail and sorting rapidly requires full understanding of procedures on part of worker. Exercises alertness and judgment in taking care of improperly addressed mail, checking for correct address, and marking for return mail that belongs elsewhere.

APTITUDE V—VERBAL

Ability to understand meanings of words and ideas associated with them, and to use them effectively. To comprehend language, to understand relationships between words, and to understand meanings of whole sentences and paragraphs. To present information or ideas clearly.

Level 1

Editor, Newspaper (print. & pub.): Writes leading or policy editorials. Must write clearly, briefly, and accurately descriptions and interpretations of events, things, and people. Must write rapidly in a grammatical, well-organized manner in order to meet deadlines with which constantly confronted. Must be able to select vocabulary and style in accordance with reading tastes of particular public for which writing. Vocabulary must be adequate for expression in political, economic, labor, social, scientific, and other specialized fields, on a non-technical basis.

Level 2

Teacher, High School (education): Teaches academic subjects to high school students. Must understand language of textbooks and related material on subject taught and be able to choose words and sentences to most effectively "put across" subjects to pupils. Must be able to handle technical terms specific to subject as well as usual and common conversational terms.

Level 3

Salesperson, General (ret. tr.): Displays, explains, and sells merchandise to customers. Uses effective questioning techniques to find out from customers make, type, size, design, and quantity of merchandise wanted. Assists customer to make a selection by suggestions and explanations. Emphasizes chief selling points of articles, slanting his conversation toward this end. Tells the customer how to use article. Must be able to use ordinary levels of speech effectively to present ideas calculated to produce desired response in customer.

APTITUDE N—NUMERICAL

Ability to perform arithmetic operations quickly and accurately.

Level 1

Mechanical Engineer (profess. & kin.): Designs tools, engines, and machines, and supervises mechanical industrial processes. Employs empirical and differential equations to solve the fundamental relationships of an operation and designs industrial equipment to conform to the requirements of an industrial process.

Level 2

Bookkeeping–Machine Operator (clerical) I: Maintains records of all financial transactions of an establishment, recording on special forms and in journals by operating a bookkeeping machine. Keeps up-to-date records of cash paid out, cash received, and similar items. Adds and checks figures in the separate journals and copies results in general ledger, adding and checking. Balances books and compiles reports at regular intervals to show receipts, expenditures, accounts payable, accounts receivable, profit and loss, and other items.

Level 3

Boilermaker (boilermaking): Fabricates and assembles boilers, tanks, vats, and other vessels made of heavy steel plate. Lays out work according to blueprints, drawings, or specifications by marking on plate all curves, lines, points, and directions for subsequent fabricating operations. Must be able to employ shop mathematics in the laying out of the work and in the calculation of dimensions.

Level 4

Counter (hat & cap): Counts and weighs bundles of fur pelts as they are received and enters weights in stock records.

APTITUDE S—SPATIAL

Ability to comprehend forms in space and understand relationships of plane and solid objects. May be used in such tasks as blueprint reading and in solving geometry problems. Frequently described as the ability to "visualize" objects of two or three dimensions, or to think visually of geometric forms.

Level 1

Dentist (profess. & kin.): Practices dentistry. Extracts, cleans, fills, and replaces teeth. Performs surgery on jaw or mouth. Makes and fits false teeth. Must have a thorough knowledge of oral anatomy and denture construction. Must be able to construct partial and complete dentures that are attractive, fit the patient's mouth precisely, and with which the patient's teeth oppose each other properly. Must be able to easily visualize relationships of forms in space in order to work with precision on teeth and gums which he observes not directly, but in dentist's mirror. Must be able to picture correctly the arteries, nerves, muscles, and tendons underlying the body surface as he performs surgical procedures.

Level 2

Machinist (mach. shop): Constructs and performs major repairs of all kinds of metal parts, tools, and machines. Shapes metal parts to precise dimensions. Observes mechanical malfunctioning of machines and equipment and makes necessary repairs on own diagnosis. Sets up (positions and aligns) machines such as lathes and shapers to perform many different cutting operations in order to achieve various angles, radii, contour types, and linear dimensions.

Level 3

Carpenter (const.): Performs general carpentry work. Must read blueprints and visualize structures to be built. Must understand the relationship and proper position of one member being fitted to the whole.

Level 4

Wrapper Layer (tobacco): Lays wrapper tobacco leaf on cigar-making machine and operates machine which cuts cigar wrapper and rolls it around filler bunch to make the cigar. Places tobacco leaf on die of soft-work cigar-making machine in such a manner as to obtain maximum cuts per leaf.

APTITUDE P—FORM PERCEPTION

Ability to perceive pertinent detail in objects or in pictorial or graphic material. To make visual comparisons and discriminations and see slight differences in shapes and shadings of figures and widths and lengths of lines.

Level 1

No bench marks.

Level 2

Draftsman, Topographical (*profess. & kin.*): Drafts, corrects, and compiles topographical maps. Works from drawings, maps, and other pictorial material. Must be able to detect slight differences in shapes, lines, and shadings so as to accurately identify and plot objects or terrain in true relationships.

Level 3

Paperhanger (*const.*): Covers interior of room with strips of wallpaper or fabric. Matches adjacent edges of figured paper. Notes detail in design of paper and matches pieces so that no discontinuity of pieces is discernible. Notes appearance of paste mixed to judge when it is of right consistency. Must be able to decide when wall has been well enough cleaned to receive new paper.

Level 4

Furniture Assembler (*furn.*): Performs hand carpentry to assemble and fasten together prefabricated parts into frames, sections, or complete articles of furniture. Must inspect point of assembly to make sure joints appear straight and clean (free from glue).

APTITUDE Q—CLERICAL PERCEPTION

Ability to perceive pertinent detail in verbal or tabular material. To observe differences in copy, to proofread words and numbers, and to avoid perceptual errors in arithmetic computation.

Level 1

Proofreader (*print. & pub.*): Reads typescript or proof of type set-up to detect and mark for correction any grammatical, typographical, or compositional errors, checking proof against original copy. Must be able to quickly and accurately detect errors not only of different kinds of symbols, such as letters and numbers, but variations in the symbols, such as type faces, styles, and sizes.

Level 2

Bookkeeping-Machine Operator (*clerical*) *I*: Keeps set of records of business transactions, using bookkeeping machine. Extracts from sales slips, invoices, purchase orders, bills, statements, etc., such information as name and address of seller or sellee, items sold or purchased, services rendered or received, and purchase or sale price. Simultaneously records this data on sheets by quickly and accurately pressing keys of bookkeeping machine. Pays constant and close attention to avoid errors in reading and transposing names and numbers involved.

Level 3

Cashier-Wrapper (ret. tr.): Acts as a cashier and wraps merchandise sold to customer. Checks amount shown on cash register with amount of sales check. (Sales person rings up amount of sale on cash register.) Compares sales ticket on merchandise with sales check to insure against under or over charges. Prepares daily receipt records.

Level 4

Machinist (mach. shop): Constructs metal parts, tools, and machines. Works from shop orders, blueprints, sketches, and applicable specifications. Checks work during operation using micrometers, scales, feeler gages, calipers, etc.

APTITUDE K—MOTOR COORDINATION

Ability to coordinate eyes and hands or fingers rapidly and accurately in making precise movements with speed. Ability to make a movement response accurately and quickly.

Level 1

No bench marks.

Level 2

Key-Punch Operator (clerical): Records statistical data on tabulating cards by operating a keyboard machine to punch a series of holes in cards, following a specified sequence. The punching is performed by "touch," the fingers striking the appropriate keys as the eyes follow the copy. Finger movements are simultaneous with visual signals and are almost more rapid than the eye of an observer can follow.

Level 3

Engine-Lathe Operator (mach. shop) II: Shapes cylindrical metal surfaces with an engine lathe, performing simple repetitive operations. Turns handwheel to feed cutting tool into workpiece. Constantly regulates hand movements to coordinate advance of tool with amount of metal removed.

Level 4

Fruit Cutter, Hand (can. & preserv.): Cuts fresh fruits and vegetables into halves, quarters, or slices with small paring knife. Worker must constantly keep eyes on items being cut and control motion of knife accordingly in order to pare to size, remove faulty spots, and avoid knife wounds.

APTITUDE F—FINGER DEXTERITY

Ability to move the fingers and manipulate small objects with the fingers rapidly or accurately.

Level 1

Surgeon (medical ser.) I: Operates upon the human body, incising the flesh with very sharp-bladed scalpels and using the fingers to manipulate organs and tissue. Finger movements must be precise and are frequently carried out with great speed when working against time because of a patient's critical condition.

Level 2

Engraver, Jewelry (jewelry): Cuts ornamental designs in jewelry. Must make precise nimble finger movements in manipulating triangular-pointed engraving tools to cut complicated but delicate designs on small objects such as pins and rings.

Level 3

Weaver (textile): Operates looms to produce cloth. Repairs breaks in warp fibers, working swiftly while loom is stopped. Ties short piece of warp fiber to one end of broken warp, using a weaver's knot, and draws it through drop wires, harnesses, and reed, using a reed hook. Nimble finger movements must be employed in tying weaver's knot, a knot that is practically invisible when completed.

APTITUDE M—MANUAL DEXTERITY

Ability to move the hands easily and skillfully. To work with the hands in placing and turning motions.

Level 1

No bench marks.

Level 2

Airplane mechanic (air trans.): Repairs all parts of airplanes except engines, using hand tools. Moves hands easily and skillfully in using hand tools and positioning workpiece. Bends hand at wrist and turns them from side to side in connecting wiring and tubing, and in holding assembly units in place in the installation process.

Level 3

Sewing-Machine Operator, Style Garment (garment): Using electrically powered sewing machine, performs miscellaneous operations on style garments. Continuous turning and placing movements of hand are required in assembling pieces to be sewed together, placing cloth under needle on machine, and guiding cloth as it is being sewed.

APTITUDE E—EYE-HAND-FOOT COORDINATION

Ability to move the hand and foot coordinately with each other in accordance with visual stimuli. (Not measured by GATB.)

Level 1

Baseball Player (amuse. & rec.): Plays big league, professional baseball. Must coordinate the movements of the hands and the feet with what the eye sees. Uses this coordination in catching, hitting, and throwing the ball. Successful playing depends on split-second eye-hand-foot coordinations taking place while the body constantly shifts position in space in relation to the ball.

Level 2

Structural-Steel Worker (const.): Works as a member of a crew engaged in raising, positioning, and joining structural-steel members such as girders, plates, and columns. Often works at great heights, balancing on ladders and scaffolds, at the same time performing skilled manual operations requiring visual coordination.

Level 3

Longshoreman (water trans.): Loads and unloads ships' cargoes. Must coordinate hand and foot motions with vision when engaging in such activities as carrying goods over narrow gangplank to and from ship; standing on boxes, ladders, or other objects to stack and arrange cargo high in the hold; and bracing and blocking objects to insure their stability during the voyage, however rough it may be.

Level 4

Paper Cutter (any ind.): Cuts paper. Holds sheets of paper against guides and sets guides. Steps on a treadle causing knife to descend through the paper. Coordinates the hand movements with what the eye sees as he holds paper against guides and steps on treadle.

APTITUDE C—COLOR DISCRIMINATION

Ability to perceive or recognize similarities or differences in colors, or in shades or other values of the same color. To identify a particular color, or to recognize harmonious or contrasting color combinations, or to match colors accurately. (Not measured by GATB.)

Level 1

Color Matcher (plastics mat.): Develops color formulas. Selects and combines appropriate dyestuffs and pigments to achieve desired color. Must be able to distinguish minute differences in shades and must have the capacity to visualize the hue and brilliance which will result from mixing the primary colors in various proportions.

Level 2

Interior Decorator (profess. & kin.): Designs interiors of rooms and other indoor areas. Must be well informed on the values of color in interior decorating and capable of choosing color schemes which are pleasing to client as well as in good taste.

Level 3

Floral Designer (ret. tr.): Makes floral designs. Must distinguish color and shade when designing and fashioning bouquets, corsages, sprays, wreaths, and in decorating buildings with flowers. For the most part works with floral designs which require the matching and contrasting of colors according to specifications but not the devising of color arrangements.

Level 4

Dye Weigher (knit goods): Weighs out powdered dyestuff, oils, acids, and chemicals called for on written order and dumps into pail for mixing. Although containers of dyestuff are numbered, worker should be able to distinguish the colors visually.

As indicated at the beginning of this section, the aptitudes that we have been considering are based on the General Aptitude Test Battery. This instrument was developed for use in the occupational counseling program of the United States Training and Employment Service and is now used throughout the State Employment Services. It is available for counseling purposes in schools and other nonprofit institutions. The GATB has been widely used and researched for many years; in fact, *The Seventh Mental Measurements Yearbook* includes more than 400 bibliographic references.[14] It was originally developed as an attempt to test significant aptitudes and to relate the obtained results to a wide range of occupations. Its present form tests nine of the eleven aptitudes just listed; neither eye-hand-foot coordination nor color discrimination is included in the test battery.

Relating test scores to occupations has been accomplished by developing *Occupational Aptitude Patterns*. The OAP's establish minimum qualifying scores on three appropriate aptitudes for specific occupations. The minimum cutting score has usually been established at the point above which two-thirds of the workers in the specific occupation would score. The normative data have been developed on results obtained by testing employed members of the various occupations. Thus, the scores obtained by a given individual can be directly compared to scores of actual workers in a specific occupation or a wide array of occupations at different skill levels. In addition to using the total test, it is possible to use various combinations of the 12 tests, called Specific Aptitude Test Batteries, to produce minimum cutting scores on two, three, or four aptitudes deemed most important for a specific occupation. Recently, reported research has expanded the number of OAP's as well as relating the OAP's to the Worker Function Groups of the *Dictionary of Occupational Titles* (which we will consider in Chapter 6). This work now provides 62 Occupational Aptitude Patterns connected to 87 of the Worker Function Groups, covering approximately 90 per cent of those occupations for which validity data exist.[15]

A well-established, frequently used test in high schools is the *Differential Aptitude Test*. Originally published in 1947, it has become very widely used, with revisions being published in 1962 and again in 1972. Standardization has been carefully developed on a nation-wide sample that purports to meet the frequent criticisms of geographic, socio-economic, or minority bias. All editions of the DAT have included tests of the following aptitudes:

Verbal reasoning
Numerical ability
Mechanical reasoning
Spelling
Language usage
Abstract reasoning
Clerical speed and accuracy
Space relations

Total testing time is somewhat more than three hours, with individual sections ranging from six to thirty minutes. Norms are available by sex and grade level for high school students.

Forms S & T, the 1972 edition, include provisions for a Career Planning Program. This service requires the completion of an additional form —a Career Planning Questionnaire—at the time the test is administered. The Career Planning Report is then prepared as a computer print-out, which compares the student's aptitude scores with stated occupational preferences, subjects and activities liked best, and educational plans.

INTERESTS

Bingham defines interests as a tendency to become absorbed in an experience and to continue it. Super[16] has suggested that there are four types of interests, primarily varying with the method of assessment. These are:

1. *Expressed interests* are verbal expressions or claims of specific interest.
2. *Manifest interests* are expressed through actions and participation.
3. *Inventoried interests* are estimates of interest based upon responses to a set of questions concerning likes and dislikes. Particularly well known illustrations of this method of assessment are the *Strong Vocational Interest Blank*[17] and the *Kuder Preference Record.*[18]
4. *Tested interests* are interests which are manifested under controlled situations.

The professional literature reveals considerable emphasis on the area of interests, with many pertinent articles of value to the reader. Gerken has emphasized the importance of interests in the educational and vocational planning process.[19] He has proposed several guidelines that are apropos for both the counselor and the teacher. McArthur and Stevens have contrasted the validity of expressed and inventoried interests as revealed through a follow-up study.[20] Ivey has considered the relationship between interests and work values.[21] Tyler discusses the development of interests in small children,[22, 23] and White has studied the impact of parental identification on the vocational interests of women.[24]

Most of the research, particularly in recent years, has dealt with inventoried interests. Most widely used in this research have been the two instruments mentioned above. The material included in the *Estimates* and in the *Dictionary* concerning the relationship of interests to occupations has been based on the work of Cottle,[25] whose factorial study of the Kuder and Strong instruments demonstrated that interest factors were bipolar in nature. The *bipolar characteristic* means that a positive preference for a specific type of activity is associated with a dislike of, or lack of interest in, a contrary type.

It would usually be assumed that people and jobs reflect patterns of interest that spread across more than one bipolar factor. Cottle perceived five bipolar factors; in other words, ten interest characteristics that fitted into pairs representing opposing ends of five continua. Research has not yet demonstrated the amount or degree of a certain interest that is associated with success in a wide variety of occupations. The material reported in *Estimates* and in the *Dictionary* is based on the assumption that interests are involved in every kind of job activity.

The interest factors proposed by Cottle are listed below in appropriate pairs. Each interest pole is illustrated with related job activities. For each occupation listed in the Qualifications Profile the two most characteristic factors are proposed.[26]

1. *Situations involving a preference for activities dealing with things and objects.*

Conducts research into motion of projectiles fired from guns. Studies rate of acceleration and velocity of projectile within gun.

2. *Situations involving a preference for activities involving business contact with people.*

Conducts financial investigations. Advises business executives and members of regulatory bodies. Serves as arbiter, advocate, or umpire in business controversies.

3. *Situations involving a preference for activities of routine, concrete, organized nature.*

Assists another worker by keeping him supplied with materials, tools, and supplies or performing routine machine operations such as feeding or unloading machine.

4. *Situations involving a preference for working for people for their presumed good, as in the social welfare sense, or for dealing with people and language in social situations.*

Assists in solving social problems of

6. *Situations involving a preference for activities concerned with people and the communication of ideas.* °

Gives individual or group instruction in instrumental or vocal music.

7. *Situations involving a preference for activities of scientific and technical nature.*

Develops tests and experiments to measure mental characteristics of human beings, standardizing by extensive trial application.

8. *Situations involving a preference for activities of an abstract and creative nature.*

Performs research to discover new or improved methods for application of mathematical theory or analysis to new or unexplored areas of scientific investigation.

9. *Situations involving a preference for activities that are nonsocial in nature, and are carried on in relation to processes, machines, and techniques.*

Tends and regulates radio equipment to transmit and receive photo-

---

° Interest in "people" may manifest itself in such situations as writing about them, portraying roles about them, and reporting events about them, without actually having personal dealings with them.

travelers, migrants, and transients. Counsels travelers to prevent incipient problems. Investigates cases and attempts to rectify motivating causes of travel, such as undesirable home conditions or personality maladjustment.

5. *Situations involving a preference vs. for activities resulting in prestige or the esteem of others.*
Writes feature articles on screen celebrities and motion picture producers, frequenting the haunts of the famous and successful and cultivating their acquaintance.

graphs, black and white sketches, and the like. Sets up photograph or material to be transmitted and adjusts controls to obtain proper transmission. Sets up equipment and makes adjustments for receiving.

0. *Situations involving a preference for activities resulting in tangible, productive satisfaction.*
Installs radios in automobiles. Completely attaches all parts; makes electrical connections; adjusts tuning. At completion of job, radio must operate properly.

Many research studies have focused on the relationship between interest and occupational choice or satisfaction. Only a few of these studies, however, have focused on the predictive validity of expressed vocational choice, which could be assumed to be identical with expressed interest. Whitney, reviewing the various studies related to expressed choice, concludes that expressed choice has as much predictive validity as do various measures of interest, aptitude, and socio-economic factors.[27] Rose and Elston tend to support this view with their conclusion that scores obtained on the Strong Vocational Interest Blank by high school seniors appear to corroborate their expressed vocational choices.[28] On the other hand, Nelson was unable to find that Kuder Preference Record scores would confirm expressed vocational choices of eleventh grade boys.[29] Whitney makes a strong point supporting the use of expressed choice when he states that an individual expressing a preference for an occupation usually does so with some awareness of both the aptitudes required in the work and the aptitudes existing in himself/herself. This type of information is beyond the scope of the best of the interest inventories.

Among the interest inventories that are extensively used, the Strong Vocational Interest Blank is the most widely recognized. Originally published in 1927, it has undergone revision with sufficient regularity to maintain currency and at the same time in such carefully planned phases that validity and reliability data appear to be undamaged. *The Seventh Mental Measurements Yearbook* now shows bibliographic references exceeding one thousand entries.[30] Recent revision has up-dated many items included in the instrument and also has provided new scales for interpreting the results.

The present form (Strong-Campbell Interest Inventory) includes 315 items grouped according to type of content, such as occupations, school subjects, activities, amusements, etc. The individual responds to each item by indicating whether he/she likes, dislikes, or is indifferent to it. There is no time limit, but most individuals complete the form in from 30 to 60 minutes. Because of the complexity of the scoring system, answer sheets must be scored by computer, and commercial scoring services are available.

The profile of the results includes different types of scores that are related to the "personality types" proposed by Holland that we considered in the previous chapter. The profile presents six "General Occupational Themes" that parallel Holland's six personality types. Seventy-three "Basic Interest Scales" are based on broad groupings relating to Holland's six types; for example, the R-Theme includes Basic Interest Scores for Agriculture, Nature, Administrative, Military Activities, and Mechanical Activities. Finally, the profile provides 124 "Occupational Scales," which show the extent of similarity between the individual's responses and those of men and women employed in the named occupation. Each of these occupational scales is also identified with the appropriate Holland code. In addition to these three types of occupationally related scales, the profile presents several additional special scales.

Previous editions of the test (usually labeled SVIB) provided separate tests and separate profiles by sex. The present SCII combines these forms, although norms for the two sexes are still maintained separately because of demonstrated differences on more than half of the items. The individual's profile does show a comparison with each sex group so that cross comparisons are possible, if desired.

The Kuder Preference Record-Vocational has been widely used, especially with high school populations, since its original publication in the mid-1930's. Two different instruments have developed from this earlier inventory—the Kuder General Interest Survey and the Kuder Occupational Interest Survey. The first of these two derivatives is primarily an up-dating and a downward extension of the original instrument. It provides 10 scores for the broad areas of outdoor, mechanical, computational, scientific, persuasive, artistic, literary, musical, social service, clerical, and a verification score. The inventory uses a forced choice system in which the individual is presented with activities arranged in a triad, among which the subject must select the one liked best and the one liked least. Norms are based on grade level and sex. Although purportedly easily interpreted, there appears to be some danger that an inexperienced counselor, or even the subject, can easily assume interpretations beyond the data actually apparent in the test scores.

The Kuder Occupational Interest Survey was developed in 1956 and revised in 1964. It provides 106 scales for men, including 77 occupational scales and 29 college major scales; and 84 scales for women, including 57 occupational scales and 27 college major scales. The format is similar to other Kuder instruments, with items presented in 100 triads. Scores are obtained by comparing the subject's responses to those of individuals in the occupation or college major. Present evidence indicates that the Kuder Occupational Interest Survey and the Strong Vocational Interest Blank do not give the same results for scales with the same or similar names. This

A Comparison of the Strong-Cambell Interest Inventory and the Kuder Occupational Interest Survey

	STRONG-CAMBELL INTEREST INVENTORY	KUDER OCCUPATIONAL INTEREST SURVEY
Format: (both pencil and paper tests)	Divided into seven parts, such as occupations, school subjects, activities, amusements, types of people. Respondent indicates *L* like, *I* indifferent, *D* dislike for most of the 325 items.	Triad format in which respondent indicates most preferred and least preferred among three alternatives included in each of the 100 items.
Rationale: (fundamentally the same except as indicated)	Employs criterion reference groups for each occupation included containing about 300 individuals, 25-55 years of age, employed for three or more years, and reporting satisfaction with their work.	The respondent's score on each occupational scale is expressed as a correlation between his/her interest pattern and the interest pattern of the given occupational group.
Range of Use: (both claim sixth grade reading difficulty)	Generally for ages 16 and over, with some students of 14 or 15 able to benefit from the inventory. Inventoried interests appear to stabilize around age 17 or 18.	Grades 11–16 and adults. Sometimes useful with younger students under certain circumstances.
Scales Reported:	a. *General Occupational Themes* based on Holland's six types, reported in terms of a standard score and an intra-sex interpretation. b. *Basic Interest Scales:* 23 clusters of items with high intercorrelations arranged according to relationship to the General Occupational Themes. c. *Occupational Scales:* 124 occupations arranged in relationship to (a) and (b). d. Other scales include academic orientation and introversion-extroversion.	a. *Occupational Scales:* 77 for men and 57 for women. b. *College Major Scales:* 29 for men, 27 for women. c. Other scales include verification scale and 8 experimental scales.

discrepancy can be explained by differences in the normative groups, but the counselor is left in an uncomfortable position when this divergence appears.

The extensive usage of the Kuder and the Strong suggests general acceptance of these two instruments even though test specialists express concerns about both. It appears likely that the technical deficiencies of the instruments may often be compounded in the interpretation of results. If counselor and subject are willing to settle for broad, general indicators or "straws in the wind," it seems likely that either instrument can provide this type of help.

The Ohio Vocational Interest Survey has been developed more recently than either the Strong or the Kuder. One of its major advantages is that it is built on the data–people–things relationship that is included in the *Dictionary of Occupational Titles* and in the Cubistic Classification System. We will consider both the *Dictionary* and the cubistic system in Chapter 6. Using the *Dictionary*-based system permits the direct translation of test results into *Dictionary*-listed occupations. The test provides scores on 24 interest scales after the individual responds to a list of 280 job activities on a five-point scale ranging from "dislike very much" to "like very much."

PERSONALITY AND TEMPERAMENT

Research focused on the relationship of personality characteristics to success in various occupations is less well developed than that associated with either aptitude or interest. Perhaps in the past, research in this area has had to wait for the development of both a theoretical framework and adequate measuring instruments.[31, 32, 33]

The earlier work developed in the *Estimates* has been incorporated into the qualifications profile of the Worker Trait Arrangement in the *Dictionary*. Again based on job analysis, an attempt has been made to emphasize the relationship between personality factors and work. Here, the approach has been to identify the persistent characteristics of a certain kind of work that require a particular kind of response from the worker. For example, both counselors and teachers work in situations that not only involve dealing with people beyond giving and receiving instructions, but also involve evaluating information against sensory or judgmental criteria. Even though neither aspect of the work can be thought to be a temperament trait, the personality characteristics that make it possible for the person to meet such work demands can be so considered.

It is important for the reader to bear in mind that the research into the relationship betwen work and personality is rudimentary at best. The material included in the *Dictionary* is essentially an educated guess based on careful observation of workers and jobs. It is, nevertheless, helpful in giving us insight into this aspect of the worker-job relationship and proposing a base on which research can later be built.

In the *Estimates,* an attempt was made to identify the two temperament traits most characteristic of jobholders in each of the 4,000 jobs included. In the *Dictionary,* each qualifications profile includes all those temperament traits that are characteristic of the group of jobs. Twelve different types of occupational situations to which workers must adjust were identified.

Listerd below are the twelve temperament characteristics. The job definition included with each trait, to illustrate the point, has been taken from the *Estimates.*[34] These definitions are essentially the same as the definitions in Volume 1 of the *Dictionary.*

1. VARCH: SITUATIONS INVOLVING A VARIETY OF DUTIES OFTEN CHARACTERIZED BY FREQUENT CHANGE.

Example: Performs general office work. Makes up and files reports. Tabulates and posts data on various record books. Takes telephone orders. Checks cash registers. Gives information to callers. Sends out bills. Checks calculations. Keeps a small set of books. Takes inventories. Adjusts complaints. Operates various office machines, such as calculator and mimeograph.

2. REPSC: SITUATIONS INVOLVING REPETITIVE OR SHORT CYCLE OPERATIONS CARRIED OUT ACCORDING TO SET PROCEDURES OR SEQUENCE.

Example: Addesses envelopes, cards, advertising literature, packages, and similar items for mailing, by hand or on typewriter.

3. USI: SITUATIONS INVOLVING DOING THINGS ONLY UNDER SPECIFIC INSTRUCTION, ALLOWING LITTLE OR NO ROOM FOR INDEPENDENT ACTION OR JUDGMENT IN WORKING OUT JOB PROBLEMS.

Example: Types on cards information concerning newly registered guests for use of hotel front-office employees.

4. DCP: SITUATIONS INVOLVING THE DIRECTION, CONTROL, AND PLANNING OF AN ENTIRE ACTIVITY OR THE ACTIVITIES OF OTHERS.

Example: Devises, installs, and supervises operation of general-accounting budget and cost systems. Supervises subordinates engaged in maintenance of accounts and records.

5. DEPL: SITUATIONS INVOLVING THE NECESSITY OF DEALING WITH PEOPLE IN ACTUAL JOB DUTIES BEYOND GIVING AND RECEIVING INSTRUCTIONS.

Example: Promotes sales and creates good will for his firm's products by preparing displays, touring the country, making speeches at retail dealers' conventions, and calling on individual merchants to advise on ways and means for increasing sales.

6. ISOL: SITUATIONS INVOLVING WORKING ALONE AND APART IN PHYSICAL ISOLATION FROM OTHERS, ALTHOUGH THE ACTIVITY MAY BE INTEGRATED WITH THAT OF OTHERS.

Example: Is stationed on high ridge or other point commanding a view of small area of forest and keeps sharp lookout for signs of fire. Lives alone and isolated for periods of 3 or 4 months.

7. INFLU: SITUATIONS INVOLVING INFLUENCING PEOPLE IN THEIR OPINIONS, ATTITUDES, OR JUDGMENTS ABOUT IDEAS OR THINGS.

Example: Writes original descriptive advertising copy, extolling the merits of a certain product for presentation to the buying public through medium of newspapers, radio, magazines, or billboard posters.

8. PUS: SITUATIONS INVOLVING PERFORMING ADEQUATELY UNDER STRESS WHEN CONFRONTED WITH THE CRITICAL OR UNEXPECTED OR WHEN TAKING RISKS.

Example: Works below the surface of the water, dressed in diving suit and helmet, to drill holes in rock for blasting purposes at the bottom of lake, harbor, or other body of water. Risk of suffocation from fouled air hose or entrapment by rotten, falling timbers is always present.

9. SJC: SITUATIONS INVOLVING THE EVALUATION (ARRIVING AT GENERALIZATIONS, JUDGMENTS, OR DECISIONS) OF INFORMATION AGAINST SENSORY OR JUDGMENTAL CRITERIA.

Example: Collects, organizes, and interprets scientific data relating to community organizations, social customs, the family, and other social phenomena for use of administrators, lawmakers, educators, and other officials engaged in the solution of social problems.

O. MVC: SITUATIONS INVOLVING THE EVALUATION (ARRIVING AT GENERALIZATIONS, JUDGMENTS, OR DECISIONS) OF INFORMATION AGAINST MEASURABLE OR VERIFIABLE CRITERIA.

Example: Assists in examining and testing metal samples to determine their physical properties. Tests samples in pressure devices, hot-acid baths, and other apparatus to determine strength, hardness, elasticity, toughness, or other properties of metals.

X. FIF: SITUATIONS INVOLVING THE INTERPRETATION OF FEELINGS, IDEAS, OR FACTS IN TERMS OF PERSONAL VIEWPOINT.

Example: Designs artistic effects for outside displays, such as street decorations, fair grounds, and building decorations, using flags, cloth, and crepe paper.

Y. STS: SITUATIONS INVOLVING THE PRECISE ATTAINMENT OF SET LIMITS, TOLERANCES, OR STANDARDS.

Example: Compounds and dispenses medicines and preparations as directed by prescriptions prepared by licensed *Physicians* and *Dentists*. Performs routine assays and tests to determine identity, purity, and strength of drugs.

Most career development theorists include in their proposals support of a relationship between personality and career choice. Holland, Roe, Super, Tiedeman, as well as others, see career choice as an expression of personality. Each also indicates that job satisfaction, one ingredient that tends to hold individuals in a given field, is largely produced through the compatibility of personality and occupation; thus, conversely, one would assume that conflict between personality and work would minimize job satisfaction and result in the individual's departure from the occupation to search for more acceptable activity.

The existence of such a relationship seems so patently obvious that each of us can, at once, conjure up illustrations—the aggressive salesman of used automobiles, the "gung-ho" marine drill instructor, the meek and fastidious bookkeeper, the "bleeding-heart" social worker, and on and on. The stereotypes that each of us holds of most occupations include personality characteristics that we assume to be representative of the incumbents of the occupational group.

It is then surprising, perhaps even disconcerting, to review the literature and discover little evidence that identifies test instruments showing a clear relationship between personality or temperament and success or satisfaction in a particular occupation. One is compelled to ask why there is so little hard evidence to support what appears to be so obvious to the naked eye of the casual observer.

Several reasons explain the lack of substantial support. One reason is that little research on the specific relationship appears to have been completed; most of the existing research is tangential to the area of our discussion. Personality theorists have focused their research on the personality structure of individuals; practitioners have focused on selection procedures or adjustment to work. Normative data for tests have usually been based on groups that are inappropriate for estimating job success or satisfaction. There is an obvious need for extensive research in the area.

A further explanation may be the range of work settings within which each occupation is performed. This range may permit sufficient flexibility to accommodate the variety of personality or temperament characteristics apparently existing in each occupation. For example, the dominant, aggressive bookkeeper might soon be assigned to leadership activities that move him toward office management responsibilities. Thus, personality incompatibility between worker and peers or worker and employer perhaps simply results in the worker seeking another employment situation that is more congenial to his/her particular personality.

One must conclude that, at present, the use of instruments measuring personality or temperament for the prediction of job satisfaction or success lacks research justification. If the concern is to measure overall personality organization as a general *sine qua non* for satisfactory adjustment to work, or to identify personality observations that might prevent satisfactory adjustment to work, then screening type testing may be appropriate.

VALUES

The concept of values is closely related to the broader and more widely used term of personality. Often the term values is juxtaposed with needs. The idea of values as representative of personality types was proposed by Spranger nearly half a century ago. He suggested that men could be classified according to their value types as theoretical, economic, social, political, aesthetic, and religious.[35] These concepts were fundamental to the development of the *Study of Values,* an inventory originally developed in the 1930's by G. W. Allport and P. E. Vernon and later revised with the assistance of G. Lindzey. Briefly described, each value type was considered to have the following characteristics:

> The *theoretical* man seeks the discovery of truth. He takes a cognitive attitude, seeks to observe and to reason and does not make judgments about beauty or utility. His interests compare to those of scientists and philosophers.
> The *economic* man seeks the useful. He is concerned with practical affairs, often represented as a business man. His focus is often upon the accumulation of wealth.
> The *aesthetic* man is primarily concerned with form and harmony— the artistic episodes of life. He judges experience from the standpoint of grace, symmetry, or fitness.
> The *social* man has greatest concern for the love of people. He is kind, sympathetic, and unselfish and primarily directed toward the altruistic and philanthropic aspects of love.
> The *political* man seeks personal power, influence, and reknown. Both competition and struggle play major roles in his life.
> The *religious* man looks upon unity as most important. He seeks understanding of the cosmos. He is often mystical and finds religious experience in the affirmation of life.

The *Study of Values* attempts to measure the relative strength of these value areas, recognizing as Spranger did, that few individuals are "pure" types, but instead are mixtures or combinations.

A more philosophic approach to values is taken by Peterson, who clarifies the term thus:

> . . . a value is a learned conception, explicit or implicit, of what is desirable. It is a hypothetical construct, a criterion upon which

choice, either by an individual or a group, is justified and also serves to motivate commitment and action. Value represents more than needs, goals, beliefs, attitudes, interests, or preferences (terms frequently confused with value), although it may be closely related to them.[36]

The focus of this definition is on the individual's view of what is desirable. Peterson points out that today's youth often receive conflicting messages about what is good and therefore encounter difficulty in developing values. The counselor often encounters youth who are seeking identity and thereby attempting to clarify their values. Peterson suggests that values are hypothetical constructs that have motivational force and that represent the desirable in the sense of what one ought to do or what is perceived as the right thing to do in the situation.

Recent attention has focused on attempts to relate values to attitudes of individuals toward work. One recent monograph of particular significance in relating values to work and career is *Decisions and Values* by M. Katz.[37]

The Work Values Inventory by Super is an attempt to assess the values that motivate individuals to work.[38] This instrument is alleged to measure fifteen value constructs. These are identified as follows:

Altruism: *Social service values and interests, work that contributes to the welfare of others.*

Esthetic: *Related to artistic interest, work that permits one to make beautiful things.*

Creativity: *Work that permits one to invent new things, design new products, develop new ideas.*

Intellectual stimulation: *Characteristic of people with abstract professional and scientific interests, opportunity for independent thinking.*

Achievement: *A liking for work that produces visible, tangible results, accomplishment in doing a job well.*

Independence: *Freedom to work in one's way and at one's own pace, usually low-level occupations.*

Prestige: *Provides respect of others, not necessarily status or power; business contact occupations may often carry this characteristic.*

Management: *Work that permits one to plan and lay out work for others to do.*

Economic returns: *Work that pays well, and thus enables one to have the things he/she wants; a materialistic value.*

Security: *This reflects a desire for assurance or certainty that one will always have a job.*

Surroundings: *This focuses on the setting in which one works; a desire for a pleasant, comfortable, work environment rather than concern about the work itself.*

Supervisory relations: A *desire for work that includes an understanding and sympathetic supervisor.*

Associates: A *desire for work that provides congenial fellow workers.*

Way of life: Work *that permits one to live as he/she chooses, and be one's own person.*

Variety: Associated *with opportunity for engaging in many different tasks.*

The Work Values Inventory appears to have considerable promise for future use, particularly with adolescents. As additional validation data are developed and reported, it seems likely that counselors may be able to use the instrument more extensively. At present, it seems safe to say that many vocational counselors give attention to the values held by the client; however, this is most frequently handled as a component of the interview and counseling process rather than through the application of an assessment instrument.

APPRAISAL OF
PSYCHOLOGICAL CHARACTERISTICS

The preceding sections of this chapter have included brief statements relative to appraisal of the particular characteristic under consideration. Detailed discussion of the topic of appraisal falls outside the purview of this book. We will look briefly at one publication that provides much assistance to counselors and others involved in the appraisal of these characteristics for vocational counseling purposes. Secondly, we will consider data from two major research projects that have attempted to relate appraisal data to occupational involvement and success.

The *Counselor's Handbook,* a 1967 publication by the Department of Labor, attempts to provide information for both counselor and counselee that is helpful in evaluating the psychological characteristics listed above and other items that we will review in subsequent chapters.[39] Part I of the *Handbook* includes interviewing guides in appraisal of interests, temperaments, and aptitude information.

The areas of interests and temperament are considered only from the viewpoint of information available by interview; no consideration is given to inventory or test data. The section devoted to interests includes material that could be used directly by the counselee in self-evaluation. Information is provided about job-worker situations, descriptive of the kinds of work that capitalize on each specific interest pattern, and about counselee life-experience situations illustrative of common activities representative of the interest pattern. Samples of job-worker situations involving the various interests patterns were included in that section of this chapter. Samples of

"Counselee Life-Experience Situations" for "Routine, Concrete, Organized" interest patterns include:

Having an assembly line job
Concentrating your attention on a machine to see that it is running properly
Canning vegetables and fruit
Knitting to pass away the time
Having established rules to work by

Temperament materials also are presented in a way that can be used directly by the counselee in self-evaluation. In viewing this material, it is important to keep in mind that the approach applied is that of evaluating the amount of tolerance in the job rather than identifying specific attributes of the individual worker. Each of the temperament characteristics, which we have previously considered, is described with illustrations of work situations involving these worker qualities. A series of questions is provided to help the individual identify the extent to which the quality exists in himself. These questions comprise "attitude clues" and "activity clues." It is proposed that these questions are illustrative of the kind of information that will help the counselee and the counselor to make some judgment about the compatibility of the work area and the counselee.

The material included in the *Counselor's Handbook* on using Aptitude Information Resources focuses primarily on the use of Occupational Aptitude Patterns (OAP), which we have already considered. Also included is additional interpretive information, which is helpful in understanding the concepts related to aptitude analysis as applied by the Department of Labor.

Part II of the *Handbook* includes information about "Counselee Appraisal Patterns Related to Fields of Work." This section represents an attempt to pull together information about occupational areas drawn from psychological, sociological, and phenomenological models. Broad areas such as public service, the sciences, engineering, and business relations are sub-divided into smaller, but still quite inclusive fields. For example, the sciences are divided into the following:

Mathematics and logical systems
Behavioral science
Life science
Earth and atmospheric science
Astronomy and space science
Physical science
Life science technicians
Physical science technicians

Each of these areas includes a brief description of the area, and the identification of relevant factors to be considered in discussion and appraisal; these factors include:

Related majors and specializations
Related course areas
Related leisure pursuits
Pertinent information (including special requirements, cultural and socio-
  logical data)
Illustrative temperament roles
Illustrative interest involvements

A major research project initiated in 1960 is now beginning to provide some data that may be helpful in appraising the relationship between psychological characteristics of individuals and the world of work. That research effort, "Project TALENT," has been frequently described in the literature by the major investigator, John C. Flanagan.[40] The original phase of this study surveyed, by test and inventory, the aptitudes, abilities, achievements, interests, and backgrounds of more than 400,000 secondary school students in the United States. The original battery of instruments required two days and was administered to students in grades 9–12 in 1,225 high schools selected as a stratified random sample of all senior high schools.[41]

The original plan proposed follow-up studies of the group at intervals of 1, 5, 10, and 20 years after graduation. The first two were completed on schedule and the third follow-up was completed 11 years after graduation (1971–1975). Data from the five-year follow-up is now available, the 11-year follow-up will be released soon, and the final review should appear in the mid-1980's. Obviously, because of length of time involved, the final studies can be expected to have great significance for vocational counseling.

Data obtained in the five-year follow-up have been published in *The Career Data Book: Results From Project TALENT's Five-Year Follow-Up Study.*[42] The data available at this time have been organized to show what individuals pursuing various specific careers were like when they were in high school. Because the time between original testing and follow-up is too short to predict either success or even tenacity in pursuing an occupation, all that is demonstrated by the data are the high school age characteristics of those pursuing an occupation, or preparation for the occupation, five years after high school graduation. The authors propose that an individual who finds that those who are pursuing a particular career field have Project TALENT scores similar to his own can conclude that the specific field is a realizable choice for himself.

Counselors, and counselees as well, will have some difficulty in making precise comparisons since many parts of the test instruments used are neither in general usage nor available to counselors. In some test areas, attempts have been made to develop translations of the scores to other instruments; for example, the appendix includes conversion tables of aptitude information to either the Differential Aptitude Test or the General Aptitude Test Battery. In other areas, such as interests, only rough approximations can be made at this time. Nevertheless, the material available can be extremely useful in helping an individual in the process of self-evaluation.

The major portion of the nearly 400-page book consists of statements describing a particular occupation and a profile of those subjects pursuing that occupation. The narrative portion includes brief statements about the occupation covering the following topics:

Importance of the work
Training
Work activities
Outcomes
Supervision, social relations
Salary, other benefits
Role of sexes
Personal characteristics of the sample
    Interests
    Information
    Abilities
    Others

The profile chart (a sample page is included) for each occupation shows, by means of a bold-face vertical mark, the mean percentile scale value for the sample in that occupation. Along with this mean score is shown the range of percentile scores on each sub-item of the middle 50 per cent of that sample. Scores are provided on each of the following items:

Interest Scales	*Ability Test*
Phys. Sci., Eng., Math	Total English
Bio. Sci., Medicine	Reading comprehension
Public service	Creativity
Literary-linguistic	Mechanical reasoning
Social service	Visualization in 3D
Artistic	Abstract reasoning
Musical	Arithmetic reasoning
Sports	Introductory math
Hunting and fishing	Arithmetic computations
Business management	
Sales	
Computation	

Office work
Mechanical-technical
Skilled trades
Farming
Labor

Information Test	Other Variables
Vocabulary	Socio-economic status
Literature	H.S. courses taken (aca.)
Music	H.S. grades
Social studies	Amt. of extracur. reading
Mathematics	Study habits and attitudes
Physical science	
Biological science	

The authors identify and discuss four major shortcomings that they see in the data reported in the volume. These include the shortness of time between original data collection and the five-year follow-up after graduation; that current occupational choices are not necessarily final; those responding to the follow-up tend to have higher scores than those not responding; and that the data may have limited generalization to other groups if those groups differ from the 1960 sample.[43]

Table 2a is a sample page from *The Career Data Book*. Based on a sample of 1,110 males indicating an intention of becoming lawyers, it shows the distribution of scores for that group. As one might expect, high interest in public service and literary-linguistic activities is shown, along with high general knowledge, and high ability in English, Reading Comprehension, and Introductory Math.

Table 2b is the corresponding page from *The Career Data Book Supplement*. These data are based not on those indicating plans to enter the occupation but on *those who were actually employed in the occupation eleven years after high school graduation*. Obviously, the use of occupational participants now increases considerably the significance of the data. A comparison of the two pages reveals striking similarities. The changes that appear in Table 2b are easily explained; for example, the public service interest score is now higher, as are the general information and ability scores. One can assume that the withdrawal rate would be heavier among those scoring low in these areas, hence the increased selectivity pushes the scores higher. In addition to providing information about those actually in the occupation, the *Supplement* also shows the mean profile (by an asterisk) for those individuals in the occupation who report themselves as satisfied.

A somewhat different study has been reported by Thorndike and Hagen, under the title of *Ten Thousand Careers*.[44] This study, too, faced many serious limitations as well as difficulties in obtaining follow-up data. Nevertheless, its methodology and results are worth considering.

TABLE 2a. *Profile for Lawyer Sample,* The Career Data Book

LAWYER: (MALE — N = 1,110)

INTEREST SCALES	20	30	40	50	60	70	80	90
Phys. sci., Eng., math.								
Bio. sci., medicine								
Public service								
Literary–linguistic								
Social service								
Artistic								
Musical								
Sports								
Hunting & fishing								
Business management								
Sales								
Computation								
Office work								
Mechanical–technical								
Skilled trades								
Farming								
Labor								

INFORMATION TEST	20	30	40	50	60	70	80	90
Vocabulary								
Literature								
Music								
Social studies								
Mathematics								
Physical science								
Biological science								

ABILITY TEST	20	30	40	50	60	70	80	90
Total English								
Reading comprehension								
Creativity								
Mechanical reasoning								
Visualization in 3D								
Abstract reasoning								
Arithmetic reasoning								
Introductory math								
Arithmetic computation								

OTHER VARIABLES	20	30	40	50	60	70	80	90
Socio-economic status								
H.S. courses taken (aca.)								
H.S. grades								
Amt. of extracur. reading								
Study habits & attitudes								

TABLE 2b. *Profile for Lawyer Sample,* The Career Data Book Supplement
LAWYER: (N = 5 PER 1000)

INTEREST SCALES	20	30	40	50	60	70	80	90
Phys. sci., Eng., Math.								
Bio. sci., medicine								
Public service								
Literary-linguistic								
Social service								
Artistic								
Musical								
Sports								
Hunting & fishing								
Business management								
Sales								
Computation								
Office work								
Mechanical-technical								
Skilled trades								
Farming								
Labor								
INFORMATION TEST	20	30	40	50	60	70	80	90
Vocabulary								
Literature								
Music								
Social studies								
Mathematics								
Physical science								
Biological science								
ABILITY TEST	20	30	40	50	60	70	80	90
Total English								
Reading comprehension								
Creativity								
Mechanical reasoning								
Visualization in 3D								
Abstract reasoning								
Arithmetic reasoning								
Introductory math								
Arithmetic computation								
OTHER VARIABLES	20	30	40	50	60	70	80	90
H.S. courses taken (aca.)								
H.S. grades								
Amt. of extracur. reading								
Study habits & attitudes								
SATISFACTION AND PAY	20	30	40	50	60	70	80	90
Pay (actual reported)								

Aspects of Occupation that Project TALENT Participants Report as Important and Most Satisfying

  Relationship of work to prior training
  How well I can do the work
  Challenging work

Aspects of Occupation that Project TALENT Participants Report as Important but Least Satisfying

  Income to start
  Quality of surroundings
  Status

(*based on 76% of individuals in occupation)

Thorndike and Hagen report a follow-up study based on 17,000 applicants for aviation cadet training who were all tested with the same form of an extensive test battery in 1943. The men, at the time of testing, were between 18 and 26, unmarried, had passed a rigorous physical exam, and had also passed a scholastic aptitude and achievement test. The qualifying test had standards that restricted successful applicants to those who would rank approximately in the upper half of a high school graduating class. The cases selected for study were drawn in eleven blocks of 500 each from each of the three testing centers in use in 1943, with the blocks of cases selected across the entire five-month period that the same battery was used. About 17,000 cases were included in the sample, from a population of approximately 75,000.

The eighteen tests were pooled into five groups when factor analysis revealed that essentially five factors were being measured. The five group scores included the following: general intellectual, numerical, perceptual-spatial, mechanical, and psychomotor. Scores were scaled so that the mean equaled zero with a standard deviation of 100.

Since the testing program was designed to be used in assigning applicants to various training programs in the army air force, it was naturally loaded with tests that stressed those characteristics believed to be significant in such selection. The reader must be aware that, although lengthy, the testing program was not equally comprehensive.

The follow-up information was sought in 1955, about twelve years after testing. About 51 per cent of the questionnaires were returned by the respondents, and information on another seven per cent was supplied by the Retail Credit organization. The remaining cases were either on active duty in military service (8 per cent), deceased (8 per cent), did not respond (11 per cent), or had no acceptable address available (14 per cent). Thus, of those eligible for inclusion, about 70 per cent responded. For each respondent, information on present occupation and work history was elicited. A *Dictionary of Occupational Titles* code was assigned according to the individual's response of job title and description. In many cases, grouping was necessary to obtain a sample of sufficient statistical size. A total of 124 different occupational categories was used in the study. Some of these were fairly large homogeneous groups; others quite small and heterogeneous. The questionnaire also provided information that permitted seven criterion scores roughly indicative of success and satisfaction: monthly earned income, number supervised, self-rated success, self-rated job satisfaction, vertical mobility, lateral mobility, and length of time in occupation.

Differences in group scores by the various occupational categories are shown in Table 3 (pp. 100–103). Thorndike and Hagen report group scores for all 124 occupational groups. Inspection of the table reveals that several occupational groups have distinctive profiles, with one or more of the group scores definitely elevated above the mean. Other occupational groups show a rather flat profile, some falling near the average on all scores, others either elevated or depressed. The intellectual composite varies more among occupational groups than any other score; this is followed by the mechanical, numerical, visual perception, and psychomotor group scores, in that order. The authors estimate that the intellectual difference is due in part to the differences in educational achievement required for admission to many professional areas, and in part to actual intellectual differences in job demands.

The study also compared the test data with measures of success within about ninety occupational groups. Although several test scores correlated significantly with reported income, it was concluded that the number of significant correlations did not exceed those that could have occurred by chance. For the most part, correlations between test score and reported income were low. Biographical data were also correlated with reported income, with differences again appearing to be a product of chance. This section of the report appears to fall short of hoped-for significance; in addition, there are several intervening variables that made true assessment of results difficult. These include the problems of clearly establishing criteria of success comparable because of geographic and other variants, test limitations emphasizing ability factors, and the question of how many of the correlations could be assumed to be zero and disregarded when checking for chance factors.

In summary, the reported study appears to have four major limitations, all previously mentioned, including restriction of sample, limited scope of test battery, heterogeneity in several occupational groups, and possibly unstable measures of success. In spite of these weaknesses, the research shows definite differences in aptitude patterns among many occupational groups and differences in personal background variables. The study fails to predict occupational success based on either test scores or biographical data, but possibly suggests the need for further study in this area before abandoning the search.

TRAINING TIME

Training time is considered as the amount of *specific vocational preparation* and the *general educational development* necessary for the worker to acquire the knowledge and ability needed for average performance in a specific job.

General educational development includes the general academic preparation obtained in elementary and secondary school and in college that does not have a specific occupational objective. It refers to aspects of education that develop reasoning and adaptability to environment, and ability to follow instructions, as well as such "tool" knowledges as language and mathematics.

TABLE 3. *Occupational Group Means on Five Score Composites* [*]

	GENERAL INTELLEC- UAL (G)	NUMERI- CAL FLUENCY (N)	VISUAL PERCEP- TION (PS)	MECHANI- CAL (M)	PSYCHO- MOTOR (PM)
1. Accountants and auditors	28	54	— 4	—46	— 16
2. Advertising agents	26	—12	34	—15	—12
3. Agricultural, miscel- laneous	13	10	— 1	—16	18
4. Airplane pilots	—16	—20	18	64	43
5. Architects	44	4	74	8	14
6. Artists and designers	— 7	—12	51	— 4	8
7. Assemblers, production	—83	—76	—46	—27	—34
8. Bricklayers	—24	— 5	—38	10	—32
9. Buyers	1	9	—18	—37	—18
10. Carpenters	—44	—17	— 4	24	— 1
11. Claim adjusters, insurance	—13	— 5	— 9	—44	—20
12. Clerical, accounting records	—28	5	— 7	—48	— 6
13. Clerical, communications	—30	4	—17	—19	—12
14. Clerical, machine operators	—30	— 6	— 1	4	—16
15. Clerical, material records	—36	— 2	—14	—31	— 6
16. Clerical, public contact	— 1	2	—11	—29	—31
17. Clergymen	13	1	—17	— 4	0
18. College professors	75	38	38	—33	1
19. Contractors	— 7	—10	—10	34	5
20. Crane operators	—66	—84	—37	—19	—29
21. Dentists	28	20	15	—19	1
22. Dispatchers, control tower operators	4	37	31	31	41
23. Draftsmen	1	—14	31	14	15
24. Drivers, bus and truck	—53	—11	—23	—14	—20
25. Earth movers	—71	—70	—22	— 3	—37
26. Electricians, structural wiring	—24	—20	—27	35	— 3
27. Electricians, instruments and equipment	—33	—43	—12	17	7
28. Electricians, power systems	—30	—41	—33	22	— 5
29. Engineers, chemical	106	42	30	19	20
30. Engineers, civil	75	31	56	36	14
31. Engineers, electrical	65	6	9	32	11
32. Engineers, industrial	44	41	34	— 4	4
33. Engineers, mechanical	93	34	44	52	23
34. Engineers, sales	57	33	35	39	40

[*] Expressed as standard scores for which mean = 0, standard deviation = 100.

TABLE 3. (Cont.)

	GENERAL INTELLEC- UAL (G)	NUMERI- CAL FLUENCY (N)	VISUAL PERCEP- TION (PS)	MECHANI- CAL (M)	PSYCHO- MOTOR (PM)
35. Engineers—train- men, RR	−50	−37	−31	21	− 1
36. Farmers, general	− 6	− 7	−29	38	−36
37. Farmers, specialized	−29	−32	−21	24	−35
38. Firemen	−29	−29	− 6	−10	15
39. Foremen	−30	−16	−17	8	− 8
40. Guards	−52	−27	−83	−36	6
41. Handicraftsmen, jewelry, etc.	6	− 4	15	26	5
42. Handicraftsmen, machinery	−12	−60	−36	− 5	−17
43. Handicraftsmen, other	−45	−22	−17	−23	− 9
44. Handicraftsmen, woodworking	−30	−29	0	35	1
45. Industrial relations specialists	45	25	22	5	11
46. Laboratory technicians, testers	− 3	− 8	4	2	5
47. Laborers	−33	−36	−13	−18	−24
48. Lawyers	39	22	− 7	−42	−21
49. Linesmen, cablemen	−61	−42	−33	1	−22
50. Machinists	−35	− 6	4	31	32
51. Machine shop specialists	−47	−45	−18	− 3	−20
52. Machine operators, fabricating	−45	−25	−25	−39	9
53. Machine operators, processing	−51	−41	−56	−13	4
54. Managers, credit	− 5	22	25	−27	0
55. Managers, directing production	19	1	17	22	3
56. Managers, financial institutions	6	33	−11	−33	− 3
57. Managers, hotel, restaurant, bar	−51	− 9	−18	−29	7
58. Managers, industrial and branch	11	20	−11	17	11
59. Managers, insurance	− 6	19	− 3	−35	−13
60. Managers, other	− 2	−12	−10	−13	−35
61. Managers, office	4	33	9	−29	11
62. Managers, personnel	33	18	13	−20	− 4
63. Managers, production	32	33	5	3	14
64. Managers, sales	− 2	10	− 4	−14	− 6
65. Managers, service or recreation	−22	− 1	−12	7	17

TABLE 3. (Cont.)

	GENERAL INTELLECTUAL (G)	NUMERICAL FLUENCY (N)	VISUAL PERCEPTION (PS)	MECHANICAL (M)	PSYCHOMOTOR (PM)
66. Managers, transportation and warehousing	− 7	24	4	−22	−18
67. Manufacturers' agents, brokers	−25	− 8	8	−25	8
68. Mechanics, appliances and cameras	−19	9	17	32	54
69. Mechanics, engine	−28	−27	−29	28	−25
70. Mechanics, kilns, boilers, etc.	−34	− 4	10	− 1	24
71. Mechanics, machines and production equipment	−50	−37	−31	21	− 1
72. Mechanics, office machines	49	1	33	35	36
73. Mechanics, vehicular	−72	−65	− 7	19	− 6
74. Medical, related and supporting	− 8	−20	−19	−16	4
75. Miners, drillers	−43	− 4	73	75	80
76. Officials, minor	−15	−17	− 9	−18	− 8
77. Optometrists	14	34	− 3	−14	15
78. Painters	−63	−12	−24	−25	−22
79. Personal service, other	−49	−42	−25	−33	−29
80. Pharmacists	29	39	− 9	− 7	15
81. Physicians	59	20	18	2	0
82. Plasterers, cement finishers	−14	−12	−14	3	9
83. Plumbers	−42	−21	−31	− 7	− 5
84. Policemen, detectives	−50	−26	−20	−32	− 4
85. Presidents, vice presidents, and secretaries	40	20	15	6	20
86. Principals, high school	25	10	−13	− 8	−24
87. Printing craftsmen	−55	−25	−18	−47	−19
88. Printing pressmen	−52	−31	−14	28	28
89. Public relations men	9	0	− 4	−32	− 9
90. Pumpmen, and related	−55	−24	−17	−11	13
91. Purchasing agents	− 8	20	12	−24	0
92. Radio and TV repairmen	−33	−37	21	2	5
93. Retail store owners, managers	−22	7	−10	−10	− 9
94. Sales clerks	−40	−22	−28	−23	− 3
95. Salesmen, insurance	− 5	8	14	−17	2
96. Salesmen, real estate	6	17	6	− 7	− 9
97. Salesmen, securities	15	27	−20	−50	−32
98. Salesmen, wholesale, chemical and pharmaceutical	5	22	11	−29	2

TABLE 3. (*Cont.*)

	GENERAL INTELLEC- UAL (G)	NUMERI- CAL FLUENCY (N)	VISUAL PERCEP- TION (PS)	MECHANI- CAL (M)	PSYCHO- MOTOR (PM)
99. Salesmen, wholesale, clothes and dry goods	−13	23	0	−51	− 9
100. Salesmen, wholesale, finance and transportation	5	25	−31	−29	−20
101. Salesmen, wholesale, food and beverages	−31	6	−20	−31	−28
102. Salesmen, wholesale, household hard goods	−21	− 8	4	−15	−15
103. Salesmen, wholesale, industrial hard goods	−36	−12	− 9	− 5	− 8
104. Salesmen, wholesale, publications and advertising	−15	− 1	− 8	−43	−17
105. Scientists, biological	33	12	25	− 7	−21
106. Scientists, physical	80	22	23	5	− 8
107. Scientists, social	64	33	21	−49	−26
108. Sheet-metal workers	−11	−55	−27	25	−24
109. Social and welfare workers	− 8	−35	−40	−67	−34
110. Specifications writers, estimators	12	2	15	6	− 3
111. Steel workers	−29	−37	−23	− 8	−31
112. Surveyors	−25	−32	40	38	8
113. Teachers, elementary	− 9	18	−27	−75	−32
114. Teachers, high school English, languages, social studies	−50	−37	−20	−102	−18
115. Teachers, high school mathematics and science	35	11	− 4	− 1	− 2
116. Teachers, high school, other	− 8	10	6	0	4
117. Telephone installers	−19	−20	5	5	− 2
118. Treasurers and comptrollers	55	96	23	−31	5
119. Undertakers	−14	23	−35	−30	−12
120. Underwriters, insurance	3	2	− 9	−31	10
121. Veterinarians	− 8	− 2	−20	−16	− 5
122. Welders, lead burners	−61	−52	−32	− 3	3
123. Wholesalers	−13	18	− 4	−23	−23
124. Writers	42	0	2	−50	−24

From: R. L. Thorndike and E. Hagen, *Ten Thousand Careers* (New York: John Wiley & Sons, Inc., 1959) pp. 27–30.

Three aspects of general educational development are considered in the *Dictionary*. These include reasoning development, mathematical development, and language development. Each of these areas is divided into six levels ranging from the most elementary to the highly theoretical and abstruse. Table 4 (pp. 106–108), reproduced from page 652 of Volume II of the *1965 Dictionary*, illustrates the three areas and the six levels of each.

Specific vocational preparation includes the time required to learn the techniques, acquire information, and develop the facility needed for average performance in a specific job. The preparation may be obtained in school, at work, or from other sources. It would include training received in any of the following situations:

    a. Vocational education
    b. Apprentice training
    c. In-plant training
    d. On-the-job training
    e. Essential experience in other related, less responsible jobs

Specific vocational preparation is divided into nine ranges of training time extending from "over 10 years" at the most advanced level downward to "short demonstration only." The nine ranges include: [45]

1. Short demonstration only
2. Anything beyond short demonstration up to and including 30 days
3. Over 30 days up to and including 3 months
4. Over 3 months up to and including 6 months
5. Over 6 months up to and including 1 year
6. Over 1 year up to and including 2 years
7. Over 2 years up to and including 4 years
8. Over 4 years up to and including 10 years
9. Over 10 years

The training time requirements, both general educational development and specific vocational preparation for all jobs defined in the *1965 Dictionary*, are listed in the *1966 Supplement* and in the *1968 Supplement 2* of the *Dictionary*. One can see there, for example, that the occupation of physicist carries a GED code of 6 and an SVP code of 8, indicating that this occupation requires the highest level of abstract and theoretical thinking and specific vocational preparation extending from four to ten years.

PHYSICAL CAPACITIES OR DEMANDS

A moment's reflection is sufficient to realize that every work situation requires some type of physical involvement of the worker; conversely, every worker brings to the work situation certain physical capacities that are utilized in the process of performing the work. Just as the physical characteristics or capacities of individuals vary, so also might one expect that the physical demands associated with different types of work would vary. Some occupations require minimum output of all types of physical activity, some require rather vigorous action of one or two types, and still others involve strenuous activity of a wide variety.

The *1965 Dictionary,* the *1966 Supplement,* and *Supplement 2* include information about physical demands. The *Dictionary* includes the material in the qualifications profile, hence the information is generalized to all occupations making up each worker trait arrangement. Both *Supplements* list physical demands for each defined occupation. The worker must possess physical capacities at least equivalent to the physical demands of the job.

Physical demands are grouped into six factors, the first of which has five degrees. Definitions of each have been taken from the *1965 Dictionary.*[46]

Physical Capacities Factors

1. Lifting, carrying, pushing, and pulling:
   These are the primary "strength" physical requirements, and, generally speaking, a person who engages in one of these activities can engage in all. Specifically, each of these activities can be described as:
   1. *Lifting:* Raising or lowering an object from one level to another (includes upward pulling).
   2. *Carrying:* Transporting an object, usually holding it in the hands or arms or on the shoulder.
   3. *Pushing:* Exerting force upon an object so that the object moves away from the force (includes slapping, striking, kicking, and treadle actions).
   4. *Pulling:* Exerting force upon an object so that the object moves toward the force (includes jerking).

The five degrees of Physical Demands Factor No. 1 are as follows:

Sedentary Work: Lifting 10 pounds maximum and occasionally lifting and/or carrying such articles as dockets, ledgers, and small tools. Although a sedentary job is defined as one which involves sitting, a certain amount of walking and standing is often necessary in carrying out job duties. Jobs are sedentary if walking and standing are required only occasionally and other sedentary criteria are met.

Light Work: Lifting 20 pounds maximum with frequent lifting and/or carrying of objects weighing up to 10 pounds. Even though the weight lifted may be only a negligible amount, a job is in this category when it requires walking or standing to a significant degree, or when it involves

TABLE 4. General Educational Development

LEVEL	REASONING DEVELOPMENT	MATHEMATICAL DEVELOPMENT	LANGUAGE DEVELOPMENT
6	Apply principles of logical or scientific thinking to a wide range of intellectual and practical problems. Deal with nonverbal symbolism (formulas, scientific equations, graphs, musical notes, etc.) in its most difficult phases. Deal with a variety of abstract and concrete variables. Apprehend the most abstruse classes of concepts.	Apply knowledge of advanced mathematical and statistical techniques such as differential and integral calculus, factor analysis, and probability determination, or work with a wide variety of theoretical mathematical concepts and make original applications of mathematical procedures, as in empirical and differential equations.	Comprehension and expression of a level to —Report, write, or edit articles for such publications as newspapers, magazines, and technical or scientific journals. Prepare and draw up deeds, leases, wills, mortgages, and contracts. —Prepare and deliver lectures on politics, economics, education, or science. —Interview, counsel, or advise such people as students, clients, or patients, in such matters as welfare eligibility, vocational rehabilitation, mental hygiene, or marital relations. —Evaluate engineering technical data to design buildings and bridges.
5	Apply principles of logical or scientific thinking to define problems, collect data, establish facts, and draw valid conclusions. Interpret an extensive variety of technical instructions, in books, manuals, and mathematical or diagrammatic form. Deal with several abstract and concrete variables.		
4	Apply principles of rational systems[1] to solve practical	Perform ordinary arithmetic, algebraic, and geometric	Comprehension and expression of a level to

problems and deal with a variety of concrete variables in situations where only limited standardization exists. Interpret a variety of instructions furnished in written, oral, diagrammatic, or schedule form	procedures in standard, practical applications.	—Transcribe dictation, make appointments for executive and handle his personal mail, interview and screen people wishing to speak to him, and write routine correspondence on own initiative. —Interview job applicants to determine work best suited for their abilities and experience, and contact employees to interest them in services of agency. —Interpret technical manuals as well as drawings and specifications, such as layouts, blueprints, and schematics.
3 Apply common sense understanding to carry out instructions furnished in written, oral, or diagrammatic form. Deal with problems involving several concrete variables in or from standardized situations.	Make arithmetic calculations involving fractions, decimals and percentages.	Comprehension and expression of a level to —File, post, and mail such material as forms, checks, receipts, and bills. —Copy data from one record to another, fill in report forms, and type all work from rough draft or corrected copy.

TABLE 4. (Cont.)

LEVEL	REASONING DEVELOPMENT	MATHEMATICAL DEVELOPMENT	LANGUAGE DEVELOPMENT
2	Apply common sense understanding to carry out detailed but uninvolved written or oral instructions. Deal with problems involving a few concrete variables in or from standardized situations.	Use arithmetic to add, subtract, multiply, and divide whole numbers.	—Interview members of household to obtain such information as age, occupation, and number of children, to be used as data for surveys, or economic studies. —Guide people on tours through historical or public buildings, describing such features as size, value, and points of interest.
1	Apply common sense understanding to carry out simple one- or two-step instructions. Deal with standardized situations with occasional or no variables in or from these situations encountered on the job.	Perform simple addition and subtraction, reading and copying of figures, or counting and recording.	Comprehension and expression of a level to —Learn job duties from oral instructions or demonstration. —Write identifying information, such as name and address of customer, weight, number, or type of product, on tags, or slips. —Request orally, or in writing, such supplies as linen, soap, or work materials.

[1] Examples of "principles of rational systems" are: Bookkeeping, internal combustion engines, electric wiring systems, house building, nursing, farm management, ship sailing.

From *Dictionary of Occupational Titles*, 1965, Volume II, Occupational Classification, page 652.

sitting most of the time with a degree of pushing and pulling of arm and/or leg controls.

Medium Work: Lifting 50 pounds maximum, with frequent lifting and carrying of objects weighing up to 25 pounds.

Heavy Work: Lifting 100 pounds maximum, with frequent lifting and carrying of objects weighing up to 50 pounds.

Very Heavy Work: Lifting objects in excess of 100 pounds, with frequent lifting and carrying of objects weighing 50 pounds or more.

2. Climbing and/or balancing:
   1. *Climbing:* Ascending or descending ladders, stairs, scaffolding, ramps, poles, ropes, and the like, using the feet and legs and/or hands and arms.
   2. *Balancing:* Maintaining body equilibrium to prevent falling when walking, standing, crouching, or running on narrow, slippery, or erratically moving surfaces; or maintaining body equilibrium when performing gymnastic feats.
3. Stooping, kneeling, crouching, and/or crawling:
   1. *Stooping:* Bending the body downward and forward by bending the spine at the waist.
   2. *Kneeling:* Bending the legs at the knees to come to rest on the knee or knees.
   3. *Crouching:* Bending the body downward and forward by bending the legs and spine.
   4. *Crawling:* Moving about on the hands and knees or hands and feet.
4. Reaching, handling, fingering, and/or feeling:
   1. *Reaching:* Extending the hands and arms in any direction.
   2. *Handling:* Seizing, holding, grasping, turning, or otherwise working with the hand or hands; fingering not involved.
   3. *Fingering:* Picking, pinching, or otherwise working with the fingers primarily (rather than with the whole hand or arm as in handling).
   4. *Feeling:* Perceiving such attributes of objects and materials as size, shape, temperature, or texture, by means of receptors in the skin, particularly those of the finger tips.
5. Talking and/or hearing:
   1. *Talking:* Expressing or exchanging ideas by means of the spoken word.
   2. *Hearing:* Perceiving the nature of sounds by the ear.
6. Seeing:
   Obtaining impressions through the eyes of the shape, size, distance, motion, color, or other characteristics of objects. The major visual functions are: 1. acuity, far and near; 2. depth perception; 3. field of vision; 4. accommodation; 5. color vision. The functions are defined as follows:
   1. *Acuity, far:* clarity of vision at 20 feet or more.
      Acuity, near: clarity of vision at 20 inches or less.
   2. *Depth perception:* three dimensional vision. The ability to judge distance and space relationships so as to see objects where and as they actually are.

3. *Field of vision:* the area that can be seen up and down or to the right or left while the eyes are fixed on a given point.
4. *Accommodation:* adjustment of the lens of the eye to bring an object into sharp focus. This item is especially important when doing near-point work at varying distances from the eye.
5. *Color vision:* the ability to identify and distinguish colors.

WORKING CONDITIONS

Working conditions are the physical surroundings of the job-worker situation that make specific demands on a worker's physical capacities. Most of us work in comfortable, well-lighted offices and give little thought to the minimal demands that our work situation imposes on us. Many other workers are confronted with specific sets of circumstances imposed by the location and nature of the work that place far heavier demands on them. For example, a blast furnace keeper in a steel mill is confronted with extreme temperatures as a normal part of the work and the miner is faced with noise, hazards, dust, and poor ventilation.

Working conditions are classified into seven factors in Volume 2 of the *1965 Dictionary,* but these are not included in the qualifications profile. These are listed in the *1966 Supplement* and in *Supplement 2* for each defined occupation. The seven factors are defined as follows: [47]

1. Inside, Outside, or Both:
   I Inside: Protection from weather conditions but not necessarily from temperature changes.
   O Outside: No effective protection from weather.
   B Both: Inside and outside.
   A job is considered "inside" if the worker spends approximately seventy-five percent or more of his time inside, and "outside" if he spends approximately seventy-five percent or more of his time outside. A job is considered "both" if the activities occur inside or outside in approximately equal amounts.
2. Extremes of Cold Plus Temperature Changes:
   1. *Extremes of Cold:* Temperature sufficiently low to cause marked bodily discomfort unless the worker is provided with exceptional protection.
   2. *Temperature Changes:* Variations in temperature which are sufficiently marked and abrupt to cause noticeable bodily reactions.
3. Extremes of Heat Plus Temperature Changes:
   1. *Extremes of Heat:* Temperature sufficiently high to cause marked bodily discomfort unless the worker is provided with exceptional protection.
   2. *Temperature Changes:* Same as 2 (2).
4. Wet and Humid:
   1. *Wet:* Contact with water or other liquids.
   2. *Humid:* Atmospheric conditions with moisture content sufficiently high to cause marked bodily discomfort.

5. Noise and Vibration:
   Sufficient noise, either constant or intermittent, to cause marked distraction or possible injury to the sense of hearing and/or sufficient vibration (production of an oscillating movement or strain on the body or its extremities from repeated motion or shock) to cause bodily harm if endured day after day.
6. Hazards:
   Situations in which the individual is exposed to the definite risk of bodily injury.
7. Fumes, Odors, Toxic Conditions, Dust, and Poor Ventilation:
   1. *Fumes:* Smoky or vaporous exhalations, usually odorous, thrown off as a result of combustion or chemical reaction.
   2. *Odors:* Noxious smells, either toxic or non-toxic.
   3. *Toxic Conditions:* Exposure to toxic dust, fumes, gases, vapors, mists, or liquids which cause general or localized disabling conditions as a result of inhalation or action on the skin.
   4. *Dust:* Air filled with small particles of any kind, such as textile dust, flour, wood, leather, feathers, etc., and inorganic dust, including silica and asbestos, which make the workplace unpleasant or are the source of occupational diseases.
   5. *Poor Ventilation:* Insufficient movement of air causing a feeling of suffocation, or exposure to drafts.

HIRING REQUIREMENTS

The previous sections of this chapter have considered the psychological and physical characteristics required of a worker by a particular occupation and the working situation in which that occupation is normally performed. These factors, as has been demonstrated, relate directly to the performance of the work and, under ordinary conditions, can usually be thought to be essential, minimal characteristics for successful execution of the job.

In addition to the above factors actually involved in accomplishing the work, a prospective worker may often encounter a variety of requirements in the process of gaining entry to the specific position. These additional requirements are often imposed by the employer in the selection of workers. The additional restrictions may or may not be relevant to successful performance in the specific work situation. Since they are obviously significant in determining whether an otherwise qualified worker will have the opportunity to engage in the occupation in a particular employment setting, they warrant some consideration and discussion. These demands are usually called hiring requirements.

That considerable discrepancy may exist between hiring requirements and actual job requirements is pointed out by Shartle,[48] who states that hiring requirements often vary directly with the supply and demand of labor, thus serving as a controlling device for the quantity of applications for employment. He also indicates that such restrictions can be considered at three levels: (a) preferred requirements—those demands imposed by the employer when workers are in oversupply; (b) minimum requirements—the demands made when workers are approximately in balance with the number of positions to be filled; and (c) actual job requirements—those demands that correspond to characteristics needed to perform the tasks, and when workers possessing these cannot be found, the job remains unfilled.

Because of the apparent relationship between the supply of workers and hiring requirements, considerable fluctuation occurs. It is, therefore, difficult to obtain accurate information that will remain valid over an extended period of time.

Many conditions contribute to the existence of hiring requirements that exceed actual job demands. Some have obvious validity and can easily be defended, whereas others appear to exist because of such extraneous factors as local practice, bias, and prejudice.

A detailed comparison of employers' hiring policies, preferences, and practices in New Haven, Connecticut, and Charlotte, North Carolina, is reported by Noland and Bakke.[49] Their data clearly show some of the characteristics considered by employers in filling various types of positions in the late 1940's.

Employers were asked the question "Which of this list of qualifications do you consider to be of *outstanding importance* in hiring workers for this type job?" In response, the following percentages were obtained in the two cities for all types of positions:

Characteristic	New Haven Employers	Charlotte Employers
Character	70	77
Sex	65	60
Personality traits	60	51
Physique	51	68
Particular experience	47	53
Education	44	52
Color	29	47
Top age	26	35

When asked if they had definite preferences for certain qualifications, the following percentages of employers indicated a positive response:

Characteristic	New Haven Employers	Charlotte Employers
Character	100	100
Personality	100	100
Physique	100	100
Nationality	100	100
Sex	90	94
Color	85	91

| Best age | 77 | 91 |
| Church attendance | 71 | 72 |

Ranked in descending order by type of occupational classification were the following *highly important* qualifications:

Common Labor

New Haven	Charlotte
Physique	Physique
Sex	Sex
Character	Character
Personality traits	Color
Top age	Top age

Production Worker

New Haven	Charlotte
Particular experience	Physique
Physique	Character
Sex	Particular experience
Character	Sex
Personality traits	Color

Clerical Worker

New Haven	Charlotte
Education	Education
Character	Character
Personality traits	Personality traits
Sex	Color
Color	Sex

Administrative and Executive

New Haven	Charlotte
Character	Character
Personality traits	Education
Education	Personality traits
Sex	Particular experience
Particular experience	Physique

Of particular significance is the information obtained from employers concerning their requirements and preferences with respect to education of workers. Table 5 (p. 114) shows the percentages of employers who either required or preferred high school graduation or more for the various types of worker classifications. Figures in parentheses indicate the percentage of employers requiring or preferring more than a high school education.

A review of these data demonstrates that employers often establish requirements that exceed those basic skills needed to perform in the job. Often requirements may be as totally unrelated as the location of the prospective worker's residence, his politics, his family status, or his religious affiliation. Although discrimination among applicants for employment because of race, color, creed, or sex has been legislated against for large sections of the world of work, such legislation is not all-inclusive. Effective implementation of such legislation will take many years. Even with the

TABLE 5. *Employers' Requirements and Preferences for High School Education or More by Worker Classification*[*]

WORKER CLASSIFICATION	NEW HAVEN		CHARLOTTE	
	REQUIRE	PREFER	REQUIRE	PREFER
Common labor	2	8(1)	—	13
Production worker	2	30(5)	12(1)	51(5)
Service and maintenance	11(5)	45(24)	18(4)	69(23)
Clerical	51(17)	90(54)	72(14)	99(49)
Administrative and executive	45(18)	78(59)	70(21)	98(57)

[*] Figures are per cent of employers; figures in parentheses indicate education beyond high school.

From: E. W. Noland and E. W. Bakke, *Workers Wanted.* New York: Harper & Brothers, 1949.

elimination of unfair practices, there will frequently remain situations where employers will seek workers with qualifications that exceed what is minimally required by the job.

NOTES

1. J. T. Gray, "Needs and Values in Three Occupations," *Personnel and Guidance Journal*, vol. 42, no. 3 (November, 1963), pp. 238–244.
2. V. H. Hewer, "What Do Theories of Vocational Choice Mean to a Counselor?" *Journal of Counseling Psychology*, vol. 10, no. 2 (Summer, 1963), pp. 118–125.
3. Department of Labor, *Dictionary of Occupational Titles,* 3rd ed. (Washington: U.S. Government Printing Office, 1965).
4. Department of Labor, United States Employment Service, *Estimates of Worker Trait Requirements for 4,000 Jobs* (Washington: U.S. Government Printing Office, 1955).
5. R. L. Thorndike, "The Prediction of Vocational Success," *Vocational Guidance Quarterly*, vol. 11, no. 3 (Spring, 1963), pp. 179–187.
6. A. B. Crawford and P. S. Burnham, *Forecasting College Achievement, Part I, General Consideration in the Measurement of Academic Promise* (New Haven: Yale University Press, 1946).
7. D. B. Stuit, *Predicting Success in Professional Schools* (Washington: American Council on Education, 1949).
8. J. N. Stalnaker, "Recognizing and Encouraging Talents," *American Psychologist*, vol. 16, no. 8 (August, 1961), pp. 516–517.
9. W. V. Bingham, *Aptitudes and Aptitude Testing* (New York: Harper & Row, Publishers, 1937).
10. D. E. Super and J. O. Crites, *Appraising Vocational Fitness through Psychological Means* (New York: Harper & Row, Publishers, 1962).
11. L. Goldman, *Using Tests in Counseling,* 2nd ed. (New York: Appleton-Century-Crofts, Inc., 1971).
12. L. J. Cronbach, *Essentials of Psychological Testing,* 3rd ed. (New York: Harper & Row, Publishers, 1970).

13. *Estimates, op. cit.*, pp. 122–129.

14. O. K. Buros (ed.), *The Seventh Mental Measurements Yearbook* (Highland Park, N.J.: The Gryphon Press, 1972). pp. 1055–1061.

15. S. E. Bemis, R. L. Bonner, T. F. Kearney and K. G. Von Lobsdorf, "Development of a New Occupational Aptitude Pattern Structure for the GATB," *Vocational Guidance Quarterly*, vol. 22, no. 2 (December, 1973), pp. 130–135; and "The New Occupational Aptitude Pattern Structure for the GATB," *Vocational Guidance Quarterly*, vol. 22, no. 3 (March, 1974), pp. 189–194.

16. D. E. Super, *The Psychology of Careers* (New York: Harper & Row, Publishers, 1957), pp. 218–219.

17. E. K. Strong, Jr., *Vocational Interests of Men and Women* (Stanford: Stanford University Press, 1943).

18. G. F. Kuder, *Revised Manual to the Kuder Preference Record* (Chicago: Science Research Associates, Inc., n.d.).

19. C. Gerken, "Interests: Some Questions We Haven't Asked," *Vocational Guidance Quarterly*, vol. 12, no. 4 (Summer, 1964), pp. 280–284.

20. C. McArthur and L. B. Stevens, "The Validation of Expressed Interests as Compared with Inventoried Interests: A Fourteen-Year Follow-up," *Journal of Applied Psychology*, vol. 39, no. 2 (April, 1955), pp. 184–189.

21. A. E. Ivey, "Interests and Work Values," *Vocational Guidance Quarterly*, vol. 11, no. 2 (Winter, 1963), pp. 121–124.

22. L. E. Tyler, "The Relationship of Interests to Abilities and Reputation among First-Grade Children," *Educational and Psychological Measurement*, vol. 11, no. 2 (Summer, 1951), pp. 255–264.

23. L. E. Tyler, "The Development of Vocational Interests: The Organization of Likes and Dislikes in Ten-Year-Old Children," *Journal of Genetic Psychology*, vol. 86 (March, 1955), pp. 33–44.

24. B. J. White, "The Relationship of Self Concept and Parental Identification to Women's Vocational Interest," *Journal of Counseling Psychology*, vol. 6, no. 3 (Fall, 1959), pp. 202–206.

25. W. C. Cottle, "A Factorial Study of Multiphasic, Strong, Kuder, and Bell Inventories Using a Population of Adult Males," *Psychometrika*, vol. 15, no. 1 (1950), pp. 25–47.

26. *Estimates, op. cit.*, pp. 136–141; and *Dictionary of Occupational Titles*, 1965, vol. II, p. 654.

27. D. R. Whitney, "Predicting From Expressed Choice: A Review," *Personnel and Guidance Journal*, vol. 48, no. 4 (December, 1969), pp. 279–286.

28. H. A. Rose and C. F. Elston, "Ask Him or Test Him?" *Vocational Guidance Quarterly*, vol. 19, no. 1 (September, 1970), pp. 28–32.

29. A. G. Nelson, "Discrepancy Between Expressed and Inventoried Vocational Interest," *Vocational Guidance Quarterly*, vol. 20, no. 1 (September, 1971), pp. 21–24.

30. O. K. Buros (ed.) *cp. cit.*, pp. 1452–1462.

31. For a different approach, see: S. Levine, "Occupation and Personality: Relationship between Social Factors of the Job and Human Orientation," *Personnel and Guidance Journal*, vol. 41, no. 7 (March, 1963), pp. 602–605.

32. F. J. Thumin, "Personality Characteristics of Diverse Occupational Groups," *Personnel and Guidance Journal*, vol. 43, no. 5 (January, 1965), pp. 468–470.

33. A. Roe, "Personality Structure and Occupational Behavior," in *Man in a*

World at Work, ed., Henry Borow (Boston: Houghton Mifflin Company, 1964), pp. 196–214.

34. *Estimates, op. cit.*, pp. 131–134.

35. E. Spranger, *Types of Men*, translated from 5th German edition. (Halle: Max Niemeyer, 1928).

36. J. A. Peterson, *Counseling and Values* (Scranton, Pennsylvania: International Textbook Company, 1970). p. 9.

37. M. Katz, *Decisions and Values* (New York: College Entrance Examination Board, 1963).

38. D. E. Super, *Work Values Inventory* (Boston: Houghton Mifflin Company, 1970).

39. U.S. Dept. of Labor, *Counselor's Handbook* (Washington: U.S. Government Printing Office, 1967).

40. J. C. Flanagan, "The First Fifteen Years of Project TALENT: Implications for Career Guidance," *Vocational Guidance Quarterly*, vol. 22, no. 1 (September, 1973), pp. 8–14; and "Some Pertinent Findings of Project TALENT," *Vocational Guidance Quarterly*, vol. 22, no. 2 (December, 1973), pp. 92–96.

41. D. V. Tiedeman, "Prologue," *Vocational Guidance Quarterly*, vol. 22, no. 2 (December, 1972), pp. 90–92.

42. J. C. Flanagan, D. V. Tiedeman, M. B. Willis, and D. H. McLaughlin, *The Career Data Book: Results from Project TALENT's Five-Year Follow-Up Study* (Palo Alto, Calif: American Institutes for Research, 1973), p. 145.

43. *Ibid.*, pp. 5–10.

44. R. L. Thorndike and E. Hagen, *Ten Thousand Careers* (New York: John Wiley and Sons, Inc., 1959), pp. 27–30.

45. *Dictionary, op. cit.*, pp. 652–653.

46. *Ibid.*, pp. 654–656.

47. *Ibid.*, p. 656.

48. C. L. Shartle, *Occupational Information, Its Development and Application*, 3rd ed., (Englewood Cliffs, N.J.: Prentice-Hall, Inc., 1959), p. 190.

49. E. W. Noland and E. W. Bakke, *Workers Wanted* (New York: Harper & Brothers, 1949).

4

Sociological and Economic Factors

The influence of a calling on the lives of those who follow it does not cease with the five o'clock whistle, but extends beyond the shop or office to every aspect of existence.

THEODORE CAPLOW[1]

Counselors and teachers, assisting youth and others in building career plans, have all too often focused attention entirely on the on-the-job aspects of the relationship between individuals and work. Such emphasis has routinely included consideration of the duties or tasks included in the occupation, the qualifications and preparation normally expected of the worker, the opportunities for entering and advancing in the field, expected earnings, working conditions, etc. No one will quarrel with the importance of these topics; however, when only these are considered, the picture is incomplete and superficial.

The relationship between individuals and their occupation is, in many ways, similar to the relationship between individuals and their marriage partner. Both partners contribute to meeting the needs of each other; both impose demands on the other. There must be adaptability, mutual interest and concern, tolerance, and acceptance, if compatability is to develop. The previous chapter considered some of the demands imposed on the worker in obtaining and maintaining employment in an occupation. This chapter will consider the influence of an occupation on other aspects of the worker's life—beyond the five o'clock whistle.[2]

Sociologists have long recognized the importance of work to the life of both the individual and the group. Their attention has often turned to the process by which the individual selects and enters a field of work. Articles by Lipsett [3] and by Musgrave [4] are illustrative of this focus. Sociological theories of vocational development have frequently stressed the occupational and educational background of parents, the influence of the educational system, and the role of error and accident.[5]

Danskin,[6] drawing from the work of Becker [7] and of Lastrucci,[8] has succintly shown some of the additional demands that work may impose on the worker. He has supplied the following tentative information about the professional dance band musician:

> The age range is 17 to 30 with 26 average. The typical musician changes jobs several times a year. There is a marked hierarchy of jobs, ranging from the occasional performer at small dances or receptions at one extreme to the staff positions in radio and TV stations and legitimate theatres at the other. In between these extremes are such positions as steady jobs in "joints" (pay low, community recognition lower), steady jobs in local bands in "respectable" clubs (better pay, more status than "joint" jobs), steady jobs in "class B name" orchestras, and steady jobs with "class A name" orchestras (good salaries and hours, recognized as successful). A musician must depend on "connections" to get jobs. To be successful financially a musician feels that he must sacrifice his artistic independence and play what the public wants (refusing to submit to the demands of the audiences, which are composed of "squares," means little chance for high prestige and income). A desire for freedom from outside interferences in his work generalizes to a feeling that he should not be bound by the ordinary conventions of society. . . .
>
> The incidence of marriage is less than would be expected. A musician's wife characteristically is attractive and undomestic. A couple rarely has more than one or two children. The cost of living is high (most rent furnished apartments by the week, eat out often, and dress well). A musician is rarely in one community more than three months, so he develops no sense of community belongingness. He works nights, sleeps mornings and often practices afternoons, so he has no time for new acquaintances, interests or hobbies. He is plagued by domestic trouble (a musician typically feels that his work takes precedence over his family, causing continual friction with his wife). The rate of divorce and separation is high. He often drinks heavily and has a good chance of contracting a venereal disease. Because of the insecurity of the job, he is always "going to" save money but rarely does. By the time he becomes professionally adjusted, the musician typically has become culturally and socially maladjusted.

Similar studies of other occupations would likewise reveal the tremendous impact that an individual's work has on personal life and that of the family.[9] The daily schedule within the household is usually established by the working hours of the "breadwinner." The extent and type of family group activities may be controlled, or at least heavily influenced, by the hours of the day devoted to work. As indicated above, the dance band musician has little time he can spend either in family activity or in community or recreational pursuits. The hours that he has free do not coincide with those of most other individuals. The teacher and the banker, on the other hand, find themselves in a work schedule that fits closely with family and friends. They work when most of their friends work, when their children are in school, when their wives are busy with homemaking or volunteer activities; and they have the same time free as do other members of the family, or friends.

Whyte [10] has written of the influence of the husband's occupation on the behavior of the wife. The following excerpt from one of his articles reveals this occupational impact:

> For the corporation wife, being "sociable" is as important as stabilizing. Like the Army wife (an analogy she detests), she must be a highly adaptable "mixer." In fact, she needs to be even more adaptable than the Army wife, for the social conditions she meets are more varied. One year she may be a member of a company community, another year a branch manager's wife, expected to integrate with the local community or, in some cases, to become a civic leader; and frequently, as the wife of the company representative, to provide a way station on the route of touring company brass.
>
> As a rule she is inextricably bound up in the corporation "family," often so much so that her entire behavior—including what and where she drinks—is subtly conditioned by the corporation. "It makes me laugh," says one wife in an eastern city dominated by one corporation. "If we were the kind to follow the Pattern, I'll tell you just what we would do. First, in a couple of years, we'd move out of Ferncrest Village (it's really pretty tacky there, you know). We wouldn't go straight to Eastmere Hills—that would look pushy at this stage of the game; we'd go to the hilly section off Scrubbs Mill Pike. About that time, we'd change from Christ Church to St. Edward's, and we'd start going to the Fortnightlys—it would be a different group entirely. Then, about ten years later, we'd finally build in Eastmere Hills." It just makes her laugh, she says, because that would be the signal to everybody that she had become a wife of the top-brass bracket. Which she probably will.

THE RULES OF THE GAME

> Few wives are as articulate as that on the social role, but intuitively they are generally superb at it; their antennae are sensitive, and the rules of the game they know by heart. Second nature to the seasoned wife, for example, are the following:
>
> Don't talk shop gossip with the Girls, particularly those who have husbands in the same department.
> Don't invite superiors in rank; let them make the first bid.

Don't turn up at the office unless you absolutely have to.

Don't get too chummy with the wives of associates your husband might soon pass on the way up.

Don't be disagreeable to any company people you meet. . . .

Be attractive. There is a strong correlation between executive success and the wife's appearance. . . .

Be a phone pal of your husband's secretary.

Never—repeat, never—get tight at a company party (it may go down in a dossier).

One rule transcends all others: Don't be too good. Keeping up with the Joneses is still important; but where, in pushier and more primitive times, it implied going substantially ahead of the Joneses, today keeping up means just that; keeping up. One can move ahead, yes—but slightly, and the timing must be exquisite.

THE ASCENDANTS

The corporation itself has a way of exploding her equable world. On one very crucial question, as a result, the rules of the game contain an inconsistency that can pose for the wife a wrenchingly tough dilemma. What is she to do if her husband begins moving up faster than his age group? In advancing the husband in the office, the corporation is quite likely to advance him socially as well; it may, for example, put him up for membership (when the company quota opens up) in one of the better local clubs; or suggest to him that, just by the way, there happens to be a good real-estate bargain in a suburb favored by the brass.

There is no easy out for the couple in such cases, and for the wife the inward tug-of-war between the social *status quo* and the prospect of advancement can be extremely poignant. As one young executive puts it, "If I go ahead as I hope, and some of our friends progress as little as I think they will, there's going to be friction. My wife can't see this. She thinks we'll hold them as friends; she is nice to everyone and thinks if you are that way, everyone will be nice to you."

The shock is not long in coming. "I must have made some terrible mistakes," laments one wife now in mid-passage. "I love people and I've made many intimate friends in the company, but since Charlie got his new job it's just been hell on us. He has so much control over their lives, and it's all gotten so complicated." In a larger community the ascendant couple would have recourse, for there exists a sort of freemasonry of success, where they can talk freely without anyone taking offense. But in the smaller community their upward course is more difficult, as, baffled and hurt, they try to hang on to their old friends and wonder why they are rebuffed.

Eventually most adjust. The price, however, is a kind of social professionalism. The wife must now learn to make "constructive" friendships, to become consciously aware of the vagaries and gradations of the social structure of business—and learn to play an entirely new role in it. "It's tough," says the wife of a thirty-five-year-old plant manager. "You have got to leave behind your old friends. You have to weigh the people you invite to parties. You have to be careful of who you send Christmas cards to and who you don't. It sounds like snobbery, but it's just something you have to do. You have to be a boss's wife."

While few young wives are aware of the sacrifice involved, the role of the boss's wife is one that they very much covet. In talking about the qualities of the ideal wife—a subject they evidently had thought over long and often—they were at no loss. In one-third of the cases, the word "gracious" came instantly to them, and in nearly all the others the descriptions spelled out the same thing. Theirs is sort of First Lady ideal, a woman who takes things as they come with grace and poise, and a measure of *noblesse oblige;* in short, the perfect boss's wife.

Shaycroft has provided further evidence that underscores the impact of father's occupation on the family.[11] Data that he has drawn from the Project TALENT study reveals the relationship between the amount of education completed within five years after high school and the socio-economic status of the individual (usually determined primarily by the occupation of the father). Shaycroft shows a direct relationship between the two items: as socio-economic status increases, the likelihood of post-secondary education increases for both males and females in his sample, even when individuals were sorted according to academic aptitude. For example, within the bottom ten per cent of academic aptitude, from 16 to 29 per cent of boys from lowest socio-economic categories dropped out of high school, whereas seven to twelve per cent of boys from top socio-economic categories withdrew. Among girls the differences were even greater.

Zafiran also has reported that the combination of an individual's educational attainment, his adult social class, and his father's occupational socio-economic status account for most of the explained variance in the respondent's occupational socio-economic status.[12] Since we have indicated above that educational attainment relates in part to father's status, we can see that father's occupation has tremendous influence on the individual's ultimate career patterns, not totally defining, but heavily contributing.

Further evidence of the relationship between a man's occupation and his family is shown by Dyer,[13] who studied the reciprocating influence between family attitudes and father's job satisfaction. His study was an attempt to determine the extent to which the father served as a bridge between the two separate social systems of occupation and family life. Dyer hypothesized that the father did, in fact, serve as such a conciliating force; he specifically proposed: (1) that the father's job satisfaction is influenced by the feelings of his wife and children toward his job; and also (2) that family members gain satisfaction about the father's job according to their perceptions of his work.

To test the first hypothesis, he ran a number of correlational studies between attitudes of various family members and father's reported job satisfaction. In general, the correlations were quite high and positive; for example, father's job satisfaction and his wife's job satisfaction correlated .61; father's job satisfaction and the combined score of wife and children correlated .81. Obviously, the correlations do not show cause and effect; they do, however, show a high relationship.

The major dissatisfaction for wife and children, in contacts outside the family itself, was lack of prestige of the father's job. When the father was asked what his family liked about his job, he generally picked the same items as did other members of the family when they were questioned— salary, steady work, regular hours, and the fact that he liked his work. Items disliked both by father and family members included poor hours, dirty work, low salary, and danger.

Recent writers have confirmed the view of Caplow quoted at the beginning of this chapter. Current references in popular magazines, as well as in the professional literature, to "blue-collar blues" and "white-collar woes" emphasize the impact of work-related difficulties on the lives of workers. The very existence of two different terms suggests that different kinds of problems affect different kinds of workers in different kinds of ways. The following quotation from *Work in America* delineates the development of social alienation.[14]

There is now convincing evidence that some blue-collar workers are carrying their work frustrations home and displacing [sic] them in extremist social and political movements or in hostility toward the government. For other workers apathy is the reaction to the same set of social circumstances. The symptoms of the blue-collar blues are part of the popular sociology in America. The middlemass, the hard-hats, the silent majority, the forgotten Americans, the Archie Bunkers as they have been variously called are characterized as alienated from their society, aggressive against people unlike themselves, distrusting of others, and harboring an inadequate sense of personal or political efficacy. Yet, contrary to popular opinion, Stanley E. Seashore and Thad J. Barnowe found that the blues are not confined to any one cohort—sex, age, income status, collar color, or any combination of these traits.[15] Rather, the blues are associated with the possessor's conditions of life at work. But adequate and equitable pay, reasonable security, safety, comfort, and convenience on the job do not insure the worker against the blues. The potent factors that impinge on the worker's values, according to Seashore and Barnowe, are those that concern his self-respect, a chance to perform well in his work, a chance for personal achievement and growth in competence, and a chance to contribute something personal and unique to his work.

Further evidence that political and social attitudes and behavior are related to work experiences and expectations comes from a recent study of blue-collar union members by Harold Sheppard and N. Herrick.[16] They found that where aspirations relating to work are not realized, it is not uncommon to find a degree of bitterness and alienation among workers that is reflected in a reduced sense of political efficacy. These "alienated" workers tend to participate less in elections and, when they do vote, tend to cast their ballots for extremist or "protest" candidates. These dissatisfied workers are far more likely than satisfied workers to believe that the lot of the average person has been getting worse. They are more authoritarian in their views (they tend to prefer strong leaders to democratically developed laws). The key variable in this study, as in the previously cited study, appears to be the nature of the tasks performed by the workers. For example, those workers with jobs that measure high on variety, autonomy, and use of skills were found to be low on measures of political and personal alienation.

. . . . .

Traditionally, lower-level white-collar jobs in both government and industry were held by high school graduates. Today, an increasing number of these jobs go to those who have attended college. But the demand for higher academic credentials has not increased the prestige, status, pay, or difficulty of the job. For example, the average weekly pay for clerical workers in 1969 was $105.00 per week, while blue-collar production workers were taking home an average of $130.00 per week.[17] It is not surprising, then, that the Survey of Working Conditions found much of the greatest work dissatisfaction in the country among young, well-educated workers who were in low-paying, dull, routine, and fractionated clerical positions. Other signs of discontent among this group include turnover rates as high as 30% annually and a 46% increase in white-collar union membership between 1955 and 1968.

The worker dissatisfactions described above express themselves in many ways, both within the work setting and away from the job. On the job, many workers report decreased productivity as a technique for protesting against the frustration and dissatisfaction encountered at work. Off the job, frustration and hostility are often expressed in various anti-social acts, including excessive drinking, barroom brawling, and extra-marital affairs. Thus, the worker's job imposes an effect on not only the life of the worker but also on the life of every member of the family.

REGULATING ADMISSION TO OCCUPATIONS

Colleges and universities with strong athletic programs have used a wide array of techniques to attract outstanding high school athletes. The military services participate vigorously, even competitively, in recruiting practices. Many occupations and professions similarly exert considerable effort to attract new entrants to the field. In some cases, the procedures used are as open and spirited as those of the military. In many other situations, however, the process is performed with subtlety and diplomatic finesse. Coxon has described the procedures used in attracting candidates to the Anglican ministry.[18] Sherlock and Cohen have considered the systems used to encourage entrants into dentistry,[19] and Curie *et al.* have discussed the impact of occupational image on potential recruits for college teaching.[20] Duncan has demonstrated that even in professional areas that recruit widely, differences may be shown in employment patterns.[21] For example, he found that professional workers who came from higher socio-economic backgrounds were more likely to be involved in private practice, whereas those who came from lower socio-economic levels were more likely to be in salaried positions.

Purpose

Many occupational groups have established various methods of restricting entrance into the occupation. Most of these regulating devices serve one or the other of two basic purposes. Some of the restrictions are established to protect the public (those outside the occupation) from incompetence and inefficiency, and thus are intended to uphold adequate standards. Other regulations are established primarily to protect the group within the occupation, particularly by maintaining the level of income by preventing an oversupply of workers.

Formal Control

Some occupations, especially many of the professions, have successfully established formal control of admission procedures. This is usually accomplished through requiring the completion of specific schooling of a particular type and duration, or by demanding that the prospective applicant serve an apprenticeship or internship of a specified period. The imposition of a lengthy training program on potential candidates controls the number of applicants in several ways: for one, a long period of preparation discourages some by reducing the attractiveness of the work; secondly, the training establishments often serve as a selective instrument, restricting the members admitted to preparatory programs.

Cottrell[22] has listed the factors that control admission to the railroad occupation of locomotive engineer. He emphasizes the importance of physical fitness, especially seeing and hearing, and the willingness to wait through an often lengthy period of "extra board" assignments before earning a position as a fireman from which the worker should, in due course (perhaps several more years) be promoted to the position of engineer. The number of men who can be listed on the "extra board" is restricted by the men with regular assignments, thus limiting not only those who might in time compete for regular assignments, but who also may ultimately qualify to move on to engineer. Movement through these steps is strictly and completely based on seniority. Thus, a job that can be learned in half a year may require anywhere from a minimum of two or three years to a maximum of a decade or more before the worker gains full admission.

Licensing and Certification

As an occupational group becomes strongly established and clearly recognized, it may successfully develop additional means of controlling admission by arranging for legally recognized bodies to have the power to issue licenses or certificates. As the group becomes more professionalized, it may reach the point at which the profession itself controls the preparatory program and the licensing procedure. This concentration of power and control evolves gradually, with the profession increasing its position because of technical complexities in the preparatory program, or in the actual practice of the profession. The position of the general public becomes, for all practical purposes, a token one, and the profession continues as a self-regulating body. This arrangement continues indefinitely unless the balance is upset because of serious abuses by the professional group, or unless the restriction of membership becomes so limited that the public welfare is endangered by a shortage of competent workers. Should either possibility occur, the public may reassert its fundamental control.

Shimberg, Esser, and Kruger have emphasized that the establishment of licensing procedures has usually been the result of special efforts by practitioners.[23] Customarily, such legislation has resulted in the creation of a regulatory board composed, either primarily or entirely, of practitioners of the occupation itself. The control exerted by such boards has sometimes been unpredictable, spasmodic, and usually in the interest of the special group. Little attention is given to broader implications of licensure and its effect on the general public. Often the usual requirements for licensing (age, sex, education, and citizenship) have no established relationship to the stated reasons for licensing. Examination procedures are frequently inadequate and lacking in professional testing procedures.

"Certification," "registration," and "licensure" are sometimes considered to be synonomous. There is, however, a significant technical difference. Certification and registration usually represent the granting of recognition of qualification or competence to certain individuals in an occupation or profession, usually by a nongovernmental agency or association as a result of completing a prescribed preparatory program, by successful completion of an examination, or by successful completion of a specified period of work experience. Licensure, on the other hand, includes a legal right to engage in an occupation, usually conferred by a governmental agency.

Shimberg, *et al.*, have examined licensing procedures in several states. They describe the use of license regulatory boards by one professional group to control a closely related occupation. For example, the licensing boards for Licensed Practical Nurses, in most states included in their study, were primarily populated by Registered Nurses who frequently voted in unison on matters related to control of the other group. Similarly, licensing boards for Dental Hygienists are almost totally made up of dentists. The report describes procedures by which the authority of such licensing boards is used by dentists to protect the economic interest of the dentists rather than the public welfare.

The examination required for certification as an over-the-road driver is administered by the prospective employer and the certificate is issued by the employer. This procedure obviously permits considerable variability in decisions relative to marginal applicants; perhaps the demand for drivers could be a major criterion.

Teacher certification programs provide a further illustration of the formal control of admission procedures to a professional area. Each state has a designated agency, usually within the Department of Public Instruction, responsible for administering certification regulations. In general, these regulations specify that only holders of appropriate teaching certificates may be employed as teachers (or in other educational positions) in approved school systems. Qualification for a teaching certificate demands completion of an educational program including both general courses and specific professional preparatory courses in approved colleges and universities. Additional practical experience in supervised teaching, internship, or practicum may sometimes be required. Certification standards usually are established through committees or commissions that include representatives from teacher groups, school administrators, teacher preparing institutions, the state regulating agency, and sometimes the general public. Once established, these certification standards have the impact of law and may be effectively enforced through control of financial support or of accreditation or recognition of the local school that employs teachers.

As one can deduce from the references used in this section, many studies citing the regulation of admission to various occupations can be found in sociological journals. Many individuals in the helping relationship—teacher, school counselor, psychologist, and social worker—will have had first hand experience in the certification process. This experience does not ordinarily provide an adequate base for understanding the publicly-recognized procedures of regulating admission such as licensure and certification, to say nothing of the covert and "informal" control procedures. Shimberg, *et al.*, have clearly emphasized the chaotic state of licensing practices. Because of local variability, accurate information, if available at all, can only be obtained from the responsible agency within the geographic area of interest to the individual.

Dental Hygienists: A dental hygienist is generally required to be at least 18 years of age, a high school graduate, and of good moral character. . . .

The critical requirement for dental hygienists is the completion of a 2- or 4-year training program approved by the state board of dental examiners or by the American Dental Hygienists Association. Some 49 out of 53 licensing jurisdictions use the examination prepared by the National Board of Dental Examiners in lieu of their own state examinations for dental hygienists. . . .

The application form used by the licensing board in Oklahoma illustrates how deeply boards probe into the affairs of applicants. In addition to the usual information such as name, address, birth date, and citizenship, the Oklahoma application requests the following:

Membership in professional societies or organizations

Height, weight, sex, and color of hair and eyes

Religion

Marital status—name of spouse

Mother's name, father's name, and their respective addresses and occupations

Name of relatives engaged in the practice of medicine or dentistry

Name of dentist with whom they expect to practice if licensed

Two character references

A declaration that the applicant has never been charged with or convicted of a felony

Whether applicant has been accused of moral turpitude in any court and the disposition of the charges

Addiction to the use of drugs, narcotics, or alcohol

Evidence of mental or nervous disorders, including sexual perversion

Any treatment for mental disorders

Other Methods of Control

Both Wilensky and Hughes have discussed the efforts of many occupations to become professions.[24,25] One factor that often prompts such groups to move toward professionalization is the desire to obtain greater control over the recruitment and selection of entrants. Both authors emphasize that few occupations undertaking such efforts succeed in winning the status that they seek. Hughes also points out that the concept of the professions is changing to include salaried professionals in bureaucratic organizations as well as those in private practice.

Many of the skilled crafts use an apprenticeship program to regulate admission. Although there is usually nationwide agreement concerning the length and content of the apprenticeship, the extent to which it is actually enforced may vary considerably depending on a number of factors. In occupational groups that are extensively organized, enforcement is more widespread than in groups that are only partially organized. With the latter groups, apprenticeships may exist in those geographic areas (often in metropolitan or highly industrialized sections) where organization is strong, and be nonexistent or spotty in areas that are not organized.

The recruitment or admission of factory workers rests primarily with the employer. The previous chapter includes a description of hiring requirements, many of which are used as regulating devices to control the number of workers. In industries in which workers are organized, the control of admission is at least shared in part by the workers' organization through such devices as the hiring hall.

Groups that exert an influence on admission to an occupation may be groups of employers or groups of workers. Where the work is essentially professional or technical, such groups are likely to be known as associations or societies.[26] If the work is primarily nonprofessional, the organization is likely to be known as a union and is probably affiliated with other similar groups.[27]

Occupational groups that have clearly established training programs for prospective entrants often use the program to assist the neophyte in developing identification with the group. Becker and Carper have shown how graduate study in the areas of physiology, engineering, and philosophy leads to identification by the entrant with the specific field.[28]

Whittaker and Olesen have described another way by which a profession attracts and holds recruits to a field.[29] They discuss the creation of a myth or legend concerning Florence Nightingale by the nursing profession and its use in building the socialization of student nurses so that they develop attitudes and values that are congruent with those established by the profession. They also show that the legend has sufficient flexibility so that it can adjust to differing training situations, with university-related training programs using different aspects of the legend than hospital-based programs.

Sherlock and Morris have described the process by which dentists are recruited, educated, and moved into the profession.[30] Myerhoff and Larson have studied the changes that have developed in the field of medicine with increased emphasis on the physician's learned skills and techniques and de-emphasis of magical accomplishments.[31] Dennison has listed factors that have an effect on the selection and development of music composers in the United States.[32]

REGULATING BEHAVIOR ON THE JOB

Regulations, either formal or informal, also exist to control the behavior of the worker on the job.[33] The existence of these restrictions is usually justified on the same grounds as those for rules related to admission—protection of the public or of the occupational group. Caplow has suggested that for certain jobs—for example, policeman and locomotive engineer—the training for the occupation consists primarily of learning the rules controlling the work, rather than learning the nature of the work itself.[34]

Codes of Ethics

Professions that are primarily self-regulating usually maintain control of occupational behavior by means of codes of ethics. Caplow points out that such codes ordinarily include five essential features:

1. The prohibition of certain acts by which the practitioner abuses the client for his own advantage.
2. The prohibition of certain other acts considered antisocial in themselves.
3. The prohibition of business procedures that give the practitioner a permanent advantage in competition with his fellows. Often, but not invariably, specifications of a minimum fee or wage.
4. Specifications of the rules of eligibility and ineligibility, together with the interdiction of activities capable of weakening the professional monopoly.
5. The claim to whatever legal exemptions are necessary to accomplish the foregoing purposes, among these being professional confidence and the right to refuse to divulge information; immunity from prosecution in the event of various accidents; and the corporate privileges of the professional society.

In recent years, working rules frequently have been included in the agreements negotiated between employers and unions. Formal statements often refer to wage rates, hiring conditions, safety rules, special equipment or tools, regulation of rest periods, responsibility for company property, etc. Although not often included in the formal statement, there is frequently unspoken agreement concerning what constitutes a reasonable day's production. The workers within a specific plant often establish a production norm that they consider reasonable. The new employee soon learns from his co-workers the standards that they expect him to meet. The resistance to incentive wage rates is usually based on the concern by the workers that the highly productive "eager beaver" will either cause the rates per unit to be lowered or the number of workers needed to be reduced. Either of these would be a threat to the occupational group.[35]

Preparatory Programs

Behavior on the job is sometimes determined by the nature of the preparatory program through which workers progress before gaining admission to the field.[36] Devereux and Weiner describe the impact of this process on the occupational behavior of nurses as they are taught to respond promptly and unquestioningly to the physician's directions.[37] Devereux and Weiner further describe the cold, unfeeling, sterile climate that often pervades hospitals as a result of teaching nurses to limit the emotional support, or "tender, loving care" that might be dispensed to the patients. They ascribe this limiting of the nurses's behavior on the job primarily to the behavioral patterns established within the institutional hierarchy of the hospital. Further limiting factors are identified as the physician's emphasis on the organic or physical problems of the patient and additionally the rigidity of a structure that prevents the nurse, in turn, from receiving emotional gratification—an opportunity to "recharge emotional batteries." This brief quotation from the Devereux-Weiner article summarizes their view of this behavioral control:

> The nurse is, therefore, frequently forced to display an excessively professional attitude, which stultifies her relationship with her patients and stunts her both professionally and emotionally. By contrast, an established physician, secure in his position, can—and usually does— unbend and act human. In fact, the truly great physician seldom displays a traditionally professional facade, even when meeting human beings professionally. The nurse, on the other hand, often cannot afford to lose her dignity as a "professional" lest she should promptly be equated with what Civil Service terminology calls "subprofessional personnel." In brief, what "respectability," as a badge of membership in the middle classes, means to the lower-middle classes, a professional attitude means to the nurse.

Simpson also has studied the procedures used by the nursing profession in professionalizing those who are inducted into the field.[38] He describes a sequential pattern in which the lay concepts of the novice are transformed into technical concepts, on-the-job training with senior colleagues exposes the student nurse to professionals who become "significant others" who are used as patterns, and finally the internalization of professional values. Meyer and Hoffman describe the effect that certain values have on occupational performance.[39] For example, a nurse who is oriented toward patients will have more contacts with patients than a colleague in the same setting whose orientation is directed toward fellow workers.

Pressure from Others

The devices by which news reporting is kept consistent with newspaper policy are described by Breed.[40] The reporter becomes aware of the newspaper's viewpoint on public affairs by reading earlier issues, talking with his colleagues and superiors, and observing the deletions and rewrites on materials which he submits for publication. The newspaper's "policy" is often unverbalized and subtle, nevertheless, the novice reporter soon learns the point of view to use in preparing his stories.

Descriptions of on-the-job behavioral control that border on the illegal and unethical are provided by Mars in studies of dock workers and hotel waiters.[41] The close-knit nature of the dock gang and the setting within which they work provide access to cargo for safe pilferage. This activity is often accomplished by cooperation within the work gang in falsifying papers, blocking the view of supervisors, serving as lookouts, etc. Gang membership often requires participation in such acts but within the limits of quantity and type of cargo taken determined by the gang itself. Similarly, Mars found that waiters in many British hotel dining rooms were expected by both management and other waiters to supplement an inadequate wage system by an institutionalized pilferage system known as "the fiddle." This consisted in many cases of an organized system, often requiring or expecting cooperation from other fellow workers, in which food or drinks by-pass the control clerk. By using hidden crockery, ambiguously written tickets, or devious methods of regaining possession of tickets, the waiter orders, and is charged for, two or three coffees that he then converts to, and collects for, four or five coffees. The additional income must usually be shared with the Head Waiter, and some compensation, often in the form of a beer, provided for any "bent" employee who assists in the fiddle. The practice appears so prevalent that management usually attempts merely to limit the opportunities for fiddles rather than completely eliminating them—an action that would ordinarily result in all of the staff leaving to accept positions elsewhere with better opportunities.

Many factors enter the work situation to exert pressure for control and conformity on the worker. These include more that the relationship between employer and employee, which in itself may impose many restrictions on worker behavior. In addition, one must consider forces emanating from fellow workers, the clientele served by the work situation, and even the general public.

Lewis has studied the factors involved in the dismissal of staff from colleges and universities, thus shedding indirect light on pressures that control behavior on the job.[42] His review of dismissals covered the period from 1916 to 1962, which he divided into three periods with breaking points at the early 30's and the middle 40's. He reports that substandard performance is not a major cause of dismissal. At least 20 per cent of those dismissed were involved in conflict with students, colleagues, or administration. During the period from 1945 to 1962, he found that the most salient reason for dismissal was the faculty member's ideological position. The impact of pressure from outside groups was also greatest during the 1945 to 1962 period.

Similarly, Wallace has found that law students who expect to enter legal practice after completion of their schooling adopt the same standards and values that are held by lawyers.[43] At the same time, fellow law school students whose career plans do not include expectancies for legal practice do not accept those standards.

Role Conflicts

Denzin and Mettlin have revealed the conflict that develops within a group when solidarity of commitment fails.[44] Recent technological advances leading to an increase in the compounding and packaging of a large assortment of drugs has reduced the need for the pharmacist's professional skill and increased the need for business competency. Pharmacists are thus caught in conflict and must either stress one or the other aspect of their image, or develop some hybridized role that serves as a compromise between the two. Montague has proposed that the medical profession may also be facing a similar conflict as a result of its move beyond the mandate that society has given.[45] He suggests that the business ethic may be replacing the older professional ethic as physicians organize into clinics and other systems to increase efficiency and decrease the traditional doctor-patient relationships.

Role conflict within the occupational structure is prevalent in many occupations. Malone, Berkowitz, and Klein have stressed the problems that nurses face and that were alluded to in the excerpt from Devereux and Weiner.[46] Sterbing has analyzed those problems encountered by the high school teacher.[47] Evan has reported the problems of the engineering technician, and Lewis those of the advertising man.[48] Lewis points out, for example, the six following types of conflict encountered in the advertising agency office:

1. Conflicts among executives on separate accounts for staff help that is scarce.
2. Conflicts between account executives and staff because staff feels that executives are too demanding.
3. Conflicts between account executives and department executives over the assignment of staff.

4. Conflicts involving differences in perspective on the part of technicians, artists, and specialists, on the one hand, and business-oriented account supervisors, on the other hand.
5. Conflicts among specialist groups regarding the relative importance of their particular function in the advertising industry.
6. Conflicts among creative groups charged with the responsibility of working up an advertising campaign for the same client.

In addition to coping with this unusual quantity of conflict on the job, the advertising man is confronted with the necessity for frequent and extensive readjustment. This is brought about by the uncertainty and unpredictability inherent in the nature of the work, the pressures of excessive demands imposed by unreasonable but influential clients, and economic insecurity that is caused by agency staff changes as clientele fluctuates in a highly fluid market.

Life Style

Numerous sociological studies in recent years have provided insight into the influence a person's occupation has on his/her entire life.[49,50] As indicated in the illustration earlier, the dance band musician's work prescribes the kind of housing in which he lives, prevents his active participation in community affairs, and helps to determine the type of woman he marries. In quite a different direction, but just as definitive, the high school teacher's work leads into active community life, restriction of some freedoms that most people take for granted, and a social position higher than many occupations that have considerably higher incomes.

The work of the Lynds[51] and of Hollingshead[52] describes clearly the social structure in the communities that they studied. Permeating the social organization of both localities was a pattern of behavioral expectations and standards geared to the occupation of the individual.

Whyte's[53] description of the new suburbia similarly emphasizes the pressures to conform placed on families who are grouped in broad occupational categories. Seventy-five per cent of the families he describes as living in the rental areas of Park Forest were involved in business administration, professional positions, or sales work. The rental units occupied were all priced within a narrow range and involved an annual turnover of approximately one-third. Recreational and social patterns, as well as buying habits, political attitudes, and religious affiliations, were all influenced, and often dictated, by the folkways of the group. One development area within the community consisted of homes that sold for about 20 or 30 per cent less than the typical residence. When asked to describe the people living in the less expensive homes, the Park Foresters usually used such phrases as "people who work with their hands more than their heads," "artisans," or "blue-collar."

Social correlates of occupational membership have been reviewed by Nosow.[54] He pointed out that continued school attendance, as well as the curriculum chosen by the youngsters, related to the father's occupation. At the high school level, for example, most children from middle-class families were still in school, whereas most children from the lowest social class had dropped out. This academic differential became even more pronounced at the college level, where research consistently showed that a much smaller proportion of children from families of manual laborers attended than did those from professional families.

Group Membership

Nosow similarly described research that demonstrated differences between occupational groups in such things as memberships in organizations and associations, with laboring groups belonging and participating less often; and in leisure-time activities, with laboring groups using public parks, fishing areas, and commercial entertainment, whereas middle-class groups engaged more in home recreational activities and in church membership and religious activities.

Nosow describes the differences found among religious denominations that are related, at least in part, to socio-economic and occupational differences. Warner reports in his study of Yankee City that the upper classes attended the Episcopal church; the upper-middle class were concentrated in the Unitarian, Baptist, Christian Science, and Congregational; the lower-middle class frequented the Congregational and Episcopal; the upper-lower class belonged to the Catholic and Methodist churches; and the lower-lower group were found in the Presbyterian, Methodist, Baptist, Congregational, and Catholic churches.[55] Nosow points out that recent growth in the Pentecostal and Holiness sects has come primarily from the working class group.

Membership in community groups and associations also carries an occupational influence. Nosow suggests that, in general, the higher an individual's social stratum, the greater the involvement in associational activity. Warner reports that more than 70 per cent of the upper class in Yankee City belonged to associations, whereas less than 40 per cent of the upper-lower class and less than 25 per cent of the lower-lower group held such memberships. He found a difference not only in the extent of memberships held but also a difference in the kinds of organizations in which affiliation was held. Hagedorn and Labovitz have confirmed similar results based on more recent studies.[56] Adams and Butler also report similar class differences.[57] Wardwell and Wood report the social pressures applied to lawyers to involve them in civic activities.[58] They point out that the community generally expects that the lawyer is available as a public servant, usually as a political office-holder of some sort; that he/she is available to

> *The company expects one of us to direct the local United Fund drive each year. It takes a lot of time but. . . .*
>
> A MIDDLE-MANAGEMENT ADMINISTRATOR
>
> *Although preacher's cars no longer need be black, a little red sports job might tend to raise some eyebrows.*
>
> A PROTESTANT MINISTER
>
> *If I didn't belong to the Country Club and live in a nice house, prospective patients might think that I'm not a very good doctor.*
>
> A PRIVATE-PRACTICE PHYSICIAN
>
> *People wouldn't trust us to handle their money if we didn't appear cautious and conservative.*
>
> A BANKER
>
> *We're expected to be ideal models for all our students— solid citizens, serious-minded, hard-working. Never attract attention by dress or behavior, stay out of bars and taverns, don't be frivolous. . . .*
>
> A HIGH SCHOOL TEACHER
>
> *One of the mistakes I made was buying an automobile in the same class as those driven by my best customers.*
>
> A GROCERY STORE OWNER

fill various community leadership roles in fund drives, reform movements, etc.; and that he/she will participate in community, law-related activities such as legal aid societies. There appear to be differences in these pressures related to the type of practice in which the lawyer engages. The individual in practice alone is more likely to become a local officeholder than one who is affiliated with an established firm.

Almost every worker can provide illustrations of control exerted on off-the-job behavior. This can result from direct, unequivocal demands made by the employer on the one hand, or the very subtle, unexpressed social pressures of public expectation, or any step between these two extremes. Public school teachers, especially in smaller communities, are often expected to maintain standards of decorum usually exceeding the established level of the community. Principals or school board members often are very explicit about what is acceptable behavior in the community; even in communities where common practice includes an occasional evening in the local tavern, principals or school board members may have difficulty in feeling that the teacher should be permitted to participate. "Loud parties," public entertainment of friends, conspicuous behavior, or other activities that draw attention to the individual in any but the most favorable circumstances may garner criticism even when the behavior falls within the limits established by "respectable" members of the community. "Successful" lawyers and physicians may encounter public expectations that require them to maintain expensive automobiles, homes, or club memberships as symbols of their professional success. Business executives and government employees are often expected to contribute generously to local United Fund campaigns.

OCCUPATIONS, PRESTIGE, AND SOCIAL STATUS

The psychological need for recognition was considered in an earlier chapter in discussing the factors that influence an individual moving toward a career. Sociologists tell us that occupational groups experience the same desires for status and position that psychologists describe in individuals.

The Struggle for Status

Boggs has reported the efforts made by technicians employed in a governmental research organization to seek advancement and thereby enhance their status.[59] The workers, although unable to break across the barrier that separated them from professional workers, placed great emphasis on the importance of advancement. When advancement by way of promotion became impossible, the workers tended to use the same value, but redefined it to mean their efforts to engage in performing higher status work within the same occupational category. When even this means of "advancement" closed, the emphasis shifted to increases in job security and pay.

Record has described the struggle of the marine radioman for status.[60] She points out the distinct dichotomy of shipboard staff into officers and crewmen. Within these two distinct groups were separate hierarchies established by long tradition, licensing requirements, and union standards. The general divisions have carried down from the days of sailing ships with an accommodation made in both categories with the advent of the steam engine. The installation of radios on board created rather extensive readjustment, reaching even as high as the ship's captain, since the ship owner could now remain in contact throughout the voyage, thus limiting the absolute control that the captain previously held. Radiomen encountered difficulty in identifying a place in the ship's stratification. On some vessels they were treated as officers, on others as crewmen, very often as marginal persons falling between the two groups. Union efforts finally won contractual and legal recognition of radiomen as officers.

The search for higher occupational status by purchasing agents has been studied by Strauss.[61] Purchasing agents show concern for their status as viewed by engineers, production managers, and general management.

Their effort toward equalizing their position with that of engineers has focused on attempts to professionalize the group. They have organized a national association, called for professional preparation programs at universities, and proposed both certification requirements and a code of ethics.
Further efforts have included moving certain parts of their work to assistants.

Occupational Prestige

Closely related to the topic of occupational status is grouping on the basis
of prestige. In considering whether prestige possesses any potential significance for improving the occupational distribution of the labor force,
Thomas concludes that it does, for two different reasons.[62] These reasons
are: (1) occupational prestige is generally recognized as an important
feature in the total appeal of occupations, and (2) the present distribution
of occupational prestige need not be accepted as either completely desirable
or unchangeable.

The importance of occupational prestige for the counselor and the
teacher can be focused primarily on: (1) recognizing the considerable variation in the amount of prestige generally given to various occupations,
and (2) recognizing the impact that such prestige values have on young
people and their parents in considering and evaluating occupations.

Occupational prestige has been defined in many ways. In some
research studies reported in the literature, specific efforts have been made to
avoid definition in order to draw from the respondents their ideas and
attitudes concerning the meaning of the term. For the purpose of this
chapter, occupational prestige will be considered to be the esteem or social
status accorded to an occupation by the general population. It is important
to recognize that the concern here is with the prestige of the occupation,
not that of the individual. Studies by Osgood and Stagner [63] and by Hartmann [64] have clearly demonstrated that these are two separate concepts.

Mills investigated the elements or symbols of prestige most admired
by various occupational classes in a middle-sized city.[65] He reported that
the only symbol commonly prized by all classes was relative income position. Executives and professional workers also emphasized amount of
education and personal refinement required in the occupations. High income groups emphasized power and influence as a symbol of prestige.
Lower paid white-collar workers emphasized the importance of the distinction between white-collar work and manual labor. Security was the most
important factor to the manual labor group.

Caplow has proposed eight items as elements in occupational prestige:[66]

1. Extent of resonsibility in the work
2. Nature of the work

3. Amount of formal education required
4. Length of training
5. Authority
6. Social class attributes of the occupation
7. Income, both amount and certainty
8. Behavior control

Caplow reports that the last item, behavior control, seems to correlate more closely with the prestige order in which occupations are ranked than any of the other items on the list. He defines this item as the "degree of control" that the person in the occupation exercises over other people. Occupations that control all other people with whom they work would rank at the top. Occupations that control people of lower status would be one step lower. Occupations that have no control over others rank next to the bottom, and occupations that not only control no others but also are controlled by workers of relatively low status are at the bottom.

Garbin and Bates also studied twenty factors that appear to influence the prestige ranking of an occupation.[67] Of the twenty factors reported, six showed positive correlations of .90 to .95 with occupational prestige. In descending order, these are as follows: regarded as desirable to associate with, intelligence required, scarcity of personnel who can do the job, interesting and challenging work, training required, and education required. Five other factors produced correlations of .80 or better. These include: work calls for originality and initiative, toil for improving others, having an influence over others, security, and opportunity for advancement. Only three factors were reported with correlation of .50 or lower. These are: dealing more with people than things (.50), safe occupation (.49), and free time (.19).

Garbin also reports another study in which he asked college freshmen to evaluate thirty professions in terms of prestige, authority, economic rewards, functional importance, and community power.[68] He states that economic reward was the most incongruous factor and that no occupation was completely congruous.

Prestige Rankings

Counts, in 1925, asked a group of 450 people ranging in maturity from high school seniors to high school teachers to rank forty-five occupations.[69] In 1946, Deeg and Paterson completed a replication of Counts' earlier study.[70] The study was replicated again in 1967 by Hakel, Hollmann, and Dunnette.[71] Table 6 compares the rankings of occupations found in these three studies that span nearly half a century. The most striking result observed is the relative stability of occupations. In 1946, only three occupations changed more than two ranks, and in 1967 eight occupations made such

TABLE 6. *Social Status Ranks of 25 Occupations as Reported in Three Studies Over 42 Years*

OCCUPATION	RANK ORDER BY COUNTS (1925)	RANK ORDER BY DEEG AND PATERSON (1946)	RANK ORDER BY HAKEL, HOLLMANN, AND DUNNETTE (1967)
Banker	1	2.5	4
Physician	2	1	1
Lawyer	3	2.5	2
Superintendent of Schools	4	4	3
Civil Engineer	5	5	5
Army Captain	6	6	8
Foreign Missionary	7	7	7
Elementary School Teacher	8	8	6
Farmer	9	12	19
Machinist	10	9	12
Traveling Salesman	11	16	13
Grocer	12	13	17
Electrician	13	11	9
Insurance Agent	14	10	10
Mail Carrier	15	14	18
Carpenter	16	15	11
Soldier	17	19	15
Plumber	18	17	16
Motorman	19	18	20
Barber	20	20	14
Truck Driver	21	21.5	21
Coal Miner	22	21.5	23
Janitor	23	23	22
Hod Carrier	24	24	24
Ditch Digger	25	25	25

The correlations between the rank order (rho) are as follows: 1925 and 1946, .97; 1946 and 1967, .93; and 1925 and 1967, .88

From: *Personnel and Guidance Journal*, vol. 46, no. 8, p. 764.

moves. The largest changes in 1967 were made by *Farmer*, which dropped seven positions, and *Barber*, which moved up six positions.

An extensive survey of prestige ranking of occupations was completed in 1947 by North and Hatt.[72] This study was based on interviews with almost 3,000 people carefully selected to assure sampling for region, size of city, age, sex, status, and race. The results of the survey showed a high degree of consistency with the earlier studies of Counts and of Deeg and Paterson. Thomas reported a rank difference coefficient of .98 computed between the occupations in common on the North-Hatt and the

Counts lists.[73] The North-Hatt study was replicated in 1963 by Hodge, Siegel, and Rossi.[74] They reported a correlation of .99 between the prestige scores obtained in 1947 and those obtained in the replication in 1963. The average prestige scores and rankings for the two studies are reported in Table 7.

A recent study by Braun and Bayer reports a replication of the early study by Deeg and Paterson.[75] With only a slight modification to update the occupational items, the list was administered to black and white students at Oakland University and to an adult group between 35 and 55 years of age, matched for sex, race, age, education, and socio-economic level. The socio-economic level of students was determined according to father's occupation. The resulting matches consisted of 40 pairs of blacks and whites, 43 pairs of males and females, 40 pairs of students and adults. The result showed high correlations, between all three matches, with the highest correlation (+.925) between blacks and whites and lowest correlation (+.816) between males and females. The total group rank order correlation with the 1947 Deeg and Paterson study produced a coefficient of +.909. No general change in occupational status was found except for minor changes such as an upward movement of carpenter, plumber, and electrician.

Other studies have shown similar tendencies for prestige values of occupations to remain relatively fixed. Inkeles and Rossi show that occupational rankings in other countries follow lines quite similar to those in the United States.[76] Similarly, Haller and Lewis suggest that something connected with the complexity of occupational structures that are visible to the participants in a social system, rather than industrialization as such, accounts for the valid parts of the intersocietal correlation in prestige rankings of translatable occupational titles.[77] Mitchell states that the problem in viewing occupational prestige in industrialized and developing countries is to determine the number and identity of dimensions of occupational prestige in the differing societies.[78] In other articles, Mitchell [79] and Gerstl and Cohen [80] report the very close prestige rankings between occupations in the United States and in the United Kingdom.

Brown reports an investigation of occupational prestige in Ethiopia.[81] He asked Ethiopian students to identify occupations generally known in that country. From this inventory he compiled a list of 90 occupations used in the study. He asked sociology students in an Ethiopian university to rank the 90 occupations. When the results were matched against the Hodge, Seigel, Rossi results (Table 7) by using the occupations common to both lists, he obtained a high coefficient of correlation (rho = +.88). Similarly, Haller, Holsinger, and Saraiva studied occupational prestige in Brazil.[82] They used the 1947 North-Hatt list with subjects in isolated Brazilian communities and in more populated, sophisticated communities. They report lower agreement with North-Hatt results in rural communities (r = +.67) than in areas described as "Euro-American" urban (r =

TABLE 7. *Prestige Ranking of Occupations in the United States, 1947–1963*

	1947		1963	
OCCUPATION	SCORE	RANKING	SCORE	RANKING
U.S. Supreme Court Justice	96	1	94	1
Physician	93	2.5	93	2
Nuclear physicist	86	18	92	3.5
Scientist	89	8	92	3.5
Government scientist	88	10.5	91	5.5
State governor	93	2.5	91	5.5
Cabinet member, fed. govt.	92	4.5	90	8
College professor	89	8	90	8
U.S. rep. in Congress	89	8	90	8
Chemist	86	18	89	11
Lawyer	86	18	89	11
Diplomat, U.S. foreign service	92	4.5	89	11
Dentist	86	18	88	14
Architect	86	18	88	14
County judge	87	13	88	14
Psychologist	85	22	87	17.5
Minister	87	13	87	17.5
Member, bd. of dir. of large corp.	86	18	87	17.5
Mayor of large city	90	6	87	17.5
Priest	86	18	86	21.5
Head of dept., state govt.	87	13	86	21.5
Civil engineer	84	23	86	21.5
Airplane pilot	83	24.5	86	21.5
Banker	88	10.5	85	24.5
Biologist	81	29	85	24.5
Sociologist	82	26.5	83	26
Instructor, public schools	79	34	82	27.5
Captain, regular army	80	31.5	82	27.5
Accountant, large business	81	29	81	29.5
Public school teacher	78	36	81	29.5
Owner of factory that employs 100 people	82	26.5	80	31.5
Building contractor	79	34	80	31.5
Artist who paints pictures exhibited in gallery	83	24.5	78	34.5
Musician in symphony orchestra	81	29	78	34.5
Author of novels	80	31.5	78	34.5
Economist	79	34	78	34.5
Official, intntl. labor union	75	40.5	77	37
Railroad engineer	77	37.5	76	39
Electrician	73	45	76	39
County agric. agent	77	37.5	76	39
Owner-operator, print shop	74	42.5	75	41.5

TABLE 7. (*Continued*)

| OCCUPATION | 1947 | | 1963 | |
	SCORE	RANKING	SCORE	RANKING
Trained machinist	73	45	75	41.5
Farm owner and operator	76	39	74	44
Undertaker	72	47	74	44
Welfare worker, city	73	45	74	44
Newspaper columnist	74	42.5	73	46
Policeman	67	55	72	47
Reporter, daily paper	71	48	71	48
Radio announcer	75	40.5	70	49.5
Bookkeeper	68	51.5	70	49.5
Tenant farmer—owns livestock and machinery, manages farm	68	51.5	69	51.5
Insurance agent	68	51.5	69	51.5
Carpenter	65	58	68	53
Manager, small store in city	69	49	67	54.5
Local official, labor union	62	62	67	54.5
Mail carrier	66	57	66	57
Railroad conductor	67	55	66	57
Traveling salesman, wholesale	68	51.5	66	57
Plumber	63	59.5	65	59
Automobile repairman	63	59.5	64	60
Playground director	67	55	63	62.5
Barber	59	66	63	62.5
Machine operator, factory	60	64.5	63	62.5
Owner-operator, lunch stand	62	62	63	62.5
Corporal, regular army	60	64.5	62	65.5
Garage mechanic	62	62	62	65.5
Truck driver	54	71	59	67
Fisherman, owns boat	58	68	58	68
Clerk in store	58	68	56	70
Milk route man	54	71	56	70
Streetcar motorman	58	68	56	70
Lumberjack	53	73	55	72.5
Restaurant cook	54	71	55	72.5
Singer in night club	52	74.5	54	74
Filling station attendant	52	74.5	51	75
Dockworker	47	81.5	50	77.5
Railroad section hand	48	79.5	50	77.5
Night watchman	47	81.5	50	77.5
Coal miner	49	77.5	50	77.5
Restaurant waiter	48	79.5	49	80.5
Taxi driver	49	77.5	49	80.5
Farm hand	50	76	48	83
Janitor	44	85.5	48	83
Bartender	44	85.5	48	83

TABLE 7. (*Continued*)

OCCUPATION	1947		1963	
	SCORE	RANKING	SCORE	RANKING
Clothes presser in laundry	46	83	45	85
Soda fountain clerk	45	84	44	86
Sharecropper—owns no livestock or equipment, does not manage farm	40	87	42	87
Garbage collector	35	88	39	88
Street sweeper	34	89	36	89
Shoe shiner	33	90	34	90
Average	70		71	

From: R. W. Hodge, P. M. Siegel, and P. H. Rossi, "Occupational Prestige in the United States, 1925–63," *American Journal of Sociology*, vol. 70, no. 3 (November 1964), pp. 290–93.

+.82). Nevertheless, the correlations demonstrate striking similarities across vast cultural differences in the prestige ranking of occupations.

Tuckman [83] and Baudler and Paterson [84] have found similar results in the ranking of occupations by women. Stefflre, Resnikoff, and Lezotte report a recent comparison of rankings by men and women that reinforces the position that sex is not an influential factor in ranking occupations.[85] Hakel, Hollmann, and Ohnesorge have examined the relationship between intelligence of occupational members and the prestige of the occupation.[86] They constructed a forced choice test to determine how well students could discriminate between occupations on the basis of the average intelligence of the occupational members. Seventy-two items were systematically constructed to represent 24 combinations of intelligence and prestige differences. Accuracy at identifying occupations with higher intelligence was significantly worse than chance because subjects relied exclusively on prestige to make their choices. The study concluded that the standing of an occupation on intelligence made no contribution to accuracy independent of occupational prestige.

The Occupational Situs

Both Super and Caplow have mentioned that the occupational label is often used in American industrialized society as the bench mark by which the individual is "placed" or classified. In early New England and the pre-Civil War South, family name and home served adequately for this purpose. With the rapid change in American culture, this has been replaced by the more widely understood occupational tag.

Reiss,[87] in an extensive description of a widely recognized study of occupational prestige, says:

Two conclusions seem inescapable from this investigation: (1) despite the fact that the social position of a person has an effect on his ratings of some occupations, the prestige status of occupations is viewed in substantially the same way by major social groupings in American society; (2) despite the relative lack of consensus on the criteria for rating a job as having excellent standing, there is almost complete agreement on the nature of the occupational prestige structure of American society, at least where the rated occupations are highly salient. It seems apparent that even if persons do not have a uniform conceptualization of the "general standing" of occupations, or a common frame of reference in terms of which they view the occupational structure, there is a convergence of their perspectives such that they perceive the occupational structure in much the same way.

Further research by Hatt led him to conclude that the 90 occupations used in the opinion poll could not be placed statistically into a single scaling system.[88] His work led him to conclude that the total list included a mixture of several subgroups that he labelled *situses*. A situs consisted of a combination of occupations that appeared to have both an internal similarity of relations with the general public and also reasonable scalability. Although he arranged his original groups on the basis of logical assignment, he later adjusted the groups until scalable patterns appeared. The scalability of each situs (when reproducibility of the scaling is possible at a satisfactory statistical level) suggests that the American occupational structure does, in fact, consist of several prestige systems that parallel one another. On the basis of this preliminary work, Hatt speculated that the following situses, which in turn include the indicated families of occupations, existed:

1. *Political*
   National
   Local
2. *Professional*
   Free professions
   Pure sciences
   Applied sciences
   Community professions

3. *Business*
   Big businesses
   Small businesses
   Labor organizations
   White-collar employees
4. *Recreation and aesthetics*
   Fine arts
   Journalism and radio
   Recreation

5. *Agriculture*
   Farming
   Farm workers
6. *Manual work*
   Skilled mechanics
   Construction trades
   Outdoor work
   Factory work
   Unskilled labor
7. *Military*
   Army
   Navy
   Marine Corps
   Coast Guard
8. *Service*
   "Official community"
   "Unofficial community"
   Personal

In essence, Hatt has proposed that within each situs there probably exists a clear-cut prestige system that is understood by those engaged in that broad area and utilized in assigning status within the field. Because situses are less well understood by outsiders, it is more difficult for them to rank the occupations than it is for the insiders. This would account for some of the minor variability noted in the various studies of prestige that cut across all of Hatt's situses.

The situs approach provides a framework useful in understanding the concept of occupational mobility to be discussed in the following section.[89] Movement to higher levels within a given situs can be presumed to occur along fairly clear patterns, whereas changes to new situses are probably undertaken with greater risk in the expectation of greater gain or satisfaction.

Prestige ratings of occupations have serious restrictions, particularly since most of the studies have included a very limited list of jobs. One might reasonably ask how comprehensive a list of twenty-five or forty-five, or even ninety, names can be. Careful study, however, indicates that the occupations usually included are reasonably representative of the world of work and, therefore, the results may have more value than first appearance would indicate.

They have one value that justifies their inclusion and, specifically, their consideration at this point. The entire emphasis of prestige ratings, by their very nature and content, is sociological in nature—showing how other people, the public in general, think of a particular occupation. One of the positions advocated in this volume is that the psychological and sociological impact of the occupation on the job holder and his family is a crucial aspect of career information. One way of helping individuals to become aware of such factors is to consider with them the consistency, over fairly long periods, of public attitudes toward selected occupations. Besides broadening the perspective with which they look at jobs, prestige ratings may help some people to develop motivation to work toward goals that they previously had considered only casually

OCCUPATIONAL MOBILITY

The Horatio Alger concept of the poor but industrious and ambitious boy who starts at the bottom and rises to the top of his career field has long been a part of the American heritage. In the dynamic, expanding, and classless society that has existed in the United States for the past two centuries, such opportunities have existed; and every community has within it examples of "self-made" successes.[90, 91]

Sociologists have assigned the term *vertical mobility* to movement from one occupational stratum to a higher or lower one. When the change is essentially one of function, and the person remains at the same level, the term *horizontal mobility* is used.

The biographies of "self-made" men often imply that the individual's success has come about through the persistent application of hard work, faithfulness, and virtue.[92] This view, of course, takes the position that only the individual was active and that the situation in which he worked was passive and inert. The stories of failures, on the other hand, all too often cast the individual in the role of the helpless, storm-tossed victim of ruthless and uncontrollable circumstances. In such a picture, we must assume that the individual is passive and the situation is all-powerful. If, however, we view man and his work as an interacting relationship, to which both contribute and from which both benefit, then both parties are seen as active. A realistic consideration of mobility must proceed from this assumption of interrelatedness.

Becker and Strauss provide an excellent discussion of the interrelationship between careers and occupational mobility.[93] They vividly compare vertical mobility to an escalator, suggesting that the mobility system carries the beginning worker from the less desirable positions at the bottom of the organization to the status positions at the top. Factors recognized as important to this movement include seniority, or time in grade, appropriate experiences or "seasoning," and unusual skills or knowledge required in the particular situation. Recognition is given to the difficulty that may be encountered when a worker attempts to move from one escalator to another —a situation that can be thought of as horizontal mobility. Unless the worker has certain special attributes that make him particularly desirable for the new position, he will probably have to undertake some sort of learning or educational experience that will qualify him for a transfer of this type.

Many fundamental premises in American society imply that each individual has access to vertical mobility and that hard work is the secret to most success. Becker and Strauss clearly delineate the many factors that can impede or prevent the smooth movement up the escalator by any particular worker. Further, many occupations do not have an escalator relationship to others and hence it is impossible for the worker to move easily into better and more responsible positions.

Career education includes concepts that also imply this "escalator" relationship within various occupational situses. Although education is presented as the admission ticket for a ride on the escalator, it is important to keep in mind that possession of educational and experiential qualifications for a position does not at all guarantee the opportunity for the holder of these assets to enter the occupation.

Form and Miller emphasize that a worker tends to remain at the same occupational level at which he started.[94] Similarly, Thomas states that, except for farmers, skilled craftsmen, proprietors, managers, and officials, the best index of a worker's eventual category of employment is his initial category.[95] The exceptions listed above are fields that usually require considerable experience in other closely related lines of work. He continues by pointing out that about three-fourths of those beginning work in the white-collar range have remained there permanently, with the same proportion holding for those in manual labor.

Miller and Form studied the work histories of a group of men in Ohio.[96] The career patterns followed by these men demonstrated clearly the relationship between father's education and father's occupation, between father's occupation and son's education, and between son's education and son's occupation. They point out that, once a worker starts at an occupational level, he tends to remain there. Factors influencing this rigidity include property inheritance, differences in occupational income, and differences in occupational equipment, outlook, and culture. The typical professional worker comes from a family in which the father had almost completed high school and was employed as a farm owner, business proprietor, manager, or official. The son or daughter finishes college, enters a professional or semiprofessional job, and remains at that level. Skilled workers come from families in which fathers had a grade school education and worked as skilled workers themselves. The children usually drop out before completing high school, work for a time at the semiskilled level, and later advance to the skilled level. Semiskilled and unskilled workers have family and educational backgrounds similar to skilled workers, but differ extensively in work histories, usually holding jobs for fairly short periods of time, with no period of stable jobs.

Empey studied the occupational aspirations of approximately one-tenth of the male seniors in public high schools in the state of Washington in 1954.[97] He determined the social class level of this group on the basis of the father's occupation. He concluded that the youths at all social levels aspire to levels higher than that attained by their fathers; however, youngsters at different levels revealed aspirations at different levels. In other words, lower level youngsters, although hoping to reach levels beyond their father's, had lower hopes than youngsters whose fathers held high occupational status.

The consensus of these studies, as well as many others appearing in the professional literature, appears to give added support to the proposal by Hatt of situses, or broad occupational groups that tend to be essentially self-contained. For the majority of workers, then, the original entry into the world of work has vast significance, for within the area or situs that he chooses will be found the escalators that will carry him upward as his career advances. Only the occasional worker will move from one area to another, and those movements appear to be predominantly at the upper or lower extremes and are not distributed regularly throughout the various levels.

As indicated above, the occupational level, and the situs or occupational group, at which the person enters employment will contribute heavily to the type of life that he will live, influencing not only his life in every aspect but also that of his wife and children.

ECONOMIC FACTORS

In this section, we will look primarily at the elements affecting the income that the worker obtains from his efforts. As Super has indicated, surprisingly little literature bears directly on the economic aspects of careers.[98] Specific statistical information on such items as wages and hours can be obtained from the Bureau of Labor Statistics and other sections of the Department of Labor. Each decennial census also provides data on earnings for a large portion of the population.

Approximately 80 per cent of the total national income in any given year can be described as occupational earnings. Although there is considerable fluctuation from year to year in gross national income because of changes in economic conditions and other factors, this relative proportion appears to hold fairly constant.

Supply and Demand Influences

Economists generally agree that over the long run in a free economy the basic determinant of occupational income is the ratio between the supply of a given quality of labor and the demand for it. In other words, wages and salaries are determined by the number of workers with a particular skill who can be induced to sell their skill at a certain rate of pay and the number of employers who desire to purchase that skill and who will make wage offers at a certain rate of pay. Any factor that tends to increase the number of workers willing to sell their skill will usually cause wage levels to go lower. Any factor that decreases the number of available workers will tend to cause wages to rise. Similarly, any factor that increases employer demand for workers will cause wages to rise, whereas any factor reducing employer demand will cause wages to fall.

In actuality, the basic supply-and-demand ratio is rarely permitted to operate with total freedom. Taussig was investigating the relationship of this ratio to occupations when he developed his hypothesis of occupational levels.[99] A number of factors exist that control, or at least restrict, the free operation of the supply-demand ratio. Some of these factors have been developed to protect the general public; others have been designed to protect or assist the specific group of workers. Some of these restricting elements are social custom; others have been established as legal regulations. All of them impede the free operation of the supply-demand ratio.

Such interference with the free operation of supply-demand interaction usually comes from one or more of three sources—the public, the employers, or the workers. Control and regulation may take the form of legislation or general practice, or sometimes, a combination of both.

Examples of interference or control emerging from the public include both legislation and social practice. Minimum wage laws and child labor regulations are typical of such action. Minimum wage laws provide a floor in covered industries below which workers cannot be paid. Obviously, this control has an influence beyond the particular industries specified in the legislation since noncovered industries must usually offer a competitive wage in order to attract workers. Child labor laws similarly restrict the number of potential workers available to the employer and thus force the proffered wages to be higher in order to attract a sufficient number of workers. Legislation specifying that workers must have specific qualifications, through licensure or otherwise, also is a restrictive factor of the same sort.

The employer can interfere with the free operation of supply and demand by engaging in certain hiring practices that limit access to the job by certain workers. At first glance, one might assume that such restrictive practices would result in limited supplies of workers and therefore produce higher wages—a situation inimical to the interests of the employer. Such restriction, however, may limit some workers to access to only a very few jobs, thus depressing the wages to be paid in those positions. Although now illegal in most work situations, such practices have not totally disappeared. In previous years, this type of control was sometimes exerted toward women workers or minority member workers. The employer can, in collusion with other employers, engage in establishment of a "prevailing" wage or a "going rate" that is offered on a "take it or leave it" basis so that the position is left unfilled if prospective workers will not accept the standard that has been established.

The worker, or his representative, also can interfere with the supply-demand equation. Worker groups can insist on establishing wage rates by negotiation—a process that assures that all involved workers will require the same wage rate for the same job, thus eliminating the possibility for single workers accepting employment at lower wage rates. Workers may also control admission to the training programs by which workers become qualified for employment. An example of this is limiting the number of apprentices admitted to a craft to a certain percentage of employed journeymen regardless of the number of unfilled positions existing in that craft.

The factors listed above establish conditions within which the supply-demand ratio must operate. Thomas has identified additional factors directly affecting the ratio itself.[100] He lists the following items that bear upon the supply of qualified labor:

1. The qualifications demanded of a given kind and grade of labor. The types of special traits required in all kinds of work are too numerous to mention. Illustrative of these factors would be specific physical or mental skills required in certain work, the amount and type of effort demanded, and the amount and type of responsibility that the work carries. Some of the occupational demands can be acquired through training programs of particular kinds—for example, development of typing skill—others are little influenced by any kind of training—for example, color discrimination. The length and difficulty of the training program may have a severe impact on the number of workers available.[101, 102]

2. The general appeal of a given kind of work. The more attractive the occupation, the greater the likelihood that a large number of potential workers will attempt to qualify for placement. The effect of some factors related to a given occupation is difficult to evaluate in terms of appeal. What is challenging and interesting to one person may be monotonous and distasteful to another. There are, however, certain characteristics which tend to be commonly evaluated. Remuneration relative to other occupations is one factor that is so identified. For many individuals, the higher the rate of pay, the more attractive the occupation. Taussig, expecting this factor to operate, started his search for restricting items when he observed that the most attractive occupations were not flooded with applicants. Obviously, other restrictions prevent large numbers from preparing for these desirable fields. Some occupations lacking in prestige and generally distasteful may require special skill and equipment. When this is the case, a high wage may be offered to attract a sufficient supply of applicants. When no special skill is needed, the wage will usually remain low, since there are usually workers available who are willing to work for a low wage.

Regularity of employment is often an attractive feature, and many workers will accept a lower wage if they can be assured that the work is steady. Another factor that adds to the general appeal of an occupation is the opportunity for advancement. Some fields are steppingstones and training jobs for other more advanced and attractive occupations. The possibility of moving ahead later to such an opportunity is often sufficient to attract a large supply of workers willing to work for a relatively low wage.

3. Other factors. (a) Workers often are reluctant to move to other geographic areas. This can affect labor supply in two ways. It may cause a surplus in an area where employment is decreasing, thus forcing wages even lower. The reluctance to move may prevent the solution of a shortage of workers in an expanding labor market, thus forcing wages still higher in an attempt to find sufficient workers. Stone and Grow have reported an interesting study of geographic mobility within the aerospace industry and suggests that earlier influences in geographic mobility may now be dwindling and newer pressures are beginning to appear.[103] (b) The long-term movement of workers from rural to urban areas in this country has provided a larger supply of unskilled and low skilled workers for the urban labor market than would exist otherwise. (c) The difficulty of transferring from one occupation to another without extensive retraining affects the labor supply in expanding fields. As the demand for low levels of skill continues to decrease and greater demands are made for skilled workers, this problem will grow in seriousness. Provision is already being made to enable workers to leave fields that are declining by accepting retraining for new and expanding fields. The more exacting and lengthy the training program required in a given occupation, the more restricted is the labor supply.

(d) Unequal access to opportunities for one's occupational choice restricts the labor supply to some extent, since training opportunities are limited and not available to all who might like to take advantage of them. Restricting factors may be due to location, cost, entrance requirements, discrimination, or other reasons. (e) Organized labor exerts influence and control on the supply of workers available. Restriction on the number of members, apprenticeship or initiation requirements, and conditions of work impose limitations on the supply of workers. The degree of influence on supply is largely in proportion to the extent to which the occupation is organized. (f) Similarly, the labor supply can be influenced by activities of employers and employers' groups. Positive influences would include such things as publicizing opportunities, providing training, and improving wages and working conditions. (g) Government employment through relief projects many influence the supply of labor by absorbing many of the less skilled workers.

In summary, one can say that there are many restrictions to the free operation of the supply-demand ratio. The items discussed above have been essentially those that bear on the supply factor. They have also assumed a constant demand for labor.

Two long-run items that influence the demand for labor can be mentioned briefly, in addition to the implication of demand-related items included above. One factor having definite effect on the demand for labor is the general status of business. When producers are confident of a continuing or increasing demand for goods or services by the public, their demand for labor goes up. If producers feel that the business cycle is headed downward toward less demand for goods or services, they reduce their demand for labor.

Technological change and progress also can have a heavy bearing on the demand for labor. This will be discussed in more detail in another chapter.

Payment of Workers

The income provided to the worker for his efforts can be categorized as follows:

Entrepreneurial withdrawal
Fees
Compensation of employees
    Salaries
    Wages

Entrepreneurial withdrawal is the income taken by the owner of a business or industry as compensation for the responsibility and risk that he has assumed in establishing and undertaking the business.

Fees constitute the income paid to the various free professions when the worker is engaged in the actual independent practice of the profession. An example is the income of lawyers and physicians in private practice. Members of most free professions may actually be employed, rather than involved in private practice. When such is the case, their income is considered as *compensation of employees.*

Employees of organizations are paid either in the form of salaries or wages. *Salary* is usually a fixed compensation regularly paid for services over a specific period of time, such as a year, quarter, month, or week. *Wages* are similarly compensation for services (usually labor) paid at short stated intervals. Salaries are usually paid to managerial, administrative, professional, clerical, and supervisory employees. Although the amount of salary may be on the basis of a year, it is often paid in installments each week or month.

Workers described as laborers, even though highly skilled, are usually paid wages. These may be based on either a time rate or a piece rate. There are definite advantages and disadvantages to each of these methods; therefore, each will be briefly considered.

Time-rate wages pay the worker a fixed rate per unit of time. The time unit ordinarily is one hour, and workers often describe their income in terms of so much an hour. The major advantages of this system are that the worker knows how much he/she is going to receive and can (within limits) work at the best speed, the amount earned is easily calculated, and the system usually improves the quality of the work performed. The disadvantages are that supervisors must be employed to assure a reasonable production from the worker, and there is no incentive in the system for the worker to work faster; for the employer, unit costs are uncertain, since the number of units produced may vary considerably even over fairly brief periods of time.

The *piece-rate system* compensates the worker in terms of the number of units produced. The advantages of this system are that the efficient worker is rewarded for his/her effort, labor costs per unit are certain, and supervisors are no longer needed, since the pay system provides the incentive to produce. The disadvantages of this system include a loss of interest on the employer's part in developing new systems, quality of work may be sacrificed to assure high production figures, inspectors may have to be employed to maintain minimum levels of quality, and equipment and machines may be given harder use by the worker attempting to earn more money, thus causing excessive wear and tear.

In many work situations, some combination of time- and piece-rate wages may be in effect. This permits the worker to gain from the advantages of both systems. He/she may also be subject to some of the disadvantages of both systems. A combination method usually provides a minimum guarantee and a bonus if the standard output established for that job is exceeded. Many workers and worker groups are suspicious of piece-rate or "incentive" systems, since they fear that the superior worker who develops a method of higher production may cause either the piece-rate to be lowered or the number of needed workers to be reduced. Every organization can point to instances when unscrupulous employers have done exactly that.

The methods of paying workers that we have just considered are essentially concerned with the cash paid to the worker for productive efforts. There are many modifications to these two basic systems. Many workers, especially wage earners, obtain part of their compensation for overtime work. In most work settings, the length of the work period for which the employee receives the basic unit of pay is specified. If he/she works for a longer period, he/she is customarily paid for this time at a higher rate. Forty hours of work per week have been established by the Fair Labor Standards Act for most employees. This law also specifies overtime pay at one and one-half times the regular hourly rate. Some work agreements require double-time pay for work at specified times such as Sundays or holidays. A common practice among employers of wage earners is to pay an additional amount to workers who are employed outside the usual work day. Thus, a factory that operates with three shifts might have three different rates for the same job, with the day shift worker being paid the base rate, the swing shift worker earning an additional shift differential, and the night shift worker being paid a still larger shift differential. Some factories avoid this practice by requiring all workers to change shifts at regular intervals.

Many workers, especially in service-type occupations such as waiters and waitresses, receive their income either partly or entirely from tips provided by the customers they serve. In such cases, the compensation is based on neither the unit of time nor unit of work. Similarly, individuals in sales positions may be paid a commission—a percentage of their total sales.

In addition to cash payments received by workers, two other methods of payment must be considered in order to see the total picture of worker reimbursement. These other factors are fringe benefits and payment in kind. Fringe benefits include indirect payment to the worker that can amount to an important part of his/her total income. Typical fringe benefits include paid vacations and holidays, and various types of insurance coverage such as medical, accident, or life. Other examples include retirement programs, supplemental unemployment income, and military or maternity leave with pay. Payment in kind includes meals provided without charge by the employer, company housing free or at a reduced rental, expense accounts, free travel, use of a company automobile, uniforms or other clothing, etc.

In recent years, several modifications of the basic wage system have appeared. Some companies have adopted a profit-sharing system, in which a certain proportion of the company's annual profit is divided among the workers, often in the form of an end-of-the-year, Christmas, or vacation bonus. Other companies have established a guaranteed annual wage by which workers are assured of a specified income regardless of number of weeks worked. Still other companies have linked wage rates to a cost-of-living index, so that wages are increased to compensate for increases in the cost of living. Presumably, such systems would also lower wages with a declining cost of living.

IMPLICATIONS OF SOCIOLOGICAL AND ECONOMIC FACTORS

The counselor, by professional preparation, is quite likely cognizant of the psychological factors through which the individual is related to his work, as described in Chapter 3. Because of lesser exposure to the fields of sociology and economics he/she is less likely to have developed familiarity with the impact of concepts from these fields on the worker. Yet these concepts may, in many cases, be the predominant influence that structures an individual's work life and greatly affects life away from work.

The purpose of this chapter is to alert the teacher and the counselor to these sociological and economic factors so that they may be incorporated in both teaching and counseling in appropriate ways, as psychological factors are now utilized.

It is important for the classroom teacher to include assessment of these influences in all classroom activities in which the individual studies the relationships between people and their work. Similarly, counseling sessions should include consideration of these topics as the counselor and the client consider the world of work.

Appraisal of the individual in terms of ability, temperament, interest, and educational achievement is utilized routinely in career development. Of equal importance are the factors beyond the individual's psychological self that shape and influence the world of work and his/her relationship to it. If it is appropriate to discuss ability as it bears on the possibilities of entering a particular field, it is equally sound to look at admission restrictions, social selectivity, and life style. Selection of career goals should include consideration of how the individual fits the occupational mold *and* how the occupation fits the individual.

Because sociological and economic factors may be more abstruse than psychological components, the counselor and the teacher may have to devote more time to determining both the existence and the occupational effect of these elements

NOTES

1. T. Caplow, *The Sociology of Work* (Minneapolis: University of Minnesota Press, 1954), p. 124.
2. R. Lyon, "Beyond the Conventional Career: Some Speculations," *Journal of Counseling Psychology*, vol. 12, no. 2 (Summer, 1965), pp. 153–158.
3. L. Lipsett, "Social Factors in Vocational Development," *Personnel and Guidance Journal*, vol. 66, no. 5 (January, 1962), pp. 432–437.
4. P. W. Musgrave, "Towards a Sociological Theory of Occupational Choice," *Sociological Review*, vol. 15, no. 1 (March, 1967), pp. 33–45.
5. T. Caplow, *op. cit.*, pp. 214–229.
6. D. G. Danskin, "Occupational Sociology in Occupational Exploration," *Personnel and Guidance Journal*, vol. 34, no. 3 (November, 1955), pp. 134–136.
7. H. S. Becker, "Some Contingencies of the Professional Dance Musician's Career," *Human Organization*, vol. 12, no. 1 (1953), pp. 22–26; and "The Professional Dance Musician and His Audience," *American Journal of Sociology*, vol. 57, no. 2 (1951), pp. 136–144.
8. C. L. Lastrucci, "The Professional Dance Musician," *Journal of Musicology*, vol. 3 (1941), pp. 168–172; and "The Status and Significance of Occupational Research," *American Sociological Review*, vol. 11, no. 1 (February, 1946), pp. 78–84.
9. A. Cohen, "Sociological Studies of Occupations as a 'Way of Life,'" *Personnel and Guidance Journal*, vol. 43, no. 3 (November, 1964), pp. 267–272.
10. W. H. Whyte, Jr., "Wives of Management," *Fortune*, vol. 44 (October, 1951), pp. 86–88, 204–213. Abridged in *Man, Work, and Society* by S. Nosow and W. H. Form, pp. 549–551 (New York: Basic Books, Inc., 1962).
11. M. Shaycroft, "Factors Affecting a Factor Affecting Career," *Vocational Guidance Quarterly*, vol. 22, no. 2 (December, 1973), pp. 96–104.
12. S. Zafiran, "A Development Model for the Occupational Socioeconomic Status of American Men," *Journal of Vocational Behavior*, vol. 5, no. 3 (December, 1974), pp. 293–305.
13. W. G. Dyer, "The Interlocking of Work and Family Social Systems among Lower Occupational Families," *Social Forces*, vol. 34, no. 1 (March, 1956), pp. 230–233.
14. *Work in America*, Report of a Special Task Force to the Secretary of Health, Education, and Welfare. (Cambridge, Mass.: The MIT Press, 1972), pp. 30–31, 39–41.
15. S. E. Seashore and T. J. Barnowe, "Demographic and Job Factors Associated with the 'Blue-Collar Blues," mimeographed, 1972.
16. H. Sheppard and N. Herrick, *Where Have All the Robots Gone?* (New York: The Free Press, 1972).
17. J. Gooding, "The Fraying White Collar," *Fortune*, December, 1970.

18. A. P. M. Coxon, "Patterns of Occupational Recruitment: The Anglican Ministry," *Sociology*, vol. 1, no. 1 (January, 1961), pp. 73–80.
19. B. Sherlock and A. Cohen, "The Strategy of Occupational Choice: Recruitment to Dentistry," *Social Forces*, vol. 44, no. 3 (March, 1966), pp. 303–313.
20. I. D. Currie, H. C. Finney, T. Hirschi, and H. C. Selvin, "Images of the Professor and Interest in the Academic Profession," *Sociology of Education*, vol. 39, no. 4 (Fall, 1966), pp. 301–323.
21. O. D. Duncan, "Social Origins of Salaried and Self-Employed Professional Workers," *Social Forces*, vol. 44, no. 2 (December, 1965), pp. 186–189.
22. W. Fred Cottrell, "Social Groupings of Railroad Employees," *The Railroader* (Stanford: Stanford University Press, 1940). Abridged in *Man, Work, and Society* by S. Nosow and W. H. Form (New York: Basic Books, Inc., 1962).
23. B. Shimberg, B. F. Esser, and D. H. Kruger, *Occupational Licensing: Practices and Policies.* (Washington, D.C.: Public Affairs Press, 1973), Chap. 1.
24. H. L. Wilensky, "The Professionalization of Everyone," *American Journal of Sociology*, vol. 70, no. 2 (September, 1965), pp. 137–158.
25. E. C. Hughes, "Professions," *Daedalus*, vol. 92, no. 4 (Fall, 1963), pp. 655–668.
26. National Research Council, *Scientific and Technical Societies of the United States and Canada* (Washington: The National Research Council, 1961).
27. U.S. Department of Labor, Bureau of Labor Statistics, *Directory of National and International Labor Unions in the United States* (Washington: U.S. Government Printing Office, 1964).
28. H. S. Becker and J. W. Carper, "The Development of Identification with an Occupation," *American Journal of Sociology*, vol. 61, no. 4 (January, 1956), pp. 289–298.
29. E. Whittaker and V. Olesen, "The Faces of Florence Nightingale: Functions of the Heroine Legend in an Occupational Sub-Culture," *Human Organization*, vol. 23, no. 2 (Summer, 1964), pp. 123–130.
30. B. J. Sherlock and R. T. Morris, "The Evolution of the Professional: A Paradigm," *Sociological Inquiry*, vol. 37, no. 1 (Winter, 1967), pp. 27–46.
31. B. G. Meyerhoff and W. L. Larson, "The Doctor as Culture Hero: The Routinization of Charisma," *Human Organization*, vol. 24, no. 3 (Fall, 1965), pp. 188–191.
32. J. N. Dennison, "The Socialization of the Artist: The American Composer," *Social Forces*, vol. 35, no. 4 (May, 1957), pp. 307–313.
33. M. Seeman and J. W. Evans, "Apprenticeship and Attitude Change," *American Journal of Sociology*, vol. 67, no. 4. (January, 1962), pp. 365–378.
34. Caplow, *op. cit.*, pp. 113–121.
35. D. Harper and F. Emmet, "Work Behavior in a Service Industry," *Social Forces*, vol. 62, no. 2 (December, 1963), pp. 216–225.
36. L. I. Pearlin, "Alienation from Work: A Study of Nursing Personnel," *American Sociological Review*, vol. 27, no. 3. (June, 1962), pp. 314–326.
37. G. Devereux and F. R. Weiner, "The Occupational Status of Nurses," *American Sociological Review*, vol. 15, no. 5 (October, 1950), pp. 628–634. Abridged in *Man, Work, and Society* by S. Nosow and W. H. Form (New York: Basic Books, Inc., 1962).
38. I. H. Simpson, "Patterns of Socialization into Professions: The Case of Student Nurses," *Sociological Inquiry*, vol. 37, no. 1 (Winter, 1967), pp. 47–54.

39. G. R. Meyer and M. J. Hoffman, "Nurses' Inner Values and Their Behavior at Work," *Nursing Research*, vol. 13, no. 3 (Summer, 1964), pp. 244–249.
40. W. Breed, "Social Control in the Newsroom: A Functional Analysis," *Social Forces*, vol. 33, no. 4 (May, 1955), pp. 326–335.
41. G. Mars, "Hotel Pilferage: A Case Study in Occupational Theft," in *The Sociology of the Workplace* by M. Warner (London: George Allen & Unwin Ltd., 1973).
42. L. S. Lewis, "The Academic Axe: Some Trends in Dismissals From Institutions of Higher Learning in America," *Social Problems*, vol. 12, no. 2 (Fall, 1964), pp. 151–158.
43. S. E. Wallace, "Reference Group Behavior in Occupational Role Socialization," *Sociology Quarterly*, vol. 7, no. 3 (Summer, 1966), pp. 366–372.
44. N. K. Denzin and C. J. Mettlin, "Incomplete Professionalization: The Case of Pharmacy," *Social Forces*, vol. 46, no. 3 (March, 1968), pp. 375–381.
45. J. B. Montague, "Medicine and the Concept of Professionalism," *Sociological Inquiry*, vol. 33, no. 1 (Winter, 1963), pp. 45–50.
46. M. Malone, N. H. Berkowitz, and M. W. Klein, "The Paradox in Nursing," *American Journal of Nursing*, vol. 61, no. 9 (September, 1961), pp. 52–55.
47. C. B. Sterbing, "Some Role Conflicts as Seen by a High School Teacher," *Human Organization*, vol. 27, no. 1 (Spring, 1968), pp. 41–44.
48. W. M. Evan, "On the Margin—The Engineering Technician," and I. Lewis, "In the Courts of Power—The Advertising Man," both in *The Human Shape of Work*, ed., P. L. Berger (New York: Macmillan Co., 1964), pp. 83–112, 113–180.
49. C. Tilly, "Occupational Rank and Grade of Residence in a Metropolis," *American Journal of Sociology*, vol. 67, no. 3 (November, 1961), pp. 323–330.
50. H. L. Wilensky, "Orderly Careers and Social Participation: The Impact of Work History on Social Integration in the Middle Mass," *American Sociological Review*, vol. 26, no. 4 (August, 1961), pp. 521–539.
51. R. S. Lynd and H. Lynd, *Middletown* (New York: Harcourt, Brace & World, Inc., 1929).
52. A. B. Hollingshead, *Elmtown's Youth* (New York: John Wiley & Sons, Inc., 1949).
53. W. H. Whyte, Jr., *The Organization Man* (Garden City, L.I., N.Y.: Doubleday & Company, Inc., 1957), pp. 339–340.
54. S. Nosow, "Social Correlates of Occupational Membership," in *Man, Work, and Society* by S. Nosow and W. H. Form (New York: Basic Books, Inc., 1962), pp. 517–533.
55. W. L. Warner and P. S. Lunt, *The Social Life of the Modern Community* (New Haven: Yale University Press, 1949), pp. 426–446.
56. R. Hagedorn and S. Labovitz, "Occupational Characteristics and Participation in Voluntary Associations," *Social Forces*, vol. 47, no. 1 (September, 1968), pp. 17–27.
57. B. N. Adams and J. E. Butler, "Occupational Status and Husband-Wife Social Participation," *Social Forces*, vol. 45, no. 4 (June, 1967), pp. 501–507.
58. W. I. Wardwell and A. L. Wood, "The Extra-Professional Role of the Lawyer," *American Journal of Sociology*, vol. 51, no. 4 (January, 1956), pp. 304–307.
59. S. T. Boggs, "The Values of Laboratory Workers: A Study of Occupational Aspirations," *Human Organization*, vol. 22, no. 3 (Fall, 1963), pp. 209–217.

60. J. C. Record, "The Marine Radioman's Struggle for Status," *American Journal of Sociology*, vol. 57, no. 4 (January, 1957), pp. 353–359.
61. G. Strauss, "Work-flow Frictions, Interfunctional Rivalry and Professionalism: A Case Study of Purchasing Agents," *Human Organization*, vol. 23, no. 2 (Summer, 1964), pp. 137–149.
62. L. Thomas, *The Occupational Structure and Education* (Englewood Cliffs, N.J.: Prentice-Hall, Inc., 1956), pp. 188–190.
63. C. E. Osgood and R. Stagner, "Analysis of a Prestige Frame of Reference by a Gradient Technique," *Journal of Applied Psychology*, vol. 25 (June, 1941), pp. 275–290.
64. G. W. Hartmann, "The Prestige of Occupations," *Personnel Journal*, vol. 13 (1934–35), pp. 142–152.
65. C. W. Mills, "The Middle Classes in Middle-Sized Cities," *American Sociological Review*, vol. 11 (October, 1946), pp. 520–529.
66. Caplow, *op. cit.*, pp. 52–57.
67. A. P. Garbin and F. L. Bates, "Occupational Prestige and Its Correlates: A Reexamination," *Social Forces*, vol. 44, no. 3 (March, 1966), pp. 295–302.
68. A. P. Garbin, "An Empirical Study of Perceived Structural Congruity and Incongruity of Status Attributes As Revealed by Evaluations of Selected Occupations," *Rocky Mountain Social Science Journal*, vol. 1, no. 1 (April, 1963), pp. 121–135.
69. G. S. Counts, "The Social Status of Occupations," *School Review*, vol. 33, no. 1 (January, 1925), pp. 16–27.
70. M. E. Deeg and D. G. Paterson, "Changes in Social Status of Occupations," *Occupations*, vol. 25, no. 4 (January, 1947), pp. 205–208.
71. M. D. Hakel, T. D. Hollmann, and M. D. Dunnette, "Stability and Change in the Social Status of Occupations Over 21 and 42 Year Periods," *Personnel and Guidance Journal*, vol. 46, no. 8 (April, 1968), pp. 762–764.
72. National Opinion Research Center, "Jobs and Occupations: A Popular Evaluation," *Opinion News*, vol. 9, no. 4 (1947), pp. 3–13.
73. Thomas, *op. cit.*, p. 176.
74. R. W. Hodge, P. M. Siegel, and P. H. Rossi, "Occupational Prestige in the United States, 1925–63," *American Journal of Sociology*, vol. 70, no. 3 (November, 1964), pp. 286–302.
75. J. Braun and F. Bayer, "Social Desirability of Occupations: Revisited," *Vocational Guidance Quarterly*, vol. 21, no. 3 (March, 1973), pp. 202–205.
76. A. Inkeles and P. H. Rossi, "National Comparisons of Occupational Prestige," *American Journal of Sociology*, vol. 61, no. 4 (January, 1956), pp. 329–339.
77. A. D. Haller and D. M. Lewis, "The Hypothesis of Intersocietal Similarity in Occupational Prestige Hierarchies," *American Journal of Sociology*, vol. 72, no. 2 (September, 1966), pp. 210–216.
78. J. C. Mitchell, "Occupational Prestige and Social System: A Problem in Comparative Sociology," *International Journal of Comparative Sociology*, vol. 5, no. 1 (March, 1964), pp. 78–90.
79. J. C. Mitchell, "The Differences in an English and an American Rating of the Prestige of Occupations," *British Journal of Sociology*, vol. 15, no. 2 (June, 1964), pp. 166–173.
80. J. Gerstl and L. K. Cohen, "Research Note: Dimensions, Situs, and Ego-

centrism in Occupational Ranking," *British Journal of Sociology*, vol. 15, no. 3 (September, 1964), pp. 254–263.

81. R. Brown, "Occupational Prestige and the Ethiopian Student," *Personnel and Guidance Journal*, vol. 48, no. 3 (November, 1969), pp. 222–228.

82. A. Haller, D. Holsinger, and H. Saraiva, "Variations in Occupational Prestige Hierarchies: Brazilian Data," *American Journal of Sociology*, vol. 77, no. 5 (March, 1972), pp. 941–956.

83. J. Tuckman, "Rankings of Women's Occupations According to Social Status, Earnings, and Working Conditions," *Occupations*, vol. 28, no. 5 (February, 1950), pp. 290–294.

84. L. Baudler and D. G. Paterson, "Social Status of Women's Occupations," *Occupations*, vol. 26, no. 7 (April, 1948), pp. 421–424.

85. B. Stefflre, A. Resnikoff, and L. Lezotte, "The Relationship of Sex to Occupational Prestige," *Personnel and Guidance Journal*, vol. 46, no. 8 (April, 1968), pp. 765–772.

86. M. Hakel, T. Hollmann, and J. Ohnesorge, "Relative Influence of Prestige as a Determiner of Intelligence Judgments for Occupations," *Journal of Vocational Behavior*, vol. 1, no. 1 (January, 1971), pp. 69–74.

87. A. J. Reiss, Jr., *Occupations and Social Status* (New York: Free Press of Glencoe, Inc., 1961).

88. P. K. Hatt, "Occupation and Social Stratification," *American Journal of Sociology*, vol. 55, no. 6 (May, 1950), pp. 533–543.

89. R. J. Murphy and R. T. Morris, "Occupational Situs, Subjective Class Identification, and Political Affiliation," *American Sociological Review*, vol. 26, no. 3 (June, 1961), pp. 383–392.

90. L. Kriesberg, "Careers, Organization Size, and Succession," *American Journal of Sociology*, vol. 68, no. 3 (November, 1962), pp. 355–359.

91. W. L. Slocum, "Occupational Careers in Organizations: A Sociological Perspective," *Personnel and Guidance Journal*, vol. 43, no. 9 (May, 1965), pp. 858–866.

92. H. J. Crockett, Jr., "The Achievement Motive and Differential Occupational Mobility in the United States," *American Sociological Review*, vol. 27, no. 2 (April, 1962), pp. 191–204.

93. H. S. Becker and A. L. Strauss, "Careers, Personality, and Adult Socialization," *American Journal of Sociology*, vol. 62, no. 3 (November, 1956), pp. 253–263.

94. W. H. Form and D. C. Miller, "Occupational Career Pattern as a Sociological Instrument," *American Journal of Sociology*, vol. 54, no. 4 (January, 1949), pp. 317–329.

95. L. G. Thomas, *The Occupational Structure and Education* (Englewood Cliffs, N.J.: Prentice-Hall, Inc., 1956), p. 402.

96. D. C. Miller and W. H. Form, *Industrial Sociology* (New York: Harper & Row, Publishers, 1951).

97. L. T. Empey, "Social Class and Occupational Aspiration: A Comparison of Absolute and Relative Measurements," *American Sociological Review*, vol. 21, no. 6 (December, 1956), pp. 703–709.

98. D. E. Super, *The Psychology of Careers* (New York: Harper & Row, Publishers, 1957).

99. F. W. Taussig, *Principles of Economics*, 1st ed. (New York: The Macmillan Co., 1911), Vol. II, ch. 47.

100. L. Thomas, *The Occupational Structure and Education* (Englewood Cliffs, N.J.: Prentice-Hall, Inc., 1956), pp. 90–99.
101. E. B. Sackett, "The Relationship of Education and Earnings," *Personnel and Guidance Journal*, vol. 42, no. 5 (January, 1964), pp. 442–447.
102. P. C. Glick and H. Miller, "Educational Level and Potential Income," *American Sociological Review*, vol. 21, no. 3 (June, 1956), pp. 307–312.
103. J. B. Stone and R. T. Grow, "Geographic Mobility in the Aero-Space Industry," *Vocational Guidance Quarterly*, vol. 17, no. 1 (September, 1968), pp. 57–63.

5

Occupational Change

The rapidity of change is one of the social phenomena of our time. Life styles are subject to pressures from evolving social attitudes, legislation, world affairs, and technology. Civil rights and equal employment opportunity legislation have opened new career fields to minority members and to women. Middle eastern oil producers indirectly have changed the size of American automobiles and caused the search for alternative energy sources to be expedited. New and better production techniques are continually sought.

The first step toward automation was taken when primitive man realized that he could fashion an instrument or tool that would increase his efficiency in performing some task. Its identity has long been lost in antiquity, but probably that first tool was as rudimentary as a conveniently located and shaped rock that was suddenly, perhaps accidentally, grasped and applied to the problem that confronted that early progenitor. From that point, man has moved irreversibly toward greater application of technology to the tasks that confront him.

DEFINITION AND MAGNITUDE OF AUTOMATION

There is widespread discussion of automation and its probable effects on American life in the years ahead. As with most issues, viewpoints are scattered along a vast continuum. One view expresses great fear that automation will result in the ultimate degradation of man, turning the few remaining workers into machines, and robbing most individuals of all means of independence and self-esteem. At the other extreme is the view that automation at least frees man from onerous and abasing tasks and makes possible a life of leisure, abundance, and social perfection. It is relatively safe to conclude that it is more likely that the truth falls somewhere between these two positions.

Automation as a term has often been applied loosely to all forms of technological change. Some individuals, for example, use the term to describe the use of any labor-saving device. Others apply the term "automation" to the use of computers in business offices or automatic equipment in the handling of materials.

Technically, the term *automation* refers to the automatic, centralized control of an integrated production system. Faunce suggests that there are four basic components in the production process in which human activity or input must be replaced by machine input in order to have automation.[1] These components include power technology, processing technology, materials-handling technology, and control. Power technology deals with the source of energy applied to the production process; processing technology refers to the tools and techniques used in the actual operation performed on the raw materials; materials-handling technology relates to the ways in which materials are moved from one process operation to another; and the control factor is concerned with the regulation of quality and quantity of output.

Technological progress in these four components occurs in two steps. First, some means of replacing human participation in the step is developed; and second, the efficiency of the substitute system is increased. Technological advancement must occur in each of the four components before any one phase can advance very far. These components in turn must develop to keep pace with the power available before it is feasible to apply a more complex power technology. With the application of mechanical or electrical power, it becomes possible to use higher-speed processing machines, which are served by conveyor belts or other transfer equipment, and controlled mechanically. This development progresses in a spiral fashion toward less human input and control, and more mechanization of input and control, ultimately reaching the level of *automation*.

Faunce states that there are three developmental phases in the movement toward automation. The first phase is the handicraft stage that exists before the application of technological change. In the second period mechanized power and processing operations occur. In the third and final phase highly developed materials-handling procedures and automatic production control are used. The unique characterization of the third stage is the linking together of the various process steps into a continuous and automatic system. Various industries progress through these three stages at different rates. For example, the manufacture of textiles in the United States moved rapidly from the craft to the mechanized stage but it still has not moved on to the automated stage. On the other hand, oil refining and electrical-power generation are examples of industries that are well advanced in the third stage. The development in each stage of the four processes of production is shown in Table 8. This material is developed from a table proposed by Faunce.[2]

Wolfbein lists ten far-reaching innovations that he proposes will reshape the world of work and the kinds of workers needed in it.[3] The reader will note that most of these innovations can be easily identified as a specific illustration of a change in one of the four processes described by Faunce. Wolfbein identifies the following innovations:

1. The electronic computer
2. Instrumentation and automatic controls
3. Numerical control of machine tools
4. Communications technology
5. Increased complexity and integration of machinery
6. Mechanization of materials-handling
7. Metal processing improvements
8. Changes in transportation
9. Power production changes
10. New products and materials

Another aspect of technological progress that bears heavily on automation is discussed by Baker.[4] He emphasizes the impact of science on life today, illustrating his point with a graph of life expectancy. Life expectancy remained relatively constant at about 20 to 25 years from the Stone Age until almost modern times. Only in this century, as experimental and scientific medicine played an increasing role in everyday life, has a staggering extension appeared, pushing life expectancy into the upper 70's. Baker demonstrates the rapid application of scientific developments to life by comparing the discovery and application dates of major scientific discoveries of recent years. The reader should note the continual narrow-

TABLE 8. *Production Processes in Stages of Technological Development*

PROCESS	CRAFT	MECHANIZED	AUTOMATED
Power source	Animate	Inanimate	Inanimate
Processing procedure	Tools, simple machines	Low-speed, special purpose machines	High-speed, multi-purpose machines
Materials handling	Nonmechanized	Simple mechanization	Automatic
Control procedure	Nonmechanized	Nonmechanized	Automatic
Worker status	Artisan	Machine operator	Machine monitor

ing of the span between these two dates for the following discoveries
listed by Baker:

Item	Discovery Date	Application Date
Electric motor	1821	1886
Vacuum tube	1882	1915
Radio broadcasting	1887	1922
X-ray tube	1895	1913
Nuclear reactor	1932	1942
Radar	1935	1940
Atomic bomb	1938	1945
Transistor	1948	1951
Solar battery	1953	1955
Stereospecific rubbers, and plastics	1955	1958

Major discoveries of the type listed here provide the base for the
products and services that make up modern life. The narrowing span
between discovery and application is, at least in part, the result of the
movement of production processes from the handicraft stage to the mechanized and automated phase. Since one scientific discovery often leads
to others in related areas and to the broad application of these to the
improvement of life, the shortening of the interval between discovery and
application indicates the increasing acceleration of change in all phases
of modern life, including the world of work.

Faunce points out that the rate at which automation occurs will have
an important bearing on the extent and gravity of the problems it produces.[5] Table 9 shows his classification of major American industries according to their progress toward automation and their per cent of employment in 1964. The industries listed in the table represented about 75 per
cent of the employed civilian labor force. Not included were governmental
workers at all levels, about 13.6 per cent; and the self-employed, about 8.9
per cent. The table shows that very few workers were employed in industries that were well along the road toward automation, only 1.45 per
cent were in advanced automated industries, and 4.53 per cent in the
second level. Within Group III (mechanized industries that may be in
various stages of movement toward automation) there were another 11.2
per cent of the workers. This left the 41 per cent in Group IV and the
two excluded groups for a total of 63.5 per cent of the 1964 workers who
were employed in situations where little, if any, movement toward automation was occurring. On the other hand, over 17 per cent were in
areas that were soon to be affected by the shift toward automation.

TABLE 9. *Level of Automation in American Industry*

I ADVANCED AUTOMATION		II BEGINNING AUTOMATION		III ADVANCED MECHANIZATION		IV BEGINNING MECHANIZATION	
INDUSTRY	% EMP. 1964	INDUSTRY	% EMP. 1964	INDUSTRY	% EMP. 1964	INDUSTRY	% EMP. 1964
Petroleum refining	0.3	Cigarettes	0.05	Agriculture	6.8	Apparel	1.9
Electric power	0.4	Ordnance and accessories	0.4	Textiles	1.3	Contract construction	4.3
Industrial chemicals, plastic, synthetics	0.7	Paper & pulp	0.3	Food processing (except milk & beverages)	1.9	Wholesale and retail trade	17.2
Cement, hydraulic	0.05	Chemicals (except ind., plastics, syn.)	0.6	Rubber	0.6	Transportation	3.5
		Glass containers	0.08	Motor vehicle	1.1	Finance & real estate (except banking)	1.9
		Milk	0.3	Aircraft & missile	0.9	Services	12.2
		Beverages	0.3	Primary metals	1.7		
		Telephone communication	1.0	Mining	0.9		
		Banking	1.1	Furniture	0.6		
		Concrete, gypsum, and plastic prod.	0.2	Printing	1.4		
		Gas utilities	0.2	Leather & leather products	0.5		
				Fabricated metal products	1.7		
				Machinery	2.3		
				Instruments	0.5		
				Insurance	1.3		
				Lumber & wood products	0.9		
				Electrical equip.	2.2		
				Tobacco mfg. (except cigarettes)	0.07		

From: W. A. Faunce, *Problems of an Industrial Society* (New York: McGraw-Hill Book Company, 1968), p. 52,

THE FEAR AND THREAT OF AUTOMATION

Margaret Mead points out that technological progress is essentially neutral, and its value in civilization depends on the people in the society that developed it.[6] She examines some of the reasons for the current concern about the impact of automation on American life. She points out that automation has caused us to recognize that our economic problems are no longer focused on production but, instead, are now problems of distribution, and that we are ill-prepared in attitude and understanding to cope with problems of this type. The difficulties of readjustment, she states, include major changes in social attitudes and values—the most difficult type of changes for a society to make. She concludes that the major concern is produced by society's emphasis on short-term disturbances and inability to focus on the long-run gain to be obtained from automation.

Snyder also has written of the concern being expressed about the effects of automation.[7] He states that the problems produced by automation will have tremendous effect on our society and that a united effort must be made cooperatively by business, labor, and the government to seek solutions that will produce the maximum gain for society. He points out four myths that he claims are being used to delay a forthright approach to solving the larger problem. These myths are as follows:

1. *Automation is not going to eliminate many jobs.* Snyder estimates that automation is actually replacing workers at the rate of 25,000 to 40,000 jobs per week. On a yearly basis that amounts to one to two million jobs per year.
2. *Automation will create jobs for workers, not only in running the machines, but also in maintaining and building them.* The fallacy here is fairly obvious. Automated processes are very costly, and unless labor costs are reduced to compensate for the expenditure for the machines there would be no reason for automating in the first place.
3. *Those who lose their jobs to automation can be easily retrained and placed in more highly skilled positions that pay more money.* Actually automation is more likely to reduce demands for skills; further, retraining may be impractical for many workers because of ability, education, or age.
4. *Workers replaced by automation can find jobs in other communities.* The evidence shows that workers who lose their jobs to automation are often the least able to move. They are lower-paid, older, less skilled. They cannot move, either for economic reasons or because psychological ties hold them to the familiar places.

Hayes also emphasizes that automation not only causes unemployment by separating workers from their jobs, but also reduces the employment opportunities for new entrants into the labor market.[8] The problem is indeed a serious one for which easy palliatives do not exist. Some relief can be obtained by introducing automated systems gradually to meet additional production demands, by reassignment of workers within their present employment situations, by shortening working hours, by improving educational opportunities, and by providing for earlier retirement. More substantial accommodation may most likely come from education for leisure, reorientation of social values related to the "ethic of work," and a greater emphasis on the welfare and well-being of all aspects of society.

Faunce points out that there is not a simple relationship between automation and unemployment.[9] Three factors that bear heavily on the employment-unemployment ratio are the general level of demand for goods and services, the size and composition of the labor force, and the productivity per man-hour of work. Production technology has an impact on only the third factor. An increase in any one factor can offset a reverse change in another. In other words, unemployment because of technological progress can be counteracted by increasing the demand for services and goods. Faunce suggests that the falling unemployment rate throughout most of the 1960's was due to this type of relationship. He warns that a decline in economic growth can cause serious imbalance in employment.

This warning was confirmed in the economic downturn of the mid-seventies when increasing inflation and decreasing productivity contributed to heavy decline in demand for consumer goods. The immediate result was a rapid increase in unemployment, especially in those areas of industry in which demand had dropped most rapidly. For example, the automobile industry experienced long periods of interrupted production during the early months of 1975.

Since the introduction of automated procedures has occurred primarily during a period of high demand, there has been less resultant unemployment than might otherwise have been expected. The majority of workers affected by technological progress toward automation has been displaced rather than disemployed. As an industry comes closer to a true state of automation, it will be increasingly difficult to absorb workers within the industry itself. The transfer and downgrading of employed workers is one of the major causes of unemployment of prospective entrants. Industry redistributes its existing crew rather than adding new workers. The percentage of young workers who are unemployed is further increased by the record number of youths who are now entering the labor market. Since increasing industrial automation will likely continue to have the most serious effect on the young entrant, additional arguments are given to the contention that careful, effective vocational guidance is crucial for each person who wishes to move into the world of work.

EDUCATIONAL ASPECTS OF AUTOMATION

Those who wrote in the late 1950's and early 1960's emphasized the unemployment threat of automation much more than those who have written since the middle or late 1960's. Kalachek, in addition to Faunce, pointed out that automation was not likely to produce the mass unemployment that was earlier feared.[10] He described the economic efforts of both government and industry, separately as well as cooperatively, to ensure high levels of employment. He further pointed to the fact that even though America was in a period of affluence, consumer demands required that production be extended greatly before consumer satiety would be reached.

In the long run, Kalachek emphasized, education would play a preponderant part in solving the problems that accompany automation. Educational achievement was progressing steadily, moving to continually higher levels. New labor entrants averaged three and one-half years more of education than retirees. Jobs were being filled with better educated people; in some cases, the educational level of job holders increased at a faster pace than the educational demands of the work performed. On the other hand, some demand for highly educated workers in automated systems was temporary in nature and fell back to a lower level as the automated processes were perfected. Complex machinery is constantly being redesigned for easier and simpler operation. As has been true in the past, the worker whose educational attainment puts him/her in a poor competitive position in job-seeking will continue in a similar and more difficult position in the future.

Rogers has emphasized the discrepancy between the general unemployment rate (about 5–7 per cent) and that for the person between ages 16–20 (about 15–20 per cent or more).[11] The rate for the age group of 20–24 is about double the national average. Within the two groups of 16–20 and 20–24, the rate is much greater for the drop-outs and for the nonwhites. He proposes the following educational approaches to solving this problem:

1. Assure every child the opportunity of attending a high school of sufficient size to provide reasonable educational choices with provision for easy transfer from one curriculum to another.
2. Provide modernized industrial arts and home arts programs for most high school students.
3. Make available work-related education to students.
4. Place major emphasis on basic skills and tools for learning and communicating, including reading, writing, oral communications, arithmetic, and human relations. Specialized skill training would be postponed until post-high school or on-the-job training.
5. Arrange for the industrial community to establish a community skills center under school auspices for youth and adults.
6. Help each youth capable of acquiring skills for self-support to finish high school and go on to the community or technical college or other specialized institution.
7. Provide instruction at all levels that will educate for an acceptance of new meanings of work and leisure.
8. Provide closer cooperation with federal sources of help.

9. Modify public viewpoints toward women's education and occupational participation.

The *Occupational Outlook Handbook* emphasizes the same impact of unemployment on the younger and less well educated workers.[12] It reports unemployment among those workers with less than four years of high school to be nearly triple in the 18–24 year group as compared with the 25–54 year group. This same proportion tends to hold at each educational level when the two age groups are compared.

AUTOMATION AND THE FUTURE

Fortune-telling is obviously beyond the scope of this volume. Nevertheless, given certain basic information and a set of agreed-on assumptions, an intelligent individual can project existing data a short distance into the future with reasonable certainty.

Continued technological progress and increasing application of automation appear to be an irreversible certainty in the years ahead. The rate of this development will obviously be related to a variety of factors, such as the population explosion, the rate and nature of urbanization, international pressures, and the extent of governmental manipulation of the national economy.

One product of the trend toward automation is likely to be a further reduction in the length of the work week. During a half century or more, our man-hour output has increased at the rate of two to three per cent per year; thus, it has nearly doubled in the past twenty-five years. The benefits of this increased productivity are transmitted to the worker either through greater income or shorter working hours, and usually by a combination of the two factors.

A further product of the movement toward automation may be the reversal of the trend toward job-specialization, according to Faunce.[13] He proposes four reasons for this possibility: first, as production becomes automated, human control becomes mainly machine-monitoring and maintenance, thus reducing the variety of tasks; second, automation calls for a new combination of remaining tasks; third, previously separate production processes will likely be combined into a single system; fourth, automation will likely cause a redistribution of employment opportunity.

It is possible that the present trend of decreased demand for unskilled and semiskilled production and clerical workers and the increased demand for professional and technical workers will continue. If so, we will ultimately have a labor force predominantly consisting of highly skilled and educated workers.

Although the early fears of union leaders that automation would produce vast unemployment have not proven true, there still continues to exist a certain degree of concern among workers whose livelihood might be so threatened. Technological change is an inevitable aspect of life, both today and in the years ahead, and workers, employers, and government will be involved in seeking ways by which such change can be accomplished with minimum disadvantage to any one party involved in the process. Weinberg has proposed five "shock absorbers" that can be used to reduce the hardship of technological change.[14] He suggests that the following steps be followed when technological change is to occur:

1. Advance notice be provided to workers, unions, and the community.
2. Coordination of manpower and technical planning within the industry in order to capitalize on gradual attrition, thus avoiding sudden layoffs,
3. Provide a variety of measures for job security or income maintenance to meet the varying needs of assorted worker groups.
4. Provide a variety of training programs to assist displaced or potentially displaced workers.
5. Assure maximum cooperation of private management with government and community agencies to find new jobs with minimum periods of unemployment for displaced workers.

CAUSES OF LONG-TERM OCCUPATIONAL TRENDS

Increasingly, counselors work with vocational problems among people who range in age from adolescence to near-retirement. Regardless of the age of the counselee, the counselor must give consideration to likely developments in the years ahead. This is crucial in the case of adolescents because a) they will be in the occupational world for many years, and b) in most cases there will be a lag between the time when the career choice process gets under way and the time when they actually move from the educational world to employment.

For the high school freshman who appears to be headed toward one of the professions, one can anticipate four years of high school, four years of college, and three to five years of professional or graduate study. Starting to work for such a teen-ager is, then, possibly ten to fifteen years away. A professional career can be projected from that point onward for an additional forty years. In such a case, present labor-market information would be of relatively little value or importance. What would be more helpful is information about the profession, its opportunities and possibilities ten or fifteen years from now, and the course the profession will likely follow for the next half century.

Current labor-market figures help adolescents concerned with long-range plans only as a base or bench mark. These data must be adjusted and evaluated in terms of the approximate time when they will be entering the labor market, if the figures are to be pertinent. A career field with a severe shortage today is not a wise choice if the shortage is apt to end before one can prepare and enter the field. What is most needed to modify present data is information about trends in the occupation being considered.

Obvious factors that have a long-term influence on occupations are technological progress, invention, and discovery.[15,16] Entire industries have come into existence as a result of the relentless march of progress. Sometimes the new discovery or invention creates a new market for itself as the public becomes familiar and accustomed to it. An example of this is air conditioning. Only a few decades old, this invention has brought with it thousands of jobs in the manufacture, distribution, sale, and maintenance of equipment. Similarly, television has created opportunities for vast numbers of workers, not only in those fields mentioned above, but also in the broad entertainment and advertising aspects of that industry. For the most part, areas such as these two have created entirely new occupations that were nonexistent before.[17]

In many areas of modern life, technological progress has resulted in improvements and refinements, in the replacing of old methods and products with new and better ways. When this happens, some occupations may be drastically reduced, and sometimes may disappear altogether, to be replaced by those related to the new technique or product.[18,19] Shortly before the turn of the century, the standard container for those staples available in the local grocery store was the wooden barrel. Such diverse items as crackers, pickles, flour, and butter were often packaged in barrels. The cooper, who made wooden barrels and kegs, was a busy man. In fact, census figures show that in 1890 there were about as many coopers as there were plumbers and pipefitters in the United States. During the fifty years after 1890, new methods of processing and packaging foods and other items led to increased use of paper and plastic products, glass jars, tin cans, and similar containers, with a resultant decrease in the use of wooden barrels. By 1940, the number of coopers was so small that census figures no longer listed the occupation. In the meantime, the number of plumbers and pipefitters had increased about four times. Many more people are now employed in the production of the newer types of packages, but a once well-established trade has practically disappeared.

A second factor having a long-term influence on occupations is a change in either the birth rate or the death rate. The sudden increase in the birth rate that occurred in the United States during and following World War II had an effect that is still influencing the world of work. An increased birth rate results in greater demands on those occupational fields that produce goods or render services. In the years immediately after the increase became apparent, those occupations serving young children were affected; for example, additional classrooms in elementary schools had to be built, and more elementary teachers were needed. As the group grew older, the impact was felt at the secondary school level and, still later, at the college level. All other occupations involved with this group were similarly influenced. As the birth rate declines, one can anticipate a decreased need for such things as baby foods, toys, elementary classrooms, and teachers.

The passing of the post-World War II baby boom demonstrates this point. By the early 1970's, the number of employed elementary teachers had begun to decline as school systems encountered significantly smaller beginning classes. As these smaller classes progress through the school grades, a comparable reduction in the number of secondary teaching positions can be expected. Emphasis in the early 1970's on zero population growth has further accentuated the decline that had been anticipated for some years.

Influences such as these can be anticipated for a considerable period in advance. For example, most youngsters enter high school at about thirteen or fourteen years of age. A drastic change in the number of babies born in a given year, therefore, will have an obvious effect on high school enrollments thirteen and fourteen years later.

Changes in death rates produce similar trends in occupations that serve the older person. As the life span is extended, more and more people become involved in catering to all the needs of older people. The numbers of retirement homes and nursing homes increase, social services increase, and more medicines and special foods are manufactured.

Changes in natural resources available for use also produce long-term trends in occupations. Coal mining and related occupations have been severely affected in recent years not only by the technological development of machinery that reduced the need for the number of miners, but also by the exhaustion of many mines in the coal regions of Kentucky and West Virginia. As the mines were depleted, or reached a level of production that was no longer profitable, they were closed down and the remaining miners were left without work. In order to work, they found it necessary to move to new locations or enter new occupations.

Control of crude oil prices by the oil-producing and exporting nations and local governmental responses with import taxes to restrict purchases of expensive foreign oil again have demonstrated how these same influences affect employment. The search for temporary alternative sources of energy to replace the unexpectedly expensive oil has renewed activity in the coal fields and expanded employment there. The higher cost of oil permits the sale of coal at higher prices, bringing back into profitable production many mines that had previously been marginal or unprofitable. Additional positions are created to expedite the search for long-range alternatives in such areas as atomic energy and, still further in the future, solar energy.

Changes in patterns of capitalizing or financing certain occupational activities have an effect on those fields and on related areas as well. An excellent example is farming. During the early years of this nation, land in large quantities for farming could be obtained by homesteading or could be purchased very cheaply. As the geographic frontier closed, land became less accessible, resulting in prices that have increased and that can be expected to increase in the future. This alone has had considerable effect on the cost of entering farming, since it is no longer possible to obtain the necessary land easily and inexpensively. Many other changes also have occurred. Efficient farming involves the use of large quantities of expensive equipment with larger and larger units of land. The development of new methods and techniques has increased the demand for more expensive seed, fertilizer, and machinery. Today the boy interested in a career as a farmer must not only solve the problem of finding the land he will need, but he must also find sources of capital that will finance the extensive expenditures necessary in starting the enterprise. He also needs a great deal more specialized education, since farming has become increasingly more scientific. Similar changes have occurred in vast areas of business and industry. In some fields, the quantity of needed capital is so great that few individuals can consider entering it. The cost of necessary office equipment for some of the professions, such as dentistry or medical specialties, must be considered by those interested in private practice in these areas.

Changes in the way of life of large segments of the population also create occupational trends.[20] Shorter working hours and an affluent society have vastly increased the demand for new types of recreational endeavors. Many occupations have developed to meet this need. Many families now own one or more boats, camping gear, expensive sports equipment, and have memberships in athletic or other clubs. All of these require people to manufacture, service, or otherwise assist in participation. Hobbies often require expensive and extensive apparatus or specialized help of various kinds.

An interesting development in recent years has occurred in the provision of services. As both families and individuals continue to demand and utilize more and more services, many occupations have been created to assist people to provide the desired services for themselves. Examples of this trend are laundromats, self-service dry-cleaning establishments, coin-operated car-washing stations, tool-rental shops, and numerous other self-service businesses.

A final factor that influences long-range trends in occupational fields is the average age of workers. Occupational opportunities in any field depend on the regular replacement of a certain portion of the workers who have withdrawn because of movement to a new field, retirement, death, or other reasons.[21] In addition to replacement, there will be openings in those fields that are growing and expanding. Most of the factors discussed thus far exert their influence primarily by increasing or decreasing the number of new positions available in a field. Without further information one would normally assume that replacement rates among occupations would tend to be relatively consistent from year to year. One item that can obviously influence this, however, is the average age of workers in those occupations. Where the age is comparatively high, the number of replacements needed because of retirement or death can be expected to be considerably greater than in occupational fields of the same size filled primarily with young workers. Both tailors and carpenters, for example, are groups whose average age is twenty or more years older than that of automobile mechanics. The proportion of replacement positions available in the first two fields, therefore, can be expected to be greater than in the latter.

CAUSES OF SHORT-TERM TRENDS

Some elements cause a new trend or distort the long-term trend in an occupational field. In general, these are transitory in nature and, therefore, of less significance than the kinds of influences discussed above. However, during the period involved, the change produced can be an extreme one and the dislocation severe. Some items in this category exert an influence on the entire economy and thus affect almost every field, whereas others may focus on a small segment of the world of work, with stress appearing in only a few occupations.

Wars and calamities can impose extensive change in short order. The expansion of military services draws men from the entire employment spectrum, often causing shortages of workers in many fields. In addition, wars ordinarily require rapid expansion in industries closely related to the war effort, such as shipbuilding, munitions, and transportation. Satisfying the need for workers in these areas can usually be done only by transferring large numbers of workers from less essential fields. Such rapid expansion in selected fields, often manned by highly skilled workers, may necessitate reorganizing skilled jobs into simpler components so that new workers can be trained to do a portion of the work in a shorter training time. The job of a machinist, for example, may be subdivided into several machine operator tasks, with workers taught to perform only specific parts of the total job.

Earthquakes, epidemics, fires, floods, and other natural disasters can similarly produce strain and stress on the organization of work in the geographic area affected. The extent to which occupational change occurs depends, naturally, on the scope and severity of the catastrophe.

Fads can produce an enormous demand for a new or different item in a brief period. The influence of a television program, a popular movie, a widely distributed magazine, or the adulation and imitation of a national figure creates demand where none existed before. Children, teen-agers, and adults are all subject to crazes and fancies in clothing, hair styles, toys, and many other items. The fickleness of fashion and the conformity pressures of "keeping up with the Joneses" expands some industries and creates others.

Seasonal variations also produce short-term trends.[22] The annual Christmas shopping season creates openings for temporary salespersons in department stores and specialty shops and adds more letter carriers to the local post office. Resort areas ordinarily expand during "the season," with staff vacancies and other auxiliary jobs. Fruit and vegetable harvesting, canning factories and other processing plants may operate on seasonal schedules because of the specific nature of the work.

Economic influences can bring about short-term changes, although the ups and downs of the business cycle ordinarily produce long-term pressures. A detailed study of the business cycle reveals that, in addition to either a long-term upward or downward slope, the pattern actually consists of many brief upward or downward zigzags within the overall incline. Each fluctuation, even though brief, can have an influence on certain occupations that may be sensitive to such alterations.[23] Other economic pressures, such as strikes, material surpluses or shortages, or temporary loss of usual markets may distort employment on a short-term basis.

When one discusses tentative career fields with a high school student, it is important to consider the possible bearing of short-term factors. Since the long-range trend has much more relevance for a lifetime career, one must evaluate with extreme caution any brief distortion of occupational opportunity short-term factors may produce.

ANTICIPATED TRENDS

As indicated earlier, attempts to predict employment opportunities any distance into the future are risky and uncertain. On the other hand, if one assumes that there will be no major change in general economic conditions, that no major war or other calamity will develop, and that general work patterns and population trends will continue in the same course, one can project trends over a short period with a fair degree of assurance.[24] Just such a service is provided by the Bureau of Labor Statistics, which, in cooperation with several other governmental agencies, regularly publishes the *Occupational Outlook Handbook*. This volume is invaluable for the teacher or counselor who wishes to assist individuals in making some assessment of short-term possibilities in various career fields. By utilizing data available from the various governmental agencies concerned with employment, the Bureau of Labor Statistics is able to provide current and reliable information about trends. Frequent revision of the *Handbook* is made to provide for continuous modification as well as addition of new information.

The effect of population factors on occupational trends has already been considered briefly. Our country has grown from a population of about 4 million in the 1790 census to over 204 million in the 1970 census. It is anticipated that the national population will approach 224 million by 1980. Although the birth rate declined and immigration restrictions reduced the flow of people into the United States in the period between World War I and World War II, the increase in the birth rate since the middle 1940's has resulted in a steady and sizable increase in population from that time on.

The increasing number of births since 1945 has not only increased the total population, but it also has produced changes in the proportions of the population found in the various age groups. Table 10 gives some indication of the changes that have occurred since 1950 and that are expected up to 1990.

Although Table 10 suggests a continuing increase in population during the projected period to 1990, the rate of growth is expected to decline in the years before 1990. This is shown in the section of the table listing figures for population under sixteen years of age. The decrease in the early years of this period appears in the 1970 figures and for the older years of this span in the 1980 figures, with 1990 showing a decline in the 16–19 and 20–24 year age groups.

Because of the increasing over-all numbers of young people who reach working age, the labor force will continue to show steady growth throughout the projected period. Actual figures for the total labor force in 1960 and 1970 were 72 million and 85.9 million workers. The projected figures for 1980, 1985, and 1990 are 101.8 million, 107.7 million, and 112.6

TABLE 10. *Total Population 1950 to 1970 and Projections to 1980 and 1990 (Numbers in Thousands)*

AGE	ACTUAL			PROJECTED	
	1950	1960	1970	1980	1990
Total	152,271	180,684	204,879	224,132	246,639
Under 16 yrs.	43,131	58,868	61,894	56,795	63,560
Under 5 yrs.	16,410	20,364	17,167	18,566	20,531
5–15 yrs.	26,721	38,504	44,727	38,229	43,029
16 yrs. & over	109,141	121,814	142,982	167,339	183,080
16–19 yrs.	8,542	10,698	15,262	16,396	13,822
20–24 yrs.	11,680	11,116	17,192	21,067	17,823
25–34 yrs.	24,036	22,911	25,257	36,962	41,791
35–44 yrs.	21,637	24,223	23,156	25,370	36,902
45–54 yrs.	17,453	20,581	23,287	22,406	24,617
55–64 yrs.	13,396	15,627	18,651	21,083	20,357
65 yrs. and over	12,397	16,658	20,177	24,051	27,768

From *Manpower Report of the President*, April, 1975, p. 308. (Projections are based on intermediate-low fertility—2.1 children per woman beginning childbearing after 1971.)

million. It is, of course, important to realize that any change in the birth rate has a delayed effect on the labor force since individuals are not considered a part of the labor force before they reach age 16.

In attempting to identify and understand trends, one must examine the situation as it existed at some point in time and then consider the changes that have occurred at selected intervals from that point to the present. Obviously, the decennial census, with its regular collection of employment data each decade, provides a logical base for such calculations. Also of significant assistance are data from the annual *Manpower Report of the President* and regularly released data from the Department of Labor. Table 11 shows comparisons of actual employment in major occupational groups for three previous dates as well as projections to dates in the future.

An inspection of Table 11 reveals that all groups, except farmers and farm laborers, have shown and project actual increases in the number of individuals employed in each category. However, if one examines the percentage distribution of the labor force, other important conclusions can be drawn. One sees that, comparatively, professional workers and clerical worker categories have increased and are expected to continue to increase in the proportion of the labor force included in these two groups. Craft workers and service workers appear to be holding relatively stable, and the other groups are decreasing in the percentage figures included in each group. The greatest decline is clearly in the farmer and farm laborer groups.

Already apparent are certain pressures that will soon exert influence on the labor force. The average schooling completed by nearly all entrants to the labor market is increasing steadily. Since World War II, the number of college graduates has increased faster than the growth of the labor force. It is estimated that about 18.5 per cent of the labor force age 25 and over in 1980 will hold college degrees, about eight per cent will have a year or more of graduate study, and more than 40 per cent will be high school graduates.

TRENDS IN THE EMPLOYMENT OF WOMEN

Tremendous change has occurred in recent decades in the employment of women in this country. Today, about 45 per cent of all women sixteen years of age and over participate in the labor force. These figures are expected to hold fairly steady until 1985.[25] Table 12 compares the actual and projected percentages of women in the labor force from 1950 to 1990. Although there are increases in almost all age groups across the years, particularly significant are the recent large increases of employed women in the 20–24 and the 25–34 age groups, since these age groups comprise those most likely to have pre-school or school-age youngsters and were previously

TABLE 11. *Employment by Major Occupational Groups: 1940, 1960, 1972, and Projections for 1980 and 1985*

| | NUMBER IN THOUSANDS | | | | | PERCENTAGE DISTRIBUTION | | | | |
| | ACTUAL | | | PROJECTED | | | | | | |
Major group	1940[a]	1960[b]	1972[c]	1980[c]	1985[c]	1940	1960	1972	1980	1985
Total employment	45,166	64,267	81,703	95,800	101,500	100.0	100.0	100.0	100.0	100.0
Professional & technical workers	3,345	7,566	11,459	15,000	17,000	7.4	11.8	14.0	15.7	16.8
Managers and adminstrators except farm	3,749	6,960	8,032	10,100	10,500	8.3	10.8	9.8	10.5	10.3
Sales workers	2,905	4,172	5,354	6,300	6,500	6.5	6.5	6.6	6.6	6.4
Clerical workers	4,612	9,539	14,247	17,900	19,700	10.2	14.8	17.4	18.7	19.4
Craft and kindred workers	5,056	8,342	10,810	12,300	13,000	11.2	13.0	13.2	12.8	12.8
Operatives	8,631	12,025	13,549	15,000	15,300	19.1	18.8	16.6	15.6	15.1
Nonfarm laborers	3,064	3,151	4,217	4,500	4,500	6.8	4.9	5.2	4.7	4.4
Service workers	5,570	8,229	10,966	12,700	13,400	12.3	12.8	13.4	13.3	13.2
Farmers and farm laborers	8,235	4,283	3,069	2,000	1,600	18.2	6.6	3.8	2.1	1.6

[a] U.S. Bureau of the Census.
[b] *Statistical Abstract of the U.S., 1960.* Table 279, p. 216. (Includes Alaska and Hawaii).
[c] *Manpower Report of The President, 1975.* Table E–9, p. 314.

inclined to postpone employment until children were well along in school. These rapid changes have resulted in the present 25–34 age group match-ing the rate of participation of the most active group of 1950. Mothers with school-age children are as likely to work today as were unmarried young women of the 1950's. A recent study of female National Merit Scholars shows that 85 per cent definitely planned on careers.[26]

Regardless of the increase in the number of women who now partici-pate in the world of work, there still remain serious problems related to that involvement. The *Manpower Report* identifies five such problems:

First, the large wage differential between male and female workers has persisted over the last two decades, although earnings for both sexes have continued to rise in absolute terms. Second, this rise in absolute earnings has benefited only a minority of women in the labor force, since nearly two-thirds of all full-time year-round female work-ers earned less than $7,000 in 1972. Third, women remain overwhelm-ingly concentrated in a relatively small number of lower paying occu-pations. Fourth, while about 1 out of every 8 families is headed by a woman, the 1974 unemployment rate for female family heads averaged about 7.0 per cent. Finally, the high levels of labor force attachment among black married women aged 25 and over reflect in considerable degree their continuing obligation to supply a substantial proportion of family income in order to help compensate for the generally low wages of their husbands.[27]

The *Manpower Report* also reveals that even though marriage still lowers the extent of labor market participation of women, its impact is less than existed in previous years. For example, in 1950 about 24 per cent of married women with husbands were employed; by 1974, this figure had increased to 43 per cent. The *Manpower Report* also points out that par-ticipation in the work force by women increases steadily with educational attainment.

TABLE 12. *Labor Force Participation Rates of Women, by Age Groups for Selected Years 1950–1990, Actual and Projected Percentages*

AGE	1950	1960	1970	1980	1990
TOTAL	33.9	37.8	43.4	45.6	46.5
16 and 17 yrs.	30.1	29.1	34.9	36.1	37.4
18 and 19 yrs.	51.3	51.1	53.7	55.0	56.3
20–24 yrs.	46.1	46.2	57.8	63.6	66.4
25–34 yrs.	34.0	36.0	45.0	50.4	51.6
35–44 yrs.	39.1	43.5	51.1	53.5	55.4
45–54 yrs.	38.0	49.8	54.4	56.6	58.3
55–64 yrs.	27.0	37.2	43.0	45.1	46.1
65 yrs. & over	9.7	10.8	9.7	9.1	8.8

Source: *Manpower Report of the President, 1975*, p. 57. Reprinted from *Handbook of Labor Statistics*, 1974, p. 31.

...As one might expect, the boys tended to prefer science and the girls English. Social Science got a somewhat better rating from the boys than the girls. What we found totally unexpected—contradicting our preconceptions when designing this question—is that in terms of liking the subject, mathematics was the only subject which exhibited no sex differences. (Grades 2–12, 1973)

...We first note that the enrollment of women in these basic courses [two elementary calculus sequences] is disproportionately low. Women comprised only about a third of the class even though women were in the majority in the freshmen class of 1971. This undoubtedly is one of the inevitable corollaries of the deficient mathematical training women receive in high school....

...We do not claim that the goal is the elimination of all measurable sex differences in all human pursuits. We all have different opinions on the extent to which that would be desirable. But we are all agreed that the many sex differences in mathematical training and attitudes described in this report are *not* the result of free and informed choice. If they were then the low enrollments and high attrition rates for women in mathematics would be a matter of less concern. The immorality of these sex differences lies precisely in the fact that they are the result of many subtle (and not so subtle) forces, restrictions, stereotypes, sex roles, parental-teacher-peer group attitudes, and other cultural and psychological constraints which we haven't begun to fully understand. Before we can hope that each individual child and young adult will make these choices freely and wisely we must work towards a society generally (and an academic program specifically) which ensures that the freedom of opportunity to become whatever that individual is truly capable of becoming, is not compromised by such a chance event as the child's sex at birth....

From J. Ernest, *Mathematics and Sex* (Santa Barbara, California: Mathematics Department, University of California, Santa Barbara, 1976), pp. 3, 11, 21–22.

Race appears to be an additional factor in the employment of women. Larger percentages of white females between ages 16 and 24 are employed; at that age level, the figures reverse, and among females from 25 onward larger percentages of blacks are employed. The 25–34 and the 35–44 age groups show more than 60 per cent of the black females employed. The presence of children is less likely to keep black females from working; for example, in 1973 about 54 per cent of black women with children under six years of age were in the labor force, compared with only 31 per cent of white women with preschool-age children.

Additional factors that influence the involvement of women in the labor force are education and level of husband's earnings. Work force involvement is directly related to the level of education completed by the women. A partial explanation of this correlation may be the general relationship between education and the level of pay—the higher an individual's education, the greater the likelihood of higher pay. Thus, eligibility for higher income may be an incentive that draws a larger proportion of higher educated women into the labor force. Equally plausible is the likelihood that women with college and professional education develop commitments to their professional field that hold them to work settings. To a lesser extent, husband's earnings tend to produce a negative relationship with presence in the labor force—the higher the husband's income the less likely for the woman to be in the labor force. During the past two decades this factor appears to be weakening although the relationship is still detectable.

A continuing problem is the wage differential between full-time year-round male and female workers. In 1972, nearly two-thirds of all such women workers earned less than $7,000, whereas more than three-fourths of the comparable male group earned more than this figure. Median incomes for women workers are indicated in Table 13. An inspection of the table confirms the overall discrepancy between male and female earnings of around 40 per cent. Although some of the differential may be accounted for by part-time employment, length of service, and differences in responsibility, it is obvious that even after adjustment for these factors a considerable gap remains. Rectifying this discrepancy requires legal action as well as attitudinal change.

Women workers are still concentrated in large numbers in a small number of occupations, as shown in Table 14. Frequently, one must conclude that there has been a continuation of the balkanization of the labor force so that women are primarily employed in "female" occupations. Oppenheimer shows increasing percentages of women employed in these occupations to an extent that largely accounts for the additional women in

TABLE 13. *Median Incomes of Full-Time Women Workers by Occupational Group, 1972*

MAJOR OCCUPATIONAL GROUP	MEDIAN INCOME	PER CENT OF MEN'S INCOME
Professional and technical workers	$8,796	68
Nonfarm managers and administrators	7,306	53
Clerical workers	6,039	63
Sales workers	4,575	40
Operatives, including transportation	5,021	58
Service workers, except private household	4,606	59
Private household	2,365	Not available
Nonfarm laborers	4,755	63

Source: *Manpower Report of the President,* 1975, p. 63. Reproduced from "Fact Sheet on the Earnings Gap," U.S. Department of Labor, Women's Bureau, 1974.

the labor force.[28] Even though almost equal proportions of men and women are professional and technical workers, the women are primarily concentrated in the fields of elementary and secondary teaching and nursing, whereas the men are scattered across the entire category. The largest area in which women are employed is the service category, where they make up more than half of the work force. Recently, the finance area has become primarily female because of the growing number of clerical positions in this industry. Government and trade are also heavily populated with female workers, predominantly employed in clerical and sales categories.

In 1940, approximately half of the employed women were either service workers or blue-collar operatives, one-third were employed as white-collar clerical-sales workers, and about 14 per cent were white-collar professional-technical workers. By 1970, there was a larger share in clerical and sales and the professional-technical portion had increased slightly, but the general distribution was still much the same. Some of the areas in

TABLE 14. *The 25 Largest Occupations of Women, 1960*

OCCUPATION	NUMBER	PER CENT OF TOTAL OCCUP.
1. Secretaries	1,423,352	97
2. Saleswomen, sales clerks (retail)	1,397,364	54
3. Private household workers	1,162,683	96
4. Teachers (elementary schools)	860,413	86
5. Bookkeepers	764,054	84
6. Waitresses	714,827	87
7. Nurses, professional	567,884	98
8. Sewers and stitchers (mfg.)	534,258	94
9. Typists	496,735	95
10. Cashiers	367,954	78
11. Cooks (except private household)	361,772	64
12. Telephone operators	341,797	96
13. Babysitters (private household)	319,735	98
14. Attendants (hospitals and other institutions)	288,268	74
15. Laundry and dry-cleaning operatives	277,396	72
16. Assemblers	270,769	44
17. Apparel and accessory operatives	270,619	75
18. Hairdressers and cosmetologists	267,050	89
19. Packers and wrappers	262,935	60
20. Stenographers	258,554	96
21. Teachers (secondary schools)	243,452	47
22. Office machine operators	227,849	74
23. Checkers, examiners, inspectors (mfg.)	215,066	45
24. Practical nurses	197,115	96
25. Kitchen workers (except household)	179,796	59

Source: U.S. Department of Commerce, Bureau of Census, 1960 Census of Population.

which change had occurred represented areas of relatively small employment. For example, in 1940 one physician in 20 was a woman; in 1970 the ratio was one in eight; in 1940, only nine per cent of real estate brokers and salespersons were female; in 1970, the figure was 36 per cent. In 1940, two and one-half per cent of bartenders were women; in 1970, 30 per cent were women. In 1940, female bus drivers were very rare; by 1970, 37 per cent of the bus drivers were women, although many were part-time, poorly paid school-bus drivers.[29] Table 15 compares the changes in the proportion of jobs held by women in nonagricultural industries over the 1940–70 period. Although the figures show steady increases in all categories, they cannot be interpreted as reflecting wider employment opportunities for women. For the most part, the figures in Table 15 can be explained by increases in job fields that have long been allocated to women. In 1970, half of all employed women were in 17 occupations, compared to 63 occupations for half of the employed men.

Even though legislation prohibits sex discrimination in employment, complete eradication of the practice may take a considerable period of time. The problem is compounded by the fact that some positions, such as elementary teaching, permit work schedules that are particularly convenient for mothers with school-age children, and other positions involve activities that capitalize on skills that women who have no significant work experience may have developed in the home, such as private household service and child-care positions. Attitudinal changes in society are generally necessary to permit women access to a wider array of employment opportunities. In addition, changes in attitudes of young women themselves would permit and encourage their consideration of wider choices. An example of one recent publication that strives to accomplish the latter

TABLE 15. *Percentage of Positions in Various Industries Filled by Women, 1940–1970*

INDUSTRY	1940	1950	1960	1970
Total (Non-Agric)	31	32	36	40
Mining	1	2	5	8
Construction	2	3	4	6
Manufacturing	23	26	25	29
Transportation	12	16	18	22
Wholesale and retail trade	30	37	40	43
Finance, insurance, real estate	34	44	49	52
Services	62	58	62	63
Other Services	21	27	32	36
Public administration	20	26	28	31
Industry not elsewhere listed	38	42	40	—

Source: *Monthly Labor Review*, May, 1974, p. 4. Reprinted from Census of Population, Industrial Characteristics, 1940, 1950, 1960, 1970.

is *I Can Be Anything: Careers and Colleges for Young Women* by J. S. Mitchell.[30]

In summary, then, one must conclude that even though social attitude and extensive legislation have supported the view of wider employment opportunities for women, actual implementation has lagged. Although discouraging to those who would hope for immediate remediation, this slowness of change is not surprising. The sudden opening of a new field to women does not mean that a supply of qualified women workers will be available immediately to assume positions there. This is especially true in occupations that require lengthy preparatory programs. Time is required to develop a pool of applicants with appropriate skills and education. Family attitudes, especially during the preschool years, will have a continuing influence on the lives of both boys and girls and hence will affect the way in which both sexes look at work opportunities for women.

Of even greater influence may be attitudes of teachers and counselors who encounter girls in the elementary and secondary school years— the awareness, exploratory, and preparatory years. Changes in sex-stereotyping of occupations can occur during these years in time to assist girls in selecting appropriate curricular choices. For example, high school courses in mathematics and science are essential for admission to postsecondary programs in technical and scientific fields. These choices are made in the early high school years; failure to select appropriate preparatory courses closes the higher level occupations in these fields.

Bingham and House recently studied the extent to which counselors are both informed and unbiased about employment opportunities for women.[31] Even though this group is generally better informed and less biased than others, it is obvious that there is room for much improvement if counselors and teachers are to help girls effectively to enlarge their occupational aspirations.

TRENDS IN EMPLOYMENT OF MINORITY GROUPS

During the late 1960's, long overdue attention was focused on the employment plight of many of America's minority groups. In many occupational fields, racial discrimination has been practiced either by actual exclusion of minority members or, if demands for workers were heavy, by using them in a "last hired—first fired" situation.

Pressures of social conscience—backed up by federal legislation— have gone a long way toward eliminating discrimination in employment policy in major industries. The gradual eradication of racial restrictions on employment does not solve the problem of minority group employment since many of such groups have been so disadvantaged educationally and environmentally that they are unprepared for employment when it becomes available.

Governmental agencies and major industries have developed a variety of cooperative plans to assist in solving these kinds of problems. In many regions, employment councils have been formed to develop local approaches to specifically local aspects of the problem. Some industries have established company transportation systems to transport minority workers from home to factory when public and private transportation systems are inadequate. Industrial representatives and executives have visited high schools and colleges to encourage minority students to prepare for positions in industry and business. Other groups have sponsored training programs, established employment centers in low income areas, or engaged in door-to-door recruiting of workers. Other companies have supported institute programs for school counselors to assist them in improving their skills in working with minority members.

Table 16 shows a comparison of the distribution of white workers and workers of other races. A significant change appears in the increase of blacks and other races in the white-collar jobs and in the decline of this group in the service and farm occupations. The economic decline of 1974 raised serious concern about the gains of blacks and other races in recent years when the unemployment figures for nonwhites were approximately double that for white workers. This trend appears to be a product of "last

TABLE 16. *Employment By Occupation Group and Race, 1964 and 1974 (Percent distribution)*

| | 1964 | | 1974 | |
| | | NEGRO AND OTHER | | NEGRO AND OTHER |
OCCUPATION GROUP	WHITE	RACES	WHITE	RACES
Total: Number				
(thousands)	61,922	7,383	76,620	9,316
Percent	100.0	100.0	100.0	100.0
White-collar workers	47.6	18.8	50.6	32.0
Professional and technical	13.0	6.8	14.8	10.4
Manager, administrator	11.7	2.6	11.2	4.1
Sales workers	6.6	1.7	6.8	2.3
Clerical workers	16.3	7.7	17.8	15.2
Blue-collar workers				
Craft and kindred	13.7	7.1	13.8	9.4
Operations	18.4	20.5	15.5	21.9
Nonfarm laborers	10.5	32.3	12.0	25.1
Service workers	4.1	13.0	4.6	8.9
Farm workers	5.8	8.4	3.6	2.7

Source: *Manpower Report of the President*, 1975, p. 34. (Percentages rounded to nearest tenth)

on—first off," and inevitably will produce a testing of the strength of deeply-entrenched seniority systems versus newly-won civil rights and equal employment opportunities.

TRENDS BY MAJOR OCCUPATIONAL GROUPS

Charts 1 and 2 show the projected percentages of change in employment expected to occur by the mid-1980's by major occupational groups and by industry. Within the major occupational groups one can see an average growth of 20 to 30 per cent, with the largest expansion occurring in the professional-technical and clerical areas. The farm jobs are expected to continue to decline. Industrially, the largest percentage growth is expected in services, finance, and government, and further contraction in agriculture.

The most useful information on trends in occupational groups is usually found in publications by the Bureau of Labor Statistics of the U.S. Department of Labor. Particularly valuable for counselors and teachers is the *Occupational Outlook Handbook*, which is published in alternate years and which usually includes the latest available information on trends.

CHART 1. *Projected Percentage Change in Employment of Workers in Major Occupational Groups, 1974–85.*

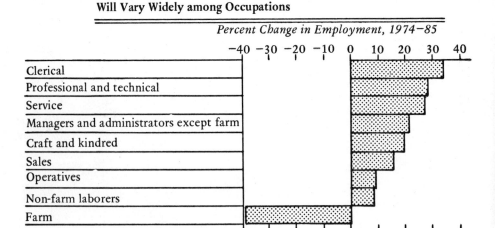

Through the Mid-1980's Employment Growth Will Vary Widely among Occupations

Source: Bureau of Labor Statistics

From: *Occupational Outlook Handbook, 1976–77,* p. 17.

Through the Mid-1980's Employment Growth Will Vary Widely, by Industry

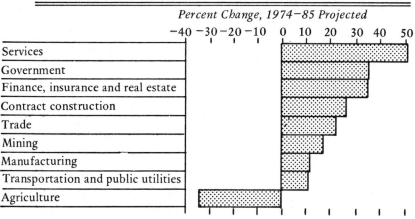

Source: Bureau of Labor Statistics

From: *Occupational Outlook Handbook, 1976–77,* p. 15.

Professional occupations may require either formal education in highly organized fields of knowledge, such as legal, teaching, ministerial, and medical; or broad general knowledge, such as that required by an editor or college president; or the creative talent of a musician, artist, or architect. Generally, these fields require college graduation, and usually advanced training beyond this level as well. Where long educational periods are not demanded, equally long periods of experience may be necessary. Many professions require a license or certificate before a person may engage in them.

The technical occupations are closely related to the professions. In fact, most of those employed in technical jobs work with engineers, scientists, and similar professional personnel. A combination of scientific knowledge and specialized education is usually necessary for employment. Educational preparation beyond high school is almost always necessary, but ordinarily the training is considerably shorter than that required by the professions. It is usually of a different type, as well.

Chart 3 compares the employment in the major professional-technical occupations in 1972. This field is expected to grow most rapidly into the mid-1980's. If 1974 estimates are realized, this group will increase by nearly 50 per cent by 1985. Chart 4 shows the steady growth that this group has reflected from 1960 onward.

Almost One-Quarter of All Professional Workers Are in Scientific and Technical Jobs

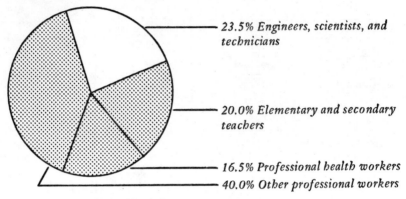

23.5% *Engineers, scientists, and technicians*

20.0% *Elementary and secondary teachers*

16.5% *Professional health workers*
40.0% *Other professional workers*

Source: Bureau of Labor Statistics

From: *Occupational Outlook Handbook, 1974–75,* p. 329.

The managerial and administrative positions are found in businesses and other organizations. These positions carry the responsibility of decision making and leadership. The category includes a broad range of people, from the president of a large corporation employing thousands of workers to the manager of the corner drugstore. Also included in the group are the proprietors—the owners and operators of businesses, factories, and other companies of any size. Overall, this group will expand at about the same rate as the total labor force. Within this group, however, salaried managers will increase much more rapidly than the field as a whole, as seen in Chart 5. This expansion is caused by the increasing dependence of business organizations and other groups on management specialists. As business becomes larger through consolidation and amalgamation, proprietors, or self-employed managers, will decline in number. In 1910, only one worker in fifteen was in an administrative position; by 1962, this ratio had increased to about one in every ten. By 1972, there were more than eight million workers in this category, representing about 9.8 per cent of the labor force. Figures for 1980 are estimated at more than ten million and are estimated to continue increasing to 10.5 million by 1985.

CHART 4. *Growth in Employment of Professional-Technical Work-*
ers, 1960-70, Projected to 1980.

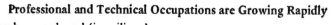
Professional and Technical Occupations are Growing Rapidly

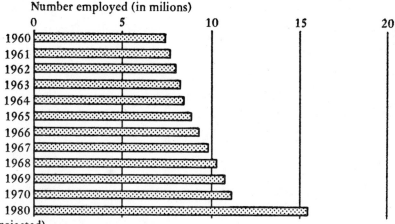

(projected)

Source: Bureau of Labor Statistics

From: *Occupational Outlook Handbook, 1972-73*, p. 26.

By 1972, the clerical field had passed 14 million workers and estimates for 1980 suggest almost 18 million persons. By 1985, this figure is
expected to increase to 19.7 million. Since the field is growing faster than
most other fields, its percentage of the labor force will increase from 17.4
in 1972 to 19.4 in 1985. More than two-thirds of the clerical workers are
women. The occupations included in the field cover a wide range of
skills, and thereby reflect considerable variation in the amount of training
and education required for the positions. Some clerical positions need no
special preparation other than short, on-the-job instruction; other positions
carry heavy responsibility and may require extensive specialized preparation or experience. Chart 6 shows the distribution of clerical workers in
the major divisions of that field as well as a comparison of the proportion
of men and women in the various divisions. Almost one-third of the total
group is composed of secretaries, stenographers, and typists.

Typical educational requirements in the clerical field are graduation
from a high school or from a short, post-secondary course in a business
college. Except for the simpler clerical jobs, some training is usually provided on the job to prepare the worker to perform the work in the particular manner preferred by the employer.

CHART 5. *Growth in Managerial Positions, 1960–70.*

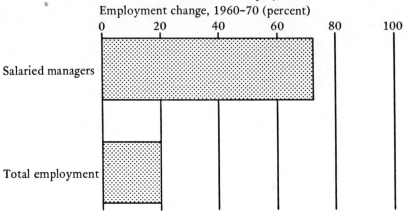

**Employment of Salaried Managers is Growing Much Faster
Than Total Employment**

Employment change, 1960–70 (percent)

Salaried managers

Total employment

Source: Bureau of Labor Statistics

From: *Occupational Outlook Handbook, 1972–73,* p. 275.

Many clerical jobs offer excellent prospects for promotion and advancement. Many of the better-paying positions require a detailed knowledge of the company and its operations, thus limiting the filling of such positions to people already employed by the organization. Other jobs lead to advanced positions, for which workers can be trained within the company.

Since the clerical field is expected to expand in the years immediately ahead, employment opportunities will result from the creation of new positions as well as from the replacement procedure of filling vacancies caused by people leaving the position. Because most clerical workers are women, the replacement rate is higher in this field than in most. We have already discussed the impact of marriage and family responsibilities on women workers, and even though these factors are holding women out of the labor force for shorter periods than was formerly true, there is still considerable turnover.

Sales occupations are expected to increase from about 5.4 million workers in 1972 to approximately 6.5 million workers in 1985. Proportionately, the field will almost hold its own with the overall increase in the labor force. The largest single division within this field is retail salesworkers, an area heavily populated by women. Chart 7 shows the distribution of workers in this field in 1972.

The sales field offers opportunities for an extremely wide range of

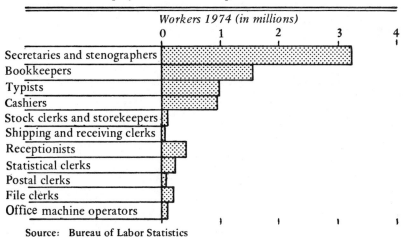

CHART 6. *Distribution of Clerical Workers by Broad Category, 1974.*

A Majority of the Approximately 15 Million Clerical Workers are Employed in These Occupations

Source: Bureau of Labor Statistics

From: *Occupational Outlook Handbook, 1976–77,* p. 81.

ability and preparation. Many positions are routine—involving little more than making change and wrapping or packaging purchases. At the other extreme are salespeople who sell highly complicated machinery or services, whose position may require extended periods of intensive training in addition to a college degree in a professional area such as engineering.

Continued population growth, expected business expansion, rising income, and new product development all exert pressure for increased sales, and thereby increased employment of sales workers. Probably the major increases in employment will come in areas other than retail sales. Since a common career path in sales work starts with retail sales experience, there will probably continue to be many replacement opportunities in this field even though only moderate expansion is expected.

The 11 million service workers in 1972 are expected to increase to 13.4 million by 1985. This increase reflects a very slight proportionate decline compared with other areas. Major influences causing increases in this field include the increased demand for hospital care and other health services, greater need for protective services as urban areas increase in size, and the more frequent use of restaurants, beauty shops, and similar services. Chart 8 shows the divisions in which most service workers are employed.

The service occupations cover a wide range of ability and educa-

CHART 7. *Distribution of Sales Workers by Broad Category, 1972.*

**Nearly 5.4 Million Workers Are
in Sales Occupations**

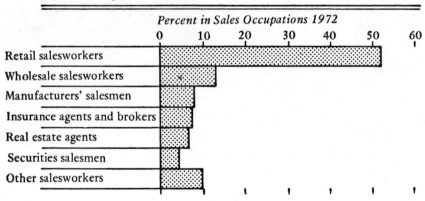

Source: Bureau of Labor Statistics

From: *Occupational Outlook Handbook, 1974–75,* p. 218.

tional background, varying from positions that require only minimal education or experience to positions that require college or professional school graduation. Some occupations require long years of on-the-job vocational training to qualify. Special personality or temperament traits or physical characteristics may be required by some of the occupations.

Craftsmen include such occupations as carpenter, tool and die maker, instrument maker, machinist, electrician, typesetter, automobile mechanic, and plumber. Industrial growth and increasing business activity, the pressures for expansion in this field, will be partially off-set by technological developments, thus holding the field to a slightly less than average expansion in the next few years. The 10.8 million workers in 1972 are expected to increase to about 13 million by 1985. Chart 9 shows the major divisions in which these workers are classified. Many of the craft occupations are entered by serving an apprenticeship, a training system that we will consider in a later chapter.

Operatives, sometimes referred to as semiskilled workers, made up the second largest group of workers in 1972, numbering about 13.5 million. Chart 10 shows the distribution of these workers. The group is expected to reach about 15.3 million by 1985. Although the growth rate is less than that for most fields, there will be many positions because of the large number included in this group. At the beginning of this chapter, we considered the impact of automation; this phenomenon is particularly relevant

CHART 8. *Distribution of Service Workers by Broad Category,*
1974.

**More Than 11 Million People Work in
Service Occupations**

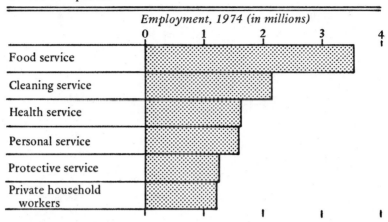

Source: Bureau of Labor Statistics

From: *Occupational Outlook Handbook, 1976–77,* p. 154.

to this group of workers because many of the jobs in this area are the ones replaced by mechanized, computer-controlled, and automated procedures.

The largest portion of the operatives group is engaged in manufacturing activities. Within this area are large components that are predominantly populated by female workers, such as garment manufacture, textile industries, and food processing.

Laborers are most frequently involved in moving, lifting, or carrying materials or tools. No appreciable increase in this field is expected in the years ahead since this work also is increasingly being handled through mechanized procedures. Some positions will be available on a replacement basis, but little growth or expansion is anticipated.

Farm workers have been declining in number for several years. This trend is expected to continue in the years ahead as farmers and farm workers increase their productive efficiency by using larger units of land and by greater application of improved farm technology. Despite the drastic reduction in the number of farmers and farm workers, there has been a steady growth in what are described as farm-related occupations, which include processing, distributing, and transporting farm products and supplies. These occupations are, of course, included in categories that we have considered earlier.

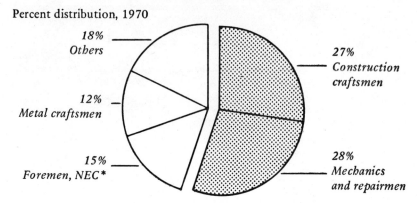

**More Than 10 Million Workers Are Employed As
Craftsmen and Foremen**

Percent distribution, 1970

*18%
Others*

*27%
Construction
craftsmen*

*12%
Metal craftsmen*

*15%
Foremen, NEC**

*28%
Mechanics
and repairmen*

*Not elsewhere classified.

Source: Bureau of Labor Statistics

From: *Occupational Outlook Handbook, 1972–73,* p. 366.

CHART 10. *Proportion of Workers in Semiskilled Jobs, 1970.*

**About 1 Worker in Every 6 is Employed
in a Semi-skilled Job**

Total employment, 1970 – 78,627,000

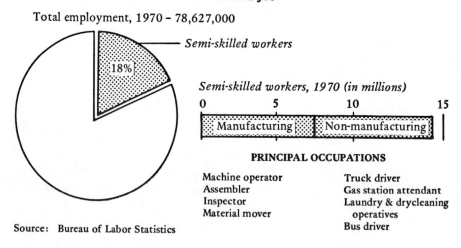

Semi-skilled workers

18%

Semi-skilled workers, 1970 (in millions)

0   5   10   15

Manufacturing   Non-manufacturing

PRINCIPAL OCCUPATIONS

Machine operator
Assembler
Inspector
Material mover

Truck driver
Gas station attendant
Laundry & drycleaning
  operatives
Bus driver

Source: Bureau of Labor Statistics

From: *Occupational Outlook Handbook, 1972–73,* p. 368.

NOTES

1. W. A. Faunce, *Problems of An Industrial Society* (New York: McGraw-Hill Book Company, 1968), pp. 42–44.
2. *Ibid.*, p. 48.
3. S. L. Wolfbein, *Occupational Information* (New York: Random House, 1968), pp. 91–93.
4. W. O. Baker, "The Dynamism of Science and Technology," in *Technology and Social Change*, ed. Eli Ginzberg (New York: Columbia University Press, 1964).
5. Faunce, *op. cit.*, pp. 51–61.
6. M. Mead, "The Challenge of Automation to Education for Human Values," in *Automation, Education, and Human Values*, ed. W. W. Brickman and S. Lehrer (New York: School and Society Books, 1966), pp. 67–70.
7. J. I. Snyder, Jr., "Epilogue: The Implications of Automation," in *Jobs, Men, and Machines: Problems of Automation*, ed. C. Markham (New York: Frederick A. Praeger, 1964), pp. 152–154.
8. A. J. Hayes, "Automation: A Real 'H' Bomb," in *Jobs, Men, and Machines: Problems of Automation*, ed. C. Markham (New York: Frederick A. Praeger, 1964), pp. 48–53.
9. Faunce, *op. cit.*, pp. 61–71.
10. E. D. Kalachek, "Automation and Full Employment," *Vocational Guidance Quarterly*, vol. 15, no. 4 (June, 1967), pp. 242–247.
11. V. M. Rogers, "Education for the World of Work," in *Automation, Education, and Human Values*, ed. W. W. Brickman and S. Lehrer (New York: School and Society Books, 1966), pp. 264–274.
12. U.S. Department of Labor, Bureau of Labor Statistics, *Occupational Outlook Handbook, 1974–75 Edition* (Washington: U.S. Government Printing Office, 1974), p. 22.
13. Faunce, *op. cit.*, pp. 162–171.
14. E. Weinberg, "Some Manpower Implications," in *Automation Management: The Social Perspective*, eds. E. L. Scott and R. W. Bolz (Athens, Ga.: The Center for the Study of Automation and Society, 1970), p. 89.
15. R. W. Fleming, "Reflections on Manpower," *Vocational Guidance Quarterly*, vol. 22, no. 3 (March, 1974), pp. 224–229.
16. C. C. Healy, "Manpower Trends: Counseling or Political Solutions," *Personnel and Guidance Journal*, vol. 51, no. 1 (September, 1972), pp. 39–44.
17. J. Diebold, "Automation: Its Implications for Counseling," *Vocational Guidance Quarterly*, vol. 11, no. 1 (Autumn, 1962), pp. 11–14.
18. ———, "Automation: Its Implications for Counseling," *Occupational Outlook Quarterly*, vol. 6, no. 3 (September, 1962), pp. 3–6.
19. R. R. Mormon, "Automation and Counseling," *Personnel and Guidance Journal*, vol. 40, no. 7 (March, 1962), pp. 594–599.
20. S. Cooper, "The Changing Composition of the American Work Force," *Occupational Outlook Quarterly*, vol. 3 (May, 1959), pp. 21–23.
21. H. Goldstein, "Estimate of Occupational Replacement Needs," *Occupations*, vol. 26, no. 7 (April, 1948), pp. 397–402.
22. W. S. Woytinsky, *Seasonal Variations in Employment in the United States* (New York: Social Science Research Council, 1939).

23. J. S. Zeisel, "Business Cycles and the Choice of a Career," *The Occupational Outlook,* vol. 2, no. 2 (May, 1958), pp. 3–8.
24. R. A. Ehrle, "Employment Counseling as an Integral Part of an Active Labor Market Policy," *Vocational Guidance Quarterly,* vol. 13, no. 4 (Summer, 1965), pp. 270–274.
25. *Manpower Report of the President, 1975.* (Washington: U.S. Government Printing Office, 1975). Table E-4, p. 310.
26. D. J. Watley and R. Kaplan, "Career or Marriage?: Aspirations and Achievements of Able Young Women," *Journal of Vocational Behavior,* vol. 1, no. 1 (January, 1971), pp. 29–43.
27. *Manpower Report, op. cit.,* p. 55.
28. V. K. Oppenheimer, *The Female Labor Force in the United States* (Berkeley: Population Monograph Series, No. 5, University of California, 1970), pp. 66–120.
29. E. Waldman and B. J. McEaddy, "Where Women Work—An Analysis by Industry and Occupation," *Monthly Labor Review,* vol. 97, no. 5 (May, 1974), pp. 3–13.
30. J. S. Mitchell, *I Can Be Anything: Careers and Colleges for Young Women* (Princeton, N.J.: College Board, 1975).
31. W. C. Bingham and E. W. House, "Counselors View Women and Work: Accuracy of Information," *Vocational Guidance Quarterly,* vol 21, no. 4 (June, 1973), pp. 262–268; and "Counselors' Attitudes Toward Women and Work," *Vocational Guidance Quarterly,* vol. 22, no. 1 (September, 1973), pp. 16–23.

PART II   Supplementary Learning Experiences

The following activities are proposed as ways in which the reader can easily test, explore, or apply the concepts and insights presented in Part II. The list is not intended to be exhaustive or comprehensive, but merely suggestive.

1. Interview two or three workers in several different occupations to determine:
   a. Training time required for the job.
   b. Important aptitudes involved.
   c. Extent to which worker interests are satisfied.
   d. Relationship of temperament, values, personality to the job.
   e. Physical characteristics required by the job.
2. Find occupations in which each of the above factors have extreme importance.
3. Interview two or three local employers to identify their hiring requirements beyond basic job skills.
4. Identify and describe two or three different methods of controlling admission to occupations.
5. Interview workers in two or three occupations to identify ways in which their occupation influences "off-the-job" behavior.
6. Interview several teenagers and adults to determine the prestige ranks they assign to various occupations. Compare the results.
7. Identify the "career escalators" that connect a group of occupations into a hierarchy.
8. Identify the factors that produce variability in economic return among a group of occupations with similar skill and training level.
9. Identify economic returns, other than salary and wages, associated with some occupations.
10. Interview workers in an industry now being automated, at least in part, to determine their attitudes toward automation.
11. Identify attitudes toward increased employment opportunities for women held by such groups as counselors, teachers, union members, production workers, etc.
12. Develop a series of lesson plans for an appropriate age group studying any of the broad areas included in this unit. Identify concepts to be taught, learning activities to be used, and methods for evaluating results.
13. Prepare a set of learning materials (posters, filmstrips, slides, audio or video tapes) presenting concepts from one area included in this unit.

PART

III

Classifying
Occupations

6

The Dictionary of Occupational Titles and a DOT-Based Classification System

The world of work continuously grows more complex. It would, in fact, be difficult, and perhaps even impossible, to identify definitively the exact number of different occupations in existence at a given time. As in an extremely complex organism, old cells die and are sloughed off, new cells replicate existing ones and replace them, other new cells develop as slight modifications of existing cells, and some new cells are totally different from any previously existing units and take on new functions. Thus, the world of work continuously and simultaneously is involved in the processes of rejuvination, homeostasis, and evolution.

Precise estimates of the number of different occupations depend on how one defines "different," since many occupations have common factors and may differ more in degree than in kind. Nevertheless, it is commonly thought that the United States has more than 20,000 occupations sufficiently varied to be thought different. Many of these occupations may be known by more than one name in different regions, or even within a given region.

If one is to help an individual learn about occupations or develop an understanding of his/her relationship to the world of work, a broad knowledge of occupations is absolutely essential. Yet, maintaining a good grasp on 20,000 constantly changing occupations is beyond the competence of most human minds. Some method of classification or grouping must be used to bring this array into manageable proportions.

Even though the number of occupations is large, many of them are related in various ways. Just as human families include brothers, sisters, and cousins, so, too, do many occupations show similar types of relationships. Classification systems are useful in understanding these relationships within the world of work.

Occupations can be grouped and classified by many systems. Each system has a special advantage or unique contribution. Since the system that is best for a specific situation or purpose depends on the goal desired, there can be no single over-all best method. The method that best achieves the goal is the best one to use. Since situations vary, the person involved in career education and career counseling must understand a variety of systems so that the best choice can be made for the desired purpose. In this chapter and the next, we will consider most of the commonly used classification systems. We will first consider the *Dictionary of Occupational Titles* and those systems directly based on its concept. In the next chapter, we will look at systems that are oriented in other ways.

Of all the publications related to counseling and teaching about occupations, the *Dictionary of Occupational Titles* has been the most widely used. It has provided classification systems for occupations, a basis for filing career materials, a method for relating beginning positions with jobs available to experienced workers, a system for identifying workers whose skills and abilities approximate those needed in shortage fields, and a brief occupational description developed from job analysis reports. Recent interest in career education has seen increased use of this valuable publication.

Originally published in 1939, the *Dictionary of Occupational Titles*, or the *DOT*, as it is usually called, was brought up-to-date by a second edition in 1949. The book was totally revised in 1965 with a new coding system and extensive new information provided in its structure. The latest revision became available in late 1976.

THE THIRD EDITION

After many years of widespread use of the 1939 and 1949 editions of the *DOT*, it became increasingly clear that thorough revision of the book was necessary. Many factors contributed to the need for revision. Among these was the rapidly changing occupational structure of the United States during the early 1960's, with the indication that the increased emphasis on technological development would accelerate during the later portion of the decade. The broad use of the book itself, no doubt, also has contributed to the need for revisions, since the *DOT* has been an important tool in a wide variety of situations not even considered in its original development.[1]

One of the most significant occurrences was the development, on an experimental basis, of the *functional classification system*. This system, originated by Fine and others, was an attempt to develop a more sophisticated code system that would provide some of the information now available about the job, in addition to assigning a number to represent an occupation.[2,3,4] The proposed coding system had three major components, based on what the worker does, the work that needs to be done, and the materials, products, subject matter, or services involved.

Extensive experimentation with the functional classification system led to many refinements and developments that were later incorporated into the third edition of the *DOT*.[5] As the coding structure of the *DOT* is discussed in the following pages, the reader will see the direct application of the functional classification system.

Simultaneously with the development and refinement of the functional classification system, the United States Employment Service was involved in the study of certain worker traits and their relationship to success in the worker's activities. The components considered by this group included: training time, aptitudes, temperaments, interests, work performed, physical capacities, working conditions, and industry. As the work progressed, a preliminary publication was issued entitled *Estimates of Worker Trait Requirements for 4,000 Jobs as Defined in the Dictionary of Occupational Titles*.[6] This volume analyzed the included jobs in terms of the components listed above, except for work performed.

The 1965 *DOT* increased the emphasis on the functional classification system and on the worker trait requirements.[7,8] Modifications of these two developments provided the major foundations on which the third edition was based. In general, there were two major changes in the third edition.[9] The first change was a revision in the major grouping of occupations, and the second was a totally new coding system based on the incorporation of an occupational grouping arrangement and a worker function arrangement. Both of these changes will be discussed in detail.

Our purpose in this chapter is to provide a general introduction and a basic understanding of the *DOT*. If a high level of competency in using the *DOT* is desired, the reader may refer to an invaluable training manual prepared by the Bureau of Employment Security.[10] The manual has been "programmed" for self-instruction and includes a detailed consideration of the *DOT* as a professional tool.

Both the 1939 and 1949 editions were based on seven major groups of occupations. The third and fourth editions use a base of nine occupational categories. As can be seen below, the major change came about as a result of substituting five specific groups for the skilled, semiskilled, and unskilled categories used in the earlier volumes.

Each major group is subdivided into what are called two-digit

DOT, 1ST AND 2ND EDITIONS		DOT, 3RD AND 4TH EDITIONS	
0	Professional and managerial occupations	0 1	Professional, technical, and managerial occupations
1	Clerical and sales occupations	2	Clerical and sales occupations
2	Service occupations	3	Service occupations
3	Agricultural, fishery, forestry, and kindred occupations	4	Farming, fishery, and forestry occupations
4,5	Skilled occupations	5	Processing occupations
6,7	Semiskilled occupations	6	Machine trade occupations
8,9	Unskilled occupations	7	Bench work occupations
		8	Structural work occupations
		9	Miscellaneous occupations

occupational divisions. Eighty-three divisions are listed, ranging from seven in the farming and structural work occupations to as many as fifteen in the professional, technical, and managerial areas. These divisions are identified by adding a digit in the second position. The two-digit divisions used in the third and fourth editions are included in Appendix A.

The two-digit occupational divisions are similarly subdivided into three-digit occupational groups by adding another digit in the third position. There are more than 600 groups. In level of specificity, the three-digit codes of the early editions and the later editions are about the same. Typical illustrations drawn from various two-digit divisions in the third and fourth editions are included in Appendix A.

Up to this point, the changes that appear in the third edition seem rather simple. The seven major groups have been changed to nine occupational categories, two-digit occupational divisions have been developed, and the industrial occupations have been reorganized into five categories that depict the type of work performed. The advantages of more descriptive grouping and elimination of such socially undesirable terms as *semi*professional, *semi*skilled, and *un*skilled are immediately obvious. Nevertheless, the occupational group arrangement constituting the first three digits of the code is essentially comparable in form to the structure used in the earlier editions. It is in the last half of the code structure that the real change occurs, and the difference is considerable. In the earlier editions, the digits to the right of the decimal point were used simply to form more specific subdivisions. In other words, the three-digit groups were broken into smaller occupational classes consisting of either specific occupations or classification titles. A totally different approach is used in the third and fourth editions.

In the third edition (1965) dictionary, the digits to the right of the decimal point make up the *worker functions arrangement*. This portion of the code system is based on the functional classification plan and assumes that every job is involved to some degree with instructions and information (*data*); with people in the form of the public, or supervisors and fellow workers (*people*); and with materials, equipment, or products (*things*).

The worker function hierarchy is essentially the same as the functional classification system. The plan used in the third edition of the *DOT* is as follows:

Data	*People*	*Things*
0 Synthesizing	0 Mentoring	0 Setting up
1 Coordinating	1 Negotiating	1 Precision working
2 Analyzing	2 Instructing	2 Operating–controlling
3 Compiling	3 Supervising	3 Driving–operating
4 Computing	4 Diverting	4 Manipulating
5 Copying	5 Persuading	5 Tending
6 Comparing	6 Speaking–signaling	6 Feeding–offbearing
7) No significant	7 Serving	7 Handling
8) relationship	8 No significant relationship	8 No significant relationship

The terms are arranged in descending order, so that as the numbers ascend the level of complexity goes down. The *DOT* code number is completed with one digit from each of these groups. The fourth digit represents the relationship of the job to *data*, the fifth represents the relationship to *people*, and the sixth digit, to *things*. Thus, a code number ending in the digits .081 represents a type of activity that demands the highest level of complexity in working with data, has no significant relationship to people, and involves the next to the highest level of complexity in dealing with things. Examples of work with a code number ending in .081 are artistic work, engineering research and design, and scientific research. A code number terminating with .288 requires working with data at the analyzing level of complexity, but has no significant relationship either to people or things. Examples of this code ending are found in corresponding and related work, and in title and contract search and analysis work. It is thus apparent that the final digits may show similar worker trait requirements in fields not at all related by the first digits.

Actually, an attempt has been made to supply two different kinds of information with the *worker functions arrangement*. First, as indicated above, the level of complexity of significant involvement with data, people, and things is represented by the appropriate digit in each position. Secondly, the use of the "8" digit for people and things and the "7 and 8" digits for data also may indicate an occupationally insignificant quantity of involvement with this factor, even though the small amount of involvement may be at a high level of complexity. This double-duty assignment occasionally leads to some confusion as well as to the possibility of misinterpretation. Thus, the earlier illustration of a code ending in .288 presents two different interpretations in both "people" and in "things." The "8" in each factor suggests that the level of complexity is very low for each factor; on the

Chart For Relating School Subjects and Occupations Through Worker Trait Groups													
AREAS AND SUBJECTS							WORKER TRAIT GROUPS						
	1	2	3	4	5	6	109	110	111	112	113	114
Language Arts Composition, Creative Writing, Journalism	◦◦		◦			◦◦			111	112	113	114
Speech, Debate, Dramatics	1					◦◦	◦		111	112	113	114
Literature	◦					6			111	112	113	114
Mathematics General Mathematics		◦◦			◦			◦◦				
Algebra, Geometry		◦◦				◦	◦					
Trigonometry, Higher Math						◦	◦					
Science Biology			◦			◦			◦			
Botany, Horticulture						◦			◦			
Chemistry						◦			◦			
Physics		◦	◦			◦	109		◦			
Earth Sciences						◦			◦			
Trade & Industry Auto Mechanics												
Auto Body & Fender Repair												
Appliances Repair												
Carpentry, Woodworking					5							
Commercial Art, etc.		2		4	5							

Number in box = If you like this subject explore this Worker Trait Group.
◦◦ = This subject is important to most occupations in this Worker Trait Group.
◦ = This subject is important to some but not most occupations in the Worker Trait Group.

From: P. Stowers, "CIS: A New Dimension for Organizing Career Information Resources," *Occupational Outlook Quarterly*, Fall, 1975.

other hand, a complex level of involvement may be required but so infrequently that it is considered insignificant. Obviously, quite different worker characteristics might be required, depending on the proper interpretation of the "8." Fortunately, the 4th edition of the *DOT* resolves this confusion.

All code numbers, then, end in a sequence of digits that represents this relationship to *data–people–things* according to the hierarchy of terms established under each of the three headings. Since there are nine headings under each of the three areas, there are theoretically many combinations into which the numbers could be grouped. In actuality, however, there are now 114 groupings. In other words, all third and fourth edition code numbers use one of 114 different three-digit sets, each of which can be translated directly to the *data–people–things* relationship. For example, the ending of .021 can be seen as requiring synthesizing–instructing–precision working levels of complexity.

The *worker traits arrangement* consists of 22 broad areas of work into which the 114 combinations can be grouped. The broad areas are designed to facilitate the use of the code numbers by providing a broad distinction among the occupations so that the user can easily find what he/she is looking for. The 22 areas are:

Art
Business relations
Clerical work
Counseling, guidance, and social work
Crafts
Education and training
Elemental work
Engineering
Entertainment
Farming, fishing, forestry
Investigating, inspecting, and testing
Law and law enforcement
Machine work
Managerial and supervisory work
Mathematics and science
Medicine and health
Merchandising
Music
Personal service
Photography and communications
Transportation
Writing

Under each of these broad areas are groups containing jobs that have common trait requirements. It is important to recognize that the same set of terminal digits might appear under several of the broad areas, as well as more than once within a broad area. In each case, the occupations could involve different kinds of tasks, each of which, however, would require the same level of complexity in dealing with data, people, and things. This is easy to understand when one recognizes the variability in the types of data or things encountered in different jobs. Samples of some of the twenty-two broad areas and the groupings included under each are listed in Appendix A. The reader's attention is directed to the fact that the .081 of our earlier illustration is included in each area used in this example and in each case represents *the same level of complexity* but not the same activity with data–people–things.

A profile has been developed for each group within each broad area. This profile indicates the training time, aptitudes, interests, temperaments, and physical demands that are characteristic worker traits required for that type of work. In addition, a statement describes the work performed, the worker requirements, clues for relating applicants and requirements, the training and methods of entry, and related classifications.

The following material, from page 232 of Volume II of the third edition, is an example of the kind of information provided in the *worker traits arrangement:*

ART   ART WORK

Art Work

.081

Work performed

Work activities in this group primarily involve the creative expression of ideas, feelings, and moods in artistic designs, objects, and arrangements. Fine arts typically involve creation and execution of such works as portraiture, sculpture, ceramics, mosaics, and murals which are produced for their own sake rather than for utilitarian considerations, and are generally characterized by the artist's freedom to choose media and technique. Commercial arts are characteristically concerned with the creation and reproduction of commercial and industrial designs involving adherence to technical requirements or functional limitations specified by the client or employer.

Worker requirements

An occupationally significant combination of aesthetic appreciation; creative imagination; artistic judgment concerning the harmony of color and line; eye-hand coordination and finger and manual dexterity to paint or draw and to use handtools when working with plaster, clay, stone, and other materials; perception of form and design; color discrimination to perceive differences in hue, shade, and value; and spatial aptitude to visualize and depict three-dimensional objects and arrangements on two-dimensional surfaces.

Clues for relating applicants and requirements

Demonstrated artistic ability, including hobbies, particularly if art work has won prizes or been sold.

Training and methods of entry

Vocational high schools and art schools or institutes awarding diplomas upon completion of 2 or 3 years of theory and practice provide preparation generally acceptable for entry positions in commercial art. Commercial artists may find employment in printing and publishing houses, greeting card companies, advertising agencies, commercial art studios, department stores, and Government agencies. Specialized skills, such as lettering, illustrating, or typography, enhance employment prospects. Advancement to responsible positions involving planning and layout work depends largely on development of artistic and technical skills through experience and on-the-job training.

Art schools offering 4 years of study, particularly those connected with colleges or universities, commonly award the degree of bachelor of fine arts which is generally considered evidence of preparation for entry into fine arts work. Preparation for fine arts work includes studying such subjects as portrait and landscape painting, sculpture, history, and English, which are not ordinarily included in preparation for commercial art work.

Related classifications

Decorating and artwork (.031; .051; .061), p. 228

Photography and motion picture camera work (.062), p. 230

Drafting and related work (.181; .281), p. 377

Artistic restoration, decoration, and related work (.281; .381), p. 234

Instructive work, fine arts, theater, music, and related fields (.028), p. 226.

Qualifications profile

GED:	5	4		
SVP:	7	8	5	
Apt:	GVN	SPQ	KFM	EC
	223	224	222	52
	13	1 3	333	41
				3

Int:	8	6		
Temp:	X	9		
Phys. Dem.:		S	L	4	6

The material included in the last section, the qualifications profile, is based on the *Estimates of Worker Trait Requirements for 4,000 Jobs as Defined in the Dictionary of Occupational Titles.* The abbreviations used represent the following terms:

GED:	General educational development
SVP:	Specific vocational preparation
Apt:	Aptitude
G:	General intelligence
V:	Verbal
N:	Numerical
S:	Spatial
P:	Form perception
Q:	Clerical perception
K:	Motor coordination
F:	Finger dexterity
M:	Manual dexterity
E:	Eye-hand-foot coordination
C:	Color perception
Int:	Interests
Temp:	Temperament
Phys. Dem.:	Physical demands

In summary, then, the coding structure consists of a group of six digits. The three digits before the decimal identify the occupational group, and the three after the decimal indicate the level of complexity of the specific job. Each digit has a specific meaning and tells the sophisticated reader something about the job. By properly translating the meaning of each digit, the reader acquires not only the two- and three-digit groupings to which the occupation belongs, but also its relationship to data, people, and things. Figure 6–1, p. 211, may help emphasize the purpose of each digit in the code number.

Volume I of the third edition is similar in content and arrangement to the corresponding volumes of the earlier editions. Basically, it consists of an alphabetical listing of job titles with definitions. Since many jobs are known by various titles, the definition is placed with the base title—that name by which the job is most frequently known. The synonymous titles, known as alternate titles, are listed alphabetically, and the reader is referred to the base title for the job definition.

The alphabetical arrangement is based on a letter system, in which the separation of a title into more than one word is ignored in placing it in the proper alphabetical sequence. Titles are listed as they are en-

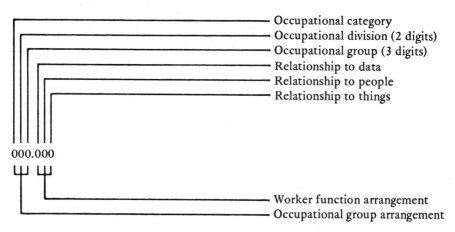

000.000

FIGURE 6–1. *Purpose of code number digits.*

countered in common usage, except where the titles have been inverted so that: (1) the same base word can be used for distinguishing several related occupations (a rough carpenter would be listed as a carpenter, rough); (2) a modifier indicating a qualifying factor that is not a usual part of the definition is placed last (a marshmallow candy maker would be listed as a candy maker, marshmallow); (3) arbitrary modifiers used to distinguish certain titles from others in the group are placed last (sales manager would be listed as manager, sales).

Each definition is also given an industrial designation, which indicates the usual industrial location of the job. If an occupation keeps its general nature regardless of the industry in which it is encountered, it is given a "type-of-activity" designation. For example, *"typist"* is encountered in many industries; rather than attempting to identify it with each, typist is assigned an industrial designation of "clerical and kindred." In general, the industrial designations follow the suggestions of the *Standard Industrial Classification Manual.*[11]

The following are samples of definitions as seen in the early pages of Volume I:

Able Seaman (water trans.) 911.884. Able-bodied seaman. Performs the following tasks on board ship: stands watch at bow or on wing of bridge to look for obstructions in path of vessel. Measures depth of water in shallow or unfamiliar waters, using lead-line, and telephones or shouts information to bridge. Turns wheel on bridge or uses emergency steering apparatus to steer vessel as directed by *Mate.* Breaks out, rigs, overhauls, and stows cargo-handling gear, stationary rigging, and running gear. Overhauls lifeboats and lifeboat gear and lowers or raises lifeboats with winch or falls. Paints and chips rust on deck or super-structure of ship. Must hold certificate issued by the Government. When working aboard vessels carrying liquid cargoes, must hold a tankerman certificate. May stow or remove cargo from ship's hold [*Longshoreman II*]. May be concerned with only one particular phase of duties as maintenance of ship's gear and decks or watch duties, and be known as *Deck-Maintenanceman; Watch-Stander.*

Accounting Clerk (clerical) 219.488. Performs variety of routine calculating, posting, and typing duties to accomplish accounting. Posts details of business transactions, such as allotments, disbursements, deductions from payrolls, pay and expense vouchers, remittances paid and due, checks, and claims. Totals accounts using adding machine. Computes and records interest charges, refunds, cost of lost or damaged goods, freight or express charges, rentals, and similar items. May type vouchers, invoices, account statements, payrolls, periodic reports, and other records. May be designated according to type of accounting performed as *Abstract-Examination Clerk* (insurance); *Accounts-Payable Clerk; Accounts-Receivable Clerk; Rent and Miscellaneous Remittance Clerk* (insurance); *Tax-Record Clerk* (light, heat, and power); *Ticket-Rebate Clerk* (motor trans.; rr. trans.). See Volume II for additional titles.

> *Additions and Betterments Clerk* (rr. trans.) Specialty clerk. Records data for improvements to existing facilities or equipment, posting items such as labor and material costs and value of salvaged materials.
>
> *Voucher Clerk* (rr. trans.) Claims clerk. Prorates cost of lost or damaged goods among interline railroad carriers. Receives claims for lost or damaged goods filed by shipper or consignee. Verifies records to substantiate claim of shipment and requests *Adjustment Clerk* (clerical) to investigate claim and to submit estimate of value of lost or damaged goods. Receives estimates and verifies records to ascertain names of carriers involved in transporting goods. Computes number of miles each carrier transported goods. Prorates and computes cost to be charged to interline carriers according to comparative mileage in transit over each railroad, using calculating machine. Records name of each interline carrier involved and amount prorated to each.

Volume II of the third edition, like its counterparts in the early editions, consists primarily of a listing of occupations according to code number. Each major group, occupational division, and three-digit occupational group is briefly described, and occupations are listed according to code number. In addition to base title and industrial designation, alternate titles also are listed.

The following excerpt from the first page (col. 1, page 33) of the *occupational group arrangement* will illustrate how this section of Volume II is composed.

OCCUPATIONAL GROUP ARRANGEMENT
OF TITLES AND CODES

$\left.\begin{matrix} 0 \\ 1 \end{matrix}\right\}$ *Professional, technical, and managerial occupations*

This category includes occupations concerned with the theoretical or practical aspects of such fields of human endeavor as art, science, engineering, education, medicine, law, business relations, and administrative, managerial, and technical work. Most of these occupations require substantial educational preparation (usually at the university, junior college, or technical institute level).

$\left.\begin{array}{l} 00 \\ 01 \end{array}\right\}$ *Occupations in architecture and engineering*

This division includes occupations concerned with the practical application of physical laws and principles of engineering and/or architecture for the development and utilization of machines, materials, instruments, structures, processes, and services. Typical specializations are research, design, construction, testing, procurement, production, operations, and sales. Also includes preparation of drawings, specifications and cost estimates, and participation in verification tests.

001. *Architectural occupations*

This group includes occupations concerned with the design and construction of buildings and related structures, and/or floating structures, according to aesthetic and functional factors.

001.081 *Architect* (profess. and kin.)

  Architect, Marine (profess. and kin.)

    Architect, naval
    Naval designer

001.168 *School-Plant Consultant* (education)

001.281 *Draftsman, Architectural* (profess. and kin.)

    Draftsman, tile and marble (profess. and kin.)

002. *Aeronautical engineering occupations*

This group includes occupations concerned with the design and construction of aircraft, spacecraft, and missiles. Accessory techniques required are those used in mechanical, electrical, electronic, and powerplant engineering. Typical specializations are aerodynamics, design, electronics, flight-testing, structural dynamics, thermo-dynamics, and weapons-control research.

002.081 *Aerodynamist* (aircraft mfg.)

    Aerodynamicist
    Aerodynamics engineer
    Aerophysics engineer
    Thermodynamics engineer (aircraft mfg.)

Aeronautical Engineer (profess. and kin.)

Aircraft Designer (aircraft mfg.)

    Airplane designer
    Design engineer, aeronautical
    Master-lay-out man
    Wind-tunnel-model-design engineer (aircraft mfg.)

Engineer, Controls (aircraft mfg.)

Engineering Designer, Aircraft

Structures (aircraft mfg.)

    Designer
    Draftsman
    Engineering designer
    Engineer, layout
    Engineer, structures

Engineer, Standards and Analysis (aircraft mfg.)

Flight Analyst (aircraft mfg.)
    Test engineer

Propulsion-Systems-Design Engineer (aircraft mfg.)

Research Engineer, Aeronautical (aircraft mfg.)

In addition to the numerical listing of occupations, Volume II also contains the *worker traits arrangement*. An excerpt of this material describing the .081 group of art work has already been quoted. The compilation of all occupations bearing the same *worker functions arrangement* code is also placed on pages succeeding the description of the worker trait group. This material appears in the same way as the earlier illustration of the .168 listing.

In addition to the two main volumes of the 1965 *DOT*, supplements have been issued that provide more valuable information to many counselors. In 1966, the first supplement, *Selected Characteristics of Occupations (Physical Demands, Working Conditions, Training Time)* was published. The supplement listed the above information for each job defined in the *DOT*. It was prepared to meet the needs of organizations and individuals concerned with manpower utilization who needed information beyond what was available in the *DOT*. The supplementary material can be used to determine job relationships in such activities as worker mobility, training, and rehabilitation.

The information included in the 1966 supplement is presented here in columnar form:

Column 1–*DOT* code number

Column 2–Page number in Volume II for worker trait group in which the job appears

Column 3–Industry designation

Column 4–Job title

Column 5–Physical demands

Column 6–Working conditions

Column 7–Training time (consisting of two parts–general educational development and specific vocational preparation)

Supplement 2 to the *Dictionary of Occupational Titles* was published in 1968. This booklet is entitled *Selected Characteristics of Occupations by Worker Traits and Physical Strength*. It includes the same information as is in the 1966 supplement and uses the same columnar format, except that the first two columns have been reversed. This reversal emphasizes the difference in organization of the two supplements. Information in the first supplement is listed in order of *DOT* code number; in the second supplement, the entries are in order of the page numbers of worker trait groups as listed in Volume II of the *DOT*.

The second supplement permits better interpretation and evaluation of certain significant job characteristics for a wide range of occupations that require similar traits and abilities. This organization is useful to the rehabilitation counselor who wishes to determine potential transferability of handicapped individuals from one job to another, while retaining the fullest possible application of their occupationally significant characteristics, experience, and remaining functional capacity. The second supplement also can be used to inform employment applicants of jobs suited to the skills they may have acquired on previous jobs; to make use of military training and experience in civilian jobs and, conversely, to use civilian experience in making military assignments; to redirect workers displaced by technological change; and to arrive at decisions concerning the kind and extent of rehabilitation or retraining needed. Caution must be taken when using Supplement 2 since the information provided is based on a composite description of the typical job and, obviously, a specific job may vary considerably from the usual pattern.

The increased use of computers to process labor-market data and the desire to capitalize on the greater precision capability provided by the computers have demonstrated the need for more detailed identification of jobs than is possible with the six-digit code structure in the third edition. In other words, a need developed to discriminate among occupations that shared the same six-digit code. Since the desire for greater specificity was primarily an "in-house" matter within the Department of Labor, it was resolved quite simply without major change to the basic structure of the *DOT*. In 1967, the Department published *Suffix Codes for Jobs Defined in the Dictionary of Occupational Titles, Third Edition*. This publication provided a simple means for changing the six-digit code to a nine-digit code by adding three digits in the seventh, eighth, and ninth positions for each job. The first job title assigned a specific six-digit code was given a suffix code of 010, the second job title with that same six-digit code was assigned a suffix code of 014, the third job title was assigned 018, and so on. Thus, occupations in the engineering series that carry the same six-digit code of 005.081 still retain those digits but also acquire differentiating digits in the seventh, eighth, and ninth positions. These occupations are now coded as follows:

005.081–010	Airport engineer
005.081–014	Civil engineer
005.081–018	Construction engineer
005.081–022	Highway engineer
005.081–026	Hydraulic engineer
005.081–030	Irrigation engineer
005.081–034	Materials engineer
005.081–038	Purification plant operator
005.081–042	Railroad engineer
005.081–046	Sanitary engineer
005.081–050	Sewage-disposal engineer
005.081–054	Structural designer
005.081–058	Structural engineer

Similarly, the desire to eliminate all sexist connotations from occupational titles led to the 1975 publication of *Job Title Revisions to Eliminate Sex- and Age-Referent Language from the Dictionary of Occupational Titles, Third Edition.* As its title indicates, this booklet provides new titles for each occupation that previously carried a title implying the performance of the work by a single sex, such as salesman, charwoman, bus boy, shop girl. Also eliminated were occupational titles carrying an age referent, such as bat boy and junior executive.

THE FOURTH EDITION*

Each succeeding edition of the *DOT* incorporates the best of previous editions with new materials so that the book continues to increase in practicality and value. The fourth edition, published in late 1976, appears to be no exception to this pattern. First glance will suggest to many

* At the time this chapter was written, the 4th edition of the *DOT* had not yet been published. These pages were prepared with the gracious assistance of Arden Nelsen and Adaline Padgett of the Division of Occupational Analysis of the Department of Labor. Both willingly shared the planning for their respective portions of the 4th edition. Without their help, these pages could not have been included in this edition.

readers that the fourth edition is a totally new approach; closer inspection, however, will reveal that the individual actually has in hand the same old *DOT* with some very useful revisions and improvements. The major changes from the third edition to the fourth edition include the following items.

1. NEW FORMAT. The material previously included in Volume I plus the first major parts of Volume II now have been combined and rearranged in a single volume. The result is a large volume quite similar in appearance and content to the 1971 edition of *The Canadian Dictionary of Occupational Titles*. The major portion of the volume is a numerical listing of occupational titles as in the former Volume II with the definitions incorporated in that listing. An obvious advantage is that the relationship between occupations previously shown in the numbering system also can be reinforced in the definition structure. For example, the tentative sample page (in Appendix A) provides the one-, two-, and three-digit definitions for "6 Machine Trades Occupations," "60 Metal Machining Occupations," and "600 Machinists and Related Occupations," immediately followed by the definitions of those occupations in the 600 group. Thus, the similarities and differences can be accentuated in characterizing each occupation. This can be seen by inspecting the entry for 600.131–010 MACHINE SHOP SUPERVISOR, TOOL, and 600.131–014 SALVAGE ENGINEER. The two occupations carry identical code numbers in the *occupational group arrangement* (600) and in the *worker functions arrangement* (131), differing only in the unique code (010 and 014), and even there by only one step.

All editions of the *DOT* contain a glossary in which specialized or unusual terms are defined to assist the reader in understanding definitions. The major difficulty consisted of not being able to identify which terms in a given definition were considered to be "specialized" or "unusual." Now, each term included in the glossary is printed in italics the first time it occurs in a definition so the reader is immediately alerted to the fact that further information is available in the glossary.

An alphabetical listing of all occupational titles, similar to the previous Volume I, is retained at the end of the current Volume I. It consists simply of an alphabetical listing with a reference to either the appropriate code number, or to the appropriate title within this alphabetical listing. The reader thus can be directed, in not more than two tries, to the proper definition information. A sample page of this arrangement also is included in Appendix A.

Under this format, the portions of the *DOT* having widest general use are combined into a single volume, thus greatly reducing the necessity of moving back and forth from one volume to another while working with the *DOT*. (The specialized materials remaining in Volume II will be discussed later.)

2. CHANGES IN CODING STRUCTURE. Readers familiar with the third edition code structure and its subsequent modification with the 1967 publication of the *Suffix Codes* will find that only minor changes have been made in the coding system, mostly of an up-dating nature. Readers familiar with the third edition six-digit code structure, but unfamiliar with the unique codes supplied by *Suffix Codes*, will need to incorporate the seventh, eighth, and ninth digit into the system they already know. The coding structure of the third edition, which has been described in earlier pages of this chapter, becomes operative for the fourth edition by adding the unique codes in the last three positions, thus changing the six-digit codes to nine-digit codes.

The change, occurring in the *worker functions arrangement* (the fourth, fifth, and sixth positions), does affect the code number for some occupations and will produce slight discrepancies in the numbers used in these positions in the third and fourth editions. As indicated in our discussion of the third edition, an attempt was made to use low level digits to reflect either low level of involvement or higher level involvement of insignificant frequency. The result was occasional blurring of intent. This has been rectified by using these digits to show only level of involvement. A minor change has thus occurred at the lower levels to reflect this change in use, eliminating the category of "no significant relationship." The digit describing the actual level is now used: the lowest digit if the level is truly low, a higher digit if the level is more complex, regardless of frequency. As a result, the worker functions arrangement has now been revised to the following:

Data		*People*		*Things*	
0	Synthesizing	0	Mentoring	0	Setting up
1	Coordinating	1	Negotiating	1	Precision working
2	Analyzing	2	Instructing	2	Operating–controlling
3	Compiling	3	Supervising	3	Driving–operating
4	Computing	4	Diverting	4	Manipulating
5	Copying	5	Persuading	5	Tending
6	Comparing	6	Speaking–signaling	6	Feeding–offbearing
		7	Serving	7	Handling
		8	Receiving instruction		

Thus, we see that the 8th digit for *People* has been changed to "Receiving instruction," and the 8th digit for *Things* and the 7th and 8th digits for *Data* have been dropped. Changes will occur in those worker functions codes where the third edition listed an "8" in either the fourth, fifth, or sixth position or a "7" in the fourth position. For example, an ACCOUNT EXECUTIVE carried a third edition code of 164.168, later revised to 164.168–010 with a suffix code; in the fourth edition the "8" in the sixth position is replaced and the code number now becomes 164.167–010.

3. USE OF TITLES WITHOUT SEX OR AGE REFERENTS. The replacement titles that were provided by the 1975 publication of *Job Title Revisions* are incorporated into the main body of the *DOT* in the fourth edition. Thus, former titles that carry either a sex or age referent will not be used.

4. DEVELOPMENT AND EXPANSION OF THE WORKER TRAITS ARRANGEMENT AS A COUNSELING INSTRUMENT. The only major component of the third edition not incorporated in Volume I of the fourth edition is the *Worker Traits Arrangement*. This material, which primarily serves a counseling function, now logically is incorporated into a separate volume. This section, as it appears in the fourth edition, reflects extensive revision and expansion of the earlier third edition content.

Research activity by the Division of Counseling and Test Development has focused for some time on the need for a more effective means of describing applicants in terminology used to describe the worker traits required by the various occupations. This effort has resulted in an interest inventory that includes 11 interest factors. These interest factors have been renamed career areas and replace the 22 work areas of the third edition. Thus, an individual's scores now identify primary and secondary interests that are directly translatable to related worker trait groups. Similarly, the level of complexity of the work, reflected in *worker functions arrangement,* also can be related to the GED/SVP educational attainment and the aptitude codes.

The major advantage of this new endeavor is the provision for direct translation of human characteristics into job characteristics via the interest and aptitude instrument developed within the Department of Labor. This is clearly a major movement forward that can enhance the growing value of the *DOT*. At the same time, this new thrust carries certain disadvantages because it fractionates still further the extensive research efforts on the relationship between tested interests and aptitudes (as demonstrated by a wide array of test instruments) and actual job performance (as evaluated by various criteria of success). The ultimate value of this new effort will be identified through practical applications in the months ahead.

USING THE *DOT*

Experienced counselors and teachers will recognize at once that the *DOT* is not a panacea to solve instantly all of the problems they encounter in career planning and counseling. In fact, the *DOT* alone probably will not solve even one problem. It is, however, a most important tool, the utility and value of which depend on the professional skill of the individual employing it.

The *DOT*, in its present form, has been developed and modified over many years, to serve a wide range of users in many different situations. Not all of these groups will use the book in the same way, or even for the same purposes. The neophyte should first attempt to understand how the tool is used in the function he/she wishes to perform and then develop skill and competence in this particular application. As one becomes more familiar with the book and its ramifications, additional insight into its other uses will ordinarily increase proficiency in using it for special purposes. Although the employment counselor will frequently be concerned with using the book to ascertain a code number for a referred worker or to develop an entry code number for a person entering the labor market, neither the counselor nor the teacher will often be concerned with this application. Even though their understanding of how the book is used for this purpose will be helpful, it will not directly advance their work with students.

Teachers and counselors will find both volumes of the *DOT* helpful in the following ways:

1. It is a useful way of helping students, in groups and individually, to develop understanding of the world of work. All students have some previously acquired knowledge of the world of work. The *DOT* can assist them in adding to their knowledge in several dimensions. Classification systems can be utilized along with the *DOT* to show both scope and depth in various occupational areas. Both Volumes I and II are particularly valuable in introductory and exploratory activities with students both in the classroom and in the counseling session. The coding structure and the data–people–things concept are especially appropriate for helping a person to form some picture of the world of work and are equally useful in helping to explore the relationship between an occupation and the rest of the working world.

2. It clearly demonstrates the interrelationships that exist in the world of work. This is of great importance in working with adolescents, who often have a concept of work as being organized into tight, unrelated compartments. Refinements in the third and fourth editions are particularly helpful in this application. The *occupational group arrangement* is directly related to the "field" concept of occupations and can be used to demonstrate this relationship. *The worker functions arrangement* clearly shows a "level" approach to occupations. Thus, promotional routes and transfer lines can be demonstrated and studied, so that the individual can see the various avenues that lead from each occupation to other parts of the world of work. The industrial designation provides further insight by relating each occupation to its industrial location.

3. The *worker traits arrangement* is helpful in showing a client or student the general qualifications needed in various occupational areas. This can help relate educational programs, as well as other types of experiences, to eventual occupational goals. Although by no means a clear road map guaranteeing arrival at a specific future goal, the information now included should help teenagers to think more clearly about their futures. In the hands of skillful counselors, the book can provide much informa-

tional and motivational food for thought as adolescents begin to explore the meaning of work and its relationship to their future lives.

4. Both the *occupational group arrangement* and the *worker functions arrangement* provide useful bases for filing career materials. Where a file is primarily intended to help the user gain a broader knowledge of the world of work, a system based on the occupational groups will often be most useful. If the basic purpose is to help the user relate self and abilities, interests, and goals to the world of work, a system based on the *worker functions arrangement* will have direct relevance.

5. It provides a basis for counselor use in assisting clients to initiate career planning on a broad foundation, and to move forward to more specific objectives as client experience and maturation justify more specific planning.

THE CUBISTIC CLASSIFICATION SYSTEM

The Cubistic classification system, proposed by D'Costa and Winefordner, is an example of direct application of *DOT* concepts.[12] This plan develops a three-dimensional approach to the *Worker Functions Arrangement* of the 1965 *DOT*. Proceeding from the idea that each job can be described in terms of its relationship to data–people–things, this notion suggests considering the world of work as a cube, with each of the three aspects constituting one dimension of the cube.

By grouping the nine levels of involvement for the data–people–things relationships into three broader classes of high, average, or low, it becomes easier to visualize. Table 17 shows this reclassification.[13] Thus, the original cube can be subdivided each direction into a $3 \times 3 \times 3$ matrix of 27 cells. Each cell can be thought to represent those occupations involving the corresponding attributes of the data–people–things relationships. Viewing the total cube head-on, the lower front left cell is designated 000 and represents those occupations with no significant relationship to any of the three factors—a theoretically and practically unused category. Similarly, the upper rear right cell is labeled 222 and would involve occupations that require the highest levels of involvement in all three areas. Figure 6–2 (p. 223) illustrates the composition of the cube and the interrelationship of the cells. Each 1965 *DOT* Worker Trait Arrangement code can be transposed into the appropriate cell label representing that degree of involvement with data, people, and things. For example, our earlier illustration of .168 encompassing a coordinating (data)—speaking/signaling (people)—no significant relationship (things) level of involvement reflects a high–average–low level represented by a code of 210 and the lower rear middle cell. All occupations involving this worker trait arrangement occupy this particular cell. Again, one might expect many different types of activities to exist within this cell, but all occupations placed there would have the same high data, average people, low things relationship.

TABLE 17. *Division of Data–People–Things Involvement into High, Average, Low Groups*

DIRECTION	H–A–L	DOT LEVELS OF INVOLVEMENT		
		DATA	PEOPLE	THINGS
COMPLEX				
	HIGH (2)	0 Synthesizing 1 Coordinating 2 Analyzing	0 Mentoring 1 Negotiating 2 Instructing 3 Supervising 4 Diverting	0 Setting-up 1 Precision Working 2 Operating–controlling 3 Driving–operating
	AVERAGE (1)	3 Compiling 4 Computing 5 Copying 6 Comparing	5 Persuading 6 Speaking–signalling 7 Serving	4 Manipulating 5 Tending 6 Feeding–offbearing 7 Handling

	LOW (0)	7 No Significant
		  Relationship
		8
			8 No Significant
			  Relationship
				8 No Significant
				  Relationship

SIMPLE				

From: D. W. Winefordner, "Orienting Students to the World of Work Using the Data–People–Things Conceptual Framework and the Ohio Vocational Interest Survey." Paper presented to APGA Convention, Las Vegas, Nevada, 1969.

FIGURE 6–2. *Data–People–Things Dimensions of the World at Work.*

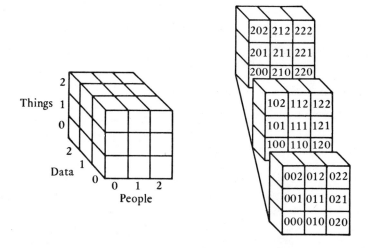

From: A. G. D'Costa, "The Development of a Vocational Interest Survey Using The Data–People–Things Model of Work." Paper presented to APGA Convention. Las Vegas, Nevada, 1969.

The Cubistic Concept has been related to the *Ohio Vocational Interest Survey,* which produces scores in terms of various job clusters, which in turn can be related to one of the cells within the cube.[14] The use of this interest inventory appears to be increasing in junior and senior high schools. One can infer that this increasing popularity may be because its results appear to translate so directly into categories that have empirical validity.

The Cubistic system has been further applied by Winefordner and others at the Appalachia Educational Laboratory as the basis for a comprehensive career information system including a filing system, guides, a keysort index, and instruments that assist students in self-evaluation. These materials are now available through commercial sources for school use.

Because of the increasing use of the *DOT*, other classification systems with a *DOT* base probably will appear.

NOTES

1. S. A. Fine, "The 1965 Edition of the Dictionary of Occupational Titles: Content, Contrasts, and Critique," *Vocational Guidance Quarterly,* vol. 17, no. 3 (March, 1969), pp. 162–172.
2. ———, "A Structure of Worker Functions," *Personnel and Guidance Journal,* vol. 34, no. 2 (October, 1955), pp. 71–72.

3. ———, "The Matching of Men and Jobs—A New Look," *Labor Market and Employment Security* (May, 1956), pp. 7–12.

4. S. A. Fine and C. A. Heinz, "The Functional Occupational Classification Structure," *Personnel and Guidance Journal*, vol. 37, no. 2 (October, 1958), pp. 180–192.

5. Department of Labor, Bureau of Employment Security, Division of Placement Methods, *Manual of Operating Instructions for Verification of Occupational Information* (Washington: U.S. Government Printing Office, 1960).

6. Department of Labor, U.S. Employment Service, *Estimates of Worker Trait Requirements for 4,000 Jobs as Defined in the Dictionary of Occupational Titles* (Washington: U.S. Government Printing Office, 1955).

7. A. B. Eckerson, "The New Dictionary of Occupational Titles," *Employment Security Review*, vol. 30, no. 2 (February, 1963).

8. ———, "The New Dictionary of Occupational Titles," *Vocational Guidance Quarterly*, vol. 12, no. 1 (Autumn, 1963), pp. 40–42.

9. Department of Labor, Bureau of Employment Security, *Dictionary of Occupational Titles*, Volumes I and II, 3rd ed. (Washington: U.S. Government Printing Office, 1965).

10. Department of Labor, Manpower Administration, Bureau of Employment Security, *Training Manual for the Dictionary of Occupational Titles (third edition) Trainee's Workbook* (Washington: U.S. Government Printing Office, 1965).

11. Bureau of the Budget, *Standard Industrial Classification Manual* (Washington: U.S. Government Printing Office, 1945).

12. A. G. D'Costa and D. W. Winefordner, "A Cubistic Model of Vocational Interests," *Vocational Guidance Quarterly*, vol. 17, no. 4 (June, 1969), pp. 242–249.

13. D. W. Winefordner, "Orienting Students to the World of Work Using the Data–People–Things Conceptual Framework and the Ohio Vocational Interest Survey." Paper presented at APGA Convention, Las Vegas, Nevada, 1969. ERIC Document Ed 029 343, CG 003 993.

14. A. G. D'Costa, D. W. Winefordner, J. G. Odgers, and P. B. Koons, Jr., *Ohio Vocational Interest Survey* (Columbus, Ohio: State Department of Education, 1967).

7

Other Classification Systems

We have already established the fact that the world of work is extremely varied and complex. The more than 20,000 occupations included in the *Dictionary of Occupational Titles* are brought together by code numbers into a classification system that has two major parts—the occupational group arrangement and the worker function arrangement. Each part, as we saw in the last chapter, is a complete, self-contained, classification system. Each part can be used, and often is, by itself for classification purposes as well as in combination to produce the code number.

If we wish to compare bench work occupations with processing occupations, we can do so by using the occupational group arrangement to identify the jobs classified in the two categories. Within these two categories, we can use the worker function arrangement if we wish to study how these two categories of occupations relate to the data–people–things concept. The occupational group arrangement permits us to be as broad as a major category or as specific as a three-digit group. Thus, we can select the classification system that provides the degree of specificity needed to accomplish our task.

In some situations, we need, or perhaps prefer, an extremely broad classification of occupations. The blue collar/white collar dichotomy is an illustration of the broadest type of classification. This structure is generally understood, widely used, and often, sufficiently specific for the situation in which it is being used. A moment's reflection, however, shows some serious disadvantages. Each category (white collar/blue collar) is so broad as to be almost meaningless; and many occupations can be classified in either division, or often in both, with equally valid arguments for the action. Nevertheless, the terminology is extremely useful in appropriate situations.

At the other extreme, one can hypothesize that groupings as specific as six-digit *DOT* numbers are too broad and general to meet the need of the moment. All secondary teachers, for example, carry the same code number, as do all secretaries, all carpenters, all accountants, etc. Yet within each occupation there may be times when a much finer distinction is desirable.

The purpose of this chapter is to identify some of the more widely used and recognized systems for classifying occupations so that the reader knows commonly-used arrangements or has sufficient knowledge to develop a system for the specific situation being confronted. Exhaustive treatment of the topic would result in a voluminous chapter with much more detail than could be justified. Obviously, many systems that have significant value for a specific situation have not been included. In this chapter, we will consider the following classification systems:

Cluster systems
Decennial census
Socio-economic
Intellectual demands
Two-dimensional systems
Industrial classification

CLUSTER SYSTEMS

The recent consideration given to Career Education has directed attention to "career clusters." These are broad groupings of occupations within which one can find an obvious inter-relationship.[1] None of the writers has suggested that the concept is new and, of course, it is not. As the previous discussion has implied, any grouping from blue collar/white collar to *DOT* code numbers can legitimately be considered as "clusters." Of major concern should be whether the list has value in a particular situation in which it will be used.

For our purposes, we will consider two different types of cluster systems and some illustrations of each type. The first of these cluster systems includes lists that have been developed primarily on an empirical basis—the categories make sense and have value to the individual or group who compiled the list.

An excellent illustration of this type of cluster system is a list developed by a group of experts working with the U.S. Office of Education on the development of the Career Education models, which we considered in Chapter 1. Career education advocates propose that the curriculum of the elementary and secondary school should be restructured so that the work of the school more closely relates to the world of work, as represented by the various clusters. The basic concept of *Career Education* is that the individual is prepared either to continue in the educational structure or to enter work in one of the clusters at an appropriate level. Therefore, the curriculum must include preparation that would make possible the movement between education and work, or vice versa. The clusters provide a structure for helping the elementary school child become familiar with the world of work and with the requirements for admission to the various areas. Similarly, the clusters can be used by junior high students and high school students for more detailed exploration, with the expectation of choice selection followed by acquisition of sufficient skill for entry positions in the cluster, or qualification for advanced education that would lead to later entry at a higher level.

The *Career Education* clusters include the following[2]:

1. Consumer and homemaking occupations
2. Health occupations
3. Public service occupations
4. Construction occupations
5. Personal service occupations
6. Transportation occupations
7. Fine arts and humanities occupations
8. Manufacturing occupations
9. Marketing and distribution occupations
10. Agri–business and natural resources occupations
11. Environmental occupations
12. Marine science occupations
13. Communications and media occupations
14. Business and office occupations
15. Hospitality and recreation occupations

The American College Testing Program has recently published materials for a *Career Planning Program*[3]. This material proposes a set of six job clusters that encompass 25 job families. Although partly based on theoretical concepts of Holland (as discussed in Chapter 2) and on interest inventory research (as discussed in Chapter 3), it appears realistic to think of the proposed cluster system as partly empirically developed. The purpose of this cluster system is to provide a base for career materials prepared as part of their *Career Planning Program*. The six clusters and their component parts include the following[4]:

Business Sales and Management Job Cluster
   A. Promotion and direct sales
   B. Management and planning
   C. Retail sales and services
Business Operations Job Cluster
   D. Clerical and secretarial work
   E. Paying, receiving, and bookkeeping

F. Office machine operation

G. Storage, dispatching, and delivery

Technologies and Trades Job Cluster

H. Human services crafts

I. Repairing and servicing home and office equipment

J. Growing and caring for plants/animals

K. Construction and maintenance

L. Transport equipment operation

M. Machine operating, servicing, and repairing

N. Engineering and other applied technologies

Natural, Social, and Medical Sciences Job Cluster

O. Natural sciences and mathematics

P. Medicine and medical technologies

Q. Social sciences and legal services

Creative and Applied Arts Job Cluster

R. Creative arts

S. Applied arts (verbal)

T. Applied arts (visual)

U. Popular entertainment

Social, Health, and Personal Services Job Cluster

V. Education and social services

W. Nursing and human care

X. Personal and household services

Y. Law enforcement and protective services

The second cluster system that we will consider was developed from a research base. For the most part, previous research that has led to "cluster" data has been based on interest inventories. Only more recently has there been an attempt to move from the theoretical writing in career development. One can expect this latter base to expand extensively in the years immediately ahead. One of the illustrations in this section shows an attempt to relate the theory proposed by Holland to one of the more widely used interest inventories—the *Strong Vocational Interest Blank*.

As described in Chapter 3, the *Strong Vocational Interest Blank* was originally developed by searching for common responses made by members of occupational groups. In other words, it was hypothesized that accountants, as a group, would tend to like the same occupations, activities, amusements, etc., and dislike or be indifferent to other items in common. Similarly, physicians would indicate common patterns of likes and dislikes. This basic concept was fundamental to the development and standardization of the instrument. Although the list was shorter for the original version of the test, ultimately well over 100 occupational keys were developed. If one can accept the assumption that occupational members will tend to respond with a similar, although not necessarily identical, pattern, it is also easy to accept the idea that one might expect some occupational keys to have large amounts of commonality—or, to be quite similar to certain occupations and very different from others. This hypothesis was studied by a statistical procedure known as factor analysis and confirmed. Somewhat oversimplified, this situation might be described by picturing the scoring key for each occupation as producing a result that can be plotted on a globe. Some of these points might be found to be quite close together, like cities of the world—Montreal, New York, Boston, and Philadelphia, for example, would obviously have more geographic relationship than any one of these cities with Munich, Vienna, or Prague. It is reasonable to think of these two groups as each representing a cluster of occupations that have certain relationships to a greater degree than with any other more distant point.

The *Strong-Campbell Interest Inventory* is the latest form of the *Strong Vocational Interest Blank*, originally published a half century ago.[5] Scores are available for six General Occupational Themes (corresponding to Holland's six occupational personalities), 23 Basic Interest Scales, and 124 Occupational Scales. The six General Occupational Themes and the related 23 Basic Interest Scales are listed here as an example of a test-developed, test-related cluster system. They include:

R–Theme (Realistic)
    Agriculture
    Nature
    Adventure
    Military activities
    Mechanical activities
I–Theme (Investigative)
    Science
    Mathematics
    Medical science
    Medical service
A–Theme (Artistic)
    Music/Dramatics
    Art
    Writing
S–Theme (Social)
    Teaching
    Social service
    Athletics
    Domestic arts
    Religious activities
E–Theme (Enterprising)
    Public speaking
    Law/Politics
    Merchandising
    Sales
    Business management
C–Theme (Conventional)
    Office practices

Holland also has developed an instrument based on his six personality types entitled *The Self-Directed Search.*[6] The items consist of activities, competencies, and occupations grouped according to Holland's six basic types. From responses to these various items, the individual can identify the primary, secondary, and tertiary types with which he/she has expressed similarity.

A companion booklet, *The Occupations Finder,* includes the more common occupations, sorted according to Holland's groupings. Keeping in mind that the six types—Realistic, Investigative, Artistic, Social, Enterprising, and Conventional—permit $6 \times 5 \times 4$ different occupational clusters, one can see a great many permutations, not all of which are presently used. For example, realistic occupations are group in the following clusters: RIA, RIS, RIE, RIC, RAI, RSE, RSC, RSI, REC, REI, RES, RCI, RCS, and RCE. Similarly, social occupations are grouped into SEC, SER, SEI, SEA, SCE, SRI, SRE, SRC, SIA, SIE, SIC, SIR, SAE, SAC, and SAI. Estimates of general educational level related to each occupation also are provided. The user is encouraged to explore other combinations of the same types; for example, if the obtained code is IRE, the individual also should look at RIE, REI, IER, and ERI.

One observes a good deal of overlap and similarity among these illustrations of cluster groups. Whether a cluster system is developed through observation and experience or by study of broadly-based interest inventory results, that commonality is to be expected. One might consider it generally reassuring to find that results based on the two different approaches confirm each other.

CENSUS CLASSIFICATION

As a part of each decennial census completed in the United States, many questions concerning occupations are asked. Such questions have been a part of the census for well over a century. The value of information about occupations across the nation collected at approximately the same time at regular ten-year intervals is obvious. No other source of information about jobs now provides such a comprehensive picture as the census.

In spite of the advantages of comprehensiveness, currency, and availability, some caution in using census data is warranted. One should keep in mind that census information is collected by enumerators whose training is necessarily brief and whose understanding of occupational names and terms may not be as extensive as desirable for the most accurate recording of information. Secondly, the enumerator usually works during the same hours that most people work; consequently, the occupational information often may be obtained from a member of the family group who may not understand precisely the nature of the breadwinner's vocation. Further, occupational titles are not defined in the classification. It is therefore possible for some distortion of information to find its way into the data. Because of the vast quantity of data, it may be relatively safe to assume that the various errors will tend to cancel one another. Nevertheless, the census is an extremely important source of information about occupations in the United States.

As the utilization of occupational information in the census has changed through the years, the method of classifying the information also has changed. In the last two or three enumerations, the modifications have been relatively minor. The latest system is that used for the 1970 Decennial Census of Population.[7]

The 1970 census classification divides the world of work into four broad areas: white collar workers, blue collar workers, farm workers, and service workers. These four areas are broken into twelve major groups, which approximately correspond to the major groups used in recent census enumeration. These, in turn, are further divided into occupational categories. Table 18 identifies the twelve major occupational groups and compares the numbers of specific categories allocated to each major group in both 1960 and 1970. An inspection of the table reveals that the number of categories has increased in all groups from 297 in 1960 to 441 in 1970. Of special significance is the greater proportionate increase in the white

TABLE 18.   *Major Occupation Groups*

AREA AND GROUP	NUMBER OF CATEGORIES	
	1960	1970
White Collar Workers		
Professional, technical, and kindred	84	124
Managers and administrators, except farms	13	24
Sales workers	9	15
Clerical and kindred workers	28	48
Blue Collar Workers		
Craftsmen and kindred workers	61	96
Operatives, except transport	53	54
Transport equipment operatives		12
Laborers, except farm	10	16
Farm Workers		
Farmers and farm managers	2	3
Farm laborers and farm foremen	4	5
Service Workers		
Service workers, except private household	28	38
Private household workers	4	6
Total	297	441

collar groups. The one new major group created in the 1970 classification is that of transport equipment operatives which, in 1960, was included under operatives and kindred workers.

Several of the major groups include subgroups that bring together closely related categories. In addition to the clustered categories arranged under these subgroupings, other categories are separately listed in each group. The subgrouping titles are recorded in Table 19.

Several examples of specific or discrete categories, as well as of clustered categories, are shown in Table 20 (p. 234). The items were selected for this table to give the reader some understanding of the scope and specificity of the occupational divisions used in the latest census classification.

In general, some of the categories are approximately as specific as the three-digit groups of the *Dictionary of Occupational Titles*. For example, there are eleven engineering numbers in the census classification and twelve such three-digit groups in the *Dictionary*. The *Dictionary* uses 45 numbers for sales occupations, compared with only 15 in the census classification; similarly the *Dictionary* uses 67 groups for service occupations, compared to 38 categories in the census. On the other hand, the *Dictionary* uses approximately 80 numbers for the professional and technical area, whereas the census uses 123.

Because of the relatively few categories, the census system is quite easy to learn. It is particularly useful in local occupational surveys or similar situations in which occupational names covering relatively broad areas are sufficient.

The major advantage of census data for the counselor or teacher is the vast wealth of information about occupations nationally or statewide. Data are automatically processed for all metropolitan areas exceeding 25,000 population, so census data also are useful as a source of information for smaller geographic areas. For communities with fewer than 25,000, the data tabulations can be secured from the Census Bureau quite inexpensively, since the charge includes only machine time and labor.

Information concerning comparative sizes of occupational groups, geographic distribution, and similar statistics are available from the census data. In addition to helping students see the broad scope of an occupational group, the census classification is particularly useful for community surveys, since such use permits direct comparison with data for larger political units.

Disadvantages and limitations have been previously mentioned, and the data should be utilized with these in mind. If the data are used for broad, general comparisons and not for detailed, specific information, the error factor is more likely to be minimized.

An understanding of the census classification system helps the individual—counselor, teacher, or student—to interpret the data reported in the census publications. Because of their scope, census data will be used frequently in studying the world of work.

TABLE 19. *Major Groups and Subgroupings*

Professional, Technical, and Kindred Workers
- Computer specialists
- Engineers
- Lawyers and judges
- Librarians, archivists, and curators
- Mathematical specialists
- Life and physical scientists
- Physicians, dentists, and related practitioners
- Nurses, dietitians, and therapists
- Health technologists and technicians
- Religious workers
- Social scientists
- Social and recreation workers
- Teachers, college and university
- Teachers, except college and university
- Engineering and science technicians
- Technicians, except health, and engineering and science
- Writers, artists, and entertainers

Managers and Administrators, except Farms

Sales Workers

Clerical and Kindred Workers
- Office machine operators
- Secretaries

Craftsmen and Kindred Workers
- Mechanics and repair

Operatives, except Transport
- Precision machine operatives
- Textile operatives

Transport Equipment Operatives

Laborers, except Farm

Farmers and Farm Managers

Farm Laborers and Farm Foremen

Service Workers, except Private Household
- Cleaning service workers
- Food service workers
- Health service workers
- Personal service workers
- Protective service workers

Private Household Workers

TABLE 20. Excerpts from Occupation Classification

TABLE 20. *Continued*

704	Conductors and motormen, urban rail transit
705	Deliverymen and routemen
706	Fork lift and tow motor operatives

SERVICE WORKERS, EXCEPT PRIVATE HOUSEHOLD

Cleaning service workers

901	Chambermaids and maids, except private household
902	Cleaners and charwomen
903	Janitors and sextons

Food service workers

910	Bartenders
911	Busboys
912	Cooks, except private household
913	Dishwashers
914	Food counter and fountain workers
915	Waiters
916	Food service workers, n.e.c. except private household

SOCIO-ECONOMIC CLASSIFICATION SYSTEMS

One of the earliest attempts to build an occupational scale or classification system is seen in the work of Taussig at Harvard in 1911.[8] As an economist, he was interested in finding reasons why his hypothesis that the most attractive jobs would attract the largest numbers of participants and consequently provide the lowest pay did not hold true. His investigation led him to consider classes in society and the impact that social status and economic factors had on occupational selection. He concluded that certain relatively distinct, clear-cut, noncompeting occupational groups existed in American society. These groups were held apart from one another and hence were largely noncompeting because of the existence of certain artificial barriers such as family differences in culture, unequal access to educational opportunities, and financial inability to take advantage of available education.

Taussig proposed that there were approximately five occupational categories, which he identified as follows:

1. The well-to-do class (higher level professional workers, salaried officials, larger proprietors).
2. The lower middle class (lower white-collar group of clerks, salesmen, small proprietors).
3. Skilled labor (primarily craftsmen).
4. Slightly skilled and semiskilled labor.
5. Day labor.

The classification proposed by Taussig was used frequently; numerous references to it can be found in the literature for about a quarter of a century.

Beckman proposed a somewhat similar scale in 1935. Working from an *a priori* basis, he used essentially three criteria in building the scale.[9]

He considered the amount of intelligence, job skills, and education or training required by the job. Like Taussig, Beckman developed a scale of five parts; however, three of the steps were subdivided into two or three subcategories. Probably the major differences between the Taussig and Beckman scales are the reversal of direction by Beckman, who started at the lower end of the scale, and the equating of skilled workers with lower level white-collar workers.

The Beckman scale includes the following levels:

I. Unskilled manual
II. Semiskilled
III. a. Skilled manual
    b. Skilled white-collar
IV. a. Subprofessional
    b. Business
    c. Minor supervisory
V. a. Professional (linguistic)
    b. Professional (scientific)
    c. Managerial and executive

Probably the most widely used classification based on socio-economic factors is the one developed by Edwards in the early 1940's.[10] Edwards published a long-range comparison of occupational statistics using his classification system. His grouping included six steps, providing separate categories for professional managerial occupations. Like Taussig, he listed the occupational groups from highest to lowest. Edwards found that Beckman's system of subcategories was useful and used it for two of his steps. The following are the Edwards classifications:

1. Professional persons
2. Proprietors, managers, and officials
    2-a. Farmers (owners and tenants)
    2-b. Wholesale and retail dealers
    2-c. Other proprietors, managers, and officials
3. Clerks and kindred workers
4. Skilled workers and foremen
5. Semiskilled workers
6. Unskilled workers
    6-a.   Farm workers
    6-b, c. Laborers, except farm
    6-d.   Servant classes

Caplow has pointed out several assumptions that must be made to form the basis for socio-economic grouping.[11] These include: (1) white-collar work is superior to manual work; (2) self-employment is superior to employment by others; (3) clean occupations are superior to dirty ones; (4) the importance of business occupations depends on the size of the business, and (5) personal service is degrading. For those who view all legitimate work as making an important and essential contribution to society, these are impossible assumptions. Well over a half century has passed since Taussig first proposed an occupational hierarchy and more than 35 years since Beckman and Edwards developed their scales. This period has been fraught with social and economic change—industrial expansion, growth and maturity of labor unions, development of automation, increased educational opportunities—and many other changes that influence values and attitudes. With these changes in mind, one might reasonably ask if the assumptions proposed by Caplow and the spread of a more democratic philosophy have negated the socio-economic classification system.

In the economic sphere there is considerable indication that, at best, the situation is clouded. One would be unable to contend that all professions have higher economic returns than all other occupations. In fact, there are several skilled and semiskilled categories in which both weekly and annual income exceed that of occupations in those categories that Edwards and Beckman placed in higher groups. On the other hand, if one compares the extremes with each other, there is obvious indication that significant differences still exist.

Similarly, in the social area it is possible to point to many developments that indicate a reduction in "class" emphasis and an increase in democratization. The rapid extension of education to more and more of our population is perhaps most illustrative of changes here.

On the other hand, studies of prestige rankings of occupations, variation of income by educational level or by type of work, occupational mobility, and other aspects of social stratification point to the continued existence of some rigidity of structure. The socio-economic scales were developed by roughly ranking occupations according to the quantity of intelligence, skill, and education involved in performing various jobs. In general, both social status and economic compensation have been, and still are, somewhat related to these factors.[12]

Although, overall, one cannot precisely peg each occupational group on a social and an economic continuum, it is, nevertheless, clear that many distinct differences do exist. Caplow's assumptions, by using the terms "superior" and "inferior," imply a difference that seems strictly vertical in nature—that is, one kind of job is better than another. This is probably true if one evaluates the positions on a single criterion, such as income, and if the evaluator holds that this single criterion is the most important factor for comparison. If, however, the differing item is not of crucial significance to the individual, or, as is likely, there are other criteria where the two jobs reverse positions, their relative position on a vertical scale is harder to ascertain. Since the socio-economic scales use only two or three criteria, one does not need to generalize to an overall position of superiority or inferiority.

The categories included in socio-economic scales have had a long period of usage and contain groups that are simply identified. The terms are not likely to be dropped and, in fact, have real value when one wishes to divide the world of work into only a few broad groupings that relate to such factors as level of training and skill required. Consequently, it would seem logical that the scales could be used advantageously in many ways to help youth gain insight into occupations. The undemocratic implication of superiority and inferiority can be minimized if one considers the grouping to be on a horizontal scale indicating differences in the characteristics involved, without adding the connotation that comes from a vertical ranking. The approach to these scales as descriptive of horizontal differences permits consideration of many other criteria for comparison, which in numerous cases may be more pertinent and important for the individual involved.

A complex society such as ours can operate only when the work of all individuals is integrated efficiently. Those involved in the professions, at one end of the socio-economic continuum, cannot perform their tasks without the contribution of the unskilled workers, at the other end. For example, one of our cities became acutely aware of this interdependence of all workers a few summers ago, when the city's garbage collectors engaged in an extended strike and withdrew their services for several July days.

INTELLECTUAL DEMANDS

As early as World War I, attention was being turned to the possibility that occupations could be ranked or classified in terms of the amount of intelligence required to perform successfully in the occupation. One of the earliest results of such effort was the development of the *Barr Scale* in 1918. In this research, Barr carefully described 121 different occupations and then asked a jury of 20 judges, consisting of graduate students in psychology and professors of economics, education, and psychology, to evaluate or rate the occupations according to the amount of intelligence required to perform the work.[13] The obtained range then was divided into 14 equal parts.

Test data obtained on enlisted personnel during World War I permitted an extensive study by Fryer.[14] From 60,000 records, involving 115 occupations, he selected the data for 3,598 cases representing 96 occupations for special attention. Using the obtained mean scores from the *Army Alpha Test*, he ranked the occupations in order. To simplify the classification procedure, he utilized a series of letter grades used by army psychologists to classify enlisted men. These included A, B, C+, C−, and

D. He later added D+ and E as additional categories. Examples of occupations as grouped by Fryer have serious limitations. These include: (1) the sample uses only enlisted men, thus excluding officers, who might be expected to have higher ability, experience, and education; (2) the selective factors of the draft prevent the group from being a typical sample of the civilian population, and (3) only abstract intelligence is measured by the test. See Table 21.

TABLE 21. *Corresponding Intelligence–Achievement Values*

(From: Fryer and Sparling)[16]			
A VERY SUPERIOR 18.0-UP MA	**B** SUPERIOR 16.5–17.9 MA	**C+** HIGH AVERAGE 15.0–16.4 MA	**C** AVERAGE 13.0–14.9 MA
High professional level	Professional level	Technical level	Skilled level
Editor Lawyer Teacher (college) Engineer Diplomat Minister Salesman Statistician Teacher (h. s.) Accountant	Writer (journalist) Physician Teacher (elementary) Salesman (insurance) Businessman (large merchant) Chemist Private secretary Office manager Factory supt. Draftsman	Stenographer Bookkeeper Nurse Office clerk Salesman (wholesale) Businessman (small merchant) Railroad clerk Teacher (gymnasium) Traffic clerk Photographer	Engineer (locomotive) Furrier Telephone operator Stock checker Handyman Policeman Auto assembler Riveter (hand) Tool & die maker Auto engine mechanic
C− LOW AVERAGE 11.0–12.9 MA	**D** INFERIOR 9.5–10.9 MA	**D−** VERY INFERIOR 7.0–9.4 MA	**E** USELESS 0.0–6.9 MA
Semiskilled and Low skilled level	Unskilled level	Lowest unskilled level	
Hospital attendant Mason Lumberman Watchman Shoemaker Sailor Structural steel worker Canvas worker Packer	Fisherman Laborer (unskilled) Loader Lifter	Laborer (simplest work)	None

A study similar to Fryer's early work was completed by Stewart, using data from World War II records.[15] From an original group of 250,000 records, she drew cases for 81,553 white enlisted men representing 227 occupations. The median score on the *Army General Classification Test* for these occupational groups was then ranked. The same limitations that apply to the study reported by Fryer also apply to Stewart's data. In studying these two reports, the restrictions must be kept in mind. Statistical treatment of the data revealed that all scores fell within 2.5 standard deviations of the mean for the total group. She consequently divided the entire range into ten categories of a half standard deviation each. Illustrations of the occupations falling in each half sigma category may be seen in Table 22 (pp. 242–43). One can observe that the lowest category includes occupations that are essentially manual labor and the highest category includes occupations that are professional or administrative in nature. The middle categories include occupations that are semiskilled, skilled, sales, and clerical.

Even though Stewart's study is most helpful in demonstrating the distribution of the medians of scores attained by the various occupational groups, attention also should be given to the overlap of ranges within the occupational groups. Super emphasized the situation that appears to prevail when he suggested: [17]

> The spread of intelligence in any one occupation is so great that it is impossible to set specific limits of minimum and maximum intelligence for any one kind of work!

If we examine the scores attained by the two occupations at the extremes of Stewart's distribution, we find that the scores earned by the top ten per cent of the lumberjacks are roughly comparable to the scores attained by the lowest ten per cent of the accountants. Thus, even at the extremes overlap is found. As we move closer to the middle of the distribution, the extent of overlap obviously becomes appreciably greater. From the evidence provided by Stewart, it appears reasonable to conclude that even though some general hierarchy of occupations according to intellectual demand does exist, the amount of overlap is so great that no completely effective categorizing of occupations can be accomplished.[18]

The *Minnesota Occupational Rating Scales* refines the approach to rating occupations according to intellectual demands by dividing "ability" or "intelligence" into several different types.[19] This, of course, permits a more precise description of the specific demands made by the occupations. Each type of ability is broken into levels. An early edition of the *Minnesota Occupational Rating Scales* used five ability areas and divided each of these into six levels. The 1953 edition lists seven areas of ability, each with four levels.

This rating system emphasizes the different characteristics required in various jobs, and the usual advantage of this approach is that it permits occupations to be grouped according to the pattern of ability level.[20] Almost one-third of the occupations rated reveal a unique pattern of traits. The other two-thirds, however, fall into one of 77 different patterns that include two or more occupations.

Like prestige ratings, classification systems based on intellectual demands have only limited use in understanding the world of work. Their most obvious value is helping clients understand that even though an intellectual hierarchy of occupations does appear to exist, it is not arranged in discrete gradations but, instead, has very extensive overlap. Before discarding this evidence entirely, one must recognize that the sample limitations have no doubt produced bias and that no evaluation of success in any category is included; each person was classified according to the civilian occupation that he claimed on entering service. If a truly representative sample could be made and if some consideration could be given to the degree of attainment within a stated occupation, the apparent overlap might be somewhat reduced.

Occupational choice should be based on a careful study of many characteristics. Attention to intellectual ratings should help teachers and counselors to point out that intellectual ability alone is not a sound criterion.

TWO-DIMENSIONAL CLASSIFICATION

An extension of the intellectual demands classification system can be seen in "the field and level" concept proposed by Hahn and MacLean.[21] This approach suggests a two-dimensional framework for classifying occupations and has undoubtedly served as the basis for considerable recent work along this line. Hahn and MacLean have implied that many occupations can be classified horizontally into fields or clusters determined by the major area of emphasis in the occupation. For example, there is a cluster of occupations that are essentially scientific in nature, another group considered mechanical, and so on. Within these clusters of occupations one might expect to find a vertical hierarchy based principally on intellectual demand, educational background, responsibility, and so on.

This concept is especially useful for vocational counselors, since it provides a useful device for helping the counselee to understand the whole occupational structure as well as relationships within specific fields.

Roe's approach within the framework of a two-dimensional system is slightly different.[22] She has proposed that horizontal (to p. 244)

TABLE 22. *Selected Occupational Groups Whose AGCT Medians Lie in Each Half-Sigma Interval From the Mean of all the Medians*

(From: Stewart)[15]

−2.5	−2.0	−1.5	−1.0	−.5	MEAN
85.3	89.9	94.5	99.1	103.7	108.3
Teamster	Marine	Tractor	Welder,	Not elsewhere	
Miner	fireman	driver	electric	classified	
Farm	Laundry	Painter,	arc	Machinist's	
worker	machine	general	Plumber	helper	
Lumberjack	operator	Foundry-	Switchman,	Foreman,	
	Laborer	man	railway	labor	
	Barber	Animation	Machine	Locomotive,	
	Shoe re-	artist	operator	fireman	
	pairman	Hospital	Hammer-	Entertainer	
	Jackhammer	orderly	smith	Meat cutter	
	operator	Baker	Student, h.s.,	Student, h.s.,	
	Groundman,	Packer,	agric.	vocational	
	telephone	supplies	Mechanic,	Cabinet maker	
	Section	Sewing	auto-	Airplane	
	hand,	machine	motive	engine	
	railway	operator	Blacksmith	mechanic	
		Truck driver	Welder,	Heat treater	
		Painter, au-	acetylene	Fire fighter	
		tomobile	Bricklayer	Engineering	
		Hoist	Blaster or	aide	
		operator	powderman	Construction	
		Construction	Small-craft	equip.	
		machine	operator	mech.	
		operator	Lineman,	Optician	
		Horse-	power	Packer, high	
		breaker	Packing case	explosives	
		Tailor	maker	Petroleum	
		Stonemason	Carpenter,	storage	
		Crane	general	technician	
		operator	Pipe fitter	Pattern maker,	
		Upholsterer	Electric	wood	
		Cook	truck	Electrician,	
		Concrete-	driver	automotive	
		mixer	Highway	Coppersmith	
		operator	mainte-	Ship fitter	
		Light	nance	Sheet metal	
		stationary	man	worker	
		fireman	Auto serv-	Electroplater	
		Warehouse-	iceman	Instrument re-	
		man	Rigger	pairman,	
		Gas & oil	Wood-	elec.	
		man	working	Steam fitter	
		Forging-	machine	Diesel	
		press	operator	mechanic	
		operator	Chauffeur		
		Longshore-	Motorcyclist		
		man	Burner,		
		Well driller	acetylene		

TABLE 22. *Continued*

+.5 112.9	+1.0 117.5	+1.5 122.1	+2.0 126.7	+2.5 131.3
Carpenter, heavy construction	Switchboard installer, telephone & tele- graph, dial	Bookkeeper, general	Writer Student, civil engi- neering	Accountant Student, mech. en- gineering
Dispatcher, motor vehicle	Stock record clerk	Chief clerk Stenographer Pharmacist	Statistical clerk	Personnel clerk
Gunsmith	Clerk, general	Typist Draftsman	Student, chem. en-	Student, medicine
Musician, instru- mental	Radio repairman	Chemical laboratory	gineering Teacher	Chemist Student,
Tool maker	Purchasing	asst.	Lawyer	elec. en-
Nurse, practical	agent Survey &	Draftsman, mech.	Student, business	gineering
Photog- rapher, portrait	instrument man Physics labor-	Investigator Reporter Tool	or public admin. Auditor	
Rodman and chainman, surveying	atory asst. Stock con- trol clerk	designer Tabulating machine	Student, dentistry	
Airplane, fabric & dope worker	Manager, production Boilermaker, layer-out	operator Addressing- embossing machine		
Multilith or multigraph work	Radio operator Linotype	operator Traffic rate clerk		
Shipping clerk	operator Student,	Clerk-typist Postal clerk		
Printer Steward	mechanics Salesman	Bookkeeping mach.		
Foreman, warehouse	Athletic instructor	operator Meat or dairy		
Bandsman, cornet or trumpet	Store manager Installer-	inspector Photographic laboratory		
Instrument repair- man, non- electrical	repairman, telephone & telegraph	technician Teletype operator Student,		
Boring mill operator	Motorcycle mechanic	sociology		
Projectionist, motion picture	Dispatcher clerk, crew			
Dentist, lab. technician	Tool dresser File clerk			
Lab. technician, V-mail or microfilm	Embalmer Brake in- spector, railway Airplane & engine mechanic Shop clerk			

groupings can be made on the basis of the primary focus of activity. The focus of an occupation may be on personal interactions, the handling or processing of natural resources, the development of knowledge, or similar factors. This has led to a series of eight groups, defined as follows:

I. *Service.* These occupations are primarily concerned with serving and attending to the personal tastes, needs, and welfare of other persons. Included are occupations in guidance, social work, domestic, and protective services.

II. *Business contact.* These occupations are primarily concerned with the face-to-face sale of commodities, investments, real estate, and services. This group includes those occupations in which selling is essentially personal and persuasive, but excludes those where selling is routine and the person-to-person contact relatively unimportant.

III. *Organization.* These are the managerial and white-collar jobs in business, industry, and government, with the occupations concerned primarily with the organization and efficient functioning of commercial enterprises and of governmental activities.

IV. *Technology.* This group includes occupations concerned with the production, maintenance, and transportation of commodities and utilities. Here are occupations in engineering, crafts, machine trades, transportation, and communication.

V. *Outdoor.* This group includes agricultural, fishing, forestry, mining, and similar occupations. These are mainly concerned with the cultivation, preservation of mineral and forest products, and other natural resources, and with animal husbandry.

VI. *Science.* These occupations are primarily concerned with scientific theory and its application under specified circumstances, other than technology.

VII. *General culture.* These occupations are concerned with the preservation and transmission of the general cultural heritage. This includes the humanities, education, journalism, correspondence, the ministry, and linguistics.

VIII. *Arts and entertainment.* These occupations are concerned with the use of special skills in the creative arts and in the field of entertainment.

The second, or vertical, dimension is based on level of function, which includes the degree of responsibility, capacity, or skill. When these three factors do not correlate with one another, Roe has given basic emphasis to the level of responsibility required in the occupation. Six levels of function have been established:

1. *Professional and managerial—independent responsibility.* This level includes innovators and creators, and top managerial and administrative people with independent responsibility. Suggested criteria for this group include:
   a. Important, independent, varied responsibility

b. Policy making

c. Education, when relevant, at the doctorate level

2. *Professional and managerial—other.* The difference between this level and the previous one is one of degree. Responsibility is generally narrower and less significant. Suggested criteria include:

   a. Medium level responsibility

   b. Policy interpretation

   c. Education at or above bachelor level but below the doctorate or its equivalent.

3. *Semiprofessional and small business.* This level is based on the following suggested criteria.

   a. Low level responsibility for others

   b. Application of policy or determination for self only

   c. Education at high school plus technical school level

4. *Skilled.* This level requires apprenticeship or other similar special training or experience.

5. *Semiskilled.* These occupations require some training and experience, but markedly less than those in level 4. There is much less autonomy and initiative permitted in level 5.

6. *Unskilled.* These occupations require no special training or education and not much more ability than that needed to follow simple directions and to engage in simple repetitive actions.

Table 23 (pp. 246–47) illustrates the use of two-dimensional classifications to provide a framework for categorizing occupations. An empty cell suggests that no occupation fits that level and group.

The two-dimensional classification system is particularly helpful when used to assist teen-agers in grasping both the scope and interrelationships in the world of work. The vastness of the occupational life of our nation is overwhelming to youth and adults alike. The suggestion that there are more than 25,000 different ways to earn a livelihood can easily create despair and frustration. Considering the world of work from the approach of Roe's classification system, however, simplifies the task and also stresses an orderliness in it.

The horizontal dimension is useful in stressing the broad areas into which occupations can be divided. Even though "primary focus" is the classification factor used for this dimension, this term embraces several characteristics of what people do, how they do it, where they do it—in general, the field in which they work. An obviously related factor in considering this dimension is an individual's interests—the kinds of things he likes and prefers. The field concept is somewhat related to the situs approach proposed by Reiss and discussed in Chapter 4.

The vertical dimension encourages consideration of such factors as ability, educational preparation, degree of responsibility, and related items. This may be extremely helpful in showing a student whose possibilities of attaining a college education are limited that the field of technology, for example, includes a long list of occupations other than engineering in which

TABLE 23: Roe's Two-Way Classification of Occupations

LEVEL	I SERVICE	II BUSINESS CONTACT	III ORGANIZATION	IV TECHNOLOGY	V OUTDOOR	VI SCIENCE	VII GENERAL CULTURAL	VIII ARTS AND ENTERTAINMENT
1 Professional & managerial (ind. responsibility)	Personal therapists Social work supervisors Counselors	Promoters	U.S. President & cabinet officers Industrial tycoons International bankers	Inventive geniuses Consulting or chief engineers Ship's commanders	Consulting specialists	Research scientists Univ., col. faculties Medical specialists Museum curators	Supreme Court justices Univ., col. faculties Prophets Scholars	Creative artists Performers, great Teachers, university equivalent Museum curators
2 Professional & managerial	Social workers Occupational therapists Probation truant officers (with training)	Promoters Public relations counselors	C.P.A.'s Business and government executives Union officials	Applied scientists Factory managers Ships' officers	Applied scientists Land owners and operators, large Landscape architects	Scientists, semi-independent Nurses Pharmacists Veterinarians	Editors Teachers, high school and elementary	Athletes Art critics Designers Music arrangers
3 Semiprofessional and small business	YMCA officials Detectives, police sergeants Welfare workers City inspectors	Salesmen; auto, bond, insurance Dealers, retail & wholesale Confidence men	Accountants, average Employment managers Owners, catering, dry-cleaning, etc.	Aviators Contractors Foremen (*DOT I*) Radio operators	County agents Farm owners Forest rangers Fish, game wardens	Technicians, medical, X-ray, museum Weather observers Chiropractors	Justices of the peace Radio announcers Reporters Librarians	Ad writers Designers Interior decorators Showmen

4 Skilled	Barbers Chefs Practical nurses Policemen	Auctioneers Buyers (*DOT* I) House canvassers	Cashiers Clerks Foremen, warehouse Salesclerks	Blacksmiths Electricians Foremen (*DOT* II) Mechanics	Laboratory testers, dairy products, etc. Miners	Technical assistants	Law clerks	Advertising artists Decorators, window, etc. Photographers
5 Semiskilled	Taxi drivers General house-workers City firemen	Peddlers	Clerks, file, stock, etc. Notaries Runners	Bulldozer operators Truck drivers	Gardeners Farm tenants Teamsters	Veterinary hospital attendants		Illustrators, greeting cards Showcard writers Stagehands
6 Unskilled	Chambermaids Hospital attendants Watchmen		Messengers	Helpers Laborers Wrappers Yardmen	Dairy hands Farm laborers Lumberjacks	Nontechnical helpers in scientific organization		

From: A. Roe, *The Psychology of Occupations*, New York: John Wiley & Sons, Inc., 1956, p. 151.

a college degree is not a prerequisite for admission. High school students sometimes reveal confusion and indecision in vocational planning because they have an interest in an area but lack knowledge of what is available in that area at the level that seems accessible to them.

The two-dimensional approach to occupations emphasizes consideration of both similarities and differences between occupations, as well as focuses attention on different factors or traits that relate directly to vocational choice. The system is useful in the classroom where the teacher may desire to develop a general concept of the world of work. It is equally useful in the counseling room where the client may be seeking help in matching abilities, interests, and ambitions with the realities of the occupational world.

A recent study by Meir attempts to determine the extent to which Roe's Primary Focus of Activity classification could be confirmed statistically.[23] Meir discovered that he could identify a graded order of levels in the fields of Service, Business, Organization, Technology, Outdoor, Science, General Culture, and Arts and Entertainment. His investigation produced two structures, one of which included Service, Organization, Business, Technology, and Outdoor. The second structure included Business, Service, General Culture, and Science. Neither system could accommodate Arts and Entertainment, but at the same time, both structures included Business and Service. Three replications produced the same results. One must conclude that, in general, Roe's two-dimensional system may have considerable validity as an overall representation of the world of work, both horizontally by area, and vertically by level. Further, as one might logically suppose, some of the areas and levels can be more clearly circumscribed than others.

The *World of Work Map for Job Families* is another example of a two-dimensional plan that facilitates understanding the relationships between occupations.[24] This proposal has developed from the research conducted by the American College Testing Program, which indicated that there are two fairly independent sets of dimensions involved in most work activities. These bipolar dimensions include a data/ideas continuum and a people/things continuum. By using one of these sets for a horizontal axis and another for a vertical axis, it is possible to visualize a "map" on which each occupational group can be plotted according to the coordinates obtained from the two bipolar continua. Thus, occupations involving considerable involvement with people and with data would be plotted in a quadrant opposite that occupied by occupations involving major contact with things and ideas; similarly, occupations involving great use of data and only moderate contact with people or things would lie opposite occupations with emphasis on ideas and only moderate contact with people or things. As the research has progressed, the "map" has been divided into 13 "regions." Twelve of these represent 30° sectors of the circle, and the 13th region is a centralized area reflecting no major relationship to any of the four extremes. The regions on the "map" can then be related to the various job clusters and job families that we considered earlier in this chapter. Two job families (X—Personal and Household Services and Y—Law Enforcement and Protective Services) are not presently plotted on the "map." The nature of these two groups might suggest a relatively weak cohesive interest, with the result that it would be difficult to assign either to one or two specific regions.

Figure 7–1 presents the *World of Work Map for Job Families*. Although specific points are plotted to represent the various job families, it should be obvious that each cluster really occupies an area, not a specific point. Thus, many job families actually may overlap into another ad-

FIGURE 7–1. *World of Work Map for Job Families.*

From: *World of Work Map For Job Families* © 1975 by the American College Testing Program.

jacent region. The plotted points must be considered to represent a general area and are not highly specific.

Closely related to the *World of Work Map* is the *Map of College Majors* also developed by American College Testing Program staff members.[25] This concept provides a means for plotting college majors along the two bipolar dimensions of people/things and data/ideas. Both "maps" are parts of the *Career Planning Program, Grades 8–11.* Figure 7–2 presents the *Map of College Majors.*

Super has proposed a classifying system that uses a field and level approach for two dimensions, but he adds a third dimension that he labels "Enterprise." [26] The added dimension covers the industrial fields in which

FIGURE 7–2. *Map of College Majors*

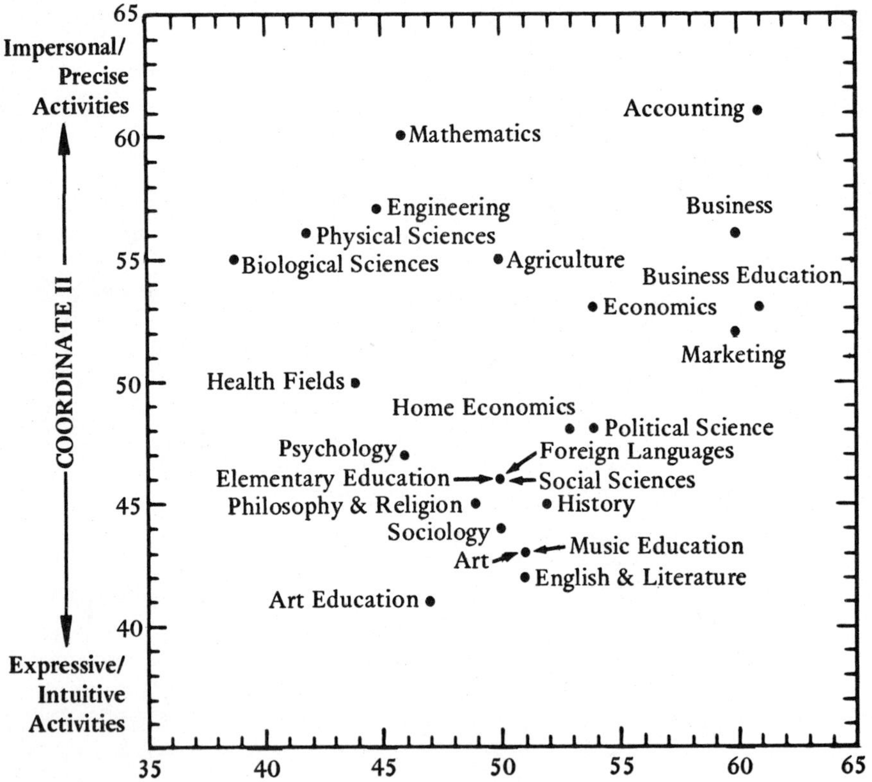

From: *Map of College Majors* (Student Profile Report) (Iowa City, Iowa: American College Testing Program, 1975).

jobs are found, such as agriculture, mining, construction, manufacture, trade, finance, transport, services, and government. The system can be visualized as a three-dimensional solid, eight categories wide (fields), six categories high (levels), and nine categories deep (enterprises). The third dimension is useful in illustrating that many jobs occur in different work settings or industries—in fact, that many industries are large and varied enough to include great numbers of different occupations. Within the classroom or counseling room this added span may generate further insights that help students to visualize work structure more broadly. Often, though, the two-dimensional system provides an adequate framework.

CLASSIFICATION BY INDUSTRY

Thus far, we have considered the world of work primarily from the standpoint of what the worker does—an occupational approach. Major attention has been given to that view of the world of work since we are usually more concerned with what the worker does than with where he works. Before we leave the subject of classification, it is appropriate to consider that the world of work also can be subdivided into categories or areas based, not on the specific tasks of the worker, but on the broader perspective of the work setting in which we find the various occupations—an industrial approach. Super's three-dimensional classification system, mentioned just above, includes as its third dimension the idea of enterprise. This roughly translates into the industrial classification and emphasizes that it is sometimes important to recognize that this dimension adds useful data.

Three classification systems include a consideration of industry. These include the *Dictionary of Occupational Titles* and the *Decennial Census Data*, both of which we have already considered, and the *Standard Industrial Classification*.

The *Standard Industrial Classification* provides an important base for much statistical data published by various governmental agencies.[27] This system provides eleven major classifications of industry, which, in turn, are divided further into 84 major groups. The major groups break into groups of closely related industries, which, in turn, subdivide into industries. Examples of the major classifications are: (1) Agriculture, forestry, and fisheries; (2) Manufacturing; and (3) Finance, insurance, and real estate.

In this chapter, we have examined several classification systems that are widely used. Each has particular advantages and disadvantages. They are important to teachers, counselors, and others because they provide a frame of reference that is helpful in understanding occupations and relationships between occupations. This, of course, is an essential ingredient in career education and career counseling.

NOTES

1. G. I. Swanson, "Career Education," in *Career Education: Perspective and Promise*, K. Goldhammer and R. E. Taylor, (eds), (Columbus, Ohio: Charles E. Merrill Publishing Company, 1972), p. 113.
2. U.S. Department of Health, Education, and Welfare, *Career Education*. HEW Publication No. (OE) 72–39, 1971.
3. American College Testing Program, *Career Planning Program, Grades 8–11* (Boston: Houghton Mifflin Company, 1974).
4. American College Testing Program, *Handbook User's Guide and Summary of Research for Career Planning Program, Grades 8–11.* (Boston: Houghton Mifflin Company, 1974), pp. 8–9.
5. *Strong-Campbell Interest Inventory.* (Stanford, California: Stanford University Press, 1974).
6. J. L. Holland, *The Self-Directed Search* (Palo Alto, Calif.: Consulting Psychologists Press, Revised 1974).
7. S. Greene, J. Priebe, and R. Morrison, "The 1970 Census of Population Occupation Classification System," *Statistical Reporter*, no. 70–76 (December, 1969), pp. 77–84.
8. F. W. Taussig, *Principles of Economics*, 1st ed. (New York: The Macmillan Co., 1911), vol. 2, ch. 47.
9. R. O. Beckman, "A New Scale for Changing Occupational Rank," *Personnel Journal*, vol. 13, no. 1 (1934–1935), pp. 25–33.
10. A. M. Edwards, *Population: Comparative Occupational Statistics for the United States, 1870–1940* (Washington: U.S. Government Printing Office, 1943).
11. T. Caplow, *The Sociology of Work* (Minneapolis: University of Minnesota Press, 1954), pp. 42–43.
12. R. Centers, *The Psychology of Social Classes* (Princeton, N.J.: Princeton University Press, 1949), p. 49.
13. F. E. Barr, "A Scale for Measuring Mental Ability in Vocations," (unpublished Master's thesis, Stanford University, 1918).
14. D. Fryer, "Occupational-Intelligence Standards," *School and Society*, vol. 16 (September, 1922), pp. 273–277.
15. N. Stewart, "A.G.C.T. Scores of Army Personnel Grouped by Occupation," *Occupations*, vol. 26, no. 1 (June, 1947), pp. 1–37.
16. D. Fryer and E. J. Sparling, "Intelligence and Occupational Adjustment," *Occupations*, vol. 12, no. 1 (October, 1934), pp. 55–63.
17. D. E. Super, *The Dynamics of Vocational Adjustment* (New York: Harper & Row, Publishers, 1942), p. 57.
18. T. W. Harrell and M. S. Harrell, "Army General Classification Test Scores for Civilian Occupations," *Educational and Psychological Measurement*, vol. 5, no. 4 (Winter, 1945), pp. 229–239.
19. D. G. Paterson, C. Gerken, and M. E. Hahn, *The Minnesota Occupational Rating Scales and Counseling Profile* (Chicago: Science Research Associates, Inc., 1953).
20. B. J. Dvorak, "Differential Occupational Ability Patterns," *Bulletin of the Minnesota Stabilization Research Institute*, vol. 3, no. 8 (1934).

21. M. E. Hahn and M. S. MacLean, *General Clinical Counseling in Educational Institutions* (New York: McGraw-Hill, Inc., 1950), pp. 73–87.
22. A. Roe, *The Psychology of Occupations* (New York: John Wiley & Sons, Inc., 1956), pp. 143–152.
23. E. I. Meir, "Empirical Test of Roe's Structure of Occupations and an Alternative Structure," *Journal of Counseling Psychology*, vol. 17, no. 1 (January, 1970), pp. 41–48.
24. G. Hanson, *ACT Research Report 67: Assessing the Career Interests of College Youth: Summary of Research and Applications.* (Iowa City, Iowa: American College Testing Program, 1974).
25. *Map of College Majors* (Student Profile Report). (Iowa City, Iowa: American College Testing Program, 1975).
26. D. E. Super, *The Psychology of Careers* (New York: Harper & Row, Publishers, 1957), p. 48.
27. U.S. Executive Office of the President, Office of Management and Budget, *Standard Industrial Classification Manual.* (Washington, D.C.: U.S. Government Printing Office, 1972).

PART III   Supplementary Learning Experiences

The following activities are proposed as ways in which the reader can easily test, explore, or apply the concepts and insights presented in Part III. The list is not intended to be exhaustive or comprehensive, but merely suggestive.

1. Select a specific occupation and attempt to identify a job family based on it.
2. Develop either the pro or con position for the following statement: Socioeconomic factors are still a viable base for classifying occupations.
3. Set up a hierarchy of occupations similar to intellectual demands using as a base social skills, physical strength, etc.
4. Using such classification systems as the Cubistic System, Primary Focus of Activity, or the *Map of the World of Work,* assign a random list of occupations to categories.
5. Using a unitary classification of occupations such as prestige level or average income, attempt to fit the list into a two- or three-dimensional system, such as the cubistic plan.   Try to account for any discrepancies.
6. Develop a lesson plan and learning materials for teaching the use of the *Dictionary of Occupational Titles* to a class at junior or senior high school.
7. Develop a lesson plan and learning materials for teaching the Cubistic system or the *World of Work Map for Job Families* to adolescents.
8. Develop plans for a group session aimed at developing increased understanding of the world of work through use of a classification system.

PART

IV

Preparing For
and Entering
the World of Work

8

Post-Secondary Educational Systems

Career education advocates envision education as a lifelong process with the individual moving back and forth from education to work to education to work again, and even, at times, combining the two. Certainly most astute viewers of the American scene would argue that the old concept of "commencement" as the end of education and the beginning of life is gone forever. The increasing complexity of life in our society, especially the impact of technological developments, requires every worker to keep abreast of change in some way. Furthermore, the changes are broader and require more than just routine up-dating—new jobs appear, old fields melt away, or are combined with others. Workers who need education to qualify originally for employment also must continue education to maintain their qualification, to master new procedures or developments, and to move to new fields that offer greater opportunity.

Time was, at least in the myths of earlier days, when the educational world was neatly compartmentalized. Only those few individuals pursuing the so-called "learned" professions went on to college or university, and high school graduation opened the door to almost every available occupation. Postcollegiate preparation in a professional or graduate school is commonly required today in many professions, and some type of postsecondary education is an admission requirement in many fields.

In this chapter, we will consider the various types of educational institutions that are involved in preparing workers. Most of these, but certainly not all, presume that the applicant has already completed a secondary school program. The lines of demarcation have become increasingly blurred in recent years, and it is no longer easy to separate the array of educationl institutions into clear-cut categories. Degree-granting institutions, which usually have had a high level of stability, are in the process of change. Even the hallowed idea of the traditional four-year program for the bachelor's degree is being re-evaluated since the recent recommendation by the Carnegie Commission that the degree be based on three years of study. Some degree-granting institutions now provide two-year programs or other specialized options that are even shorter. Many two-year schools offer plans that permit the student to transfer to a degree program, as well as a course of study that may directly parallel that offered in a trade school.

The categories we are using in this chapter must be viewed as approximations that have a loose, general fit but are not suitable for clearly classifying all institutions. We will consider the following groups:

Colleges and universities
Nonbaccalaureate schools
Community colleges/Junior colleges
Trade and vocational schools

COLLEGES AND UNIVERSITIES

From the early colonial beginnings of this country, there has been a continuing and increasing emphasis on the acquisition of as much formal education as possible. The history of our national development is studded with events that demonstrate this trend—including the founding of colleges almost with the beginning of the colonies, the "old deluder Satan" act of the Massachusetts Bay Colony establishing compulsory schooling in the towns,[1] the Northwest Ordinance providing land for support of local schools,[2] the Morrill Act establishing land grant colleges and universities,[3] the Kalamazoo decision endorsing tax support for secondary schools,[4] and the GI Bill, which has sent thousands of veterans on to higher education[5]— to name only a few.

As our society has increased in complexity and become more dependent on technological development, the need for education beyond minimal levels also has become more apparent. Although the legal school-leaving age is still set at fifteen or sixteen in most states, the majority of youngsters now stay in school beyond this point. The proportion completing high school has increased steadily—in recent years doubling almost every decade. Not too long ago, the high school graduate was considered to have a very real educational advantage on entering the labor market, and many employers gave priority in hiring to such individuals. More recently, high school graduation is considered as minimal educational preparation, and the person who desires to be in a position of advantage in the labor market now thinks of further preparation beyond high school.

We can expect the school-leaving age to continue to rise in all industrialized societies, since the increasing complexity of living makes more education for the typical citizen imperative. Further, the old idea of "completing one's education with graduation from high school or college" is now obsolete. The impact of technology on the world of work will emphasize a pattern in which individuals regularly return to school for either new or refresher training.

During the decades of the 1950's and 1960's, enrollments in colleges and universities increased regularly and in some institutions rapidly. This expansion was caused, in part, by the increased emphasis on the importance of advanced education as well as by the postwar baby boom that followed World War II. By the mid-1970's, the high school graduating classes had begun to decrease, thus partially reducing the pressure on higher educational institutions. Although the general recognition of advantages accruing with advanced education has continued, some changes in perception appear to be developing that are bringing further adjustments to colleges and universities. By the early 1970's, the student activist movement had faltered and had begun to decline; nevertheless, its search for alternative life styles and alternative educational patterns had a residual effect.[6] Many high school graduates are now including in their educational plans the option of delaying the start of college or interrupting their college program to engage in work or travel. Some colleges are proposing programs that facilitate "laying out" after the second year. The expansion of educational programs in community colleges and in other settings has had an impact on the traditional four-year, residential colleges and universities. Declining enrollments, linked with rapidly increasing instructional costs, may produce further changes, and some degree-granting schools may find it necessary to reorganize or even close by the late 1970's. Except for isolated cases of continued growth, the tremendous clamor for admission to colleges, heard everywhere a decade ago, has subsided. Many schools will elect to meet changing circumstances in different ways—by eliminating programs, launching new programs, moving to open admissions, or restricting enrollments.[7]

Kinds of Programs

The myriad of degree programs extant in colleges and universities has developed in many ways from numberless roots. Some of these, like Topsy, have "just growed"; others have originated from legislated prescriptions, pressures of professional groups, public insistance, or national emergencies. Higher education in America has followed a pattern permitting more flexibility and more breadth than ordinarily encountered in the rest of the world. One result has obviously been greater variations in the nature and quality of educational programs as well as in size and organization of the institutions. Because of this dispersion, any general statement is subject to exceptions in one or many schools.

In general, programs leading to a bachelor's degree are most frequently about four years in length. Recent years have shown movement in both directions from that base point with programs in some technical areas, such as pharmacy or engineering, tending to climb upward toward five years. At the same time, there has been increasing pressure to recognize the improved quality of secondary education in America by reducing the bachelor's degree to a three-year program. Advocates of this proposal were recently heartened when the Carnegie Commission endorsed this plan. Bersi reports on 243 such institutions that had shortened degree programs in 1973.[8]

Unlike most of the rest of the world, American colleges and universities view college study as a cumulative process with students earning credits, course by course, on a time period base that may be a quarter, semester, term, or trimester. Degrees are most frequently granted when the requisite number of credits has been attained with a satisfactory level of quality. Most institutions use a letter-grading system, some use a numerical system, and a very few, usually small colleges, use a narrative report system. The pass/fail grading system has been adopted by very few schools on "an across the board" basis; however, many schools use it as an adjunct or supplementary plan, permitting students to take a restricted number of hours, ordinarily outside of their basic program, with pass/fail grades.

Programs may range from the broad, liberal arts option originally developed to produce the "educated man" in early American colleges to the narrow, intense, professional preparation requiring almost all of the student's allotted schedule. Most matriculations fall between these extremes and provide that part of the student's time be devoted to broad, foundational, or enriching study and part of the work be focused on a subject or area major or professional specialty. Except in those programs controlled by law, licensure or certification requirements, or professional organizations, the degree of variation is probably greater than most people realize. The plan used at "alma mater" is not necessarily the pattern accepted universally.

Admissions Requirements

The restriction of admission by a school, either because of its desire to maintain a student body size that it considers desirable or because it wishes to limit its faculty or facilities, at once creates a competition among applicants. If the school has a generally favorable reputation the competitive-ness is accentuated and the school's "prestige" status is enhanced. Unfortunately, many prospective applicants and their parents assume that limitation of enrollment automatically reflects a quality educational program. Often one can find academic opportunities of equal quality at nearby public or private institutions that have not yet enforced limited admission policies. Hills, Gladney, and Klock have discussed several issues related to selective admission.[9] They point out that many institutions admit on the basis of predicted success, thus utilizing some prediction formula, often based on high school rank, college admissions tests, and other data.

Again, generalizations are risky. Different institutions are moving in opposite directions on admission policies for various reasons. Some schools are establishing enrollment ceilings as a means of maintaining what the school views as an ideal size for its purpose, faculty, and facilities. Often, when such ceilings are set, admission requirements may become more specific in order to narrow the range of clientele served by the school. Other institutions have moved in exactly the opposite direction with some schools now adhering to a policy of open admissions, under which anyone with a high school diploma or other basic qualification may be permitted to enroll. Many institutions, even before the recent emphasis on career education, had established means by which individuals whose schooling had been earlier interrupted at high school graduation, or before, could qualify for admission on the basis of significant employment, examination results, or other criteria. For the most part, it seems that higher education is in a period of opening up, increasing flexibility, and recognizing a broader array of publics to be served.

For many years, a number of colleges and universities have asked applicants to submit information on examination results as a part of their application materials. With the recent rapid expansion in the quantity of applicants, many additional schools, including junior colleges as well as four-year schools, are now requiring test results. It is reasonable to assume that the list of schools that require this information will continue to increase.

Colleges and universities require test scores for many reasons. Most large schools serve students who are drawn from wide geographic regions, often nationwide or worldwide. In such a broad area, considerable difference in academic standards of high schools can be anticipated; as a result, high school grades are difficult to compare, and the college or university may elect to require test scores in order to provide some uniform basis on which applicants' potential ability can be compared. Other schools may seek to serve a particular type of student. For example, they may choose to focus on the development of writing skill; such schools would be anxious to identify those students who have high verbal skill. Some schools, in which enrollment restrictions limit the number of students, may wish to give priority to only the most able students; such a school may feel that a uniform testing program will provide the information it needs to select the students it wishes to admit. On the other hand, some schools may wish to diversify the group it admits and may use test results as an additional means of assuring the variety it wishes to include in its student body.[10] Many schools base their financial aid programs on consideration of ability, and thus require scholarship applicants to submit test scores for this purpose.

Because the use of testing programs is likely to expand rapidly in the years ahead, it is imperative that teachers and counselors who discuss college plans with high school students be familiar with the general operation of such programs. In this way, students can be informed of the necessary procedures in sufficient time to meet the requirements of the colleges and universities in which they are interested. Two widely used programs—the College Entrance Examination Board program (CEEB) and the American College Testing program (ACT)—will be considered briefly here. Approximately 850 schools now require a CEEB examination, and about 500 others require the ACT. A sizable number permit the student to submit results from either examination program.

The Scholastic Aptitude Test, administered by the CEEB, is completed by many candidates for college admission each school year. The examination takes about three hours and measures verbal and mathematical abilities. The verbal portion of the test focuses on ability to read with understanding and to reason with verbal material. The mathematical portion emphasizes reasoning ability with various kinds of problems. Test items in both portions are multiple-choice. The scores are based on a range from 200 to 800, with a standard deviation of 100 and a standard error of measurement of about thirty points. The different administrations of the test are equated to provide for the time differential; thus students who take the test in a late administration do not have an advantage that otherwise might occur. The test is normally taken during the senior year, although many juniors also take it. Studies show that an average gain of about thirty points can be expected between a junior and senior administration; individual students, of course, may vary widely in either direction from this average.

The Preliminary Scholastic Aptitude Test is a modified version of the Scholastic Aptitude Test developed for guidance use with high school juniors. It is a two-hour, multiple-choice examination, providing scores ranging from 20 to 80 in parallel with the 200–800 range of the SAT. This test was developed to provide juniors with an indication of the kinds of scores they are likely to make on the SAT, a year before the SAT is usually taken. Thus, three years of high school grades and PSAT scores can be used by the student, with the help of his/her counselor or teachers, to begin to develop realistic plans for college. This permits the time needed to acquire information about the schools in which the student is interested and to evaluate more precisely possibilities for admission and for success if admitted. Since the CEEB publishes information provided by participating schools showing the distribution of entering freshmen classes according to class rank, residence, and SAT scores, the student can use these materials with available personal data in the evaluation.

College Board Achievement Tests cover the following subjects:

English
    English composition
    Literature
History and social studies
    American history and social studies
    European history and world cultures
Mathematics
    Mathematics level I
    Mathematics level II
Foreign languages
    French, German, Russian and Spanish
    Hebrew
    Latin
Sciences
    Biology
    Chemistry
    Physics

The College Board Achievement Tests on this list are administered about five times each year. Each test is one hour in length. The tests are designed to measure knowledge of facts about the subject and ability to reason with those facts to solve problems appropriate to the subject area. The language tests measure vocabulary and syntax. Scores, like those of the SAT, are standardized on a range of 200 to 800. The Achievement Tests required by a particular school may vary considerably; thus, the student should check with the prospective schools to determine which tests should be taken. Some colleges and universities use other forms of the CEEB Achievement Tests for placement purposes, to determine appropriate courses or sections in which the student should start his college work. When so used, the tests are given by the individual school at the beginning of the academic year.

The College Level Examination Program is one method used by many colleges and universities to determine if an applicant qualifies for advance standing and college credit. The program consists of a group of achievement tests more difficult than those we have just discussed. The basic assumption of this program is that there are many ways in which an applicant might acquire the knowledge or competencies taught in beginning level college courses. Many high schools now provide advanced study for highly motivated students; some students undertake self-teaching projects because of interest or other reasons; tutorial assistance may push other students beyond the levels usually accomplished in high school; and some students may acquire these skills through travel, employment, or other out-of-school activity. Assuming that many colleges would willingly recognize such claims for advance standing as legitimate if properly documented, the CEEB established the CLEP plan. This program enables the student to move ahead to an appropriate level in those areas in which advance skill has been developed and to obtain credit for the by-passed courses. CEEB reports at least two separate studies demonstrating that students given CLEP advanced standing do as well or better in advanced courses as students who have completed the usual prerequisite courses.

The College Scholarship Service is another program operated by the CEEB. This service is designed to simplify the process of providing family financial information to colleges and universities by applicants for financial aid. It provides a Parents' Confidential Statement that the applicant's parent completes, describing the family's financial situation. The report is analyzed by the CSS and a copy of the form and the analysis are forwarded to the schools specified by the applicant. With an increasing number of schools considering financial need in their determination of students to receive aid, the service reduces the number of forms that must be completed by the families of those students applying. This service is used by scholarship program sponsors as well as by financial aid officers in colleges and universities.

The American College Testing Program is an admissions, scholarship, guidance, and placement test battery.[11] It consists of four tests, each about forty-five minutes in length, covering English, mathematics, the social studies, and the natural sciences. The total score provides a general estimate of ability to succeed in college, and scores on the English and mathematics sections also can be used for placement. The English test is primarily concerned with appropriateness and effectiveness of expression. The mathematics test focuses on general mathematical reasoning ability and familiarity with the skills and concepts taught in high school mathematics. The other two tests check ability to reason and to solve problems in the social studies and natural sciences, as well as knowledge of sources of information related to these two fields.

The ACT scores are reported to the schools specified by the student. Scores are reported for each section and for the composite, with standard scores ranging from 1 to 36, with a mean of approximately 17.4 and a standard deviation of about 6.4. The norm sample is based on twelfth-graders across the country. The norms for administration later in the year are adjusted to equate them to the early administration, to provide for the increases in scores that would be expected on the later tests.

In addition to the examination portion, the ACT Assessment Program includes a questionnaire section that provides supplementary self-reported data about the student. These items include the rank order of factors the student considers important to college choice; the student's special educational needs and interests; the student's self-reported subject grades, high school rank, and grade-point index; extracurricular activities; and optional background information.

Both CEEB and ACT have developed profile sheets, explanatory booklets, and other information that can be easily used and properly understood by students and their parents. In addition, both provide reporting systems for counselors and college admissions offices that provide high quality information in an extremely usable format.

Although there has been some recent decline in the number of institutions requiring applicants to submit either SAT or ACT scores, there is likely to be a reversal of this trend in the near future. Recent legislation, frequently referred to as "the Buckley Amendment," now requires that all materials in a student's record be open to the student or his/her parents. Unless specifically waiving the right, the student can read each recommendation, faculty comment, or similar written data forwarded to the institution to which the student is applying. One can expect that the result will be recommendations consisting primarily of bland generalizations rather than the more specific and descriptive statements frequently found before the legislation became effective in October, 1974.

Factors To Consider In Choosing a College

School administrators, teachers, and counselors can anticipate a greater demand for accurate, usable information about college preparation in the years ahead. Inevitably, concerned students and parents will expect greater effort by the secondary school to assist its graduates in preparing for college and in gaining admission. This will likely require planning over a longer period as well as developing more extensive information about available institutions and greater staff involvement in the transitional process.[12] If we add to the picture the factors of greater mobility in our population and the rapidity of change that will occur in the colleges, the complexity of the problem is accentuated even more.

Since institutions of higher education come in an almost limitless variety of size, kind, and purpose, one can find almost as many individual differences here as among people. One can properly conclude, then, that specific schools will better fit the particular needs of certain students than will others. If an appropriate matching process is to occur, accurate information is imperative.

Many high school students assume that there is one perfect college that exactly fits their needs and personality. Such a romantic notion is comparable to similar ideas on finding the one perfect mate that often are prevalent in the same age group. It is more likely that for most individuals there are several colleges or universities that will suit each equally well.

Berdie has pointed out that universities are very complex institutions and often students in the same school may view it quite differently.[13] Ivey, Miller, and Goldstein also have reported different perceptions of the college situation by staff and students.[14]

Even a student who is motivated to make careful educational plans may feel frustrated when confronted with an array of educational institutions numbering in the thousands and varying in many important characteristics that can have tremendous effects on the future. Just as the occupational world is too vast to consider job by job, so, too, is the range of colleges and universities. Some methodical approach is necessary to help the student understand the educational world. Since it can be assumed that it is impossible to study every school, some procedure must be applied that will help identify certain institutions for careful consideration.

Although the selection of a few schools for final consideration by a specific student depends on a great many factors, several general characteristics can be used in reducing the number of schools to be studied in detail. Among these are the following:

1. *Size*—Institutions vary in size from less than 100 students to giant urban universities with enrollments of 80,000 students. Usually schools can be divided into three general groups—small (those with less than 1,000 students), medium (1,000 to about 4,000), and large (over 4,000).
2. *Type of school*—A school may be tax-supported, church-supported, or independent of both church and state.
3. *School environment*—The location of the school by geographic region may be of importance because of distance from home or other factors. Similarly, another consideration is whether the school is located in an essentially rural area, a small city, or a metropolitan area.
4. *Admission requirements*—Some institutions may attempt to control their size by increasing admission requirements; others may limit their services to particular groups of prospective students. In the past, tax-supported institutions have usually been able to accept most applicants from accredited high schools in their governmental areas.
5. *Type of student body*—Some schools enroll only men, others only women, others are coeducational.
6. *Expenses and financial aid available*—The cost of higher education varies extensively.[15] Generally, costs will be lower in a tax-supported school than in a private school. There are, of course, many exceptions to this situation, especially when private schools receive generous help from a church affiliation or other supporting body. One must consider not only basic tuition charges, but also such items as living expenses, additional fees, and travel expenses. Some schools, with relatively high tuition fees, provide numerous endowment and scholarship programs that may materially reduce total costs. Others have work programs that enable a student to earn a major portion of the funds needed. Loan funds from which a student may borrow are becoming increasingly available at many schools.

7. *Type of program*—One of the first items for a student to consider is preference for a general education or a specialized education. If primarily interested in a broad general education, he/she will find this available in the majority of higher educational institutions in this country. If, however, the student is interested in combining this with some specialization or wishes the major study to be specialized, this factor becomes quite important. No university offers a complete range of specialization. If the student has settled on one particular subject area, he/she must look closely to determine what schools have the specialized program. Failure to do so can be costly in both time and money, since a transfer to another school for a specialized program may well result in a loss of credits and a lack of needed prerequisites for the program desired. The variety of course offerings, in both breadth and depth, may be important to many students whose interests are other than general in nature. The extent of accreditation also should be considered.

8. *Student-faculty ratio*—In the past, this ratio has often been used to provide a rough index of the amount of individual assistance that might be available to the prospective student. In many ways this is a most deceptive item and is probably of very limited value. Some programs can be handled more effectively when the number of students per faculty member is relatively high; other programs, because of their nature, require a much lower ratio. Computation of the figure is also difficult since one cannot tell if the student figure is based on full-time students only, equivalent full-time students, or total enrolled students; similarly, the faculty figure may include administrative staff, research staff, or others whose teaching involvement may be minimal or none. Even if these problems in computation could be resolved, it is still difficult to evaluate whether a student-faculty ratio of 10 to 1 where the faculty member is a beginning instructor is better than one of 20 to 1 where the teacher is a recognized authority in the field. With increased enrollments and greater utilization of such techniques as closed-circuit television, team teaching, and programmed learning, one can expect this index to become less important as an evaluative device.

9. *Student activities and social life*—The small, rural boarding school may provide a total program of activities, since the student's entire day is spent in the institutional environment. Other schools, at the opposite extreme, may operate primarily as day schools, without any provision of living or recreational facilities and other out-of-class activities. Most schools fall somewhere near the middle of this continuum.[16] Obviously, schools vary in the extent to which they accept responsibility or encourage student activities and social life as a part of the total college life of the student. Students also vary in the extent to which such programs are important to them.

10. *Campus facilities*—Although it is possible for a small school to provide a really outstanding education in the most rudimentary plant, and for a school with luxurious accommodations to offer only a mediocre learning experience, this usually does not happen. Certainly there are minimal levels of adequacy that bear directly on the school's ability to perform its educational function. Unless the needed tools, equipment,

and buildings are available, the program will probably be impaired to some extent.

Many additional factors can be considered by the student in the preliminary selection process. In some cases, such items as the availability of military training, extent of campus housing, fraternities and sororities, placement facilities, and the success of graduates may be of greater importance than the items enumerated above. Certainly there are particular items that may be of relatively less importance to a specific student. Probably one of the first factors for a student to decide is the type of education desired; then he/she should decide which of the items above, or others, apply to the situation. These selected factors then can be utilized in completing the preliminary screening.

Accreditation

Much of our time is spent in a world in which regulation and control are very obvious, as in speed limits, vehicle inspection stickers, building permits, social security numbers, and consumer protection agencies. We sometimes forget the ancient warning of *caveat emptor*. The undertaking of a commitment to a college education, in terms of time, effort, and money, is so great that both student and parent need to be more fully assured that value will be received than is usually the case. Accreditation is one means by which the potential purchaser of a college education can have some assurance about the quality of the purchase.

Accreditation of colleges and universities is usually accomplished by two different kinds of organizations. In some academic areas, programs are evaluated by established groups or agencies formed by the appropriate professional organization into which graduates of the program ultimately will be received. The second type of accrediting agency is an association of educational institutions organized on a geographic basis, either national or regional. The National Council for the Accreditation of Teacher Education (NCATE) is an example of the first type and the North Central Association of Colleges and Secondary Schools is an example of the second type.

Many prospective students or their parents raise questions to counselors about the ranking of a college or university or of a specific department or section within the school. It is often difficult to convince them that such rankings are not made by the accrediting agencies or other national groups. Generally, the accrediting groups simply list schools that meet certain levels of standards. Occasionally, this listing is arranged into appropriate groupings related to the scope of the program, the areas included, or similar factors, but a numerical listing in order of quality is seldom made. The variety of programs among schools, even in highly specialized subject areas, precludes the possibility of such ranking in terms of quality.

Public conviction that such rankings exist stems primarily from two sources. Many loyal alumni remember their alma mater as "the best in the country," "tops in such and such," or "highly recognized." Such evaluation is, of course, subjective and not based on comparative criteria. Secondly, many popular magazines, newspapers, and Sunday supplements run feature stories based on the judgment of a single person or a panel of "experts" who often purport to evaluate the relative quality of institutions in various subject fields and by type of school or other category. Again, the published judgments may be made by individuals who are highly knowledgeable and who have a wide acquaintance with many schools; nevertheless, the reports are subjective in nature and not based on detailed study of the type and scope that justify a precise ranking.

Accreditation must be understood by the prospective student. The accreditation process is usually quite involved, relatively expensive, and highly demanding of large amounts of faculty time to prepare materials, reports, and other studies for review. If a school has been accredited by a recognized agency, this indicates that the school has demonstrated to the satisfaction of that agency that it meets the minimum standards established by the agency. If the school is not accredited, one cannot automatically assume that it falls short of the minimum standards. There are sometimes valid reasons why a school with high quality and standards is not accredited, including the desire of the school to maintain a position of independence, the newness of the program, or a reluctance to expend the time and funds required to establish accreditation.

Financial Aid

With the cost of higher education continuing to rise, more people want to know about sources of financial assistance available to students or prospective students.[17] Each college or university has an established office or appointed official responsible for this phase of its operation. Almost every school has some type of financial assistance available to its students, and information about such resources can be obtained directly from the school itself.

In addition to the financial aid programs administered by a specific school, there have appeared in recent years an increasing number of scholarships not directly committed to a specific institution. It is usually much more difficult to obtain information about these possible reservoirs of help. One of the most comprehensive sources of information about such aid is *Scholarships, Fellowships, and Loans*[18] by Feingold. Volume 5 of the series appeared in 1971. Each volume includes some revision of information appearing in earlier volumes because of changes that have occurred in programs previously described. The major portion of each volume is devoted to a listing of new sources of aid. The information provided is of obvious value to the school counselor or other person concerned with helping teenagers make appropriate college plans.

Scholarships, Fellowships, Grants and Loans is another publication providing helpful information for counselors and others attempting to aid students who seek financial assistance for college study.[19] This book is part of the College Blue Book series. Its information is not only for the beginning college student but also for advanced students at every level up to the post-doctorate. Further examples of publications of this type include the National Register of Scholarships and Fellowships[20] and Barron's Handbook of American College Financial Aid.[21] Feingold also has published a bibliography of financial aid information called Student Aid Planning in the Space Age: A Selected Bibliography.[22]

Recent federal legislation has underwritten a program entitled Basic Educational Opportunity Grants. Participants must be at least half-time students. The grants are open to eligible students enrolled in college, vocational, and technical schools. The amount provided each grantee varies. In 1975–1976, the average grant was about $800 per student, with a ceiling of $1400. Repayment is not required.

Many high school students assume that the only sources of financial assistance for a college program are their parents or a scholarship program.[23] Schools are changing the procedures for granting scholarships and more and more awards are limited in amount and granted on the basis of need. The expansion of loan funds available to students has helped to offset the restriction of scholarship funds. Students and parents may hesitate to consider loan funds as a means of financing a college education, even though they are probably purchasing a home on this system and may regularly use this procedure to replace the family automobile. With colleges encouraging the use of loan funds, there has been an increase in their use in recent years.

Federal funding has supplied some money to colleges and universities to provide loans to students. The program is revised regularly. In general, the intent is to make available supplementary amounts that will permit students to initiate or continue college-level study when the student does not have sufficient personal financial resources. At present, the program is known as National Direct Student Loans. Eligibility is determined by the college loan officer. The maximum yearly loan for an undergraduate in 1975 was $2,500, with a $5,000 total for the bachelor's degree. Graduate level students have a $10,000 ceiling. Repayment begins nine months after students discontinue their studies and the interest rate is 3 per cent per year.

Local banks often are willing to make educational loans for college attendance. School counselors can easily determine local practice. Several states have established state loan funds or provisions for guaranteeing loans made by local banks. Where state law does not already provide access to such funds, federally insured student loans are available. Maximums are usually $2,500 per year and $7,500 total. The interest rate is usually 7 per cent and repayment begins within a year after discontinuing study.

Most colleges have loan funds of their own, in addition to the federal funds, which they administer. Additional sources of loans include those sponsored by such organizations as church groups, fraternal societies, corporations, and others.

Students should not overlook the possibility that at least a portion of college expenses can be met by their own earnings. The high school student who decides early to go to college has from then until actual entrance to accumulate the funds that will be needed. Summer vacation periods, as well as part-time jobs, offer many opportunities for employment that will permit saving for college. Even though it is probably true that academic standards in college are more demanding than ever of a student's time and effort, there are still many hours per week that could be used to earn part of his/her support. Both college admissions officers and high school counselors frequently advise students against part-time work, especially during the first year in school. The basic intent of such advice, of course, is to encourage the new college student to focus undivided attention on academic adjustment and progress. Nevertheless, there is little evidence to support the position that part-time work interferes with academic progress. Every campus offers numerous opportunities for the student who wishes such help. In addition, the summer vacation period permits many students to accumulate funds to be used in the following year.

Some students may be interested in work-study programs offered by various colleges. In these programs, students alternate periods of full-time study with periods of full-time employment. The basic purpose of the employment is to provide experience related to the field of study; however, the income obtained is obviously of help to the student who is seeking support for study.

External Degree Programs

Career education advocates contend that there should be a close relationship between the formal educational experiences encountered in schools and colleges and those found outside the walls and campuses of those institutions. They point out that it is foolish to assume that the only learning with significance occurs within the classroom, since every individual's experience establishes the truth of the contrary. Finally, inasmuch as significant educational experiences do occur outside the school, should not students receive "credit" or other school recognition for those valuable benefits?

The external degree program recognizes the validity of these arguments and provides a response that is receiving increasing attention across the nation. Although the earliest program appeared almost fifteen years ago, the rapid expansion of these plans has occurred since 1970. By the mid-70's, more than half of the states had one or more institutions with established external degree programs.

The external degree has been defined by Houle in this way: [24]

> An external degree is one awarded to an individual on the basis of some preparation (devised by himself or by an institution) which is not centered on traditional patterns of residential college or university study.

The major portion of a student's work for this degree occurs off campus and in varying ways. The Career Education Project has identified the following benefits of external degree study: [25]

The Assessment and Accreditation of Previous Learning Experiences. External degree programs have established methods for assessing college-level knowledge acquired through formal course work and/or independent learning. For example, a teacher's aide might receive college credits for teaching experience as well as for any special training received.

The Opportunity to Devise and Direct One's Own Study Program. While most external degree programs have basic requirements that influence the nature of the learning that occurs, many programs allow students considerable flexibility in choosing studies that fit their interests, abilities, and goals.

The Flexibility to Learn in a Variety of Educational Settings. External degree programs recognize not only traditional classroom learning but also independent study, field work, on-the-job training, private tutorials, and everyday jobs. This kind of flexibility makes it easier to pursue personal learning interests, to obtain actual experience within your field of academic interest, and to avoid giving up present employment to devote more time to studies.

Flexible Scheduling. Unlike traditional courses in colleges and universities, most external degree study is done off-campus at the student's convenience.

Potentially Inexpensive Education. Depending on the program a student selects, the cost of an external degree can be comparable to or *considerably less than* the cost of a degree at a traditional college. In addition, advanced standing credits can further reduce the cost by decreasing the amount of time required to earn a degree.

Individual Attention. Students in most external degree programs are assigned to or select a faculty advisor with whom they have frequent contact either personally or through correspondence. Such *frequent,* one-to-one academic counseling is often not provided in the traditional system of higher education.

Relatively Open Admissions Policy. One intent of external degree programs is to make higher education available to people who have traditionally been denied access to it. Recognizing that this group of people may qualify in different ways from high-school-age applicants, most programs employ flexible admissions criteria.

Even though the type of program obviously by-passes many of the usual characteristics of traditional college study, it does place a large responsibility on the student. It assumes that the student can organize an individual schedule for learning activities, can continue the learning process without immediate feedback from faculty or other students, can plan a program comprehensive enough to achieve the goals desired, and can locate and use appropriate resources. Clearly, these assumptions require a highly motivated, self-directing, persistent individual.

Many institutions offer external degrees at the associate and bachelor's level. A few offer master's level programs and some even have doctoral programs. Accreditation of these programs varies with the institutions offering them. In many cases, the schools are recognized members of regional accrediting organizations and offer their regular degrees in an external program. This would be a fully accredited program. Other institutions have not held regional accreditation and therefore have not had time to obtain such recognition even if it is being sought. We have previously considered the fact that accreditation may or may not be important in a particular situation.

Just as traditional programs can vary extensively in quality and value, so, too, can external degree programs. In both settings, one major ingredient of quality education is the effort of the individual.

SOURCES OF INFORMATION
ABOUT COLLEGES AND UNIVERSITIES

Obviously, the most precise and up-to-date information about a specific school can be obtained only from the institution itself. Colleges and universities, because of changes in enrollments, rapid advances in science and other fields of learning, and greater financial resources, as well as other causes, are in a turmoil of growth, expansion, revision, and change in general. Consequently, every other source of information must be considered as possibly obsolete because of changes that might have occurred since the data were obtained. The schools are too numerous and the time required to obtain specific answers too long to consider individual contact with each higher educational institution. Once a tentative list of schools has been developed by the prospective student, such contact is essential.

Careful reading and study of the catalog and other publications of each institution is similarly impossible. First, there are probably very few comprehensive collections of all available college catalogs. Secondly, the immense amount of time needed to accomplish such a survey is too much for a single student to undertake. The student should, however, recognize that, next to a direct contact with the school itself, the catalog and other publications are probably the best sources of accurate information—barring changes that have occurred since publication. Further, there are many questions that are likely to occur to an investigating student which even a carefully prepared catalog cannot answer. For example, the bulletin usually will be unable to describe the specific instructors with whom the student will study, the particular nature of the student body, the general life style within which the student will operate, and the overall climate of student attitudes, interests, and expectancies.

Because of the scope of the problem, the prospective student and parents, teachers, and counselor often must rely on secondary sources of information about schools, at least during the preliminary phases of the screening process. This inevitably leads to one of the guides or directories that offer condensed descriptions of the schools, usually including information about the pertinent factors listed above. Although sketchy and incomplete, the data are ordinarily sufficient for preliminary purposes. A number of such guides are available, and copies of several should be found in the high school library and in the counselor's office. Because up-to-date information is crucial, the latest edition always should be used, and always with the caution that even this may be out of date for a specific item concerning a particular school.

State offices of education and the United States Office of Education usually can provide information about available directories, if such information is not found in local library resources. Publishers usually keep school counselors informed of revisions and new publications in this field, since they are the most frequent users. Since many directories serve a specific purpose, they should, in most cases, be considered as supplementary resources. More than one directory should be available in every high school.

To illustrate the variety of directories available, three commonly used volumes will be described briefly.

1. BARRON'S PROFILES OF AMERICAN COLLEGES.[26] This publication is frequently revised and presently consists of two volumes. It appears both in an inexpensive paperback edition as well as a standard hard-cover issue. Information is included for almost 1,500 regionally accredited colleges and universities.

Volume 1 is entitled *Descriptions of the Colleges* and provides brief statements about the following items:

Student Life: Drop-out rates, geographic distribution, racial and religious composition, regulations, activities, etc.

Campus Environment: Size of plant, outstanding facilities, accommodations, library, etc.

Program of Study: Programs, degrees awarded, majors, special programs, three-year degree, required courses, etc.

Costs. Tuition, room and board, books, fees, etc.

Financial Aid: Scholarships, loans, work, how to qualify, etc.

Admissions: SAT and ACT scores of freshmen, required courses and examinations, application procedures, deadlines.

College Selector: Arranges schools by degree of competitiveness.

Volume 2 is entitled *Index to Major Areas of Study* and provides information about the same institutions presented in a different format. Information is arranged according to the following headings:

Program of Study: Majors and concentrations at each school is shown; data are arranged in tabular form.

Alternative Education: Schools offering alternative programs are identified, including those with work-study, independent study, pass/fail, experimental programs, etc.

College Selector: Like Volume I, information is provided showing degree of competitiveness for admission and average annual cost.

The information provided in these two volumes is also arranged in four separate volumes for the Northeast, South, Midwest, and Western regions of the country.

2. LOVEJOY'S COLLEGE GUIDE.[27]   This volume is authored by Clarence E. Lovejoy and is published by Simon and Schuster, Inc.   The author publishes a monthly supplement, which provides information about developments between revisions of the *Guide*.

The major portion of the book includes descriptive material for more than 2,300 institutions of higher education, including practically all of the degree-granting four-year institutions as well as a large number of junior colleges, technical institutions, and special schools.   One helpful section in the volume includes a chapter entitled *Career Curricula—Guidance and Clues*.   This lists institutions offering programs in 435 career fields.

Each included institution is "rated" in one of eight categories, as follows:

1. Senior institutions with regional accreditation.
2. Senior institutions without regional accreditation, but may have approval and recognition of a state university or agency.
J1. Institutions with regional accreditation that do not confer baccalaureate degrees—usually junior, terminal, or community colleges, or technical institutes.
J2. Institutions like those in (J1) without regional accreditation.
G. Graduate institutions.

P. Institutions that might be classified in (2) or (J2) but that have professional accreditation by one or more of the accrediting bodies.

R. Institutions whose student body almost entirely comprises students studying for the Roman Catholic priesthood or as clergy or missionaries of other faiths.

S. Special institutions at the level of higher education with unusual, usually nondegree, programs.

Although the categories described above are listed as "ratings," they are more descriptive of the type or purpose of the school; and the rating category is not necessarily indicative of quality, except in a very general sense.

For institutions in the first two categories, the following information is usually provided:

Rating; name of institution; city; street address; environment, *i.e.*, urban, rural; reference to mileage to nearest well-known center; whether coed; publicly controlled or private; major characteristics, whether liberal arts college, university, technological institute, teacher training, etc.; when established; any previous names or mergers; number of students, men and women; number of volumes in library; faculty-to-student ratio; when freshmen and transfer students are admitted during the year, and whether tests of College Entrance Examination Board or other tests are mandatory or optional, or whether admission is granted on secondary school graduation, transcript, and recommendation; if institution has chapter of Phi Beta Kappa and when established, Tau Beta Pi, Sigma Xi; whether approved by American Association of University Women; accreditation regionally by one of the six constituted bodies; accreditation professionally and by which of the accrediting bodies.

Tuition costs; board and room charges and other institutional costs and fees; typical expenses for a year; whether dormitories, dining halls, and cafeteria are available; whether apartments or trailers, huts, "prefabs," etc., are available for married students; number of national and local fraternities and sororities, and whether students are permitted to live in chapter houses; scholarships, number and/or amount in money; whether participating in College Scholarship Service; loan funds, average loan and interest rate; proportion of students earning all or part of way; noteworthy athletic programs, for instance, whether solely intramural or whether football has been abolished.

Various schools, colleges, and main divisions of the institution; degrees offered, including professional and graduate degrees; whether associate degrees are available for affiliated lower divisions and junior colleges; whether acceleration permits earning degrees in less than four years; whether cooperative, alternating work-and-study programs are utilized, perhaps prolonging degree; new educational programs, unusual developments, and special curricula features; location and distance of subordinate or branch campuses; whether Summer Session is operated and number of weeks; whether institution has Reserve Officers Training Corps of the Army, Navy, and Air Force.

3. AMERICAN UNIVERSITIES AND COLLEGES.[28]   This book is published by the American Council on Education every four years.   Unlike *Lovejoy's Guide,* which includes junior colleges, technical schools, and other varieties of institutions, this volume includes only four-year, bachelor's-degree-granting schools.   About 1,400 institutions are included in the 1973 edition, all of which are accredited by a professional association or by a regional accrediting agency.   The emphasis is toward the student who wishes to earn a bachelor's degree in a usual four-year program.

The volume includes a listing of accredited schools for professional preparation in each of the following areas: Architecture, Art, Business, Chemistry, Dentistry, Dental Hygiene, Engineering, Forestry, Journalism and Communications, Landscape Architecture, Law, Medicine, Allied Medical Services, Health-Related Professions, Music, Nursing, Optometry, Osteopathy, Pharmacy, Psychology, Public Health, Social Work, Speech Pathology and Audiology, Teacher Education, Theology, Veterinary Medicine.

The major portion of *American Universities and Colleges* is devoted to institutional exhibits, which consist of abstracts of materials submitted by the schools themselves in response to a lengthy questionnaire.   The submitted material has been organized into a brief, self-explanatory format. The included information is usually for the academic year previous to the year of publication; in other words, the 1973 volume includes data based essentially on the 1971–72 year.   Fee information is listed for the 1972–73 school year.

The institutional information includes a preliminary descriptive paragraph, which gives some information on origin of the institution, degrees granted, and unique features.   The remainder of the material is included under the following major headings: Accreditation, History, Governing Board, Calendar, Characteristics of Freshmen, Admission, Degree Requirements, Schools and Teaching Staff '71–'72, Special Academic Programs, Graduate Work, Degrees Conferred, Fees '72–'73, Student Financial Aid '71–'72, Enrollment, Foreign Students '71–'72, Student Life, Publications, Library, Finances '71–'72, Buildings and Grounds, Administration.

The section on Divisions and Teaching Staff can be most useful to the prospective student and his teacher or counselor.   Since the staff sizes provide a basis for rough estimate of the general size of the program in that particular division, certainly comparisons within the institution can reasonably be made.   Since the staff is reported by rank—that is, professor, associate professor, assistant professor, instructor, and part-time staff—it is possible to draw some tentative conclusions about the emphasis on the subject in the school, although caution must certainly be used in applying these figures.

Other well known directories that provide comparable information about colleges and universities include *The College Blue Book* [29] and the *Counselors' Comparative Guide to American Colleges.* [30] The first of these is a four-volume publication providing a vast quantity of information; it is also available in regional editions. The second includes schools with programs less than two years in length up to the baccalaureate.

Computer-assisted college selection on a wide scale seems simply a matter of time. The knowledge and technical hardware already exist for the implementation of an effective, nationwide service. Some private programs are already available on a fee basis.

Most presently existing systems have deficiencies in either the range of information about institutions or in the system for obtaining personal information. Improvement of these two aspects under present conditions is costly, and serious efforts toward perfection in either could result in costs that cause the system to be unmarketable. Anticipated refinements in equipment and procedures should provide rapid improvement in the use of this technology with resulting benefits to clients in the immediate future.

Information about colleges and universities can, of course, be obtained from former students and others who may be acquainted with a particular school. Some institutions appoint state or regional representatives from its alumni group to serve as information resources for prospective students.

When a prospective student has selected a group of schools in which he/she feels a genuine interest, he/she should consider visiting each school. Such a trip should, if possible, be completed when the school is in session, to assure some insight into the types of student, the general nature of the school, its typical class procedures, and similar factors that cannot be observed during a vacation period. Only an actual visit to the campus permits evaluation of many factors that are important in making the final choice.

NONBACCALAUREATE SCHOOLS

The greatest change in American education in the last few years has occurred with the rapid expansion of post-secondary schools offering programs shorter than the traditional baccalaureate degree. The major portion of this growth has been the development of community colleges across the country. There also has been an increase in the number of vocational schools. For convenience, we will consider first the community college and junior college and then look at trade and vocational schools.

Community Colleges and Junior Colleges

Junior colleges have existed in this country for many years. Some states, California, for example, have included junior colleges as an integral part of the statewide education program for at least forty years. Of more recent origin is the community college now found in most states. The two institutions are increasingly serving the same purposes and are therefore largely synonymous.

The junior college originally was developed essentially as a downward thrust of the college or university. Often established in populated areas not conveniently close to baccalaureate institutions, the junior college provided a means of delivering the first two years of several degree programs to students who, for varying reasons, could not attend a residential college or university. Since the curriculum consisted largely of introductory, or at least lower level, college courses, it needed neither elaborate facilities nor senior faculty members. Costs were often considerably less than those charged at four-year campuses. The underlying idea was that the increased accessibility and the lesser costs would permit greater numbers of high school graduates to undertake baccalaureate programs, which could then be completed by transfer.

For twenty years after World War II, the expanded interest in college programs added further pressure for the development of new postsecondary opportunities for education. Changing interests, vocational goals, and life styles, as well as increased mobility, new teaching procedures and other factors led to the creation of an institution somewhat different from the junior college. The junior college function of bringing the college or university to "Main Street" was usually incorporated in the structure, but ordinarily as only one part of a broader program serving a much wider segment of the community population. Thus, the community college often is considered to be an upward thrust of the secondary school, incorporating extensive offerings not necessarily leading to the traditional baccalaureate degree. Instead, many community college programs were designed to be terminal in nature, sometimes vocationally oriented, but also based on local needs and interests. Many junior colleges, during the same period, moved to meet more effectively a wider range of local needs, and hence the two titles are now often used almost interchangeably and one would be hard pressed to establish clear-cut differential criteria. Probably they are now more commonly known as community colleges or as two-year colleges.

To illustrate the rate of expansion that has occurred in a brief period by schools of this type, we can note that in 1959 there were 390 accredited, two-year public institutions with a total enrollment of 551,760 students. By 1969, the number of such schools had increased to 794 with an enrollment of 2,051,493. The number of schools had more than doubled and their collective enrollment had expanded nearly four-fold. More than two-thirds of these institutions are public, supported largely by tax funds, either state or local, or some combination of the two. Most of the remaining third are church-supported institutions, and less than 100 are independent, nonprofit schools operating under a self-perpetuating board of trustees.

Whether called community college or junior college, most of the public institutions, as well as most of the independent schools, provide a four-part program that includes: (a) the traditional college-related program for students who plan to transfer to a four-year institution to complete a baccalaureate degree; (b) a technical–terminal program to prepare students to enter employment upon completion of the two-year, or less, curriculum; (c) short courses of various sorts needed locally for retraining or further education; and (d) an adult education program of either formal or informal courses. The church-supported schools normally include the first two types of programs, but less often the latter two. A few of the private schools offer only a two-year liberal arts program that provides for transfer to another institution.

Among the four types of programs, the greatest expansion has been in the technical–terminal area. This growth of the occupationally-oriented part of the curriculum will increase the significance of the institution as a part of the educational plans for students who are not interested in the formal four-year degree programs of the traditional baccalaureate institution. Its significance in the educational structure will be further enhanced as the concepts of career education are more widely adopted. It is entirely logical that this school can be expected to become the local skills center that will provide basic employment competencies through training and/or retraining programs. In some geographic areas, it will assume the role of the area vocational school. The place of the two-year school in American education is now firmly established; one should not expect, however, that these schools will assume a uniform organization, curriculum, or clientele. One of their greatest advantages may well be the flexibility that permits their response to local needs and interests.[31, 32, 33, 34]

The two-year transfer programs and those technical-terminal programs that extend over two academic years customarily provide for the granting of an "Associate in Arts" degree upon satisfactory completion. Programs that ordinarily are completed in less than this amount of time recognize successful completion with a certificate or other credential.

As with baccalaureate institutions, variation in admission requirements is common. Schools offering only college-related programs often may establish entrance requirements parallel to those used by the schools to which their graduates transfer. Technical–terminal programs are more likely to have skill-based or experience-based requirements and unlikely to specify particular academic records as prerequisites for admission. Terminal programs and adult education programs often operate on a totally open admission plan within the community served by the school. As a generalization, admission requirements usually are less stringent in the two-year schools than in the four-year schools, in keeping with the broader educational function of the two-year school.

Factors previously listed for consideration in identifying possible four-year schools for a particular student have less significance for non-baccalaureate institutions. Some students will have a special interest in certain two-year schools with college-related programs for many different reasons, such as church affiliation, family ties, special programs available, geographic location, or other reasons. In these situations, the student may need the same kind of assistance in planning that other college-bound students require. Often the choice may be based on local accessibility or a similar reason, and obtaining the information needed to aid the student may be easy.

Responsibility for accreditation of two-year schools rests primarily with state and regional agencies. Originally, accreditation was focused on the state department of education, the state university, or an organization of colleges within the state. In recent years, there has been a trend toward establishing regional accreditation, and most schools are moving toward such recognition if it has not already been acquired.

Financial aid at institutions that basically emphasize college-related programs is usually structured in a fashion similar to that at four-year schools. Schools that emphasize other programs often have different plans for financial aid of students. Since students who attend two-year schools often reside at home, one of the biggest expenses in college attendance is drastically reduced. Furthermore, because many schools are heavily tax-supported, tuition and fees are frequently modest. Some programs that lead to specific employment opportunities may be further subsidized with private, local, state, or federal funds.

As is true of baccalaureate institutions, the most reliable source of information about any school is the school itself. Direct contact with appropriate officials is most likely to result in up-to-date correct answers to questions. The next best source of information is the bulletin or other publications of the school—also subject to the inevitable time lag and the danger that change has occurred. Finally, there are several guides or directories that bring together information about schools in this group.

Three directories will serve as illustrations of the type of information available about the two-year schools. Other directories also provide similar data.

Lovejoy's College Guide (listed in the previous section of this chapter) includes most two-year schools in the United States.[35] *Lovejoy's* places such schools in one of two categories according to the existence of regional accreditation for the school. The presentation for each school is somewhat briefer than that included for baccalaureate institutions.

Barron's Guide to the Two-Year Colleges is a two-volume publication parallel to the *Profiles of American Colleges*.[36] The first volume (*College Descriptions*) provides basic information about such factors as admission requirements, enrollment figures, religious affiliation, student-teacher ratio, campus size, atmosphere and housing, financial aid, and academic programs. The second volume (*Occupational Program Selector*) arranges information according to program and presents data in tabular form. If the student knows the program in which he/she is interested, this volume permits ready comparison of those institutions offering that program. If he/she knows the names of the schools offering the program of interest, Volume I will supply brief descriptions.

American Junior Colleges, now in its 9th edition, is published by the American Council on Education as a companion volume to *American Universities and Colleges*.[37] The information in each volume is presented in approximately parallel form. In addition to information about such general items as history, control, buildings and grounds, and administration, the following academic items are included: calendar, admission, programs, teaching staff, degrees, special facilities, enrollments, and student life. The presentations also include financial information on fees, student aid, and institutional finances. This volume now includes only institutions that have established at least regional accreditation.

Trade and Vocational Schools

One by-product of the increased emphasis on career education and alternative educational programs has been greater attention focused on vocational preparation. During periods of economic down-turn, high unemployment rates, and general uncertainty, there is a frequent upsurge in vocational school enrollment. Some of this is a search for security or a grasping for any help that might assure employment or even an opportunity for employment.

The increasing importance of specialized, post-high school education has already been discussed; one great change has been the expansion of public education into the field through the community colleges. A technical society, growing constantly more complex, underscores a continuing need for expanded opportunities for such preparation.[38] The increasing emphasis on more varied forms of post-secondary education and the continuing technological thrust of our society undoubtedly will encourage many youth and adults to seek specialized education of one sort or another, often in vocational and technical schools, either public or private.[39]

In many states, the expansion of the community college program or the establishment of publicly supported technical schools has met the major need in specialized education. Such expansion has not been uniform across the nation, however. Some states have established area vocational schools; other states have established programs of post-secondary specialized education through contractual arrangements with local secondary schools, universities, or other agencies equipped to offer vocational training to groups of students. Part of the impetus producing these rapid changes has come from the Vocational Education Amendments enacted by Congress, which broadened and redefined vocational education.

Since we have already considered both four-year and two-year schools in previous sections of this chapter, we are concerned here with schools whose programs generally are shorter than those offered by community colleges. Obviously, there is considerable overlap, since it has already been pointed out that one type of program offered by two-year schools is the short-course program to meet local needs. Having recognized that some four-year schools offer two-year courses and that some two-year schools offer short courses, let us focus our discussion on institutions that cannot properly be placed in the two-year classification. Some schools within the group are publicly supported by local, regional, or state tax units. Most, however, are private, proprietary schools; the extent of this aspect of education is often surprising. Wilms points out that there are more than 10,000 such schools in the United States, enrolling more than 3,000,000 students annually and producing gross revenues beyond $2.5 billion dollars annually.[40]

Obtaining accurate, usable information about a vocational school is often much more difficult than finding similar information about a degree-granting institution.[41] Several reasons contribute to this. Teachers and counselors, having been professionally prepared in colleges and universities, are more aware of the baccalaureate schools. Intercollegiate athletics and other activities publicize the colleges and universities locally, regionally, and nationally. The prestige or status occupations in society mostly require college educations and focus public attention on schools providing such education. In addition, vocational schools usually offer shorter training programs in less conspicuous quarters, have often been in existence for shorter periods, and rarely attract public attention.

Private proprietary vocational schools, like any other type of business, can include establishments that do their best to deliver a quality product for the lowest possible price, shoddy merchandise at exorbitant prices, or something between these two extremes. Belitsky suggests that private vocational schools provide an excellent opportunity for motivating and preparing unemployed older workers who do not expect to be able to return to their former occupations.[42] Ressing, on the other hand, emphasizes the importance of care and caution in dealing with private vocational schools.[43] He urges prospective students, before enrolling for training in such an institution, to check first with potential employers by asking such questions as these:

a. Would you hire graduates of this school?
b. How many did you hire last year?

c. Were they hired because of their training?

d. Did the training make a difference in their starting salary?

Of the approximately 10,000 private proprietary vocational schools in the United States, Wilms points out that about one-third are "beauty" or cosmetology schools, one-third are trade and technical schools, and one-third are business schools and correspondence schools. Although the correspondence schools make up less than one-tenth of the total group, they enroll two-thirds of the students and generate more than one-half of the total income.

Wilms has recently reported a research study that bears significantly on the status of private vocational schools.[44] Funded by the National Institute of Education, his study sampled 4,800 students and graduates of 50 public and proprietary schools in San Francisco, Chicago, Boston, and Miami in six occupations—accounting, programming, electronic technician training, dental assisting, secretarial, and cosmetology. He reports that both groups of schools tend to serve the least advantaged of the students in post-secondary education; yet even so, the proprietary students were "the least advantaged of the least advantaged," more likely to be high school dropouts or products of general or vocational curricula, more likely from an ethnic minority group and having lower verbal skills than public school counterparts. He explains the paradox of least advantaged students paying high fees for education that is almost free in the public schools by pointing to the single-purpose nature of the private school, which has a shorter, more intensive program, with more flexible starting dates, and which is more actively advertised. The study reached 85 per cent of all graduates in the six occupational programs for the years of 1970–71 and 1972–73; personal and telephone interviews were held with each of the 2,270 graduates in the group. On the basis of these interviews, Wilms reports the following findings:

a. Little or no difference was found in the occupational success of public and proprietary graduates.

b. Only two out of ten graduates from both groups who trained for professional or technical-level jobs ever got them. Most became clerks or took low paying unrelated jobs.

c. Almost eight out of ten graduates in both types of schools who prepared for lower-level clerical or service jobs got them, but except for secretaries barely earned the federal minimum wage.

d. Neither type of school fully compensated for less-advantaged students' backgrounds.

e. Proprietary graduates were generally less satisfied with their training than their public school counterparts, and had paid 20 times more for it.

Wilms recommends that federal and state governments should be more actively engaged in protecting consumers of vocational programs in both public and proprietary schools by: (1) insuring that potential students have access to reliable information on the school's educational program; (2) developing standards for vocational program effectiveness; (3) insuring that all schools adhere to Truth-in-Advertising requirements; (4) auditing information given to prospective students to insure accuracy; (5) insuring that graduates of occupational programs receive equal pay for equal work; (6) encouraging experimentation on ways to best use our institutional resources for post-secondary occupational training; and finally, (7) encouraging both kinds of schools to evaluate objectives of programs and how they are being met.

The need for current, reliable, and useful information about vocational schools is emphasized in several of the recommendations, clearly underscoring the greater difficulty in obtaining it. Publications similar to the catalog or bulletin of the college or community college are unusual rather than customary. Information is often in the form of brochures, briefs, flyers or other sketchy statements. In vocational schools, new programs are established and old programs disappear more rapidly than in traditional two-year and four-year institutions, which, of course, affects routine publication of informational materials. The counselor who needs current information about vocational schools may find it helpful to check with the state office of education about opportunities within his/her state. Additional sources of information include the American Vocational Association in Washington, D.C., and the Center for Research in Vocational and Technical Education at the Ohio State University, Columbus, Ohio. Information also may be obtained from:

Association of Independent Colleges and Schools
1730 M Street, N.W., Washington, D.C.

National Association of Trade and Technical Schools
2021 L Street, N.W., Washington, D.C.

National Home Study Council
1601 18th Street, Washington, D.C.

The National Vocational Guidance Association has recently published an excellent guide for prospective vocational students entitled *How to Select a Private Vocational School.*[45]

An example of a directory for vocational schools is *Lovejoy's Career and Vocational School Guide,* 4th edition.[46] Information is classified by type of school, arranged geographically.

A new publication, *The National Guidance Handbook,* is intended to provide information about available vocational and technical education and also to relate that training to occupational fields.[47] The volume describes 146 available vocational–technical programs. There are additional chapters on career planning, general trends, apprenticeship information, and an indication of the availability of the training programs in the various states.

Many factors point to an increased use of both kinds of vocational schools—public and proprietary. It is, therefore, of great importance that teachers, counselors, and others be able to assist intelligently individuals who can benefit from such preparation to find the kind of training that is appropriate for their needs and plans.

Local school systems now frequently provide an array of educational opportunities directed toward the post-secondary age group. Like the Danish Folk School, these programs are usually quite informal, often of brief duration, and ordinarily developed in response to expressed local needs. Adult education programs appear to be expanding into many new communities as well as providing a broader range of courses in established programs. Courses may be of several types, such as basic education, vocational education, cultural, or avocational and recreational.

NOTES

1. Massachusetts Bay Assembly, 1647.
2. "Ordinance for the Government of the Territory of the United States Northwest of the River Ohio," 1787.
3. First Morrill Act, 1862.
4. Charles Stuart, et al., vs. School District No. 1 of the Village of Kalamazoo, 30 Michigan, pp. 39ff.
5. Public Laws 16 and 346, 1944.
6. M. Hecht and L. Traub, *Alternatives to College* (Riverside, N.J.: MacMillan Information, 1974).
7. W. W. Willingham, *The Source Book for Higher Education* (Princeton, N.J.: College Entrance Examination Board, 1974).
8. R. M. Bersi, *Restructuring the Baccalaureate: A Focus on Time-Shortened Degree Programs in the United States* (Washington, D.C.: American Association of State Colleges and Universities, 1973).
9. J. R. Hills, M. B. Gladney, and J. A. Klock, "Nine Critical Questions About Selective College Admissions," *Personnel and Guidance Journal*, vol. 45, no. 7 (March, 1967), pp. 640–647.
10. E. Douvan and C. Kaye, "Motivational Factors in College Entrance," in *The American College*, ed. R. Nevitt Sanford. (New York: John Wiley & Sons, Inc., 1962), pp. 199–224.
11. *Highlights of the ACT Technical Report* (Iowa City, Iowa: The American College Testing Program, 1973).
12. J. S. Hammond III, "Bringing Order into the Selection of a College," *Personnel and Guidance Journal*, vol. 43, no. 7 (March, 1965), pp. 661–664.
13. R. F. Berdie, "A University is a Many-Faceted Thing," *Personnel and Guidance Journal*, vol. 45, no. 8 (April, 1967), pp. 768–775.
14. A. E. Ivey, C. D. Miller, and A. D. Goldstein, "Differential Perceptions of College Environment: Student Personnel Staff and Students," *Personnel and Guidance Journal*, vol. 46, no. 1 (September, 1967), pp. 17–21.
15. *Financing a College Education—A Guide for Counselors*, 1974–75 (New

York: College Scholarship Service, College Entrance Examination Board, 1973).

16. C. R. Pace and G. C. Stern, "An Approach to the Measurement of Psychological Characteristics of College Environments," *Journal of Educational Psychology*, vol. 49, no. 5 (October, 1958), pp. 269–277.

17. *Student Financial Aid Manual for Colleges and Universities.* (Washington: American College Personnel Association, 1960).

18. N. Feingold, *Scholarships, Fellowships, and Loans*, 5 Vols. (Cambridge, Mass.: Bellman Publishing Co., 1949–1971).

19. L. Mathies and E. Dixon, *Scholarships, Fellowships, Grants and Loans* (Riverside, N.J.: MacMillan Information, 1974).

20. J. L. Angel, *National Register of Scholarships and Fellowships*, (New York: World Trade Academy Press, 1971).

21. N. C. Prioa, *Barron's Handbook of American College Financial Aid*, Revised Edition (Woodbury, N.Y.: Barron's Educational Series, 1974).

22. N. Feingold, *Student Aid Planning in the Space Age: A Selected Bibliography* (Washington, D.C.: B'nai B'rith Vocational Service, 1971).

23. R. B. Kimball, "Do Scholarships Help?" *Personnel and Guidance Journal*, vol. 46, no. 8 (April, 1968), pp. 782–785.

24. C. O. Houle, *The External Degree* (San Francisco: Jossey-Bass, 1973), pp. 14–15.

25. Career Education Project, *External Degree Study: A New Route to Careers* (Newton, Mass.: Education Development Center, 1975), pp. 6–7.

26. *Barron's Profiles of American Colleges* (Woodbury, N.Y.: Barron's Educational Series, 1973).

27. C. E. Lovejoy, *Lovejoy's College Guide*, 12th edition (New York: Simon and Schuster, Inc., 1974).

28. W. T. Furniss, *American Universities and Colleges*, 11th edition (Washington, D.C.: American Council on Education, 1973).

29. *The College Blue Book*, 14th edition (Riverside, N.J.: MacMillan Information, 1972).

30. J. Cass and M. Birnbaum, *Counselors' Comparative Guide to American Colleges*, 6th edition (New York: Harper and Row, 1974).

31. J. M. Richards, Jr., L. P. Rand, and L. M. Rand, "Regional Differences in Junior Colleges," *Personnel and Guidance Journal*, vol. 45, no. 10 (June, 1967), pp. 987–992.

32. D. P. Hoyt, "Description and Prediction of Diversity Among Junior Colleges," *Personnel and Guidance Journal*, vol. 46, no. 10 (June, 1968), pp. 997–1004.

33. L. S. Simon, "The Cooling-Out Function of the Junior College," *Personnel and Guidance Journal*, vol. 45, no. 10 (June, 1967), pp. 973–978.

34. C. E. Blocker and D. M. Anthony, "Social Status and Prestige in the Selection of a Program of Study in the Community-Junior College," *Personnel and Guidance Journal*, vol. 46, no. 10 (June, 1968), pp. 1005–1009.

35. C. E. Lovejoy, *op. cit.*

36. *Barron's Guide to the Two-Year Colleges* (Woodbury, N.Y.: Barron's Educational Series, 1974).

37. E. J. Gleazer, *American Junior Colleges*, 9th edition (Washington, D.C.: American Council on Education, 1975).

38. K. Hoyt, "A Challenge to Vocational Guidance: The Specialty Oriented Stu-

dent," *Vocational Guidance Quarterly*, vol. 11, no. 3 (Spring, 1963), pp. 192–198.

39. P. A. Perrone, "Technicians: Somewhere In-Between," *Vocational Guidance Quarterly*, vol. 13, no. 2 (Winter, 1964), pp. 137–141.

40. W. W. Wilms, "Protecting the Vocational Ed. Consumer," *The Research Reporter*, vol. 9, no. 1, 1975.

41. P. Crawford, "Counselor Responsibility in Investigating Private Vocational Schools," *Vocational Guidance Quarterly*, vol. 17, no. 3 (March, 1969), pp. 173–177.

42. A. H. Belitsky, "Private Vocational Schools: An Underutilized Training Resource," *Vocational Guidance Quarterly*, vol. 19, no. 2 (December, 1970), pp. 127–130.

43. A. H. Ressing, "The Uncertain Promise of Private Vocational Training," *Vocational Guidance Quarterly*, vol. 23, no. 1 (September, 1974), pp. 6–8.

44. W. W. Wilms, *op. cit.*

45. G. D. Pitts, *How to Select a Private Vocational School* (Washington, D.C.: National Vocational Guidance Association, 1974).

46. C. E. Lovejoy, *Lovejoy's Career and Vocational School Guide*, 4th edition (New York: Simon and Schuster, 1973).

47. *The National Guidance Handbook—A Guide to Vocational Education Programs* (Chicago: Science Research Associates, 1975).

9

Career Preparation Outside the Classroom

Recent emphasis on the concept of career education has increased attention on the acquisition of usable job skills. Early discussions of this idea envisioned easy transfer back and forth from education to work. The models currently being developed—school-based, experience-based, community-based, and residence-based—include the provision for skill-building as an antecedent to entrance to full-time employment. Even the experience-based plan, which essentially emphasizes the employment setting as the primary factor and the classroom as a secondary component, presupposes the existence of marketable skills. These models emphasize the role of the classroom as a preparatory laboratory for participation in the world of work.

It would, however, be extremely short-sighted and simplistic to assume that all preparation and training for employment occurs within the school house. In this chapter, we will examine some typical programs providing preparation for employment that have varying amounts of relationship to the school itself.

Many young people today, as well as in the past, graduate from high school without having acquired the marketable skill described by the career education advocates as essential for easy transfer to the world of work. In addition, many others, for various reasons, have already withdrawn from formal schooling. Large numbers of both groups find continuing their education impossible or undesirable because of personal preferences, family finances, or other factors. Many people may also lack the motivation or academic skills necessary for success in the programs that we considered in the previous chapter. Even among those who have the academic accomplishments, the resources, and the aspiration to continue formal education, there are some for whom the programs we will consider here might be more advantageous.

If the concept of career education flourishes and expands in the late 1970's and into the 1980's, it will provide the incentive for the development of many more preparatory programs similar to the ones we will consider here. If we develop a wider approach to vocational preparation to meet a broader array of needs within our society, out-of-school preparation programs can be expected to expand. For example, Pearl and Riessman suggest that present occupational structures do not provide sufficient opportunities for the poor.[1] They propose that: existing job situations be restructured, the specific job demands be identified, the job role be reconceptualized, and mechanisms for training new workers be developed through either innovative or traditional preparatory methods.

In this chapter, we will consider five preparatory programs. The first two involve some school-related activity. The next two do not have any direct involvement with formal schooling, and the last type provides its own "built-in" educational system. The five topics are:

1. Work experience programs
2. Apprenticeship
3. On-the-job training
4. CETA and government-related programs
5. Military training

WORK EXPERIENCE PROGRAMS

Many secondary schools now include in their curricula opportunities for students to combine study in the classroom with experience in an employment situation. These opportunities vary slightly from school to school and are known by a range of titles, such as cooperative work experience, distributive education, office practice, job experience, and diversified training. The programs are usually incorporated into the vocational curriculum of the school.[2,3,4,5]

The general purpose of the programs is to prepare selected students for employment while they complete their high school education. As a result of successful participation, a student graduates with his/her class, thereby completing a basic general education and, at the same time, being prepared for full-time employment in his/her chosen occupation.[6,7,8]

Operationally, these programs depart somewhat from traditional high school instructional procedures. Often students in the group are involved in widely varied occupations; in fact, one of the titles used for this type of program—*Diversified Cooperative Education*—stresses the variety. The program involves the harmonious cooperation of the high school and local employers, who divide instructional and supervisory responsibilities according to their unique abilities to assist the student in gaining occupational competence. In general, then, this is a school-community program of vocational instruction that uses the training and educational resources, facilities, and personnel of both the local school and the community.[9,10,11]

The program is expected to accomplish the following things:

1. The student establishes an occupational objective consistent with abilities and interests.
2. The student develops manipulative skills necessary for full-time employment as a worker or as an apprentice in his/her chosen occupation.
3. The student acquires related and technical information necessary for intelligent occupational practice.
4. The student develops appropriate attitudes and personal characteristics enhancing adjustment, success, and progress in the occupational field.
5. The student becomes increasingly mature in his/her relationship to school, economic, social, and home life.

The specific objectives can be thought of in terms of: (1) the job skills that the student will need to master, (2) the knowledge that must be gained in order to perform the work with intelligence and judgment, and (3) the personal and social traits one must develop in order to get along well on the job and in the community.[12,13]

Borow has succinctly emphasized the goals of the work experience program with the following statement:[14]

> Broadly speaking, three goals of vocational education are pursued in the work experience aspect of cooperative education programs. First, the student learns the characteristic skills, duties, and practical understandings associated with the occupation to which he is assigned through a training station. These are cognitive learnings. Secondly, he acquires what we call a work ethos, a set of attitudes, rules of etiquette, and interpersonal skills involving relations with fellow workers, supervisors, and clients. In short, he learns how society, and especially his place of work, expects him to "play the game." It is astonishing to what degree the school and the community assume that any student who is making the transition from school to employment has somehow mastered work protocol and the repertoire of unwritten and informal, yet highly critical, situational skills. It may be noted, parenthetically, that among culturally disadvantaged youth it is the utter lack of an acceptable work ethos quite as fully as inadequate training in the formal duties of the job that makes the work situation seem so bewildering and terrifying and which so frequently predisposes such

novices to almost certain failure. Thirdly, the school youth enrolled in a cooperative education program may come to know better what manner of person he is—what strengths, limitations, aspirations, and personal values characterize him. These personal attributes are, as a matter of fact, frequently shaped and fortified by the work experience itself. If a student is the fortunate beneficiary of wise and sensitive supervision, he will learn to see himself psychologically mirrored in the work situation. Thus, his experience on the training station will serve to build his self-identity as worker-to-be.

The instruction in job skills is provided by the employer, through work experience under actual employment conditions, according to a program developed jointly by the school representative and the employer. Students usually work a minimum of fifteen hours per week, most of which are scheduled during the regular school day.

The typical work experience program permits a student, usually in the junior or senior year, to attend classes half of the time and work in an assigned employment position the other half. In a few large city systems, the student spends one week in school and the following week at work, alternating with a fellow student who is on a reverse schedule. The most frequent situation, however, has the student in school in the morning and on the job in the afternoon. The student is supervised by the employer in the work assignment, but a staff member of the school serves as liaison agent between the school and the employer and maintains close contact with both the student and the employer. The student earns academic credit for the work assignment as a part of the school's vocational curriculum.

All participants in the program are enrolled in a related study class, which meets for at least one regular class period each school day. The class is conducted and supervised by the school staff member responsible for the program—usually designated as a coordinator. Most of the instruction is technical in nature and has a direct relationship to the student's work assignment. The study is designed to provide the trainees with information that will help them make sound judgments in their work. Because the students in the class are usually in a wide range of occupational assignments, they have a similar variety of individual training plans; so the class work is necessarily provided on an individual basis, using special instructional materials.

General information for beginning workers is included in the study class. Subjects covered usually include units on employer-employee relations, social security provisions, money management, income tax problems, personality and work, and labor organizations. This material usually is provided to all students in the program and often is called "general related" instruction. Some schools arrange their program so that each day includes one period of general related instruction and another period of specialized or individual instruction.

The development of desirable personal-social traits needed by young workers is more difficult to approach directly. Although the general related instruction helps to meet this objective, the direct contact with the employment assignment also contributes. Finally, the coordinator helps to accomplish the development of the desired traits through individual contacts with the student.

The work experience is totally realistic, since it has every characteristic of a regular job, including pay. The student has an opportunity to face the same situations that every worker encounters, with the added advantage of having a coordinator to assist him in making the adjustments or solving the problems encountered in his position.

Students who enroll in the work experience program are normally placed in an assignment appropriate to their vocational aims. Because of limited placement possibilities, distances involved, or other factors, the relationship between assignment and vocational goal may be only indirect. Even in such a situation, participation in the program has many advantages for youth not contemplating further formal education. They are provided an opportunity to gain insight into the working situation and their responsibility in it. They must adjust to the employer, fellow workers, the public related to the job, and the demands of the work situation. They come to know the importance of punctuality, cooperation, responsibility, paths for advancement, and similar factors that lie beyond simple vocational skill. It is not unusual for participants, on the completion of their schooling, to accept full-time employment with the companies in which they were placed for work experience, although such an arrangement is not included in the original placement.

The major advantages of the work experience program are, then, immediately obvious. The experience is totally realistic, without any of the artificialities thought by students to exist in the school setting. There is a direct relationship between school and work, with the study course serving as the connecting link. The participant gains an additional advantage later, since he can claim actual experience when he seeks full-time placement.

Inevitably, there are also some disadvantages to the program. Sometimes it is not possible to arrange ideal placement, which would provide the maximum in training and in experience. Some employers are primarily concerned with obtaining inexpensive workers, when they should be fundamentally interested in training them. Similarly, students may enter the programs principally for the financial benefits, rather than for vocational preparation. Some communities do not have available employment settings that offer a wide range of experiences. Some schools may have such strict admission requirements that the student who most needs the assistance of the program is ineligible to participate.[15] Because of the time consumed in field supervision, consultation with employers, and observation of student workers on the job, each coordinator can effectively handle only a limited number of students; consequently, the program is rarely as extensive as it should be to meet the needs of most non-college-bound students in a given high school.

Although rarely used to the fullest extent, the work experience program appears to offer an opportunity for most secondary schools to render a service to both students and community by helping students prepare themselves realistically for post-school employment.[16,17] Closer cooperation between the coordinator and the school counselor should bring more effective selection and placement in the program and more satisfying results to student, school, and community.

Career education advocates point to the work experience program as illustrative of the close school-community cooperation considered essential for effective career education. They suggest that all students, from high school entrance onward, should have related experience in the work setting. This should be part-time, perhaps even intermittent, not necessarily for pay, but clearly significant and participatory. Early assignments would be expected to be essentially exploratory in purpose, whereas later assignments would be considered more preparatory in nature, providing a practical laboratory experience with maximum realism. Extending over several school years and incorporating a variety of work assignments, such a program would clearly provide students with a better understanding of the world of work as well as with a set of marketable skills. Inevitably, the school and local employers would be drawn together into cooperative relationships of mutual benefit.

Implementation of a full-scale program involving all upper level students would necessitate major change in the educational program; but fundamentally, that is what career education is all about. Other countries have already adopted versions of this kind of activity with obvious benefits for participating students. Several high level governmental and industrial leaders have recently suggested that Child Labor laws should be revised and possibly modified to encourage and permit more work participation by school-age individuals. One can only agree that exploration and preparation would both be enhanced if students could actively share in work experiences.

APPRENTICESHIP

The use of apprenticeships for transmitting knowledge and skills to new workers dates back at least to the Middle Ages.[18] The various guilds of skilled craftsmen developed the regular practice of indenturing young workers to master craftsmen. During the period of indenture—often seven years—the young worker served or worked for the master; in return, the master provided food and lodging for the boy—usually in the master's own home—and taught him the skills and secrets of the craft. Upon successful completion of his indenture, the worker was accepted by the guild as a journeyman or independent craftsman. As the practice of his craft grew and expanded, he in turn later became a master and took into his shop apprentices to whom he taught the necessary skills.

The general use of apprenticeships has continued since those early days. The experience of Ben Franklin, who was an apprentice printer under his older brother, is part of our own colonial history. During the 1800's, as our industrial development mushroomed, thousands of workers were attracted to our country from Europe. Many were already skilled craftsmen, and for nearly a century immigration provided the major source of supply of the mechanics and craftsmen needed to operate our growing industries. Following World War I, changes in immigration laws seriously restricted the movement of many European skilled workers to this country, thus necessitating the development of other sources of labor that this country needed in increasing numbers.

The National Apprenticeship Program was established by Congress in 1937 with the support of both labor and management organizations. The Fitzgerald Act authorized the Secretary of Labor to set up standards to guide industry in employing and training apprentices; to bring management and labor together to work out plans for training apprentices; to appoint such national committees as needed; and to promote general acceptance of the standards and procedures agreed on.

The agency later known as the Bureau of Apprenticeship was created to put the program into effect. A committee representing management, labor, and government was appointed, known as the Federal Committee on Apprenticeship, to develop standards and policies.

A basic policy of the Bureau of Apprenticeship has been that programs for employment and training of apprentices should be jointly developed by and mutually satisfactory to both employers and employees. Because apprenticeship programs exist in a wide range of trades, the standards recommended by the Federal Committee on Apprenticeship are quite general, thus permitting the employer and employee groups in the various trades to work out the details for the training programs.[19] Under the provisions of the Bureau of Apprenticeship, an apprentice is a person at least sixteen years of age who works under a written agreement registered with a state apprenticeship council (or with the Bureau of Apprenticeship if there is no state council). The regulation provides for not less than 4,000 hours of reasonably continuous employment for the person, and for his participation in an approved schedule of work experiences supplemented by at least 144 hours per year of related classroom instruction. (In 1973, a one-year apprenticeship was established for prosthetic technicians.)

The Bureau has established certain basic standards under which an apprenticeship program can function. These include the following:

1. An apprenticeable occupation usually requires 4,000 hours or more—at least two years—of employment to learn.
2. The employment must be organized into a schedule of work processes to be learned so that the worker will have experience in all phases of the work in the apprenticeship. This prevents assignment to only one or a few specific details for the period of training, and is intended to assure the development of skill and knowledge in all aspects of the work.
3. A progressively increasing wage scale for the apprentice starting at about half the regular journeyman's rate.
4. Related classroom instruction should amount to at least 144 hours per year.
5. A written agreement, including the terms and conditions of employment and training of each apprentice, is registered with the State Apprenticeship Council.
6. The State Apprenticeship Council provides review of local apprenticeships.
7. Programs are established jointly by employer and employees.
8. Adequate supervision and records are required for all programs.
9. Full and fair opportunity to apply for apprenticeship is provided, with selection made on the basis of qualifications alone without discrimination.
10. Periodic evaluation of the apprentice's progress is made, both in job performance and in related instruction.
11. Recognition of successful completion is provided.

According to the Bureau of Apprenticeship,[20] a well-planned, properly supervised apprenticeship can provide the following benefits:

1. Provide the most efficient way to train all-around craftsmen to meet present and future needs.
2. Assure an adequate supply of skilled tradesmen, in relation to employment opportunities.
3. Assure the community of competent craftsmen, skilled in all branches of their trades.
4. Assure the consuming public of those quality products and services that only trained hands and minds can produce.
5. Increase the individual worker's productivity.
6. Give the individual worker a greater sense of security.
7. Improve employer-employee relations.
8. Eliminate close supervision because the craftsman is trained to use initiative, imagination, and ability in planning and performing work.
9. Provide a source of future supervision.
10. Provide the versatility necessary to meet changing conditions.
11. Attract capable young people to the industry.
12. Generally raise skill levels in the industry.

For the young worker entering employment, apprenticeship holds these important values:[21]

1. The opportunity to develop the highest skills, creating a greater demand for his/her services throughout industry, and assuring greater economic security and a higher standard of living.
2. Further training and education—with pay.
3. Assurance of a wage while serving an apprenticeship, with regular increases.
4. Opportunity for employment and advancement.
5. Recognition as a skilled craftsman in his/her chosen trade.

Friend has recently re-emphasized some advantages that accrue to the individual who decides to pursue apprenticeship training, rather than to attend college.[22] He particularly delineates the financial difference between the two situations. The college student not only earns no income during the usual four-year degree program, but also expends money for school expenses and maintenance. For many students, these two items could easily total several thousand dollars per year. On the other hand, the apprentice not only pays little or nothing for his training, but also is actually being paid at a rate representing a major fraction of the pay for a skilled journeyman. Thus, at the end of the same four-year period, he has a favorable balance in terms of expenditures for training as well as in earnings during that same period. The difference is great enough to require the college student to invest many years in employment before "catching up" financially.

State departments of labor were asked to establish apprenticeship councils at the state level. Such councils were intended to serve as liaison agencies between federal and local levels and to encourage cooperation of state agencies and employers and employee groups within the state. Where formed, these groups included an equal number of representatives of employers and employees, and representatives from appropriate state agencies. The state organization, using standards recommended by the federal committee as guides, set up state standards and procedures to be followed by industry within the state in employing and training apprentices. Once established and recognized by the bureau, the state council becomes a part of the national apprenticeship program.

In some industries, national employer groups and national trade unions have appointed apprenticeship committees. These committees meet as joint management-labor groups to develop national apprenticeship standards and to encourage establishments of training programs in accordance with the adopted standards. These organizations grow out of specific industries and are concerned with programs within that specific industry; they are, therefore, independent of the Bureau of Apprenticeship. The usual practice has been for a close relationship to develop between the national committees and the federal bureau, with each assisting the other through the sharing of information and consultation.

Both the federal and state organizations are primarily concerned with the establishment and development of standards. The actual employment and training of apprentices occurs at the local level. Local joint apprenticeship committees are established to organize the development of standards for employment and training of all apprentices in the specific trade by employers who are members of the local groups and other employers who subscribe to the program.

Qualifications for employment, such as age, education, aptitude, wages, hours of work, the term of the apprenticeship, the schedule of job processes, and the amount of class time required, are usually spelled out in detail in the local standards. Also included are procedures for executing and registering the agreement and methods of supervising apprentices at work and at school. The classroom instruction is provided by local and state vocational schools. The local committee often serves as an advisory group in developing an appropriate program of instruction.

The local program specifies the way in which applicants are selected and employed. Often there are more applicants than openings. Frequently, sons or daughters of workers in the industry are given first opportunity if they can meet the established standards. A person who has had previous trade training in school or in military service also may have a better chance of acceptance; and if the previous training is of sufficient quality, the training period may be shortened.

Approximately 300 apprenticeable occupations are listed, under about 90 trade classifications. The training period ranges from two to six years, with the most common period being three to four years. The trade classifications include the following:

Aircraft fabricator	Candymaker
Airplane mechanic	Canvas maker
Asbestos worker	Carman
Automobile body repairman	Carpenter
Automobile mechanic	Cement mason
Baker	Cook
Barber	Cooper
Blacksmith	Cosmetician
Boilermaker	Dairy products maker
Bookbinder	Dental technician
Brewer	Designer-draftsman
Bricklayer	Dry cleaner-spotter-presser
Butcher	Electrician
Cabinetmaker	Electroplater

Electrotyper	Photoengraver
Engraver	Photographer
Fabric cutter	Plasterer
Farm equipment mechanic	Plate printer
Floor coverer	Plumber-pipefitter
Foundryman	Pottery worker
Furrier	Printer
Glazier-glassworker	Printing pressman
Heat treater	Rigger
Ironworker	River pilot
Jeweler	Roofer
Lather	Rotogravure engraver
Leadburner	Sheet metalworker
Leatherworker	Sign and pictorial painter
Lithographer	Silversmith
Machinist	Stationary engineer
Mailer	Stereotyper
Maintenance mechanic	Stoneworker
Marking-device maker	Stonemason
Mattress maker (custom)	Stone mounter
Metal polisher and buffer	Tailor
Miller	Telephone worker
Millwright	Terrazzo worker
Modelmaker	Textile technician-mechanic
Musical instrument mechanic	Tile setter
Operating engineer	Tool and die maker
Optical technician	Upholsterer
Orthopedic technician	Wallpaper craftsman
Paint maker	Wire weaver
Painter and decorator	Wood carver
Patternmaker	

At the end of 1972, the latest year for which apprenticeship figures are presently available, 264,122 individuals were registered in apprentice training programs. During that year, slightly more than 53,000 persons completed their training, and another 57,000 withdrew or cancelled their participation. The three largest apprenticeship fields include occupations in construction, metalworking, and printing. Within these three fields, the approximate numbers completing training in 1972 were 28,488 in construction, 8,830 in metalworking, and 2,706 in the printing trades. Thus, these three areas accounted for more than 40,000 of the new entrants; the remaining 13,000 were scattered across all other fields.

If one compares this total group of apprentices in training, amounting to only a little more than a quarter of a million, to the 1972 total labor force of approximately 89 million, it is obvious that the apprenticeship program involves a very small portion of the total work force. Its importance, however, far exceeds its small proportional representation. A recent monograph emphasizes that this group provides the core of the skilled work force.[23]

Even though there is no movement toward restricting trades to apprentice-trained journeymen, there does appear to be general recognition that the apprentice training program needs to be expanded in both quantity and quality.[24] One difficulty in increasing the number of apprenticeship positions is the cost of training apprentices. This cost is borne primarily by the individual employer, but he may not derive the benefits if the apprentice goes elsewhere for employment when qualified as a journeyman. Possible solutions to the cost problem include the development of trust funds, use of tax credits or other subsidy for the sponsor, and the development of subsidized pre-apprenticeship training programs.

Training programs can be improved, according to the above-mentioned monograph, by basing the content and sequence on an analysis of the required performance, by using more tests and examinations in the training process, by improving the supervision of training, and by increasing the flexibility of the related training programs.

Foltman has identified four underlying principles for the apprenticeship system of the future.[25] He includes the following points:

1. *Voluntarism with some government guidance.* The present pattern of voluntary cooperation by labor and management should be continued, with government serving as a friendly but active third partner.
2. *Flexibility in defining standards and in implementation.* Several standards cited earlier in this section have been in existence for the past forty years. Two examples are the two-year minimum for an apprenticeship and the 144 hours per year of related training. No one questions that an apprenticeship must be long enough to assure mastery of the skills by an apprentice; but there is no special magic in a two-year minimum. In fact, a one-year program was approved in 1973 for the first time. Similarly, reasons for adjusting the related time may be providing for the use of learning modules, self-instruction units, mastery learning, dual enrollment in community college courses, and similar learning resources that are now commonly available.
3. *Broad application to a wide range of occupations and industries.* Many fields have long been excluded from apprenticeship programs, including such areas as sales and retailing, managerial, clerical, professional, and scientific occupations. Extension of apprenticeship programs into such areas is recommended, as is broadening the base for training by including nonunion employers.
4. *Emphasis on quality and quantity.* Even though there is a real need for expanding the number of workers who complete vocational preparation by the apprenticeship route, this expansion can only take place if the quality of training is maintained and enhanced. This requires the

identification and preparation of high quality instructors who not only have technical skill in the craft but also are competent teachers.

Career education, with its emphasis on the interrelationship of education and work, will find a strong ally in the apprenticeship training program. Both areas can be expected to reinforce each other since both are built on a common, fundamental principle.

ON-THE-JOB TRAINING

Some employment situations require neither specialized educational preparation nor specific vocational experience as a prerequisite. The absence of such requirements means that the worker operations either can be learned readily in a brief demonstration period, or are such that only a minimal general education is sufficient to prepare the worker. Such a conclusion is not always precise. The employer may prefer, for a variety of reasons, to hire inexperienced workers who can be trained as desired.[26,27]

Frequently, large companies employ training directors and extensive staffs who operate elaborate programs, including class instruction, to prepare new employees for the assignments they will be given. Such companies prefer to start with totally inexperienced workers so that they can be taught the exact procedure to follow on the job. Previous experience may have taught the worker different techniques or methods that the employer wishes to avoid. The employer prevents such "contamination" by providing a training program. In some cases, such a supervised training program may be quite lengthy and detailed.

More commonly, employers offer on-the-job training when the basic essentials of production can be learned in a relatively brief period of time, so that the worker is soon assigned to the task for which he/she was employed. Where the basic operation is performed by a team or crew of skilled workers, the new employee may be assigned to a skilled worker or to a team as a helper, where he/she learns a complex task by observing and assisting skilled practitioners for a specified period. Some employers may rotate the beginner, so that he/she serves a period with several teams involved in different aspects of the work, thus becoming familiar with several phases before assignment to a specific job. Frequently, however, the rotation does not give the trainee comprehensive preparation in all parts of the work.

This type of training is often found in occupational fields that involve apprenticeship. On-the-job training frequently lacks the careful organization involved in apprenticeship, thus resulting in a worker who may not have the thorough preparation that goes with the latter.[28]

COMPREHENSIVE EMPLOYMENT
AND TRAINING ACT

The Comprehensive Employment and Training Act became law in December, 1973. Now usually referred to as CETA, this legislation frequently has been described as a landmark for at least two reasons. First, it is one of the more significant applications of special revenue sharing, under which the federal government provides funds to state and local governmental units but under which policy and decision making occur at the state and local level. Secondly, CETA is a significant act because it reversed the direction of national manpower program design and operation by clearly establishing a decentralized approach.[29]

Any major change in governmental policy or procedure requires considerable time, great effort, and attitudes of patience and forbearance to accomplish. This is especially true when, like CETA, the new direction involves changes in many existing programs that touch the lives of a great many individuals. The conditions of the time demanded full-scale, intensive operation of the programs included in the law before the necessary machinery and procedures for effective implementation could be established. One must recognize that many months must pass before judgment and evaluation can be made.

The major thrust of CETA is to establish a legal framework by which federal funds can be made available to state and local governmental units to provide a variety of manpower services to local citizens according to programs determined by those governmental units. Such a move maximizes the opportunity for state and local governmental units to deal with local manpower training and employment problems in a creative, realistic manner; to meet needs without overemphasizing program procedures; and to adjust rapidly to changing situations. On the other hand, it allows state and local officials to deal ineptly with problems, to squander and misuse funds, and to create bureaucratic structures if they are inclined to disregard their responsibilities. One can safely predict that CETA will spawn programs of both types—some areas will enjoy innovative activities of excellent quality and minimal per capita cost, others will encounter the opposite.

The law provides for the recognition of "prime sponsors"—the appropriate governmental unit that is responsible for receipt of the federal monies and for execution of the program.[30] Ordinarily, this would be a state government; it can also be either a local governmental unit, or a combination of local units. Through the use of planning councils, recommendations are made regarding program plans, basic goals, policies, and procedures, monitoring of programs, and analysis of needs for other programs and services. Final responsibility rests with the prime sponsor, except for those activities and programs specifically identified in other portions of the law.

It is extremely important to recognize the degree to which almost total control is allocated to the prime sponsor. Programs obviously will vary, and sometimes greatly, from the geographic unit of one prime sponsor to that of another, even though located in contiguous areas. Counselors, and others in helping relationships, must keep abreast of developments and programs in the prime sponsor areas in which their clientele reside, including nature and scope of available services, elegibility requirements, etc.

The law also provides for the establishment of a State Manpower Service Council in states in which the state itself is a prime sponsor. The membership of this group consists of representatives from localities with approved comprehensive manpower plans, the state board of vocational education, the state employment agency, representatives of organized labor, business and industry, community-based organizations, appropriate state agencies, and the general public. This council is responsible for review, coordination, and monitoring of programs by state agencies and the prime sponsors.

The law includes several distinct sections or titles that provide for special programs or spell out particular provisions or policies. We will consider briefly some of the major portions.

Title II of CETA provides funds for public employment programs. This section is intended to provide unemployed and underemployed persons with transitional employment in jobs providing needed public services to facilitate their movement into employment or training not supported by the law. This portion of the law is restricted geographically to areas designated as having substantial unemployment. Within such an area, an eligible resident must have been unemployed for at least 30 days. Programs developed to provide such transitional employment must be designed with a view toward:

1. Developing new careers; or
2. Providing opportunities for career advancement; or
3. Providing opportunities for continued training, including on-the-job training; or
4. Providing transitional public service employment that will enable individuals so employed to move into public or private employment or training not supported by CETA.

In general, the purpose of Title II is to develop and identify jobs in the public sector that not only meet public needs but also provide the incumbent with employment experiences or training that will enhance the likelihood of moving on to either training or employment outside the province of the act. Many special assurances must be satisfied by the prime sponsor in establishing such programs to guarantee special consideration to target groups, avoidance of abuse of the plan, etc.

Title III spells out certain federal responsibilities. One federal responsibility is the identification of "special target groups" that need help in gaining training and employment. These groups include youth, offenders, persons of limited English-speaking ability, older workers, and other special groups with similar disadvantages in the labor market. In addition to the special target groups, consideration is given to meeting employment needs of other special groups, including Indian and native Alaskan communities as well as migrant and seasonal farm workers. Title III also specifies the provision of the following types of services:

1. Programs to provide part-time employment, on-the job training, and useful work experience for students from low income families who are in grades nine to twelve and need earnings to permit resumption or continuation of attendance in school.
2. Programs to provide unemployed, underemployed, or low income persons (age sixteen and over) with useful work and training to assist in developing maximum occupational potential and to obtain regular competitive employment.
3. Jobs for economically disadvantaged youth during the summer months.
4. Special programs involving work activities directed to the needs of those chronically unemployed poor who have poor employment prospects and who are unable to secure appropriate employment or training.
5. Special programs that provide unemployed or low income persons with jobs leading to career opportunities in programs designed to improve the physical, social, economic, or cultural condition of the community.
6. Special services when required for middle-aged and older men and women who are unemployed as a result of the closing of a plant or factory or a permanent large scale reduction in the work force of a locality.
7. Other manpower programs conducted by community-based organizations.

Title III also designates responsibility to the Secretary of Labor to develop both a comprehensive system of labor market information and a nationwide computerized "job bank" with adequate means for matching existing skills with employment needs throughout the country.

Several special programs, related to this title, were established immediately after passage of the legislation. Such programs include the National On-The-Job Program, which provides on-the-job experience in addition to classroom preparation for unemployed and underemployed persons. During 1974 and 1975, most of this training focused on skilled trade areas such as construction and machine tool making, and semiskilled fields such as automobile industry, dental laboratories, and processing operations. Another program is the Apprentice Outreach program, designed to provide recruitment, referral, and placement services for individuals, primarily minority group members, who wish to enter skilled occupations through the apprenticeship route. A further example is the Journeyman Training Program, designed to assist individuals, primarily minority group members who are ineligible for apprenticeships because of age, to enter employment training in fields usually structured on apprenticeship lines, such as the building and construction trades.

The extensive training programs developed under the Manpower Development and Training Act, which has now been eliminated by the passage of CETA, probably will be continued under the provisions of Title III. Prime sponsors in several states already have moved to contract with the institutions providing MDTA instructional programs to assure continuity for much of the MDTA classroom activity.

Title IV provides for the continuity of the Job Corps. Originally established under the provisions of the Economic Opportunity Act of 1964, the Job Corps was designed to assist the most underprivileged of our youth by removing them from stultifying home environments and providing training and supportive services in new surroundings to help them make the transition to a productive life. It was intended for individuals who had dropped out of school, who had the least educational and vocational skills, and who were in greatest need of remediation.[31, 32, 33] Between 1965 and 1975, approximately 550,000 young men and women, ages 16 to 21, had enrolled in the job training and basic education provided in the residential and nonresidential Job Corps centers.

In 1974, there were 61 Job Corps centers in operation with a capacity of approximately 22,000. Of these, 27 were civilian conservation centers located in national parks and forests throughout the country and providing basic education and vocational education slanted toward the construction trades. The other 34 Job Corps centers were located in or near large urban areas and were operated by business firms, educational organizations, or state government agencies. Educational and vocational programs covered a wide array of occupations. All centers provide the following services:

1. Intensive individual and group counseling intended to improve the enrollee's self-concept and to raise motivation and expectation.[34, 35]
2. Medical attention and the fundamentals of personal health care.
3. Remedial education for enrollees, 45 per cent of whom are either illiterate or poor readers on enrollment.
4. Vocational training geared to realistic standards, which prepare enrollees for employment on completion.
5. Activities designed to develop behavior patterns that will improve enrollees' chances of obtaining and keeping a job.
6. Courses leading to a high school equivalency certificate.
7. Opportunities for learning and assuming the responsibilities of a contributing member of society.

The educational program is organized to meet the needs of enrollees and is comprised of reading, mathematics, the "world of work," an advanced general education program, and health education. Some centers offer supplementary programs of physical education, driver education, language and study skills, English as a second language, home and family living, and tutorial programs. The advanced general education program provides the information and knowledge required to pass the High School General Educational Development test for high school equivalency; about 4,000 enrollees successfully pass the GED and receive certificates each year. Beyond that, more than 600 Corps members entered college in 1974. The vocational preparatory program uses instructors supplied by trade union organizations and may include on-the-job training with local governments or private employers.

The placement record for the Job Corps has been consistently bright. In the 1974 fiscal year, 69 per cent of the terminees available for placement received job placements. Others were placed in regular school work, other training programs or entered the Armed Services. Overall, the total of 32,589 placements represents 94 per cent of all terminees available for placement.[36]

Many programs, which were previously federally funded and have provided various training opportunities, are now in a state of reorganization and restructuring. MDTA training programs are one example of this type of reappraisal. Funding is not provided directly for the continuation of these training centers in the CETA legislation. Congress apparently intended that such programs as were needed in specific geographic areas could be continued through contractual arrangements between CETA prime sponsors and training institutions. If such contracts are not established, MDTA programs would, of necessity, have to secure other local or regional support, or disband. Another program that will continue in areas in which contracts can be developed between the program and the prime sponsor is the Neighborhood Youth Corps. In the past, this program offered a three-pronged approach to training and employment problems faced by youth, especially in urban areas. One component provided an in-school program for high school age youth, another provided summer employment for school age youth to enhance the chances of returning to school in the subsequent term, and the third aspect was an out-of-school program aimed at the school drop-out.[37,38,39,40] Continuation of the program will depend on local and state arrangements.

Outside the purview of CETA is another federally funded program providing both employment and training placement. This is the Work Incentive Program revised extensively in 1973 and now often referred to as WIN II. The program requires certain recipients of Aid to Families with Dependent Children (often described as Welfare recipients) to register for work and/or training. At the time of registration, an appraisal of potential for employment is made and an employability plan is developed. Training may include on-the-job training, institutional training, work experience, public service employment, referral to other training programs, or referral for job placement. Although training is provided in the program, employment is emphasized. To encourage expansion of placement opportunities for WIN II program participants, tax credits to employers reduce costs and make participants attractive potential employees.

The decentralization of manpower programs brought about by CETA will obviously lead to extensive variation in the nature of such resources from one geographic area to another. Not only will the variety of programs increase, but also frequent change and readjustment will become a basic characteristic. Any guide or directory of such opportunities is likely to be out-of-date as soon as it is printed. Counselors and others must develop contacts with the local agencies and the appropriate prime sponsors to assure their being knowledgable of local programs.

MILITARY TRAINING

A further opportunity for preparation for employment is found in the programs offered by the various military services. Now that all branches of military service depend on volunteers, many opportunities for specialized training have been developed as inducement for enlisting. Counselors need to keep abreast of new opportunities available to young men and women. Literature describing programs in the various branches of service is available at recruiting stations or by writing directly to the branch.

Each of the services provides training through on-the-job assignment or through specialized school; often a combination of both is used to provide the level of training desired by the service involved. For example, on completing basic training in the army, a young man or woman may be given an on-the-job assignment, or may be sent to a service school and assigned either to a leadership course or a specialist course. Similarly, in the air force, after completing basic training, he/she is sent either to on-the-job training or to a technical school.

Obviously, the curriculum and training provided in the special technical schools operated by the military services are designed to develop the skills needed by them. Consequently, the training specifically prepares the individual for a career field in that branch of service. Since many of the military career fields have some relationship to similar assignments in civilian life, the training acquired in service often can be used later in the civilian world of work. The degree to which transfer of training from military to civilian work is possible will vary considerably, with almost total applicability in some areas and relatively little carry-over in other fields. In general, the degree of usefulness is probably less than that pictured by active recruiting agents and that hoped for by naïve enlistees. In some career fields, the quality of training available in military service equals or exceeds what can be acquired in civilian life.

In addition to the career training offered through on-the-job training and service schools, the military encourages members to study voluntarily in off-duty hours.[41] Bartlett, for example, points out that the military services operate thirty correspondence school centers, which offer more than 2,000 courses that have been taken by more than one million service personnel.[42] The services also hold contracts with fifty colleges and universities for 6,000 additional correspondence courses.

Qualified military personnel may obtain tuition aid amounting to as much as three-fourths of the cost of tuition if they enroll in classes conducted by civilian schools. Such courses are usually offered by schools located near the military base to which the person is assigned. Arrangements exist for such courses both overseas and in the United States.

Berry and Nelson have demonstrated some of the reasons for the emphasis placed on educational programs by all military services.[43] Their recent study of marine corps personnel shows that enlistees who have completed high school do better than those who drop out of school. Among the dropout group, those who finish their schooling after enlistment do better than those who do not finish.

NOTES

1. A. Pearl and F. Riessman, *New Careers for the Poor* (New York: Free Press, 1965).
2. U.S. Department of Health, Education, and Welfare, Office of Eductaion, *A Look Ahead in Secondary Education* (Report of the Second Commission on Life Adjustment Education for Youth, Bulletin No. 4) (Washington: U.S. Government Printing Office, 1954), p. 87.
3. ———, *Education for a Changing World of Work* (Report of Panel of Consultants on Vocational Education) (Washington: U.S. Government Printing Office, 1963).
4. ———, *Digest of Annual Reports of State Boards for Vocational Education* (Washington: U.S. Government Printing Office, 1963).
5. L. M. Lessinger, "Role for Honest Work and Socially Valued Service in the Formal Educational Process," *Journal of Secondary Education*, vol. 44 (December, 1967), pp. 339–343.
6. C. A. Weber, "The Role of Work Experience," in *A Basic Text for Guidance Workers*, ed. C. E. Erickson (Englewood Cliffs, N.J.: Prentice-Hall, Inc., 1947), p. 355.
7. L. D. Mason, "School-Work Programs: The Vocational Education Act in Action," *Clearing House*, vol. 42 (January, 1968), pp. 294–296.
8. A. W. Silver, "Toward a Work-School Curriculum," *Journal of Teacher Education*, vol. 18 (Summer, 1967), pp. 211–215.
9. E. Murray, "Work: A Neglected Resource for Students," *Personnel and Guidance Journal*, vol. 41, no. 3 (November, 1962), pp. 229–233.
10. G. Venn, "Remedy for Ghetto Unrest," *American Education*, vol. 4 (May, 1968), pp. 23–24.
11. D. U. Levine, "Work Study Programs for Alienated High School Students," *Journal of Secondary Education*, vol. 41 (December, 1966), pp. 371–378.

12. R. La Jeunesse and O. Hansen, "Personalized Education," *Phi Delta Kappan,* vol. 48, no. 4 (December, 1966), pp. 169–170.
13. G. Venn, "Learning Beyond the Classroom," *American Vocational Journal,* vol. 42, no. 1 (September, 1967), pp. 14–16.
14. H. Borow, "Vocational Education, Guided Work Experience, and Career Development," an address delivered at The National Conference on Cooperative Vocational Education: Implications of the 1968 Amendments (Minneapolis, Minnesota, February 26–28, 1969).
15. N. A. Jones, "Work Activity Programs for Delinquents," *Vocational Guidance Quarterly,* vol. 13, no. 1 (Autumn, 1964), pp. 45–49.
16. R. J. Havighurst and L. J. Stiles, "National Policy for Alienated Youth," *Phi Delta Kappan,* vol. 42, no. 7 (April, 1961), pp. 283–291.
17. H. J. De Planta, "Follow Up of a Work-Experience Program," *Balance Sheet,* vol. 49 (May, 1968), pp. 404–405.
18. U.S. Department of Labor, Bureau of Apprenticeship, *Apprenticeship, Past and Present* (Washington: U.S. Government Printing Office, 1955).
19. ———, *Apprentice Training—An Investment in Manpower* (Washington: U.S. Goverment Printing Office, 1957).
20. ———, *The National Apprenticeship Program* (Washington: U.S. Government Printing Office, 1964).
21. E. E. Goshen, "Apprenticeship: A Sure Road to Skills," *Occupational Outlook Quarterly,* vol. 8, no. 1 (February, 1964), pp. 16–20.
22. B. L. Friend, "Apprenticeships in the '70's," *Vocational Guidance Quarterly,* vol. 20, no. 4 (June, 1972), pp. 291–293.
23. *Apprenticeship Training in the 1970's: Report of a Conference,* Manpower Research Monograph No. 37 (Washington, D.C.: U.S. Government Printing Office, 1974), p. VII.
24. G. Strauss, "Alternative Approaches to Improving Apprenticeship Effectiveness," *Apprenticeship Training in the 1970's* (Washington, D.C.: U.S. Govment Printing Office, 1974).
25. F. F. Foltman, "Implications for Action," *Apprenticeship Training in the 1970's.* (Washington, D.C.: U.S. Government Printing Office, 1974).
26. H. C. Carr and M. A. Young, "Industry-Education Cooperation," *Vocational Guidance Quarterly,* vol. 15, no. 4 (June, 1967), pp. 302–304.
27. E. Riessman, "New Anti-Poverty Ideology," *Teachers College Record,* vol. 68, (November, 1966), pp. 107–119.
28. D. Bell, "The 'Invisible' Unemployed," in *Man, Work, and Society,* eds. S. Nosow and W. H. Form (New York: Basic Books, Inc., 1962), pp. 149–156.
29. *Manpower Report of the President, 1974* (Washington, D.C.: U.S. Government Printing Office, 1974), pp. 191–242.
30. *Manpower Report of the President, 1975* (Washington, D.C.: U.S. Government Printing Office, 1975), pp. 79–104.
31. F. Parker, "Salvaging School Failures: The Job Corps Acts," *Phi Delta Kappan,* vol. 49 (March, 1968), pp. 362–368.
32. B. B. Washington, "Education in League With the Future: the Job Corps," *National Association of Women Deans and Counselors' Journal,* vol. 29 (Summer, 1966), pp. 184–187.
33. H. B. Wood, "Job Corps New Look in Education," *American School Board Journal,* vol. 152 (June, 1966), pp. 19–20.

34. D. Gottlieb, "Poor Youth Do Want To Be Middle Class But It's Not Easy," *Personnel and Guidance Journal*, vol. 46, no. 2 (October, 1967), pp. 116–122.

35. B. R. Shoemaker, "National Need for Residential Vocational Schools," *American Vocational Journal*, vol. 43 (October, 1968), pp. 14–17.

36. *Manpower Report of the President, 1975* (Washington, D.C.: U.S. Government Printing Office, 1975), pp. 98–100.

37. G. Arnstein, ". . . to the Advantage of Secondary Education: A Discussion of the Neighborhood Youth Corps," *National Association of Secondary School Principals' Bulletin*, vol. 50, no. 311 (September, 1966), pp. 22–36.

38. B. M. Hill and H. Lieberman, Jr., "Youth Corps Counseling," *Vocational Guidance Quarterly*, vol. 15, no. 4 (June, 1967), pp. 257–261.

39. E. E. Ruff, "Guidance as Viewed Through the Neighborhood Youth Corps," *National Association of Secondary School Principals' Bulletin*, vol. 50, no. 1 (September, 1966), pp. 37–42.

40. R. H. Saxton, "Three Years of the Neighborhood Youth Corps," *Children*, vol. 14 (July, 1967), pp. 156–161.

41. H. F. Clark and H. S. Sloan, *Classrooms in the Military* (New York: Bureau of Publications, Teachers College, Columbia University, 1964).

42. L. M. Bartlett, "Education in the Department of Defense: Unrecognized Giant," *College and University*, vol. 43 (Summer, 1968), pp. 390–400.

43. N. H. Berry and P. D. Nelson, "The Fate of School Dropouts in the Marine Corps," *Personnel and Guidance Journal*, vol. 45, no. 1 (September, 1966), pp. 20–23.

10

Placement Services

Increased attention on career education has re-emphasized the importance of placement services in both instructional institutions and in comprehensive counseling programs. The fundamental concept in career education, that the individual, having reached school-leaving age, is henceforth prepared to continue to advanced educational levels or to enter employment, certainly underscores the essential nature of a service that can help the individual follow either fork of that road—advanced education or employment. The corollary concept, that one should also be able to move easily from work back to school and then return to work again, further underscores a new and expanded emphasis on placement services. Obviously, placement services must serve not only the individual who wishes to move from school to job, or vice versa, but also the person who wishes to move from one job to another or from one educational situation to another.

The two preceding chapters have dealt directly with post-secondary education and/or practical experience as preparation for employment. This chapter is concerned with helping the individual, whether student, client, patient, or employee, to take that next step toward either further education or employment.

EDUCATIONAL PLACEMENT

In most communities, movement from one educational level to another within the public school system is an automatic process. Youngsters entering kindergarten or first grade are ordinarily assigned to an elementary school on the basis of the location of their home. Similarly, as they move on to junior high school, assignment normally is based on geographic proximity, with all pupils from one elementary school moving together to the junior high school that serves that area. In a few communities, minor variations may bring about a better balance in the educational system; occasionally, a student who lives in an overlapping zone between two junior high schools may have the opportunity to choose the school he/she will attend. The point is, however, that at this educational level a pupil is customarily assigned to the school.

Much the same situation prevails as the junior high-schooler moves on to senior high school. Small communities often have only one high school, to which all junior high schools transfer their graduates. In larger communities served by more than one high school, assignment is also usually based on proximity to the school. Since the typical American high school offers a comprehensive program, there is little reason to be concerned about appropriate matching of individual and school.

Although the trend in this country has been away from special-purpose high schools, several cities do maintain schools of this type. They vary in purpose and function. Many so-called technical or manual training high schools are now comprehensive high schools that simply have retained their former names through tradition; others may still provide special programs that serve students from a larger geographic area than that served by other high schools in the system. Similarly, some city schools offer special emphasis in such areas as art, music, science, and vocational preparation. Obviously such schools, where they exist, serve a special purpose and, therefore, a special clientele. One might expect questions about placement, in these situations, to be a problem at the scondary level. In actuality, where special-purpose schools exist as an integral part of a total school system, the selection and referral techniques are so routine in operation that special consideration of placement as discussed in this chapter is not generally applicable. Eligibility for admission, or the procedures for establishing eligibility, are clearly understood by all school personnel involved, and appropriate assignment of a student to such a school can ordinarily be mutually resolved by school personnel, parents, and student. When entrance to a specialized high school is an option of the student and his/her parents, the remainder of this section is pertinent.

For the vast majority of secondary students, school placement services become important only as students approach the legal school-leaving age or as they near completion of the secondary program. At this point, it becomes necessary to complete plans that will fit future needs and long-range goals.

The function of placement service as the student moves from school to employment is considered in the next section of this chapter. This section is concerned with the responsibility of the school in assisting the student who desires to continue formal training beyond the secondary school. This responsibility is readily accepted by most schools. Unfortunately, in some schools it may be given only lip service or, at best, an erratic, informal effort is made to send transcripts to whichever schools the student requests. Such slipshod efforts fail to help the students as effectively as they deserve, and may easily result in disappointment for both students and their parents, with resulting disintegration of the school's public relations. If the school accepts as its obligation a full effort to assist every student to attain the maximum personal development of life, it must accept as a corollary the provision of an efficient placement service that enables the student to move to the next educational level with the minimum of frustration and difficulty.

The theories of vocational choice described briefly in Chapter 2 emphasize that selection of a career is a process extending from an individual's childhood through the educational years, and often well beyond. Increasingly, school guidance services are being organized on this concept of the developmental process. Effective placement can be made only by the application of that same concept. In fact, selection and placement are so interrelated that the student may be best served when no attempt is made to separate the two. Many activities that on the surface appear to be primarily concerned with career selection inevitably carry overtones of placement, and vice versa. For example, consideration of any career field involves attention to training facilities, and this leads to consideration of factors such as availability, costs, and entrance requirements.

Chapter 8 noted the expansion of higher education in America, especially with the spread of the community colleges, area vocational schools, and other public and private vocational and technical schools. This increased array of educational opportunities, as well as changes in societal attitudes toward higher education, changes in birth-rates, and other factors, have all combined to broaden the educational perspectives of many people. Only a decade ago, many high school juniors and seniors considered only the option of enrollment in college, and both they and their parents were often deeply concerned about the possibilities of gaining entry to one of the colleges of their choice.

Even though the pressures that encouraged some students to apply to certain schools prematurely and perhaps unwisely generally have subsided, the importance of long-range cooperative planning involving students, parents, and school has not diminished. In many ways, the broader educational opportunities now available suggest the greater need for careful planning to assure most effective use of available resources. One can easily understand that increasing the number of choice options does not necessarily increase the odds of making an appropriate choice; in fact, statisticians would suggest that the opposite is more likely to happen.

The material to be presented next was prepared with college choice clearly predominant. Its value is not diminished by recognizing that the proposed schedule has pertinence whether one is considering a choice of college or an alternative educational option. The reader is urged to use the broader view.

The American School Counselors Association has suggested a time-table for a family to follow in helping its children plan for college.[1] The timetable includes the following:

EIGHTH GRADE:

1. Visit the school counselor to discuss the results of the scholastic aptitude tests taken by the student to determine whether he has college level ability.
2. Help the student plan his ninth grade program carefully to include the science, mathematics, and language courses suggested for college preparatory work.

NINTH GRADE:

1. Begin to read catalogs and learn about the different types of schools.
2. Help the student plan his high school program with his counselor.

TENTH GRADE:

1. Continue to read college catalogs and study the sections on entrance requirements.
2. Suggest that the student seek further guidance from his counselor.

ELEVENTH GRADE:

1. Visit college campuses, attend college information conferences, talk with admissions counselors, consider the faculty, courses offered, size of classes, size and location of colleges, tuition and fees.
2. Have the student take the aptitude and vocational interest tests recommended by the counselor.
3. Have the student take the *Preliminary Scholastic Aptitude Test* (PSAT).

TWELFTH GRADE:

1. Apply to those colleges in which the student is interested and to which he is eligible for admission.
   . . . Choosing the *right* college for your son or daughter is a major decision involving both home and school and requires conscientious study and planning by all concerned.

This schedule implies that questions related to placement will begin to arise at least as early as the ninth grade, as parents and students begin to read college catalogs. Both the teacher and the counselor should be prepared to provide assistance in these early phases of planning.

Although many staff members may be involved in the process that leads to final selection and application to the schools of one's choice, probably the student and his/her parents are best served if there is some centralization in the processing of applications and in the preparing of any information required.

Hatch and Dressel point out that some schools have established educational placement offices to prepare the information sought by schools, colleges, and universities.[2] Whether this is an appropriate responsibility in a specific school is an administrative decision that should be based on all factors pertinent to the situation. In any case, it is necessary to bring together the preparation of materials into one location—often the guidance office. If properly organized, much of the work can be handled by clerical staff. A system of regular advance screening of classes to determine which students anticipate further schooling (if such information is not already available through counseling staff activities) would permit routine collection of the usual information needed to complete application forms. If the counseling staff has been involved in the long-range planning process with the student, the guidance office records should be sufficiently complete to make the development of a separate set unnecessary.

In those secondary schools where large numbers of students plan to continue their education, it may sometimes be more efficient to assign one of the counseling staff to maintain contacts with those institutions in which students are most interested. Such centralization tends to assure that someone is currently informed of the changing requirements and conditions in the various schools in which students may be interested.

Recognition also must be given to the process of educational placement for adults. Increasingly our society is recognizing that education is a life-long process. Large numbers of adult workers are returning to school to up-grade their skills or to develop new skills because of technological changes that occur in the world of work, for example. Rehabilitation counselors, neighborhood center workers, and others who counsel adults are likely to be involved in educational placement services. The need for careful consideration of the individual's needs and goals, the availability of appropriate institutions providing the desired preparation, an understanding of the nature of the educational institution, and assistance in arranging admission are factors that are crucial, not only for the graduating high school senior, but also for the forty-year-old amputee who must prepare for a new vocation.

JOB PLACEMENT

Public employment services designed to help people find appropriate jobs have existed in this country for over a century. New York City organized a municipal service as early as 1834, and San Francisco established one in 1868. By the turn of the century many cities had followed the same pattern.

The various state employment agencies, which ordinarily have offices in all major cities, serve all areas of each state. Their responsibilities are clearly established, with general uniformity from state to state. The services that they provide include:

1. *Placement.* Applicants are registered, classified, selected, and referred to prospective employers. Orders for workers are received, and applicants' qualifications are matched with the employer's specifications so that referrals can be made.
2. *Counseling.* Applicants without previous work records or with inadequate experience are provided assistance through aptitude testing and counseling, so that appropriate classification and referral can be made.
3. *Service to veterans.* Each office is charged with providing special assistance to veterans seeking employment.
4. *Service to handicapped applicants.* Each office is also responsible for providing placement assistance to the handicapped.
5. *Collection of labor market information.* Changes and trends in the local employment situation are regularly assessed; pooling this information at the state and federal level increases the service available to those seeking work, as well as providing a current picture of employment across the nation.
6. *Cooperation with community agencies.* The local office helps to keep the public informed, attracts applicants and possible employers, and maintains close contact with local employment conditions.

Statistical information is sometimes helpful in trying to grasp the size and scope of an agency's operation. The Employment Service reported, for example, that its total number of nonagricultural placement transactions exceeded 4.9 million in 1974. During that same year, they dealt with 13.3 million applicants, of whom 3.3 million were placed in jobs, another million received job counseling, and nearly another million were provided job testing.[3]

The Job Bank, operated by the Employment Service, is an example of the application of computerized storage and retrieval of information to the area of job information. Basically, the Job Bank provides a network for the interchange of information about available jobs listed in the Employment Service Offices in 150 major metropolitan areas. Archerd and Ausmus have described the functioning of this program as well as other services available through the Employment Service Offices.[4]

Because of the specific responsibilities assigned to the local public employment agency, it offers many services and advantages to the person attempting to obtain employment. Its continual involvement in placement and collection of local labor market information gives its staff a knowledge of local employment conditions and opportunities that cannot be matched elsewhere. Liaison with other local offices through the state provides useful information on employment opportunities at both a statewide and nationwide level. The services of the local office are available without charge to applicants seeking work, who will be served by a professional staff concerned with matching applicants' abilities to employers' requests.

The services of the public employment agency are available to, and frequently utilized by, special service organizations involved in rehabilitation or assistance to particular groups of adults, such as veterans, the physically handicapped, the disadvantaged, and others. Cooperative agreements exist, for example, between employment offices and Veterans Administration hospitals to expedite job placement of discharged patients. Other agencies have established their own placement services because of the special characteristics or needs of the clientele served by those agencies.[5]

The Comprehensive Employment and Training Act allocates certain responsibilities related to placement to the appropriate prime sponsor or its designated subagencies. Local or regional offices probably will develop to help provide special services to the special groups identified by CETA, including youth, older workers, and offenders. Because of the CETA emphasis on decentralization, it appears unlikely that a uniform national pattern will emerge to convey these services. Regional or even local variation probably will prevail; over time, some patterns will prove to be superior and then will become models for reorganization of less efficient plans.

In addition to the public employment offices located throughout the country, many metropolitan areas have commercial, or private, employment agencies. Like other profit-making businesses, they vary in size, scope, clientele, and quality. All charge a fee for their services, often based on a percentage of the salary for the position in which the applicant is placed. Since no fee (or, at most, a modest registration charge) is paid until placement occurs, applicants can anticipate that the agency will make strenuous effort to place them as quickly as possible. Many private agencies specialize in a particular occupational field; for example, many agencies restrict their efforts to educational positions and others focus on technical occupations. Some large private placement agencies operate branch offices in other localities and work cooperatively, and some provide testing and/or counseling services for their clientele. A variant of the private placement office can be seen in the placement services operated for or by a specific professional group; for example, many metropolitan areas include a registry for nurses who accept private cases.

PLACEMENT AND THE SCHOOL

The dearth of information about placement services in the schools has been noted by several authors.[6] Odell has recounted his early experience in the Employment Service involving the development of a demonstration project on School-Employment Service relations in 1939.[7] He also suggests that the Employment Service and the schools drew apart during the 1960's as the Employment Service concentrated its efforts on the hardcore unemployed and the disadvantaged, and the schools became preoccupied with a post-

Sputnik pursuit of excellence. He now sees the two groups reuniting their efforts to create effective placement services for all individuals.

Herr and Cramer have pointed out the school counselor's involvement in placement in the following statement:[8]

> If placement is viewed as a transition process for the student as well as a point in time, the school counselor can help him prepare himself psychologically for placement. This may require role-playing interview situations, assistance in completing or recognizing the importance of employment applications, or provision of information about jobs available in the local setting. It will also involve support and follow-up while the individual is moving through the placement process. In some cases, the school counselor must lend strength to individual students who encounter initial rebuffs until their confidence and self-esteem are reinforced through being accepted by a firm.
>
> To be effective in the placement process, it is obvious that the school counselor will need to communicate with persons outside the school active in placement—personnel or training people in business and industry, employment service counselors, rehabilitation counselors, and others. Such communication will require that the school counselor be able to talk knowledgeably about the competence level, goals, and characteristics of persons to be placed, as well as to secure information about openings which is relevant, accurate, and localized.

The school has several available options in organizing a placement service ranging from transferring full responsibility to the local public Employment Service Office to retaining total responsibility within the school itself. We will consider each option briefly.

The major arguments for full use of the local public employment agency to meet placement needs of the local school usually are these: [9]

1. The state employment service, including the local office, is set up uniquely for placement services, with a trained staff, close contact with employers, and current and accurate local information on the labor market.
2. It is uneconomical to operate two parallel systems.
3. Development of a competing placement service within the school would arouse ill will among the public, who would oppose duplication.
4. The state employment service is where workers go to get a new job, so this facility might just as well be available in looking for a first job.

In spite of the above points, a strong argument can be made in support of job placement services within the school.[10,11] Advocates of this position usually bring out the following points:

1. The school is responsible for the adjustment of the individual. Changing from the classroom to the job is part of the adjustment of the individual.
2. Placement, to be best, should be made with consideration of the indi-

vidual's previous experience and abilities. The school is in the best position to know these.

3. If the school provides vocational education, it should logically include placement as a part of the total process.

Additional arguments can be marshalled to support the position that the school should be involved in placement activities.[12,13] It is commonplace among books describing guidance programs for secondary schools to consider placement as an essential guidance service.[14,15] If educational placement can be accomplished most effectively over an extended period of work with the individual, certainly the same is true of job placement.

Of special importance in school placement activities is the opportunity to help students obtain part-time and vacation employment. Valuable experience, as well as a more realistic understanding of the relationship of worker to job, can be acquired by teen-agers who engage in work after school hours, on Saturdays, or during summer vacation. Such opportunities can be capitalized on by the school guidance program if students are helped to use their job experience as an aid in career planning. Often part-time placements can be arranged that give the student exploratory experiences that have direct relationship to career fields in which he is interested. Even when this is not possible, the student can expect to profit in various ways from participation in work experience. Hipp has described the advantages to students when a high school organizes a placement office for part-time job placement.[16] In addition to the obvious benefit of practical work experience, he includes experience in completing application forms and experience in job interviews.

Andrews[17] points out some reasons that young people encounter temporary failure in obtaining and holding jobs. Some of the reasons listed include: unsatisfactory appearance, attitude, and behavior; unrealistic wage demands; insufficient training; insistence on job though unqualified; impatience and unwillingness to adapt to entry requirements; insistence on own concept of job duties; and ignorance of labor market facts. Many of these problems, prevalent in many young inexperienced jobseekers, can be alleviated or even eliminated by an effective combination of counseling and placement. The recognition and eradication of possible problems is more likely to occur in the school setting, where the young person is better known and where time for counseling is available.

If the school assumes that the student needs special assistance as major changes are encountered in the educational experience—such as moving to junior high school and on to senior high—it is certainly logical to expect that help will be needed in moving from school to job. The school can strongly contend that the student will learn most effectively if the change from school to job is correlated with experiences in the school that have been organized to prepare and assist in making the transfer. A school placement program would presumably provide this assistance. The discussion of the work experience program in the previous chapter pointed out that a major advantage of the program was the availability of the coordinator as a liaison between school and employer, thus helping the student adjust to the demands of the work situation. The placement officer could serve this function for students not enrolled in the school's work experience program.

Perhaps the strongest argument of all in support of placement services within the school is the basic philosophic position that must be taken by each agency in order to perform its responsibility to society. The employment service has a primary responsibility for meeting manpower needs. The school must, if it meets its share of the responsibility, give preeminence to the long-range development of the individual.[18] It must consider the individual as a unique person with particular needs and goals, and its actions should be to maximize the development of that person. Frequently there may be no conflcit in these two positions; nevertheless, conflict is possible.

To some extent, the question of whether the school should be involved in placement services is an academic question, since inevitably it is involved. In every school, staff members are contacted by employers seeking applicants for positions. Probably this happens most frequently in the vocational departments of the school, where commercial and shop teachers are asked to recommend possible candidates for existing vacancies. The basic question is whether the school wishes to continue an informal, unorganized placement service, or whether it prefers to recognize a responsibility to all students who may seek work, regardless of the curriculum in which they are enrolled, and to organize a program to meet the needs of all students.

If the school moves to establish placement services, it has four possible options—a decentralized program, a centralized program, a combination of these two, or a cooperative program with the public employment service.

The *decentralized plan* places responsibility at the lowest functional level. In a small school system involving only one high school, this probably would simply extend the informal placement efforts in which teachers or school departments already engage. In large school systems with more than one high school, placement would operate at the school level. The advantages are that students are in familiar surroundings, with staff members who probably already know them well, so little or no delay is involved in the referral process. The disadvantages of such a system are also obvious. The program serves a smaller group of students and may not be able to supply the best applicants; little time is available for developing employer contacts and making follow-up; there is duplication of effort among the schools in the system; employers are uncertain about which school staff member to contact, or they must make several calls to reach the proper person without a central clearinghouse.

In a *centralized program*, a single office is established that develops pertinent information about students desiring placement and to which employers may send notification of job openings. The advantages are convenience and efficiency, with the likelihood of better staff, uniform policies, and better community relations. The disadvantages are that student records are not as readily available, and the student is usually not personally known by the staff.

Larger school systems may find advantage in developing some *combination* of the two basic systems, in order to capitalize on local situations or to meet particular needs that may exist within the system. For example, a school system might establish a central office for employer contacts but use separate school offices for developing student records, or a central office might be used to coordinate the activities in the various schools.

A *cooperative program* involving both a school placement service and the local public employment service may provide the best opportunity to secure the advantages of each, as well as to minimize the disadvantages.[19] Several variations are possible in building such a service. The appointment by both agencies of liaison persons, who work together to accomplish the desired goals, is probably the first step. Both offices can focus on those parts of the work they can best handle, information can be shared as needed, and skills can be developed mutually.[20,21] The likelihood of having a program that meets local needs seems greater when the two agencies can effectively combine their efforts.

Odell, Pritchard, and Sinick agree that a cooperative plan offers many mutual advantages to both school and Employment Service and also increases the provision of effective service.[22] Odell suggests that schools could improve their basic lack of occupational information by drawing on the services of the Local Employment Service Office, which has much local information at hand. He further describes a suggested arrangement by which an Employment Service Counselor might be placed in a school assignment, either part-time or full-time, to assist both in placement and occupational information and in vocational guidance of students, and to provide access to Employment Service operations such as the Job Bank. Pritchard emphasizes that placement programs need to be school-based and community-linked as well as to provide opportunity for follow through —helping the individual adjust to the job and develop in it.

Post-secondary schools also are involved in placement, and many of them operate placement offices for their students and alumni. Typically, these offices operate as a part of the services provided by the educational institution and charge either no fee or a very modest registration charge. In some cases, the services provided are as minimal as the fee charged, with the agency serving primarily as a depository for confidential placement papers. Many placement offices, on the other hand, are exemplary models that could be used as patterns by other private and public placement offices. Some, on large university campuses, use computer printout systems to notify registered students of companies that offer the kinds of

ACTIVITIES OF THE PLACEMENT COUNSELOR
IN ONE GUIDANCE DEPARTMENT

1. Conduct a voluntary job registration of all students in the school system over age 14 and most recent graduates and dropouts.
2. Provide job guidance, placement and personalized follow-up of these students. Placements may be part-time, temporary, vacation, or permanent, based on the individual's needs, desires, and opportunities.
3. Solicit job openings by personal visitation, telephone, or mail.
4. Set up and maintain the forms, procedures, and records.
5. Confer with counselors, teachers, parents, and administrators.
6. Give talks to ninth and tenth grade groups to explain program.
7. Visit senior English classes to explain how programs can help students.
8. Orient new teachers to objectives and explain how the program can help provide better teaching.
9. Receive, evaluate, file, and pass on a continuous flow of current occupational materials.
10. Develop group guidance activities on job findings.
11. Coordinate the Career Conference Program.
12. Interview an average of six students or employers daily.
13. Compile a directory of where students are employed.
14. Regularly prepare and send out news releases for area papers.
15. Visit homerooms of seniors to explain the placement service.
16. Maintain contact with local service clubs and Chamber of Commerce in order to expand occupational surveys.
17. Make follow-up contacts of students placed in jobs.
18. In cooperation with guidance staff, prepare a resource book on community services.

Adapted from *Job Placement Primer* (Indianapolis: Indiana State Department of Public Instruction, 1975), pp. 13–14.

employment opportunities that are compatible with the students' registered preferences.

Bottoms and Thalleen have described a plan used by state-supported technical schools to assist their students in placement.[23] Unlike the typical college or university placement plan in which employers are scheduled throughout the year to interview students for prospective employment, the Georgia schools set up "Career-day" sessions, in which representatives from employing industries describe opportunities in their different companies, after which students then can select the representatives they wish to interview for a job.

Florida has been developing a program in which para-professionals are prepared to work as counselor-aides in school systems. One major activity in which the para-professional is prepared is placement and follow-up. Given a more flexible schedule and more mobility than the school-based counselor, the para-professional can devote time to cultivating employer contacts, developing new placement opportunities, maintaining liaison with public and private employment services, and assisting in the transition from school to work.

Although a single, best model for a school placement service has not yet materialized, it is apparent that every secondary and post-secondary educational institution must provide more adequate placement services than has previously been true. Within each school, the responsibility for effective placement must be assumed, and the structure for meeting that obligation must be clearly understood by students, faculty, and the public.

One indication of the attention being directed to the placement and transitional relationship between school and work is seen in a recent study by Ferrin and Arbeiter.[24] This report, entitled *Bridging the Gap: A Study of Education-to-Work Linkages*, focuses on the barriers that interfere with transition and on mechanisms that might smooth the passage. Their recommendations are far-ranging, including work experience for all students, establishment of Community Education and Work Councils, revision of licensing and certification procedures, and the use of competency-based preparatory and qualifying procedures.

REGULATIONS AFFECTING EMPLOYMENT

The school, and its staff, often finds itself in a frustrating and baffling situation when it discovers that often it can give the least placement help to those who most need it. This refers, of course, to the student who decides to leave or drop out of school before graduation. The school dropout is not a rare and isolated problem; on the contrary, about a third of a million young people over the age of sixteen drop out of school each year before graduating. Another sizable group, age sixteen or under, also leave each year. These young people encounter more difficult problems in finding employment than do their classmates who stay on until graduation. They are much more likely to be unemployed than their classmates and to remain unemployed for longer periods of time.

The school dropout not only faces the handicap of fewer years of education than the classmate who stays in school, but also often has made a poor academic record while in school and frequently was limited severely in either reading or arithmetic, or both. He/she rarely was involved in extracurricular activities and often failed one or more subjects. He/she often comes from a family that is unable to help build positive attitudes toward either school or work.

In addition to these complications that make placement difficult, the dropout is faced with further restrictions as a result of regulations that limit the employment of youngsters of school age. Although the basic in-tent of the laws is to provide needed protection for young people, an additional product is to restrict still further the possibilities for placement for the school dropout. If the school counselor is to provide the assistance that the dropout desperately needs, it is essential that he/she be thoroughly familiar with regulations—federal, state, and local—that bear on the employment of minors.

In addition to school dropouts, every secondary school has a size-able group of students who wish to engage in part-time work. In some cases, the student seeks work because of real financial need and responsi-bilities; in other cases, the income is to acquire a car or to save for college or some other project. In still other cases, the student may wish to work because he/she has time to spare or because many friends are so engaged. Whatever the reason, finding work will involve consideration of the previously mentioned regulations. The counselor must be aware of perti-nent restrictions if he/she is to help make placement possible.

Many of the regulations that control or restrict the employment of minors are included in the provisions of the Fair Labor Standards Act. The child labor provisions of the act apply to any employer who employs a minor in interstate or foreign commerce or in the production of goods for such commerce, or to a producer, manufacturer, or dealer who ships goods or delivers goods for shipment in interstate or foreign commerce. The act prohibits the employment in the above situations of any oppressive child labor, which it defines as the employment of children under the minimum age set forth for the various types of work described in the act.

Employers can protect themselves from unintentional violation of the minimum age provisions by obtaining and keeping on file an age or employment certificate for each minor employed, showing the minor to be of the age established for the occupation in which employed. Such a certificate should be obtained and placed on file before the minor starts to work. Age or employment certificates issued under state child labor laws are accepted as proof of age in all states except Alaska, Idaho, Mississippi, South Carolina, and Texas. In Alaska, special arrangements for proof of age have been made; in the other four states, federal certificates of age are issued.

An age certificate is a statement showing a minor's age, issued by a public official on the basis of the best available documentary evidence of age, and usually carrying the signatures of the minor and the issuing officer. The certificates usually are issued by a representative of a state labor or education department or by a local school official. The certificate may have different names in different states—such as age certificate, em-ployment certificate, work permit, or working papers. It has the double purpose of protecting minors from harmful employment as defined in the act, and of protecting the employer from unintentional violation of the minimum age provisions of the act by furnishing reliable proof of age of minors employed in the establishment. Employers should obtain such a certificate for each minor claiming to be under eighteen years of age before employing him/her in any occupation, and for minors claiming to be eighteen or nineteen years of age before employing them in any of the occupations declared hazardous.

The minimum ages defined by the act vary according to the type of employment. Sixteen is the minimum age for most jobs, and during school hours for any employment, including agriculture. There are a few jobs, under specified conditions and outside of school hours, for which fourteen is the minimum age. Children under fourteen years of age may not be employed at any time in any occupation under the act.

Children who are fourteen or fifteen years of age may be employed in occupations that do not require a sixteen- or eighteen-year age minimum, provided they are employed only outside of school hours and under the following conditions:

a. Maximum of three hours on any school day and eight hours on any non-school day.
b. Maximum of 18 hours in a week during any part of which school is in session, and 40 hours in other weeks. A week is interpreted as a payroll week, not necessarily a calendar week.
c. All work must be performed between 7 A.M. and 7 P.M.

Sixteen years of age is the minimum for any of the following occupations except for those that are declared hazardous and require an eighteen-year age minimum:

a. Manufacturing, mining, or processing occupations; occupations requiring the performance of any duties in workrooms or workplaces where goods are manufactured, mined, or otherwise processed.
b. Public messenger service.
c. Operation or tending of any power-driven machinery other than office machines.
d. Occupations in connection with: (1) transportation of persons or property by rail, highway, air, water, pipeline, or other means: (2) warehousing and storage; (3) communications and public utilities; (4) construction, including demolition and repair, including such office work or sales work that involves any duties on any train, boat, or other media of transportation or at the actual site of construction operations, but not including office or sales work, which does not involve such duties.

Eighteen years of age is the minimum for all occupations that are found and declared by the Secretary of Labor to be particularly hazardous for minors between sixteen and eighteen years of age. Examples of hazardous occupations are:

a. Occupations in or about plants manufacturing or storing explosives or articles containing explosive components.
b. Occupations of motor-driven equipment driver and helper.
c. Coal-mine occupations.

d. Logging occupations and occupations in the operation of any sawmill, lath mills, shingle mill, or cooperage-stock mill.
e. Occupations involved in the operation of power-driven woodworking machines.
f. Occupations involving exposure to radioactive substances and to ionizing radiations.
g. Occupations involved in the operation of elevators and other power-driven hoisting apparatus.
h. Occupations involved in the operation of power-driven metal forming, punching, and shearing machines.
i. Occupations in connection with mining, other than coal.
j. Occupations in slaughtering and meat packing establishments and in rendering plants.
k. Occupations involved in the operation of bakery machines.
l. Occupations involved in the operation of paper-products machines.
m. Occupations involved in the manufacture of brick, tile, and kindred products.
n. Occupations involved in the operation of circular saws, band saws, and guillotine shears.
o. Occupations involved in wrecking, demolition, and shipbreaking operations.

Exemptions specified by the act include:

a. Employment of children in agriculture outside of school hours in the school district where such employees are living while they are so employed.
b. Employment of children as actors or performers in motion picture, theatrical, radio, or television productions.
c. Employment of children under 16 years of age by their parents in occupations other than manufacturing or mining or occupations found by the Secretary of Labor to be particularly hazardous for the employment of children between the ages of 16 and 18 years.
d. Employment of children engaged in the delivery of newspapers to the consumer.

In those states where state laws set higher standards, the higher state regulations must be observed by employers. Such regulations may restrict hours of employment more rigidly than the federal regulation, or may even add other occupations to the list in which employment is restricted. Metropolitan areas also may have additional restrictions that go beyond those established by the state. Some cities and states publish brochures that describe the additional regulations in effect there; where such data have not already been compiled, the counselor should collect the information for his own use. Figure 10–1, entitled *Your State Law*, is provided as a sample work sheet that a counselor might use to summarize the regulations with which he/she needs familiarity.

FIGURE 10–1. Your State Law

MINIMUM AGE	FOR BOYS	FOR GIRLS
For employment during school hours	_____	_____
For employment outside school hours	_____	_____
For factory employment at any time	_____	_____
For work in hazardous occupations	_____	_____

Which occupations are considered hazardous?

_____

_____

_____

_____

MAXIMUM HOURS OF WORK	FOR GIRLS	FOR BOYS
For minors under 18: hours a day	_____	_____
days a week	_____	_____
hours a week	_____	_____
For minors 16 and 17 attending school:		
hours on schooldays	_____	_____
hours a week	_____	_____
For minors 14 and 15 attending school:		
hours on schooldays	_____	_____
hours a week	_____	_____

NIGHTWORK

For minors 16 to 18:

prohibited between_____P.M. and_____A.M. for boys

prohibited between_____P.M. and_____A.M. for girls

For minors under 16:

prohibited between_____P.M. and_____A.M. for boys

prohibited between_____P.M. and_____A.M. for girls

EMPLOYMENT CERTIFICATES

Required for minors under_____years

Obtained from:_____

Required by:_____

SCHOOL LEAVING AGE

_____Years in_____(State);_____years in_____(City)

Are there any minimum ages set for occupations in your particular area? Check with your city hall.

Local Ordinances

	MINIMUM AGES	
OCCUPATIONS	FOR BOYS	FOR GIRLS
_____	_____	_____
_____	_____	_____
_____	_____	_____
_____	_____	_____
_____	_____	_____

NOTES

1. American School Counselors Association, *How About College?—A Guide for Parents of College Bound Students* (Washington, D.C.: American Personnel and Guidance Association, 1959).
2. R. N. Hatch and P. L. Dressel, *Guidance Services in the Secondary Schools* (Dubuque, Iowa: William C. Brown, Publishers, 1953).
3. *Manpower Report of the President,* 1975 (Washington, D.C.: U.S. Government Printing Office, 1975), p. 112.
4. M. Archerd and N. Ausmus, "New Resources in the Employment Service for Counselors and Jobseekers," *Vocational Guidance Quarterly,* vol. 21, no. 2 (December, 1972), pp. 144–148.
5. T. Flannagan, "What Ever Happened to Job Placement?" *Vocational Guidance Quarterly,* vol. 22, no. 3 (March, 1974), pp. 209–213.
6. R. Campbell, G. Walz, J. Miller, and S. Kriger, *Career Guidance, A Handbook of Methods.* (Columbus, Ohio: Charles E. Merrill Publishing Company, 1973), p. 202.
7. C. Odell, D. Pritchard, and D. Sinick, "Whose Job is Job Placement?" *Vocational Guidance Quarterly,* vol. 23, no. 2 (December, 1974), pp. 138–145.
8. E. L. Herr and S. H. Cramer, *Vocational Guidance and Career Development in the Schools: Toward a Systems Approach* (Boston: Houghton Mifflin Company, 1972), p. 215.
9. "Suggested Guidelines for Further Coordination of Educational Institutions and Employment Services," sponsored by National Vocational Guidance Association, *Vocational Guidance Quarterly,* vol. 13, no. 3 (Spring, 1965), pp. 215–220.
10. L. L. Lerner, "Placement by Public Schools," *Occupations,* vol. 27, no. 5 (February, 1949), pp. 322–325.
11. D. Sinick, "Placement's Place in Guidance and Counseling," *Personnel and Guidance Journal,* vol. 34, no. 1 (September, 1955), pp. 36–41.
12. W. J. De Gregorio, "I Need to Find a Job," *Vocational Guidance Quarterly,* vol. 15, no. 1 (September, 1966), pp. 29–31.
13. G. Bottoms and M. Oelke, "Needed Student Personnel Services in Area Vocational-Technical Schools," *Vocational Guidance Quarterly,* vol. 15, no. 2 (December, 1966), pp. 101–105.
14. S. S. Olshansky, "Vocational Guidance as Continuum," *Personnel and Guidance Journal,* vol. 31, no. 9 (May, 1953), p. 540.
15. B. J. Novak, "What Place for Placement?" *Occupations,* vol. 30, no. 4 (January, 1952), pp. 258–260.
16. E. Hipp, "Job Placement: Organize and Advertise," *Personnel and Guidance Journal,* vol. 51, no. 8 (April, 1973), pp. 561–562.
17. M. E. Andrews, *Providing School Placement Services* (Chicago: Science Research Associates, Inc., 1957).
18. N. D. Stevens, "A Concept of Placement Readiness," *Vocational Guidance Quarterly,* vol. 10, no. 3 (Spring, 1962), pp. 143–147.
19. C. E. Odell, "School-Employment Service Cooperation," *Personnel and Guidance Journal,* vol. 32, no. 1 (September, 1953), pp. 9–13.
20. R. A. Ehrle, "Vocational Planning Information Available to Employment

Service Counselors," *Vocational Guidance Quarterly*, vol. 13, no. 2 (Winter, 1964), pp. 91–94.

21. J. E. Rossmann and E. M. Prebonich, "School Counselor-Employment Service Relations: The Minnesota Report," *Vocational Guidance Quarterly*, vol. 16, no. 4 (June, 1968), pp. 258–263.

22. C. Odell, D. Pritchard, and D. Sinick, *op. cit.*, pp. 140–142.

23. G. Bottoms and W. Thalleen, "Tech Days: Georgia's State-Wide Job Placement Program for Area Vocational-Technical Schools," *Vocational Guidance Quarterly*, vol. 18, no. 1 (September, 1969), pp. 10–14.

24. R. I. Ferrin and S. Arbeiter, *Bridging the Gap: A Study of Education-to-Work Linkages* (New York: College Entrance Examination Board, 1975).

PART IV   *Supplementary Learning Experiences*

The following activities are proposed as ways in which the reader can easily test, explore, or apply the concepts and insights presented in Part IV. The list is not intended to be exhaustive or comprehensive, but merely suggestive.

1. Select two or three colleges in various size groups and identify differences in admission requirements, costs, programs, etc.
2. Visit a community college or a technical school to determine scope of program, purpose, type of student body, etc.
3. Visit two vocational schools to determine admission requirements, costs, nature of program, placement services, etc.
4. Interview apprentices in two or three different occupations to determine nature of program, quality of experience, satisfaction of workers, etc.
5. Interview military recruiters to identify nature of opportunities for vocational preparation.
6. Interview State Employment service workers to identify services available, effectiveness, demand for help, etc.
7. Interview a private employment agency to determine costs, extent of service, etc.
8. Investigate university placement services.
9. Interview high school personnel who are involved in job placement of high school students.
10. Determine where in your community under-age workers find employment.
11. Assist an individual in securing a position.

PART
V

Materials Describing the World of Work

11

Occupational Information Sources and Media

Simply put, occupational information consists of facts about jobs. Occupational information helps individuals gain insight and understanding about the world of work. It can be used in industry to develop and revise personnel plans, in government as a basis for program formulation, and in education to test curriculum adequacy. We are concerned here with its use in the classroom and in the counseling office in activities that create awareness, encourage exploration, facilitate decision-making, enhance preparation, or increase employability.

Frequently, printed occupational information has focused on what the worker does and related matters; rarely has it included psychological and sociological information. Even if one accepts the limited scope of most occupational information, one must still be constantly wary of misinformation, distortion, inaccuracy, and obsolescence. This is not to say that people who prepare occupational publications are careless and inaccurate. Just as a person's photograph, even though taken under ideal conditions with the best equipment by the most skilled photographer, soon becomes out of date and inadequately reflects how the individual really appears, so, too, does occupational information soon reflect inaccurately the nature of the occupation.

It is essential for those who use occupational materials to keep in mind the dynamic, constantly changing nature of the world of work. Only if occupations and the world of work were static and unchanging would information acquired last month or last year still be accurate today. Since even the most stable occupations are undergoing constant metamorphosis, one cannot expect materials to remain current except for quite brief periods of time.

Further, the society in which we live is highly volatile, constantly interacting, and producing impacts on the world of work. Our population is now much more mobile than previously, goals and aspirations have changed, even values have been revised and reoriented. All of these factors affect the way in which people look at and evaluate jobs.

Finally, one must recognize the infinite possibility of variation that can occur within a single occupation as it is encountered in numberless situations across a country as vast as the United States. One might reasonably expect that, given the opportunity to study intimately a specific occupation in a thousand random situations scattered about the country, the variations and permutations within that occupation would form what would resemble the normal, bell-shaped curve of the statistician. Thus, what is most frequently presented as representative of the occupation is the mean or median of the distribution—the picture that is most typical of the total range. We have, then, information that is generalized or representative but that we often attempt to use in a specialized or specific situation. The result is no more satisfying than if we tried to force all American men to wear size 8 shoes because the average American male wears that size. Information that is nationally available will ordinarily be broadly based and only generally applicable, and thereby often in need of validation when utilized locally.

Hopke has summarized some of the changes and innovations that can be expected in occupational information materials in the next few years.[1] He anticipates the continuation of rapid occupational change as the bench mark of the times and suggests that these changes will necessitate production of larger quantities of information. A wider range of materials seems likely to meet the need for information on opportunities for women, the culturally disadvantaged, minority groups, and other special groups. Materials with diversified reading levels from elementary grades through college are likely to be produced. Mechanized processing will provide wider variation of types of material that will have general utility. Revision can be expected to be more frequent and more rapidly accomplished. A greater amount of information based on local or regional areas also appears likely in the future.

OCCUPATIONAL INFORMATION MEDIA

Kunze reports a "spectrum of occupational information data" developed by Thompson.[2] This scale ranges from abstract printed materials to actual work experience across ten points. These points include the following:

1. Publications (books, monographs, etc.)
2. Audio-Visual Aids (films, tapes, slides, etc.)
3. Programmed Instructional Materials (books, workbooks, etc.)
4. Computer-Based Systems (storage, retrieval mechanized systems)
5. Interviews with Experts (direct questioning of occupational representatives)
6. Simulated Situations (career games, role playing, etc.)
7. Synthetically Created Work Environments (artificial reproduction of work settings)
8. Direct Observation (visits to work sites)
9. Directed Exploratory Experiences (work samples, evaluation tasks, etc.)
10. On-the-Job Tryout (casual work or work-study programs).

Visualizing this continuum suggests that Thompson's ten points can be categorized into three broad groups. Points 1, 2, and most of 3 include primarily materials that are encountered in a passive situation, most frequently related to the school library or media center. Points 4–7 are more animated and require the individual to interact with other individuals or with equipment and structured situations in a classroom or laboratory setting. Points 8–10 require active, "hands on" involvement with tools, equipment, and workers in a field-based work setting.

In this chapter and the next, we will consider the first major group, including Thompson's first three points. These materials are very extensive and lend themselves readily to the traditional school setting. Advantages in cost, convenience, flexibility, and familiarity suggest that they will continue to be heavily used by teachers, media specialists, counselors, and others. In Chapter 13, we will examine the second and third broad groups consisting of the laboratory and field-based activities. Most of these are newer, less familiar, often more difficult to implement, but nevertheless filled with the promise of greater efficiency, increased realism, and better learning and application.

In addition to the types and sources of materials considered in this and subsequent chapters, there is additional occupational information that the counselor should seek out if he is to be effective in assisting his client. Overs labels this hidden information "covert occupational information." [3] He describes "overt information" as information that is available in published form or that would be published without question if anyone were interested in publishing it. On the other hand, "covert information" includes knowledge of informal practices that circumvent established, proclaimed policies. It is generally unwritten and usually modifies or contradicts what is written about a specific job or work situation. It is usually not expressed verbally but instead is demonstrated by the actions of company employing officials. Departures from stated official policies can be in either direction; that is, toward a more restrictive position than policy indicates, or toward a more lenient stance. Obviously, the counselor needs to know of such discrepancies if the client is to be provided maximum assistance. Overs suggests that several sources are available to the counselor to learn "covert information," including reports from other clients, informal talks with significant administrators, observations of employment outcomes, other professional contacts, and information from social conversations, newspapers, and miscellaneous contacts.

Occupational materials come in a wide variety of forms. Although there is no total unanimity on a system of categories, some consideration of the terms used to describe frequently encountered items may be helpful.

The classification structure developed by the Career Information Review Service Committee of the National Vocational Guidance Association is probably most widely accepted. These definitions are used in describing the listings that appear in the *NVGA Bibliography of Current Career Literature*,[4] as well as those listed in the *Vocational Guidance Quarterly* under the regular feature heading of "Current Career Literature." The terms and definitions proposed by the committee are:

A—*Career Fiction:* An account, portrayed through the experiences of one or more fictional characters, of an occupation which may encompass duties, qualifications, preparations, conditions, and nature of work and advancement.

B—*Biography:* An account of the life of a successful man or woman in a given field of endeavor, portraying the problems faced by this person in preparing for and advancing in his career.

C—*Single job information:* This includes information related to a single occupation and may be either brief or comprehensive.

D—*Jobs in specific business or industry:* This includes information describing a specific business, industry, or service and the major occupations represented in it.

E—*Job family information:* This includes career or job family information or series presenting information about a broad field of work encompassing a wide range of occupations which have some relationship such as similar interests, aptitudes, and abilities.

F—*Recruitment literature:* The purpose of this material is to recruit youth into a specific occupation or career field. Examples could include publications by educational institutions describing their programs, by professional organizations, trade associations, or armed forces.

G—*Orientation—World of work:* This includes broadly based material designed to provide the reader with some understanding of relationships among very general groups of occupations.

H—*Special groups:* These materials are designed for primary use by a particular group such as women, minority groups, the disadvantaged.

I—*Bibliography:* This item includes printed lists of materials concerned with career information.

J—*Directory:* This material consists of alphabetical or grouped lists of institutions offering educational or training programs.

K—Financial assistance: This includes information about financial support for training programs at any level.

L—Other: This miscellaneous category is for any other type of career material not classified in one of the listed groups including special studies, general reviews, technical reports, charts, posters, etc.

A review of the types of occupational materials defined above reveals that some may be as brief as a single page, and others may be as long as an entire book. Since each client or student has unique needs, the counselor and teacher will obviously require knowledge of a wide range of materials for many occupational fields. The student who is just beginning to explore the world of work is more likely to need access to a wide array of short descriptive statements such as those found in a brief or abstract. On the other hand, the client who is moving toward an appropriate choice may be anxious to read a lengthy description, such as that found in a monograph, in order to answer some of the many specific questions he/she may have about the occupation. Further discussion of the use of these materials will be included in Chapters 14, 15, and 16.

An excellent publication prepared by Hansen provides a review of sources and media presently being used by local schools, both large and small.[5] The reader who wishes more detail as well as a description of the many practices now extant is urged to consult this reference. Particularly helpful are the second chapter, which focuses on developmental and sequential practices and programs in various school systems, and Chapter Three, which looks at school community projects.

GRASS ROOTS SOURCES OF INFORMATION

Fundamentally, there are only two basic or primary sources of information about the worker and what he does. One of these is the worker himself; the other is the worker's employer. In some occupational fields, a third primary source might be added; this would be the governmental agency involved in licensing or certifying workers or in controlling worker activity in some other way.

Basic data about jobs are obtained from these sources in three ways —by job analysis, by community survey, or by follow-up survey. All three methodologies are appropriately used to obtain local information—a most significant component of any occupational information file or library. If such information has not already been developed by the local Employment Service Office or other agency, a counselor or teacher may have no alternative to undertaking the task. Our purpose in this volume extends only to a familiarization level; therefore, we will examine each method only briefly.

Job Analysis

At least four approaches to job analysis are widely recognized and used in this country, according to a recent publication by the Department of Labor.[6] These approaches are:

1. Department of Labor methodology
2. Functional Job Analysis developed by Dr. Sidney Fine of the W. E. Upjohn Institute for Employment Research
3. Health Services Mobility Study developed by Dr. Eleanor Gilpatrick
4. Position Analysis Questionnaire developed by Dr. Ernest J. McCormick of the Purdue University Occupational Research Center

Of the four techniques, the Department of Labor system is probably basic to the other three, as well as being more widely used. We will focus our attention here on it; however, each of the other methods has unique advantages that should be considered by anyone contemplating this approach to the study of occupations.

The Employment Service defines job analysis as the activity involved with determining what the worker does in relation to Data, People, and Things; the methodologies and techniques employed; the materials, products, subject matter, and services involved; machines, tools, equipment, and work aids used; and the traits required of the worker for satisfactory performance.

We can deduce from this definition that job analysis is a process of observing jobs being performed and reporting pertinent facts. Its development occurred primarily for industrial purposes beyond our immediate concern. However, from an industrial viewpoint, job analysis is important because it provides knowledge about the requirement for the job, thus helping determine the qualifications needed by workers. It also is used in industry to determine the best way to perform a task or job as a means of seeing the worker in relation to the specific task performed. In other words, industrial use of job analysis largely focuses on improving the technical proficiency of workers and perfecting techniques for hiring workers. The technique of job analysis is important to us because it is the only accurate source of knowledge about the nature and demands of a job and the qualifications essential for a worker to perform that task.

In job analysis, the emphasis is on the job—what the worker does, and what he needs to do it. To determine these facts, the job is studied as it is being performed by the worker. It is important, therefore, to focus on the job rather than on the worker, who may actually be a distracting element in understanding the job. One can, for example, easily stray from determining what aptitudes are needed to perform a task, to considering what aptitudes the worker has. In job analysis, the second consideration is irrelevant and falls in the area of worker analysis.

Counselors and teachers may only rarely engage in job analysis; in fact, many may never be directly involved. Nevertheless, it is important to understand that process, so that information produced by job analysis can be used effectively with clients and students. As indicated earlier, one must be aware that the job analysis method may be the only way to obtain accurate, up-to-date information about local jobs. On occasion, the need for accurate local information may be important enough to justify applying job analysis to secure the data. Since proficiency in job analysis is not easily developed—a week or two of intensive formal training, followed by many weeks of practical experience are usually necessary—neither counselors nor teachers will likely use the technique extensively. They will find it helpful in understanding occupational information and in understanding differences between jobs.

We have already used some aspects of job analysis information as we considered the psychological and physical traits of the worker in Chapter 3 and the worker functions and work fields included in the *Dictionary of Occupational Titles* in Chapter 6. Those earlier considerations may now simplify our study of job analysis. Keeping in mind that both jobs and the reasons for studying them are subject to frequent change, we can then accept the idea that component items included in job analysis might be expected to change wth circumstances and purposes.

At present, five categories of information are included in a complete analysis of a job.[7] These categories and a brief description of each one are listed in *Job Analysis for Human Resource Management* as follows:

1. *Worker Functions:* *All jobs involve a relationship to Data, People, and Things in some degree. These relationships are expressed by 24 Worker Functions, and a combination of the highest functions which the worker performs in relation to Data, People, and Things expresses the total level of complexity of the job.*

2. *Work Fields:* *Work Fields are organizations of specific methods either (1) characteristics of machines, tools, equipment, or work aids, and directed at common technological objectives, or (2) characteristics of the techniques designed to fulfill socio-economic purposes. There are 99 Work Fields which have been organized for purposes of classifying all the jobs. . . . The Work Fields have been organized into groupings [which are] more or less similar technologically or socio-economically in overall objectives, that is, the getting of materials and making of products, the processing of information, and the providing of services. . . .*

3. *Machines, Tools, Equipment, and Work Aids:* *These are examples of the instruments and devices which are used to carry out the specific methods. . . . [Precise definitions are given for each of the separate parts of this category.]*

4. *Materials, Products, Subject Matter, and Services:* *These include: (a) basic materials being processed, such as fabric, metal, or wood; (b) final products being made, such as automobiles and baskets; (c) knowledge being dealt with or applied, such as insurance or physics; (d) types of services, such as barbering or dental services. . . .*

5. *Worker Traits:* *The requirements made upon the worker are expressed by Worker Trait factors. These are reflected in the following components: (1) Training Time, (2) Aptitudes, (3) Temperaments, (4) Interests, and (5) Physical Demands. This body of job information provides a sharper focus on the type of work involved and the traits demands made on the individual worker concerned, and is extremely helpful in counseling, job development, training, and other activities directed toward full manpower utilization.* [Detailed discussion of each of these traits is included in Chapter 3 and need not be repeated here.]

Although our major concern here with job analysis is based on providing accurate information, it is easy to see many related applications of the procedure. These would include providing a base for building training programs for potential workers, job restructuring to provide opportunities both for entry workers as well as more challenging activities for higher level workers, and developing career ladders that permit promotion of workers to more advanced levels.

Community Survey

Job analysis, as described above, is obviously intended to answer questions about a specific job. Sometimes, however, one is not so much interested in acquiring information about a particular job as in developing a general picture of the total work situation in the community or other geographic area. In this case, the questions are more likely to be related to what jobs exist, and where they are.

At least part of this information can be acquired from the latest decennial census, if those data can still be considered current. Such a source can probably be safely used in most communities during about the first third of each decade, then with diminishing confidence in each succeeding year.

If one decides that census data are not current or available in sufficient detail, he/she then may wish to consider a community survey as a method of acquiring the desired information. Zapoleon[8] has prepared a detailed statement describing the procedures to follow in developing and completing a community survey. The statement includes more than seventy steps to be taken in accomplishing the task, and it is usually considered the basic reference on this topic. So that the reader may understand the general procedures followed in such a project, the major topic headings are briefly described here:

a. *Preliminary planning:* Defining the needs, listing the purposes, obtaining and examining available material bearing on the problem; finding a sponsor.
b. *Determining scope, content, and method:* Defining the geographic area;

sex, race, and age groups; occupational groups to be included; deciding on nature of information sought and whether it can best be obtained from employers or from residents at home; deciding between mailed questionnaire and interview.

c. *Preparing work plan and budget:* Estimating number to be contacted, and number needed to obtain and tabulate information; preparing a budget.

d. *Preparing forms:* Preparing questionnaire, testing it, coding items, preparing written instructions.

e. *Introducing the survey:* Presenting plans to sponsor, arranging for publicity and public cooperation.

f. *Directing survey personnel:* Selecting personnel needed, training workers.

g. *Collecting the data:* Preparing lists of contacts to be made, supplying interviewers with assignments, checking incoming data for completeness.

h. *Editing and tabulating data:* Checking each item, tabulating information.

i. *Interpreting data and preparing report:* Assembling tabulations and other data, organizing for interpretation, outlining report, preparing final report, reproducing report.

j. *Using report:* Distributing to key persons, publicizing findings, planning for revision.

The need for local surveys to develop information specifically pertinent to the locality has been emphasized by Mitchell [9] and by Smith.[10] The literature includes several illustrations of community surveys that can be used. Among those available are studies of Toms River by Ames;[11] of Middletown by Brochard, Beilin, and Thompson;[12] of Pasadena by Leis;[13] and of Santa Cruz County by Elder.[14]

Nonschool counseling agencies find the community survey particularly applicable to their clientele. Since most of these agencies serve adults whose vocational problem is their immediate relationship to their jobs, it is frequently crucial to have available current and accurate information that reflects the scope of occupations in the locality. Obviously, successful occupational relocation or readjustment necessitates knowledge of reasonable options that exist within the area. The importance of community surveys is emphasized by the fact that the Social Security Administration authorizes the collection of such data when needed to provide a basis for proper discussions in disability award hearings.

Follow-up Survey

A third source of occupational information has more direct relevance to curriculum evaluation and revision but, nevertheless, provides data that have great value within a specific school. This source is the follow-up survey of previous students. When properly executed, such a study permits a school to reach some decisions regarding the effectiveness of its program in assisting its pupils to meet successfully the problems they encounter after leaving school. Information obtained about career experiences should be pertinent for those students about to complete their schooling. To be completely realistic, the study should include dropouts as well as those who have completed the program. Because of possible biases that can result from incomplete returns, every effort should be made to secure as near total returns as possible.

Procedurally, one would organize a follow-up study in the same way as a community survey. Zapoleon's recommendations would, therefore, be an appropriate guide. Further help, particularly with suggested forms that might be used, can be found in Hoppock.[15]

Rothney and his associates have contributed specific suggestions on improving various follow-up procedures.[16, 17, 18] Kornhauser and Sheatley have proposed techniques for improving the questionnaire and interview procedures utilized in follow-up studies.[19] Putnam has discussed the use of community resources,[20] and Cleland has proposed the use of visual aids.[21]

Several professional journals include summaries of results obtained in various follow-up studies. These are useful to the reader not only in providing specific information about the group studied, but also as a model for developing a study appropriate to his/her own situation. A complete tabulation of such studies lies outside the scope of this volume.

Most journal reports of follow-up studies describe school-based projects. The use of this procedure in out-of-school counseling agencies is equally appropriate. Like the community survey, this technique lends itself to the specific needs of the clientele served by the agency. Although the results of such a study would automatically reflect the effectiveness of the agencies' service, the major value should lie in the useful information produced that can be used by and with clients. Only minor modifications in procedure are needed to change the school follow-up study to an agency follow-up study.

SOURCES OF PUBLISHED
OCCUPATIONAL INFORMATION

Occupational information is acquired and developed by means of one of the three techniques described above. It is processed and published by numerous agencies and companies—in fact, so many that some categorization of such sources is essential in order to use them most effectively. No attempt will be made in this volume to provide an exhaustive list of occupational materials. The *Vocational Guidance Quarterly* publishes in each issue a special feature entitled "Current Career Literature," which lists recently published materials available to the counselor. The publications are classified according to the categories listed earlier. The identification and listing of these publications is a most worthy professional contribution by the members of the Career Information Review Service Committee of the National Vocational Guidance Association.

Government Agencies

Most federal agencies publish materials that relate directly to occupations. If the publication is free, it can be obtained directly from the agency that produced it. If the material is sold, it can be obtained either from the agency itself or from the Superintendent of Documents, U.S. Government Printing Office. Since most government publications are sold, the latter source is usually the better one. Arrangements for purchase can be made in any of three ways: (1) the price of each item can be included with the order (although, since many of the items are very inexpensive, this can be awkward and inconvenient); (2) coupons can be purchased in quantity, and then used as scrip to pay for small purchases; or (3) funds in the amount of $25 or more may be placed on deposit, and then arrangements made to charge purchases against this credit until the funds are exhausted. Most users will usually find one of the last two methods convenient for their purposes. One cannot order materials from the Government Printing Office and expect to be billed for them. Because a tremendous number of publications are handled by this agency, the purchaser must be careful to provide the exact title of the item desired as well as the name of the agency responsible for its publication.

Since the output of the Government Printing Office is so extensive, it is difficult to keep abreast of new items that might have value for the counselor or teacher. A monthly catalog is published that lists all materials published during the previous month. Although the only way to be certain of identifying each government publication that has pertinence to the field is to check each issue of the catalog carefully, this becomes an arduous and time-consuming task. For most counselors, it is more convenient to be placed on the mailing list of agencies that produce the major portion of occupational materials, or to obtain regularly the price lists of materials (available from either the agency or the Superintendent of Documents) published by those agencies. Even though this will not be as comprehensive, it will help the counselor to be aware of most of the materials issued by government agencies.

The reader who has even a modest understanding of the various governmental departments and their function and purposes can deduce the subject areas of materials likely to be available from those agencies. To provide some picture of the scope of pertinent government agencies, some of those that publish more extensively are listed below, with a very brief statement of the kinds of materials available from each.

DEPARTMENT OF AGRICULTURE. Many brochures and pamphlets are available concerning various careers in the field of agriculture and closely related fields. There are also materials available describing opportunities in the department itself.

DEPARTMENT OF COMMERCE. Many publications are available related to various aspects of business. Since the Bureau of the Census is a part of this department, all census publications can be obtained here.

DEPARTMENT OF DEFENSE. Each of the armed forces publishes handbooks describing career opportunities within that specific branch of service. Designed primarily for recruiting purposes, each book provides an indication of the relationship of each military specialty to civilian work.

DEPARTMENT OF HEALTH, EDUCATION, AND WELFARE. Career opportunities in the health occupations, particularly those opportunities within the agency, are described in a series of pamphlets. Other publications related to the fields of rehabilitation and education also are available.

DEPARTMENT OF INTERIOR. Information about career fields within the department are described in various publications. Most of the materials are related to professional careers.

DEPARTMENT OF LABOR. Many sections of this large department are extremely active in publishing materials that can be used advantageously by counselors and by teachers. Many publications mentioned in earlier chapters come from this source, such as the *Dictionary of Occupational Titles* and the *Occupational Outlook Handbook*. The price list of publications from this agency is one that all counselors should have on hand.

DEPARTMENT OF STATE. Information about careers within the department and in the foreign service is available.

DEPARTMENT OF THE TREASURY. Publications describing careers in the Coast Guard are available from this agency.

OTHER FEDERAL AGENCIES. Many agencies, such as the Civil Service Commission, National Science Foundation, National Aeronautics and Space Administration, and the Small Business Administration publish materials related to their areas of emphasis.

STATE GOVERNMENT AGENCIES. Many state agencies, particularly the offices of public instruction and the employment services, publish materials that have direct relevance to counselors. Inquiries should usually be made directly to the appropriate office.

Commercial Publishers

Many commercial printing companies publish materials that contain information directly related to occupations. Several companies publish series of pamphlets, monographs, or booklets designed specifically to provide occupational information. A list is included in Appendix B.

Several publishers have issued series of books with career emphases.[22] Some of these are detailed descriptions of occupational fields; others are essentially career fiction or biographical in nature. Publishers having series of such books available are included in Appendix B.

Professional and Industrial Organizations

A variety of occupational materials is available from the professional groups that are active in career fields. Some of these groups have prepared and published excellent monographs and other materials of real help to the counselor or teacher. The Department of Commerce has published a *Directory of National Associations of Businessmen*, which provides a list of most of the groups that can be classified under this heading. The Department of Labor publishes a similar directory of labor unions.

Since the materials published by these groups may be designed to serve the special interests of the sponsoring group, the counselor should evaluate the materials carefully before using them with students. Publications, if slanted, could be in either direction—emphasizing the advantages of the work in order to recruit and attract others to the field, or concentrating on the disadvantages or restrictions in order to limit the number of entrants attracted to the field. Some decline has recently been noted in this area of publication.[23]

Private Companies

A number of private companies in a variety of industries such as retail merchandising, banking, steel production, and chemical production publish occupational materials. Ordinarily, this is done by large nationwide corporations whose basic purpose is to use the materials in recruiting potential career workers. Some of the publications tend to emphasize the benefits that accrue to the worker. On the other hand, the materials often are prepared with copious illustrations and information that make them most useful. The kinds of items available from these sources also vary widely, from brief pamphlets to substantial hardback books.

Educational Institutions

A number of universities and other educational institutions have prepared materials that describe opportunities in career fields for which the specific school provides preparation. Some of these are brief, four-page abstracts, others are collections of such briefs, and a few are extensive publications covering several fields in depth.

Some of the larger state universities have prepared briefs that are compiled in a hardback binder, copies of which are placed in all of the high schools served by that institution. Many briefs are kept up-to-date by recording the name of the person to whom the binder is issued and sending regular replacement materials as new publications appear or as older ones are revised. Usually the principal or the counselor is responsible for maintaining the folder.

Trade and technical schools often prepare descriptions of the fields for which they offer training; frequently the materials are specifically focused on the area within which the school places most of its graduates.

A few degree-granting schools prepare lists of occupations into which their graduates have gone. These are sometimes prepared according to the area of the student's academic major—for example, a list of occupations into which English majors have been placed. Such publications are especially useful to teachers and counselors who attempt to answer students' questions about the kind of work for which they will be prepared when they select a particular major field.

Periodicals

One often encounters articles in the popular national magazines that are pertinent to the field of career information. Many of these articles have been prepared as human interest or feature stories, but may be highly useful in helping a student understand an occupational field.

A number of popular magazines are aimed at particular reader groups and include career materials of special interest to those groups. For example, *Glamour, Mademoiselle,* and *Seventeen* all serve the teen-age girl. Each of these frequently includes articles focused on career information for this group. Some even include career departments as a regular feature.

Publications of professional or industrial groups, such as *National Business Woman* or *Zontian,* include career information directed to girls or women or to other groups served by those periodicals.

There are, of course, several periodicals related to the field of counseling and guidance that include up-to-date career information. Examples of these include *Guidance Newsletter, Journal of College Placement, Per-*

sonnel and Guidance Journal, and the *Vocational Guidance Quarterly.* Most of these often will be available in the professional library.

A few periodicals, such as the *Monthly Labor Review* and the *Occupational Outlook Quarterly,* are government periodicals publishing specific materials that are career-oriented.

Audio-Visual Materials

Many films and filmstrips are highly useful in presenting career information. The old Chinese proverb "A picture is worth a thousand words" should not be disregarded in helping youth to gain insight into those career fields not easily accessible for direct contact. One may often acquire more understanding of what a worker does and how he/she does it from an eleven-minute film than from many hours of reading. In addition to films, there are tapes containing career information.

Since films are costly to produce and many have a more limited usage than printed materials, the teacher and counselor may wish to rent these materials, rather than purchase them. Career films can be obtained from many film-rental centers. Most schools regularly use such services through the facilities of city or state educational departments or the visual instruction center of nearby universities. Counselors and teachers usually can consult the catalog of such centers or other guides to audio-visual materials to determine what is available. The school media specialist often will have information about materials that have been released since publication of the various guides or catalogs.

Audio-visual materials often serve as the core for the many multimedia approaches that are now available to schools and agencies. Some indication of the phenomenal growth in this area is seen in the well established trend of school systems to employ media specialists. Responsible for an overwhelming array of materials and devices for effective use of the material, these specialists can be of great help to the counselor in finding and using audio-visual materials as well as the more traditional printed library resources.

Counselors should utilize a wide range of information sources to keep abreast of developments in this rapidly growing field. Commercial companies and professional groups often produce audio-visual materials pertinent to the counselor. One helpful source is a regular monthly feature in the *Vocational Guidance Quarterly* entitled "Current Career Films." The previously mentioned monograph by Hansen also includes an extensive discussion of multi-media approaches,[24] some of which we will consider in Chapter 13.

As is true of printed materials, films may soon become out of date or inappropriate for particular students. Care should be exercised in selecting all career materials, to assure currency and appropriateness.

Laramore has described a project in which counselors made audio-tapes and slides of jobs for use with high school students in Maryland.[25] Many school systems now own portable video taping equipment that can be applied to the preparation of local career information. The lack of professional quality found in commercially prepared films may often be compensated for by the local interest and local color that a "home made" production can incorporate. Johnson, Korn, and Dunn report a study in which they demonstrated that presentation of occupational information by use of a locally prepared slide-tape format was more effective than presenting the same information either orally or in a written format.[26]

SOURCES OF PERSONAL-SOCIAL INFORMATION

We have used the term "educational information" to describe materials about facilities and programs by means of which the individual develops marketable skills and knowledge. Most of Part IV was concerned with this general topic. Similarly, we have used "occupational information" to refer to materials that describe jobs and occupations.

The term "personal-social information" is used ordinarily to refer to materials whose function is to help the individual understand self and others better so that interpersonal relations can be more effective. This area often includes such topics as understanding oneself, understanding others, making friends, social skills and manners, personal appearance, family relationships, and economic planning. We are frequently reminded by an unending barrage of television commercials, magazine advertisements, and other media devices, of the crucial importance of using the proper deodorant and hair grooming preparation, of wearing fashionable clothes, and of borrowing money from the most advantageous source for the car, home, boat, or other item that will assure our social success. Although our mass media undoubtedly exploit the advertising budgets of the suppliers of these commodities and services, it is clear that career success does involve the application of personal-social information.

Self-understanding and interpersonal relations touch all aspects of the individual's life, not just one's vocational life. Within the school setting, attention is provided to these topics at all levels and in many parts of the curriculum. In fact, almost every subject area has applications that relate, at least in part, to the personal-social area. The health teacher is concerned with body care and grooming; the physical education teacher will focus on these as well as on social interaction through games and physical activities; the social studies teacher will devote time to understanding others, boy-girl relations, etc. Many others on the school staff have direct involvement in this area. Outside the school, numerous agencies deal with various aspects of this vast area; for example, character building agencies, family relations agencies, financial and material assistance agencies, psychological and psychiatric aid agencies, recreation agencies, and religious agencies.

One might justifiably ask why the counselor need be concerned with the personal-social area, when so many are already focusing on the topic. To a large extent, the question answers itself. Since the counselor is concerned with helping the individual develop and implement career plans, anything that bears on that development and implementation must be reckoned with. Obviously, this includes the personal-social area.

Within the school setting, the counselor has many colleagues who have special competencies in various aspects of this broad area. He/she should, of course, seek the assistance of those individuals wherever possible. Similarly, many specialists in the various community social agencies can provide special skills. Counselors, both within the school and in nonschool agencies, should utilize appropriate resource individuals as needed, regardless of their location. Counselors in both settings should develop a community resources file if such a directory does not already exist and should determine the other kinds of resources that already exist, either within their agency or in other accessible locations. For example, the school counselor may find that faculty colleagues have already accumulated an array of pamphlets, brochures, booklets, even books on those personal-social topics that relate to the subject area for which they have responsibility. Needless duplication would be a waste of both funds and effort. Other staff members who have not organized collections of materials may be especially knowledgeable about either general sources of pertinent materials or specific items appropriate for a particular need.

INDEXES

As one surveys the wide range of sources from which career information emanates, one is led to conclude that it is difficult to keep abreast of current publication—and so it is. Effective proctoring of the various sources requires close attention to a number of publications designed to notify interested individuals that new materials are available. The regular listing of recently released materials in *Vocational Guidance Quarterly* already has been identified.

Supplementary to this type of listing is a series of indexes published by commercial publishers, public service agencies, and professional organizations. These indexes usually are printed at regular intervals, four or more times yearly, and include lists of those articles, pamphlets, or other materials related to the field. Many counselors find this type of service especially helpful in keeping abreast of materials that appear from sources outside the channels routinely checked by the counselor. Illustrative of this type of publication are the following:

Career Index. Published by Chronicle Guidance Publications, Inc., Moravia, N.Y. 13118

Counselor's Information Services. Published by B'nai B'rith Career and Counseling Service, 1640 Rhode Island Ave. N.W., Washington, D.C. 20036

Inform. Published by National Career Information Center (APGA), 1607 New Hampshire Ave. N.W., Washington, D.C. 20009

Cumulative indexes have certain inherent advantages, particularly in terms of comprehensiveness. On the other hand, publication lag and the fact that such books appear on a two- or three-year cycle create serious problems of timeliness. Two examples of this type of publication are the *NVGA Bibliography* previously mentioned and Forrester's *Occupational Literature*.[27,28]

Many agencies and publishers of career information also produce materials related to the personal-social area. School librarians and other media specialists can be especially helpful to the counselor in identifying sources of suitable materials for the group or individual with whom the counselor is working. Norris, Zeran, Hatch, and Engelkes have identified a comprehensive list of sources and items classified according to the following topics: Understanding oneself, Understanding others, Family relations, Sex education and human sexuality, Health-good health practices, Drug education, Venereal Disease control, Personal appearance, Manners and etiquette, Social skills, Financial planning, and Leisure time.[29]

SOURCES—SOCIOLOGICAL, PSYCHOLOGICAL, ECONOMIC

Only very limited assistance can be given at this time to the counselor who is seeking materials on the sociological, psychological, and economic aspects of career fields.[30] There is a tremendous need for interdisciplinary research in which counselors and counselor educators work with members of the basic disciplines to develop knowledge that will help us all to acquire further insight into these aspects of work and their influence on the worker and his/her family. Much of the present material dealing with these areas is exploratory and often incomplete. Nevertheless, enough has been done to demonstrate the importance of extending the coverage of these areas.

At the present time, more sociological articles are appearing than either economic or psychological ones. These, of course, are concentrated primarily in the professional journals on sociology. The counselor who wishes to expand knowledge of these aspects will find it helpful to include several sociological journals in a basic program of professional reading.

Overs and Deutsch have compiled a series of abstracts of sociological studies that bear directly on the individual and his work.[31] The counselor who becomes familiar with this excellent volume will gain invaluable understanding of the specific occupations included in the various abstracts. Further, the kind of information provided should help the counselor frame questions about the sociological aspects of other occupations that may be of immediate concern to a client.

Economic information is currently available from various government publications, especially those of the Bureau of Labor Statistics in the Department of Labor. The *Monthly Labor Review* and the *Occupational Outlook Quarterly* are most useful for many counselors.

NOTES

1. W. E. Hopke, "A New Look at Occupational Information," *Vocational Guidance Quarterly*, vol. 15, no. 1 (September, 1966), pp. 18–25.
2. K. R. Kunze, "Industry Resources Available to Counselors," *Vocational Guidance Quarterly*, vol. 16, no. 2 (December, 1967), pp. 137–142.
3. R. P. Overs, "Covert Occupational Information," *Vocational Guidance Quarterly*, vol. 16, no. 1 (September, 1967), pp. 7–12.
4. NVGA Career Information Review Service Committee, *NVGA Bibliography of Current Occupational Literature* (Washington: National Vocational Guidance Association, 1973).
5. L. Hansen, *Career Guidance Practices in School and Community* (Washington, D.C.: National Vocational Guidance Association, 1970).
6. Department of Labor, Manpower Administration, *Job Analysis for Human Resources Management: A Review of Selected Research and Development.* Manpower Research Monograph No. 36. (Washington, D.C.: U.S. Government Printing Office, 1974).
7. *Ibid.*, pp. 6–7.
8. M. W. Zapoleon, *Community Occupational Surveys*, U.S. Office of Education, Vocational Division, Bulletin No. 223 (Washington: U.S. Government Printing Office, 1942).
9. J. P. Mitchell, "Vocational Guidance and Skills of the Work Force," *Personnel and Guidance Journal*, vol. 35, no. 1 (September, 1956), p. 7.
10. J. A. Smith, "Developing Local Occupational Information," *Vocational Guidance Quarterly*, vol. 2, no. 2 (Winter, 1953), pp. 59–61.
11. D. A. Ames, "Toms River Surveys Its Needs," *Personnel and Guidance Journal*, vol. 31, no. 5 (January, 1953), p. 227.
12. J. H. Brochard, H. Beilin, and A. S. Thompson, *Middletown Occupational Handbook* (New York: Teachers College, Columbia University, 1954).
13. W. W. Leis, "Pasadena's Occupational Survey Features Segments and Cycles," *Vocational Guidance Quarterly*, vol. 4, no. 3 (Spring, 1956), pp. 110–112.
14. L. A. Elder, "An Inservice Community Occupational Survey," *Vocational Guidance Quarterly*, vol. 17, no. 3 (March, 1969), pp. 185–188.
15. R. Hoppock, *Occupational Information* 4th ed., (New York: McGraw-Hill Book Company, 1976), pp. 164–165, 266–267.

16. J. W. M. Rothney and R. L. Mooren, "Sampling Problems in Follow-up Research," *Personnel and Guidance Journal*, vol. 30, no. 9 (May, 1952), pp. 573–579.

17. R. L. Mooren and J. W. M. Rothney, "Personalizing the Follow-up Study," *Personnel and Guidance Journal*, vol. 34, no. 7 (March, 1956), pp. 409–412.

18. R. M. Jackson and J. W. M. Rothney, "A Comparative Study of the Mailed Questionnaire and the Interview in Follow-up Studies," *Personnel and Guidance Journal*, vol. 39, no. 7 (March, 1961), pp. 569–571.

19. A. Kornhauser and P. B. Sheatley, "Questionnaire Construction and Interview Procedure," in *Research Methods in Social Relations*, eds. C. Sellitz and others (New York: Holt, Rinehart & Winston, Inc., 1962), pp. 546–587.

20. J. A. Putnam, "Use of Community Resources in a Follow-up Study," *Personnel and Guidance Journal*, vol. 32, no. 7 (March, 1954), p. 409.

21. H. L. Cleland, "A Follow-up Survey through Visual Aids," *Occupations*, vol. 19, no. 5 (February, 1941), pp. 331–334.

22. K. A. Haebich, *Vocations in Biography and Fiction* (Chicago: American Library Association, 1962).

23. H. Mathis and L. Mathis, "Career Information Publications of Professional Societies and Trade Associations," *Vocational Guidance Quarterly*, vol. 19, no. 3 (March, 1971), pp. 211–214.

24. L. Hansen, *op. cit.*, Chapter 4.

25. D. Laramore, "Counselors Make Occupational Information Packages," *Vocational Guidance Quarterly*, vol. 19, no. 3 (March, 1971), pp. 220–224.

26. W. F. Johnson, T. A. Korn, D. J. Dunn, "Comparing Three Methods of Presenting Occupational Information," *Vocational Guidance Quarterly*, vol. 24, no. 1 (September, 1975), pp. 62–66.

27. NVGA Career Information Review Service Committee, *op. cit.*

28. G. Forrester, *Occupational Literature: An Annotated Bibliography* (New York: H. W. Wilson Co., 1971).

29. W. Norris, F. Zeran, R. Hatch, and J. Engelkes, *The Information Service in Guidance*, third edition (Chicago: Rand McNally and Co., 1972), Chapter 7, pp. 253–296.

30. J. Samler, "Psycho-Social Aspects of Work: A Critique of Occupational Information," *Personnel and Guidance Journal*, vol. 39, no. 6 (Feb., 1961), pp. 458–465.

31. R. Overs and E. Deutsch, *Abstracts of Sociological Studies of Occupations* (Milwaukee: Curative Workshop of Milwaukee, 1968).

12
Collecting, Evaluating, and Filing Printed Career Information

All agencies that work with adolescents and adults in the process of vocational choice and planning will find frequent need of a wide range of printed career materials. Since many of the materials will be used with many students, it is generally agreed that a collection of these items should be compiled in advance, so that they will be available for use as needed. This chapter is concerned with some of the basic concepts pertinent to the collection, evaluation, and filing of printed materials for a career resources center.

Many reasons can be marshalled that argue against any attempt to collect everything that provides information about careers. Such considerations as space needed for storage, cost, and degree of utilization are sufficient to rule out such an extravagant approach. Careful selection is necessary to assure the acquisition of pertinent and useful materials.

Among the changes that have occurred in the past decade is the transformation of the school library into a learning resources center or a media center. Technological developments now have made possible the inclusion of much material in a variety of forms, both printed and non-printed, as well as an assortment of equipment used in applying the materials. With increasing frequency, this vital area of the school is staffed by a highly competent, thoroughly-trained media specialist.

Fortunate, indeed, is the school counselor who finds such a colleague in his/her school. Here is an ally, fully knowledgeable about the material and equipment in that center, as well as totally dedicated to helping students and staff use those resources. The media specialist has been taught the principles and procedures for collecting, evaluating, filing, and using the entire gamut of materials included in the center. He/she can be of immense help to the counselor in the activities described in this chapter and the next. The media specialist usually is the resident expert for finding the materials needed by the counselor, and a close working alliance should be built for the mutual advantage of both.

Since many counselors work in nonschool settings, and some work in schools without broadly trained media specialists, the remainder of this chapter is written from the viewpoint that assumes the counselor must either take sole responsibility or major leadership in developing and operating a career resources center.

CRITERIA FOR COLLECTING MATERIALS

Attention must be given to several factors in the process of collecting career information. The following items should be considered before undertaking the collection process:

1. The group that will make major use of the materials
2. The nature of the community
3. The staff that will utilize the materials
4. How the materials will be used
5. Existing materials already available
6. Auxiliary local resources
7. Funds available

1. THE GROUP THAT WILL MAKE MAJOR USE OF THE MATERIALS. Obviously different materials would be used in a junior high school, where students are only beginning to explore concepts about the world of work, than in a vocational rehabilitation center for adults. Even where the differences are less extreme than this, materials should be appropriate to the specific group. Within a school, the grade levels to be served by the career resources center will provide some basis for selection. If materials are to be used primarily by junior high school students, a different emphasis would be needed than if students from grades seven through twelve were expected to use the collection, or if only senior high school students were involved. The grade level of the group will provide at least a rough indication of the level of reading skill—a factor that relates to both length and reading difficulty level of prospective materials. Even within a grade level, there are differences that might modify the selection of materials. A junior high school that serves students likely to withdraw from school as soon as the dropout age is reached would want to use different materials than the junior high school with a negligible dropout rate. The range of ability and interest in the group also will influence the choice of materials. One might hypothesize the narrowest range of materials would be appropriate only in a senior high school where *all* the students come from a middle-class background, *all* are of relatively high academic ability, and *all* are definitely planning to go on to college. Since few such schools exist, most will have to select materials on a fairly broad base, considering the students served by that school.

Most nonschool agencies can almost automatically assume a broad range of interest, ability, and academic background in the clients they serve. These variations will necessitate planning to select as broad a range of career materials as needed. If the agency exists to serve a specific group, its needs must be considered in choosing materials.

2. THE NATURE OF THE COMMUNITY. A knowledge of the community in which the school or agency is situated will provide additional information about the group that will use the career information library. Although the growing mobility of Americans decreases the likelihood that they will remain within the community throughout their lives, the range and scope of occupations within the community may well provide the framework for the evaluation and consideration of career fields by students and their parents. That is, it will be more difficult to stimulate students to consider a wide range of occupational choice if they have grown up in a stable community dominated by a single industry, than if the town has many businesses and factories and the population is constantly changing. Pamphlets and monographs related to agricultural careers would certainly be appropriate in rural schools, but of quite limited value in a school in most of our congested urban areas. Descriptions of opportunities in the textile manufacturing industry would be of interest and use in Tennessee schools, but of little value in Montana; information on the shipbuilding industry would have pertinence along both coasts of our country, but little relevance in the midwestern plains states.

The socio-economic range within the community and the extent to which community attitudes encourage educational achievement and individual development also are factors to be considered.

3. THE STAFF THAT WILL UTILIZE THE MATERIALS. Logically, the materials to be used only by the counselor would differ from those to be used by a group of teachers. The teachers' broader range of experiences and knowledge about career fields would probably necessitate a wider range of materials.

Use of some items—for example, the *Dictionary of Occupational Titles*—presupposes some understanding of the organizational structure of the world of work and of the volume itself, as well as the theoretical and philosophic basis for the book. If materials are purchased that lie beyond the competency of the staff that will use them, they will likely be misused or left unused. For example, almost every school counselor has encountered both students and teachers who interpret scores on the *Kuder Preference Record* as indicative of ability or aptitude, when it claims only to be a manifestation of interests and preferences. This misconception often creates difficulties in helping youth to understand their personal characteristics. Similarly, misuse or misinterpretation of career materials can be a disservice.

4. How the Materials Will Be Used. Closely related to who uses the career resources center is the question of how the materials are to be used. If career materials will be used only by the counselor and only in individual counseling concerning vocational plans, a wide range of items in single or duplicate copies will probably be most appropriate. On the other hand, if materials are to be used for instructional purposes in a group guidance or classroom setting, the range of materials will probably be narrowed, in order to have available the number of copies needed for the group to use. Similarly, if class or group use is anticipated—for example, in a junior high school careers class—the durability of binding may become a more important factor than would normally be the case, so the person responsible for collecting materials may need to give more attention to this requirement. Between these two extremes are the needs of small groups—group counseling, special interest groups, a career club, or others—who may need multiple copies or material in depth in certain fields.

5. Existing Materials Already Available. Even if a counselor were newly appointed in a school that had never previously had a counselor, it would usually be fallacious to assume that the school had no career material on hand. Probably the only time this is likely to be true is when a new school is opened. Whether or not he/she finds a file of career information in his/her office, the counselor should check with the school librarian to learn what pertinent materials are in the library. Although difficult to imagine, it is possible to have a school library that does not include anything related to careers.

An additional reservoir of career materials may be found in the resource materials collected by teachers for their use in the classroom. Many teachers have encountered inquiries by students concerning the relationship between subject area and possible career fields. The classroom book shelves are a likely source of career materials. Beyond these general materials, some classroom teachers may have developed additional files or collections of career materials for their classes. This is particularly likely in those subject areas that have a direct and obvious career relationship. Examples of people to consult would be industrial arts teachers, commercial teachers, home economics teachers, and the coordinator of diversified education classes.

If the school has a curriculum materials center or a professional library for its staff, it is likely that appropriate materials will be available there. Sometimes nonteaching staff, such as the school nurse, may have available materials related to a specific occupation.

6. Auxiliary Local Resources. In almost every community are agencies that work with youth or adults, and hence might have materials that relate to their problems, including career information materials. The local public library is a most likely location for materials of this type. The counselor who is responsible for collecting materials for the school or agency should certainly check with the local library, not only to determine the extent of present holdings in the library, but also to develop some coordination in making future acquisitions, so that the two sources supplement rather than duplicate one another. Other local resources that may have materials would be 4-H clubs, youth centers, YMCA and YWCA, and churches or other groups that operate active youth or adult programs.

7. Funds Available. Obviously, plans for obtaining career information will be influenced by the amount of money available. Rarely does a school, or any other agency, have an unlimited budget; consequently, the development of a basic library of materials may have to be planned over a period of time. The individual responsible for the development of the library should be sure that there are sufficient funds to make a reasonable start, and that there will be continuing appropriations in future budgets for extending the project as well as replacing out-of-date items.

Some schools have found that the financial support of a career resources center is a public service project that often has appeal to one or more of the local service clubs. If a service club wishes to help start the project but does not want to be committed to future support, the school should be prepared to provide the funds for subsequent years before initiating the undertaking. A library that is not maintained with regular replacements is soon filled with out-of-date material, which is worse than no material at all.

In many states, funds for initiating or extending a career resources center in a school can be obtained through the state department of education.

INITIATING A COLLECTION OF
CAREER MATERIALS

It is axiomatic that the counselor should focus first on meeting the greatest need. Considering the first two or three items on the list above should help concentrate attention on the group to be served. Since student bodies, even within the same school system, or clients in an agency may be expected to vary considerably, one will develop a more useful library on this basis than if one simply duplicates the materials of a counselor in a nearby school or agency.

If a guidance advisory committee has been named in the school, discussion with this group may help clarify the nature of the general student group and the areas of student needs that should be given priority. If such a committee does not exist, the counselor can seek similar aid from a representative group of faculty members.

A school that includes many students who will complete their formal education at this level must have career materials to serve them. Since this may be their last chance for such help, these students may warrant some priority. In other schools, most students may be college bound. Here, emphasis should first be given to educational information about colleges and to materials related to occupational fields requiring college training.

Since a career resources center in any school should serve all students, the principle of greatest need must sometimes be modified by considering how widely usable the materials will be. The counselor will inevitably confront the decision of selecting materials that serve one or the other of these major purposes. Some reasonable balance between the two is the most sensible choice. How far one can go in selecting materials to fill students' unmet needs in these two different directions will, of course, depend primarily on the amount of funds available to start the program.

Once the counselor has collected the materials that are urgently needed to meet the most pressing needs apparent within the group, it is logical to move toward the development of breadth of materials next. The extent or range of materials to be considered obviously is based on the range within the group. After these two needs have been met, at least minimally, one then may move toward acquiring materials related to specialized fields or adding depth to already selected areas.

In summary, then, the counselor should ordinarily assign priority in selecting materials in the following order: (1) attempt to meet the most urgent needs within the group, (2) select materials likely to have the broadest use or appeal within the group, and (3) select specialized materials or those that provide depth in areas of greatest interest.

Because of the variability to be expected in each situation, it is impossible to spell out specifically how each counselor should proceed. There are, however, certain preliminary steps that may help the counselor select the most appropriate materials for local needs. Those steps are considered next. Like an intelligent consumer in any other field, one is more likely to make wise expenditures if one has a fairly good idea of what is available and of comparable costs for various materials. With these two general items of information, the counselor then should be able to make the best use of available funds.[1]

The following steps, not necessarily in this specific order, should be taken by the counselor to gain familiarity with what is currently available (for specific references, see the previous chapter):

1. Subscribe to some of the indexes listing occupational materials. Since these do not completely overlap one another, it often is wise to subscribe to at least two, if possible.
2. Request price lists from federal and state agencies that publish materials related to areas pertinent to the counselor's group. One also may wish to check with the local or other nearby library to determine if it subscribes to the Government Printing Office's *Monthly Catalog*. If so, he/she may want to check this periodically for useful publications. He/she also should arrange to purchase government materials as described in the previous chapter.
3. Obtain some of the more recent bibliographies of occupational materials, such as the *NVGA Bibliography*,[2] Forrester's,[3] or *Career Index*.[4]
4. Check recent professional publications, such as *Vocational Guidance Quarterly*, for appropriate materials.
5. Obtain price lists from commercial publishers who have materials directly related to occupations. (One may wish to collaborate later with the school librarian and the local public librarian in developing resources of career fiction, biographical career materials, and similar books available from other publishers.)
6. Ascertain from appropriate professional organizations and societies, private industries, industrial associations, and private companies what materials they have that are approprite for his/her group.[5]
7. Contact educational institutions for publications. Many schools have career materials available, as well as such items as catalogs and bulletins. Among higher educational institutions, the counselor in a secondary school would probably first contact the colleges within the state or immediate geographic area, and then those out-of-state institutions to which students from the school regularly go. Materials from trade and technical schools usually would be requested on the basis of the schools in which students express an interest.
8. Determine which general items or basic resource volumes are essential for immediate use. These might include one or more sets of the latest *Dictionary of Occupational Titles*, the latest issue of *Occupational Outlook Handbook*, and annual subscriptions to *Occupational Outlook Quarterly* and appropriate educational directories.

Once the counselor has completed these steps, he/she has available the basic information needed to make appropriate purchases in light of the needs being met, with the funds at hand.[6] If funds are sufficient, one should hold some in reserve to purchase new materials as they appear, or to obtain materials for special needs that develop during the year.

Maintaining and expanding a collection of career information is an unending task. The counselor must continuously strive to keep materials current. Since the world of work is constantly changing, and sometimes extremely rapidly, one must provide for some system of regularly assessing the appropriateness of materials on hand. This usually can be handled most easily by scheduling time, at least annually, to review materials. Currency must be the determining factor in deciding whether to retain material in the file. If an item no longer presents an accurate picture, it must be discarded, regardless of how much "life" appears to be left in the binding. Materials related to highly volatile fields should be checked more frequently than once a year.

As the materials are regularly checked for currency, they also should be checked to ascertain losses. Career materials can be expected to disappear, so provision for replacement is necessary. A basic expectation in developing such a file is that the materials will be used by students, hopefully on an extensive basis. When this occurs, some loss is inevitable and should be anticipated. Stringent security measures to minimize loss of materials probably will result in decreased usage—a far higher price to pay. Reasonable care should be given to protect and assure the return of materials, but this should not become the primary issue.

In addition to replacing obsolete and lost items in the library, the counselor should expand it to meet new and anticipated needs. The various indexes, bibliographies, and price lists will help the counselor know what is available or may soon be available. One should then have little difficulty in developing a list of items to be purchased as soon as funds are on hand.

The present trend in many schools and colleges to employ professionally trained media specialists should be of great assistance to the counselor in collecting appropriate materials. Close cooperation between counselor and the media specialist is essential. Many schools are now assigning primary responsibility for the acquisition of materials to this specialist.

EVALUATING CAREER INFORMATION

Evaluation is an integral part of building a good career resources center.[7, 8, 9] No counselor would make indiscriminate personal purchases—a dozen shirts from a local department store, for example—without specifying size, color, style, quality, and material. Casual or careless accumulation of career information can easily result in a "wardrobe" as ludicrous and useless as the foolish shirt order. The wise consumer wants to be assured that the purchase meets present needs before a commitment to buy is made. If one buys a "grabbag" item, one recognizes the risk of funds involved with a high possibility of little return for the money. This premise is just as appropriate in collecting career information.[10]

The seven factors discussed at the beginning of this chapter obviously bear on the evaluation of career information and should be basic to the consideration of material. A counselor always should keep in mind the group that will use the materials, and the needs of that group.[11] Further, one must remember the staff that will use the materials and the ways in which the materials will be used. Finally, one must remain aware of the costs of the various desired items in relation to the funds available.

Additionally, each possible acquisition should be measured against these criteria: accuracy, currency, usability, reader appeal, and thoroughness.

1. ACCURACY. Even if the item being evaluated meets all other criteria, it is valueless if it fails this one. The material must depict the occupation fairly and correctly, if the reader is to be able to draw inferences and conclusions that will help in understanding the field. Inaccuracies will inevitably be misleading and could result in choices and decisions built on fallacy rather than fact. The material should be forthright and honest and should describe the occupation as it is. Precise determination of absolute accuracy probably is an impossibility, considering the variation that exists across the country, and even locally sometimes, in any particular occupation. No publication can take into account all of these differences; usually it strives toward the median or mode of the distribution—the area of typicality. Nevertheless, gross inaccuracies or information that is accurate in only a limited sense or narrow geographic area must be avoided.

Many occupational materials published in the past failed to provide any adequate basis that the counselor could use to evaluate the material in terms of accuracy. The counselor was forced to use his/her own knowledge of the particular occupation as a basis for judgment, and in most cases this was not extensive enough to provide a really useful measurement. It seems reasonable to expect the publisher who wants to serve both counselor and client to include within a publication information that will help the counselor judge its accuracy. As a minimum, this would include an indication of how the information was collected, the size of the sample on which it is based, and its location and extent of dispersion, identification of the person who collected the information and prepared the publication, and his/her competency in unbiased reporting, and the dates when the data were obtained.

Since most published data are presumably based on a fairly large geographic area, the counselor needs to check not only the general accuracy for the occupation across the country, but also the degree of precision with which the local situation is pictured. When the necessary information needed to determine accuracy is not included, the counselor has little recourse other than matching the information against such sources as the *Occupational Outlook Handbook* and other Department of Labor publications that are developed, for the most part, on careful job analyses with relatively large samples.

2. CURRENCY. This criterion is closely related to accuracy. It is listed as a separate factor to emphasize its importance. Accuracy tends to stress precision; currency adds a time factor. In other words, as we evaluate career information, we must ask the question, is it accurate *now?*

Change is constant in the world of work. Unfortunately, the *rate* of change is not constant; hence, we cannot automatically adjust for this evolution by adding a common quantity to material prepared some time ago. The rate of change not only varies between occupations, it also varies within occupations. Many of the characteristics of human growth are applicable to the world of work. The rate of growth may progress through spurts and plateaus during childhood and adolescence, and slow down or cease when one reaches maturity. Even then physical change does not cease for the human; neither does it for an occupation.

At any given point, an occupation either may be holding relatively constant or may be involved in very rapid, perhaps even extreme, change, or it may be someplace between these two rates. For example, the present impact of automation is producing extensive change in many of the manufacturing occupations.

It is difficult for the counselor to predict precisely or estimate the degree to which an occupation is caught up in this change at a given moment. The best basis for judgment probably lies in an unending effort to keep abreast of developments and anticipated changes across the entire spectrum of the world of work.[12] Publications from the Bureau of Labor Statistics will be of some help in this task, as will materials that keep the counselor informed of economic and technical developments, such as reliable weekly news magazines and other publications of various types.

3. USABILITY. At least during the preliminary period of collecting career materials, preference should be given to materials that concern the more common occupations, since they are usually of greatest interest to the greatest number.

Similarly, some materials are so organized and prepared that they are of value to a variety of students or clients whose purpose in utilizing them may range from casual perusal to serious study. Such materials are obviously more useful than ones that apply only to a narrow situation. It may also be that certain publications can be used advantageously by a broader group of the staff, and perhaps even used in a wider variety of situations. When this appears likely, first purchases should include those that have a wide usability. Later purchases then may include materials that serve a narrower group or have more limited application.

The counselor should be aware that the range and quantity of materials generally available do not correlate very highly with this factor of usability or general applicability. Some occupations, particularly several of the professions, have relatively extensive representation in the literature, even though they are fields into which very few actually enter. On the other hand, many heavily populated occupations have a very limited coverage in the literature. The counselor should not be misled by this imbalance in availability; rather, he/she should first search out and include materials that relate to occupations in which many students may be interested.

4. READER APPEAL. Materials that are attractive are more likely to be used by more readers than materials with an uninviting format. This is probably true to an even greater extent when the users are adolescents. A readable type face arranged in a pleasing layout, accompanied by an appealing use of color and illustrations, will result in greater use of the materials.

In addition to general appearance, consideration should be given to the style of writing and the general level of reading difficulty. This latter item often is overlooked in selecting materials, with the result that many career resources centers have much material of a reading difficulty level inappropriate for the group the library is intended to serve. Many monographs have a reading level at an upper high school grade level, far beyond the actual reading ability of most junior high-schoolers and numerous high school students or adults with limited education.

5. THOROUGHNESS. Occasionally, in evaluating career materials for selection, a counselor will have a special purpose in mind and will be seeking material to fit that purpose. Ordinarily, however, the counselor is concerned with selecting materials that will have general application for the group using the resources center. In the latter case thoroughness should be considered as material is evaluated.

To a large extent, thoroughness must be appraised in terms of the group that is to utilize the career resources center. Thoroughness of coverage is crucial for upper educational years and later, when users are seriously involved in actual choices and decisions. At this point the counselee or client should have available all information that will help him/her see clearly the occupation being considered.

If the users are mainly junior high school age or lower, thoroughness should be defined in terms of appropriateness for this group. Since they normally will be concerned only with exploration, they usually will not need, or even be able to use, the amount of detail and specificity that may be desirable with older clients.

In earlier chapters, we considered that occupational materials frequently concentrate on the so-called economic aspects of work and overlook the sociological and psychological factors. The counselor should constantly watch for materials with the added thoroughness that provides the reader insight into the demands that the work makes on the individual, and the way it affects his/her life and that of the family.

The National Vocational Guidance Association has long been involved in efforts to upgrade and improve all types of career materials. The association has published standards for preparing and evaluating both printed and nonprinted career materials for nearly half a century. The latest edition, published in 1971, proposes detailed criteria for individual occupations, occupational fields or families, and occupations found within an industry, arranged by the three media categories of printed materials, films, and filmstrips. This issue is entitled *Guidelines for the Preparation and Evaluation of Career Information Media: Films, Filmstrips and Printed Material.*[13]

Although prepared primarily for those who write or produce career information, it is valuable to those who purchase or use those materials. Anyone who regularly selects or uses any of these three types of career information media can use the criteria proposed for evaluating the materials being considered.

To familiarize the reader with the major thrust of this document, we will list the main points recommended for inclusion under the headings of content and of style and format. These include the following:

Content

1. The nature of the occupation/occupational field/industry and its importance
2. Work performed in a single occupation, the variety of jobs in the occupational field or industry
3. Work settings
4. Potential personal rewards in the occupation/occupational field/industry
5. Entry requirements
6. Advancement possibilities
7. Outlook, including technological, economic, and demographic factors that will influence future employment opportunities
8. Related occupations
9. Licensing requirements and/or membership in unions and professional societies
10. Personal qualifications needed for success

Style and Format

1. Vocabulary
2. Format
3. Illustrations and graphic displays
4. Dating and revisions
5. Freedom from bias
6. Credit assignments
7. Additional sources of information
8. Training and education
9. Sources of financial aid
10. Opportunities for experience and exploration

Although the *Guidelines* are the most complete "checklist" presently available, the reader should be aware that the list is, by no means, all-inclusive. It also is important to keep in mind earlier emphasis on the significance of sociological and economic factors and the frequent difficulty in obtaining these kinds of data. Further, the counselor should always be cognizant of local needs and situations that may have overriding importance compared to the usual situation elsewhere.

Since useful evaluation must consider factors that relate to the specific situations in which career materials are to be used, it is not feasible to have materials evaluated in a pre-packaged arrangement when published, except in very general terms. One example of a "general" evaluation can be seen in each issue of the *Vocational Guidance Quarterly*, in which the Career Information Review Service Committee of the National Vocational Guidance Association regularly reports on recently printed career literature. The information provides the name, source, publication date, size, and cost of the item. In addition, a three-item code consisting of a capital letter *A* through *L*, a number from *1* to *3*, and a small letter *a* through *c* is affixed. The capital letter refers to the type of publication ranging from *A, Career Fiction* to *L, Other*, as described in the previous chapter. The numbers describe the extent to which the material adheres to the *Guidelines*, according to the following scale:

1. Highly recommended (maximum adherence to NVGA Guidelines)
2. Recommended (general adherence to NVGA Guidelines)
3. Useful (limited in scope; does not adhere to NVGA Guidelines but contains authentic, objective, timely, and helpful information)
4. Not recommended (this classification is used by the Review Committee but items so evaluated are not listed in the *Vocational Guidance Quarterly*)

The small letters indicate the difficulty of vocabulary used in the publication as follows:

a. Advanced
b. Moderate
c. Easy

Thus, an item carrying a code of *C2b* is considered to be a piece of single job information, with general adherence to NVGA Guidelines, with moderate vocabulary.

Obviously, this type of categorization is of some help to the counselor or teacher by indicating both what is available and the general over-all quality of the item. It is still necessary to appraise the material in terms of the situation and the individuals with whom the items will be used. If this requirement is to be met, there is no alternative to a personal assessment of every piece of material.

A brief checklist may be a convenience for maintaining a record of the evaluation of a particular publication. This can be maintained in a file for later reference as needed. Ideally, such a checklist should include those factors important in the local situation as well as other basic bibliographic information.

FILING PRINTED CAREER INFORMATION

Once obtained and evaluated, printed career materials must be maintained in some manner that facilitates retrieval and use by those for whom the materials were acquired. We will consider five aspects of this topic, including:

Basic criteria for selecting a filing system
Operational decisions that affect a career resources center
Filing educational materials
Filing unbound occupational materials
Filing bound occupational materials

Basic Criteria

At least four factors must be considered as plans are made to develop a career resources center: accessibility, attractiveness, ease of operation, and adaptability.

ACCESSIBILITY. If career materials are conveniently located, more people will use them.[14] If they are to be used in a school, consideration should be given to student traffic flow and a location that is available to the greatest number of students for the maximum period of time. The time factor also should be considered. In a school, career materials should be available not only at all times during the regular school day, but also for reasonable periods of time before and after school hours.

LeMay and Warnath asked college students where they would most prefer to have an occupational library located.[15] The most frequent response was the student union, recommended by 43 per cent of their sample. The site recommended next was the library, suggested by 23 per cent. Only 2 per cent suggested the counseling center, the location most frequently used on college and university campuses.

Although confidentiality is not a major consideration, it should, of course, be possible for the student or client to have access to career materials without feeling conspicuous. In general, it would be most desirable if the materials were at least as accessible as any other instructional or resource materials regularly used by students in the school.

In nonschool settings the problem of accessibility is likely to be a lesser one, since the number of individuals seeking to use the materials will probably be considerably fewer and the hours materials are available will usually coincide with the operating hours of the agencies involved.

ATTRACTIVENESS. The setting in which career information is maintained should be one that is inviting to users, and that stimulates their interest and desire for use. Furnishings should be tasteful and selected to encourage both casual browsing and serious study. There should be sufficient space so that students or clients will feel that they can use the materials easily and conveniently without interfering with others.

Posters, bulletin boards, and other visual displays can be used to stimulate interest. These devices should be adequately maintained and regularly changed.

EASE OF OPERATION. Career materials probably will be used more if they are filed so that the user can find items without help. If the filing system is easily understood and the materials so placed that the user can be self-sufficient, he/she will likely sample what is available. If the client finds that obtaining what he/she wants is simple, he/she is likely to be encouraged to explore further.

Obviously, clients or students with upper high school or college background might be expected to operate relatively complex systems. Upper elementary students, or others with limited experience in general library procedures, may need a simpler system if they are to use the materials independently. At any educational level, however, increasing complexity is likely to result in decreasing use. Perhaps the basic rule to follow is to select the filing system that is easiest for the user and is compatible with the range and variety of available material.

ADAPTABILITY. We have considered the importance of collecting career materials to fit the needs of the group that the resources center is intended to serve. Similarly, the filing system also should be "tailor-made" to fit those needs. Because variations can be expected among various groups, the filing system should have enough flexibility to expand in areas that call for such stretching and to contract in those areas in which the need is little or nonexistent. For example, if a senior high school is heavily populated with college-bound students, the filing system should be adaptable enough to permit heavy emphasis on occupational materials in the professions and related areas and educational materials from institutions of higher learning. This probably means that the filing system can be contracted in another area—agricultural, perhaps, if our illustrative school is in an urban area.

Adaptability, in terms of adjusting to a specific student body, is an advantageous factor. However, adaptability is a desired characteristic for other reasons, too. Student bodies may change in nature as time passes; if the filing system is flexible, the change in materials collected and retained can be accommodated easily. Further, changes in economic conditions, in technical developments, or in other influencing factors may make it advantageous to enlarge the system to include new or expanding areas. Finally, the mere fact that most collections of career information materials require several years to develop to a comprehensive level emphasizes the importance of adaptability in the filing system.

Operational Decisions

In addition to the general criteria discussed above, several administrative factors bear directly on the development of a career resources center. Most of these have to be considered and at least tentative answers obtained before a final decision on a filing plan or system can be reached. Topics that need attention include:

1. Responsibility
2. Staff
3. Facilities
4. Location
5. Security
6. Budget
7. Publicity
8. Operating policies

1. RESPONSIBILITY. One of the first decisions that should be made is to determine who is to have responsibility for the development and maintenance of the career resources center. In a nonschool agency, this can usually be resolved quite easily by assigning responsibility to the person who takes leadership in the vocational counseling provided by the agency. If the agency is a large counseling center, each counselor may take primary responsibility for different phases of the program related to his/her activity —one of which would be the career resources center; others might be the testing program, and the research activities.

Within a school setting, other factors must be assessed. If a new school is being opened, the problem can be considered along with several others that relate to the development of guidance services in the school. If a guidance committee has been established in the school, it obviously should be involved in this decision. If a director of guidance is employed, the choice may be either for him/her to take personal responsibility or to assign it to a member of the guidance staff for basic leadership responsibility.

The more typical situation involves developing such a resource in an already existing school. Here the problem may be complicated if various staff members already are dealing with the problem, or parts of it, on a piecemeal basis. For example, as indicated above, most school media centers will include some materials related to careers. If the center does in fact have some career materials on hand and the media specialist is involved in this area, he/she should be included in the decision of basic responsibility. In other schools, where an organized guidance program may not previously have existed, it is quite possible that some members of the instructional staff already have accumulated some materials to help meet student needs in this area. In most cases, such overt expressions of interest in guidance activities would lead an administrator to include these individuals on the guidance committee, where the problem can be considered and resolved in terms of how best to meet all the student needs in the school.

Although one can generally assume that a collection of career information materials in a school media center has been developed to meet different uses than those found in the counselor's office, one cannot automatically assume that responsibility for the materials should be taken from the librarian or media specialist and given to the counselor. The decision should be based on all the factors in the local situation. One would expect the counselor, the media specialist, and the teacher to work closely together to find the solution that is best for that particular school. It may, in fact, often be that some kind of joint responsibility will offer the best opportunity to provide the broadest service possible. Such joint responsibility might best be vested in the guidance committee, with specific assignment to one person—perhaps a member of the guidance staff—to take the leadership in maintaining the coordination and development needed. In this area, as in all parts of the guidance program, good working relationships among all members of the school staff are essential if the program is to be most effective. To assure consistent effort in developing and maintaining an adequate file of career information, it is essential that responsibility for this task be clearly assigned.

2. STAFF. Problems of staffing depend, in part, on the size and scope of the anticipated career resources center, the extent to which the clientele who will use the materials can operate independently, and the volume of acquisitions, as well as general usage of the materials and other factors. Professional people will be needed for at least part of the staff. Decisions about materials to be purchased, classification and evaluation, periodic review, and general supervision must all be put in responsible hands. At the high school or college level, there are certainly many competent students who can handle much of the routine activity, under supervision, including filing, checking out materials, and preparing cards for new acquisitions. Whenever possible, professional staff should be used for activities that require professional judgment and training. If the task can be accomplished as well by clerical or student help, such arrangements should be made.

3. FACILITIES. The decision to develop a career resources center carries with it the assumption that necessary facilities and equipment can be provided. The following will be needed: a considerable quantity of shelf space, filing cabinets for unbound materials, furniture such as study tables and chairs, a table or desk for checking materials in and out and for processing new materials, small card files for record keeping, display racks for new booklets, and bulletin boards.

It is not necessary to have elaborate and expensive equipment in order to operate effectively. On the other hand, a miscellaneous array of furniture and equipment that is not compatible with the basic purpose of the career resources center will not provide the desirable stimulus for student use. In most schools or agencies, the equipment needed to initiate the operation is probably already available. If it is not on hand, the initial budget must provide for the purchase of whatever equipment is essential for launching the project.

4. LOCATION. Several local factors bear on the location of the career resources center, not the least of which is available space. The problem is likely to be simple when a new school is being opened. If adequate, long-range planning has gone into the development of the building, it is probable that a room has been set aside to meet this need. The size depends on such factors as expected traffic, size of the collection to be maintained, and the extent to which materials will be used on the spot. If ideal conditions exist, there will be a room of adequate size, with direct access from the outer office of the guidance suite. Such a room can be readily available at all times to clients and others wishing to utilize the materials, as well as to counselors who wish to introduce counselees to the materials. Some supervision also is possible by the clerical or receptionist staff, whose work space is likely to be in the outer office.

If it is expected that students will use career information materials, the library obviously should not be placed in the counselor's inner office since the materials would be inaccessible whenever he/she is busy with a client. Similarly, locating the resources in a classroom would be a poor choice.

One major advantage in placing career information in the school media center is that this location usually provides maximum student access to the materials. There is also a serious disadvantage in this, however, since it usually impedes the use of the file by the student and counselor together during the counseling process. Two factors are involved here: first, the location may be some distance from the counselor's office in a large school; second, it is difficult for the student and counselor to use materials together when other students are using the room for study or other school purposes, and counselees may sometimes prefer more privacy than a school media center arrangement permits.

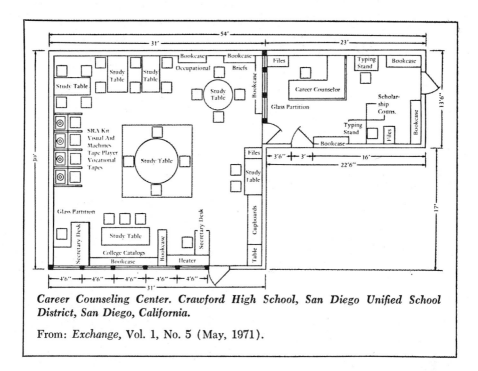

Career Counseling Center. Crawford High School, San Diego Unified School District, San Diego, California.

From: *Exchange*, Vol. 1, No. 5 (May, 1971).

5. SECURITY. Many considerations carry more priority than security. In fact, every effort should be made to provide clients maximum access to the materials on file. The system for obtaining and using career information materials should be made as simple and as easy as possible. Without doubt, efforts to simplify the system may well result in some losses that could have been prevented by more stringent security measures. Generally, though, the losses will not be excessive and probably should be accepted as part of the operating costs. Nevertheless, some minimum provisions need to be made to provide some protection for more expensive items, such as bound directories.

6. BUDGET. Establishing an adequate career resources center involves considerable expense; additional funds are needed regularly thereafter to maintain and expand it. Unless the school or agency is willing to accept this double responsibility, it should think carefully before making the original investment. The amounts needed for both purposes depend on many factors, thus preventing any particular amount being specified as sufficient for the project. At one time, when the availability of good commercial publications was limited, there was a fairly wide range of free materials that were obtained by counselors. Although there are still many free and inexpensive publications that the counselor will find useful, there has been a great expansion in the preparation of materials by commercial publishers. Often these are more useful than the free ones.

As indicated previously, many schools find the support of the career

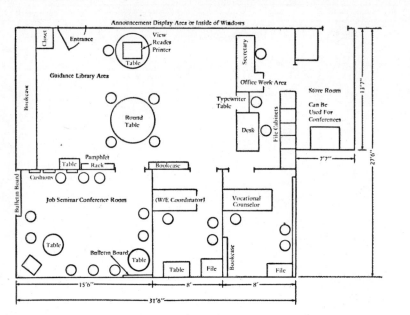

Career Development Center. Room 114, Mount Miguel High School, Grossmont Union High School District, Spring Valley, California

From: *Exchange,* Vol. 1, No. 5 (May, 1971).

resources center to be a project attractive to many local service clubs, which may be seeking some worthwhile way to assist the school. It would probably be wise administrative policy to provide basic or minimal support within the regular school budget, and to use such outside support for increased or expanded services. Since assurance of continued support may be difficult to obtain, provision for continuity should probably be based on school support. If an outside organization wishes to assist in establishing such a library, it may be able to provide the additional amount needed at the beginning to launch a worthwhile program. Obviously, the selection and purchase of materials should be left up to the person assigned the task of developing the library.

7. **Publicity.** A career resources center is meant to be used. Thus, provision should be made to keep potential users continually informed of its availability. All agencies that work with adolescents are aware of the constant changes in their clientele as a result of maturation alone. Each school, for example, starts a new class each year. This necessitates some plan for informing this group, as well as familiarizing those who have been around before but who had not previously established contact. In most settings, the need for this communicative effort is a continuous one. Plans should be developed that will permit a constant flow of information to

prospective clients. Many agencies, schools particularly, may wish to publicize the center on a broad scale. For instance, regular notification by the school to the community at large may help both parents and other school patrons know about the services available.

8. OPERATING POLICIES. Many problems cannot be anticipated, so it is necessary for someone or some group to be assigned the responsibility for solving such problems as may arise. Even though the general operating framework of the career resources center can be determined ahead of time, there must be provision for flexibility and modification to fit the needs of the group served. Someone must be responsible for establishing procedures and for making changes as needed.

FILING EDUCATIONAL MATERIALS

Most career information places primary emphasis on either the educational and training aspects or on the various occupations themselves. This book follows a similar approach and first considers the matter of filing educational materials. Three general topics will be considered: (1) training directories, (2) school catalogs and bulletins, and (3) miscellaneous educational materials and information.

One essential ingredient in every career resources center is a collection of training or educational directories such as those discussed in Chapter 8. The number and scope needed will, of course, vary with the age and educational range of the users and the breadth of their anticipated educational plans. Even the most modest of libraries should include at least one directory for each general educational level. Most libraries, especially those serving senior high schools, should provide more than one.

In most career resources centers, these volumes will be more frequently used than any others and so it may be necessary to establish different procedures for using these items. For example, it may be necessary to limit borrowing to overnight periods only, so that the volumes will always be available during the normal working day. It also may be wise to confine their use to the career information room during the day, so that counselors and students, as well as others, will have access to them as needed. If general student usage is heavy, it may even be advantageous to place duplicate copies of one or two of the more frequently used directories in the media center.

Within the career resources center, the educational directories usually can be handled best by establishing a conveniently located shelf and placing all directories together. If the center includes several directories, it may help to section the shelf according to educational level—for example. a section for college and university directories, one for trade and vocational schools, etc. In some settings, it may be more appropriate to place the directories with other publications from the kinds of schools included in the directories—that is, the vocational school directories might be located with vocational school bulletins. Ordinarily, the centralized location will be more convenient and will permit more efficient use.

School catalogs and bulletins can be organized either on shelves or in filing cabinets. In either case, it usually will be desirable to separate them according to broad categories of schools—such as professional schools, four-year colleges and universities, community colleges, vocational-technical-trade schools, and others. Since most professional schools are related to a college or university, it may be advantageous to combine the first two categories. In fact, if it is anticipated that the range of schools regularly included will not be extensive, it may even be desirable to combine the first three categories so that only two groupings are used, with a general label such as "academic" for one group and "vocational-technical-trade" for the other.

Materials from the "academic" institutions can be arranged in filing cases or on shelves, depending on which is available. If filing cases are used, a separate folder should be made for each institution. If the collection is not extensive, a simple alphabetical arrangement probably will be most satisfactory. If the number of items is fairly large, it may be better to arrange the folders alphabetically by states. The face of the folder can be used for listing the contents, to assist in maintaining a complete file and in identifying lost or strayed items.

If shelf space is assigned for "academic" materials, it usually will be more convenient to place materials in pamphlet boxes with the same alphabetical or alphabetical-by-state sequence. Since the larger institutions often publish many bulletins, a separate box can be used for these schools. Schools that publish only a single catalog can be grouped. Again, for ease of use, it will be helpful to list the contents of each box on the back.

Materials from the vocational-technical-trade schools can be arranged in either of the methods described above for the academic institutions. In addition, another alternative is often preferred. These publications can be arranged according to the occupation for which training is provided. Since many schools of this type are likely to be single-purpose institutions, there often is an advantage in this system. It brings together in a single section all barber schools, for example. When this system is used, the occupational headings are often arranged alphabetically or according to *DOT* number, with each school placed alphabetically within this category. Single folders can be used for each school, or if the number is small, single folders or pamphlet boxes can be used for each occupational category. If this system is used, a cross-referencing system will have to be used for schools that offer programs in more than one occupational area. In either the file or shelf system, a reference can be made easily by using a card with the occupational heading and a listing of appropriate schools that are filed under other headings, and the heading under which the school in question is filed.

A card file is sometimes recommended to identify what is available in the file of educational institutions. Such a file can be arranged in several ways—alphabetically, geographically, or occupationally. Unless the collection of materials is quite large, this may not be essential, since directories can provide the same information without the time and effort of compiling and maintaining a card file.

Provision also must be made to file other miscellaneous materials that relate directly to educational institutions, such as data about scholarships. Although the information available in *Scholarships, Fellowships, and Loans*[16] described in Chapter 8 is so extensive that it covers several volumes, it is not exhaustive. Certainly every high school that sends graduates on to college will have at least occasional need for additional information about scholarships and other types of financial aid. This need can best be handled by establishing a card file of scholarship information. Since some scholarships are related to specific schools and others can be used generally, information should be classified under both of these headings, as well as under an occupational listing if the scholarship is restricted to those preparing for a particular field. Each card should include at least information on the name of the scholarship, the amount, eligibility requirements, and where and how to apply. Most schools will want to limit the school section of the file to those institutions most frequently chosen by their students. Similarly, the general file might be restricted to those items for which local students would be eligible. The scope of this file obviously is related to the number of users of the career resources center who are making serious plans for further schooling and who are interested in and need additional financial assistance.

Other items to be grouped with educational materials might include information about how to study in college, orientation information, and similar general materials published by schools or other sources. How it can best be incorporated into the career resources center will depend on the amount of such material, the extent to which it will be used, and other factors.

FILING SYSTEMS FOR UNBOUND OCCUPATIONAL MATERIALS

One major problem in establishing a career resources center is selecting a filing system for occupational materials. Since these materials make up a major portion of the total center, the filing system must be organized to meet the general principles discussed at the beginning of this chapter. In addition to accessibility, attractiveness, ease of operation, and adaptability, other factors should also be included, if possible. For example, the system must be simple enough to be used easily by the clientele it is to serve. It also must be able to handle several different types of materials—job oriented, industry oriented, locally developed, and nationally or state developed.

A decision about the filing system to be used should be reached before any attempt is made to collect materials, so that all acquisitions can be incorporated into the file as soon as they arrive. If this decision is delayed until materials are on hand, the task of organizing them into usable order becomes a formidable one. Since no system yet devised serves all purposes ideally, a compromise choice is necessary, the selection should be made in terms of the factors most important in the local situation.

Most occupational materials are published as unbound pamphlets, briefs, or monographs. Obviously, these must be handled differently than bound items. Consideration will be given to methods of dealing with these unbound items first.

Many attempts have been made to organize unbound materials into some meaningful system. Several systems are in use today, and no one method is generally preferred over others. Alphabetical, coded, and other systems will be considered briefly.

Filing systems can be developed locally to meet the needs of a particular agency, or they can be obtained commercially. Which procedure should be followed depends on such factors as available funds, staff time, special local needs, and suitability of commercial systems. Several of the commercial systems take a variety of forms. Some publishers, for example, sell a set of gummed labels and directions for developing the file; others supply printed folders with directions and cross-reference cards, or a complete kit including the filing system and an assortment of occupational materials. The ready-made occupational file has the advantage of saving time, with the possible disadvantage of including materials that have limited use in a local situation. Rarely will a "kit" be complete enough to fit all local situations; consequently, regular additions will need to be made to keep it up to date and most useful. When such a kit is purchased, one should be selected that can be adjusted to local needs.

ALPHABETICAL. The simplest method of filing unbound occupational materials is in a series of folders, each labeled with the name of an occupation, in alphabetical order. In schools where unorganized occupational materials have accumulated over a period of time, an alphabetical system is often the solution.

A simple alphabetical system has certain obvious advantages. First, it is the easiest system to operate and therefore is usable at low educational levels, or by clients whose educational background is limited. Second, an alphabetical system is totally adjustable to local conditions, since the number of folders included can be fitted exactly to the materials to be used in the file. As new materials are obtained on occupations not previously included, the file is expanded easily by simply labeling new folders with the names of the occupations to be added. Third, it requires no "key" or index to help find materials, and they can be filed or found easily and rapidly.

Where it is expected that the ultimate size of the file will not exceed one or two file drawers, the alphabetical system will usually be more efficient than any other method.

As the occupational file grows larger, the simple alphabetical system becomes less efficient. As the file expands, the problem of alternate titles becomes a serious one. For example, if a student is curious about a legal career, he/she might find material filed under any one or several of these headings: advocate, attorney, barrister, counselor-at-law, jurist, lawyer, or solicitor. If we assume that most neophytes are unfamiliar with some of the alternate titles, it is likely that materials filed under those headings will not be seen. Even if we simplify the problem by narrowing the choice to titles most likely to be recognized, we face the same dilemma with "attorney" and "lawyer." A client is likely to look for either title, and may not think of the other. If we have only a drawer or two of materials, he/she may inspect each folder label for possible alternatives, but this is unlikely if the file system is large. The only feasible solution to the problem actually adds to its complexity. To be sure that clients will locate the material in the file, regardless of the title under which it is placed, it becomes necessary to set up folders for each title that they might use and organize a cross-reference system that will direct them to the folder or folders in which material can be found.

A further criticism of the simple alphabetical system is that it does not provide any way by which occupational groups or families can be identified. Occupations that actually may be very closely related often are filed far apart because of alphabetical order.

Agencies that feel that an alphabetical plan best fits their needs must seek a satisfactory solution to these disadvantages. One way is to move from the simple alphabetical plan, which is usually homemade, to an organized or structured alphabetical plan, which can be either homemade or obtained commercially. Such a plan usually incorporates a set or fixed number of folders in which materials are placed and a cross-reference system, which may be internal, as described above, or external with listings on cards or in a booklet.

An example of a structured alphabetical system is the *Bennett Occupations Filing Plan.*[17] This plan uses nearly 400 headings for folders in which materials are placed and nearly 700 more cross-reference headings for folder-sized cards. The folders and cards are filed alphabetically to provide an internal cross-reference system. Labels for the folders are printed in red, cross-reference cards in blue. In addition to the basic filing system, an additional fifty-seven headings are provided for supplementary materials under such titles as apprenticeships, job satisfaction, and part-time and summer jobs. A manual that includes the alphabetical list of headings and cross-references also has been developed as part of the system.

The first ten folders and cross-reference cards are labeled as follows:

1. *ABLE SEAMAN*. See WATER TRANSPORTATION.
2. Abrasive and polishing products industries. See CERAMICS INDUSTRIES.
3. *ACCOUNTING*. See also OFFICE WORK.
4. Acoustics. See SCIENTIFIC WORK—PHYSICAL SCIENCES.
5. *ACTING*. See also DANCING AND SKATING; MOTION PICTURE INDUSTRY; MUSIC; PUPPETRY; THEATRICAL WORK.
6. Actuarial work. See INSURANCE WORK.
7. Adult education. See TEACHING—ADULT EDUCATION.
8. *ADVERTISING*. See also PRINTING AND PUBLISHING; RETAIL TRADE; SELLING.
9. Aerial mapping. See PHOTOGRAPHY.
10. Aerial navigation. See AIR TRANSPORTATION.

CODED. The *Dictionary of Occupational Titles* has served as a logical base for filing career materials since the first edition appeared in 1939. At one time, a system was proposed based on the literal translation of the *DOT* coding system into a filing plan. With more than 7,000 code numbers in the 1939 edition, it is obvious that such a plan is far too detailed for practical application. Nevertheless, the *DOT* provides an obviously useful base for filing career materials. Consequently, it has frequently served as the model for building filing systems, both privately developed and commercially prepared. One widely used plan of this type is the *Chronicle Plan for Filing Unbound Occupational Information.*[18]

The *Chronicle Plan* was originally based on the 1939 *Dictionary of Occupational Titles*. It followed the general coding structure, with folders divided into the three subdivisions of major category, occupational division, and specific occupational title. Folders with different colored tabs cut into thirds were used, thus making easy identification possible.

The *Chronicle Plan* has been revised to keep in step with the 1965 revision of the *DOT*. It still includes a system of folders divided into major occupational categories, major divisions, and specific jobs within each subdivision. Tabs are used to distinguish between the three subdivisions. The major occupational category and major division folders correspond to the major occupational categories and major divisions of the *DOT* classification. Selected specific jobs have been included in the third subdivision; these are identified by the first three digits of the corresponding *DOT* code number. This group of folders can be easily expanded or contracted to fit specific local needs.

The first ten titles that appear in the revised *Chronicle Plan* are listed below. The chart also indicates whether a title is printed on a left-cut, center-cut, or right-cut folder to correspond with the appropriate subdivision to which it belongs.

The system includes an alphabetical cross-reference, as well as a cross-reference for the worker functions coding represented in the digits to the right of the decimal in the *DOT* coding system.

Folder position				
1	2	3	Code	*Group Arrangement*
			0	
X			1	PROFESSIONAL, TECHNICAL, AND MANAGERIAL
	X		00	ARCHITECTURE AND ENGINEERING
		X	001	Architectural
		X	002	Aeronautical engineering
		X	003	Electrical engineering
		X	005	Civil engineering
		X	006	Ceramic engineering
		X	007	Mechanical engineering
		X	008	Chemical engineering
		X	010	Mining and petroleum engineering

There are two major advantages in a system such as the *Chronicle Plan*. First, the system is tied directly to a classification system that is probably more widely used and known than any other. The *DOT* has been in existence for more than a third of a century, and during that time has been utilized in schools, employment offices, military services, industry, and almost every place where job classification is important. In addition, many publishers of occupational materials have coded their products with *DOT* numbers. A second advantage of a *DOT*-based plan is its flexibility; it can be expanded in areas where many folders are needed, or contracted in areas of little interest or paucity of material.

The major criticism aimed at such a plan relates to the first advantage listed. Some contend that the plan requires special knowledge and training to operate. It must be admitted that most individuals will find the system somewhat complicated at first encounter, especially if they are exploring on their own. If we assume that most users will be introduced to the file system by a counselor or someone who understands it, this complaint soon falls, since the method is easily explained and readily grasped. Some agencies, where users frequently initiate contact with the file without assistance, have found it helpful to place a placard nearby explaining how to use the file. Another criticism of the system is that it does not group occupations by job family. Systems built on the 1965 *DOT* will in part answer this fault, but will create a different set of problems.

The *Career Information Kit* is another widely used coded plan.[19] This system has gone through a number of revisions and adaptations. Originally the publishers issued a coded alphabetical plan; later this was modified to a *DOT*-based system. More recently it has been adjusted again, so that it now includes job families and provides an index based on the Dewey decimal system. It provides about 200 folders categorized into ten major groups.

The major advantage claimed for this system is its base of job families. Even though it does help the user see certain relationships among jobs that cut across different areas, one may justifiably ask whether a filing system should perform this function. Perceptions of this sort probably can be better developed in other ways—in the classroom or in the counseling session.

Since very little published material is coded on a job family basis, it becomes difficult to add items to such a file. This problem can be avoided when the kit is purchased as a self-contained package, or when it is intended that materials from only a single publisher will be added to the file. Probably neither is a wise procedure to follow.

The *Careers Desk-Top Kit* is an attempt to provide a condensed supplement to the regular occupational file.[20] It includes brief sketches of a fairly wide range of occupations organized in a portable box only six inches by nine inches by nineteen inches. The *Desk-Top Kit* can be used easily by the counselor at his/her desk or by students or clients seated at other tables or desks. The material included is filed according to a system based on the 1965 *DOT*.

OTHER SYSTEMS. Through the years, a number of proposals have been made for other methods of filing unbound occupational information. Such plans have frequently been based either on areas of interest or academic subject areas. In the first case, it has been fairly common to tie the filing system to an interest inventory, usually the *Kuder General Interest Survey Form E*. In the second case, either high school subjects or college major areas are used as a base for filing.[21]

The major advantage of such plans is fairly obvious, since the filing plan is tied directly to a base that is easily understood by the users of the file. It is very simple to consider a *Kuder General Interest* profile, for example, and ascertain the area or areas of highest interest and then turn to a filing system that lists jobs in this same type of classification. On the surface, such a system appears to make sense and appeals to the user.

There are two serious disadvantages in such plans, either of which can prevent their adoption. First, interest factors or academic subjects are unrealistic bases for classifying occupations, simply because most fields of work do not have or require a special or unique interest pattern that can be used to differentiate the work from other fields. Probably only a minority of occupations can be clearly tied to one or a combination of interest traits; instead, many occupations require a broad generalized interest pattern, or accommodate easily to a variety of specialized patterns. Similarly, many occupations do not relate closely or specifically with any one academic area or subject. Attempts to fit the majority of occupations, which in reality are "neutral," into such a system become artificial and meaningless. If fields without obvious ties are left out, the user does not have access to large areas that might be important to consider; if they are forced into categories that do not truly fit, the user might be misled. Inevitably, either base would require extensive cross-referencing, and the system would soon become cumbersome and inefficient.

The second disadvantage is the danger that classification by either subject matter or interest area will mislead the user, by placing undue emphasis on the base system (either interest or subject) as the primary factor in making a vocational choice. Both counselors and teachers want an individual to consider many factors as he/she moves toward a choice. Filing materials according to one of these factors can place greater emphasis on that factor than is warranted.

Filing Bound Occupational Materials

Filing bound occupational information usually does not present the problems encountered with unbound materials. For one thing, probably fewer items are published in bound form; second, counselors, teachers, and other personnel are more accustomed to working with bound materials.

If all occupational materials are to be located separately—in the guidance suite, for example—a simple plan for shelf filing usually can be developed to fit the system used for unbound materials. For most users it will be easier if the two types of materials are set up under the same general filing plan. Shelf space can be readily organized in this fashion. Since many of the bound items—such as the *Occupational Outlook Handbook*, for example—include information that cuts across many occupations, a "general" shelf will have to be established in addition to the specific areas.

If the occupational information is to be located where other books and materials are maintained—in a school media center, perhaps—other questions must be resolved. Within a media center the basic question of separating the occupational materials must be faced. If it is decided that this will be done, a system such as that described above can be utilized in whatever space within the center is assigned for career information materials. Items to be filed in this area should be labeled with some identification mark, to alert librarians and assistants to return them to the special shelf rather than to incorporate them into the usual library system. When bound materials are kept in the school media center and unbound items are in a file in the guidance division, center materials still can be grouped together by slightly modifying whatever system is in general use within the center. Forrester[22] suggests that if the Dewey decimal system is used in a school library, the career materials can be marked with a "V" preceding the regular classification number. Items so marked can then be shelved together on a "Vocational Shelf" arranged in regular library classification sequence.

Should it be decided that bound materials will be placed in the general media center and not separated from general center materials, some card index system must be developed to help users find the occupational materials.[23] This is probably the least satisfactory system, but occasionally local conditions may require it. In any case, the unbound file should include cross-reference to any bound material, regardless of where the bound material is shelved. This can usually be handled easily by including a card in each folder that lists the items, by title and location, to which the user is being referred.

In summary, emphasis should be focused on the development of a system that best fits both local conditions and the group that is to use the materials. Any system that does this offers maximum advantage.

NOTES

1. A. H. Brayfield and G. T. Mickelson, "Disparities in Occupational Information Coverage," *Occupations*, vol. 29, no. 7 (April, 1951), pp. 506–508.
2. NVGA Career Information Review Service Committee, NVGA *Bibliography of Current Occupational Literature* (Washington: National Vocational Guidance Association, 1973).
3. G. Forrester, *Occupational Literature: An Annotated Bibliography* 1971 ed., (New York: H. W. Wilson Co., 1971).
4. *Career Index* (Moravia, N.Y.: Chronicle Guidance Publications, Inc., annual).
5. H. F. and L. R. Mathis, "Occupational Literature Published by Professional Societies and Trade Associations," *Vocational Guidance Quarterly*, vol. 10, no. 1 (Autumn, 1961), pp. 70–72.
6. W. F. Dobberstein, "Free Occupational Information: How Much? How Good?" *Vocational Guidance Quarterly*, vol. 12, no. 2 (Winter, 1963), pp. 141–142.
7. R. Hoppock, *Occupational Information* (New York: McGraw-Hill, Inc., 1967), ch. 5.
8. W. Norris, F. R. Zeran, R. N. Hatch, and J. R. Engelkes, *The Information Service in Guidance: for Career Development and Planning*, 3rd edition (Chicago, Ill.: Rand McNally and Company, 1972), pp. 193–200.
9. S. G. Weinrach, "How To Evaluate Career Information Materials," *The School Counselor*, vol. 22, no. 1 (Sept., 1974), pp. 53–57.
10. D. E. Watson, R. M. Rundquist, and W. C. Cottle, "What's Wrong with Occupational Materials?" *Journal of Counseling Psychology*, vol. 6, no. 4 (Winter, 1959), pp. 288–291.
11. H. J. Peters and S. F. Angus, "New Challenges in the Riddle of Occupational Information," *Vocational Guidance Quarterly*, vol. 13, no. 3 (Spring, 1965), pp. 179–183.

12. R. Scherini and B. A. Kirk, "Keeping Current on Occupational Information," *Vocational Guidance Quarterly*, vol. 11, no. 2 (Winter, 1963), pp. 96–98.

13. National Vocational Guidance Association, *Guidelines for the Preparation and Evaluation of Career Information Media: Films, Filmstrips and Printed Material* (Washington, D.C.: NVGA, 1971).

14. I. M. Wilstach, "Career Guidance Center," *Vocational Guidance Quarterly*, vol. 10, no. 4 (Summer, 1962), pp. 245–247.

15. M. L. LeMay and C. F. Warnath, "Student Opinion on the Location of Occupational Information on a University Campus," *Personnel and Guidance Journal*, vol. 45, no. 8 (April, 1967), pp. 821–823.

16. N. Feingold, *Scholarships, Fellowships, and Loans* (Arlington, Mass.: Bellman Publishing Co., 1949–72).

17. *Bennett Occupations Filing Plan* (Danville, Illinois: Interstate Printers and Publishers, 1968).

18. *The Chronicle Plan for Filing Unbound Occupational Information* (Moravia, N.Y.: Chronicle Guidance Publications, Inc., 1965).

19. *Career Information Kit* 1965 ed., (Chicago: Science Research Associates, Inc.).

20. *Careers Desk-Top Kit* (Largo, Florida: Careers, Inc., 1967).

21. J. H. Brochard, *School Subjects and Jobs* (Chicago: Science Research Associates, Inc., 1961).

22. G. Forrester, *Methods of Vocational Guidance* (Boston: D. C. Heath & Company, 1951), p. 416.

23. R. Shosteck, *What to Read Guide* (Washington: B'nai B'rith Vocational Service Bureau, 1956).

13

Mechanized, Computerized, and Direct Contact Information Systems

In the past, the term *career information* has been essentially synonymous with *printed and audio-visual career information.* Two factors now clearly suggest that in the next decade the emphasis will be on the middle and upper ranges of Thompson's Spectrum of Occupational Information Media.[1]

The continuing development and diversification of computer hardware in our modern technological society will produce greater application of mechanization and computerization to career information. As computers decrease in cost and size and increase in power and flexibility, their use will rise almost geometrically. Obviously, they can be applied directly to Thompson's steps 4, 6, and 7 in computerized storage and retrieval systems, in simulated situations, and in synthetically created work environments.

Secondly, the increasing acceptance and application of career education concepts, especially those emphasizing the closer relationship between school and community, will enlarge the opportunities for direct contact by career-planning individuals with the reality of the work site. Whether our concern is with a youth making a tentative vocational choice, an adult involved in a delayed choice, or another adult now contemplating changing career plans, direct contact through observation, exploratory experiences, or actual tryout obviously will enhance the decision-making process. Use of these out-of-school resources soon should be easier and their existence more plentiful.

Some people may want to argue whether these modern techniques are appropriate for counselors and teachers to use. Actually, the issue is almost irrelevant. Instead, the major issue is how can these procedures best be used to maximize the effectiveness of teacher and counselor. Our society insists that physicians be as up-to-date as implanted peacemakers and would seriously challenge the doctor who advocated only home remedies. Similarly, every professional area is expected to use newly developed methods that offer promise. Walz has stressed the idea that technology carries the potential to enable counselors to reach new goals and to accomplish old goals in new ways.[2] He further describes five levels at which technology is used in guidance, ranging from ignoring it as something unneeded, to an integrative approach that accepts technology but continues to seek the best usage and application.

In this chapter, we will consider each of the nonprint media aspects of Thompson's spectrum. In some of these areas only exploratory work has been undertaken, and our discussion, of necessity, will be brief. In other areas, both hardware and software are developed and available for implementation. Most steps fall between the two extremes and demonstrate considerable existing development as well as much room for further advancement.

MECHANIZED SYSTEMS

The application of the microfilm aperture card, and its necessary corollary equipment of a microfilm reader and a microfilm printer, to the delivery of career information occurred almost simultaneously on opposite coasts. One system entitled Vocational Information for Education and Work (VIEW) was developed by the Department of Education in San Diego, California.[3, 4] The other, entitled Vocational Guidance in Education (VOGUE), was developed by the Bureau of Occupational Education Research of the New York State Education Department.[5]

The VIEW system was developed to serve high schools and junior colleges within the geographic and political unit of San Diego County. It was expected that the system would overcome the following weaknesses that had been encountered and reported by school counselors: (a) occupational information lacking in authenticity and realism, (b) lack of currency and local application of career material, and (c) difficulty in filing and retrieving data.

Although our concern here deals essentially with the third of these three weaknesses, a brief summary of efforts to deal with the first two may be helpful. Six secondary schools were used in a pilot project to obtain student evaluation of existing occupational information. These evaluations identified the kinds of data most useful to high school age youth. It was then possible to rewrite occupational briefs from general sources that provided a broad, national picture of the occupation, emphasizing aspects that were particularly interesting or relevant as indicated by the youths themselves. Local experts and sources, such as employment office analysts, industrial personnel workers, management level consultants, curriculum and guidance experts, were used to develop local and regional information about the same occupations, written in the same style and format of the general occupational brief.

Two four-page occupational briefs were prepared for each occupation. The first brief was general and national in nature; the second emphasized local and regional information. Each four-page brief then was transferred to a standard microfilm aperture card into which was punched additional information about the occupation that could be used in sorting and listing according to individual characteristics or needs. As data become obsolete, a new brief is prepared, master microfilm cards are made, and copies are distributed to users to replace the out-of-date card.

Use of the card by the client and the counselor requires either a microfilm reader-scanner or a microfilm reader-printer. Both are relatively inexpensive and simple machines that are easily operated. The reader-scanner projects the information on a viewing screen, where it can be easily read by the user. If the occupational brief contains material that the user wishes to study further, the reader-printer can be used to reproduce the microfilm brief on an eight-and-one-half by eleven-inch paper print-out. An unlimited number of print-outs can be produced from an aperture card at modest cost.

The microfilm aperture card can be stored more easily than most printed occupational material. It can be kept up to date more easily and less expensively than the usual printed briefs. Further, users may easily obtain print-out copies for their individual use if desired.

The VOGUE system was developed in New York to meet the needs of school counselors who, like their California colleagues, indicated that they wanted occupational materials that were appropriate for the clients, both regionally and nationally oriented, up to date, and related to local opportunities. The experimental phase of the program involved a variety of educational institutions and three methods of disseminating occupational information. Microfilm aperture cards were prepared for a variety of occupations, with one card providing information for one occupation. These cards could be used either with a reader-scanner or with a reader-printer. The same "occupational guides" placed on the microfilm aperture cards were also prepared in standard size and incorporated in loose-leaf notebooks so that experimental comparisons might be made of the two methods of presentation.

The advantages of a microfilm aperture system have been clearly established and focus primarily on content and delivery system.[6] Provision within the system for developing the basic information for relatively small areas, such as states or smaller units, permits preparing information to meet the needs and interests of the user group within that area. Information aimed at a particular geographic area can deal specifically with conditions in that area, whereas printed career information, based on the concept of national or wider usage, must deal with broader, less definite data. Writing style, reading difficulty, and content information can be adjusted to meet the particular users within that smaller specific area. The delivery system carries the advantages of economy, compactness, versatility, ease of updating, speed and accuracy in filming and retrieving, and adaptability to computer use.[7] Childers and Whitfield identify the following points about each claimed advantage:

1. *Economy*—Up to nine pages of career information can be included on a single microfilm aperture card, capable of being viewed repeatedly. Microfilm can be processed and disseminated quickly and inexpensively.
2. *Compactness*—Since one card 3″ × 7″ holds the equivalent of nine regular sized sheets of information, one small filing cabinet holds the equivalent of a much larger storage unit.
3. *Versatility*—The users can study the information projected on a viewing screen, or print a regular sized copy for personal use, as many times as desired.
4. *Updating*—When updating is required, a new card can be prepared by retyping only pages on which correction is needed. New microfilm cards then can be prepared and issued immediately to users of the system.
5. *Filing and Retrieving*—Since the basic card accommodates to data processing equipment, it can be filed and retrieved by this equipment. The card can be punched to carry additional information that can be used for selective retrieval. Of course, the card can be hand-filed, if desired.
6. *Computer Adaptability*—As indicated, the card can be used in a computerized system to supplement computer data with no difficulty in combining the two systems. The system can be used alone, without computer, if desired.

Nearly three-fourths of the states have used or are presently using some form of the VIEW system. Typical of the more advanced applications is the system used in Pennsylvania, named Pennscript. In this project, the state has been divided into 18 areas for which localized labor market information is available. Occupations included in the deck are 260 of the most common occupations requiring educational preparation ranging from the eighth grade to beyond the Master's degree. A VIEW (or Pennscript) deck of 260 cards has been developed for each of the 18 labor market areas. Any school within each area can have a deck of aperture cards for that area.

In addition to the basic 260 cards, two additional decks have been developed in Pennsylvania. One of these is a 50-card deck prepared in Spanish for Spanish-speaking residents of southeastern Pennsylvania. The second deck of nearly 200 cards has been prepared with a third grade reading level for use by educable mentally retarded individuals. In addition to the basic use of Pennscript in the state's schools, it also is being used by correctional institutions in rehabilitation programs for offenders. Present plans provide for updating local information on an annual basis.

Effective application of a plan such as Pennscript requires commitment by the state educational agency or its designate to provide the services needed to operate such a plan. These include personnel to write the scripts and to prepare and distribute cards to cooperating schools. Regular revision and updating must be maintained. In addition, counselors and teachers must be taught through in-service workshops, newsletters, staff meetings, and in other ways, to use the system properly. Some states have invested generously in equipment and original preparation of scripts but have failed to provide either updating or staff training; the result has been poor use of its investment. The system, properly used, provides an excellent step beyond the printed or audio-visual material that generally includes national information.

COMPUTERIZED SYSTEMS

Computers are an integral part of the operational hardware used by business, industry, and government. Our monthly bank statements, department store billings, magazine subscriptions, and tax forms are processed by computers. Serious consideration is being given to computerizing health records of all our citizens for greatest availability in case of medical emergencies. Such complex operations as space exploration would be impossible were it not for computerized control of much of the mission. It is only logical to expect the use of computers in counseling. Unfortunately, such use sometimes is viewed either with an aura of magical mysticism or with defensive suspicion that machines are going to control human lives. Since computers are man-made and man-controlled, neither view is valid. Instead, they should be looked on in the same way that we view the many machines we daily use to increase efficiency, to save time or labor or cost, or to accomplish many things that otherwise would be difficult, if not impossible.

Frederick has proposed a three-by-four-cell chart (see Table 24) that provides an excellent theoretical base for conceptualizing the ways in which computers can be used in counseling.[8] The vertical levels of the chart represent the extent of computer use and the horizontal categories identify the user or user groups. The cells indicate the interaction at that level with the specific user group. Our concern in this chapter is primarily focused at Level II in all three cells since we are considering the storage and retrieval of information. Level III involves the use of information in

TABLE 24. *Student Decision Modes*

COMPUTER INVOLVEMENTS / USER GROUP	A. STUDENT ALONE	B. STUDENT–COUNSELOR	C. COUNSELOR–STUDENT
I Noncomputer	No outside assistance in problem solution.	Personal problem solving, student utilizes counselor as a reference and information resource.	Counselor guidance in helping student "fix" on appropriate problem-solving behavior.
II Computer as search tool	Student actively controls the inquiry or information gathering process (student interactive).	"Student interactive" with information provided by computer through counselor.	Counselor guides problem examination and accesses the computer.
III Computer as search tool with question resolution capability	Student solves problem on basis of information provided by the computer through questioning student and filling gaps in information.	Student queries both computer and counselor, computer queries both student and counselor and provides "fill-in" information for each.	Counselor guides problem examination, queries both student and computer, computer queries both counselor and student, and provides "fill-in" information for each.
IV Human–computer interaction	Student–computer interactive where both query; and student formulates decisions without assistance.	Student and counselor interact with computer so computer adaptively queries both and provides "fill-in" information for use by student. Student may seek assistance but essentially guides himself.	Counselor and student interact with computer, computer adaptively questions both and provides "fill-in" information for use in a counselor-guided decision situation.

solving problems and thus is primarily "counseling." Level IV is a very sophisticated interchange between user and machine and, at least at present, must be considered only in the theoretical or developmental stage. Examples of Level II projects are quite well developed and some are operational. Level III projects are approaching the operational phase and can be expected to be applicable during the late 70's. Level IV probably will not be practical until the middle or end of the next decade.

In simplest terms, the computer is merely a device in which innumerable pieces of information can be stored by use of a magnetic tape. The user transmits his inquiry and receives his reply by means of a terminal, somewhat similar to a typewriter, which has been connected to the computer. The inquiry is typed via the keyboard into the system and the response may be returned either by means of a typed print-out or by appearing on a screen similar to a television picture tube. Since the distance between the terminal and the computer is unimportant, it is possible to plan a system with several terminals connected to a computer within the same building or an array of widely scattered terminals connected to a remote computer. The reaction time of the computer is so rapid that many terminals can be used simultaneously and appear to receive answers at the same time, although in actuality the responses are made in sequence. Maintaining accuracy of information is quite simple and is accomplished by recording revised data on the tape, which is then immediately available to users at any terminal station.

Several computerized systems have been developed to the operational stage. Harris states that at least 30 computer-based guidance informational systems have been designed and are at least partially developed.[9] She has identified two major types of systems that have been labeled as indirect and direct inquiry. Indirect inquiry systems operate simply and usually are based on a questionnaire completed by the user. The computer provides responses, such as a list of colleges, occupations, or financial assistance opportunities, that best fit the inquirer's stated specifications. Ordinarily, there is a delay between completion of questionnaire and receipt of response—sometimes a week or two in length. The user probably employs the system only once and is likely to be unaware of the narrowing effect his/her various questionnaire answers may have on the final computer response. The indirect inquiry system uses only computer capabilities for storage, interrelating, and retrieving data.

The second type of system is the direct inquiry system, as in Levels III and IV of Frederick's classification. In these programs, the user interacts directly with the comupter via a terminal. The user receives immediate response, has considerable control over the program, is aware of the effect of the choices, and usually can individualize the situation to meet his/her own needs. In addition, the system usually provides for repeated use.

Harris has summarized the available research studies on the effect of computer use on students. Consistently, the studies have shown favorable response to use of computers. Much work remains, not only in developing and perfecting systems, but also in researching effective means of application. The discussion of cost feasibility reported by Harris suggests that it is difficult to obtain precise data in this area. Several programs, including two that we will consider, report hourly user costs ranging from three to six dollars. This range is sufficiently modest to permit rapid expansion of computer use.

We will consider three systems as representative of the state of the art—one developed to serve a single school system, one that is a statewide system, and one that offers nationwide service. These systems include the Computerized Vocational Information Service (CVIS) of Willowbrook High School, the Oregon Career Information System (CIS), and the System of Interactive Guidance and Information (SIGI) developed and marketed by Educational Testing Service.

Willowbrook High School, just west of Chicago, has developed a single-school computerized vocational information system. The hardware consists of an IBM 360-30 computer connected to terminal stations, which consist of an IBM 1053 typewriter and an IBM 2260 cathode ray tube. The user input is made by means of the typewriter and responses are returned via the cathode ray tube with printouts simultaneously made by the typewriter for later reference.[10]

The vocational information stored in the computer is classified according to the two dimensional system proposed by Roe, which we considered in Chapter 7. This arranges the occupational world into eight areas—service, business contact, organization, technology, outdoor, science, general cultural, and arts or entertainment. Each occupational area in turn is divided into six levels according to the amount of training required or degree of responsibility assumed by the worker.[11] Information about approximately 400 occupations is stored in the computer.

The computer also stores cumulative class rank, composite achievement and ability test scores, and *Kuder Preference Record* scores for each student according to an assigned student number. These data are used by the computer as the individual students use the system.

A student using the system is first asked his/her student number, thus recalling personal data stored in the computer. A prepared script then helps the student through a limited self-analysis. Questions are asked about ability, school achievement, relations with fellow students, and multiple choice responses are checked against the personal data stored in the computer. If his/her recollections are confirmed, the machine proceeds. If that memory is faulty, it reports the data it has, or refers the student to the counselor. A further question asks about post-high school educational plans, which again are matched against personal data in the computer and the student is supported or discouraged in his/her choice. (Discrepancies lead to referral to the counselor and the computer provides the counselor with a list of students whom it has "referred.") The student next is asked to choose one of the previously mentioned areas of interest. This is matched for consistency with Kuder Preference Record scores. A combination of educational goal and area of interest identifies the cell within the Roe classification that relates to these two factors. The computer then presents a list of suggested occupations representative of this cell. The student may reject the list and ask for another or may explore any of the occupations on the list. He/she explores the listed occupations by typing the number of the occupation about which information is desired. The computer provides a fifty-word definition on the screen. If more information is desired, one asks for an occupational brief, which is typed out by the typewriter. This includes references to additional sources for further information. One may go on to other occupations within the same list or may move to other cells by identifying a different area of interest.

Further career information can be incorporated into the system to provide users, who express interest in Level I and II occupations, information about college decisions, suggested colleges, and scholarship aid. Students expressing interest in Levels III and IV can be given information about trade and technical schools, local training programs, and apprenticeship programs. Students exploring occupations in Levels V and VI can be provided information about local companies who hire high school graduates or dropouts in the field of interest.

As seen from this description, CVIS is a sophisticated information-retrieval system that can deliver a large amount of valuable data to the user, who is assumed to be in the career decision process. The system, as do all other similar computer-based systems, assumes that the likelihood of sound decisions is enhanced by the availablity of adequate information about possible options.

Harris estimates the annual cost (1973) for operating CVIS at $18,000. This figure provides six terminals and two printers in the computer system, which serves 3,450 students. On this basis, the annual per student cost is less than six dollars.

The Oregon Career Information Service operates on a statewide basis using a consortium of four computers located in geographically separated educational settings.[12] Each user school is connected to its nearest computer by a teletype terminal and telephone lines. The services were made available to 140,000 users during the 1974–75 school year. The system is primarily designed to provide a single, efficient informational source that relates career opportunities and decisions with post-secondary educational opportunities and choices. In addition to the computerized aspects of the program, provisions exist for a needle-sort system for an exploratory self-reporting exercise and printouts of the stored information available in book form.

Major information components of the program include the following five parts:

1. *Quest*—A 25-item questionnaire allows the user to match presently seen interests, aptitudes, and abilities with possible occupations.
2. *Description File*—This section stores and retrieves information on 225 occupations, representing 95% of Oregon's employment. A 300-word description of job duties, working conditions, hiring requirements, and local, state, and national employment prospects is included for each. One part of this file indicates where visits may be made and individuals who may be contacted for further information about the occupation. The information is localized for seven geographic regions of the state.
3. *Preparation File*—This section provides information for each listed occupation, including ways to prepare for the occupation, licensing requirements, and a cross-reference to appropriate post-secondary educational training.
4. *Program File*—Information is provided here on 125 post-secondary educational programs in Oregon. A user may request information on a particular program and receive a description of degrees offered, specialties, program objectives, courses, and Oregon schools providing the program.
5. *School File*—Information on 150 of Oregon's two- and four-year colleges and licensed proprietary institutions. Users may compare three schools at a time on 65 different topics.

During the early period of statewide application (the 1974–75 school year), problems consisted of overcoming counselor resistance to using machines, being sure that users knew how to operate the relatively simple system, and identifying the best sequence for using the various files. Costs in the system include delivery system costs and information development costs. These costs are met by charging a user fee to all participating institutions (high schools, community colleges, correctional institutions, vocational rehabilitation offices, Youth Manpower offices, and four-year colleges). In 1974–75, the fee charged was $1.20 per user up to 3200 users, and $0.48 for each user over 3200. Preliminary data indicate that the average user employs the equipment two or three times per year for 20 to 30 minutes per use. On this basis, the annual per student cost is estimated to be approximately two dollars.

The System of Interactive Guidance and Information (SIGI) reached the field-testing stage during the 1974–76 period and should be generally available thereafter.[13] Five two-year colleges were used for the two-year field test. The system is primarily designed to help students who are in or about to enter community and junior colleges to make informed and rational career decisions. In addition to information-retrieval, the system provides a way for the student user to examine personal values, explore options, and formulate tentative plans.

Oregon Career Information System (CIS):
Sample Computer Printouts

CIS
HELLO; PLEASE ENTER YOUR NAME, THEN PUNCH THE 'RETURN' KEY.
?
  WENDY ARNOLD

WHICH AREA ARE YOU IN:
LANE COUNTY? (TYPE IN 'LANE').
PORTLAND METROPOLITAN AREA? (TYPE IN 'PORT').
COOS-CURRY COUNTIES? (TYPE IN 'COOS').
OTHER AREA? (TYPE IN 'AREA').
?
  LANE

HELLO WENDY,
HOW DO YOU WANT TO START?
IF YOU FILLED OUT THE QUESTIONNAIRE IN YOUR HANDBOOK,
      TYPE IN: 'QUEST.'
IF THERE ARE OCCUPATIONS, EDUCATIONAL PROGRAMS,
OR SCHOOLS YOU WANT INFORMATION ABOUT,
      TYPE IN: 'INFO.'

?
  INFO

THREE KINDS OF INFORMATION ARE STORED IN THE COMPUTER:
— — —OCCUPATIONS: LOCAL, STATE, AND NATIONAL LABOR MARKET
      INFORMATION THAT IS CONTINUOUSLY UPDATED.
              TYPE IN 'DESC' AND A 4-DIGIT OCCUPATION CODE
              (E.G.: DESC 1684). YOU MAY ALSO FIND OCCUPATIONAL
              BIBLIOGRAPHIES (BIB), VISITS (VISIT), EXPLORER
              POSTS (XPLOR), AND WAYS TO PREPARE FOR OCCUPA-
              TIONS (PREP).

— — — EDUCATION AND TRAINING PROGRAMS: LISTS OF COURSES,
      DEGREES, SCHOOLS, AND ON-THE-JOB TRAINING.
              TYPE IN 'PROG' AND A 3-DIGIT PROGRAM CODE
              (E.G.: PROG 131)

— — — SCHOOLS: SERVICES AND COSTS OF SCHOOLS.
              TYPE IN 'SCH'

YOU CAN FIND CODE LISTS IN YOUR HANDBOOK.

?

  From: Oregon Career Information System (CIS).

Sample of a Description Statement for an Occupation

DESC FOR 8456   ELEMENTARY & SECONDARY TEACHERS

ELEMENTARY AND SECONDARY TEACHERS DEVELOP AND PLAN TEACHING
MATERIALS AND PROVIDE CLASSROOM INSTRUCTION TO STUDENTS.
ELEMENTARY TEACHERS NORMALLY WORK WITH ONE GROUP OF PUPILS
DURING THE ENTIRE SCHOOL DAY.   (DOT# 092.228–010) SECONDARY
TEACHERS USUALLY SPECIALIZE IN A PARTICULAR SUBJECT AREA
SUCH AS ENGLISH, MATH OR SOCIAL STUDIES. (DOT# 191.228–018)
————APTITUDES: THE ABILITY TO RELATE WELL WITH PEOPLE AND TO
ORGANIZE MATERIALS AND IDEAS.
————WORK SETTING: USUALLY WORK AT LEAST 40 HOURS A WEEK WHICH
INCLUDES PREPARING, PLANNING, AND SUPERVISING ACTIVITIES.
MANY WORK 9 MONTHS A YEAR AND TAKE COURSE WORK OR HOLD PART-
TIME JOBS AFTER SCHOOL AND DURING THE SUMMER.
————HIRING PRACTICES: A COLLEGE DEGREE AND AN OREGON TEACHING
CERTIFICATE.   TRAINING: AVAILABLE AT UNIVERSITIES, COLLEGES
AND COMMUNITY COLLEGES.   SEE PREP 8456 FOR DETAILS.

————CURRENT EMPLOYMENT: AROUND 27,000 TEACHERS EMPLOYED IN
OREGON.   APPROXIMATELY 5% ARE EMPLOYED IN PRIVATE SCHOOLS.
TEACHERS WORK IN ALL AREAS OF THE STATE AND ARE FAIRLY EVEN-
LY DISTRIBUTED WITH POPULATION.
————WAGES: VARY WITH SCHOOL DISTRICTS, BUT RANGE FROM AN
AVERAGE ENTRY WAGE OF $7,900/YR (A BACHELOR'S DEGREE AND
NO EXPERIENCE), TO AN AVERAGE MAXIMUM WAGE OF $13,900/YR
(MASTER'S + 45 HOURS).
————OUTLOOK: SURPLUS OF APPLICANTS.   STUDIES FORECAST LITTLE
DEMAND NATIONALLY OR IN OREGON.   THE OUTLOOK WILL DEPEND
UPON REPLACEMENT OF THOSE TEACHERS CURRENTLY EMPLOYED, EX-
PANSION OF THE STUDENT POPULATION, AND UPON FINANCIAL SUP-
PORT.   CURRENTLY LOW TEACHER TURNOVER RATE AND DECREASED
SUPPORT OF LOCAL SCHOOL BUDGETS HAVE REDUCED THE NUMBER OF
AVAILABLE POSITIONS.   PROSPECTS MAY IMPROVE IF SCHOOL BUDG-
ETS ARE INCREASED TO EXPAND SPECIAL PROGRAMS, REDUCE CLASS
SIZES, AND INCREASE STAFFING.   A 1975 SURVEY BY THE OREGON
TEACHERS' STANDARDS AND PRACTICES COMMITTEE LISTED THE FOL-
LOWING AREAS AS HAVING A 50%-PLUS CHANCE OF EMPLOYMENT:
SPECIAL EDUCATION, HOME ECONOMICS, ADVANCED MATH, MUSIC, P.E.,
PHYSICAL SCIENCES & TEACHING THOSE WITH HEARING DEFECTS.   AREAS
WITH LESS THAN A 50% CHANCE INCLUDE: ART, BUSINESS, FOREIGN
LANGUAGE, INDUSTRIAL ARTS, SOCIAL STUDIES, BIOLOGY & SPEECH.

From: Oregon Career Information System (CIS).

Sample of a Preparation Statement for an Occupation

PREP FOR 8456   ELEMENTARY & SECONDARY TEACHERS

————SKILLS: CAPACITY FOR UNDERSTANDING & GUIDING STUDENTS
IN THE LEARNING PROCESS; FAMILIARITY WITH LEARNING TECHNIQUES USED IN
COMMUNICATING & GENERATING KNOWLEDGE; ABILITY TO PRESENT
SUBJECT MATTER EFFECTIVELY ON A GROUP OR INDIVIDUAL BASIS;
KNOWLEDGE OF THE TECHNICAL PROCESS OF EVALUATION.
————PREPARATION: ALL PUBLIC SCHOOL TEACHERS MUST BE CERTI-
FIED BY THE STATE DEPARTMENT OF EDUCATION. THERE ARE TWO
KINDS OF CERTIFICATES IN OREGON—BASIC & STANDARD. ENTRY
LEVEL TEACHERS, BOTH ELEMENTARY & SECONDARY, EARN A BASIC
CERTIFICATE BY COMPLETING A BACHELOR'S DEGREE AT AN ACCRED-
ITED SCHOOL. ELEMENTARY TEACHERS MAY TEACH WITHOUT A STAND-
ARD CERTIFICATE BUT SECONDARY TEACHERS EVENTUALLY HAVE TO
OBTAIN IT EITHER BY COMPLETING A PLANNED FIFTH YEAR PROGRAM
OR A MASTER'S DEGREE PROGRAM. ELEMENTARY TEACHERS COMPLETE
A BACHELOR'S DEGREE IN ELEMENTARY EDUCATION (SEE PROG 234)
BEFORE BEING CERTIFIED. SECONDARY TEACHERS COMPLETE A BACH-
ELOR'S DEGREE IN THE SUBJECT FIELD OR 'NORM' THEY HOPE TO
TEACH (SEE PROG 236).
————TIPS: PROSPECTIVE SECONDARY TEACHERS MAY IMPROVE EM-
PLOYMENT CHANCES BY TAKING COURSEWORK IN MORE THAN ONE
TEACHING AREA. THE SECOND TEACHING AREA DOES NOT HAVE TO
INCLUDE ENOUGH COURSEWORK FOR CERTIFICATION BUT IT SHOULD
BE ENOUGH TO PROVIDE THE NECESSARY KNOWLEDGE & CONFIDENCE
TO TEACH THE SUBJECT. IF A PROSPECTIVE TEACHER CAN SUPER-
VISE AT LEAST ONE STUDENT ACTIVITY, PLACEMENT OPPORTUNITIES
ARE IMPROVED. COLLEGE ACTIVITIES THAT PROVIDE GOOD TRAINING
& EXPERIENCE INCLUDE INTERCOLLEGIATE & INTRAMURAL SPORTS,
JOURNALISM, ART, DRAMATICS, BAND & STUDENT GOVERNMENT. VOL-
UNTEER WORK AS TEACHER AIDES OR TUTORS MAY BE HELPFUL. WILL-
INGNESS TO LOCATE ANYWHERE IN THE STATE MAY IMPROVE EMPLOY-
MENT PROSPECTS. ADVANCEMENT IN THE TEACHING PROFESSION USU-
ALLY RESULTS IN SALARY ADVANCES IF YOU TEACH IN THE SAME
SCHOOL SYSTEM FOR MORE THAN ONE YEAR. SECONDARY TEACHERS MAY
ADVANCE TO SUPERVISORY & ADMINISTRATIVE POSITIONS. BOTH
AREAS REQUIRE SEVERAL YEARS OF TEACHING EXPERIENCE & ADDI-
TIONAL COURSEWORK (SEE PROG 231). OTHERS BECOME INTERESTED IN
COUNSELING (SEE PROG 238). MANY TEACHERS STAY IN THE PROFESSION
AS CLASSROOM TEACHERS.

From: Oregon Career Information System (CIS).

The system is designed to operate on a Digital Equipment Corporation PDP-11 minicomputer, which can typically operate with up to 17
terminals. The terminal includes a cathode-ray tube and a keyboard.
The cathode-ray screen presents information to the student, or a choice of
what to do next, or sometimes it serves as a spokesperson for the student in
trying out or modifying values, goals, or plans.

The SIGI system consists of six major subsystems entitled Values,

Locate, Compare, Prediction, Planning, and Strategy. These subsystems are described briefly in Table 25 (p. 398). On first encounter, the student goes through an overview of the entire system sampling all of the subsystems. Thereafter, the student is free to use any subsystem at any time. He/she encounters continual emphasis on values as a major element in career decision-making. The six subsystems involve:

1. VALUES. Students are asked to weigh each of ten values in terms of its importance to them. They can then compare the ten weights and adjust them if they wish. They are next "tested" with hypothetical value dilemmas to help them interpret their value judgments. Then they are confronted with any inconsistencies between the original weights and those indicated in the dilemma game. Finally, they are asked to distribute a fixed sum of 40 points across their ten values to produce a profile of their "examined values."

2. LOCATE. The students are asked in this subsystem to use their weights on any five values at a time. Usually the students start with values carrying the heaviest weights, but this is not necessary. The computer responds with a list of occupations that meet or exceed the value specifications selected by the students.

3. COMPARE. Using occupations either from the LOCATE subsystem or any others included in SIGI in groups of three, students can ask specific questions about such topics as work activities, entry requirements, income, personal satisfactions, etc. The occupational information is nationally based, and periodically up-dated in the computer.

4. PREDICTION. This subsystem provides students with probability statements based on marks obtained by previous students in the specific institution. The statements reveal their chances of acquiring a given mark in the "key" course of a given program. The data are locally-based for each institution and are built on items that are predictive for each of the included courses.

5. PLANNING. This subsystem shows the students what requirements must be met to enter any occupation being considered. They can decide if they are able and willing to meet those specifications. If they are undecided, they are shown both rewards and risks related to trying the program for a semester.

6. STRATEGY. This section compares values, occupational information, and predictions for three occupations at a time. Students are provided a rating of the opportunity of each occupation providing the reward represented by each value. The computer multiplies the value by the opportunity rating to produce an overall desirability index. This desirability index is matched against probability of successful entry, and the students can then examine their choices in terms of relative risks and rewards.

Two other systems, at present less operational than the three previously discussed, will be considered briefly. These systems include the

TABLE 25.   SIGI^{TM} at a Glance

- *Is an interactive computer-based aid to career decision making . . .*
- *Serves primarily students in, or about to enter, two-year and four-year colleges . . .*
- *Complements the work of guidance counselors . . .*
- *Uses the PDP-11 family of computers and cathode-ray tube terminals . . .*
- *Operates under the RSTS/E time-sharing monitor and is programmed in BASIC-PLUS . . .*
- *Includes six interrelated subsystems listed below. (Each subsystem raises a major question and helps the student answer it. These questions and answers form distinctive steps in decision making.)*

SUBSYSTEM	WHAT THE STUDENT DOES	QUESTIONS ANSWERED
Introduction	Learns concepts and uses of major sections listed below.	Where do you stand now in your career decision making? What help do you need?
I. VALUES	Examines 10 occupational values and weights importance of each one.	What satisfactions do you want in an occupation? What are you willing to give up?
II. LOCATE	Puts in specifications on 5 values at a time and gets lists of occupations that meet specifications.	Where can you find what you want? What occupations should you look into?
III. COMPARE	Asks pointed questions and gets specific information about occupations of interest.	What would you like to know about occupations that you are considering? Should you reduce your list?
IV. PREDICTION	Finds out probabilities of getting various marks in key courses of preparatory programs for occupations.	Can you make the grade? What are your chances of success in preparing for each occupation you are considering?
V. PLANNING	Gets displays of program for entering each occupation, licensing or certification requirements, and sources of financial aid.	How do you get from here to there? What steps do you take to enter an occupation you are considering?
VI. STRATEGY	Evaluates occupations in terms of the rewards they offer and the risks of trying to enter them.	Which occupations fit your values best? How do you decide between an occupation that is highly desirable but risky and one that is less desirable but easier to prepare for?

From Katz, M. *SIGI: A Computer-based System of Interactive Guidance & Information.* Copyright © 1974, 1975 by Educational Testing Service. All rights reserved. Reprinted by permission.

Education and Career Exploration System (ECES) and Information System for Vocational Decisions (ISVD).

The Education and Career Exploration System (ECES) has been described by Minor, Myers, and Super,[14] and by Bohn and Super.[15] This system attempts to relate understanding of self to understanding of the external environment. The purposes of the system include helping the student by: (a) broadening knowledge of self and of occupational alternatives, (b) providing a system for exploring educational and curricular preferences without occupational restriction, (c) providing a means of focusing a search for appropriate educational institutions. This system helps the counselor by relieving him/her of maintaining an occupational resources center and by bringing to the counseling session students who are better prepared for decision making.

The career information aspect of the system is based on three phases: the first provides the student with an occupational information bank that can be used for browsing, exploring, and clarification; the second phase provides general educational information; and the third phase presents specific information about post-high school educational institutions. The student can enter any one of the phases and can move back and forth from one to another. Personal data that are stored in the computer include a record of high school grades, a prediction of highest educational attainment, inventoried interest scores, and self-concept data including the student's own estimate of ability and interest. The student's personal data can be related to the occupational areas he/she explores with the computer.

Phase I of the information bank uses a modification of Roe's classification, retaining the eight fields or areas, but using only four levels of educational requirements. The student can browse by indicating to the computer the kinds of activities and work conditions that appear appealing. The computer retrieves names and definitions of compatible occupations. The student then indicates the occupations that appeal and the computer responds with a statement relating these occupations to his/her personal data, and a list of fields not mentioned but compatible with computerized personal data. The system provides further clarification by giving the student opportunity to explore more deeply. This is done by providing information about duties performed, training requirements, work situation, competition, career growth potential, etc. He/she becomes familiar with the nature of the work through a problem-solving situation representative of the work performed. Responses and reactions are matched against personal data, previous responses, and similar data to adapt to individual needs. The computer provides printout summaries of the responses to each occupation, of the relationship of personal data to the occupation considered, and of the frequency with which specific school courses are recommended for the occupation. These printout reports can, if the student wishes, be used with parents or counselor.

Phase II is designed for students who plan to continue education beyond high school. This phase can be entered from either a vocational orientation developed in Phase I or from a curricular preference approach. The student may name the major areas of study which appeal most, thus leading to courses or programs offered by various types of post-high school institutions. One also is provided other related areas of study that might be of interest and with relationships between curricular and vocational preferences.

The third phase helps the student narrow the search for an educational institution by considering factors such as preferred geographic location, size, type, etc. Printouts provide further data on possible schools, including degree of selectivity, availability of ROTC, residence facilities, costs, etc. Selection of schools considered can come from the student's expressed career or educational aspirations, or he/she can query the computer directly about any specific school that interests him/her.

Tiedeman and his colleagues have developed a system of similar sophistication entitled Information System for Vocational Decisions.[16] The system is based on the assumption that forming a career involves a set of decisions that are made over a span of time encompassing the person's lifetime. For the high schooler or young adult, these decisions are made in the context of education, vocation, military service, and family. Each of these areas, in turn, breaks into subcategories. For example, the educational context includes choice of secondary school curriculum, choice of post-secondary education, choice of collegiate major, choice of a graduate school, choice of a graduate specialization, and choices related to the further refining of occupational location by both job and position emphases.

Operationally, the system will place banks of data in the computer for each of the context areas of education, vocation, military service, and family. These data will be both present- and future-oriented and range from the general to the specific. They will include material from the local job market as well as regional and national data. A fifth file will carry data about the users in two parts. One part will include characteristics of individuals generally and the relationship among these characteristics, choices, and later success. The other part of the file will be the private educational and occupational history of the user.

The computer routines will be used primarily for three user applications—review, exploration, and clarification. The review routine provides for call-up and comparison of previous statements about what was then a future event but now has passed so that the user may check how prior expectations were fulfilled. It is expected that this routine will help the user gain insight and learn how intuition guides actions. The exploration routine permits the user to browse through data files, to compare personal characteristics with comparative data of others and their preferred alternatives, and to suggest alternatives on the basis of this comparison. The objective is the emergence of a set of alternatives and the basis on which those choices are preferred. The clarification routine queries the user about the depth of knowledge concerning his favored alternatives and the understanding of future alternatives that are likely linked with present preferences. The objective here is to reduce the user's doubt and ignorance regarding next actions.

Harris predicts that in the future the computer will become increasingly significant as a guidance tool.[17] She bases this prediction on the demonstrated capability of presently developed hardware, the continuing emphasis on accountability and on career guidance, and the increasing evidence of cost feasibility. Further, she anticipates that future systems will be designed to emphasize a sequential career development approach rather than the present emphasis on the decision-making phase.

INTERVIEWS WITH EXPERTS

Every elementary and secondary teacher or counselor already has encountered problems of credibility when discussing career options outside the educational structure. Even the teacher who may have long years of significant involvement in a noneducational field is just as likely to meet the attitude of "how can you know about that job, you're a teacher!" Attempting to dispel that point of view may well be as futile as tilting at windmills. Fortunately, the solution is near at hand and can be applied to the advantage of all concerned. The logical step is to enlist the assistance of someone with that aura of credibility—someone engaged in the field and thereby an automatic "expert."

Teachers, especially elementary teachers, have long followed the custom of using community resource individuals to supplement and amplify the classroom learning experience. We are concerned here with essentially that same practice, using someone with special knowledge who comes, ordinarily, from beyond the school campus.

Interviews with experts are appropriate experiences in the career development process at all steps from the awareness level onward. Obviously, they should be adjusted to the level of development of the individuals involved, and other steps should be taken to make the experience valuable. In the awareness and early exploratory phases of career development such interviews, undoubtedly, can be best utilized with groups of students. The career day and career conference programs are examples of such activities; we will consider these shortly. As the student progresses toward a tentative decision, it would be most useful for him/her to confer individually with such a resource person.

Career Day

On "career day," groups of students are given an opportunity for direct contact with representatives of selected occupations in which they have indicated an interest.

The exact form of the career day varies considerably among the many schools using this technique. Typically, the school operates the program during a half day of school time. Some schools occasionally arrange the program for an evening.

The career day program is designed to provide the students with pertinent and accurate information about specific fields of work. If properly organized, it can help them broaden concepts and understanding of fields in which they have some interest. It also gives them contact with at least one individual from whom they may be able to obtain further information if interest continues and expands.

Student involvement throughout the planning and presentation of a career day program is essential if the program is to be effective. Many schools develop such programs through the student council or similar student government groups. If such a group does not exist, an advisory committee of representative students can be used to assure student participation.

Although many schools schedule the career day late in the spring, a strong case can be made for holding it much earlier in the school year. Ideally, the career day should serve as a stimulus for students, encouraging them to give attention to the development of career plans and to become involved in the process of exploration. If this is the major goal of the career day, it probably should be scheduled early in the year, so that the rest of the year will be available for exploration, reading, conferences, and counseling. A date not later than the middle of the fall term provides sufficient time for the pre-conference activities and still leaves the maximum amount of time for the student, teacher, and counselor to capitalize on the event.

Once the date has been fixed, the next question concerns the best part of the day for the program. Whether morning or afternoon is chosen depends largely on the local situation, the normal school schedule, and which portion of the day best lends itself to the objectives of the program.

Consideration should be given to an evening program if the school wishes to include parents in the activity. There are, of course, many obvious advantages to a schedule that permits the maximum number of parents to be included, and this is more likely to occur outside the usual work day. If parents are to be involved, such participation must be included in the planning from the very beginning, and student attitude toward such involvement must be developed. Including parents in the career day is based on our assumption that the development of sound career plans by youth involves the adults in the immediate environment—parents, teachers, and counselors.

Career day programs sometimes have been criticized because the occupations included have not been representative of student interest. This is likely to occur only when student interests have been disregarded in developing the program. One way to prevent this is to begin planning with an indication of interest areas by the students who will be involved in the program. Each student may be asked simply to indicate the occupations he/she would most like to have included in a career day program. Sometimes a checklist is used, on which the student indicates from three to five preferences. The list can be compiled from a survey of occupations into which students from the school in question most frequently go, or from an "armchair" listing of the occupations most prevalent in the geographic area. Space always should be provided on any checklist for the students to add occupations not listed.

It is rarely possible to include all occupations listed by students in a single school. A tally of the checklists, however, will indicate areas in which student interest is sufficient to plan for one or more groups. Frequently one can meet specialized interests by grouping on a broader base than the student response. For example, if only a few indicate interest in carpentry, stone-masonry, and painting, these can be logically grouped as construction trades. Where student interest is too small to include the requested occupations, the students making the requests should be helped to obtain the desired information in other ways.

Once student interests have been inventoried and tallied, the groups to be included can be easily identified. Every effort should be made to cover the entire range of student interests. One occupational area—the professions, for example—should not dominate the program. Securing speakers for each area is a difficult and time-consuming process. Members of the faculty may be helpful in suggesting resources or speakers in some areas. Often local service clubs can suggest individuals who might discuss particular fields. Speakers for craft and manufacturing areas may be found by consulting with local union representatives or with local employers. Representatives from professional and managerial fields often have greater control of their own time schedules and may find it easier to arrange their calendars so that they can participate. The problem of finding available representatives from the "blue-collar" fields is a further reason for scheduling the program outside the usual working day.

Speakers should be sought who can fairly present their occupations to interested students. Breadth and years of experience in the field may not necessarily be of major concern, particularly of a field in which changes have recently occurred. They can be assisted in preparing for their participation by being given appropriate materials well before the scheduled day. Pamphlets, booklets, pages from the *Occupational Outlook Handbook,* and similar materials may be useful in broadening the individual's perspective of his own field. Student groups—the advisory committee, perhaps—can prepare lists of questions that students are likely to ask in the actual program, so that the speakers can anticipate some of the topics about which they might be questioned. The person responsible for the program should be sure that the participating speakers clearly understand their roles in the day's activity. If special equipment of any kind is needed, these arrangements must be made in advance. Sufficient time in each session should be planned for student questions.

Publicity about the program should be carefully organized within the school, to stimulate student interest and to build and maintain that interest as the time for the program approaches. The usual channels of communication, such as the daily bulletin, school newspaper, or bulletin boards, can be employed to provide students with basic information. Whether parents are invited to participate or not, the community should be informed of the event through ordinary news media, including information about its purpose and scope and its value for the student body. Participants, particularly occupational representatives, ought to be recognized for their contribution to the project.

Since the program is basically a learning activity, students should be properly prepared for their part. If students are provided ample opportunity to read and study material about the occupations in which they are interested before the career day program, they will be in a better position to ask appropriate questions and, thereby, to make better use of the speakers' limited time. Groups of students can be encouraged to prepare questions in advance and to complete other preparatory steps that will enhance the effectiveness of the program. Serious advance preparation also may help to alleviate the "carnival" air that sometimes surrounds the career day program.

Faculty members also should be prepared for their parts in the program. They can add to its smooth operation by introducing speakers in the various groups, helping move groups efficiently to assigned locations, and assuming responsibility for specific groups.

The organization of a career day program is complex. As much of the detail work as possible should be completed in advance so that the activity will run more smoothly. Once students have indicated their interests on the inventory and the areas to be included in the program have been identified, it is possible to establish a schedule for each student to visit the groups most appropriate for him/her, and to see that groups where multiple sessions are needed can be balanced. Each student should be informed in advance of his/her schedule for the day and a duplicate filed, to provide for the occasional forgetful one. Rooms should be assigned with the sizes of the groups in mind.

Soon after the program has been held, it should be evaluated by all participants to determine whether such a program should be used in subsequent years, and, if so, how it should be modified to improve its effectiveness. Ideally, evaluation should include reactions from students, faculty members, and occupational representatives. Probably most schools use a brief evaluation form for gathering reactions from students and from speakers. The form for students can be quite brief, providing space for a general reaction to the total program as well as for specific reactions to each session. Students can be expected to respond to items concerning the general quality of each session, the effectiveness of the speaker in providing them useful information, and the value of the session to other students. Speakers should be asked to react to student interest, extent to which the general organization succeeded in accomplishing the goals, whether time allocated was adequate, and willingness to participate again. Both groups should be asked for suggestions for modification or change. Faculty members also can be queried by questionnaire, or if possible, during discussion time in a faculty meeting.

Follow-up of the program is just as crucial as is preparation of students beforehand. Many opportunities for follow-up exist in every school situation; these should be identified and capitalized on. Several of the classes in which students are enrolled naturally lend themselves to further discussion of the topics in the program. Others, such as English classes, can be used for stimulating student thought and reaction through assigned papers, preparation of letters, role-playing interviews, and similar activities. Counselors should follow up such programs with student interviews to help them obtain further information, discuss tentative career choices, arrange for visits to businesses, industries, or advanced schools, or develop further plans that help develop career plans. The career day program should be used so that the maximum benefit accrues to all of the participating students.

Career Conference

Some schools have developed the career conference instead of scheduling a special career day. Arranging a special day obviously interrupts the normal school activity and sometimes carries with it a "holiday" atmosphere that can interfere with its basic purpose. In some schools the career day is advantageous because it briefly concentrates the attention of the entire school, and sometimes even the community, on the school's commitment to career planning. In other schools a single day's effort is more effective because of local situations.

If a school prefers not to interrupt its schedule, a series of career conferences can be arranged within the framework of the regular school calendar. Basically, the career conference is a segment of the career day program, in which an occupational representative is brought together with a group of interested students to discuss a specific field.[18, 19] Often a series of these, extending over a considerable period of time, can be strung together to provide the same coverage as the career day program.

Organizing and developing a series of career conferences involves the same steps as those described for the career day program. The major difference between the two activities is simply that the career day puts the whole program into a single day or portion of a day, whereas the career conferences may number one or two a day over a period of a month or more, depending on the number of occupations to be included.

The flexibility provided in a series of career conferences has certain definite advantages.[20,21] Individual student scheduling is likely to be easy since students can be scheduled for the number of conferences in which they indicate an interest. Under the career day plan it is difficult to avoid the lock-step regimentation of scheduling all students for the number of sessions included in the program. Some students may be seriously interested in exploring only one or two areas, whereas others may be anxious to participate in five or six conferences. The students included in career conferences are more likely to be truly interested in the area being discussed, with the increased possibility that the session will be more profitable for them. Secondly, the flexible schedule also may make it easier to obtain occupational representatives who can do the best job of presenting information about their fields.

The flexibility of scheduling can, however, create certain problems that must be dealt with cooperatively by school administration and faculty. Establishing a series of career conferences during the school day will inevitably raise some conflicts for students and necessitate choice between the regularly assigned class and the scheduled conference. Although this problem cannot be entirely eliminated, it can be reduced somewhat by arranging the conference schedule so that all periods of the day are treated as fairly as possible; thus, no one class encounters continuous absences over a prolonged period.[22]

Follow-up and evaluation of the career conference are just as important as for the career day program. Usually the same techniques can be used.

"Post-High School Education" Programs

Many high schools have developed programs or special days that have been labeled "College Day" or some similar title. These programs resemble the career day, except that speakers are drawn from educational institutions. Historically, these programs have developed because school and college officials recognize that high school students need an opportunity to discuss post-high school educational plans with representatives of institutions in which they might be interested. Numerous high schools set aside a special day or time when the representatives of the various schools are invited to meet with interested students. The program has developed in an attempt to meet student need without disrupting the school day by allowing college representatives to drop in at various times during the school year.

Some schools attempt to combine the activities of the college day and the career day. Ordinarily this is not a wise procedure, because it attempts to concentrate too much into a limited amount of time, and consideration of both broad areas in a single activity is more likely to be con-fusing rather than helpful. Occasionally schools have attempted to combine the two activities because of small student body. Rather than mix the two, such schools might better serve their students by joining with other nearby schools to conduct two separate programs.

As the name implies, many schools invite only college representa-tives to participate in their college day programs. Since every school has students whose future plans do not include college, only a portion of the student group is served by such a program. It seems wise, in this period of increased emphasis on post-high school education of many types, to rename the day with some more inclusive term that will permit representa-tives from technical schools, trade and vocational schools, and other similar institutions to be involved in it.

Although many high schools have overlooked the importance of parental involvement in career days, they have for some reason often pro-vided for this in programs related to colleges. Consequently, many of these sessions have been properly labeled "College Night" and held in the evening, to permit parents to attend with the youngsters. Scheduling both types of activities outside regular working hours might encourage greater participation by parents and result in a closer working relationship between school and parent.

The format of these programs is quite similar to that used in career day programs, and the organization and development of such programs should be similar.

Some of the same kinds of problems will develop in an "education day" program as in a career day. One of the most obvious is the wide disparity in student interest. Since most institutional representatives must travel a considerable distance to participate in a local "education day," it must be determined how many interested students are needed to justify their participation. The extent of student interest can be determined fairly accurately if it has been assessed by an inventory. Another alterna-tive is a cooperative program among nearby schools, so that there can be some pooling of students whose interests are in institutions only occasion-ally selected by the student bodies generally. School A might invite a representative from Institution X and include students from Schools B and C in its program. Similarly, School B might invite Institution Y and stu-dents from Schools A and C.

A second problem often develops unnecessarily. If students have not previously been prepared for participation, institutional representatives may find that their time is being spent in explaining such terms as "semes-ter hours," "grade points," "prerequisities," rather than discussing the topic for which they have come. If terminology is explained and colleges and other schools discussed before representatives are invited in, students will be ready to ask appropriate questions.

A further, and partially insoluble, difficulty may be encountered in

the usual "education day." Student questions to the institutional representative can, of course, cover the entire range of the institution's program.
It is difficult for any representative to be equally versed in all phases of an
extensive educational program; consequently, he/she may not always be
able to provide the precise information desired by the student.

Many schools have developed a modified version of the "education
day" that is particularly advantageous. This involves asking recent alumni
of the local school to be institutional representatives. The major advantages are quite obvious: (1) the former students arouse personal interest
among the listeners, since they are probably known to them, (2) their
experiences will be accepted by the student groups, and (3) their concerns
and problems will have meaning for them.

Two difficulties often arise when a group of alumni are scheduled
for such a program. One problem is arranging an appropriate time for
the program. The obvious solution is to find a time that is a vacation
period for most surrounding post-high school institutions but is regularly
scheduled for the local school. Such periods are most likely to occur either
at the Christmas holiday period or at the term break. Both of these times
have disadvantages, since the first occurs when the local students may be
more interested in their own holiday than in educational plans, and the
second often coincides with the examination period in the local school. If
an appropriate time can be found without local conflict when alumni are
available, such a program can offer much to the local students. The second
problem relates to the breadth of knowledge that the former student has of
the new school and the difficulty in answering questions about areas in
which information is limited. Again, this problem can be partially resolved if the school counselor helps the panel of alumni prepare for the
program by discussing with them the types of questions that may be raised
and by providing them access to local copies of school catalogs and
similar sources.

SIMULATION AND SYNTHETIC
WORK ENVIRONMENTS

In this section, we are concerned with providing experiences, through
artificial means, that are intended to assist the student or client understand
more completely the decision-making process or the nature of a work
situation. By no means limited to the school setting, this type of experience
can often be encountered in the classroom or learning situation.

Simulation has long been recognized by teachers as an effective
means of teaching both simple and complex skills. Obviously, simulation
offers counselors a comparable opportunity to transmit or develop insight
into demands imposed on workers, the nature of the work environment,

skills needed by workers to complete certain jobs successfully, and similar aspects of employment. Strangely, the procedure remains underdeveloped as it relates to counseling and career development activities.

A common example of simulation is the fire drill encountered by every elementary school pupil. The military services have used the technique extensively with infiltration courses, obstacle courses, and combat training. A more sophisticated example of simulation is the Link Trainer, a device encountered by many who have qualified for a pilot's license. Recently developed devices for preparing instructors of driver education are further examples. One such device consists of a trailer fitted out with sixteen stations, each equipped with the gauges, foot pedals, and steering wheel typical of the driver's seat in an ordinary automobile. Via sound film, students are presented situations they might meet while driving. Their responses can be monitored so that they learn appropriate behavior for each incident. The advantages are obvious—a wider range of experiences, including apparent collisions and other "accidents," can be safely undergone than could be included in the usual "on-the-road" portion of driver education.

The *Life Career Game*, developed by Coleman and Boocock, is an example of gaming and simulation applied to the career development process.[23] The game, appropriate for adolescents, permits each player to make decisions about education, occupation, family, and leisure activity for one of four youths, expected to be somewhat similar to the players themselves. Each "round" of the game corresponds to a year of life and presents new problems to deal with. Boocock points out that the game permits players to experience how decisions are interrelated, how success is affected by various factors, and how educational and occupational opportunities are available to different kinds of people. Barbula has modified the game and developed additional materials to broaden the age span across grades six to eight.[24] The original game is available through Academic Games Associates, Johns Hopkins University.

Parker Brothers has developed a game entitled *Careers*, which is available commercially. Although intended as entertainment, the game does include aspects that make it an appropriate device for motivating interest in the career development process. The rules require each player to set individual goals in the areas of fame, fortune, and happiness, and to attempt to satisfy those goals through various occupational choices.

Many high schools have developed "Civil Service Commissions" of various types to provide students job experience through applying for the various helper positions in classrooms, laboratories, and elsewhere in school. These programs usually require completion of an application form, sometimes a job interview, supervisory reports from the responsible faculty member, and similar job-related experiences. Leonard has reported on the use of this technique with inner city elementary school pupils.[25]

Krumboltz has written about using vocational problem-solving experience as a means of increasing career exploration and interest.[26]   Hamilton and Krumboltz report an experimental study using such materials with 10th grade students to determine how realistic the kit needs to be.[27]   Their experimental group, using more lifelike equipment, expressed greater enjoyment, wanted more information about the job, and signed up to try more kits than the control group.   Lack of sufficient data prevented determination of statistical significance, however.   Out of this research has come the publication of 20 *Job Experience Kits* by Science Research Associates.   Each *Kit* presents tasks similar to those found in the specific occupation.   The students or clients are involved in problem-solving activities in these tasks so that they develop some "feel" for what the worker does. An attempt has been made to assure that the problem is representative of those encountered by the worker, that student interest is maintained, and that reading skill is not an influencing factor.

For some jobs, students are asked to do certain tasks using typical tools.   The *Kit* for accountant, for example, asks the user to examine the books of a businessman who feels that his business is not earning as much money as it should.   The student must examine certain records, returned checks, and a bank statement to determine if errors or other improper procedures have been followed.

Johnson reports the use of similar devices in X-ray and medical laboratory technology.[28]   The use of the materials was found to produce interest in both occupations among girls in the 9th and 11th grades.

Synthetic work environments also have been used frequently in teaching situations but rarely in career development and counseling.   Their appropriateness for career-related activities is so obvious that one is compelled to speculate about the lack of use.   Again, one can hope that increased emphasis on career education will lead counselors to prospect in what appears to be an area ripe for development.   We are concerned here with providing occupational experiences, either simulated or real, in an artificial setting.   Like simulated activities, this group of experiences offers the opportunity to develop insight and understanding as well as skills.   The boundary line between synthetic and real work environment is blurred, and a sharp distinction between the two would be difficult to establish at times.   Generally, one can assign to the synthetic work environments category those unpaid occupational experiences that are carried out in settings other than the usual or customary site and for purposes other than the usual or customary.   The setting ordinarily will be a school or some other learning center, and the objective ordinarily will be for attitudinal or skill learning purposes.

Elementary teachers frequently have used this technique to enhance classroom learning activities; for example, the class establishes a "store" through which it acquires commonly used supplies such as paper, crayons, pencils, paste; or perhaps a "bank," in which each student maintains a small savings account.   Fundamentally, the teacher's objectives focus primarily on sharpening mathematical and communication skills and on building understanding of basic economic and social agencies. The experience also provides an opportunity for developing awareness of occupations directly related to the project and, even at second and third grade levels, for helping students assess the extent to which they like that type of activity.

High school vocational education classes also have used the technique extensively to teach specific vocational skills. Many trade and industry departments assign construction craft students to a class project involving the complete building of a home that then is sold to provide the materials for next year's similar project. In the construction process, the students, under proper faculty supervision, actually do the work of a carpenter, an electrician, a plasterer, a plumber, a painter, a mason, etc. School projects of this type provide abundant opportunities for youngsters in the awareness and exploratory phase to learn more about the activities of such crafts. Commercial departments in many high schools routinely provide experiences that are prototypes of actual employment settings. Students in practical nursing programs engage in bed-making and other patient care services using a manikin in a "laboratory" classroom.

Almost every elementary and secondary counselor can find within the confines of the school numerous activities similar to those identified above that can be used effectively in career development. A little ingenuity and consultation with teachers will uncover unlimited comparable possibilities.

Just beyond the school is another cluster of corresponding activities that can be equated to synthetic work environment experiences. One illustration from the activity or extra curricular category is Junior Achievement —an organization found in many communities and ordinarily sponsored by out-of-school groups. The program primarily helps youngsters acquire business "experience" by forming "companies" in which each participant actually invests personal funds. Materials then are purchased and a "product" is manufactured by the company. The participants then develop a marketing plan, often door-to-door selling, in which each participant engages. The profits are divided among share-holders and the company either continues the cycle or dissolves itself.

DIRECT EXPERIENCES—OBSERVATION, EXPLORATORY, AND TRYOUT

We will now consider the use of direct contact with workers in natural work settings as the final form of career information media. The advantages of such a technique are immediately apparent. The credibility of reality is always difficult to contest. The student or client is able to see things as they are and to develop impressions and insights that would be impossible to foster in other ways. At the same time, one is compelled to realize that this tremendous advantage also can operate in a negative fashion. Inexperienced observers and participants are not always able to see things as they really are and misunderstandings then can develop. Further, the specimen situation may be atypical for various reasons and thus misconceptions are created. Both difficulties can be counteracted by increasing the number and the time factor for direct contact; if this corrective measure cannot be applied, then the contacts used must truly be representative. Jepsen reports an experiment in which he presented career materials based on a videotaped field trip to two classes and nationally produced printed materials about the same occupations to two other classes.[29] Both groups were provided with an introductory filmstrip and discussion was used with both groups. He states that the classes using the videotaped field trip reported more accurate images of the occupations than did the control group.

As the world of work has become more complex, many occupations have been removed from public view, so that most students have little opportunity to go "behind the scenes" and actually see how and where certain types of work are performed. The perceptions they have may be developed on limited information and consequently may be quite unrealistic.

The field trip or industry tour provides many students their first chance to have direct contact with this side of the world of work. Such a trip can be highly motivating to students, encouraging them to explore further both the world of work and their own future plans.[30]

The group involved and the purposes to be accomplished are important in planning a field trip of this type. If the group consists of younger students and the purpose is to arouse interest and insight into how people earn their living, the tour probably should be limited to samples of occupations most frequently encountered in the local community. On the other hand, a group of sophomores or juniors in the vocational curriculum will be interested in a different type of trip. They will be anxious to see working conditions, tools and equipment used, actual work processes, company organizations, and similar items that specifically relate to particular occupations. A high school class in occupations may be interested in exploring, but at a much different level from the elementary group.

Most local businesses and industries recognize the educational value of an industry tour or field trip and accept the chance to participate as an opportunity for community service or public relations. In fact, many companies are asked so frequently to permit such tours that they have arranged regular schedules, trained personnel to conduct the tours, and sometimes even prepared special exhibits, displays, or films to help visitors understand what they see on such trips.

Teachers and counselors who arrange such visits should be aware that a tour through a plant by a group of students is costly to the company, since it disrupts work schedules as well as requires the time of the guide or other personnel. To make this contribution by the employer worthwhile, the student group should be adequately prepared for the trip. Students should understand the purposes of the visit and also should be told what they should watch for, so that the trip will be as meaningful as possible. Ordinarily, the company also should know ahead of time the nature of the group and the purpose of the trip, so that the group can be best served. The planning should provide time for adequate discussion soon after the tour. This follow-up permits clarification of any misunderstanding and allows the group to share its observations and reactions, hence reinforcing the learning that has occurred.

Industry tours involve several administrative problems. These usually focus on scheduling, transportation, and liability. Any industrial visit usually requires more time than a single school period, so the difficulty of scheduling at the school is inevitable. Arrangements for a longer period require close cooperation with the school administration and other teachers. Advance planning usually can reduce these difficulties to a minimum, but it seldom eliminates them. Transportation for a group may necessitate the scheduling of buses or other vehicles, with consequent cost and the complexity of arrangements.

The individual visit by a single student to a specific industry or business may offer one of the best opportunities to gain insight into a field in which he/she is seriously interested.[31] Such a visit often is arranged for an entire working day, and usually the visiting student is assigned to a worker with whom the entire day is spent. Such a visit provides maximum opportunity to see a variety of aspects of the job, and to question the worker about what he/she is doing, as well as why and how. The student may have an opportunity to spend time with two or three workers in the course of the day. This provides a chance to become familiar with the workers' attitude toward their work, opportunities for advancement, and work stability, among other things.[32]

The use of the individual industry visit is one way in which the career day program can be supplemented for many students. It should be restricted to students who would find such a visit most helpful in developing plans. Arranging such visits will be time-consuming for both school personnel and for the cooperating industry, but the benefits to the student usually will more than repay the effort involved.

To a large extent, one can safely generalize that group visits, especially for younger students, are primarily focused on the building of awareness, whereas individual visits are clearly oriented toward the exploration and decision-making phases of development. During the decision-making and preparatory phases, visits to post-secondary educational institutions serve a function similar to that of the industry or business tour at an earlier age.

Increased attention to post-high school education in recent years has been accompanied by an increase in the number of visits made by high school students to institutions of higher learning. Such visits have been helpful to both the prospective student and the college or university.

The secondary school is inevitably involved in helping students make appropriate choices of schools. Once admitted, students will often find greater academic pressures; consequently, it becomes even more important that the original selection of a school be a wise one. A visit to the campus is one way for the prospective student to learn about the institution being considered. First-hand observation can answer questions that can be resolved in no other way. If the visit can be arranged when classes are in session one has the opportunity to see members of the student body and learn of their interests, goals, backgrounds, social life, living facilities, and similar factors that cannot be fully assessed by reading college catalogs or viewing films of the school.

Many colleges and universities have recognized the importance of such visits as a part of the educational planning of high school students, and have developed programs such as "Day on Campus," in which students from secondary schools are invited to participate in a day's program on campus. If a formal program is scheduled, it usually provides an opportunity to talk with representatives of the curricular areas in which the visitors are interested, to visit educational facilities and housing units, and to talk to one or two students from their home schools. Even though such a mass program has obvious disadvantages, it does at least permit the student to gain some feeling of the institution and its various programs.

From the standpoint of the prospective student, the ideal visit should be made when he/she is not part of a mass inundation, so that he/she can see a typical cross-section of campus life. Individual school tours require more effort for the local counselor or teacher to arrange, but usually can be handled without insurmountable problems.

Usually the local school can arrange trips only to nearby institutions and only when there is a large enough group of students to justify the staff time required. A group of students on such a trip of course should be accompanied by a counselor or other staff member. Naturally, the number of staff days that can be allotted to such activities is limited. Where distance is too great or only a single student is interested in a specific school, the counselor should work with student and parent to encourage a family visit to the campus as a substitute for a school-sponsored visit.

Although the school visit is often considered in making plans for students who are college-bound, it is just as important for students whose interests lie in other educational directions. The same arrangements can and should be made for students interested in vocational schools and other noncollegiate institutions. In fact, many arguments can be raised that these visits are even more crucial; for example, many vocational schools provide limited facilities for student activities and housing, so that a student may be forced to make individual arrangements to a greater extent than on many college campuses. Some preview of what is available may be helpful in making more appropriate plans.

Using work samples and evaluative tasks is well established in industrial personnel offices as a means of properly classifying and assigning a new employee. Many companies allocate large sums of money for professional staff and develop elaborate facilities in which these pre-employment, exploratory exercises can be conducted and evaluated. Such behavior clearly is based on the premise that these procedures are effective in identifying potentially successful employees. If this premise is correct, then using a similar technique in the exploratory and decision-making phase also should be valuable. By using work samples and evaluative tasks, an individual could have a clearer concept of the employment situation and could use the preparatory period more adequately to build skills and competencies of value in the job. Unfortunately, little has been done to develop this technique as a media system.

Hansen describes the efforts of Whittier Union High School District to use the procedure, as reported by Eisen.[33] The project, in addition to the traditional work experience program, includes a component designed to serve large numbers of students who wish to sample various occupations. This component includes a two-week experience in sales and merchandising, a Christmas vacation work experience, and a released time try-out program. Assignments, usually about three weeks in length, can be any place in the community. In one school year (1965–66), more than 2,000 students participated in the program.

In Chapter 9, we considered preparatory programs including work experience programs, apprenticeships, and on-the-job training. Our concern there was with the vocational preparatory aspects of these experiences, a narrower consideration than our focus here.

Work experience programs can be exploratory, general, or vocational preparatory. Exploratory programs aim at helping the student understand various types of work, work settings, tools and equipment used by workers, demands placed on workers, and similar factors. General work experience programs are designed to assist students develop attitudes and skills that are not narrowly vocational in nature, including punctuality, dependability, acceptance of supervision, inter-personal relations, and similar characteristics that apply to all work situations. The Whittier Union program mentioned above illustrates both the exploratory and general models.

Many career education proponents urge the incorporation of unpaid work experience into all education from early high school onward. Certainly the early years of such involvement would be principally oriented toward the exploratory and general patterns. Hansen describes several special applications of work experience programs and brief employment opportunities in addition to the Whittier Union program. An extensive bibliography of relatively recent references on the use of the work experience program can be found in Campbell, Walz, Miller, and Kriger.[34]

Many permutations of the work experience program, which can be developed either for individual students or for groups of students, provide direct contact with the realities of the work setting. These include such activities as prevocational courses, independent study, and participation in volunteer work. Each vehicle permits exposure for varying periods of time on either an intensive or extensive basis to the settings in which workers perform their daily activities. This flexibility to meet individual needs is one of the major advantages of direct contact programs.

Using direct contact experiences to help students or other clients better understand the world of work is clearly more complicated than using printed materials, audio-visual materials, or school-based simulation. Complicating factors include locating and developing suitable sites, maintaining liaison with the employer and providing appropriate supervision for the client, resolving problems of transportation, coordinating the experience with other parts of the individual's schedule such as other classes and school responsibilities, and clarifying liability and responsibility when the client is away from the school or counseling site. No doubt, one or more of these factors has been the retardant that has prevented extensive use of what is clearly the most relevant and meaningful way to acquire knowledge about work. Until increased acceptance of career education principles brings school and employer into a cooperative relationship, the counselor, teacher, coordinator, and placement officer must carry an extra load to seek out and develop these vital experiences for their clientele.

Not to be overlooked as instruments for learning about jobs and their interrelationship to workers are the casual work experiences of nearly every adolescent. Included in this category are summer vacation jobs, part-time jobs during the school year or briefer vacation-period jobs, and the incidental experiences with a paper route, child care, or similar episode. Barzelay describes a summer work program designed to provide high school students with a better understanding of the business world.[35]

In summary, as we review the Spectrum of Occupational Information Data proposed by Thompson and described in Chapter 11, we can see a high level of development and availability of those devices categorized at the lower end of the scale, including publications and audio-visual aids. However, by the time one reaches the midpoint of that spectrum and turns to such devices as simulated situations, synthetic work environments, and direct experiences, we find ourselves in territory that is mostly unexplored and only slightly developed. This area can be expected to undergo that development in the next few years.

NOTES

1. K. R. Kunze, "Industry Resources Available to Counselors," *Vocational Guidance Quarterly*, vol. 16, no. 2 (December, 1967), pp. 137–142.
2. G. R. Walz, "Technology in Guidance: A Conceptual Overview," *Personnel and Guidance Journal*, vol. 49, no. 3 (November, 1970), pp. 175–182.
3. G. Pierson, R. Hoover, and E. Whitfield, "A Regional Career Information Center," *Vocational Guidance Quarterly*, vol. 15, no. 3 (March, 1967), pp. 162–169.
4. M. Gerstein and R. Hoover, "VIEW—Vocational Information for Education and Work," *Personnel and Guidance Journal*, vol. 45, no. 6 (February, 1967), pp. 593–596.
5. G. DuBato, "VOGUE: A Demonstration System of Occupational Information for Career Guidance," *Vocational Guidance Quarterly*, vol. 17, no. 2 (December, 1968), pp. 117–119.
6. E. A. Whitfield and G. A. Glaeser, "The Microfilm Approach to Disseminating Vocational Information: An Evaluation," *Vocational Guidance Quarterly*, vol. 18, no. 2 (December, 1969), pp. 82–86.
7. R. D. Childers and E. A. Whitfield, *VIEW—An Implementation Guide*, Career Decision-Making Program (Charleston, West Va.: Appalachia Educational Laboratory, Inc., 1974).
8. F. Frederick, "Adjunct Roles of Data Processing Devices in Computer Assisted Counseling," unpublished paper presented at AERA Convention, Atlantic City, 1968.
9. J. Harris, "The Computer: Guidance Tool of the Future," *Journal of Counseling Psychology*, vol. 21, no. 4 (July, 1974), pp. 331–339.
10. J. Harris, "The Computerization of Vocational Information," *Vocational Guidance Quarterly*, vol. 17, no. 1 (September, 1968), pp. 12–20.
11. A. Roe, *The Psychology of Occupations* (New York: John Wiley and Sons, Inc., 1956), pp. 143–152.
12. P. Franklin, "The Oregon Career Information System," a paper presented at the Conference on Consumer Protection in Post-Secondary Education, Knoxville, TN, 1974.
13. "Field Trials Start for Computer-Based Guidance System," *ETS Developments*, vol. 21, no. 4 (Fall, 1974).
14. F. Minor, R. Myers, and D. Super, "An Experimental Computer-Based Educational and Career Exploration System," *Personnel and Guidance Journal*, vol. 47, no. 6 (February, 1969), pp. 564–569.
15. M. Bohn, Jr. and D. Super, "The Computer in Counseling and Guidance Programs," *Educational Technology*, vol. 9, no. 3 (March, 1969), pp. 29–31.
16. D. Tiedeman and G. Dudley, *Information System for Vocational Decisions* (Cambridge, Mass.: Harvard Graduate School of Education, Project Report No. 9, 1967).
17. Harris, *op. cit.*
18. L. S. Hansen, *Career Guidance Practices In School and Community* (Washington, D.C.: National Vocational Guidance Association, 1970), pp. 57–62.
19. C. Demain and G. S. DuBato, "CC–LSD: Career Conferences—Let Students Do It," *Vocational Guidance Quarterly*, vol. 19, no. 2 (December, 1970), pp. 141–144.

20. F. A. Plotsky and R. Goad, "Encouraging Women Through a Career Conference," *Personnel and Guidance Journal*, vol. 52, no. 7 (March, 1974), pp. 486–488.

21. R. Hoppock, "How to Conduct an Occupational Group Conference With an Alumnus," *Vocational Guidance Quarterly*, vol. 18, no. 4 (June, 1970), pp. 311–312.

22. W. A. Rubenfeld, "Weekly Group Conferences on Careers," *Personnel and Guidance Journal*, vol. 33, no. 4 (December, 1954), pp. 223–225.

23. S. S. Boocock, "The Life Career Game," *Personnel and Guidance Journal*, vol. 46, no. 5 (January, 1967), pp. 328–334.

24. M. Barbula, *Life Career Game* (San Diego: San Diego County Department of Education, 1967).

25. G. E. Leonard, *Developmental Career Guidance In Action* (Detroit: Wayne State University and Detroit Public Schools, 1968).

26. J. D. Krumboltz, *Vocational Problem-Solving Experiences for Stimulating Career Exploration and Interest.* Final Report. (Stanford: Stanford University, 1967.)

27. J. A. Hamilton and J. D. Krumboltz, "Simulated Work Experience: How Realistic Should It Be?" *Personnel and Guidance Journal*, vol. 48, no. 1 (September, 1969), pp. 39–44.

28. R. G. Johnson, "Job Simulations to Promote Vocational Interests," *Vocational Guidance Quarterly*, vol. 20, no. 1 (September, 1971), pp. 25–30.

29. D. A. Jepsen, "The Impact of Video-Taped Occupational Field Trips on Occupational Knowledge," *Vocational Guidance Quarterly*, vol. 21, no. 1 (September, 1972), pp. 54–62.

30. R. G. Hughes, "See for Yourself: A Doing Approach to Vocational Guidance," *Vocational Guidance Quarterly*, vol. 13, no. 4 (Summer, 1965), pp. 283–286.

31. W. D. McKenney, "Another Slant on Career Day," *Occupations*, vol. 30, no. 7 (April, 1952), pp. 534–535.

32. F. Broadley, "Job Observation Changes—an Unrealistic Choice," *Vocational Guidance Quarterly*, vol. 13, no. 2 (Winter, 1964), pp. 145.

33. N. Eisen, "Exploratory Work Experience Education," reported in *Career Guidance Practices in School and Community*, L. S. Hansen, author (Washington, D.C.: National Vocational Guidance Association, 1970), pp. 68–69.

34. R. E. Campbell, G. R. Walz, J. V. Miller, and S. F. Kriger, *Career Guidance: A Handbook of Methods* (Columbus, Ohio: Charles E. Merrill Publishing Company, 1973), pp. 114–120.

35. R. Barzelay, "Giving Summer Jobs a New Dimension," *Manpower*, vol. 2, no. 5 (1970), pp. 21–24.

PART V   Supplementary Learning Experiences

The following activities are proposed as ways in which the reader can easily test, explore, or apply the concepts and insights presented in Part V. The list is not intended to be exhaustive or comprehensive, but merely suggestive.

1. Select an occupation and prepare a job analysis from actual observation of two or three workers.
2. Follow up some graduates from a high school who graduated five or ten years ago; determine the extent to which they feel high school did or did not prepare them for their present activities.
3. Evaluate the printed career material for a specific occupation relative to its use with a specific group.
4. Review two or three occupational films.
5. A high school junior boy or girl expresses interest in the occupation of _____. Select the printed career materials that would be appropriate for use.
6. Explore the possibilities of creating a synthetic work situation or a job simulation for that 11th grade student.
7. Identify ten adults you know who could serve as an "expert" with elementary or secondary students exploring occupations.
8. Interview a large firm to ascertain entry jobs and how information about these jobs is provided to possible applicants.

PART

VI

Using Career
Information

14

The Familiarizing and Exploring Stages

The close relationship between *career education* and *career information* was discussed in the opening pages of this book. In the words of Hoyt, *career education* is defined as the total effort of public education and the community aimed at helping all individuals become familiar with the values of a work-oriented society, to integrate these values into their personal value systems, and to implement these values into their lives in such a way that work becomes possible, meaningful, and satisfying to each individual.[1] *Career information* was defined in this book as valid and usable materials about the world of work that are appropriate for assisting the individual seeking vocational guidance. These materials describe: the world of work; its structure and organization; the demands that work imposes on the individual and the rewards and benefits it bestows on him/her; how and where one prepares to enter the field; and the educational, personal, and experience requirements one must meet to enter, remain, or advance in the job. Thus, we see that career education is impossible without career information, and career information is useful in a career education context.

General consensus exists that pursuing the goal of work that is possible, meaningful, and satisfying is a long process. Evans, and others, contend that the action is life-long.[2] All agree that many years are consumed during which the individual goes through a succession of stages, phases, or periods in transition from a child to an adult who is meaningfully and satisfyingly employed.

Both career education and career development are broader concepts than career information. As indicated above in Hoyt's words, career education is a total effort of education and community, thus implying a restructuring of the educational effort to produce the result he proposes. Career development involves efforts and activities beyond the use of career information, such as assessment, appraisal, clarification of values, motivations, family ambitions, etc. In both concepts, however, career information is an essential ingredient.

We can approach the use of career information materials using either the language and concepts of career education, as described briefly in Chapter 1, or the language and concepts of career development theorists, as described in Chapter 2. The two are actually so close together that it would be difficult to use one ladder exclusively. Thus, we think of career education as embodying the idea of the individual's career development moving through awareness to exploration to decision to preparation to employment. Super, as a career development theorist using the life stages concept, speaks of growth, exploration (fantasy, tentative, realistic), and establishment (trial and stable). Marland, describing the Comprehensive Career Education Matrix developed by the Ohio State Center for Vocational and Technical Education, appears to use concepts from both areas.[3] He describes the eight elements of career education identified by the center as:

1. Career Awareness—knowledge of the total spectrum of careers.
2. Self-Awareness—knowledge of the components that make up self.
3. Appreciations, Attitudes—life roles; feelings toward self and others in respect to society and economics.
4. Decision-Making Skills—applying information to rational processes in order to reach decisions.
5. Economic Awareness—perception of processes in production, distribution, and consumption.
6. Skill Awareness and Beginning Competence—skills in ways in which man extends his behavior.
7. Employability Skills—social and communication skills appropriate to career placement.
8. Educational Awareness—perception of the relationship between education and life roles.

Many career education advocates agree that within the educational structure, the elementary school years (K–6) should focus primarily on career awareness, the middle school and junior high school years (perhaps 7–10) should focus on career exploration, and the later high school and post-high school years (11–12 and beyond) should focus on career preparation. Thus, the decision stage would overlap and provide the transition between the exploration period and the preparation years. Decision is used here in a developmental sense—the individual gradually clarifies and identifies career objectives over considerable time; very rarely, if ever, is this a brief process like the butterfly emerging from its cocoon.

Variation in physical growth and development has long been recognized and accepted. Infants are born with different birth weights; they begin to crawl, walk, and talk at different ages; puberty is entered and completed at diverse times. Psychological, attitudinal, and skill development probably are even far more varied than physical development. In addition, these areas lack the discrete bifurcation that is so apparent in physical development—once acquired, the ability to walk and talk are maintained and enhanced and the child rarely regresses to the earlier stage. Not so in other areas, in which change, adaptation, readjustment, and revision are the routine pattern of development. For example, after brief observation or examination, we can state confidently that a child is in the crawling stage, or is beginning to form words into sentences, or is now pubescent. But on the other hand, we would be hard pressed to identify clearly and precisely the exact state of his/her career development. Nevertheless, broad generalizations are possible; and it is with these that we must work most of the time, keeping in mind that anomalies are both possible and likely. When these irregularities or variants occur, they require individualized attention.

Just as we recognize an age range within which most individuals begin to walk or to talk, so, too, can we assume that there is a career development period in which most individuals are gaining an awareness of the world of work, and a subsequent period in which exploration is the primary focus. This does not imply that "awareness" stops on one day and "exploration" begins the next, but rather that the focus or major emphasis moves gradually from one to the other, with the earlier stages very rarely becoming totally dormant. In fact, almost everyone can identify someone who, while nearing retirement, has suddenly become "aware" of a new occupational opportunity and restructured a work life to capitalize on the new opportunity.

Many career development specialists and career education advocates now agree about the career-related objectives and activities of the elementary school years or the awareness years. For example, in 1970, Smith stated that there existed a mandate to the vocational guidance program in the elementary grades to provide experiences by which youngsters could:[4]

1. Expand knowledge of the magnitude of the world of work.
2. Appreciate broad dimensions of work.
3. Systematically diminish distortion about occupations.
4. Understand factors that cause change and affect work and workers.
5. Identify, understand, and interpret significance of interests, capacities, and values as dominant factors in the career process.
6. Establish meaningful relationships between education and future occupational endeavors.
7. Acquire more effective decision-making skills.

Similarly, in 1972, Goldhammer and Taylor took the following position:[5]

> The career development program at the elementary level should be informational and orientational in nature. The effect should be directed toward expanding the student's awareness of self and of the occupational structure. More specific objectives toward which career exploration programs should be directed are given as follows:
>
> > First, students learn to know themselves in their immediate environment and begin to relate to the broader environment beyond the family and school.
> >
> > Second, students develop identifications with workers, fathers, mothers, or other significant persons.
> >
> > Third, students acquire simple manual and mental skills in the performance of a number of work tasks.
> >
> > Fourth, students at the upper elementary level become aware of factors that may have an impact upon their future.
> >
> > Fifth, students acquire satisfactions in the task of learning itself.
> >
> > Sixth, students learn to get along and work with peers.

Isaacson, in earlier editions in 1965 and 1971, had written:

> The elementary teacher participates in the vocational choice process by:
>
> 1. Providing a broad, basic knowledge of the world of work.
> 2. Developing a healthy attitude toward all forms of work.
> 3. Developing some understanding of the individual's role in vocational choice and how the process of choice proceeds.
> 4. Developing the child's self-concept.
> 5. Helping parents to see and accept their role in the development of the youngster.

We will use these five points as the basis of our discussion of career development in the awareness years. Before turning to that consideration, let us first look at the relationships among the team involved in providing those services.

RELATIONSHIP OF TEACHER AND COUNSELOR

Detailed consideration of the role, function, and relationship of the teacher and the counselor lies outside the province of this book. Excellent discussions of this topic can be found in several books concentrating on the organization and administration of guidance services, as well as in books dealing more broadly with public school administration. It is important that we recognize that a team approach is essential if the interests of students, school, and community are to be served effectively. Recent articles by both Roberts [6] and Clapsaddle [7] have demonstrated that teachers alone are not prepared or able to carry out the career development activities of the elementary school. Our discussion of teacher-counselor relationships is not intended to exclude other team members who may be found in some school systems. Since the majority of schools presently provide only teachers and counselors for career development activities, our discussion has been limited to these two groups.

The fundamental function of the school is to provide instruction. All other activities in the school are designed to help accomplish this function with maximum effectiveness. The underlying purpose is to create an opportunity for the optimum development of the individual. This basic purpose is usually interpreted broadly with the recognition that the classroom alone cannot bring about this optimum development. To accomplish this, other activities and personnel are brought into the operation of the school.

Ordinarily, school personnel are classified, according to the function they primarily perform, into three categories—administrative, instructional, or service. The administrative staff is responsible for the planning, executing, evaluating, and interpreting activities of the school. It provides the leadership that helps create the situation in which individual development is to occur. The instructional staff is responsible for inculcating skills, knowledge, and behavior that is important to the development of the individual. The service staff, including counselors, is responsible for activities that aid the individual youngster in the maximum development of his potentialities. The three functions performed by school personnel pervade the entire structure and operation of the school. That is to say, each staff member is usually involved, to some extent, in all of the functions, although one can usually identify the area in which he/she has primary responsibility and others in which he/she has only secondary involvement. Accomplishing the goals of the school requires the close cooperation of all staff members. Each function will be weakened by the failure of any part of the organization.

Within this general structure, the teacher, whose primary function is instruction, and the counselor, whose primary function is service, must work closely together if each student is to gain the maximum growth in career development. Both teacher and counselor are inevitably involved in this process; neither alone can do all that must be accomplished. Each can contribute uniquely to the process. At the same time, while the work of each complements that of the other, it is not easily divided into two discrete units. Rather, one would expect to find in most school settings some variability in actual roles, since the skills and proficiency of each will determine how they can best work together.

In the past few years, as guidance and pupil personnel services have expanded in our schools, two contradictory and fallacious positions have developed concerning the relationship of teacher and counselor. One position implies total overlap in the work of the two, and suggests that a good teacher can perform all of the guidance services needed by the students in a school. This position has been supported by such slogans as "Every teacher a guidance worker," and "Guidance is just good teaching." This is an indefensible position because of the student load that each teacher carries in his/her instructional responsibilities and the lack of specialized preparation in such crucial guidance activities as psychometrics and counseling techniques.

The other position implies a false dichotomy, with the suggestion that the teacher has responsibility for instructional activities only, and the counselor has responsibility exclusively for guidance services. One could, with considerable effort and resultant inefficiency, perhaps bring about such a division of activity. If carried out, it would be most undesirable, since many guidance activities can be more effectively accomplished through instructional techniques and services; similarly, many instructional goals can be best accomplished through guidance activities. Further, even though specialized skills are certainly required in both functions, neither the teacher nor the counselor is totally lacking in the basic skills of the other. This is particularly obvious when one recognizes that almost all school counselors, because of state certification requirements or local hiring practices, formerly worked as teachers; and, second, that many states encourage or require teachers to have at least an introductory course in guidance.

The author maintains that both of these extreme positions are erroneous and that, instead, both counselor and teacher are involved in instructional and guidance responsibilities. The teacher plays a crucial role in the guidance activities of the school. No other staff member has as much direct contact with the student. No one else is in as strategic a position to observe individual growth and development and to see the first glimmerings of interest in new areas or the beginnings of concern about future problems. No one else has as many opportunities for brief informal contacts with the student and for encouragement to explore new areas or to open new vistas. The teacher's daily contact with the student does more to develop and influence the student's attitude toward the school than anything done by all the rest of the staff. It is in this contact that the opportunity is greatest to create a working climate in which each student can feel that he/she has the chance to grow and develop as an individual. The teacher, then, is instrumental not only in giving instruction, but also in obtaining information about the individual, establishing a favorable working environment, identifying students who need special help, building attitudes toward the guidance program and other services of the school, and participating with the counselor in the guidance program.

The counselor, on the other hand, makes many direct contributions to the instructional program. He/she is able to provide the teacher with additional information about the students, so that the teacher can adjust the instructional program to meet their needs and characteristics. He/she can help the teacher with students whose problems cause them to be disruptive influences in the classroom. The counselor's frequent contacts with parents help the teacher by providing opportunity to interpret the instructional program of the school to the community. He/she works directly with most of the students in the school in a counseling relationship or in other aspects of the guidance program, thereby helping them to work more effectively in the instructional program.

Recent years have brought considerable clarification to the role of the counselor in the educational setting. A recent statement by the American School Counselor Association shows the involvement of the counselor not only with the student, but also with the teacher, the parent, and the community at large.[8] The Association identifies the responsibilities of school counselors to:

1. Assist each pupil to meet the need to understand himself in relation to the social and psychological world in which he lives. This implies helping each pupil to understand his aptitudes, interests, attitudes, abilities, opportunities for self-fulfillment, and the interrelationships between these.

2. Assist each pupil to meet the need of accepting (defined as being able to behave consistent with) his aptitudes, interests, attitudes, abilities, and opportunities for self-fulfillment.

3. Assist each pupil to meet the need to develop personal decision-making competency. Included is the responsibility for assuring that the pupil's opportunities for self-understanding and self-fulfillment are not restricted by the group consideration and processes inherent in schools.

4. Assist all members of the school staff to understand the importance of the individual pupil and to provide information, material, and consultive assistance aimed at supporting their efforts to understand him.

5. Determine the influence of the school program on pupil educational and psycho-social development, and convey such information to other staff members.

6. Inform other staff members of significant changes in the school and non-school environments which have implications for instruction and for the psycho-social well-being of pupils, and participate in related program development.

7. Assist parents to understand the developmental progress of their child, his needs, and environmental opportunities, for purposes of increasing their ability to contribute to his development.

8. Interpret to the community the importance of consideration for the individual and the contribution of the school counseling program to that end.

9. Promote the community nonschool opportunities necessary for student development.

10. Use and/or promote community resources designed to meet unusual or extreme needs of youngsters which are beyond the responsibility of the school.

The concept of levels or echelons of guidance responsibilities has been proposed by Warters [9] and by Foster, [10] and more recently by Hollis and Hollis. [11] This approach suggests that the first level consists of guidance activities conducted by the professional teacher within the classroom. This includes establishing a feeling of security, promoting the feeling of belonging within the peer group, encouraging a broader understanding of self, and developing competencies in the subject area. The second echelon may involve teacher or counselor or both working with the individual toward decisions of long-range concern beyond what can be done within the classroom. Problems of tentative educational and vocational choice often fall within this area. Whether teacher or counselor is involved depends primarily on the qualifications of the teacher, the time needed by the student, and the time the teacher has available. The third echelon is mainly the responsibility of the counselor. Here the individual's need requires work with a professional counselor over an extended period of time. At the fourth echelon, the individual's need requires referral to a specialist such as a psychologist or psychiatrist.

Both teacher and counselor are involved, then, in the first three levels of guidance. So it seems logical to conclude that both the instructional and guidance functions of the school are best served when counselor and teacher work together cooperatively. Both the instructional and guidance functions are deeply and extensively involved in the career development process. Continuous teamwork between the two is necessary if this portion of individual development is to be advanced effectively. Within the school at least three situations bear on the individual as he/she is involved in the career development process. These include the individual in the formal, structured group in the classroom; the individual in other group situations that may or may not be formal and structured; and the individual in the face-to-face contact of the counseling relationship. In the first situation, we would expect the teacher to make the major, but not the exclusive, contribution; in the second, both teacher and counselor should be continuously involved; and in the third, the counselor should make the major, but not the exclusive, contribution. The specific involvements should be worked out in terms of personal qualifications, available time, and other factors related to the local situation.

BUILDING A BROAD BASIC KNOWLEDGE
OF THE WORLD OF WORK

Even before the child's first day in school, awareness of the world of work has already begun to develop. Casual observation of preschoolers at play soon demonstrates the ease with which they assume a variety of work roles —policeman, cowboy, firefighter, physician, nurse, etc. A walk through the toy department or a glance at preschool picture books further confirms the early emphasis on occupational roles. Consequently, even in the earliest primary years, the child has a readiness for considering "world of work" material. Herr, recognizing the high regard that youngsters hold for work, stresses that a crucial issue is preserving these positive attitudes toward work so that they may become foundational for more realistic attitudes and understanding.[12]

Within the larger objective of helping the elementary school youngster understand the world about him/her is the responsibility for helping to widen horizons and understanding of the world of work. Although much of this concern with how people earn a living is primarily aimed at helping the pupil develop insight into the society of which he/she is a part, the fact that this goal is so often approached along the "occupations" avenue helps the youngster develop some understanding of the significance of work. At each grade level of the elementary school many opportunities exist for the teacher to help the youngster learn more about the wide range of occupations.[13] Every effort should be made to assure each youngster ample opportunity to develop both breadth and depth of awareness of the world of work. Information that helps the developing mind grasp relationships between jobs, and between people and jobs, will contribute more to the decision-making process in which the individual will ultimately be involved than will isolated, factual information.[14]

Since this goal of developing knowledge of the world of work is pertinent at all educational levels, it is not necessary for the elementary teacher to feel that all of the task must be accomplished before the child moves to another level. Rather, emphasis should be directed toward stimulating the youngster's curiosity about jobs so that he/she will continue to acquire this kind of knowledge. As he/she moves through the elementary school, he/she hopefully will develop some concept of why people work, and of what some jobs demand of the worker in the way of skills, knowledge, and special qualifications. Within the elementary grades, the pupil also should be introduced to the dynamic nature of the world of work, so that he/she will soon grasp the idea of the constancy of change and the effect of change on the worker and his job.

Hoyt, Pinson, Laramore, and Mangum point out that the substantive content of career education can be integrated into the basic skills content of the elementary school curriculum.[15] They suggest that one problem encountered in attempts to incorporate career education concepts into the elementary curriculum is the uncertainty of elementary teachers regarding what those concepts really are. The following quotation indicates the teachers' response to this uncertainty:

> The substantive content of career education consists in part of basic information regarding occupations, the world of work, career development, and the nature of work. In part, the substantive content of

career education consists of career education concepts that pupils should have assimilated by the time they leave the elementary school. Such concepts grow out of the basic knowledge referred to above. Essentially, it is a matter of translating major generalizations concerning work, occupations, careers, and career development into terms that can serve as teacher goals. Many such concepts can and have been developed around a wide variety of areas. The following list, while not comprehensive, illustrates the kinds of career education concepts that can be formulated for use in the elementary school.

Concepts Related to the Role of Work in Life and Society

1. At least some people must work if society is to survive.
2. Society is dependent upon the work of many people.
3. All work needed by society is honorable and dignified.
4. Trained, experienced, productive workers are most useful and more in demand than untrained, inexperienced, or nonproductive workers.
5. Man's work determines his standard of living.
6. Work provides opportunities for one to enhance his dignity and worth.
7. There is a relationship between the commitment to education and work and the availability and enjoyment of leisure time.
8. The individual's perception of people affects his ability to work cooperatively.
9. Job satisfaction is dependent on harmonious relationships between a worker and his work environment.
10. The economic system structures incentives for man to work.
11. Our economic system influences work opportunity.
12. Job specialization creates interdependency.

Concepts Related to the Nature of the World of Work

1. Some workers produce goods; others produce services.
2. There is a wide variety of occupations that may be classified in several ways.
3. There are job clusters within occupational areas, as well as across occupational areas.
4. Any career area has different levels of responsibility.
5. Society enacts laws to protect the individual as a producer and consumer of goods and services.
6. The customs, traditions, and attitudes of society affect the world of work.
7. Technological developments cause a continual change in the emergence and disappearance of jobs.
8. The pace of technological development has been accelerated in recent times.
9. Man must learn to use technology to his advantage.

Concepts Related to Work Values

1. People work for various rewards and satisfactions.
2. Work that is enjoyed by some people is disliked by others.
3. Work means different things to different people.
4. Generally, those workers who are trained, experienced, and productive find their work satisfying.
5. Occupations and lifestyles are interrelated.
6. Persons need to be recognized as having dignity and worth.
7. The individual's perception of his environment affects his attitudes toward work.

Concepts Related to Education and the World of Work

1. Education and work are interrelated.
2. Different kinds of work require varying degrees and types of educational preparation.
3. Basic education enhances job performance.
4. There are both specific and general knowledges for each career area.
5. There are many training routes to job entry.
6. Workers may need vocational retraining several times in the course of a lifetime.
7. Knowledge and skills in different subjects relate to performance in different work roles.

Concepts Related to Career Development and Career Decision Making

1. Every individual can have a meaningful, rewarding career.
2. Individuals differ in their interests, aptitudes, abilities, values, and attitudes; and occupations differ in their requirements and prospects.
3. Career planning should be a priviledge and responsibility of the individual.
4. The understanding, acceptance, and development of self is a lifelong process and is constantly changed and influenced by life experiences.
5. Environment and individual potential interact to influence career development.
6. Hobbies and interests may lead to a vocation.
7. Occupational supply and demand has an impact on career planning.
8. Work experience facilitates career decision making.
9. Individuals can learn to perform adequately in a variety of occupations.
10. Every career requires some special preparation.
11. Job characteristics and individuals must be flexible in a changing society.

12. A person's relationships with other people, with his employer, and with society affect his own career, as well as the careers of others.

Concepts Related to Work Habits

1. A worker must understand not only his job, but also his employer's rules, regulations, policies and procedures.
2. There are identifiable attitudes and behaviors which enable one to obtain and hold a job.

Several state departments of education have begun to develop materials, lesson guides, and other resources for classroom teachers to use in developing concepts such as those proposed by Hoyt and his group. Typical of this type of publication is the *Career Education Curriculum Guide* published by the Indiana State Department of Public Instruction in 1973 . A sample page is included as Table 26.[16] This page is selected from the K-2

TABLE 26. Sample Page from **Career Education Curriculum Guide**
AWARENESS STAGE

LEVEL: K-2	SUBJECT AREA: LANGUAGE ARTS	CONCEPT CLUSTER: WORK
LEARNING OBJECTIVES	LEARNING EXPERIENCES	MATERIALS AND RESOURCES
Students will be able to name six different jobs in a circus.	1. The class will construct a circus train and display different employees and animals (possible bulletin board).	Library books Theatrical Make-up Film: "Circus People," A-V Center, Indiana University
Students will be able to verbalize about the differences between acrobats and clowns, etc.	2. Have students role-play different jobs in a circus.	
Students will be able to verbalize on some of the special problems involved with a nomadic life.	3. Students will illustrate themselves as circus people.	
	4. Students will draw self-outlines on kraft paper and dress as circus performers (clown, acrobat, etc.).	

TABLE 26. *Continued*

LEVEL: K–2	SUBJECT AREA: LANGUAGE ARTS	CONCEPT CLUSTER: WORK
LEARNING OBJECTIVES	LEARNING EXPERIENCES	MATERIALS AND RESOURCES
	5. The class will put on a "circus" for parents including a ring master, clowns, acrobats, tumblers, tight-rope walkers, elephants and trainers, lions and tamer, horses and trainer, etc.	
Students will become aware of the many careers in the postal department.	Title: Postal Service	Film: "The Mailman," Encyclopaedia Britannica Films
	1. Have a mail carrier visit the classroom and explain his duties and the necessity of a well-addressed letter.	
Students will be able to verbalize about the path a letter follows from writer to the addressee.		Envelopes
		Rubber Stamp
	2. Take a field trip to post office.	Resource person (mailman)
Students will become familiar with the necessary parts of an address on an envelope.	3. Have students role-play as mail carriers.	
Students will observe that different workers have varying responsibilities within the same career area.	4. The class will build a mock post office in the classroom with letters stamped and delivered by students.	
	5. Students will write and address letters.	
	6. Students will write letters to pen pals in other schools.	

grade level and lists learning objectives, learning experiences, and materials and resources that can be used by the lower grade primary teacher.

Leonard reports the use of a unit on life in a medieval town as a means of identifying the variety of occupations needed to sustain life in that community.[17] Forsyth describes a class session in which elementary youngsters identify workers who wear a particular hat on the job.[18] Many of the concepts proposed by Hoyt, *et al.*, could be included in such a lesson plan. Estill suggests establishing a school post office to help youngsters understand occupations related to this service.[19] Similarly, Leonard also reports the development of a classroom "popcorn factory" in which students sell shares to raise capital and then prepare and market popcorn in a simulated work experience.[20] All of these activities broaden the child's basic knowledge of work.

DEVELOPING A HEALTHY ATTITUDE TOWARD ALL FORMS OF WORK

The intricate relationship and interdependency of jobs within the world of work is a unique characteristic of modern society. There are few occupations in our country that do not depend on many others in the process of accomplishing their goals. Similarly, there are very few occupations that could suddenly be removed from the scene without seriously disrupting occupational activities in many other fields. In other words, all kinds of work are essential for the maintenance and improvement of our society. Youngsters should be introduced early to the concept that all work contributes in its own way and is an important part of that society.

Many myths and attitudes impede the development of respect for all kinds of work. Unfortunately, the school has sometimes contributed to these fallacies rather than helped to overcome them. This is not surprising because the teaching profession is drawn primarily from the middle class group and brings to the classroom ideas and concepts typical of the middle class. The family backgrounds and previous experiences of teachers have made them more familiar with white-collar workers than with skilled and semiskilled workers. The youngsters with whom they work in the classroom may be drawn from a much wider sociological spectrum, with attitudes and viewpoints quite different from those of the teacher. The teacher should carefully avoid developing or supporting biases and prejudices toward various types of work. Instead, he/she should teach that all work is important and that the worker who uses unique skills and abilities effectively in any field makes an important contribution to all members of society.

Several recent studies have looked at the vocational values held by elementary school children. For example, Cooker reports differences across both grade level and sex on values held concerning altruism, control, and money.[21] He reports fourth, fifth, and sixth grade girls scoring higher on altruism as a vocational value and boys in those grades scoring higher on control and money. Hales and Fenner found similar differences across sex but no differences across social classes.[22]

Wernick decribes the use of an adult from the community as a nucleus for building classroom activities that not only involve basic learning skills, but also develop attitudes toward a wide range of occupations.[23] The T4C project in New Jersey places a complete set of hand tools in the elementary classroom along with a set of learning guides for 47 different learning episodes.[24] These experiences help the child "feel" the role of the various workers who us those tools in their jobs. Rost relates the building of a "career pyramid" by selecting any occupation suggested by an elementary class member and then constructing the pyramid of jobs, identified by the class members, that support that job.[25]

DEVELOPING AWARENESS OF SELF—
A SELF-CONCEPT

We can reasonably assume that the major purpose of the school is the maximum development of the individual. Sometimes we interpret this narrowly to mean the maximum intellectual or academic development of the pupil; consequently, we focus the effort of the school on the learning experiences that are subject-matter oriented. The acquisition and application of knowledge are crucial for the survival of both the individual and the nation, since all future development, technologically and economically, depends on these things. This is, however, too narrow an approach. At all educational levels, we must concern ourselves not only with helping the individual to learn about the world, but also about himself/herself.

Even before the youngster reaches the adolescent years, when he/she will become increasingly involved in the development of self-concept, he/she will have many opportunities for self-exploration that will contribute to understanding of self as a person. The elementary classroom as a self-contained unit provides innumerable opportunities in which the individual can come to see self and begin to grasp what he/she is like and why he/she does some things. If the process of insight and self-understanding is fostered early, the pupil benefits not only as he/she moves toward better relationships with self and with others, but also in many other ways. For example, as one understands self better, one will likely understand others better. It is an easy step from there to an understanding of how different kinds of people can make different contributions to their group as a result of special knowledge, skill, or experience.

Using career-oriented materials in the elementary classroom may help many children build positive self-concepts. Too often success in the classroom may be based on activities that are academically oriented but have less direct relationship to the world of work. Of course, it is important for academically able youngsters to experience success; but all youngsters should have those experiences. Learning that is related to the "real world" and solving problems in that world is likely to have greater value for the child than an activity that is carried out to please the teacher. Cross has proposed that every child needs a human "home base," someone they can depend on to be available and understanding, and one who doesn't have to be impressed.[26] Further, he suggests that teachers must provide a secure place for every child with the other children in the classroom and that all school personnel must work toward the goal of building a sense of membership in the school within each child.

Hansen has proposed a career development model that is incorporated into the school curriculum.[27] She assumes that career development *is* self-development; in other words, a process of developing and implementing a self-concept satisfying both the individual and society. By providing for exploration of self, particularly in educational and vocational pursuits, the system suggests that vocational maturation will develop. Hansen identifies objectives for this approach that parallel those we have been considering. These goals propose that students will:

1. Be aware of their own preferred life styles and work values.
2. Exercise some control over their own lives through conscious choice and planning.
3. Be familiar with the occupational options available to them.
4. Know the educational paths to preferred occupations and the financial requirements for entry.
5. Be familiar with the process of career decision making.
6. Know the major resources available in the school and community and be able to use them.
7. Be able to organize and synthesize knowledge of self and the world of work and to develop strategies.

The *Career Education Curriculum Guide* lists both learning objectives and learning experiences that focus on the development of the self-concept in the elementary years. For example, at the grade 3–5 level, learning objectives in the language arts area include the following statement:[28]

Students will be able to identify different types of careers and relate these careers to their individual differences and interests.

Suggested learning experiences propose that each child present an imaginary story about his/her life after school including career choice to the class. The ensuing discussion determines if the student can relate present interests to the identified career choice. Further objectives in this area include defining success, identifying success experiences encountered by the student, and identifying personal characteristics that make him/her unique. To accomplish these goals, the *Guide* proposes appropriate class activities that draw on the skills being developed in language arts.

Bender has suggested that simplified job application forms for various classroom assignments can be used to help youngsters understand themselves.[29] He proposes that the forms become more complex as the grade level advances, with more specific inquiry about interests and other personal attributes. By using students in a variety of work assignments, the youngsters become aware of the differences in their own interests and abilities; they find some jobs easy, others difficult; some jobs fun, others boring.

FOSTERING UNDERSTANDING OF THE INDIVIDUAL'S ROLE IN CAREER DEVELOPMENT

Elementary youngsters bring to the classroom attitudes and ideas that have developed as a result of the interaction of their background or environment and their experiences.[30] Since both are necessarily limited in the early years of elementary school, they reflect primarily attitudes of the adults with whom they have contact. Thus, in many ways their ideas and concepts may well be a generation out of date, since they reflect parental attitudes. During each generation, tremendous changes occur, especially in areas such as the world of work. Few sociologists would contend that ours is a totally free and open society with every person having complete opportunity to advance socially and occupationally according to abilities and desires. Nevertheless, in recent years many provisions have been developed that strengthen the possibilities for such opportunities. Examples of such legislation are legion, and many have been discussed earlier—including the numerous education bills approved by Congress, which provide loan funds, expansion of educational opportunities, and retraining situations.

Early in the elementary school, each child should be helped to grasp the idea that much of what happens to him/her in the future will be of his/her own making and will depend to a large extent on how he/she uses abilities in the opportunities encountered. Long before entering school, each child will have made fantasy occupational choices such as cowboy, policeman, pilot, or astronaut.[31] During early school years, he/she will have matured to the point at which he/she can recognize that these are fantasy choices and nothing more. As this realization develops, one can comprehend what factors are involved in the choices to be faced as one completes an educational program. One should understand the extent to which all choices that are made—recreational activities, hobbies, reading materials, clubs, and others—ultimately influence major choices and decisions. One also should realize that vocational choice is always an evolving and changing choice and that this is true throughout the entire life span.

In many ways, this section is a logical outgrowth or product of the previous sections of this chapter. In other words, if elementary school students are helped to develop an awareness of an increasingly broader world of work and also to develop a more acute sensitivity to themselves as individuals with differing interests, abilities, and motivations, one might reasonably expect some balancing of one area against the other to occur. Two opposing dangers exist that underscore the importance of giving attention to this goal at the elementary level. One danger is assuming that an automatic connection between work and self will be made; this leaves too much to chance. The other danger is that elementary students may attempt to move too far toward closure and make precipitous choices prematurely. The goal, and a crucial one, lies between these two extremes. Students should be taught early that they do make decisions that affect their lives. This involves at least two aspects; namely, how decisions are made, and, once made, how those personal choices influence their lives.

Tiedeman speaks of career development as involving an "unarticulated sense of something a person is trying to create or produce" and a sense of responsibility and initiative as he/she works to express that choice.[32] He identifies this "sense of agency" on the part of the individual as the primary concern of guidance. That is, the individual student helped in this process can develop a more meaningful life for the mutual advantage of self and society. Emphasizing the importance of teaching the how and why of decision making, Tiedeman says:

> . . . the counselor violates the integrity of his pupils' individual freedom and responsibility if he tries to influence their choices while keeping them ignorant of the basic processes of knowing.

Hoyt, *et al.*, suggest three questions that the mature individual can answer about himself/herself.[33] These questions are: "What is important to me?" "What is possible for me?" and "What is probable for me?" Recognizing that elementary age children cannot be expected to provide mature answers to these questions, they proposed that beginning to seek answers can help the child understand how decisions will influence life. Even though great change probably will occur before the child enters the labor market, grappling with questions of this type will help increase self-confidence and a sense of agency.

Thompson and Parker report a study in which fifth graders were taught a unit based on learning objectives related to occupations.[34] They found the youngsters gained insight and knowledge of work from the unit. They could identify better reasons for working, and could identify a broader range of occupations after the unit, thus apparently understanding better the system by which individuals move into occupations.

HELPING PARENTS SEE, ACCEPT, AND
ACTIVATE THEIR ROLE IN CAREER DEVELOPMENT

The recent emergence of career education has re-emphasized a reality that often has been overlooked or ignored: that the school is not the sole agent responsible for the development of the child. Career education concepts stress the role of the rest of the community, clearly including the family as well as other adults. School personnel, including teacher and counselor, have a responsibility to create with these others a cooperative working relationship to maximize the opportunity for the child to develop.

Almost every parent wants the best for his/her child. Confusion often develops, however, in determining what is best and how it can be obtained. Consequently, parents often err in one of two opposite directions —either by rigidly controlling a youngster's development, or by permitting too much freedom through an attitude of *laissez faire* or indifference.

The first of these approaches can so severely restrict the child that he/she fails to develop the independence and freedom of choice that ultimately must be exercised if one is to find satisfaction as a mature, self-directing adult. If the parent, worthy though his/her motives may be, makes too many decisions and permits the child too few, the youngster may react either by rebellion and resentment or by resignation and apathy. Either reaction impedes normal development as an individual, and hence has a negative impact on self-concept.

Parental ambition for a youngster also may affect how he/she looks at the world, and at occupations specifically. Deprecating one's own work in an effort to motivate the child toward something "better" may not help the youngster to develop a base for decision making in which the crucial factors can be weighed objectively. Parental pressures that push a child of limited ability toward academically competitive areas are just as harmful and wasteful as those that encourage academically able children to leave school and go to work as soon as possible.

Similarly, parental attitudes toward various occupational fields may influence the child's view of these fields.[35] This is particularly true of attitudes that certain jobs are "men's work" or "women's work." The impact of such attitudes by parents and by society generally has become all too evident when we examine the distribution of the sexes in certain occupational fields.

The elementary teacher has a special advantage in his/her relationship to the parents of the children in the class. As indicated, the teacher often is the first adult outside the family circle to spend a considerable period of each day with the youngster. The parent accepts the teacher in this role and usually recognizes the concern and interest that the teacher shares in the development of the child. This closer relationship between teacher and parent makes it possible for the teacher to help the parent see how his/her behavior and attitudes relate to the child's behavior in school, and in turn to his/her ultimate development as an individual. The teacher can help the parent discover how he/she can be most helpful in the maturational process.

In Chapter 13, we considered the use of parents as an information resource to help youngsters learn about occupations. Almost every elementary teacher already uses the variety of job holders within the parental group in this way. The value of this simple activity should not be discounted.[36] It provides an opportunity for the other children in the class to learn about a particular job by listening to Johnny's mother or Mary's father tell about what they do, how, and why. It also may help Johnny and Mary to see their parent's work from a different viewpoint than the random, end-of-the-day remarks that, until now, may be the major basis for their view. Many peripheral values in school-home relationships also may accrue from such activity. There are, of course, numerous ways in which the school can involve parents in classroom activities as well as in school functions outside the classroom. If these are organized to maximize contact between the participating parents and children, both their own and others, many opportunities to learn adult roles, attitudes, and values will ensue.

Both teacher and counselor can help parents see the unlimited opportunities within the home for children to learn about work. Unfortunately, many parents have developed the attitude that parental success is accomplished by making the life of their children easier than the life they experienced as children. Such a distorted view prevents capitalizing on the home-based circumstances to learn about work. The assignment of regular home tasks to each child helps the child to learn necessary work-related attitudes such as punctuality, reliability, efficiency, and responsibility. It also helps him learn the rewards of work—satisfaction in a job well done, service to others, a feeling of worth and accomplishment, comradeship with fellow workers. Some families have found advantage in developing family projects such as do-it-yourself home improvements, gardening projects, or similar tasks that also teach much about work and also create family togetherness and other by-products.

Parents sometimes may be unaware of the attitude toward work that they reflect in the family setting. Teachers and counselors can help parents identify the extent to which they emphasize the negative aspects of their job, such as the boredom, weariness, discontent, conflict, pressure, and competitiveness in the conversation of the family circle. If only these aspects are revealed, the child will have difficulty in seeing the positive values that the job provides. Children whose classroom view of work seems heavily negative may be reflecting parental comments and behavior of this type, and the parents may be unaware of the impact of their words and actions. Elementary youngsters are not yet mature enough to recognize that for every job holder the advantages of the job exceed the disadvantages, especially if they are taught only the latter. Parental work values are the primary base on which the youngster begins to build a personal view toward work.

The family also can provide many decision-making experiences that will help the child build these essential skills. Daily living in every home provides such opportunities. Parents can help the child build self-confidence as well as responsibility by helping make choices rather than usurping decisions. As the child makes decisions, he/she learns the consequences of good and bad choices. Study after study has consistently shown that parents exercise more influence on the eventual educational and vocational choice of children than any other adult. Thus, if parents view occupations in limited ways, the child is likely to do so as well. Parents who see only a few occupations as suitable for their daughters limit girls' ability to see wider opportunities. Parents who insist that their children follow parental patterns or ambitions may build frustration, dissatisfaction, and failure.

In summarizing the broad general goals of building career awareness during the elementary years, it is important to emphasize once again that the basic purpose is not to help the child find an occupation at this time. It is, instead, to prepare the child for involvement in a process that will extend for the rest of his/her life as he/she seeks and engages in occupational activities.

THE EXPLORING YEARS

The strengthening and enforcement of child labor laws in this country have given added emphasis to the general public attitude that all youth should be encouraged to continue their education as far as possible. The trend toward larger percentages of our youth completing secondary school is clear. Already, throughout the country, minimum school dropout age requirements and employment restrictions keep almost all youth in school at least through the junior high school years. One can expect that present pressures to keep them in school for longer periods not only will continue, but also will increase, with the result that minimal numbers of youth will withdraw before the high school years have been completed.

As the pressures for more education keep a greater proportion of youth in school for longer periods, one might conclude that the use of career information materials in the middle or junior high school would more and more follow the pattern of the elementary school, with primary emphasis on foundational activities for later choices. Prognostication is a difficult and tricky business; one cannot be sure that the anticipated changes will occur. Further, the trend toward a longer period of education may affect schools in various geographic areas in quite different ways. For example, in a school in which the student body changes drastically as a result of population shifts to suburban areas and replacement by minority groups, greater numbers of students may plan to terminate educational programs early.

One cannot, then, simply extend and expand the elementary school career information to the next school and be assured that the application is appropriate. Our knowledge of adolescents provides some basis for the development of activities that meet general needs of this age group. Careful attention to the students can be expected to indicate special activities that will be suitable for them.[37]

For most youth, the middle school years are stormy and hectic. During this period, they enter adolescence and begin to move toward greater independence and self-direction. The awareness of self becomes more pronounced, and the youth's concept of self as an individual independent of parents and family takes shape. As this distinctiveness of self becomes more apparent, the adolescent inevitably moves toward a view of self in terms of the world of work.[38] Many of the career information activities of the middle school must be keyed to this transitional phase, to provide the adolescent an opportunity to try out self-concept and to modify, refine, and expand his/her view of self as a person. In fact, the junior high school came into being largely as an effort to provide this opportunity for tryout and exploration, and it is at this level in most school systems that the pupil encounters the first opportunity to make educational choices. In addition to the curriculum, the junior high school also provides clubs and other activities that serve the purpose of exploration.

At the time most pupils enter middle or junior high school, they are still many years removed from full-time activity in the world of work. The majority of these pupils are, similarly, still many years away from such activity when they move on to high school. Nevertheless, they are on their way toward the world of work, and most of the students during these years become aware of this fact, thus creating a greater concern with the occupational world and their personal relationship to it. Although they are, for the most part, still concerned with work in the future, the realization of their future involvement enhances their awareness of it and focuses their attention on it to a much greater extent than previously.[39] Students who are likely to be school dropouts may already have passed this point and may be concerned with thoughts of work in an immediate and specific sense.

The curriculum of the middle or junior high school helps the pupil see some relationship between educational choice and future occupation. Some of the courses obviously lead to further study, in preparation for long educational programs in college and professional school; others lead toward programs to be completed during high school, and more directly toward work; a few others may relate to work in the very near future. Orientation programs at the junior high school level help the individual see more clearly the routes followed by various educational programs and the relationship between the courses studied and future work. This relationship becomes particularly apparent to the student as he/she prepares to leave the school and to enter high school, where a specific curriculum must be selected.

By middle or junior high school age, many youngsters have had such casual work experiences as babysitting and newspaper routes. Even though these occasional bits of employment have little direct vocational significance, they do provide further contact with the world of work. Incidental employment not only helps the youngster gain some insight into why and how people earn a living, but it also makes him/her more aware of an ultimate relationship to work. This new awareness usually stimulates concern for information about occupations generally. Often involvement in casual work provides an opportunity to encounter some of the experiences of adult workers—for example, receiving a pay check and deciding how to use the money.

Progressing from elementary school to the next educational level does not conclude the individual's involvement in the activities we have considered as "career awareness." Certainly these learning experiences must project on into the distant future. On the other hand, it would be equally foolish to imply that one must gain middle or junior high school status before engaging in any exploratory activities. These inexact divisions according to school level are only for convenience and not for precise or exact labeling. Anyone familiar with human development in these pre-adult years easily recognizes that growth and maturation are much easier to see in retrospect over time than in day-by-day measurements. Therefore, the shifting of emphasis from "awareness" to "exploration" is a gradual one and occurs imperceptably.

Each of the goals of the awareness years is equally important in this next stage of development. The ingredients that change are greater individual responsibility, ability to deal with more abstract information both in depth and quantity, involvement in educational choices, and increasing psychological and physical maturation.

Career education proponents suggest that the career awareness activities of the elementary years will have provided sufficient breadth of understanding of the world of work so that the youngster now can explore occupations in some depth. The cluster concept that groups almost all occupations into 15 different groups in one suggested approach. Of course, other classification systems also would be appropriate to use with this age group. Three examples that can be applied advantageously are Roe's Primary Focus of Activity system, the Cubistic classification system, and the ACT Map of the World of Work. These systems have been discussed in earlier chapters. By incorporating consideration of level of responsibility, degree of involvement with data-people-things, and the people/things, data/ideas relationships, each system provides a frame of reference that helps the individual capitalize on self-knowledge while exploring the world of work. Since the ultimate goal of both career education and career guidance is the development and execution of appropriate career choices, it is beneficial to use techniques that will maximize that thrust at each step.

In the middle and junior high school years, most youngsters encounter their first real choice of educational options. Many counselors and teachers have developed orientation programs to help students understand the elective courses among which they may chose. Often, such programs focus on explanations of course content, with insufficient attention given to the long-run significance of selecting a particular course. Since one reason for the existence of this intermediate unit in the school system is to prepare students to make appropriate educational choices, every effort must be made to direct this attention to the choices available and the consequences of choosing each. For most students at this level, the most significant educational choice will be the selection of the high school curriculum to be followed when they move to that school. Both career education and career guidance stress the importance of adequately preparing the student and the student's parents for the choice.

Johnson and Myrick have described a program that assists students in building decision-making skills.[40] The system, called MOLD—Making of Life Decisions, is a simulation plan for middle school age students. The plan simulates local job market and educational facilities information and motivates students by involvement in the decision-making process. The student makes decisions for himself/herself and is provided feedback of the probable consequences of that choice. The steps involved in the program include:

1. The student completes a personal profile sheet including estimates of ability and interest.
2. He/she participates in small group procedures that assist in self-appraisal.
3. He/she explores career fields and makes a tentative choice.
4. He/she tentatively plans on paper the next year of life—education, jobs, leisure time, home.
5. He/she receives feedback on the decisions based on probability tables.
6. He/she revises the plans on the basis of the new information.

The various curriculum guides developed by local or state offices also identify a range of exploratory activities appropriate for use with this age group. These activities usually concentrate on the goals we have already considered. An example of a page from such a guide is included in Table 27.[41]

Goldhammer and Taylor describe two programs developed in Oregon school districts to maximize the exploratory activities in junior high school.[42] These include SUTOE (Self-Understanding Through Occupational Exploration) and CORE (Careers Oriented Relevant Education).

TABLE 27. *Sample Page from* Career Education Curriculum Guide

EXPLORATORY STAGE

LEVEL: 6–8	SUBJECT AREA: GUIDANCE	CONCEPT CLUSTER: DEVELOPMENTAL PROCESS
LEARNING OBJECTIVES	LEARNING EXPERIENCES	MATERIALS AND RESOURCES
Students will experience making decisions and identify endings for open-ended situations.	Divide the students into small groups. Each group will be given a card with a "what would you do if" situation printed on it. The card will explain the situation up to a certain point and the students will make a decision on the problem, then make up an ending. Each group will role-play the final situation in front of the class and explain why they decided to end it as they did. Each group will also discuss how their decisions would affect the future of each character in the group.	*Discovering Yourself,* by Marjorie Cosgrove Pamphlet: "Coping With" Series, American Guidance Service
Students will make decisions, evaluate their decisions, and make judgments as to why a decision was made.	1. Have each student select a number. He will be that number. List the ways he might be used during a day. 2. Have each student state a wage they would like to receive at their age. List what they would do with their money. Decide if this is a reasonable wage.	*Discovering Yourself,* by Marjorie Cosgrove
The student will draw up a tentative plan for his high school program. He will identify his personal	1. The student will complete a self-appraisal inventory, the "Goal Selecting Methods" form, or any	*My Educational Plans* by Harold Munson "Goal Selecting Methods" (App. A)

TABLE 27. Continued

LEVEL: 6-8	SUBJECT AREA: GUIDANCE	CONCEPT CLUSTER: DEVELOPMENTAL PROCESS
LEARNING OBJECTIVES	LEARNING EXPERIENCES	MATERIALS AND RESOURCES
interests and personal goals and be able to relate his tentative high school program to his uniqueness.	other device useful in defining his areas of interests. 2. Invite a counselor to come to the class to explain high school programs offered and terms such as semesters, units, majors, minors, electives, and qualifications for graduation. 3. Using an appropriate form, have the student complete a tentative program of classes for high school. 4. The students will take their forms home to the parents for their opinion and discussion.	Counselor Filmstrip: "Roles and Goals," Argus Communications Four-year tentative schedule form

The programs include the development of discussion groups for students and faculty, curricula revision, work experience, and expanded counseling facilities.

RESOURCES FOR CLASSES AND GROUPS

An abundance of resources exist that can be used with groups to enrich the study of career information. Since individuals differ in the ways they learn, extensive use of varied resources should be made to assure the most effective results.[43] For the most part, the resources discussed here are other than the primary ones discussed in Chapters 11 and 13. Some, but by no means all, of the resources considered at this point can be classified as primary ones. They can contribute to the study of career information by helping bring it to life for the student seeking to extend his/her understanding of the world of work. We will consider briefly the wide range of auxiliary resources under four headings: audio-visual materials, publications, school resources, and community resources.

Audio-Visual Materials

Each person's world is already crammed with sights and sounds; in addition, there is a vast store of others that can be selected to help learn about careers. When properly prepared and utilized, they can provide a maximum of information in a very brief period. The range of use is almost endless, since A-V materials can be used to stimulate interest, to explore broad areas briefly, to study minute segments intensively, to provide knowledge of topics not ordinarily physically accessible, or to supplement information obtained directly through other techniques.

The motion picture is probably the most useful A-V material, since it ordinarily permits optimum simultaneous use of the senses of sight and hearing. Its range of flexibility can meet the varied needs of the observer. It can provide a realistic picture of the worker on the job, showing the work setting, the actual task of the worker, the equipment and tools used and the product that results.[44, 45] It is a field trip in reverse, bringing the worker to the student. It can be rerun in part or in full for further consideration of specific details.

At least two major disadvantages are associated with motion pictures. One is the problem of staleness. Many occupations are subject to very rapid change, and almost any occupation can be caught up suddenly in vast revision because of technological progress or other factors. Also, constant evolution and modification affect all occupations. In addition, irrelevant factors sometimes may cause a film to appear to be out-of-date, thus causing the viewer to mistrust the motion picture although its basic message is still appropriate. The changing hemline of women's skirts, for instance, may date a film so clearly that its basic value is destroyed.

A further disadvantage of motion pictures is cost. Films are expensive either to purchase or to rent. If they are to be used extensively, an ample budget must be provided. In most situations, the occasional use of a specific film does not justify outright purchase. In these circumstances, arrangements can easily be made to rent the film from an A-V center.

Many companies prepare career-related films, so that new films regularly become available. Each A-V center maintains a catalog listing the films available there. In addition, one can consult the *Educational Film Guide* [46] to determine what films on a given topic are in general use. Besides films specifically prepared for career information purposes, many others produced for other reasons are usable. The films may show the processing of a particular product, or seek to develop a company's public image, or introduce a new product, or recruit workers to a shortage field, for example.

A teacher or counselor will find many uses for motion pictures related to career information. They can be used in the classroom related to regular or special units of work, in career conferences, in assemblies, as preparation for industry tours, or as summaries of such trips. Although less often used this way, they also can be appropriately shown to an individual seeking information at some point in the career development process.

Filmstrips or slides have many of the advantages of films. Additionally, they offer greater flexibility in showing than do motion pictures, since a specific scene can be held as long as desired for discussion.

Filmstrips or slides, like all visual aids, can become out of date. The user should preview all materials carefully before showing them to a group.

Filmstrips and slides can be acquired economically either by direct purchase or rental. In addition, slides can be easily made locally. This can be a real advantage, since alumni or students can be used in the pictures to help develop human interest. Commercially prepared filmstrips can be found by consulting either the *Filmstrip Guide* [47] or the *Educators' Guide to Free Slidefilms*. [48]

Using strips and slides corresponds to the use of motion pictures, and the same preparation and procedures should be followed.

Recordings, either on tape or on disc, are readily available and can be used advantageously. Many commercially prepared filmstrips are accompanied by recordings. Locally prepared strips or slides can also be enhanced by recording a narrative on tape or disc.

Recordings used alone are ordinarily less desirable than other devices, since no visual stimulation is provided. In certain situations, however, a recording can be most effective. Examples include taping an interview with a worker in a particular field for later use with other students, or taping an assembly program or panel discussion related to career information.

Both radio and television offer many programs that have a direct relationship to career information. The extensive programming of local and network stations in both media include numerous references to the world of work, both in entertainment and public service programs. Besides the offerings of commercial stations, many programs are prepared by educational stations, with the student in mind as the basic consumer.

Displays and bulletin boards, if properly used, can stimulate interest and transmit information. These devices provide a convenient vehicle for sharing items from magazines and newspapers, as well as calling attention to new monographs and books. Local industries frequently publish display materials that can demonstrate career opportunities within the locality. Displayed items should be appropriate to the group's interests and needs and should contribute to the basic purpose of learning more about the world of work. Often groups of students can prepare and maintain such materials.

Publications

The school newspaper offers almost unlimited opportunity for passing information to students, arousing their interest, informing them of services that are available, or in other ways involving them in acquiring career information. It has many built-in advantages and should be used regularly to communicate with the student body.

The news columns of the newspaper can be used to inform the students of career conferences, scheduled field trips, visits to the school of industrial or educational representatives, and other newsworthy events that relate to career information. Feature pages are logical spots for stories of continuing interest, such as reports from recent graduates, or new career books available. Many aspects of career information lend themselves to a regular column presentation; for example, nearby colleges can be described in a continuing series, as can be various jobs available locally, or nearby nonacademic training programs.

Special issues can be utilized to inform students of a major activity such as a "Career Day." Details of the event and supplementary information about the topics to be included in the program can be published, so that students may participate more intelligently in the event.

Local or nearby daily newspapers also provide additional access to student readers.[49] Already rich with information about what is happening in the local community, many also carry special business or financial pages that feature stories about employment opportunities or new and expanding business or industry. The classified advertisements are a convenient barometer of job openings in the community and can be used with students to help build realistic concepts of the local world of work.

Besides being an excellent source of local information, the newspaper usually provides adequate coverage of stories centering on school activities. This offers a means of keeping parents and other school patrons informed about aspects of the school program that relate to career education and information. Special events in the school always warrant coverage in the local press. This coverage keeps the community informed and can lead to closer cooperation among school, student, and parent—a most desirable by-product if realistic career plans are ultimately to evolve.

Many schools regularly prepare a student handbook. Intended basically as an orientation device for new students, it has considerable potential as an instrument for transmitting educational information and materials about services available to students. Most handbooks include a section that presents the various curricula offered in the school. To be of maximum utility for the student and parents, this section should include a discussion of the educational and vocational goals to which each curriculum leads. Examples of employment opportunities, further schooling available, and future advanced career fields should be discussed here. A brief survey of occupational fields related to each school subject also could be included.

The handbook is probably more effective if arrangements are made for its use in a series of orientation sessions for new students, either within the framework of regularly scheduled classes or in special groups created specifically to help students adjust to their new environment. Group discussion of the contents should emphasize the importance of the information in the book.

School Resources

Even the most circumscribed and isolated school often has resources of which most staff members are unaware. This is especially true of career information resources and often occurs because no one has attempted to determine and evaluate the existing sources of information.

Useful resources are the educational and occupational experiences of the school staff. A simple inventory of the institutions attended by staff members often will reveal a fairly adequate representation of many nearby colleges and universities—often including the schools in which most of the college-bound students ultimately will enroll. Obviously, a staff member who has attended "school X" can help students who are interested in that institution. Such information can be used to supplement the routine data available in catalogs and in the various directories. Impressions of types of students, institutional goals and standards, student life, living accommodations, standards of dress, major activities, and similar information that usually can not be accurately assessed from the printed page are particularly helpful.

Similarly, the typical school staff will have encountered a wide variety of part-time or full-time work experience during their high school and college years and later. In addition to their direct experiences will be additional occupations with which they have had indirect contact through family, close friends, or other personal contact.

Another "built-in" resource often overlooked is the student body itself. Many young people have had opportunities to observe or experience a specific occupation or a group of occupations, or they have become knowledgeable in some other way. Munger reports the development of a "speakers bureau" as an outgrowth of student observations of limited occupational insight on the part of other classmates.[50]

Community Resources

Outside the school, but within the local community, are many resources that can be used in building insight into and understanding of career fields.[51] Almost everyone is a potential resource who can be used to help students. Many local agencies recognize a responsibility in this area and are willing to assist the school in activities related to career choice.

The development and maintenance of a complete file of community resources falls outside the domain of this volume, since it has many uses beyond the specific area of utilizing career information. The existence and use of such a file is absolutely essential to an effective guidance program. Detailed discussion of appropriate procedures can be found in books that relate to the general field of guidance or personnel services, such as those by Hollis and Hollis,[52] and Miller.[53]

Schools that maintain a file of community resources will have on hand an extensive listing of agencies and individuals that can be used in a variety of ways. Schools that do not have such a file may want to consider some of the following resources that they will find available nearby.

Local businesses and industries already have, in most cases, close ties with the school. They have a continuing interest in the products of the local school, since this is often their main source of employees, particularly for positions that do not require post-high school training. Because of this natural relationship, they are usually interested in cooperating in any possible way to improve the quality of those products. This provides the school with an entree to representatives of local businesses and industries who might be able to inform students about their fields of activity. Local professional groups also may be anxious to render the same kind of service to interested students.

Local service clubs, whose members are drawn from the businesses, industries, and professions mentioned above, also are frequently anxious to provide assistance to the school or to specific students in problems related to career information. It is fairly common for service clubs to provide financial assistance for career information libraries. They also are helpful in organizing career day conferences or community occupational surveys. Members often are encouraged to make themselves available to students to discuss career opportunities in their fields.

Some service clubs make special efforts to provide assistance in this field. Rotary International, for example, maintains a vocational service committe that focuses on career information activities in each of its local clubs.

If the school does not maintain a list of the service clubs in its locality, such a list, including officers, usually can be obtained from the local chamber of commerce or the local library.

Local representatives or officials of labor unions can be useful sources of information for students interested in fields represented by such groups.

They are particularly helpful in providing data on training requirements and opportunities, union membership requirements and benefits, and similar information that may help the student acquire a more complete picture.

Government offices located in community, at the local, state, or national level, often can provide information that will assist students. Civil service opportunities and requirements are areas that can be covered by such representatives. Some agencies such as county extension offices and employment services already are involved, by the nature of their work, in career information activities. These resources that should not be overlooked by the school. Cooperation with such agencies will increase the effectiveness of both the school and the agency involved.

Every community, regardless of size, includes some social agencies that are involved in career information activities. Particularly likely to be involved are agencies whose services are directed primarily at youth, such as Boy Scouts, Girl Scouts, YMCA, YWCA, and 4-H clubs. Many of these agencies serve the same youth group as the school. Special projects that they may develop related to career information can be of genuine assistance to the school. They also may have access to information in specialized fields that can help the school in its task. Other social agencies that are more broadly based in the community may be particularly helpful in resolving family or financial problems that may be interfering with the vocational development of specific students.

Many churches organize special activity programs for school-age youth. Often these programs are developed around the concerns and problems of the age group involved; for teen-agers, this inevitably includes career-related problems. Many churches support or maintain church-related colleges or other educational institutions that may be of particular significance to members of the church's youth group. Some churches include as staff members professionals who devote their efforts to the youth groups. These persons can be helpful in reaching special groups or individuals. A number of churches operate summer camping programs for school-age youth, thus providing an additional means of reaching young people.

The importance of the local library to the career information program already has been mentioned. Cooperation with the library often will lead to a more comprehensive collection of career information materials, as well as to the development of special services that will be of assistance to school-age youth.

Many resources cut across more than one of the categories we have considered. In many ways, these may be the most valuable of all. For example, combining both school and community resources are the many prevocational programs developing in many junior high schools. These programs provide a school-based course in which students have extensive opportunities to participate in exploratory observations of workers on the job. Often patterned after a plan used in Swedish schools for many years, the program immerses the student in a series of direct contact experiences in which the reality of the work setting is thoroughly sampled. Such exploratory observations can be adapted to provide a concentration of settings in a single field or a group of closely related occupations or a broad sampling across many fields.

Teachers and counselors can obtain assistance in learning about typical programs that are developing across the nation by using the ERIC system, which has been mentioned earlier. This system provides a depository for descriptions of programs, samples of materials, and other items that have direct, practical relevance for the persons seeking "how to do it" ideas.

NOTES

1. K. B. Hoyt, R. N. Evans, E. F. Mackin, G. L. Mangum, *Career Education: What It Is and How To Do It,* 2nd ed. (Salt Lake City, Utah: Olympus Publishing Company, 1974), p. 15.
2. *Ibid.*
3. S. P. Marland, Jr., *Career Education* (New York: McGraw-Hill Book Company, 1974), pp. 100–102.
4. E. D. Smith, "Vocational Aspects of Elementary School Guidance Programs: Objectives and Activities," *Vocational Guidance Quarterly,* vol. 18, no. 4 (June, 1970), pp. 273–279.
5. K. Goldhammer and R. E. Taylor, *Caerer Education: Perspective and Promise* (Columbus, Ohio: Charles E. Merrill Publishing Company, 1972), pp. 216–217.
6. N. J. Roberts, "Establishing a Need for a Vocational Guidance Program at the Elementary and Middle School Level," *Elementary School Guidance and Counseling,* vol. 6, no. 4 (May, 1971), pp. 252–257.
7. D. K. Clapsaddle, "Career Development and Teacher Inservice Preparation," *Elementary School Guidance and Counseling,* vol. 8, no. 2 (December, 1973), pp. 92–97.
8. American School Counselor Association, "Tentative Statement of Policy for Secondary School Counselors," *Personnel and Guidance Journal,* vol. 42, no. 2 (October, 1963), pp. 195–196.
9. J. Warters, *High School Personnel Work Today,* 2nd edition (New York: McGraw-Hill, Inc., 1956), pp. 159–161.
10. C. R. Foster, *Guidance for Today's Schools* (Boston: Ginn and Company, 1957), pp. 71–73.
11. J. W. and L. U. Hollis, *Organizing for Effective Guidance* (Chicago: Science Research Associates, Inc., 1965), pp. 31–32.
12. E. L. Herr, *Decision-making and Vocational Development* (Boston: Houghton Mifflin Company, 1970).
13. W. W. Tennyson and L. P. Monnens, "The World of Work Through Elementary Readers," *Vocational Guidance Quarterly,* vol. 12, no. 2 (Winter, 1963), pp. 85–88.

14. G. Kaback, "Occupational Information in Elementary Education: What Counselors Do–What Counselors Would Like to Do," *Vocational Guidance Quarterly*, vol. 16, no. 3 (March, 1968), pp. 203–206.
15. K. B. Hoyt, N. M. Pinson, D. Laramore, and G. L. Mangum, *Career Education and the Elementary School Teacher* (Salt Lake City, Utah: Olympus Publishing Company, 1973), pp. 41–42.
16. *Career Education Curriculum Guide* (Indianapolis, Indiana: Indiana State Department of Public Instruction, 1973), p. 30.
17. G. E. Leonard, "Career Guidance in the Elementary School," *Elementary School Guidance and Counseling*, vol. 6, no. 4 (May, 1972), pp. 283–286.
18. L. B. Forsyth, "The Hat Exhibit," in G. E. Leonard, "Career Guidance in the Elementary School," *Elementary School Guidance and Counseling*, vol. 7, no. 1 (October, 1972), pp. 51–54.
19. K. Estill, "Post Office–A Career Guidance Unit," in G. E. Leonard, "Career Guidance in the Elementary School," *Elementary School Guidance and Counseling*, vol. 8, no. 2 (December, 1973), pp. 128–29.
20. G. E. Leonard, "Career Guidance in the Elementary School," *Elementary School Guidance and Counseling*, vol. 6, no. 3 (March, 1972), pp. 198–201.
21. P. G. Cooker, "Vocational Values of Children in Grades Four, Five, and Six," *Elementary School Guidance and Counseling*, vol. 8, no. 2 (December, 1973), pp. 112–118.
22. L. W. Hales and B. J. Fenner, "Sex and Social Class Differences in Work Values," *Elementary School Guidance and Counseling*, vol. 8, no. 1 (October, 1973), pp. 26–32.
23. W. Wernick, "The ABLE Model," in G. E. Leonard, "Career Guidance in the Elementary School," *Elementary School Guidance and Counseling*, vol. 7, no. 2 (December, 1972), pp. 150–155.
24. G. E. Leonard, "Career Guidance in the Elementary School," *Elementary School Guidance and Counseling*, vol. 7, no. 3 (March, 1972), pp. 234–237.
25. P. Rost, "The Career Pyramid," in G. E. Leonard, "Career Guidance in the Elementary School," *Elementary School Guidance and Counseling*, vol. 8, no. 1 (October, 1973), pp. 50–53.
26. F. R. Cross, *Elementary School Careers Education* (Columbus, Ohio: Charles E. Merrill Publishing Company, 1974), p. 56.
27. L. S. Hansen, "A Model for Career Development Through Curriculum," *Personnel and Guidance Journal*, vol. 51, no. 4 (December, 1972), pp. 243–250.
28. *Career Education Curriculum Guide, op. cit.*, p. 18.
29. R. C. Bender, "Vocational Development in the Elementary School: A Framework for Implementation," *The School Counselor*, vol. 21, no. 2 (November, 1973), pp. 116–120.
30. B. Nachmann, "Childhood Experience and Vocational Choice in Law, Dentistry, and Social Work," *Journal of Counseling Psychology*, vol. 7, no. 4 (Winter, 1960), pp. 243–250.
31. R. C. Nelson, "The World of Work in the 'Fantasy Stage' of Development," *Elementary School Guidance and Counseling*, vol. 2, no. 1 (October, 1967), pp. 222–224.
32. D. V. Tiedeman, "The Agony of Choice: Guidance for Career Decisions" in R. C. Pucinski and S. P. Hirsch (eds), *The Courage to Change: New Di-*

rections for Career Education (Englewood Cliffs, N.J.: Prentice-Hall Inc., 1971), p. 124.

33. Hoyt, Pinson, Laramore, and Mangum, *op. cit.*, pp. 79–81.

34. C. L. Thompson and J. L. Parker, "Fifth Graders View the Work World Scene," *Elementary School Guidance and Counseling*, vol. 5, no. 4 (May, 1971), pp. 281–288.

35. W. B. Barbe and N. S. Chambers, "Career Requirements of Gifted Elementary Children and Their Parents," *Vocational Guidance Quarterly*, vol. 11, no. 2 (Winter, 1963), pp. 137–140.

36. G. E. Leonard, "Career Guidance in the Elementary School," *Elementary School Guidance and Counseling*, vol. 9, no. 1 (October, 1974), pp. 48–51; and vol. 9, no. 2 (December, 1974), pp. 149–150.

37. B. E. Shertzer and S. C. Stone, "Junior High School Guidance: Problems and Potentialities," *Vocational Guidance Quarterly*, vol. 12, no. 4 (Summer, 1964), pp. 255–260.

38. R. Leonard, "Vocational Guidance in Junior High: One School's Answer," *Vocational Guidance Quarterly*, vol. 17, no. 3 (March, 1969), pp. 221–222.

39. D. Anderson and R. Heimann, "Vocational Maturity of Junior High School Girls," *Vocational Guidance Quarterly*, vol. 15, no. 3 (March, 1967), pp. 191–195.

40. R. H. Johnson and R. D. Myrick, "MOLD: A New Approach to Career Decision-Making," *Vocational Guidance Quarterly*, vol. 21, no. 1 (September, 1972), pp. 48–52.

41. *Career Education Curriculum Guide, op. cit.*, p. 129.

42. Goldhammer and Taylor, *op. cit.*, pp. 236–237.

43. W. M. Lifton, "Counseling Theory and the Use of Educational Media," *Vocational Guidance Quarterly*, vol. 13, no. 2 (Winter, 1964), pp. 77–82.

44. E. L. Higgins and D. Brown, "Motion Pictures: A Source of Vocational Information," *Vocational Guidance Quarterly*, vol. 12, no. 1 (Autumn, 1963), pp. 68–71.

45. D. Laramore, "Jobs on Film," *Vocational Guidance Quarterly*, vol. 17, no. 2 (December, 1968), pp. 87–90.

46. *Educational Film Guide*, Standard Catalog Series (New York: H. W. Wilson Co.), published annually with monthly supplements.

47. *Filmstrip Guide* (New York: H. W. Wilson Co.), published annually with monthly supplements.

48. *Educators' Guide to Free Slidefilms* (Randolph, Wis.: Educators Progress Service), published annually.

49. K. Gutsch and R. Logan III, "Newspapers as a Means of Disseminating Occupational Information," *Vocational Guidance Quarterly*, vol. 15, no. 3 (March, 1967), pp. 186–190.

50. D. Munger, "The Occupational Speakers' Bureau," *Vocational Guidance Quarterly*, vol. 15, no. 4 (June, 1967), pp. 265–266.

51. A. H. Ryden, "Diamonds at your Doorstep," *Vocational Guidance Quarterly*, vol. 13, no. 2 (Winter, 1964), pp. 131–133.

52. Hollis and Hollis, *op. cit.*, pp. 217–245.

53. C. H. Miller, *Guidance Services* (New York: Harper and Row, Publishers, 1965), pp. 22–45.

15

The Decision-Making and Preparing Stages

The idea of individual differences assures us that each person will grow at his/her own pace. Therefore, we must expect the same variation in the rate of career development that we encounter in other areas of human maturation. The American educational system provides considerable latitude for this diversity of growth; nevertheless, the passage of time and progression through the grades brings all individuals to certain crucial points in their educational experience. Choices and decisions must be made, and the individual must pursue the consequences of each decision.

A fundamental goal of the guidance program is to alert the student to each impending decision sufficiently far enough in advance to permit the student, and parents whenever appropriate, to prepare for a wise choice. Only rarely does the elementary or middle school student face educational and vocational decisions of major importance. These situations ordinarily begin to occur near the end of middle or junior high school and then appear with increasing frequency for the next several years. In the previous chapter, we considered the importance of teaching the elementary youngster how to make decisions so that readiness for decision making would be developed before the time for action. The patterns of human development and educational organization coincide in a way that confronts the high school age student with a continuous network of situations in which decisions must be made. Many of these situations are organized in a branching lattice fashion, often without overlapping options. To illustrate, let us hypothesize that a student at point A must choose between two options (A_1 and A_2); if he/she chooses A_1, he/she will be confronted at point B with choices among three options—B_1, B_2, and B_3; however, if he/she chooses A_2 originally, the choices at point B will be among a different set of options—B_4, B_5, B_6, and B_7. In turn, each option will provide a differing arrangement of choices at point C. Occasionally, a given option would be common to two or more branches, so that "switching over" may occur easily at those points; elsewhere, however, it is difficult, costly, and time-consuming.

CAREER DEVELOPMENT AND CAREER EDUCATION IN HIGH SCHOOL

Career development specialists and career education advocates both agree that the high school years ideally should include for each student the following:

1. Maximum opportunity to make educational, vocational, and personal decisions.
2. Maximum opportunity to identify the consequences of each decision, not just at the immediate point, or even at the next point, but as far into the future as possible.
3. Maximum flexibility in program to permit those students who recognize erroneous choices to move to more appropriate paths with minimum loss.
4. An educational program that prepares each student with the skills and competencies that permit either entry into the world of work or continued appropriate education for later entry, always relating the realities of now to the expected realities in the life of the student beyond school years.

Hoyt and his associates suggest that when an effective career awareness and career exploration program operates in the pre-high school years, three groups of students will be found in the high school.[1] These three groups include: students preparing for careers that require at least a baccalaureate degree; students preparing for careers that require additional preparation at less than baccalaureate level; and students preparing for careers to be entered with no post-secondary preparation.

Hoyt, *et al.*, continue by emphasizing some of the changes that must occur in the high school if these three groups of students are to pursue the educational program that will best prepare them. Suggested changes include:

1. A system in which students can move easily from school to work and back to school, with most students involved in some type of program that combines work participation and classroom study.
2. Replacing the present time base of semester or term as the criterion for determining educational achievement with a performance criterion.
3. Recognition that learning also occurs outside the school and permitting the establishment of credit for appropriate learning acquired outside the school.

4. An extended program that includes day and evening classes on a year-long basis.
5. A curricular structure with great flexibility to permit a wide variety of choice.

Parnell, as Oregon State Superintendent of Public Instruction, was one of the first to participate in the development of a statewide policy for implementing career education. He, too, has emphasized that certain changes must transpire in the high school if effective career education is to occur.[2] The changes he identifies as necessary are somewhat different from Hoyt's, but they aim in the same direction. He proposes that the following must take place:

1. Schools must move from the traditional curricular tracks to new tracks developed on a career cluster concept. Parnell views this not so much as the development of new curricula as the reorganization of present curricular modules into a new structure that permits a student to choose a career cluster on entry and to pursue that goal throughout the school years.
2. Areas of the high school curriculum described as general education must be "infused" with unlimited illustrations from the world of work so that the student is continually aware of the relationship between studies and eventual employment.
3. Most specific vocational preparation for careers not requiring bacca-laureate preparation should be concentrated largely in post-secondary institutions and programs such as community colleges, apprenticeship programs, on-the-job training, and private vocational schools.
4. Each school must build strong, schoolwide guidance and counseling programs. The emphasis of the elementary guidance program should be on early identification of potential problems so that prevention can be stressed rather than later remedial efforts. Secondary programs should aim toward assisting all students to set broad goals and choose lifestyles.

It is obvious that the kinds of educational changes proposed both by Hoyt and Parnell are major in scope and, if they occur, probably will evolve slowly. Sudden, drastic remodeling is unlikely to take place on a nation-wide basis. Clearly, some states and many communities are already moving in these or in parallel directions. Even in high schools where change is not yet apparent, much can be done by teachers and counselors to help students develop and implement effective career decisions.

The involvement of students in choosing among elective courses, at least in high school, if not earlier, almost inevitably produces some consideration of occupational goals. The necessity of completing a schedule for the subsequent year provides the teacher and counselor adequate opportunity to direct student attention to the larger issue of career decisions.

Continuation of the exploratory activities initiated at earlier levels can be expected, with major attention at the high school level on narrowing and clarifying the student's goal. Specific identification should not be expected for most high school students; fuzziest of all are likely to be the plans of students definitely expecting to pursue a baccalaureate program. The refining of choice to the point of naming a specific goal is not a function of age, grade level, or ability, but rather should be directly related to the imminence of entry into the world of work. That choice should precede the entry point by sufficient time to acquire the specialized training required by the chosen occupation. For example, the scientific and technical professions generally require a specific and detailed baccalaureate program for admission; that college program often specifies a preparatory program heavily loaded with high school mathematics and science. A decision to move toward occupations in this general cluster would have to be made early enough in high school to assure completion of these preparatory courses. On the other hand, some professional occupations require specialization only in the final year or two of college. In these fields, the student could remain "unfocused" until the college sophomore year and still encounter no delay in preparation.

From the junior high school years onward, the amount of time available for developing specificity of choice may be determined more by factors related to the occupational areas than those involving the individual. The teacher and the counselor have a most crucial responsibility in the career development process: to help students develop awareness of these vital pre-entry points. Unless the individual is willing to sacrifice the time needed to "make up" missed prerequisites, the opportunity to choose a general area is lost when the student passes the point at which the first required prerequisite ordinarily is started.

This condition of variability provides an overwhelming argument in support of proposals to reorder the high school curriculum along occupational cluster groupings. Such an organization would greatly reduce the risk of students passing key points unaware that a crucial choice must be made at that time. The cluster concept would incorporate in its structure the preparatory steps related to the occupations within the structure, permitting the specification to develop in a gradual and orderly manner.

Obviously, the high school student is closer to entry than is the middle or junior high school student. The emphasis in these years, therefore, will be directed toward refining career goals in terms of the three broad groupings suggested by Hoyt, et al.[3] Accepting these groupings further requires that students who indicate post-secondary educational plans be assisted in developing "back-up" plans for occupational entrance at a lower level if those educational plans do not eventuate. It is logical to expect the teacher to be involved in the continuing exploratory aspects of the process, primarily in group settings. Meanwhile, the counselor is supplementing these teacher activities, as well as giving major attention to the decision-making activities, both in group and individual settings.

The counselor has responsibilities beyond group and individual counseling with students. Brown, Feit, and Forestandi describe the additional responsibilities of consultation and coordination.[4] Similarly, Gerler points out that many programs to familiarize teachers with career education concepts and practices fail because no provision has been made for follow-up.[5] This follow-up help can be supplied by the counselor who, in group and individual sessions with teachers, helps expand and improve teacher efforts as well as directs the program toward the needs of the local students.

Cleary has identified some of the problems that will inevitably be encountered as high schools move toward wider adoption of career education practices.[6] Concerned about the pressure for more specificity during the high school years, she directs attention to our present psychometric shortcomings, which prevent accurate appraisal of aptitudes and interest— two areas of information vital to the decision-making student. Jobs in our society are so complex, she continues, that we are unable to provide exact specifications required by various jobs so that matching individual and job can be most effective. Finally, Cleary stresses the need to re-educate teachers to include career education concepts in their instructional activities and to up-grade counselors in their use of appraisal procedures and career information materials. Certainly these problems exist, and their eradication will not occur suddenly; but then neither will the installation of effective career education and career development approaches. One can hope that the gradual growth of career education will provide the time needed to overcome the shortcomings.

Marland describes the Skyline High School complex in the Dallas, Texas, school system as a possible prototype of the career-oriented high school of the future.[7] The complex includes the high school; a Center for Career Development, which offers special occupational courses; and a Center for Community Services, which offers an adult education program. All three programs focus on career development, with a curriculum organized on the career cluster concept.

The Skyline Career curriculum includes the following clusters:

Business and management technology
Study of man and his environment
Computer technology
World languages
Horticulture
Higher sciences
Higher mathematics
Metal technology

World of construction
Electronic sciences
Advanced English, speech, and journalism
Climate control technology
Aeronautics
Transportation services
Plastics technology
Aesthetics
Dramatic arts
Photographic arts
Graphic technologies
Advanced music
Television arts
World of fashion
Beauty culture
Food management
Child and youth-related professions
Health, medical, and dental technologies

For each career cluster, career competencies and behavioral objectives have been developed. Student evaluation is based on the competency with which he/she completes the behavioral objectives. Since, at present, the one school serves the entire city of Dallas, it is possible for students to enroll at Skyline on either a full-time basis or part-time, with the remainder of their time spent in their home high school.

Our discussion in this and previous chapters has established that both teachers and counselors are continuously involved in career education and career development at both elementary and secondary levels. Each has differing but sometimes overlapping responsibilities. In addition, the career education concept includes the involvement and cooperation of many out-of-school people, such as employers, union leaders, civic officials, and others. As career education is developed in each school system, there will be increasing need for coordination and leadership. Hoyt already has written of the necessity for an individual to be assigned this responsibility.[8] He suggests the development of a preparatory program at the advanced graduate level for individuals with competency in career development, curriculum, the teaching/learning process, economics, sociology, and vocational education. This person's position would be at a high administrative level. This administrator would have sufficient authority and influence to implement the changes and collaborative efforts needed to accomplish the transition to and development of a career education program. Kehas has described what often happens when a teacher or counselor, working at the operational level, is simply designated as "coordinator."[9] Lacking authority to redirect efforts, the individual simply becomes a disseminator of information.

Until leadership of the type described by Hoyt can be developed and placed in school systems, teachers and counselors must depend on their mutual assistance and cooperation and on the leadership that over-worked school administrators can divert from their other activities and responsibilities. Even under these conditions, much can be done by each teacher and counselor to improve career development in the school.

CAREER DEVELOPMENT IN CLASSROOMS AND GROUPS

Let us first consider high school situations in which the teacher is likely to carry major responsibility. We will give most of our attention to classroom and group-related activities. We must not think only of the classroom, however, when considering the teacher's involvement in career development. Nor should we think that only the teacher works with students in groups. The counselor often may teach a class or lead a group, and the teacher often is involved with a student in a one-to-one counseling relationship.

As indicated earlier, the development of the self-concept is a continuing process that begins with the individual's first awareness of self as a person and continues to death. Continuous though this process is, there are periods of particular intensity. The years of secondary school make up one of these periods, in which the individual is deeply involved in learning to understand self, the relationship to others, and to the world.

Super has described how the school becomes involved in the exploration of self.[10] The school provides the principal setting in which the elementary and early secondary student encounters the world outside the close family circle. In this setting, he/she usually establishes the first prolonged contacts with adults and with peers who are not a part of the family group. It is entirely normal to select some of these people as "models" and "ideals." As he/she experiments with the different roles perceived as possibilities, he/she encounters varying degrees of gratification and satisfaction. Some of the roles played sometimes may be at variance or even in conflict with the roles that would be encouraged and approved within the family circle. Thus, inevitably, the school setting helps the student to broaden his/her development.

Obviously, this objective is met in part with each contact between student and teacher. Every staff member has an impact on the student, and thereby influences the development of the self-concept each time a student-staff relationship occurs.[11] Other career development objectives are satisfied through activities within regular subject-matter classes, through specially organized guidance or career classes, through special group activities, and through individual counseling. Let us now consider the use of career materials in regular and special classes.

Many secondary schools, both junior and senior high, attempt to assist their students in the career development process by using portions of regular academic classes for special units related to the general area of educational and vocational planning. There are certain obvious advantages to such an approach. First, the administrative difficulties of staffing and scheduling are eliminated, since the work is simply incorporated into a regular course. Second, if a required course is used, all students at a given grade level are reached automatically, thus providing the broad coverage that the administrator usually desires. Third, use of certain courses for special units leads to involvement of those teachers in the guidance program of the school.

As is true in most other situations, advantages often have compensating disadvantages. Attaching a special guidance unit to a subject-matter class may solve the staffing problem, but in an unfortunate way. The subject-matter teacher may lack interest in teaching the special unit and, even more likely, may lack any preparation or background for such teaching, with the result that he/she will feel both unhappy and threatened. Subject-matter teachers, naturally, have such an affinity for their own subject area and see so much in their own field that they consider useful or needed by students that they often are reluctant to give up any sizable portion of that subject time for a special unit. Similarly, even though scheduling problems are resolved by the special unit, designating time in one subject area for a special unit may cause difficulties with accrediting agencies, or may result in student deficiencies in that subject area.

Even though a guidance unit in freshman English will reach all freshmen enrolled in that course, this may not be the best or most appropriate time to present the unit to all freshmen. Individual differences in development and in personal plans may make the unit appropriate for some seventh- and eighth-grade students and perhaps even premature for some eleventh-graders. Placing the course arbitrarily at a given grade level may meet the needs of the average students, but may fall seriously short for the others. Because the personal variable is so pertinent to this problem, only a careful analysis of the students in the school can determine if the group has sufficient homogeneity for this approach.

Teacher involvement in the guidance program is both highly desirable and essential. This position has been taken a number of times throughout this volume. It is possible, however, that teacher involvement can be obtained in a number of better ways than usurping class time.

All in all, the balancing of the advantages and disadvantages of using subject-matter time for guidance units must be resolved by the administrator. Resolving the problem requires careful consideration of many factors, including assessment of student needs, teacher abilities and interests, guidance staff utilization, and various other components.

Guidance units incorporated into regularly scheduled courses may be either general or specialized in nature. A general guidance unit usually is complete in and of itself, with little or no direct connection to the subject area into which it is inserted. A specialized guidance unit usually has a direct relationship to the subject area.

General guidance units may be found at any grade level of the secondary school. Because of the desire to reach all students at that level, they are usually attached to such courses as English or social studies. Also, the objectives of these courses are usually broad enough, especially in content, to make them more amenable to such adaptation.

At the upper junior high and lower senior high levels, the general units most frequently are related to such broad topics as "orientation to school," "educational and vocational planning," or "personal adjustment." In the upper grades, they may, instead, deal with "selecting a college," "applying for a job," "military service," or with some similar topic appropriate for the person about to complete high school work. The duration of such units may vary from one to four weeks, with the most frequent span covering two or three weeks.

The purposes of these general guidance units vary considerably. Usually the purpose is to encourage and stimulate occupational exploration and to help students see the relationship between school and later careers. When the purpose is limited in this way, there is usually a reasonable chance that the unit will be successful. If, on the other hand, the school attempts to meet its total obligation for helping in career development through such a unit, the project is doomed to failure, since the total process is too large to be handled in such a manner. Provision should be made for close cooperation between teacher and counselor, so that the counselor can assist the teacher in developing and presenting the unit, and so that the unit can lead to individual counseling for students for whom it is appropriate.

Specialized units frequently are career-oriented, and therefore often focus on the career opportunities that relate to a specific subject area. Such units logically are a part of high school courses that have obvious career implications. They also may be just as relevant in courses that have broader, fundamental, general education value, since few occupations are filled any longer by workers with only a specialized preparation. Too often in the past, such specialized units have concentrated on the related specialities and have overlooked the broader application that each subject may have. Thus, the noncollege-bound student may feel that, since college preparation is necessary to become a chemist or a physicist, science holds no opportunity for him/her. Understanding the interrelationships of occupations should help the teacher see the broader implications and provide opportunity for students to grasp the vast range of openings at various levels in all fields.

A series of charts included in a recent revision of *The Teacher's Role in Career Development* by Tennyson, Soldahl, and Mueller demonstrates the scope, in both area and level, of occupations related to various subject fields.[12] Table 28 (pp. 468–69) from that publication is typical.[13] The categories at the left are educational levels usually required; the areas across the top are similar to the primary focus classification discussed in Chapter 7.

Subject-matter teachers can find a broad range of materials available for use in specialized units. Many of the sources, and the indexes leading to further sources of career information, already have been considered in Chapter 11.

Career-oriented units not only help the student from the broad standpoint of career development, but also serve a special purpose in stimulating interest in a specific course. Close cooperation between teacher and counselor will be helpful to both and will provide maximum value to the student.

Career education advocates staunchly support the idea of teacher involvement in the career development process. They contend that the activities we have just described inevitably include a degree of artificiality because the unit is "laid on" the ordinary subject-matter instructional efforts of the teacher. They propose that more could be accomplished if

---

Goal 11: Extend knowledge and understanding of the world of work, career clusters, or similar content sources regarding career information.

Strategy 11a: Develop a chart or illustration of the 15 USOE career clusters with their corresponding families of occupations and/or other career information.

Strategy 11b: Interview persons such as employers, personnel managers, organization representatives, and state employment counselors to determine educational, occupational, and personal-social requirements for various occupations; identify from sources in print occupational requirements information; compare the interview information with that of printed sources.

Strategy 11c: Select an occupation and locate in the *Dictionary of Occupational Titles* related jobs to the occupation selected. Explore further, jobs related in career information sources, such as the *Occupational Outlook Handbook*, and the like.

Strategy 11d: Identify in various career clusters those jobs/occupations for which one's chosen academic major or minor can prepare one.

From: L. McKinney, E. Dozier, D. Harmon, J. Lynn and J. Meighan, *Career Education Personnel Development* (Columbus, Ohio: Center for Vocational Education, The Ohio State University, 1975), pp. 15–16.

TABLE 28. *Careers Related to Science*

LEVELS	SERVICE	BUSINESS, CLERICAL, AND SALES	SCIENCE AND TECHNOLOGY	OUTDOOR	GENERAL CULTURE	ARTS AND ENTER-TAINMENT
I B.A. or above	Occupational therapist Psychologist Psychiatrist Dietician	Sales engineer Mfg., electronic equip.	Anthropologist Chemist Medical technologist Astronautic engineer Physicist Engineer Mathematician Physician Biologist Botanist Veterinarian Pharmacist Nurse Dentist Chiropractor	Agronomist Wildlife specialist Range management specialist Horticulturist County agent Landscape architect	Curator Science teacher Phys. ed. teacher	
II High school plus technical	Mortician	Pharmaceutical salesman Medical secretary Chemical secretary	Biological research aide Dental technician Dental hygienist Optometrist	Floriculturist Nurseryman Tree surgeon Fish culturist Soil conservationist		Botanical artist

	Salesman, scientific supplies and equip.	Medical technician Weather observer Practical nurse Embalmer	
III High school plus graduate	Masseur	Taxidermist Glass blower Dry cleaner Textile technician Lab. technician	Landscape gardener Poultryman Truck gardener Apiarist	
IV Less than high school graduate		Veterinary hosp. att. Zoo caretaker Nurse's aide	Lumber inspector Nursery employee	Animal trainer Photographic technician

Source: *The Teacher's Role in Career Development* (see note 12).

the attention to career-related aspects were totally infused into the day-by-day classroom activities. This would require the teacher continually to relate subject matter to the world of work, to use illustrations from work wherever possible, and to orient classroom learning to post-school plans of the students. No one can argue successfully against that position. Its successful implementation necessitates major curricular revision and joint effort by teacher, counselor, and administrator. In the interim, the classroom teacher can use career units advantageously.

For many years, a number of schools have included regular courses on careers in their curriculum, under various titles.[14] These courses often are called "Careers" or "Occupations." They are sometimes taught at either the ninth- or twelfth-grade level. Grade placement of such a course always has been a difficult problem. Placement at the ninth grade permits maximum opportunity for educational planning after that grade, but the students at this point often feel so far removed from the world of work that motivation may be difficult. If the course is taught at the twelfth-grade level, the student is more likely to see its pertinence to his/her own life, but the course may occur too late in the educational career to permit capitalizing on it effectively. The difficulties at either level can be met best if the course is developed to meet the needs of the students involved. Obviously, the ninth-grader is likely to be more concerned with exploring occupations broadly, as they affect educational planning for the years ahead, whereas the senior is more apt to be confronted with the specifics of job-seeking and preparation for entrance into the world of work.

Organized classes in careers permit more extensive consideration of the topic than is possible in the short unit studied in another class. Nevertheless, the course cannot be of maximum value to the student if it is approached in textbook fashion with the aim of thorough familiarization in depth with the world of work. The goal of such a course should be to maximize self-actualization through the development of concepts appropriate to the student's level of maturity and proximity to the world of work.[15]

One advantage of an organized course in "Occupations" or "Careers" is that it can be closely tied to the school's total guidance program and properly staffed. In some schools, the course is taught by a member of the guidance staff, whose academic preparation may be more appropriate for teaching such a course than that of a subject-area teacher. Even though such an arrangement lets the guidance staff members become better acquainted with the students they serve by having classroom contact with them, it also reduces the time they will have available for individual counseling and other guidance activities.

A regularly scheduled course taught by a guidance staff member may offer the best opportunity to meet the individual needs of the students enrolled. It should be possible to relate class activities to individual counseling and to develop an approach based on both group procedures and individual counseling, with the student being involved in both phases to whatever extent is appropriate. When this dual approach can be arranged, the student will have the maximum opportunity to benefit.

A regularly scheduled class does not necessarily meet all the needs of the students. In some schools, unfortunately, the instructor may be the one with free time at the scheduled hour, rather than the one best qualified to teach the course. Because process is just as important as content in this type of course, such a procedure is an even greater mistake than assigning a teacher a course outside his/her field.

Further, the adoption of an organized course may lead a school faculty to assume that it has met its responsibility for helping students in the career development process. When this happens, the course becomes a "one shot" effort, and the basic axiom that career choice and development should start in the early years and continue throughout one's life is disregarded.

Another aspect of this problem occurs when the "Careers" course is organized on the premise that each participating student will make a "career choice" during the course. This approach disregards the developmental aspect of career development and may lead the student to the unwarranted view that a vocational choice is static and permanent rather than dynamic and flexible. Even in adulthood, the possibility of modification and revision of choice—because of change in self-concept, technological developments, and other factors—is so likely for most people that any implication of early permanent choice not only is misleading but also is likely to make later adjustment difficult. A much more realistic approach is to help the student see vocational choice as a continuing series of choices, each of which is likely to be revised, thus leading to a new choice that may similarly be modified.

A final disadvantage can exist in the regularly scheduled "Careers" course if it focuses only on the occupational aspects and disregards the educational factors. Educational and vocational planning and development are so closely interrelated, both during formal schooling and later, that it is inappropriate to consider one without the other. This is especially important in a society in which we can expect increasing numbers of adults to need continuing education and retraining beyond the regular school years, to prepare them for occupations that did not exist when they were in school. As automation and other technological changes eliminate and modify existing occupations and create new ones, more adults become involved in further education to fit them for new jobs. The school can serve this group better if it helps them accept and understand the inevitability of change, rather than leading them toward a specific niche as a definite and final goal.

Concern for the career development of the individual should have a natural and normal place within any classroom. Each member of the instructional staff has a responsibility to this area of student growth and maturity. This responsibility probably can be met best by an awareness by all staff members and a concerted effort by all, led by the administration and the guidance staff, to develop an approach that permeates the school program with sufficient breadth and depth to meet the varying needs of all students.

Group procedures may enable the school, or other agency, to work with all or many of these students collectively on certain aspects of their development. The commonality of the problem may make it easier for many students to become involved with members of their peer group in seeking information or understanding that will help them resolve their problems. Frequently youngsters are more apt to discuss their problems with peers than with adults. This attitude also may lead them to accept suggestions and reactions from the peer group that they would be inclined to resist from adults. The recognition that others of their peers face similar problems and uncertainties may help them obtain a different perspective of their own concerns, and this may encourage more independence and initiative on their part in seeking information and solution. In addition, an inevitable sharing of knowledge and information leads to a broader foundation for ultimate decision making.

Certain disadvantages or limitations exist in group procedures, and care must be taken to assure the accrual of advantages and the avoidance of negative experiences. It is possible that one individual within the group may be ahead of the others in personally acquiring the information or resolution that the group is seeking. Even though no loss may come as a part of the group, his/her personal progress may be slowed by group participation. It also is possible for specific individual problems to be overlooked or side-tracked while the group focuses on a broader, more general concern. Thus, the individual does not acquire what he/she had hoped to gain, or the rest of the group marks time while attention is given to the individual's specific concern. Finally, there is always the possibility of loss of status by an individual within the group, since it may be difficult to develop a totally accepting group. An individual who is open and honest may reveal information about self that results in loss of "face" within the group. Even when this does not occur, some participants may limit their role in a group because of the threat of such loss.

Overall, much can be gained by use of group procedures as a part of the vocational choice process. Group procedures do not replace individual counseling, but may contribute to the total effectiveness of counseling and to the maximum development of the individual.

This chapter is based on the premise that group methods supply an essential ingredient in the career development process. Individual counseling alone cannot accomplish all that is desirable. Individual and group methods, when properly coordinated, can contribute more than either method alone. Even the most extensive use of career information in classes and in other groups cannot solve an individual's problem as effectively as individual counseling. Each process makes a unique contribution to development; therefore, each school should provide maximum opportunity for each student to become involved in career planning through class activities and out-of-class groups as well as through individual counseling.

Even though a school goes to great pains in providing career information in class situations, this does not justify its disregarding out-of-class group activities. Class activities usually are oriented toward the general needs of the class, even in schools that make every effort to individualize instruction. Within each class, we can expect to find some individuals whose particular needs scatter around the general mean for the class. Some individuals will obviously be farther from the mean than others. For those whose needs are quite different from the majority, the general class activity will have less significance than for the rest. In many situations, these special needs can be met more adequately by out-of-class groups. For example, within a typical class of ninth- or tenth-graders, students who are already planning to terminate their formal education shortly are confronted with quite different career questions than students who anticipate continuing to graduation or beyond. A senior class unit on how to apply for a job is of no help to the early dropout, who expects to be gone from school before then. Unless he/she can be helped before leaving school, the unit is wasted. Further, he/she may need help in acquiring information about the specific job opportunities available locally to young workers with limited education. However, exploration of this topic in sufficient depth to be meaningful to a potential dropout is not of crucial importance to the rest of the group.

Learning occurs in a variety of ways for each individual, and for some one method or technique is more helpful than another. For this reason, out-of-class activities may provide an approach that would be ineffective in the classroom setting. This may be true for the potential dropout or for the student at the far end of the ability and interest continuum who has become disenchanted with the classroom, where activities are generally pitched far above or below him/her. Group experiences outside the classroom may, then, produce more effective results. Even for the well-adjusted youngster who participates well in the classroom setting, the out-of-class activity may provide enough change of pace to result in increased learning.

Healy has described a plan for using groups in a career counseling procedure based on Super's theory of career development.[16] He has used five two-hour group sessions that permit the participant to identify what he/she wants from work and what he/she can offer to it, to examine different goals and means of reaching those goals, to select career possibilities appropriate to important goals, to make plans for acquiring training or entrance, to begin execution of plans, and to evaluate personal progress toward career goals. Daane also has described a similar group-oriented program entitled *Vocational Exploration Group*.[17]

In Chapter 13, we considered many techniques that can be used with groups of individuals in the decision-making stage. These techniques include such activities as career days and career conferences, simulation, synthetic work experience, visits to business and industry, and try-out experiences. All of these techniques, properly used with appropriate students, will enhance individual career development.

Materials such as the previously mentioned *Career Education Curriculum Guide* provide suggestions that are useful for teachers and counselors working with classes and groups. A sample page for those working with decision-making students is included in Table 29.[18]

TABLE 29. *Sample Page from* Career Education Curriculum Guide

LEVEL: 11–12	SUBJECT AREA: SOCIOLOGY	CONCEPT CLUSTER: DEVELOPMENTAL PROCESS
LEARNING OBJECTIVES	LEARNING EXPERIENCES	MATERIALS AND RESOURCES
Students will be able to identify experiences that will facilitate a smooth transition from school into the world of work.	1. Help students identify educational and training opportunities in the community and state. (A state map could be constructed indicating the location and type of education and training.) 2. By "brainstorming," have students describe an experience or experiences that have influenced their ideas about education and vocations. 3. In cooperation with the guidance department, administer and discuss the results of Super's Work Values Inventory with interested students. 4. Present to class taped interviews of school dropouts discussing frustrations they encounter on looking for and holding a job without a salable skill.	Super's Work Values Inventory (App. J) Filmstrips: "Dropping Out: Road to Nowhere" "Four Who Quit" "I Wish I'd Known That Before I Went to College" "Preparing for the World of Work" "What You Should Know Before You Go to Work" "Who Should Go to College" Guidance Associates (App. F)

TABLE 29. *Continued*

LEVEL: 11–12	SUBJECT AREA: SOCIOLOGY	CONCEPT CLUSTER: DEVELOPMENTAL PROCESS
LEARNING OBJECTIVES	LEARNING EXPERIENCES	MATERIALS AND RESOURCES
	5. Show educational and vocational subject matter film and filmstrips.	
	6. Assign students an essay entitled, "What I would like to be doing in ten years." Follow-up at the end of the year with a similar assignment entitled "What I think I'll be doing in ten years." Return both essays for comparison.	

Also available are materials prepared by commercial publishers oriented particularly toward classroom and group career development activities. Examples of these include the *Career Planning Program,* grades 8–11.[19] This material includes assessment materials integrated with career guidance components intended to fit into the developmental approach to career development across grades 8 through 11. These materials are coordinated with a subsequent package entitled *Career Planning Program,* grades 12–13, which focuses more specifically on the needs of students about to complete high school and who anticipate pursuing programs in vocational or technical schools or community colleges or instead plan to enter the world of work.[20] A further illustration of similar materials commercially prepared for use in classes or groups is the *Career Education Guide.*[21] These materials are arranged in four levels, extending from kindergarten through adult; each level emphasizes awareness, aptitudes and attitudes, skills and initial exploration, and exploration and decision-making. Less comprehensive than these two programs, and designed for use with secondary school classes and groups, is *My Career Guidebook,* second edition.[22]

The Polaroid Company has prepared *Career Field Guides,* primarily for internal use to teach employees about accessible careers within the company but also applicable for high school students contemplating employment with that company.[23] Johnson has described a plan for establishing an information center through which school counselors can obtain current information about employment and preparation programs.[24]

COUNSELING—DEFINITION AND PRINCIPLES

Counseling has been described as a relationship between a counselee and a professionally competent counselor, with the purpose of assisting the counselee to integrate and apply understanding of self and the present situation so that he/she can make the wisest and most appropriate decisions and adjustments.

Wrenn has prepared a similar definition with his statement: [25]

> Counseling is a dynamic and purposeful relationship between two people in which procedures vary with the nature of the student's need but in which there is always mutual participation by counselor and student wtih the focus upon self-clarification and self-determination by the student.

Stefflre has proposed a definition that emphasizes the same general position.[26] He says:

> Counseling denotes a professional relationship between a trained counselor and a client. This relationship is usually person-to-person, although it may sometimes involve more than two people, and it is designed to help the client understand and clarify his view of his life space so that he may make meaningful and informed choices consonant with his essential nature in those areas where choices are available to him.

Tyler has proposed certain principles that underlie the counseling process.[27] These five principles are listed below.

1. COUNSELING IS MORE THAN ADVICE GIVING. Each definition cited above has indicated that the purpose of counseling is to help the individual understand self and the existing situation. This implies that he/she is a self-directing individual, capable of making decisions, and that the counselor's task is to help assess the factors involved and the way he/she looks at those factors. There is no implication that the counselor should either tell the counselee what to do or what he/she would do if he/she were the counselee. To do either violates respect for the individual and his/her right to be self-directing; the advice-giver must assume that he/she knows and understands the individual and the situation better than the person. The counselor, who hopefully has some knowledge of personality development, knows that he/she does not have the super-human power that would validate that assumption.

Many people who do not understand counseling equate it with advice-giving. This suggests that the counselor is a kind of fortune-telling authority who, in some way, can read the future and manipulate people and events so that everyone lives happily ever after. Such an implication is both untrue and distasteful.

2. Counseling Involves Something More Than the Solution to an Immediate Problem. If counseling were concerned only with the immediate problem confronting the counselee, the work of the counselor could be compared with that of the firefighter whose job is to put out the current fire. This implies that the counseling relationship is an unending one, since every individual is continuously confronted by a series of choices, problems, and decisions. Each time an incident occurred, one would have to consult a counselor before resolving the situation.

The counselor's work, on the contrary, is directed toward helping the individual to be self-directing, to face problems and situations, and to find solutions independently. In many ways, the counselor's task with each client is to work himself/herself out of a job—to progress to the point at which the counselee terminates the relationship because he/she feels able to go forward alone.

3. Counseling Concerns Itself With Attitudes Rather Than With Actions. The definitions indicate that the counselor is concerned with helping the individual to understand self. The emphasis is on the individual's attitudes and feelings. The basic question is not one of deciding what should be done in a specific situation; that will be resolved as the counselee gains insight into self, particularly into attitudes, and faces the question of how and why he/she feels as he/she does. As this area is clarified, the alternatives available in the situation at the moment will become more apparent and an appropriate choice of action will more likely be made.

We must assume that a person's behavior is consistent with his/her self-concept—that one behaves in terms of the way in which one views oneself. Suggesting or advising some change in behavior deals only superficially with a symptom, rather than with the cause of behavior. It is unlikely that the individual could accomplish the behavioral change on such a casual basis; even if one tried, one would not get at the factors that are producing the unsatisfying action. To change these in a manner that will be helpful to the counselee, he/she must first deal with the underlying causes; this means considering and realigning the way he/she looks at self.

4. Emotional Rather Than Purely Intellectual Attitudes Are the Raw Materials of the Counseling Process. Being able to talk about one's behavior does not really lead to change in actions unless the individual is able to change the way he/she feels about them. Popular magazines and other mass media have given many people a knowledge of psychological terms, so that they can discuss such forms of behavior as "rationalization" and "projection" and even identify such behavior in themselves and others. Such cursory knowledge of one's own behavior does not result in change unless the individual is able to penetrate to more depth and explore the feelings behind the action. It is the counselor's task to help the client explore those underlying feelings by creating a situation in which the client feels safe.

5. COUNSELING INEVITABLY INVOLVES RELATIONSHIPS BETWEEN PEOPLE, ALTHOUGH IT MAY SEEM TO BE PURELY AN AFFAIR OF THE ONE INDIVIDUAL WHO IS UNDERGOING IT. By its very nature, counseling establishes a relationship between client and counselor. In fact, unless that relationship is established, counseling cannot really occur. This state is often referred to as *rapport*. The ingredients of this condition involve, for the counselor, an acceptance of the client as an individual, an interest in him/her and his/her concerns, and an ability to "feel" or empathize with him/her. The counselee must recognize that here is a person who is interested and accepting, and one whom he/she trusts sufficiently to reveal thoughts and feelings about problems. Within the counseling room, he/she finds no need to maintain the defenses and pretenses that are used with other individuals— here is a person who seems to understand and to be with him/her in feelings, even though the person sees him/her as he/she "really" is. As the client finds no need to maintain a façade in order to be accepted, he/she is able to examine feelings and actions toward self and others, and inevitably makes changes in attitudes and behaviors that bear on relationships with other people. These changes do not necessarily occur only in the counseling room, but also often between counseling sessions as the client reflects on the counseling relationship. The important factor is that the situation in the counseling room brings about the change.

In a recent edition of *The Work of the Counselor,* Tyler has proposed that most counseling cases can be classified either as *choice* cases or as *change* cases, with some falling between the two categories into a *doubtful* class.[28] In a *choice* case, the counselor decides that the client's present possibilities are sufficient to offer alternative choices that are likely to lead to rewarding and satisfying development. In a *change* case, the counselor must decide that viable alternatives are not now available to the client and he/she must first be helped to change behavior or situation so that more promising possibilities for constructive action can be opened up. A case might be classified as *doubtful* when the counselor needs more understanding of the client and the situation in order to classify him/her.

The *choice* case may need help from the counselor either to make a comprehensive survey of possibilities or to make a commitment or decision. The *change* case will need help from the counselor either to remove an obstacle to a possible choice, or to create new possibilities. The *doubtful* case will need help in creating a structure to replace present confusion. Tyler proposes that these early decisions by the counselor will, in large part, determine the counseling strategies that will be used by the counselor in assisting the client. For example, if a comprehensive survey seems needed, the counselor may undertake an exploratory interview, develop a testing program, gather other pertinent data, discuss the data, and help the client gain insight and understanding. If the counselor decides the situation calls for creation of new possibilities he/she may refer for medical treatment, or use educational planning, social innovation, and similar techniques along with interviews.

Finally, in our attempt to identify the nature of counseling, it may be helpful to contrast it with psychotherapy and with instruction—two areas with which counseling is often confused by the layman. Stefflre[29] has attempted to differentiate these three areas in the following statement:

> The distinction between counseling and psychotherapy cannot be made with complete clarity and satisfaction. At the same time an attempt must be made to at least distinguish the master's level school counselor and the psychoanalyst as well as many intermediate positions. The total length of training for school counselors is presently averaging about one year of graduate work, and of that probably less than half is psychological in nature. Can we not make it clear to these counselors that they are not trained as therapists? The position of this chapter is that at least the extremes of differences between counseling and psychotherapy can be identified. While it is true that "tall" cannot be distinguished from "short" when men are roughly five-foot-nine, it is equally clear that five-foot-two is different from six-foot-five. An attempt to distinguish between these two activities—counseling and psychotherapy—is made particularly difficult by the prestige structure in American academic circles. In general, education is less valued than psychology as a discipline. Since education departments train most counselors, counseling does not have the prestige of psychotherapy. As a consequence master's level school counselors like to think of themselves as counseling psychologists, counseling psychologists sometimes like to think of themselves as clinical psychologists, and clinical psychologists like to muddy the distinction with psychiatry. Although snobbery—and professional psychopathy—make these distinctions difficult, the distinctions themselves are not without value.
>
> In attempting to point to some differences between counseling and psychotherapy, we can now look at the several elements we have considered and compare the two activities with regard to their position on various continua. (1) Counseling tends to be concerned with instrumental behavior, with role problems, with situations, with choices which must be made, and with actions which must be taken. Goals of counseling are more limited than those of psychotherapy, but this does not mean that these limited goals are unimportant or that changes in immediate behavior may not have lasting global effects. (2) Counselors deal with normal individuals. (The distinction between "normal" and "neurotic" is as fraught with difficulties, of course, as the distinction between counseling and psychotherapy.) (3) The practitioner of counseling may be trained at the doctoral level with a two-year internship as would be his counterpart in clinical psychology.

Many counselors, however, are trained at less than a doctoral level or at the doctoral level but with relatively little psychology and little or no formal supervised internship. These people because of the prestige rank of psychology and because of their own confused role concepts may quickly come to think of themselves as psychotherapists. Although they have difficulty making the distinction, there is no reason why more objective observers should. (4) The setting in which counseling takes place is most apt to be an educational setting or a community agency, although counselors may work in a medical setting or in a private practice. (5) The methods used will indicate that counseling shows more concern than psychotherapy with present events than with those of the past, more concern with cognition than with affect, more concern with clarity than with ambiguity.

There seems to be no litmus paper which will distinguish counseling from psychotherapy as it changes from blue to red. Combinations of clues, however, may be helpful in distinguishing the two activities. If we see an interview relationship in which the professional person is trained at less than a doctoral level (or at a doctoral level without a formal two-year internship), if he is dealing with a normal client, if he is dealing with him in an educational setting, if he is primarily concerned with conscious processes, and if his goals are to help the client play one of his life roles more effectively by making better choices, we can say that counseling is going on. On the other hand, if the practitioner has been trained primarily in clinical psychology, if his client seems quite disturbed, if they are working in a medical setting, if the goals are to reconstruct the personality of the client, and if the methods are characterized by ambiguity, intense emotion, and concern for unconscious processes, we may more appropriately label the activity as psychotherapy.

Counseling Distinguished From Instruction

If to a counseling practitioner the thunder on the left is representative of psychotherapy, the thunder on the right is representative of instruction. There are educational theorists who see little distinction between counseling and teaching. Certainly in a broad sense their goals may be much the same since both are concerned with helping an individual develop to the point where he can assume responsibilities for himself and live a satisfying life. More narrowly, however, the goals of counseling are more determined by the needs of the individual as he sees them, whereas the goals of instruction are more apt to be societally determined. The most permissive and student-centered teacher of an algebra class has some views as to what should be covered in an instructional situation because society has, to some extent, defined those goals, but in the counseling situation the counselor has less preconception about what will be needed to help the individual.

With regard to the client (or student) instruction is thought to be for all. With regard to counseling, there are those who think counseling should be given to everyone, but frequently it happens that counseling is only given to those who voluntarily request it or perhaps to those seen as "needing" it.

The practitioner of teaching has been trained in specific instructional techniques and subject matter, while hopefully the counselor has had additional training in interviewing, psychometrics, occupational information, and other competencies required by his specialized role. It would seem to be true, however, that often teachers do counseling and sometimes counselors do teaching. The wisdom of having the same person play both roles can be questioned because the teacher as required to be judgmental and to operate as a representative of an educational institution with certain responsibilities determined by the function of that institution, whereas the counselor has primary responsibility to the individual and so can be less judgmental. Part of this confusion stems from the fact that educational institutions in America have two purposes—the developmental and the screening. They have the job of helping a student grow, but they also have the job of acting as gatekeeper to certain occupations and roles. This screening function, which is now being performed by the educational institution, would seem to inhibit the kind of relationship which is thought to be most helpful in counseling. The counseling, then, particularly if it concerns individual educational problems, may be difficult to distinguish from instruction.

The methods of teaching are more apt to be group methods, and the methods of counseling are more apt to be individual methods. However, teachers may teach one student at a time, and this tutoring function has long been recognized and valued, while more and more counselors are experimenting with group procedures.

If we see an individual in a group being dealt with by a teacher with some societally determined preconception as to the goals of the interaction, we are apt to call this activity instruction rather than counseling.

The discussion and quotations above indicate that counseling can touch many aspects of the client's life. We are concerned here primarily with involvement in the career development process. Restriction of our discussion to this area in no way is an attempt to narrow our interpretation or definition of counseling; rather, it is done in order to focus on the immediate concern of this volume.

The use of career information in counseling relates directly to the theories of vocational choice considered in Chapter 2. The reader who is not thoroughly conversant with those theories may find it helpful to review them briefly before proceeding with this chapter—particularly those of Hoppock, Super, and Holland.

Buehler has proposed five psychological life stages.[30] These include: the *Growth Stage*, which extends up to about age fourteen; the *Exploratory*

Stage, which extends from about fifteen to about twenty-five; the *Establishment Stage,* which ranges from about twenty-five to about forty-five; the *Maintenance Stage,* which extends from forty-five to about sixty-five, and the *Decline Stage,* which extends from about sixty-five to death.

Super has discussed the relationship between the life stages and vocational development.[31] He emphasizes that individuals enter the various stages at different chronological ages; some people have completed the exploratory phase and entered the establishment stage by their early twenties; others may still be groping and searching in the exploratory stage in their thirties or beyond. Super also emphasizes that the life stages apply to all other aspects of life in addition to the vocational. For example, the exploratory stage is concerned with the search for self-understanding, for a mate, and for a position in the community, as well as for an occupation.

Career information is used in the counseling relationship in all five life stages, although to a lesser extent in the growth, maintenance, and decline stages than in either the exploratory or establishment stage.

During the growth period, primary attention is focused on the physical and intellectual growth of the individual. The school years within this period obviously include attention to the world of work and the individual's future relationship to it. Much of this activity will be in a group setting, as discussed in the previous chapter. The transition from one stage to another is gradual, however, and certain exploratory activities will be initiated long before the individual is fully launched in the second phase. Some of these activities may well occur in the counseling relationship, as discussed in the next section.

Similarly, the maintenance and decline stages involve occasional counseling contacts for some individuals focused on vocational development, as the person finds that he/she must reorient work activities either because of physical changes or because of technological or other factors. The change from lifetime career to tapering-off employment often is not an easy change to make. Recent trends in technological development also indicate an increasing likelihood that many workers will change positions with increasing frequency in the years ahead, as automation and similar influences either change or eliminate the positions they may have held for many years. Counseling often may be the vehicle used to effect the change that comes to such workers. Likewise, as life is extended by medical progress and retirement age is lowered through the processes mentioned above, more workers may need counseling help in making the transition from employment to retirement.

The very names of the exploratory stage and the establishment stage indicate the extent to which these two periods are involved in career development. During these two periods counseling is most deeply involved in the career choice process. Most of our attention in the remaining portions of this chapter will be devoted to the consideration of this relationship.

COUNSELING USES OF CAREER INFORMATION

Each definition of counseling in the previous section emphasizes that a function of counseling is to help the individual understand self and understand the situation in which he/she is in or expects to be in. The reason for the stress on self and situational understanding is apparent in the latter portion of each definition. This understanding provides the basis for decision making—self-determination, as stated in Wrenn's definition.

Career counseling helps bring about the client's increased understanding of the relationship between self and present or anticipated environment. The counselor has several aims in working with a client. One may be effecting changes in client behavior, accelerating career development, stimulating the desire for self-direction, or building needed skills for future personal planning. Regardless of which aim has momentary emphasis, the counselor often will use career information in assisting the client toward vocational maturity.

Throughout this book, we have proceeded on the assumption that career development is a lifelong process, a series of choices selected sequentially as the most workable alternatives at specific times among the choices available to the individual. Each choice, whether overtly selected or submissively accepted, provides part of the base on which the next choice in the sequence is made. Each decision that is made affects the individual's future in two contradictory ways, since it both narrows and simultaneously opens or broadens the range of future choices. For example, the college-entering freshman who elects to enter a school of engineering restricts future choices by eliminating possibilities in the humanities, the sciences, agriculture, and other fields entered through other schools. At the same time, he/she opens a band of future choices that will require selecting among several types of engineering; later he/she will be faced with deciding whether to look toward research, practical applications, business administration, teaching, or other choices, and still later with a choice of the company in which to begin professional employment. This choice, too, for most individuals is only the first of many that are a part of total career development.

Since the counselor may encounter the client at any point in this lifelong process, he/she must be prepared to meet a variety of situations. The counseling assistance needed by a junior high school student just beginning to think of a vocational future is likely to be very different from that needed by the graduating high school senior about to enroll in a local technical school.[32,33] The needs of a college sophomore are likely to be very different from those of the fifty-year-old adult who has been displaced by automation.[34] Although the basic purposes of counseling in these situations—self-clarification leading toward self-determination—remains constant, the techniques used by the counselor obviously will vary according to the individual client's needs. Thus, the use of career information in vocational counseling will be based similarly on the client, the situation, and the need.[35] The counselor's decisions about whether to use career materials, and if so, when, which ones, and how, cannot be automatically prescribed. These choices must be made by a professionally competent counselor within the framework of the counseling relationship with a specific client at a specific time.[36] Although it is impossible to lay out in cookbook fashion which ingredients to combine for certain results, it is possible to consider various ways and situations in which career materials are used.

We can approach the use of career materials in counseling either from the purpose of the counselor in using the materials, or from an analysis of the client's primary problem at the time of counseling. Of course, a close relationship exists between the two approaches, since one would expect the counselor's choice of technique and response to be appropriate to the presenting situation. Let us look at both approaches sequentially, considering first the various ways that career information is used in the counseling process, and then looking at some of the specific types of "problems" that may involve the use of career materials.

Again, we must keep in mind the assumption that we are dealing with a process extending over considerable time, not an event of a day or week's duration. Continuing emphasis on career education's developmental and lifelong aspects will help both clients and counselor, as well as the public at large, to grasp the significance of the time factor.

Many authors concur in the viewpoint that four major functions of career information in counseling can be identified. Although there is some variation in the names applied to these functions, in general they can be thought of as *motivational, instructional, adjustive,* and *distributive.* Let us consider each function briefly.

MOTIVATIONAL USES. Many sources suggest that career materials can be used to arouse or to stimulate the counselee. Within the educational setting it is easy to envision this type of activity, since it logically fits into the exploratory life stage discussed above. The client at any age level who is just beginning to think about how he/she can relate to the world of work in the future often is confused and finds it difficult to grasp any sort of structure. He/she may, for example, imagine self engaged in some professional or technical field, but at the same time have no conception of how to proceed into that field. Career materials that describe the extent and nature of the education leading to that field afford some clarification. The high school freshman who dreams of engineering may move from fantasy toward reality as he/she learns something of the college program taken by engineering students and contemplates the prerequisite curriculum crammed with mathematics and science.

Similarly, the student who anticipates completing education with high school graduation, or even sooner, may be helped to become realistic by considering career materials describing employment opportunities in the fields being scanned, as well as some of the extrinsic benefits. The goal here is not to convince the client that more education is the solution to the problem—it very well may not be. The goal is to assist him/her to see as accurately as possible what he/she wants and what that desire will cost in effort, finance, and other resources, so that the result—self-determination—has an opportunity to develop.

An even simpler motivational use of career materials is to encourage the individual to begin vocational planning. This may start with helping him/her realize that each person has some degree of self-determination, the amount usually specified by the individual. Junior high school students often can be seen at this stage of development. Brief vocational biographies may motivate them as they enter the exploratory phase.

Counselors with clients who have been technologically displaced or who are physically handicapped may encounter similar problems in helping them understand what they can do to alter the unpleasant situation in which they find themselves. Being older, such clients may more likely have fixed values and self-concepts that are more rigid than those of adolescents. Career materials that help them become aware of alternative fields may be highly motivational. Such materials may provide the "handle" they need to start restructuring a situation previously considered hopeless and confusing.

INSTRUCTIONAL USES. Probably the most common function of career information in the counseling relationship is to inform or teach the client about the occupation being discussed. At this point, the work of the teacher and of the counselor are in close conjunction. The teacher, with primary concern for a group of students, must focus mainly on the general area; the counselor, with basic concern for one particular student, can concentrate on the specific areas in which that student expresses interest.

Obviously, the depth and scope of the instructional use of career materials will vary according to the individual and his/her needs and desires. The early adolescent may be more concerned at the moment with acquiring some grasp of the broad range of occupations and less interested in detailed study of one or two. Occupational briefs, abstracts, and surveys may be of more use with this client than the longer, more detailed monographs or books. As this individual continues exploratory activities, we can expect him/her to reach a point, probably much later, when he/she will want to peruse materials that held no interest before. At this point, the same kinds of items selected previously will not provide the help sought. He/she is now ready for a more intensive study of a specific field or two. Monographs and books, as well as visits to observe workers on the job, may be appropriate and useful now.

There are numerous opportunities throughout each student's educational career for the teacher and counselor to collaborate in fulfilling this function. Very often, the teacher's classroom activity can be utilized as a starting point that will lead to further exploration with the counselor. This follow-up can be developed either in individual counseling or in group counseling. Such movement from the classroom to the counseling room should be a natural and normal outgrowth of the relationship between teacher and counselor, providing the maximum opportunity to meet the individual needs of each student. The counselor can play a useful role as a resource person for the classroom activity, thus making the transition from classroom to counseling room easier.

The instructional use of career materials by the counselor provides many opportunities to help the counselee acquire some insight into the vocational choice process as a *process*. Clients can be easily helped, during early educational years, to develop the concept of tentative choice based on broad areas rather than specific occupation, and to see the impact of additional educational experiences, broadening personal observations, and family influences in modifying tentative plans. If the counselor can help the client with career materials that are appropriate and with the opportunity to discuss those materials, he/she can help immeasurably in the type of planning that ultimately results in self-determination.

Baer and Roeber include in this category the evaluative function of career information in counseling.[37] They define this function as checking the accuracy of the counselee's knowledge and understanding of an occupation or family of occupations. This is, of course, an important aspect of the instructional use of career materials. Obviously, a counselee can not make appropriate decisions when he/she either lacks needed information or possesses inaccurate information. In many situations, misconception or inaccuracy may be even more dangerous, since the client may act on it and become committed to a course of action that later is difficult to undo. The self-clarification aspect of counseling involves not only the client's understanding of personal strengths and weaknesses, but also an understanding of the present and anticipated environment. This latter area certainly includes the world of work. It is essential that the counselor have a broad and current knowledge of as much of the world of work as possible, if he/she is to help the counselee become aware of misconceptions and misunderstandings that might become a basis for wrong action. Having at hand adequate career materials that client and counselor can consider together is probably the most effective way to eliminate such misinformation. To be most useful, the materials must be up to date and include a range of materials to meet the varying needs of the clients using them.

ADJUSTIVE USES. The adjustive function of career information in the counseling process is used to help the counselee develop a more appropriate balance between self and tentative career plans. The "self" in the previous sentence includes all of the inputs that the individual brings to the vocational development process—abilities, limitations, resources, potential experiences, and other things. Those individual characteristics set certain limits within which career success and satisfaction are more likely to occur. If career goals demand abilities beyond the individual's range, the chances for success are limited.

Clear and precise evaluation of one's total self is not an easy process, and there are innumerable opportunities to go astray. It is not at all surprising that many, in fact probably all, people have less than an exact picture of themselves. In many cases, such "photographic distortions" within the self-concept not only may cause no difficulty in vocational choice, but also may actually increase the potential for success. On the other hand, many distortions of reality may be located in what can be called pressure points or friction points. These distortions can cause not only unhappiness and dissatisfaction, but disaster as well. The readjustive process is one of helping the individual deal with distortions that are likely to be troublesome.

Distortion of reality can occur in any aspect of the self-concept. Since it is natural for most of us to want to think as well of ourselves as possible, the danger of an inflated view of one's potential is easy to acquire. In terms of vocational planning, this view easily can lead the individual to select a goal that appears beyond the likelihood of attainment.[38] On the other hand, a person may underrate potential and thus select a goal that does not provide the challenge and opportunity that he/she is capable of matching.

Career materials will be invaluable to the counselor who is helping a client in the adjustive function, since accurate, up-to-date materials can provide the basic criteria against which the individual can measure self. Not only does the situation call for materials and experiences that clearly set forth the demands and requirements for success in the field, but also for materials and experiences that will help the client assess the psychological and sociological factors related to the occupation.

The counselor will find printed materials and experiential situations particularly useful since the client is more likely to be able to measure self against these standards than against information that the counselor might relate orally, because of the personal relationship between counselor and client. The client should be able to feel at all times that the counselor is "with" him/her, rather than "against" him/her. If the counselor draws on personal knowledge to quote standards or requirements, he/she assumes a position that the client may feel is one of authority and opposition. However, if he/she helps the client find appropriate information in reliable sources and experiences he/she remains "with" the client, and is thereby in a better position to interpret feelings and reactions.

DISTRIBUTIVE USES. The functions of career information discussed up to this point are concerned primarily with selecting a career field and preparing for that field; this function is basically focused on entrance into employment or the placement activity.

It is generally recognized that the principle of individual differences applies to occupational fields just as it does to people. In other words, there are tremendous differences between jobs or positions that carry the same occupational title. Although the basic skills and competencies required of high school English teachers are pretty much the same, there are likely to be wide differences in the specific work of any two English teachers. These differences may be due to differing standards in the two schools, differing facilities, students, communities, working conditions, administrators, colleagues, and numerous other factors. The counselor here is concerned with helping the client who is about to enter the world of work select a work situation compatible with needs, drives, and ambitions. He/she recognizes the truth in the old adage about "being in the right church but in the wrong pew." That is, a counselee might make an appropriate career choice in terms of all of the factors that should be considered, but find that all his/her careful planning has gone for naught if he/she selects a working situation that is incompatible. For example, the neophyte English teacher whose family background has been entirely in a large city and who completes professional preparation in a metropolitan university may find considerable difficulty in adjusting to a teaching assignment in a small rural school far from any urban area.

Career materials used in counseling as the client approaches the placement situation may help in recognizing problems of this type and thus avoiding what might prove to be a disappointing and disillusioning experience. No doubt, many workers have abandoned a career field toward which they have worked for many years because of an inappropriate placement. The loss to the individual and to society could have been avoided by considering possible problems at the proper time.

Each individual is unique, with an individual set of values, hopes, ambitions, worries, problems, and limitations. He/she brings these to the counseling session as well as to every other human encounter. It is reasonable, then, to expect that every counseling situation is unique—and so it is. Because of this unique characteristic, it is not possible to classify clients into discrete categories that can be easily labeled and for which prescriptive action can be identified. Each counselee must be recognized as an individual in his/her own right and dealt with by the counselor, using the best professional judgment and highest professional competencies.

Nevertheless, when clients are considered within a broad framework, many counselors, who are extensively involved in career counseling, find some recurrence of general problems. These recurrent themes or problems will be considered in this section.

Roughly categorized, the career choice problems that often bring clients to the counselor's office include:

1. Goal orientation problems
2. Motivational problems
3. Inability to operate the system

We will consider some of the problems that can be classified in each group and examine the role of the counselor in each situation. It is our intention only to introduce the topic at this point, since extensive discussion of counseling technique falls outside the scope of this book.

GOAL ORIENTATION PROBLEMS. In general, we can place in this category situations that involve the client's inability either to move toward an appropriate vocational choice, or having so moved, to retain confidence in the choice that has been made. Although rarely clear-cut, these situations are of three broad types. These include no choice, indecisive choice, and inappropriate choice.

Many clients, particularly during high school and early college years, seek out the vocational counselor's help because they think they should have a vocational goal and feel they have no clear commitment.[39] Many pressures bear on the client to produce this reaction; for example, parental encouragement to name a goal and selection by peers of vocational goals and educational plans. Our society is so vocationally oriented that it is difficult for the adolescent to recognize that this is a state through which almost everyone passes at one time or another. We commonly ask children what they expect to do when they grow up and accept with a smile the fantasy choice with which they respond. With increasing maturity the youth comes to recognize that the response given so glibly in childhood is a fantasy choice, and he/she feels dissatisfied, possibly insecure, when he/she is unable to face the question with a response that can be given with conviction. In looking at the world of work, he/she finds it so complex that there seems to be no way to proceed.

The counselor can develop some structure by helping him/her gain more understanding of self and of the world of work.[40] The first area involves continuing self-study and evaluation through the use of appropriate appraisal methods. The second aspect obviously involves career information. The materials and the methods used should be selected according to the individual's situation. Often one may find some consideration of the broad organization of the world of work helpful in making some sense out of this area. The counselor may want to use one of the classification systems such as Roe's two-dimensional system as a basis for guiding the client's preliminary perusal of the world of work. This may help in grasping the interrelationship of ability, educational preparation, and responsibility within the various occupational fields and may lead, in time, to the tentative identification of several broad areas that deserve further exploration. At this point, appropriate pamphlets and briefs may be considered together. Remembering that we are concerned here with a process and not an event, we would expect a considerable period of time, including several counseling sessions, to pass as the client gradually moves from indecision and uncertainty to preliminary, tentative choices and on, ultimately, to more clearly defined plans.

The use of computers and other media systems as proposed and discussed in Chapter 13 provides opportunity for the client to acquire career information and apply it within the context of the self concept.[41, 42] In this way, the client can proceed at his/her own pace to explore and make preliminary decisions. With such systems at his/her disposal, the counselor obviously can play a far different role in the decision-making process than is possible without such assistance.

Closely related to the problem of no vocational choice is the situation in which the counselee feels frustrated and uncertain because of indecision. He/she makes a tentative choice, but soon finds that he/she is vacillating between that field and another one that looks equally attractive. The insecurity that is felt, and the inability to discard either possibility, often brings him/her to the counselor for help. The counselor's role here, as in the first situation, is one of providing a climate in which the individual feels safe to look at self and at the world of work with sufficient opportunity to develop some integration. If the alternatives are so disparate that some choice must be made between them to prevent loss of educational time, it may be appropriate to consider both further self-evaluation and career information. Career materials will be useful if the client's knowledge of the fields is limited; they will be of limited help if the basic problem is reluctance or uncertainty in making a decision.

A third type of problem is the counselee who has selected what appears to be an inappropriate goal. This often takes the form of a client selecting a field for which he/she appears to lack prerequisite abilities. It is possible, of course, for the inappropriateness to be related to factors other than excessive ambition.

The problem of inappropriateness is especially vexatious, since the counselor must recognize that, in the last analysis, this diagnosis can rarely be made with certainty; the nearest that one can usually come is to use a modifier such as "apparent." Exact diagnosis, even if it were necessary, is not possible now and likely never will be, because our instruments for psychological evaluation are not precise enough to give us a specific and pinpointed description of the various characteristics of every individual. Secondly, the various occupations have enough individual difference to accommodate a wide range of human difference. Finally, we do not yet know enough about any occupational field to be able to list completely and exactly which personal qualifications are absolute essentials for success in that field. In most situations, the best that the counselor can do is to make a prediction based on actuarial data. Even if the figures indicate that the chances are only five in one hundred for success, the counselor must still face the fact that this particular client may be one of those five.

The counselor should recognize that the selection of an apparently inappropriate choice may be symptomatic of conflict either within the client or between the client and others. Such conflict may surface in career choices that either are over-demanding or far below identified abilities. Whether an outgrowth of attitude toward self or relationships with others, the client must resolve that situation before progress can be made in career planning. Career information may not be a significant aspect in working through this quandary unless the pressure leading to the choice is based on a misunderstanding of occupational requirements by the client, parents, or significant others. Even though this may be the case, the counselor should first help the client examine those basic relationships before assuming that sufficient insight into occupational demands will solve the problem.

The experienced counselor recognizes that clients sometimes may seek assistance in career planning when they really want help with a different problem. He/she must assume neither that there is another problem that must be ferreted out nor that the presenting problem is the only concern the client holds. The apparently inappropriate choice is more likely to suggest an underlying problem than the other two categories, but it cannot be assumed that a problem is lurking beneath the surface.

The counselor's responsibility is not to save the client from what appears to be a mistake. He/she does, however, have the responsibility to help the client obtain all the information needed to make the best possible decision. After that has been done, the client, as a free individual, has a right to whatever decision he/she makes.

Career materials often are important tools for the counselor in helping the client. They can supplement the information obtained from appraisal devices. The counselor's objective is not only to provide the climate in which the client freely can consider the problem, but also to assist in acquiring the necessary information, both about self and about occupational requirements, so that he/she will have the knowledge on which a decision can be based. Both aspects are crucial to the ultimate resolution of the problem that has brought him/her to the counselor. Unless he/she feels free to discuss self and the dilemma, he/she will not continue the counseling relationship. Unless he/she has access to the information needed, he/she is unlikely to arrive at a solution. Again, the amount and nature of the career materials must be determined according to the client's needs.

Arbitrary admission requirements have been established in many occupational fields. When a client is interested in one of these fields, it may occasionally be possible for the counselor to be more certain of an estimate of inappropriateness. For example, the boy who expresses interest in engineering, but cannot seem to grasp introductory algebra, can be shown the scope of mathematics in the preparation of engineers. Career materials thus can be utilized in the counseling relationship to help the client assess more accurately the requirements in the field being contemplated. The counselor must recognize that this confrontation sometimes is too great a threat for the client to handle. When this occurs, the person will respond with some type of inappropriate behavior. The counselor's task is to help him/her feel safe enough in the situation so that he/she can look at the problem and its ramifications and seek alternatives that offer more promise. The counselor's knowledge of career information is thus a vital resource at this point.

Just as a client can base actions and choices on faulty evaluation of self, so also can he/she operate from a base of misinformation about an occupational field. In fact, misinformation about so many occupations is so extensive that it is not at all surprising to find clients who are basing decisions on it.[43] Such faulty perception often is aided by our mass media. Television shows, magazine stories, and other materials, designed basically to entertain, also influence the attitudes and beliefs an individual may have toward various occupational fields. These influences can be either positive or negative, thus giving the client an unduly favorable attitude or an inclination of dislike.[44, 45]

Stereotypes and misconceptions held by family members or peers also may influence attitudes toward occupational fields.[46] Every counselor has encountered the boy and girl of modest ability whose parents have taught them that no respectable occupation can be entered without a college degree.

Stereotypes are easily developed on limited experience, a difficulty that can plague anyone—including the counselor. Since it often is easier to identify another person's misconceptions than one's own, the counselor should guard against restricting attitudes that may be held toward various occupations. If these exist, they are likely to influence the counselees with whom the counselor works.[47]

Accurate and comprehensive career information, not only of the printed variety, but also including occupational observations and visits to members of the occupation, may provide a base for the client and counselor to use in developing a broad, accurate view of the occupation. Pamphlets, films, and direct contact with workers in the field may be of especially great help to the counselor in helping the client to develop a broad view, rather than to feel that his/her stereotype is simply being opposed by another one of a different kind. The counseling session should provide a situation in which new facts and information can be dealt with freely and openly without any need for defensiveness.

The "self-clarification and self-determination" of Wrenn's definition and the "making of meaningful and informed choices consonant with his essential nature in those areas where choices are available to him" of Stefflre's definition underscore the counselor's responsibility to the client in assisting to obtain the breadth of information needed to make reasonable choices. Many clients who come to the counselor for help are attempting to make decisions on a base of information too narrow to permit an effective choice. In this situation, the client's greatest need may be for help in broadening perspective, based on information and resources that the counselor can help utilize. To a large extent, this lack of information is only another aspect of the problem of misinformation and can be handled by the counselor in similar ways.

MOTIVATIONAL PROBLEMS. In this category we can group three situations in which the client is uninterested in career planning. In the simplest case, the individual is immobilized because of inability to identify his/her own strengths and abilities, or to see how these are applicable to the world of work. This situation shades off into the "no choice" problem that we have already discussed. The "no choice" problem can be dealt with easily, as indicated earlier.

On the other hand, the cause of motivational problems probably is more deep-seated and such simple treatment is insufficient. Counselors are aware that underlying any client's stated problem may be physical, psychological, or cultural factors of serious importance. Motivational problems are most likely to be rooted in these areas. Until that basic situation is dealt with effectively, career materials will be of limited value to the client.

Sometimes the unmotivated client has a physical problem that needs attention. Often the client and the client's family can be totally unaware that a problem exists and needs attention. Lethargy can be produced by mononucleosis, incipient diabetes, chemical imbalance, malnutrition, or any of several other physical causes. Teachers, with regular contact with students, may be in a better position to observe the behavioral change that occurs with physical problems than the counselor, who may have only infrequent contact with a client. Any hint of a physical problem should lead to referral to the client's physician.

Similarly, psychological problems may impede the normal career development process of some adolescents and post-adolescents. Counseling or even therapy may be appropriate before attention to future planning can be effective.

We often overlook the likelihood of cultural or sociological conflict as a possible deterrent to career planning. America is a highly mobile society; large numbers of our population change residence each year. When a family moves from one setting to a relatively comparable location, the readjustment is usually made with minimum difficulty. Many families, however, may transfer to a setting totally different from anything previously experienced by family members. Any move from a rural to urban setting involves such change; if a regional transfer also is involved, the change becomes even more complex. The radical change in language, customs, and life-style may lead to cultural or sociological conflict.

Mobility and relocation are not the only factors of this type that can influence career development. Dissatisfaction among many young people with the family life-style often may lead to the search for an alternative style that is more compatible with the values held by the young person. A reaction against all work is not unusual while the individual sorts out what is important. Similarly, young people reared in family settings where ethnic or religious customs and values are viewed by the young person as restrictive also may be involved in conflict and uncertainty.

Farmer has described a situation of this type frequently encountered by counselors today.[48] She describes the home-career conflict faced by many girls and young women whose families have emphasized either that "woman's place is in the home" or narrow stereotypes of appropriate fields for women. Modern technological advances, economic realities, and social attitudes make these views anachronistic; nevertheless, the earlier attitudes are not easily overcome.

SYSTEM-RELATED PROBLEMS. The problems that fit into this category often may surface as the individual attempts to move from the exploratory and preparatory stages to actual employment. The problems have existed earlier but both client and counselor may easily overlook items that fall in this group. In general, we are placing here items that demonstrate either a misunderstanding or an inability on the part of the client to operate the procedures involved in moving into a job. The client may need the help of a counselor to identify what is wrong.

Simple examples of this type of problem are unsatisfactory appearance, attire, attitude, or behavior. High school or post-secondary students often may be unaware that employers' attitudes toward dress and personal appearance are crucial in employee selection. Although many preparatory programs include attention to employer requirements to prepare students for this transition, it is not a universal practice. Further, individuals who terminate preparation early may need the most help.

Further illustrations of this type of problem encountered by the counselor include unrealistic wage or working condition expectations, unwillingness to adapt to entry level requirements, insistence on a position beyond the individual's skill or preparation, and an ignorance of the realities of the work situation.

In many of these situations, the client can be helped by more personal counseling before career planning is actively pursued. In some situations, access to the various media systems will provide the client the undertanding of work that is needed to bring problems into proper perspective.

This brief consideration of the special problems brought to the vocational counselor should make it apparent that the conuselor can help many clients only if he/she has an extensive knowledge of the world of work, and especially, a broad knowledge of the resources through which the client can obtain the information that is crucial for the decisions and choices that confront the client. When a counselee comes to the counselor with a problem that involves only attitudes and behavior toward self or others, it often may be true that the counselor's responsibility in the situation is only to help the client clarify attitudes so that he/she understands self better. But when the problem can be solved only by acquiring a broader base of information and knowledge, as is almost always true in problems related to career development, the counselor has the added responsibility of helping the client acquire that knowledge. In the area with which this volume is concerned, this means that the counselor's role in self-clarification extends beyond the client to include the world in which he/she lives or can reasonably expect to live. A large part of this environment bears on a relationship to the world of work. How the counselor and client proceed to develop this broader perspective will depend on many of the factors previously discussed. Sometimes the best approach will be within the classroom with a teacher, sometimes in a group situation led either by a teacher or a counselor; at other times it will be within the counseling relationship, or perhaps through some combination of these approaches.

GENERAL FACTORS IN USING CAREER
INFORMATION IN COUNSELING

In this section, we will attempt to pull together some of the principles that apply to the use of career information in the counseling situation. These principles provide a review of some of the factors that bear on what is considered as appropriate usage of career information in counseling.

TIMING. Earlier literature has given considerable attention to the importance of timing in the use of career information. The significance of this factor is axiomatic. Assuming that the counseling process is a specialized aspect of the learning process, we can take the position that the general principles of learning also apply to counseling.

Sinick has emphasized three factors that relate to the use of career information with clients, all of which are essentially based on principles of learning.[49] He has proposed that timing, client readiness, and client participation are crucial to its successful use. He uses the term "timing" to show a relationship betwen individual diagnosis or evaluation and the use of career materials. Brayfield [50] has similarly emphasized that the use of career information always should be preceded by self-study and evaluation. Even though this position is generally sound, strict adherence to it will force the counselor into many unnecessary dilemmas, since there will be occasional counseling situations that call for the use of career information when consideration of the strengths and weaknesses of the client is not feasible or appropriate.

Rather than stressing the idea of self-study preceding the consideration of career material, it probably is more useful for the counselor to view these as two parallel and interacting activities that, over a period of time, are carried on more or less simultaneously. Emphasis on self-evaluation before utilization of career information implies an *event* approach to career development, rather than the *process* approach that we have considered. If we accept the *process* viewpoint, we must recognize that the developmental aspects of the total procedure will not always be identical for every individual. Forcing each counseling relationship to conform to a pattern unnecessarily and unwisely restricts the counselor from providing the maximum assistance to the client. The counselor must work from the position that both self-evaluation and career information are essential components in the total process, each to be utilized at the time and in the manner that will help the counselee develop the maximum amount of insight and understanding.

The principles of readiness and client participation proposed by Sinick, as mentioned above, have direct bearing on the use of career information. The counselor must evaluate continuously the extent to which the client is ready to handle the information and to grapple with the problems to be faced. As in any other learning situation, if the learner is confronted with a problem too soon, or if the exposure is unduly delayed, learning will be less effective than when the learner faces the problem with maximum readiness. Similarly, the active involvement of the learner in problem solving results in more effective learning.

AMOUNT OF HELP. The counselor often is caught between the dangers of providing too much help and failing to provide enough. On the one hand, he/she runs the risk that a paternalistic approach will stunt or reduce the problem-solving ability of the client, and thus retard the development of independent self-direction, which is the basic goal in counseling. On the other hand, the counselor who does not provide enough help forces the client to act only on those resources that he/she is able to find alone, thus developing a problem-solving technique that is faulty and inadequate. Either result is unsatisfactory for both counselor and client. Yet, the space between these two extremes is sometimes uncomfortably narrow, so the counselor must continually question personal actions to maintain an effective balance. The difficulty is further accentuated because the zone between these two extremes varies for each counselee; for example, what for one client would be a paternalistic approach for another client would be a limiting approach. Likewise, individual clients vary in their needs from time to time, so that what is minimum help at one session might be excessive at another.

The counselor must judge the amount of help needed by the client *at this time*. He/she must acquire the skill to reach this judgment within tolerable limits, providing just enough help to maximize the self-directing forces of the client.

In using career materials, the counselor must recognize that his/her knowledge of sources of information usually will be greater than the client's. He/she must draw on those sources in terms of the client's needs, attempting to provide enough help in finding and using materials so that the client can grapple successfully with the problem he/she faces.[51] Rarely will the counselor need to flood the client with a mass of material. Instead, adroit selection of limited materials or experiences usually will be more helpful.

SELECTION OF PROPER MATERIALS AND EXPERIENCES. Closely related to the amount of help provided to the client is the kind of help. A folder on a common occupation in a well-maintained career information resource center will include a broad spectrum of materials, all of which deal with that specific occupation. These materials probably extend from quite simple, brief abstracts to lengthy and detailed monographs. Each has a purpose and a range of clientele for which it is appropriate. Many materials in the file are probably outside the scope of any one counselee.

In addition to the printed matter available in the file drawer, the counselor must review the other types of materials and media systems available to assist the client. Are there appropriate films that should be viewed? What "experts" in that career field are near at hand? Would a visit to the employment site of a worker help develop insight? Can simulation help or would a try-out experience be of more use?

The counselor must, again, make several judgments as he/she assists a client in selecting appropriate materials for consideration. One basic factor is the nature of the problem the client faces *at this time*. If we accept the *process* viewpoint, we assume that the client is involved in an activity extending over time. The immediate problem is urgent; obviously, or he/she would not have come to the counselor for help. But it is erroneous to assume that the counselor and client must chart a lifetime career, reduce it to writing, and seal it with signatures in blood—all before the end of the day! Recognition that vocational development is accomplished step by step should help the counselor and the client focus on the present step.

Secondly, the counselor will need to judge the amount of motivation that is pushing the counselee toward a resolution of the concern. Materials and experiences will need to be selected with that judgment as a basis. Obviously, the client who is feeling the first spark of concern about career planning will be better served by less material than will the one who has reached the point at which he/she is seriously interested in an intensive exploration of one or two fields to which has been given considerable thought.

Thirdly, the counselor should keep in mind the reading level of the client and the ability to understand and absorb the materials. Where reading ability is limited, selection of easier printed materials is obviously essential. When age and experience of the client do not coincide with the reading level of the material, it also may be necessary for the counselor to provide extra assistance to the client in considering the information.

DISCUSSION OF MATERIALS AND EXPERIENCES WITH CLIENTS. Giving a client printed career materials to read and expecting the client to incorporate their contents into his/her thinking and behavior usually is unrealistic. Similarly, it probably is unwise to "assign" certain readings to the client with the expectation that he/she will return to "recite" what has been learned. It is more plausible to expect that career materials will be most helpful if the counseling relationship, in which the client feels that the counselor is with him/her in feeling and understanding, is extended to include their use. There is no reason why client and counselor cannot study and consider printed materials together as co-workers, seeking the information needed in the problem-solving process. This process can include a wide range of activities, such as reading materials together, or to one another, discussing information, and comparing statements from different sources. The counselor's aim must be to help the client acquire the needed information.

Computerized systems (such as those discussed in Chapter 13) that will supplement the activities of the counselor promise to be particularly useful in helping the client to acquire basic career information and to assimilate it within a meaningful frame of reference. Systems already in operation have demonstrated that it is possible to provide the client this assistance at the cognitive or intellectual level. Computerized techniques that deal effectively with the emotional or affective level have not yet been developed.

Similarly, exposing the client to certain appropriate experiences does not routinely result in the acquisition of the understanding and insights desired. Discussion between client and counselor is necessary to clarify observations, reinforce concepts, and plan for further experiences. Often these discussions must occur over time in order to help the client derive maximum benefits from the activities in which he/she has participated.

The total counseling process is concerned with the acquisition of information and understanding about the client's self and the environment, present and future, so that he/she can develop the insights needed for self-determination. The use of career materials and experiences in the counseling interview should provide opportunity for the client to express feelings and attitudes toward those materials. The vocational choice process is not conducted solely on the intellectual plane. The client's emotions are essential parts of him/her, and their expression within the counseling relationship will help the client understand them as a part of self. Feelings toward statements or viewpoints expressed in career materials will similarly help him/her grow in self-understanding.

Finally, in considering the use of career materials and experiences in counseling, we must recognize that the professional judgment of the counselor is a necessary ingredient to the counseling relationship. Although there are many tools and techniques used by the counselor, the selection of the appropriate one at any given moment must be based on professional judgment, which has to be built on professional competence and a sincere interest in the client.

IMPLEMENTING CAREER PLANS

Time and again our discussion has shown that the development of career education concepts will change the role of the classroom teacher. It also will change the duties and activities of the counselor. One major criticism of today's educational system, according to career education supporters, is that the educational structure gives major attention to preparing the student for the next step in the educational process. This attitude fails to recognize that once school-leaving age is attained, or shortly thereafter, many students discontinue classroom learning and enter the world of work. Thus, continually fewer individuals are being served by this focus on the next educational step.

Counselors in educational settings often are guilty of the same preoccupation with students who are preparing for the next educational step. In many high schools, for example, counselors devote an inordinate amount of time arranging student conferences with college representatives, administering college admissions examinations, helping students learn about colleges, helping students complete college admissions forms and requests for financial aid, and writing letters of recommendation to the various colleges. Even though these activities serve a minor portion of the student body, they may require most of the counselor's available time.

The National Vocational Guidance Association, as long ago as 1937, defined vocational guidance as the process of assisting an individual to select, prepare for, enter, and advance in a vocation.[52] In the intervening years, most counselors have concentrated their attention on the first two parts of that definition. Career education now requires that appropriate attention be given to the last two parts of that definition.

Hansen and Tennyson have proposed a new emphasis on career management that would involve the counselor in a consultative role with the client on a life span basis.[53] In this proposal, the client's responsibility to direct and plan his/her future is central. Further, the concept that each person can succeed and be satisfied by many different occupations is emphasized, thus encouraging client choice and the opening of broader options. Such a position clearly stresses the continuing involvement of the counselor far beyond the planning and preparing stages of career choice.

In Chapter 10, we considered both educational and employment placement activities. It is no longer sufficient for the counselor to be familiar with these services so that the client can be properly referred. The counselor also must become more involved in this process, not necessarily taking on additional functions, but certainly assuring that the client is properly served if this phase is handled by others. In many situations, the counselor will be the one to walk this extra mile with the client.

Whether we prefer to deal with the concepts of vocational guidance, career development, career education, or career management, we see in all the common factor of the counselor involved in the lifelong career of the client. At almost every point, career materials or experiences will be used by the counselor, the teacher, and most of all by the client.

NOTES

1. K. B. Hoyt, R. N. Evans, E. F. Mackin, and G. L. Mangum, *Career Education: What It Is and How To Do It* (Salt Lake City, Utah: Olympus Publishing Company, 1972), pp. 90–92.
2. D. Parnell, "The Career Cluster Approach in Secondary Education," in K. Goldhammer and R. E. Taylor (eds.), *Career Education: Perspective and Promise* (Columbus, Ohio: Charles E. Merrill Publishing Company, 1972), pp. 55–61.
3. Hoyt, *et al.*, *op. cit.*
4. D. Brown, S. Feit, R. Forestandi, "Career Education: The Counselor's Role," *The School Counselor*, vol. 20, no. 3 (January, 1973), pp. 193–196.
5. E. R. Gerler, Jr., "Career Education Workshops: A Follow-up Role for Counselors," *The School Counselor*, vol. 22, no. 4 (March, 1975), pp. 250–254.
6. T. A. Cleary, "New Directions for Career Planning," in L. McClure and C. Buan (eds.), *Essays on Career Education* (Portland, Oregon: Northwest Regional Educational Laboratory, 1973), pp. 39–53.
7. S. P. Marland, Jr., *Career Education* (New York: McGraw-Hill Book Company, 1974), pp. 172–186.
8. K. B. Hoyt, "Career Education and Counselor Education," *Counselor Education and Supervision*, vol. 15, no. 1 (September, 1975), pp. 6–11.
9. C. D. Kehas, "From the Editor," *Counselor Education and Supervision*, vol. 15, no. 1 (September, 1975), p. 2.
10. D. E. Super, *The Psychology of Careers* (New York: Harper and Row, Publishers, 1957), p. 87.
11. A. Pruitt, "Teacher Involvement in the Curriculum and Career Guidance," *Vocational Guidance Quarterly*, vol. 17, no. 3 (March, 1969), pp. 189–193.
12. W. W. Tennyson, T. A. Soldahl, and C. Mueller, *The Teacher's Role in Career*

Development, revised edition, (Washington, D.C.: National Vocational Guidance Association, 1965).

13. *Ibid.*, p. 85.

14. L. A. Johnson and R. Martin, "A Careers Course," *Personnel and Guidance Journal*, vol. 51, no. 10 (June, 1973), pp. 733–734.

15. D. G. Andersen and A. A. Binnie, "Effects of a Group Vocational Guidance Class with Community College Students," *Vocational Guidance Quarterly*, vol. 20, no. 2 (December, 1971), pp. 123–128.

16. C. C. Healy, "Toward A Replicable Method of Group Career Counseling," *Vocational Guidance Quarterly*, vol. 21, no. 3 (March, 1973), pp. 214–221.

17. C. J. Daane, *Vocational Exploration Group: Theory and Research* (Washington: Manpower Administration, Dept. of Labor, 1972).

18. *Career Education Curriculum Guide* (Indianapolis, Ind.: Indiana State Department of Public Instruction, 1973), p. 184.

19. *Career Planning Program*, grades 8–11 (Boston: Houghton-Mifflin Company, 1974).

20. *Career Planning Program*, grades 12–13 (Boston: Houghton-Mifflin Company, 1974).

21. *Career Education Guide* (Chicago: Science Research Associates, 1973).

22. H. S. Belman and B. E. Shertzer, *My Career Guidebook*, 2nd edition (Beverly Hills, California: Bruce Publishers, 1974).

23. H. G. Pearson, "Career Fields in Industry for the High School Graduate," *Vocational Guidance Quarterly*, vol. 18, no. 2 (December, 1969), pp. 87–90.

24. B. B. Johnson, "An Occupational Information Center for Education-Industry," *Vocational Guidance Quarterly*, vol. 18, no. 1 (September, 1969), pp. 41–44.

25. C. G. Wrenn, *Student Personnel Work in College* (New York: The Ronald Press Company, 1951), p. 60.

26. B. Stefflre, *Theories of Counseling* (New York: McGraw-Hill Book Co., 1965), p. 15.

27. Leona E. Tyler, *The Work of the Counselor*, 1953 edition. Reprinted by permission of Prentice-Hall, Inc., Englewood Cliffs, New Jersey. Pp. 14–19.

28. ———, *The Work of the Counselor*, 3rd edition (New York: Appleton-Century-Crofts, Inc., 1969), pp. 67–72.

29. Stefflre, *op. cit.*, pp. 23–25.

30. C. Buehler, *Der Menschliche Lebenslauf als Psychologisches Problem* (Leipzig: Hertzel, 1933).

31. D. E. Super, *The Psychology of Careers* (New York: Harper and Row, Publishers, 1957), p. 72.

32. R. C. Nelson, "Early Versus Developmental Vocational Choice," *Vocational Guidance Quarterly*, vol. 11, no. 1 (Autumn, 1962), pp. 23–27.

33. ———, "Knowledge and Interests Concerning Sixteen Occupations Among Elementary And Secondary School Students," unpublished Doctoral dissertation (Athens, Ohio: Ohio University, 1962).

34. M. P. Sanborn, "Vocational Choice, College Choice, and Scholastic Success of Superior Students," *Vocational Guidance Quarterly*, vol. 13, no. 3 (Spring, 1965), pp. 161–168.

35. D. H. Pritchard, "The Occupational Exploration Process: Some Operational Inplications," *Personnel and Guidance Journal*, vol. 40, no. 8 (April, 1962), pp. 674–680.

36. M. A. Kiesow, "A Professional Approach to the Information Function in Counselor Education," *Counselor Education and Supervision,* vol. 2, no. 3 (Spring, 1963), pp. 131–136.
37. M. F. Baer and E. C. Roeber, *Occupational Information,* 1st edition (Chicago: Science Research Associates, Inc., 1951), pp. 466–470.
38. A. G. Rezler, "Counseling the Marginal College-Bound Student," *Vocational Guidance Quarterly,* vol. 13, no. 2 (Winter, 1964), pp. 115–19.
39. D. E. Super, "Goal Specificity in the Vocational Counseling of Future College Students," *Personnel and Guidance Journal,* vol. 43, no. 2 (October, 1964), pp. 127–134.
40. D. C. Beardslee and D. D. O'Dowd, "Students and the Occupational World," in R. N. Sanford (ed.), *The American College* (New York: John Wiley & Sons, Inc., 1962), pp. 597–626.
41. F. Minor, R. Myers, and D. Super, "An Experimental Computer-Based Educational and Career Exploration System," *Personnel and Guidance Journal,* vol. 47, no. 6 (February, 1969), pp. 564–569.
42. D. Tiedeman and G. Dudley, *Information System for Vocational Decisions* (Cambridge, Mass.: Harvard Graduate School of Education, Project Report No. 9, 1967).
43. L. G. Lukens, "The Nurse Stereotype Must Go," *Vocational Guidance Quarterly,* vol. 13, no. 2 (Winter, 1964), pp. 95–99.
44. W. J. Dipboye and W. F. Anderson, "Occupational Stereotypes and Manifest Needs of High School Students," *Journal of Counseling Psychology,* vol. 8, no. 4 (Winter, 1961), pp. 296–304.
45. D. H. Blocher and R. A. Schutz, "Relationship Among Self-Descriptions, Occupational Stereotypes, and Vocational Preferences," *Journal of Counseling Psychology,* vol. 8, no. 4 (Winter, 1961), pp. 314–317.
46. R. A. Schutz and D. H. Blocher, "Self-Concepts and Stereotypes of Vocational Preferences," *Vocational Guidance Quarterly,* vol. 8, no. 4 (Summer, 1960), pp. 241–244.
47. G. G. Gonyea, "Dimensions of Job Perceptions," *Journal of Counseling Psychology,* vol. 8, no. 4 (Winter, 1961), pp. 305–313.
48. H. S. Farmer, "Helping Women to Resolve the Home-Career Conflict," *Personnel and Guidance Journal,* vol. 49, no. 10 (June, 1971), pp. 759–801.
49. D. Sinick, "Occupational Information in the Counseling Interview," *Vocational Guidance Quarterly,* vol. 14, no. 4 (Summer, 1956), pp. 145–149.
50. A. H. Brayfield, "Dissemination of Occupational Information," *Occupations,* vol. 30, no. 6 (March, 1951), pp. 411–413.
51. E. Ginzberg, "Guidance—Limited or Unlimited," *Personnel and Guidance Journal,* vol. 38, no. 9 (May, 1960), p. 712.
52. Report of the Committee of the National Vocational Guidance Association, "The Principles and Practices of Educational and Vocational Guidance," *Occupations,* vol. 15, no. 8 (May, 1937), pp. 772–778.
53. L. S. Hansen and W. W. Tennyson, "Career Management Model for Counselor Involvement," *Personnel and Guidance Journal,* vol. 53, no. 9 (May, 1975), pp. 638–645.

16

Realigning Career Goals

In modern western civilization, we think of adolescence and early adulthood as the period in which the transition from preparation to employment occurs. The theories of vocational development, which we considered in Chapter 2, without exception are based on the premise that this transition is a process that begins in early childhood and extends beyond age sixteen, when the individual enters the world of work, encounters a variety of tryout experiences, and establishes himself/herself in a career. He/she proceeds with this career pattern with various degrees of "success," hopefully achieving satisfaction and recognition, but possibly only managing to "keep even," and in some cases experiencing failure and frustration. The long maintenance period gradually shades off into retirement and withdrawal from work "to enjoy the rewards so richly deserved."

This fairly common pattern can be observed in certain parts of our society with frequent regularity. It is, however, by no means a universal model. Delay or readjustment often occur; their causes are numerous, and any one of them can require extensive revision in the pattern just described.

Some of the more obvious reasons for delay or postponement of career plans include the following:

MILITARY SERVICE. Selective service and military obligation have interrupted and postponed preparation for and entrance into civilian careers for a large number of youth during the past three decades. The young person who elects to enter military service generally faces at least a three-year interruption of civilian life. If he/she elects to apply for a special branch of service or for a special type of assignment within that branch, he/she may well be committing oneself for four or five years, or even longer.

MARRIAGE AND CHILD REARING. Super has referred to the double-track career pattern followed by many women.[1] In this situation, women enter work after completing their education and remain there until the birth of their first child; then they customarily withdraw from employment until the youngest child is well along in school . After this, they again return to employment until they reach retirement. Many young women modify this pattern in a variety of ways, perhaps most frequently by marrying earlier and either interrupting their education or completing their education without moving on to employment.

LIMITATION OF OPPORTUNITY. Although we like to picture our society as an open one providing each person with maximal opportunities for self-actualization, this is not true for everyone. Poverty, cultural or social disadvantage, isolation, institutional confinement, physical or intellectual deficiency, disease, or disability may limit the individual's opportunities. Any one of these factors may prevent the individual from acquiring a minimal education, or making the transition from education to employment.

PERSONAL CIRCUMSTANCES. Many factors that postpone or impede career plans can be placed under this miscellaneous heading. Problems of health or financial circumstances may cause unplanned interruptions. Family situations such as an ill or invalid parent may cause a loyal daughter to "stay home" and provide the needed care. "Helping out" temporarily in the family business or farm may interrupt or postpone other career plans.

Similarly, a variety of reasons may necessitate revision and readjustment of activities and goals in mid-career. Some of the more obvious causes of such realignment include the following:

(a) *Physical Disability.* Changes in the physical condition of the person may force a change in career. Such physical change can be a sudden event brought about by accident or unexpected serious illness. It may be a gradual deterioration that reduces the person's physical stamina or strength to a point below that required for continuation in the position.

(b) *Psychological Change.* Unwillingness by the individual to continue in a situation that the person finds onerous or distasteful may cause an adjustment in career plans. Such withdrawal may occur because the demands are too great, the competition too pressing, or because a previously challenging activity has become routine and monotonous. Thus, the person may be seeking an easier, more leisurely situation, or just the opposite, may desire new, more exacting challenges.

(c) *Personal Factors.* Changes in the individual's family or personal situation can necessitate major readjustment in the career pattern. For example, the acquisition of additional dependents such as more children, handicapped or elderly parents, or similar obligations may require greater economic return. Early retirement may lead an individual to seek a new career field. Career military personnel may retire after twenty years of service; other occupational fields offer similar opportunities.[2] A person may have met the requirements for retirement eligibility by the late thirties or early forties and wish to seek a new field in which to be productive. The death of a spouse may change established life patterns and cause a widow to seek entrance into work.

(d) *Technological Change.* We considered the impact of automation and technical change in Chapter 5. Obviously, the abolition of certain occupations by technical improvements or by shifts in consumer demand means that large numbers of workers must move to new employment.

Any of the factors discussed above can result in major change in the life style of the individual and can produce the need for revising career patterns. At one time, society tended to be profligate with its human resources and callous in accepting any responsibility for assisting individuals whose abilities or experiences prevented self-sufficiency. It was just assumed that the feudal baron would care for his serfs and the factory owner would find some simpler task when the faithful worker could no longer meet the demands of the job. In more recent years, society has admitted that this is not sufficient, and increasing attention has been given to provide more adequate assistance not only to meet minimum human needs for food, lodging, and clothing, but also to recognize and meet the needs for participation and involvement in productive activity.

NEWER CONCEPTS OF REHABILITATION

Each factor described above creates special problems in the career development of the individual that may necessitate assistance beyond that traditionally available in the school. Most people would agree that the teacher and school counselor, by virtue of their setting and their special preparation, are best situated to provide maximum assistance in the career development of the child and adolescent. They also are often at a disadvantage in dealing with the kinds of special problems listed above.

The past decade has seen a rapid growth in agencies and services designed to focus on these special problem areas. In some situations, the agencies can and do work closely with the educational structure. In other situations, more can be accomplished by maintaining separate operations that complement each other. Increasingly, society must recognize that career development is a long-range continuous process that is not and cannot be terminated with completion of vocational preparation. Continuing services must be provided for those who have been delayed in the process or who must make some sizable readjustment if we really have concern for the goal of self-actualization.

The term *rehabilitation* is rapidly being broadened in concept and now is applied to the overcoming of many kinds of disabling human problems, including physical disability, mental illness, mental retardation, alcoholism, drug addiction, undereducation, delinquency, and crime.[3] Specifically, rehabilitation may refer to special services such as education, physical functioning, psychological adjustment, social adaptation, vocational capabilities, or recreational activities. The term has recently been broadened to include the services needed by people who have been caught in the web of poverty, undereducation, and prejudice.

Vocational rehabilitation traditionally has referred to the process of returning a handicapped worker to a state of reemployability. In at least two major ways this concept is unnecessarily narrow. First, it implies that a person must have acquired certain marketable skills before eligibility for help can be established; secondly, the idea of employability as a product of the service may make ineligible for help those for whom employability may be uncertain or unlikely. Fortunately, there has been some movement toward reducing both of these restrictions, so that persons with handicaps who have never worked may qualify and even those for whom assistance may result in greater self-esteem and self-satisfaction without clear certainty of employment may be included. More recognition is now being given to the impact of disability on family life as well as on the individual. This has placed greater emphasis on the need for independence, self-regard and integration within the total society rather than on separation and isolation from it.

The federal–state relationship in rehabilitation services permits a certain degree of flexibility in state programs, but at the same time establishes some amount of parallel structure. State laws covering rehabilitation programs must accept terminology that conforms to that used in the federal legislation. Thus, each state accepts a common definition of "eligibility" for rehabilitation. This definition includes:

> (a.) "Eligible" or "eligibility," when used in relation to an individual's qualification for vocational rehabilitation services, refers to a certification that (1) a physical or mental disability is present; (2) a substantial handicap to employment exists; and (3) vocational rehabilitation services may reasonably be expected to render the individual fit to engage in a gainful occupation.

This definition does broaden access to such service by eliminating the necessity of establishing the loss of a previously existing skill. Nevertheless, parts 2 and 3 of the definition clearly retain the job-oriented purpose of vocational rehabilitation. A narrow interpretation of these two aspects can be used to withhold services from many individuals who could benefit from such assistance ever though ultimate placement in employment might be highly uncertain.

A somewhat more generous definition of rehabilitation has been proposed by Hutchison.[4] He states:

Rehabilitation may be understood to be the strengthening of the disabled person to the maximum individually attainable degree of physical, mental, social, occupational and economic efficiency.

Allan emphasized the broad approach to the concept when he said:[5]

If we are to define rehabilitation properly in the light of its objectives rather than applied services, rehabilitation is making a person aware of his potential and then providing him with the means of attaining that potential.

These definitions clearly move the process of rehabilitation into the general frame of reference on which this volume is based. The goals of career counseling and rehabilitation are synonymous. It is, thus, totally logical to accept the need for special services to overcome special problems encountered by some individuals as they move toward the attainment of their potential.

Dilley has underscored the lack of general public understanding of rehabilitation agencies and services.[6] He administered a questionnaire asking for information about existing rehabilitation services to service club members in two Wisconsin counties. The results showed very limited understanding of the existing agencies and the services they performed. A public education effort was undertaken in one county over a six-month period with a retest of the group after that time. Unfortunately, little change in understanding was observed.

Usdane has provided summary information of those rehabilitated through state and federal efforts in a single year. He lists the following characteristics of that group:

Age: 30 of every 100 were age 45 and over.
       20 of every 100 were under age 20.
       50 of every 100 were between 20 and 44.
Sex: 30 of every 100 were women.
Education: 40 of every 100 had never been to high school.
               7 of every 100 had at least one year of college.
Major disability: 36 of every 100 had either an amputation or an orthopedic impairment.
               12 of every 100 were mentally ill.
               10 of every 100 were blind or visually handicapped.
               7 of every 100 had a hearing or speech impairment.
               6 of every 100 were mentally retarded.
               5 of every 100 had a cardiac defect.
Earnings at acceptance: 80 of every 100 had no earnings when accepted.
Dependents: 13 of every 100 had 1 dependent.
               9 of every 100 had 2 dependents.

8 of every 100 had 3 dependents.

16 of every 100 had 4 or more dependents.

Major occupation following rehabilitation:

24 of every 100 entered skilled or semiskilled occupations.

20 of every 100 entered service occupations.

16 of every 100 entered sales or clerical occupations.

8 of every 100 entered professional or managerial occupations.

7 of every 100 entered unskilled occupations.

7 of every 100 entered agricultural occupations.

3 of every 100 entered sheltered workshops.

Figures for subsequent years can be presumed to be approximately comparable. These data serve as a powerful argument in support of the need for adequate rehabilitation services. For example, more than two out of every three cases are younger than 45 years of age; therefore, they can be expected to have twenty or more years of useful work life if rehabilitation successfully returns them to employment. More than four out of every five completing rehabilitation entered employment in the regular economy.

It is important to distinguish between disability and handicap. Almost every person has a disability of one sort or another. For example, so many people wear eye glasses in our society that one seldom thinks of them as having a disability. If a disability is severe or extensive enough to limit the individual's employment opportunities, we may refer to him/her as being vocationally handicapped.[8]

Obviously, disability may appear at birth or any time thereafter. One can expect that a number of youngsters within the school suffer from disabilities that may be handicaps. Because these youth face special problems in making vocational plans, they may need special help in either developing or executing realistic career objectives.[9] Disability also can occur any time during adulthood and result in handicaps that may require special services in readjustment.

ECONOMICS OF DISABILITY AND DISADVANTAGE

In simplest terms, if even one individual has a vocational handicap that restricts his/her ability to participate effectively in the world of work, there is economic loss to both individual and family as well as to society generally. In addition, there is likely to be even greater social and psychological loss suffered by the individual because of how he/she sees self and how others see and treat him/her. When one has some grasp of the extent of disability, the economic and personal loss appears gigantic. The National Health Survey estimated that at any given time in the fiscal years of 1960 and 1961, more than 40 percent of the population in this country was suffering from potentially disabling chronic diseases or impairments.[10]

Most of these people did not report handicap or a condition interfering with activity. Nevertheless, of this group, more than ten per cent did report such handicap. The report indicates that at that time, more than 14 million people suffered major activity limitation. One should note that this study focused on health factors and did not consider disabling factors of a social, educational, or other nonphysical nature. Thus, we must conclude that the extent of handicap must exceed this figure considerably. The Rehabilitation Service Administration indicates that a goal of 250,000 successful cases of rehabilitation yearly still would fall somewhat short of the annual number who join the handicapped group.

Conley has pointed out that many disabled people successfully overcome the vocational limitations of a physical handicap but that many individuals are confronted with the compounding effect of physical handicap, educational handicap, and racial discrimination.[11] He points out that the most obvious losses incurred by society are reduction of national income and the expenditure of resources for special medical, custodial, and nursing care. The consequences borne by the individual and his/her family are: reduced after-taxes income, reduced services within the family, the costs of special care or services that they must support, and the effect of the disability on the psychic well-being of the individual. The rest of society also suffers loss since they face the loss of taxes that would be paid by the individual, plus the expenditure of taxes or charitable funds that are used to provide special services to the handicapped.

Conley has estimated that about 4.4 million persons are excluded from the working population due to physical or mental limitations. Of these, about three million are under age 65. Another 300,000 are unemployable because of disability.[12] Thus, about eight per cent of the population is nonproductive. These figures are probably conservatively low since large groups of disabled individuals were excluded from the survey on which these estimates were based. In addition to these figures, the economic loss must include figures for reduced income because some people were not able to work up to their effective levels. Conley estimates that another three and a half million people fall into this catgory.

With this many individuals involved, the humanitarian arguments for effective rehabilitation are at least as strong as those on which many other social programs are based, such as unemployment compensation, old age retirement and survivors' benefits, medical assistance, and others. Conley has recognized the humanitarian aspect accompanying provision of necessary rehabilitation services in these words:[13]

> How can we set a value on the self-respect of a rehabilitant able at last to support himself and his family, or in the elimination of his despair, frustration, bitterness, and grief—felt more perhaps because of the effect of his disability on his family than on himself? No longer are the friends and families of rehabilitants compelled to stand sadly

and sympathetically by, desiring but perhaps not able to help, or perhaps embittered at the burden thrust upon them. Even strangers, humanitarian enough to feel uncomfortable in the presence of the indigent disabled, or in the mere knowledge of their existence, now feel relief as this burden is lifted from their consciences.

If one considers only the economic aspect of disability and rehabilitation, the advantages accruing from effective services are at once apparent. For example, in the single year of 1971, approximately 770 million dollars were added to the national economy by the earnings of the 291,272 individuals who had been rehabilitated in the previous fiscal year. The average weekly earnings for this group at the time they entered a rehabilitation program was $15.95. Upon completion of the rehabilitation program, their weekly average earnings increased nearly 4½ times.

In fiscal year 1973, a total of $729,655,641 was expended for rehabilitation services. During that year, 360,726 individuals were declared rehabilitated. The average cost per rehabilitation was $2,023. For fiscal 1974, the figures again are comparable. Total expenditures amounted to $809,633,614, and 1,201,661 people received services. In that year, 345,288 individuals were declared rehabilitated at an average cost of $2,345 each. An additional 16,000 persons were rehabilitated under the provisions of two closely related programs, the Beneficiary Rehabilitation Program and the Supplemental Security Income Program. Thus, it would be fair to consider total rehabilitations as exceeding 361,000 people.

The federal agency, Rehabilitation Services Administration, estimates that each person rehabilitated repays the cost of that rehabilitation in taxes in about three years after the program is completed. As previously indicated, the average age of rehabilitation clients suggests that each works many more than three years.

The funding for each state's Vocational Rehabilitation agency is provided on a shared basis. The formula used is a four-to-one ratio; in other words, of every $100 spent for rehabilitation services, the state supplies $20 and the federal government $80. The state first must indicate the availability of its funds, and then the federal dollars are allocated. In spite of the generous matching formula, many dollars authorized for rehabilitation remain unexpended because some states do not appropriate enough to permit claiming their full entitlement. Nevertheless, in the half century of the program's life, more than three million individuals have been returned to productive employment.

CAREER PLANNING NEEDS OF SPECIAL GROUPS

If we accept the broad definition of rehabilitation as the process of making a person aware of his/her potential and then providing the means of attaining that potential, we can see at once that vocational rehabilitation may be a crucial service for several large groups. For the most part, these are groups whose career development has been interfered with, necessitating realignment of plans. These groups include the physically handicapped, school dropouts, welfare and poverty clients, inmates of correctional facilities, veterans, wives or widows entering the labor market late, and senior citizens.[14, 15] Career planning for these groups is different from that of the usual maturing adolescent. Detailed consideration of career planning and counseling in rehabilitation requires a volume in itself. Our goal here is simply to accent those commonalities in the use of career information whether the counselor works in an educational setting with normal adolescents and young adults, or whether he/she is employed in another agency that focuses on one of the groups encountering special career problems. In all cases, the client needs help in developing understanding of self and of the world of work, and of how the two can be advantageously integrated to the mutual satisfaction of the individual and society.

In counseling with the physically handicapped, the counselor needs knowledge about work beyond that required in counseling most groups. His/her knowledge will be crucial in identifying occupational activities that can be performed by an individual whose physical disability limits some or many actions. Physically disabled people encounter a lengthy sequence of problems when they attempt to place themselves vocationally. Almost inevitably, the physical handicap, by definition, restricts the number of vocational opportunities. Additionally, the person encounters the public stereotype that equates certain types of disability with specific occupations; for example, blind people manufacture and sell brooms. Some employment possibilities will be closed by the requirements of the work or the possible danger to the disabled person or fellow workers.

Successful vocational rehabilitation of a physically handicapped person involves placement in a position in which he/she can compete with nonhandicapped workers as though no disability existed. Probably no job demands the total physical capacity of a normal human being. In fact, most occupations require only a very limited portion of it. Occupations requiring only physical abilities that the handicapped individual still possesses may provide an area in which he/she successfully can work and compete.[16] A consideration of the occupations demanding only abilities that the individual possesses to an extent greater than most other people may even put him/her at an advantage. For example, if a certain job requires the worker to work only at a desk, where one remains throughout the work period, the ability or inability to walk is irrelevant to the performance of the work. Such an illustration is, of course, an oversimplification. Successful placement of the physically handicapped requires an extensive study of the abilities, interests, ambitions, and motivations of the individual and an extensive and thorough knowledge of the world of work.

The counselor of the physically handicapped also needs special medical knowledge in order to understand the physical impact of most disabilities. The counselor also must be equipped to deal with the emotional problems that often are produced by physical disability and to help the client deal with these problems in preparing to work. Thoroman has stressed the greater likelihood of inconsistency between desire and ability for the physically handicapped.[17]

The persistent raising of educational standards as part of employer hiring requirements places the school dropout under constantly increasing disadvantage. The lack of a school diploma is often sufficient to bar him/her from many job opportunities in which actual job requirements may be well within his/her scope. When one adds to limited educational background the additional problems of emotional handicap and cultural and social deprivation that often accompany school withdrawal, it is easy to recognize the need that this group has for rehabilitation services.

One recent report of rehabilitation services for school dropouts emphasizes the need for pre-employment vocational experience.[18] The unsatisfactory educational experience coupled with other concomitant factors often make it impossible for the dropout to meet the basic job-holding requirements of punctuality, regularity, persistence, reasonable inter-personal relations, and acceptance of direction and supervision. Before there is any possibility of success at work, the individual must be taught how to meet these requirements that may be totally unrelated to the skills involved in the work. Using sheltered workshops or similar training situations may be necessary before any attempt at job placement can be made. Special training programs, such as those considered in Chapter 9, may be useful for the acquisition of such characteristics. The counselor needs extensive knowledge of such training situations as well as special skills in dealing with alienated and hostile youth whose life often has been bitter and frustrating.

The counselor who deals with welfare or impoverished clients often is confronted with problems similar to those met by the counselor of the school dropout, except that time has increased the depth of the clients' frustration and alienation. Often, this group suffers from multiple disabilities that may be educational and social as well as physical and mental.[19, 20]

Several recent reports have focused on the need for special services to overcome the disability encountered by this group.[21, 22, 23] McWhorter and Lamonte point out that about 75 per cent of their welfare group had a physical or mental disability and in practically all cases there were emotional disturbances. Often, such clients have given up hope of independent self-support for themselves and their families. The use of special vocational training situations along with special courses or tutorial help has consistently produced results in ultimate job placement. Such projects often require team efforts of social case workers, vocational counselors, and other specialists. The counselor often needs special knowledge of training situations that are appropriate for the individual, or he/she must have the initiative to establish such programs.[24]

Inmates of correctional and penal institutions often have been labeled as society's forgotten men and women. The extension of rehabilitation services to this group is occurring gradually. The Comprehensive Employment and Training Act, which we considered in Chapter 9, is an example of specific legislation that recognizes the needs of this group and that provides assistance and training to increase employability. CETA, of course, focuses on offenders who have "paid their debt to society" and have been released. Forward-looking institutions recognize that there is no valid reason for such rehabilitation to be delayed until the person is released; consequently, many correctional facilities now employ rehabilitation-type counselors who help inmates make educational and vocational plans and who arrange training programs that can be initiated during the period of incarceration.

The problems extant among inmates are comparable to problems encountered by the groups we have considered in the paragraphs above. Inmates, too, often have physical, mental, or emotional disabilities, often compounded by social maladjustment, cultural deprivation, and confinement. Upon release, they often can expect reentrance into society to be complicated not only by these factors, but also by commonly held attitudes of suspicion and distrust of anyone with a criminal record. The counselor must deal with all of these complexities. Special skills in placement and follow-up, often beyond the competency of over-worked parole officers, are needed for the successful rehabilitation of inmates. A few states now recognize this need and provide for it.

The veteran who has incurred a disability in service is eligible for special rehabilitation programs provided by the Veterans Administration. Such services include extensive medical and therapeutic services as well as counseling, appropriate training programs, and assistance in entering employment when the training is completed. The disabled veteran who wishes to participate in vocational rehabilitation is required to complete counseling in order to assure careful thought and planning in the development of appropriate and realistic career goals. In general, the comments made above about the physically handicapped apply to the disabled veteran except for the additional special programs provided for this group.

Vocational counseling is available for the nondisabled veteran. Originally established under the World War II legislation called the "G.I. Bill," it has been continued since that time without interruption for veterans who entered service before the recently fixed cut-off date. The veteran group is comprised of individuals whose career plans had to be postponed. In many cases, military service and resulting veteran benefits have provided an opportunity for up-grading career plans beyond the level that might otherwise have been possible. The large influx of veterans into colleges immediately after World War II and the continuing flow of veterans into advanced education illustrate this up-grading.

Perhaps the veterans who seek vocational counseling can best be typified by the phrase "young men in a hurry." They strongly feel the urgency to complete their educations as rapidly as possible in order to enter employment. Often they feel that they have been marking time in the service and they are anxious to recoup as much of the time as possible. Their haste often causes them to feel irritated by the time involved in most preparatory programs and they may seek ways to shorten or accelerate the programs if possible. Because of their additional maturity, they may find problems in adjusting to the nonveteran population in the training program.[25, 26] Their eagerness to make up "lost time" may cause them to undertake loads that are unrealistic; on the other hand, their maturity and motivation very often may enable them to carry such loads successfully. Veterans who were employed before entrance into service are faced with the choice of returning to their former occupation or capitalizing on educational benefits in order to open new areas of opportunity.

Of all the groups with special career problems, the group that has seen greatest change in the last decade is women. Even so, the changes experienced thus far probably are only indicative of the changes to occur in the next decade.

Changing social attitudes, growing partly from the civil rights movement of the '60's, have helped focus attention on the biases and prejudices that have restricted the career development of many women. The 1972 Equal Employment Opportunity Act, the proposal of the Equal Rights Amendment, and Title IX of the Education Amendments of 1972 have all served to suggest the opening of many new career fields, as well as to encourage many women to consider fields already open but only sparsely populated by women.

Changing life styles also have had an impact on women's relationship to the world of work. As discussed in Chapter 5, women in our society are now bearing fewer children and doing so at an earlier age than in the past. The result is that a woman's children are all in school and partially independent or even out of school and totally independent when she is still young enough to have many active years remaining. She may choose to enter or return to employment or she may elect to become involved in a variety of nonpaid activities that may be equally valuable to her and to her community. Certainly many of these volunteer activities are as demanding and as rewarding as most paid positions, and, as pointed out in Chapter 2, should be considered as "work" since they produce goods and services valued by others.

Cooperman has called attention to the fact that 40 per cent of the women who are employed have no husband, and among the remaining 60 per cent, a majority report economic necessity as the major reason for their employment.[27] For many of these two groups of women, earlier decisions, such as interrupting or postponing education, have had a heavy impact on their present plans and opportunities.

Clearly there are at least three distinctly different types of problems related to counseling women about careers. First, there is the need to assist girls and young women toward a broader view of the world of work so that career choices can be made more appropriately, maximizing the use of ability, interests, values, and ambitions, and minimizing the worn-out stereotypes of "women's work." Secondly, there is the need to help women with already acquired skills to reenter the world of work at levels compatible with previously developed competencies plus other vocational assets that may have been developed since previous employment. Thirdly, there is the problem faced by the woman whose previous employment, if any, may have been at an entry level, and who now chooses to seek employment. If her nonemployed years did not involve the development of salable skills through volunteer experiences or independent study, she may be confronted with a choice between starting with an entry level position or acquiring skills through an educational program of some kind. Eyde has pointed to the need to increase vocational counseling available to girls to assist them in building career plans unrestricted by old stereotypes and attitudinal restrictions.[28] She further suggests the need for counselors to keep informed of changing job conditions so that women can prepare adequately for the future. Haener insists that counselors must assume the responsibility for bringing about the changes in attitudes that would eliminate sex stereotyping of occupational opportunity.[29] Clearly, there are special needs faced by women in any of the three problem situations mentioned above. Clarification of goals, evaluation of self in terms of motivations, values, abilities and interests, and insight into the world of work may all be necessary considerations if effective career counseling is to transpire.

Some effective approaches to problems of this type have been developed. Lacy, for example, reports a project in which women over age 35, either unemployed or underemployed, and young women college graduates without previous work experience have been prepared in a ten–week training program for positions in social agencies.[30] Many colleges and universities have developed plans by which interrupted educational programs can be resumed. Several have even established external degree programs that permit a woman to establish credit for skills and knowledge already acquired and to develop an educational program compatible with her needs, time strictures, of other factors that might limit class attendance.

Torvald: Before all else you are a wife and mother.
Nora: That I no longer believe. I believe that before all else, I
          am a human being, just as much as you are—or at least that
          I should try to become one.

Henrik Ibsen, *A Doll's House,* (1879).

A recent project funded by the National Institute of Education to develop a model for community-based career education has dealt specifically with the problems encountered by women.[31] Their clientele, mostly women, ranged in age from 16 to 75 and were neither working nor attending school on a full-time basis. Many of these clients reported similar needs, including:

1. A better understanding of their own interests, abilities, values, and goals.
2. Facts about career trends, opportunities, and requirements.
3. Information about the available educational and skill-training opportunities.
4. Information about sources of help in such related problem areas as financial support, discrimination, child care, and testing.
5. Help in developing and implementing career plans.

The project developed a program to provide career counseling services to its clientele via telephone, using trained paraprofessionals. Out of this project has come a series of valuable monographs and bibliographies that may well serve as benchmarks for the development and extension of similar services across the country. These include self-teaching booklets for use by the client, as well as "how to" booklets describing how to establish a program, develop materials and a resource center, attract clientele, and evaluate services provided.

More than 18 million people in this country are over 65 years of age. Present estimates indicate that if our total population grows to 250 million by the year 2000 and if our present proportion of older people continues to increase, we will have about 36 million people eligible for benefits under the Social Security system, most of them over age 65.[32] Many factors will encourage large numbers of this group to continue working or to return to some form of employment. These factors include inadequate retirement and pension programs, continuing inflationary economic trends, continuing physical strength and good health, and the desire to be busy in some productive way. Often, artificial restrictions imposed on older citizens either by legislation related to retirement benefits or by employer's hiring requirements may seriously hamper their efforts to work. At the same time, many individuals in this group possess skills and knowledge acquired from a lifetime of work that have great value. Both society and the individual gain if ways can be found to use those resources. The counselor may have to search for new fields of endeavor or new opportunities in which the individual can apply those competencies. Like many women whose family responsibilities limit the time available for work, this group, too, may often prefer less than full-time work. The possibility for part-time employment, job-sharing, and flexible scheduling may warrant exploration.

TRENDS IN REHABILITATION

Several clear-cut trends indicate an expansion of rehabilitation services in the years ahead. The generally accepted broader definition of the term includes more groups who are eligible for services. A greater social awareness on the part of the general public creates pressure to extend services to more groups of people who need such help. The basic philosophy of career education—the continual intertwining of education and work—encourages providing counseling services and career planning to all desiring such assistance.

In 1960, approximately 88,000 persons were rehabilitated. By 1967, the figure was over 208,000, and by 1974 the number had increased to more than 345,000.[33]

Legislation passed in 1965 opened the door for extending services to the severely disabled by providing for the evaluation of the extent of their disabilities over a prolonged time. Such evaluation can be stretched over eighteen months if necessary, thus allowing a generous opportunity to decide whether rehabilitation is a realistic possibility for the individual.

Again in 1968, legislation was passed that extended to the disadvantaged the opportunity for vocational aptitude evaluation and work adjustment assistance by rehabilitation agencies. Both the 1965 and 1968 legislation clearly indicate a congressional desire to provide needed services under a broad interpretation of eligibility.

As services are extended to the disadvantaged, an inevitable product will be closer cooperation between rehabilitation and social welfare agencies. Resolution of the problems of poverty and disadvantage will require such liaison. Already teamwork is being established between rehabilitation agencies and such groups as neighborhood service organizations, model city projects, and similar groups.

Similarly, it is reasonable to expect closer cooperation between schools and rehabilitation agencies to permit earlier identification of school age youth who will need rehabilitation prior to employment. Such cooperation should permit the development of better counseling and job planning.

The expansion of state and federal programs providing services to more individuals also will increase the demand for professional rehabilitation workers. One can expect increased support for preparatory programs for these workers in order to increase their numbers and their competency.

Finally, it can be expected that the number of sheltered workshops will expand drastically. Two factors will produce this increase. First, a greater number of rehabilitation clients, such as the disadvantaged and the school dropout, will need such workshops as a site for pre-employment experience and training. Secondly, as services are extended to individuals whose disabilities are more extensive and restrictive, these workshops may become employment sites for this group since placement opportunities elsewhere may be difficult to develop.

Efforts are presently under way to review and revise the various state rehabilitation agencies so that they will be able to extend their services to all individuals in need of such help. If this goal is accomplished, it will offer hope and opportunity to a portion of our population that often has been overlooked or neglected. At that point, we may truly be nearer the point at which each individual, handicapped or not, has the opportunity to develop a career that includes the ingredients for maximizing self-actualization.

NOTES

1. D. Super, *The Psychology of Careers* (New York: Harper and Row Publishers, 1957), pp. 76–78.
2. C. A. Ullmann, "Second Careers for Military Retirees," *Vocational Guidance Quarterly*, vol. 20, no. 2 (December, 1971), pp. 96–102.
3. R. Strauss, "Social Change and the Rehabilitation Concept," in M. B. Sussman (ed.) *Sociology and Rehabilitation* (Washington, D.C.: American Sociological Association, 1965).
4. J. Hutchison, "The Vocational Rehabilitation Program and Its Relationship to the Social Security Program," in J. G. Cull and R. E. Hardy, *Understanding Disability for Social and Rehabilitation Services* (Springfield, Ill.: Charles C. Thomas, Publishers, 1973), p. 43.
5. W. Allan, *Rehabilitation: A Community Challenge* (New York: John Wiley and Sons, Inc., 1958), p. 1.
6. J. Dilley, "Our Handicapped Efforts to Help the Handicapped," *Vocational Guidance Quarterly*, vol. 15, no. 4 (June, 1967), pp. 297–301.
7. W. Usdane, "Introduction," in *Sociology and Rehabilitation*, ed. M. B. Sussman, published by American Sociological Association, 1965, p. XVI.
8. U.S. Department of Health, Education, and Welfare, Public Health Service, *Chronic Conditions Causing Limitations of Activities* (Washington: U.S. Government Printing Office, 1962).
9. I. Ratchick and F. Koenig, *Guidance and the Physically Handicapped Child* (Chicago: Science Research Associates, Inc., 1963).
10. U.S. Public Health Service, *Health Statistics from the U.S. National Health Survey*, Series B, No. 36 (Washington: U.S. Government Printing Office, 1962).
11. R. Conley, *The Economics of Vocational Rehabilitation* (Baltimore: The Johns Hopkins Press, 1965), chapter 2.
12. *Ibid.*, p. 20.
13. *Ibid.*, p. 84
14. J. Samler, "A Second Look at Careers," *Vocational Guidance Quarterly*, vol. 20, no. 2 (December, 1971), pp. 112–118.
15. H. L. Sheppard, "The Emerging Pattern of Second Careers," *Vocational Guidance Quarterly*, vol. 20, no. 2 (December, 1971), pp. 89–95.

16. D. Sinick, "Using Occupational Information With the Handicapped," *Vocational Guidance Quarterly*, vol. 12, no. 4 (Summer, 1964), pp. 275–277.
17. E. Thoroman, *The Vocational Counseling of Adults and Young Adults* (Boston: Houghton Mifflin Company, 1968), chapter 7.
18. C. Benney, E. Glynn, E. Adams, and J. Sloma, "Rehabilitating the School Drop Out," *Rehabilitation Record*, vol. 6, no. 5 (September–October, 1965), pp. 1–5.
19. V. Calia, "The Culturally Deprived Client: A Re-formulation of the Counselor's Role," *Journal of Counseling Psychology*, vol. 13, no. 1 (Spring, 1966), pp. 100–105.
20. R. Peterson, "Rehabilitation of the Culturally Different: A Model of the Individual in Cultural Change," *Personnel and Guidance Journal*, vol. 45, no. 10 (June, 1967), pp. 1001–1007.
21. C. Grigg and R. Wilson, "The Welfare Client's Rehabilitation," *Rehabilitation Record*, vol. 8, no. 1 (January–February, 1967), pp. 23–25.
22. C. McWhorter and A. Lamonte, "Special Help for Special People," *Rehabilitation Record*, vol. 8, no. 1 (January–February, 1967), pp. 26–30.
23. L. Harris, "The Poverty Client Looks at the Professional," *Rehabilitation Record*, vol. 10, no. 1 (January–February, 1969), pp. 27–28.
24. A. Heilbrun, Jr., and B. Jordan, "Vocational Rehabilitation of the Socially Disadvantaged: Demographic and Intellectual Correlates of Outcome," *Personnel and Guidance Journal*, vol. 47, no. 3 (November, 1968), pp. 213–217.
25. Thoroman, *op. cit.*, chapter 5.
26. E. R. Myers, "Counseling Today's Veterans: A Program and Its Implications," *Personnel and Guidance Journal*, vol. 52, no. 4 (December, 1973), pp. 233–238.
27. I. G. Cooperman, "Second Careers—War Wives and Widows," *Vocational Guidance Quarterly*, vol. 20, no. 2 (December, 1971), pp. 103–111.
28. L. D. Eyde, "Eliminating Barriers to Career Development of Women," *Personnel and Guidance Journal*, vol. 49, no. 1 (September, 1970), pp. 24–28.
29. D. Haener, "The Working Woman: Can Counselors Take the Heat?" *Personnel and Guidance Journal*, vol. 51, no. 2 (October, 1972), pp. 109–112.
30. C. L. Lacy, "An Experimental Project to Prepare Mature Women for Work in Community Social Agencies," *Vocational Guidance Quarterly*, vol. 18, no. 4 (June, 1970), pp. 285–288.
31. Career Educational Project, *Women and the World of Work* (Newton Centre, Mass.: Education Development Center, 1975).
32. B. Schneider, *The Older Worker* (Berkeley: University of California Press, 1962), pp. 88–89.
33. Rehabilitation Services Administration, *State Vocational Rehabilitation Agency Program Data, 1974* (Washington, D.C.: HEW, Office of Human Development, 1975), p. 2.

PART VI   Supplementary Learning Experiences

The following activities are proposed as ways in which the reader can easily test, explore, or apply the concepts and insights presented in Part VI. The list is not intended to be exhaustive or comprehensive, but merely suggestive.

1. Prepare a case study folder for a high school or college student involved in career planning.
2. Prepare a plan for group consideration of career planning materials for a specific grade or age level.
3. Identify rehabilitation resources available in your community and determine how they can assist the age level in which you are interested.
4. Prepare a unit on career materials for use in a subject course that you teach.
5. Interview two or three individuals who are representative of a special group (high school dropouts, older women entering employment, etc.) to identify the special needs they have for assistance in going to work.

Appendix A
Dictionary of Occupational Titles, 3rd and 4th Editions

TWO-DIGIT OCCUPATIONAL DIVISIONS

PROFESSIONAL, TECHNICAL, AND MANAGERIAL OCCUPATIONS

00 ⎫
01 ⎬   Occupations in architecture and engineering

- 02   Occupations in mathematics and physical sciences
- 04   Occupations in life sciences
- 05   Occupations in social sciences
- 07   Occupations in medicine and health
- 09   Occupations in education
- 10   Occupations in museum, library, and archival sciences
- 11   Occupations in law and jurisprudence
- 12   Occupations in religion and theology
- 13   Occupations in writing
- 14   Occupations in art
- 15   Occupations in entertainment and recreation
- 16   Occupations in administrative specializations
- 18   Managers and officials, n.e.c.
- 19   Miscellaneous professional, technical, and managerial occupations

CLERICAL AND SALES OCCUPATIONS

- 20   Stenography, typing, filing, and related occupations
- 21   Computing and account-recording occupations
- 22   Material and production-recording occupations

23	Information and message distribution occupations
24	Miscellaneous clerical occupations
25	Salesman, services
26 27 28	} Salesmen and salespersons, commodities
29	Merchandising occupations, except salesmen

SERVICE OCCUPATIONS

30	Domestic service occupations
31	Food and beverage preparation and service occupations
32	Lodging and related service occupations
33	Barbering, cosmetology, and related service occupations
34	Amusement and recreation service occupations
35	Miscellaneous personal service occupations
36	Apparel and furnishings service occupations
37	Protective service occupations
38	Building and related service occupations

FARMING, FISHERY, FORESTRY, AND RELATED OCCUPATIONS

40	Plant farming occupations
41	Animal farming occupations
42	Miscellaneous farming and related occupations
43	Fishery and related occupations
44	Forestry occupations
45	Hunting, trapping, and related occupations
46	Agricultural service occupations

PROCESSING OCCUPATIONS

50	Occupations in processing of metal
51	Ore refining and foundry occupations
52	Occupations in processing of food, tobacco, and related products
53	Occupations in processing of paper and related materials
54	Occupations in processing of petroleum, coal, natural and manufactured gas, and related products
55	Occupations in processing of chemicals, plastics, synthetics, rubber, paint, and related products
56	Occupations in processing of wood and wood products
57	Occupations in processing of stone, clay, glass, and related products
58	Occupations in processing of leather, textiles, and related products
59	Processing occupations, n.e.c.

MACHINE TRADES OCCUPATIONS

| 60 | Metal machining occupations |
| 61 | Metal working occupations, n.e.c. |

62 ⎫
63 ⎭ Mechanics and machinery repairmen

64   Paperworking occupations
65   Printing occupations
66   Wood machining occupations
67   Occupations in machining stone, clay, glass, and related materials
68   Textile occupations
69   Machine trades occupations, n.e.c.

Bench Work Occupations

70   Occupations in fabrication, assembly, and repair of metal products, n.e.c.
71   Occupations in fabrication and repair of scientific and medical apparatus, photographic and optical goods, watches and clocks, and related products
72   Occupations in assembly and repair of electrical equipment
73   Occupations in fabrication and repair of products made from assorted materials
74   Painting, decorating, and related occupations
75   Occupations in fabrication and repair of plastics, synthetics, rubber, and related products
76   Occupations in fabrication and repair of wood products
77   Occupations in fabrication and repair of sand, stone, clay, and glass products
78   Occupations in fabrication and repair of textile, leather, and related products
79   Bench work occupations, n.e.c.

Structural Work Occupations

80   Occupations in metal fabricating, n.e.c.
81   Welders, flame cutters, and related occupations
82   Electrical assembling, installing, and repairing occupations
84   Painting, plastering, waterproofing, cementing, and related occupations
85   Excavating, grading, paving, and related occupations
86   Construction occupations, n.e.c.
89   Structural work occupations, n.e.c.

Miscellaneous Occupations

90   Motor freight occupations
91   Transportation occupations, n.e.c.
92   Packaging and materials handling occupations
93   Occupations in extraction of minerals
94   Occupations in logging
95   Occupations in production and distribution of utilities
96   Amusement, recreation, and motion picture occupations, n.e.c.
97   Occupations in graphic art work

ILLUSTRATIONS OF THREE-DIGIT
OCCUPATIONAL GROUPS

00 OCCUPATIONS IN ARCHITECTURE AND ENGINEERING

001. Architectural occupations
002. Aeronautical engineering occupations
003. Electrical engineering occupations
005. Civil engineering occupations
006. Ceramic engineering occupations
007. Mechanical engineering occupations
008. Chemical engineering occupations
010. Mining and petroleum engineering occupations
011. Metallurgy and metallurgical engineering occupations
012. Industrial engineering occupations
013. Agricultural engineering occupations
014. Marine engineering occupations
015. Nuclear engineering occupations
017. Draftsmen, n.e.c.
018. Surveyors, n.e.c.
019. Occupations in architecture and engineering, n.e.c.

09 OCCUPATIONS IN EDUCATION

090. Occupations in college and university education
091. Occupations in secondary school education
092. Occupations in primary school and kindergarten education
094. Occupations in education of the handicapped
096. Home economists and farm advisers
097. Occupations in vocational education, n.e.c.
099. Occupations in education, n.e.c.

20 STENOGRAPHY, TYPING, FILING, AND RELATED OCCUPATIONS

201. Secretaries
202. Stenographers
203. Typists
204. Correspondence clerks
205. Personnel clerks
206. File clerks
207. Duplicating-machine operators
208. Miscellaneous office machine operators
209. Stenography, typing, filing, and related occupations, n.e.c.

33 BARBERING, COSMETOLOGY, AND RELATED SERVICE OCCUPATIONS

330. Barbers
331. Manicurists

332. Hairdressers and cosmetologists
333. Make-up occupations
334. Masseurs and related occupations
335. Bath attendants
338. Embalmers and related occupations
339. Barbering, cosmetology, and related service occupations, n.e.c.

51 ORE REFINING AND FOUNDRY OCCUPATIONS

510. Mixing and related occupations
511. Separating, filtering, and related occupations
512. Melting occupations
513. Roasting occupations
514. Pouring and casting occupations
515. Crushing and grinding occupations
518. Molders, coremakers, and related occupations
519. Ore refining and foundry occupations, n.e.c.

68 TEXTILE OCCUPATIONS

680. Carding, combing, drawing, and related occupations
681. Twisting, beaming, warping, and related occupations
682. Spinning occupations
683. Weavers and related occupations
684. Hosiery knitting occupations
685. Knitting occupations, except hosiery
686. Punching, cutting, forming, and related occupations
689. Textile occupations, n.e.c.

86 CONSTRUCTION OCCUPATIONS, N.E.C.

860. Carpenters and related occupations
861. Brick and stone masons and tile setters
862. Plumbers, gas fitters, steam fitters, and related occupations
863. Asbestos and insulation workers
864. Floor laying and finishing occupations
865. Glaziers and related occupations
866. Roofers and related occupations
869. Miscellaneous construction occupations, n.e.c.

97 OCCUPATIONS IN GRAPHIC ART WORK

970. Art work occupations, brush, spray, or pen
971. Photoengraving occupations
972. Lithographers and related occupations
973. Hand compositors, typesetters, and related occupations
974. Electrotypers and related occupations
975. Stereotypers and related occupations

976. Darkroom occupations, n.e.c.
977. Bookbinders and related occupations
979. Occupations in graphic art work, n.e.c.

DICTIONARY OF OCCUPATIONAL TITLES,
3rd EDITION

SAMPLES OF GROUPS INCLUDED IN
THE 22 BROAD AREAS

ENGINEERING

.081	Engineering research and design
.151	Sales engineering
.168	Engineering, scientific, and technical coordination
.181	Drafting and related work
.281	
.181	Technical work, engineering and related fields
.281	
.187	Engineering and related work
.188	Industrial engineering and related work
.288	
.188	Surveying, prospecting, and related work
.288	
.188	Technical writing and related work
.288	

MATHEMATICS AND SCIENCE

.021	Health physics
.081	Scientific research
.088	Social science, psychological, and related research
.088	Mathematics, physical sciences, and related research
.188	
.168	Engineering, scientific, and technical coordination
.181	
.281	Materials analysis and related work
.381	
.188	Accounting, auditing, and related work
.288	
.384	Technical work, science and related fields

SAMPLE PAGE: *DOT*, 4th EDITION, NUMERICAL LISTING

6 MACHINE TRADES OCCUPATIONS

This category includes occupations concerned with feeding, tending, operating, controlling, and setting up machines to cut, bore, bill, abrade, print, and similarly work such materials as metal, paper, wood, and stone. Throughout this category, the overall relationship of the worker to the machine is of prime importance. At the more complex levels, the important aspects of the work include understanding machine functions, reading blueprints, making mathematical computations, and exercising judgment to attain conformance to specifications. Coordination of the eyes and hands is the most significant factor at the lower levels. Disassembly, repair, reassembly, installation, and maintenance of machines and mechanical equipment, and weaving, knitting, spinning, and similarly working textiles are included in this category.

60 Metal Machining Occupations

This division includes occupations concerned with shaping metal parts or products by removing excess materials from stock of object, primarily by such means as cutting, boring, milling, abrading, and planing. Includes laying out, job setting, repairing, fitting, and assembly. The machining of plastics is also included when the methods applied to the machining of metal are used.

600 Machinists and Related Occupations   This group includes occupations concerned with shaping metal parts by milling, turning, planing, abrading, boring, chipping, sawing, and shaving with a variety of metalworking machines. Includes laying out, job setting, fitting, assembling, and repairing. Occupations primarily concerned with machine shop tools are included in Group 601 and machining gears in Group 602.

600.131–010 Machine Shop Supervisor, Tool (mach. shop)   Supervises and coordinates activities of workers engaged in custom-machining of metal workpieces, applying knowledge of machine shop procedures, variety of machine-tool setup and operating techniques, and custom-machining methods. May supervise workers in related processes such as metal-forming, welding, or assembly. Performs duties as described under FOREMAN (any ind.).

600.131–014 Salvage Engineer (mach. mfg.) Supervises and coordinates activities of workers engaged in reworking rejected ball bearings: Disassembles and inspects races, faceways, cups, cones, retainers, and bearings. Diagnoses imperfections, such as parts not within tolerance, scratches, burrs, rust, or dirt and determines if part can be reworked or should be rejected. Assigns bearings to assistants to be reworked, advises them on problems involving bearing salvage, and trains workers in principles and practices of salvaging rejects. Inspects reworked bearings and components, using special go–no-go gages, calipers, and micrometers. May operate lathes to turn, bore, face, and polish raceways, and perform related operations to rework bearings.

600.280–010 Experimental Mechanic (motor. & bicycles) development mechanic. Sets up and operates variety of machines to fabricate experimental motorcycles or components to meet operating and endurance standards required by blueprints, sketches, or oral instructions: Assembles motorcycle or components, using handtools. Positions and clamps motorcycle on test rack. Attaches test equipment, such as tachometers, thermocouples, pressure and strain gages, flow and velocity meters, to motorcycles, using handtools. Operates motorcycle at specified speeds and loads, and records meter and instrument readings on test records form. Disassembles motorcycle and analyzes cause of defect in components, such as exhaust system, frame, hydraulic fork, spring, or wheels, using handtools or power tools, calipers, micrometers, gages, and other measuring instruments. Operates drill press, engine lathe, milling machine, or other machines to fabricate experimental motorcycle parts for testing, and jigs and fixtures used to secure test equipment to motorcycle. Test rides motorcycle to verify performance and durability of motorcycle components. Compiles and submits report to engineering department to show results of tests and recommendations for design or material changes.

600.280–018 Instrument Maker (any ind.) II mechanical technician; parts mechanic; precision-instrument and tool maker; precision-mechanical-instrument maker. Fabricates, modifies, or repairs mechanical instruments or mechanical assemblies of electrical or electronic instruments, such as chronometric timing devices, barographs, thermostats, seismographs, and servomechanisms, following blueprints and engineering sketches and using machine tools, welding and heat-treating equipment, precision measuring instruments, and handtools: Lays out cutting lines of structural parts, such as brackets, fittings, and housing on stock, such as silver, nickel, platinum, steel, ivory, and plastic using square, rule, and scribe. Cuts and shapes parts, using machine tools, such as lathes, drill presses, punch presses, milling machines, grinders, brakes, and lapping and polishing machines [MACHINIST I (mach. shop)]. Anneals and tempers metal parts

[HEAT TREATER I (heat treat.)]. Assembles parts in jig and brazes or welds [BRAZER, FURNACE (welding); WELDER, SPOT I (welding)]. Fits and installs precision components, such as timing devices, springs, balance mechanisms, and gear trains in housing, using jeweler's lathe, tweezers, loupe, and handtools. Verifies dimensions of parts and installation of components, using measuring instruments, such as micrometer, calipers, and electronic gages. Coats assembled instrument with protective finish, such as lacquer or enamel, using spray gun. May set up and operate machines to fabricate dies for punch presses [DIE MAKER, BENCH, STAMPING (mach. shop)].

600.280-014 INSTRUMENT BUILDER (INST. & APP.) Sets up and operates machines, such as lathes, drill presses, and milling machines, to machine prototype fixtures, tools, and templates, and assembles, tests, and calibrates mechanical, electrical, and electronic devices, such as control panels, thermostatic switch boxes, and valve assemblies: Reads blueprints, sketches, and wiring diagrams, and follows oral instructions to determine parts, tools, test equipment, and sequence of operations required. Confers with engineers to determine materials, specifications, and sequences to be used. Requisitions parts and tools. Sets up and operates machines, such as lathes, drill

•   •   •

[*text continues on next page of* DOT]

SAMPLE PAGE: *DOT*, FOURTH EDITION, ALPHABETICAL LISTING

ALPHABETICAL INDEX OF OCCUPATIONAL TITLES

a and e mechanic (aircraft mfg.; air trans.) see AIRCRAFT AND ENGINE MECHANIC
ABALONE DIVER (fish.) see FISHER, DIVING
abalone gatherer (fish.) see FISHER, ABALONE
able bodied seaman (water trans.) see ABLE SEAMAN
ABLE SEAMAN (water trans.) 911.884-010
ABOYEUR (hotel & rest.) see FOOD ORDER EXPEDITER
ABRASIVE COATING MACHINE OPERATOR (abrasive and polish prod.) 574.782-010

ABRASIVE GRADER (optical goods) 570.782–010

ABRASIVE GRADER HELPER (optical goods) 570.886–010

ABRASIVE GRINDER (abrasive & polish prod.) 673.885–010

ABRASIVE MIXER (abrasive & polish prod.) 570.885–010

ABRASIVE MIXER HELPER (abrasive & polish. prod.) 570.886–010

ABRASIVE STONE CUTTER, HAND (abrasive & polish prod.) 776.884–010

ABRASIVE WHEEL MOLDER (abrasive & polish. prod.) 575.885–010

ABSORBER OUTSIDE HELPER (chem.) see under CHEMICAL OPERATOR II

ABSORPTION AND ADSORPTION ENGINEER (profess. & kin.) see under CHEMICAL ENGINEER

ABSORPTION OPERATOR (chem.; coal tar prod.) 551.782–010

ABSORPTION PLANT OPERATOR (petrol. refin.) see REFINERY OPERATOR

ABSORPTION PLANT OPERATOR HELPER (petrol. refin.) see REFINERY OPERATOR HELPER

ABSTRACT CHECKER (insurance) see INSURANCE CHECKER

abstract clerk (profess & kin.) see ABSTRACTOR

ABSTRACT EXAMINATION CLERK (insurance) see ACCOUNTING CLERK (clerical)

abstract maker (profess. & kin.) see ABSTRACTOR I

abstractor (insurance) see WORKSHEET CLERK

ABSTRACTOR (profess. & kin.) I 119.288–005

abstractor (profess. & kin.) II see TITLE EXAMINER

abstract searcher (profess. & kin.) see ABSTRACTOR I

abstract writer (profess. & kin.) see ABSTRACTOR I

ACADEMIC DEAN (education) 090.118–010

academic vice president (education) see ACADEMIC DEAN

ACCELERATOR OPERATOR (profess. & kin.) 015.181–010

access clerk (banking) see SAFE DEPOSIT CLERK

ACCESSORIES INSPECTOR (tex. prod., n.e.c·) see SEAT PACK INSPECTOR

ACCESSORIES REPAIRER (loco. & car. bldg. & rep.) see ELECTRICIAN, LOCOMOTIVE

ACCIDENT AND SICKNESS CLAIM EXAMINER (insurance) see CLAIM EXAMINER II

ACCIDENT AND SICKNESS UNDERWRITER (insurance) see UNDERWRITER

ACCIDENT PREVENTION SQUAD POLICE OFFICER (gov. ser.) 375.268–010 see under POLICE OFFICER

ACCIDENT REPORT CLERK (clerical) see PERSONNEL CLERK

ACCOMPANIST (amuse. & rec.) see MUSICIAN, INSTRUMENTAL

ACCORDION MAKER (musical inst.) 730.281–010

ACCORDIAN REPAIRER (any ind.) 730.281–014

ACCORDION TUNER (any ind.) 730.381–010

ACCOUNT ANALYST (banking) 219.388–014

ACCOUNTANT (profess. & kin.) 160.188–010

ACCOUNTANT, BUDGET (profess. & kin.) 160.188–014 see under AC-COUNTANT

ACCOUNTANT, COST (profess. & kin.) 160.188–018 under ACCOUN-TANT

ACCOUNTANT, MACHINE PROCESSING (profess. & kin.) 160.188–022 see under ACCOUNTANT

ACCOUNTANT, PROPERTY (profess. & kin.) 160.188–026 see under ACCOUNTANT

ACCOUNTANT, SYSTEMS (profess. & kin.) 160.188–030 see under AC-COUNTANT

ACCOUNTANT, TAX (profess. & kin.) 160.188–034 see under ACCOUN-TANT

ACCOUNTANT, CERTIFIED PUBLIC (profess. & kin) (T)

ACCOUNTANT (profess. & kin.) I (T)

ACCOUNTANT (profess. & kin.) II (T)

account application clerk (clerical) see NEW ACCOUNT CLERK

ACCOUNT CHECKER (clerical) see ACCOUNTING CLERK

ACCOUNT CLASSIFICATION CLERK (clerical) 210.388–010 see under BOOKKEEPER II

account clerk (clerical) see BOOKKEEPING MACHINE OPERATOR I; BOOKKEEPING MACHINE OPERATOR II

account executive (finan. inst.) see SALES AGENT, SECURITIES

ACCOUNT EXECUTIVE (profess. & kin.) 164.168–010

account executive (radio. & t.v. broad.) see SALES REPRESENTATIVE, RADIO & TELEVISION TIME

ACCOUNT INFORMATION CLERK (light, heat, & power) 210.368–010

ACCOUNTING CLERK (clerical) 219.488–010

ACCOUNTING CLERK, PAYROLL (banking) see ACCOUNTING CLERK (clerical)

ACCOUNTING CLERK, TRUST (banking) see ACCOUNTING CLERK (clerical)

ACCOUNTING MACHINE SERVICER (any ind.) see OFFICE MA-CHINE SERVICER

accounting system expert (profess. & kin.) see ACCOUNTANT, SYSTEMS under ACCOUNTANT

account representative (profess. & kin.) see ACCOUNT EXECUTIVE

ACCOUNTS PAYABLE BOOKKEEPER (clerical) see BOOKKEEPER II

ACCOUNTS PAYABLE CLERK (clerical) see ACCOUNTING CLERK

ACCOUNTS RECEIVABLE BALANCING CLERK (clerical) see BAL-ANCE CLERK

ACCOUNTS RECEIVABLE BOOKKEEPER (clerical) see BOOKKEEPER II

ACCOUNTS RECEIVABLE CLERK (clerical) see ACCOUNTING CLERK

accounts supervisor (any ind.) see MANAGER, CREDIT AND COLLECTION

accumulator (clerical) see RECEIVING CHECKER

ACCURAY TESTER (paper & pulp) 539.485-010

ACETALDEHYDE CONVERTER OPERATOR (chem.) see CATALYTIC CONVERTER OPERATOR

ACETONE BUTTON PASTER (button) 734.887-010

ACETONER (garment) 686.886-010

ACETONE RECOVERY WORKER (synthetic fibers) 552.885-010

ACETYLENE CYLINER PACKING MIXER (comp. & liquified gases) 549.885-010

ACETYLENE PLANT OPERATOR (comp. & liquified gases) 549.885-014

ACID ADJUSTER (elec. equip.) 727.884-010

ACID BATH MIXER (textile) see CHEMICAL MIXER (knit goods; textile)

acid blower (explosives) see NITRATING ACID MIXER

ACID BOTTLER (elec. equip.) 559.885-010

acid bottling machine operator (elec. equip.) see ACID BOTTLER

acid changer (elec. equip.) see ACID DUMPER

ACID CONCENTRATION PLANT EQUIPMENT ENGINEER (any ind.) see STATIONARY ENGINEER

ACID CONDITIONER (ore dress., smelt., & refin.) see COTTRELL TREATER

ACID CRANE OPERATOR (iron & steel) see ELECTRIC BRIDGE OR GANTRY CRANE OPERATOR (any ind.) or ELECTRIC MONORAIL CRANE OPERATOR (any ind.)

ACID CUTTER (conc. prod.) see LABORER, CONCRETE PLANT

acid dipper (any ind.) see METAL CLEANER, IMMERSION

ACID DUMPER (elec. equip.) 727.887-010

ACID ETCH MACHINE OPERATOR (electronics) see APERTURE MASK PROCESSING EQUIPMENT OPERATOR

ACID EXTRACTOR (coke prod.) 558.782-010

ACID FILLER (elec. equip.) 727.887-014

Appendix B
Sources of
Career Materials

The following companies publish series of pamphlets, monographs, or booklets intended to provide occupational information:

Arco Publishing Company, Inc., 219 Park Ave. So., New York, N.Y. 10003

Bellman Publishing Co., Box 172, Cambridge, Mass. 02138

B'nai B'rith Career and Counseling Service, 1640 Rhode Island Ave., N.W., Washington, D.C. 20036

Careers, Inc., Largo, Fla. 33540

Catalyst, 6 E. 82 St., New York, N.Y. 10028

Chronicle Guidance Publications, Moravia, N.Y. 13118

Finney Company, 3350 Gorham Ave., Minneapolis, Minn. 55426

The Guidance Centre, 371 Bloor St. W., Toronto, Ontario, Canada

Institute for Research, 610 So. Federal St., Chicago, Ill. 60605

Julian Messner, 1 West 39 St., New York, N.Y. 10018

Personnel Services, Inc., Box 306, Jaffrey, N.H. 03452

Research Publishing Co., Box 1474, Madison, Wisc. 53701

Richards Rosen Press, 29 E. 21 St., New York, N.Y. 10010

Science Research Associates, Inc., 259 E. Erie, Chicago, Ill. 60611

Vocational Guidance Manuals, 235 East 45 St., New York, N.Y. 10017

Western Personnel Institute, 10th and Dartmouth, Claremont, Calif. 91711

World Trade Academy Press, 50 E. 42 St., New York, N.Y. 10017

The following companies have series of books that are intended to provide occupational information:

American Liberty Press Publications, Inc., 746 W. Winnebago St., Milwaukee, Wisc. 53205

Chilton Books, 525 Locust St., Philadelphia, Pa. 19106

Dodd, Mead & Co., 79 Madison Ave., New York, N.Y. 10016

E. P. Dutton & Co., Inc., 201 Park Ave. S., New York, N.Y. 10003

Interstate Printers and Publishers, Inc., Danville, Ill. 61832

J. B. Lippincott Co., Philadelphia, Pa., 19105

David McKay Co., Inc., 750 Third Ave., New York, N.Y. 10017

The Macmillan Co., 866 Third Ave., New York, N.Y. 10022

Julian Messner, Inc., 1 West 39 St., New York, N.Y. 10018

Popular Library, Inc., 355 Lexington Ave., New York, N.Y. 10017

G. P. Putnam's Sons, 200 Madison Ave., New York, N.Y. 10016

Random House, 457 Madison Ave., New York, N.Y. 10022

Richards Rosen Press, Inc., 29 E. 21 St., New York, N.Y. 10010

Henry A. Walck, Inc., 19 Union Square West, New York, N.Y. 10003

Name Index

Cleland, H. L., 342, 352
Cohen, A., 124, 155–56
Cohen, L. K., 140, 158–59
Coleman, 409
Conley, R., 509–10, 518
Cooker, P. G., 436–37, 456
Cooper, S., 195
Cooperman, I. G., 514, 519
Cosgrove, M., 447
Cottle, W. C., 80–82, 115, 382
Cottrell, W. F., 124–25, 156
Counts, G. S., 138–39, 158
Coxon, A. P. M., 124, 156
Cramer, S. H., 318, 328
Crawford, A. B., 114
Crawford, P., 288
Crites, J. O., 71, 114
Crockett, H. J., Jr., 159
Cronbach, L. J., 114
Cross, F. R., 438, 456
Curie, I. D., 124, 156

Daane, C. J., 473, 501
Danskin, D. G., 155
D'Costa, A. G., 221, 233–34
Deeg, M. E., 138–40, 158
De Gregorio, W. J., 328
Demain, C., 417
Dennison, J. N., 128–29, 156
Denzin, N. K., 132, 157
De Planta, H. J., 309
Deutsch, E., 350–52
Devereux, G., 130, 132, 157
Diebold, J., 195
Dilley, J., 507, 518
Dipboye, W. J., 502
Dixon, E., 287
Dobberstein, W. F., 382
Douvan, E., 286
Dozier, E., 467
Dressel, P. L., 315, 328
Du Bato, G. S., 417
Dudley, G., 417, 502
Duncan, O. D., 124, 156
Dunn, D. J., 348, 352
Dunnette, M. D., 138–39, 158
Dvorak, B. J., 252
Dyer, W. G., 121–22, 155

Eckerson, A. B., 224
Edison, T., 8
Edwards, A. M., 236–37, 252
Ehrle, R. A., 196, 329
Eisen, N., 415, 418
Elder, L. A., 341, 351
Elton, C. F., 82, 115
Emerson, R. W., 8
Emmet, F., 156
Empey, L. T., 147, 159
Engelkes, J. R., 7, 26, 350, 352, 382
Ernest, J., 180
Esser, B. F., 127, 156
Estill, K., 436, 456
Evan, W. M., 132, 157
Evans, J. W., 157
Evans, R. N., 423, 455, 500
Eyde, L. D., 515, 519

Farmer, H. S., 494, 502
Faunce, W. A., 162–65, 167, 169, 195
Feingold, N., 269, 287, 383
Feit, S., 462, 500
Fenner, B. J., 437, 456
Ferrin, R. I., 323, 329
Field, F. L., 62
Fine, S., 338
Fine, S. A., 203, 223–24
Finney, H. C., 156
Flanagan, J. C., 12, 27, 93, 116
Flannagan, T., 328
Fleming, R. W., 195
Foltman, F. F., 300, 309
Forestandi, R., 462, 500
Form, W. H., 146–47, 156, 159
Forrester, G., 350, 352, 359, 381–83
Forsyth, L. B., 436, 456
Foster, C. R., 430, 455
Franklin, P., 417
Frederick, F., 388, 390, 417
Freud, S., 7–9
Friend, B. L., 297, 309
Froehlich, C. P., 26
Fryer, D., 238, 240, 252
Furniss, W. T., 287

Garbin, A. P., 138, 158
Gaymer, R., 5, 26
Gerken, C., 80, 115, 252
Gerler, E. R., Jr., 462, 500
Gerstl, J., 140, 158–59
Gibran, K., 8
Gilpatrick, E., 338
Ginsburg, S. W., 46–48, 61
Ginzberg, E., 32, 46–48, 61, 502
Gladney, M. B., 261, 286
Glaeser, G. A., 417
Gleazer, E. J., 287
Glick, P. C., Jr., 63, 160
Glynn, E., 519
Goad, R., 418
Goldhammer, K., 426, 446, 455, 457
Goldman, L., 71, 114
Goldstein, A. D., 266, 286
Goldstein, H., 195
Gonyea, G. G., 502
Gooding, J., 155
Goshen, E. E., 309
Gottlieb, D., 310
Gray, J. T., 114
Greene, S., 252
Grigg, A. E., 59–60
Grigg, C., 519
Grow, R. T., 150, 160
Gutsch, K., 457
Gysbers, N. C., 22, 27

Haebich, K. A., 352
Haener, D., 515, 519
Hagedorn, R., 134, 157
Hagen, D., 62
Hagen, E., 95, 98–103, 116
Hahn, M. E., 241, 252–53
Hakel, M. D., 138–39, 143, 158–59
Hales, L. W., 437, 456
Haller, A. D., 140, 143, 158–59

Hamilton, J. A., 410, 418
Hammond, J. S. III, 286
Hansen, L. S., 337, 347, 351–52, 415–17, 438, 456, 499–500, 502
Hansen, O., 309
Hanson, G., 253
Harmon, D., 467
Harper, D., 156
Harrell, M. S., 252
Harrell, T. W., 252
Harris, J., 390–92, 401, 417
Harris, L., 519
Hartmann, G. W., 137, 158
Hatch, R. N., 7, 26, 315, 328, 350, 352, 382
Hatt, P. K., 139–40, 143–45, 147, 159
Havighurst, R. J., 309
Hayes, A. J., 166–67, 195
Healy, C. C., 195, 473, 501
Hecht, M., 286
Hedahl, B., 42
Hefzallah, I. M., 27
Helbrun, A., Jr., 519
Heimann, R., 457
Heinz, C. A., 224
Helstein, R., 7
Herma, J. L., 46–48, 61
Herr, E. L., 17, 27, 318, 328, 431, 455
Herrick, N., 155
Hewer, V. H., 60, 69, 114
Higgins, E. L., 457
Hill, B. M., 310
Hill, W. G., 28
Hills, J. R., 261, 286
Hilton, T. L., 63
Hipp, E., 319, 328
Hirschi, T., 156
Hodge, R. W., 140–43, 158
Hoffman, M. J., 130–31, 157
Hoffman, S. D., 4, 26
Holland, J. L., 32, 37–42, 60, 83, 88, 227–30, 252, 481
Hollingshead, A. B., 133, 157
Hollis, J. W., 430, 453, 455, 457
Hollis, L. U., 430, 453, 455, 457
Hollmann, T. D., 138–39, 143, 158–59
Holsinger, D., 140, 143, 159
Hoover, R., 417
Hopke, W. E., 334, 351
Hoppock, R., 32–37, 60–61, 67, 342, 351, 382, 418, 481
Houle, C. O., 272, 287
House, E. W., 184, 196
Hoyt, D. P., 287
Hoyt, K. B., 27, 287–88, 423–24, 431–34, 436, 440, 455–57, 459–61, 463–64, 500
Hughes, E. C., 127–28, 156
Hughes, H. M., Jr., 42
Hughes, R. G., 418
Hutchison, J., 506–507, 518

Ibsen, H., 515
Ingersoll, 8
Inkeles, A., 140, 158
Isaacson, L. E., 426
Ivey, A. E., 80, 115, 266, 286

Jackson, R. M., 352
Jepsen, D. A., 412, 418

Johnson, B. B., 475, 501
Johnson, L. A., 500
Johnson, R. G., 410, 418
Johnson, R. H., 446, 457
Johnson, W. F., 348, 352
Jones, N. A., 309
Jordan, B., 519

Kaback, G., 456
Kahn, R., 11
Kalachek, E. D., 167–68, 195
Kaplan, R., 196
Katz, M., 90, 116, 398
Kaye, C., 286
Kearney, T. F., 115
Kehas, C. D., 62, 463–64, 500
Kiesow, M. A., 502
Kimball, R. B., 287
Kirk, B. A., 383
Klein, M. W., 132, 157
Klock, J. A., 261, 286
Koenig, F., 518
Kohout, V. A., 60
Koons, P. B., Jr., 224
Korn, T. A., 348, 352
Kornhauser, A., 342, 352
Kriesberg, L., 159
Kriger, S. F., 328, 416, 418
Kruger, D. H., 127, 156
Krumboltz, J. D., 57, 62, 409–10, 418
Kuder, G. F., 115
Kunze, K. R., 334, 351, 417

Labovitz, S., 134, 157
Lacey, D. W., 42
Lacy, C. L., 515, 519
La Jeunesse, R., 309
Lamonte, A., 512, 519
Laramore, D., 348, 352, 431–34, 456–57
Larson, W. L., 128, 156
Lastrucci, C. L., 155
Laycock, S. R., 12, 27
Lee, D. L., 42
Leis, W. W., 341, 351
Le May, M. L., 366, 383
Leonard, G. E., 409, 418, 435–36, 456–57
Leonard, R., 457
Lerner, L. L., 328
Lessinger, L. M., 308
Levine, D. U., 309
Lewis, D. M., 140, 158
Lewis, L. S., 131–33, 157
Lezotte, L., 143, 159
Lieberman, H., Jr., 310
Lifton, W. M., 457
Lindzey, G., 89
Lipsett, L., 62, 155
Livy, 8
Logan, R. III, 457
Lovejoy, C. E., 275, 287–88
Lukens, L. G., 502
Lunt, P. S., 157
Luther, M., 9
Lutz, S. W., 60
Lynd, H., 133, 157

Lynd, R. S., 133, 157
Lynn, J., 467
Lyon, R., 155

McArthur, C., 80, 115
McCormick, E. J., 338
McEaddy, B. J., 196
McKenney, W. D., 418
Mackin, E. F., 450, 500
McKinney, L., 467
McLaughlin, D. H., 116
MacLean, M. S., 241, 253
McWhorter, C., 512, 519
Malone, M., 132, 157
Maloney, W. P., 27
Mangum, G. L., 431–34, 455–57, 500
Marland, S. P., Jr., 14, 27, 424, 455, 462–63, 500
Mars, G., 131, 157
Martin, R., 500
Marx, K., 9
Maslow, A. H., 32, 43, 60
Mason, L. D., 308
Mathies, L., 287
Mathis, H. F., 352, 382
Mathis, L. R., 352, 382
Mayo, E., 9
Mead, M., 166, 195
Meadow, L., 63
Meadows, D. H., 26
Meadows, D. L., 26
Meighan, J., 467
Meir, E. I., 248, 253
Mettlin, C. J., 132, 157
Meyer, G. R., 130–31, 157
Mickelson, G. T., 382
Miller, A. W., Jr., 57, 62
Miller, C. D., 266, 286
Miller, C. H., 22, 28, 453, 457
Miller, D. C., 146–47, 159
Miller, H., 160
Miller, J. S., 59–60
Miller, J. V., 328, 416, 418
Mills, C. W., 137, 158
Minor, F., 399, 417, 502
Mitchell, J. C., 140, 158
Mitchell, J. P., 341, 351
Mitchell, J. S., 184, 196
Monnens, L. P., 455
Montague, J. B., 132, 157
Mooney, R. L., 12, 27
Moore, E. J., 22, 27
Mooren, R. L., 352
Mormon, R. R., 195
Morris, R. T., 128, 156, 159
Morrison, R., 252
Morrison, R. F., 42
Morrow, J. M., Jr., 42
Mueller, C., 467, 500–501
Munger, D., 452, 457
Munson, H., 447
Murphy, R. J., 159
Murray, E., 308
Murray, H. A., 39, 61
Musgrave, P. W., 155
Myerhoff, B. G., 128, 156
Myers, E. R., 519

Myers, R., 399, 417, 502
Myrick, R. D., 446, 457

Nachmann, B., 456
Nelson, A. G., 82, 115
Nelson, P. D., 308, 310
Nichols, R. C., 60, 456, 501
Noeth, R. J., 12, 27
Noland, E. W., 112–14, 116
Norris, W., 7, 26, 350, 352, 382
North, C. C., 139–40, 143
Nosow, S., 134, 156–57
Novak, B. J., 328

Odell, C., 317–18, 321, 328–29
Odgers, J. G., 224
O'Dowd, D. D., 502
Oelke, M., 328
O'Hara, R. P., 55, 62
Ohnesorge, J., 143, 159
Olesen, V., 128, 156
Olshansky, S. S., 328
Oppenheimer, V. K., 196
Osgood, C. E., 137, 158
Osipow, S. H., 32, 55, 57–58, 60, 62
Osler, 8
Overs R. P., 28, 33–36, 350–52

Pace, C. R., 287
Parker, F., 309
Parker, J. L., 440, 457
Parnell, D., 460, 500
Paterson, D. G., 138–40, 143, 158–59, 252
Pearl, A., 290, 308
Pearlin, L. I., 156
Pearson, H. G., 501
Perrone, P. A., 288
Peters, H. J., 382
Peterson, J. A., 89–90, 116
Peterson, R., 519
Pierson, G., 417
Pietrofesa, J. J., 32, 60
Pinson, N. M., 431–34, 456–57
Pitts, G. D., 288
Plotsky, F. A., 418
Prebonich, E. M., 329
Prediger, D. J., 12, 27
Priebe, J., 252
Prioa, N. C., 287
Pritchard, D. H., 321, 328–29, 501
Pruit, A., 500
Putnam, J. A., 342, 352

Quey, R. L., 5, 26

Ramsey, C. E., 62
Randers, J., 26
Ratchick, I., 518
Rauner, T. M., 27
Record, J. C., 136, 158
Reiss, A. J., Jr., 143–44, 159, 245
Remmers, H. H., 12, 27
Resnikoff, A., 143, 159
Ressing, A. H., 283–84, 288
Rezler, A. G., 502
Riessman, F., 290, 308–309
Roberts, N. J., 427, 455

Subject Index

Counselor-aides, 322–23
Counselor's Comparative Guide to American Colleges, 278
Counselor's Handbook, 91–93
Cubistic classification system, 85, 221–23, 445

Death rate, influence of on occupations, 171–72
Decennial census, 177, 230, 340
Department of Labor, 215, 219, 338, 344–45, 361
Dictionary of Occupational Titles (DOT), 69–72, 79–81, 85–86, 98, 104–108, 110, 201–25, 232, 251, 339, 355, 378–79, 467
  quoted, 521–32
  supplements to, 214–15
Differential Aptitude Test, 79, 94
Directory of National Associations of Businessmen, 345
Disability:
  economics of, 508–510
  vs. handicap, 508
Dropouts, 17, 443
  career planning and, 511–12
  problems of, 323–24

Economic factors, 148–54
  implications of, 154–55
Education. *See also* College; Community college; Junior college.
  automation and, 167–69
  information on, 21, 258–78
  post-secondary, 257–86
  relationship of to socio-economic status, 121
  relationship of with work, 30
Education Amendments of 1972, 514
Education and Career Exploration System, 399–400
Educational Film Guide, 449
Educational information:
  colleges and universities, 258–78
  filing, 373–75
  junior colleges, 278–82
  vocational schools, 278, 282–86
Educational placement, 311–27
Educator's Guide to Free Slidefilms, 450
Elementary school, 458
  career awareness and, 424–26, 431–42, 445
Employers' requirements, 111–14
Employment. *See* Career; Work.
Employment agencies, 315–17
Employment certificate, 324–25
Employment outlook, 186
Entrepreneurial withdrawal, 151–52
Equal Employment Opportunity Act, 514
Equal Rights Amendment, 514
Estimates of Worker Trait Requirements for 4,000 Jobs, 70, 80, 85–86, 203, 210
Ethics, of some occupations, 129–30, 132
External degree programs, college, 271–73

Fair Labor Standards Act, 324
Fees, as payment for work, 151–52
Field trip, 412–14
Filing systems, 376–81. *See also* Career information, filing; Educational information, filing; Occupational information, filing.

alphabetical, 376–80
  other, 380–81
Films, 347–48. *See also* Audio-visual aids.
Filmstrip Guide, 450
Financial aid:
  for college study, 264, 266, 269
  for junior college, 281
  location of information on, 375
Follow-up survey, 337, 341–42
Functional classification system, 203
Future Shock, 4

General Aptitude Test Battery, 71, 78–79, 94
General educational development, 99, 104
G.I. Bill, 513
Government, career information and, 454
Government Printing Office, 343, 359
Group counseling, 486
Group membership, occupations and, 134–36
Guidance, 21–22. *See also* Counseling; Vocational guidance.
  defined, 22
  goal of, 458
Guidance counselor. *See* Counseling; Counselor.
Guidance departments, high school, 317–23
  activities of, 322, 470
  teacher involvement in, 465
Guidelines for Preparation and Evaluation of Career Information Media, 364–65

Handicap, vs. disability, 508
Handicapped workers, 485, 506, 518–11
  career planning and, 511
  legislation and, 517
  placement of, 316–17
Hazardous occupations, age limits and, 325–26
High school:
  career education in, 459–67, 475
  career-oriented, 462–63
  career preparation and, 424
  guidance departments in, 317–23, 470
  placement services and, 312, 317–23
  special-purpose, 312
  technical, 312
  tests used in, 79–80, 82, 84, 93–94
Hiring requirements, 69, 111–14
Horizontal mobility, 146, 150
How to Select a Private Vocational School, 285

Income, occupational, 148–49, 151–54
Industrial Revolution, 4
Industry:
  career education and, 13–14
  career information and, 453
Industry tour, 412–14, 474
Information, personal-social, sources of, 348–49
Information, sources of. *See also* Career information; College information; Job information; Scholarship information
  economic, 350–51
  psychological, 350–51
  social, 350–51
Information System for Vocational Decisions, 399–400
Inmates, career planning and, 511, 513
Intellectual demands, 238–41

Specific Aptitude Test Batteries, 79
Standard Industrial Classification Manual, 211–12, 251
States, career education and, 16
Status:
   women and, 10
   work and, 8, 10
Status, social:
   occupations and, 136–37
   struggle for, 136–37
Strong-Campbell Interest Inventory, 82–84, 229
Strong Vocational Interest Blank, 39, 80, 82–83, 85, 228–29
Student Aid Planning in the Space Age, 270
Student records, 265
Students. *See* College; Community college; Elementary school; High School; Junior High School.
Suffix Codes for Jobs Defined in the DOT, 215–16
Supplementary Security Income Program, 510
Supply and demand, influences of, 148–51
System of Interactive Guidance and Information, 391, 393, 397–98
Systems analysis, career education and, 13–14

Tapes. *See* Audio-visual aids.
Teacher:
   occupational choice and, 30
   place of in guidance, 23–26
   role of, 428, 430, 434, 441–42, 461–65, 470
Teacher's Role in Career Development, 467–69
Technical occupations, 187–88
Technical schools, 282–86
   occupational information and, 346
Technological progress, the *DOT* and, 202–203
Temperaments, 70, 85–89, 92
Ten Thousand Careers, 95
Tests:
   for college admission, 261–65
   for high school equivalency, 306
Theories of career development, 29–64
Three-digit occupational divisions, 204, 225, 232
Time-rate wages, 152
Training, types of, 104
Training programs, 7
Training time, 70, 99, 104
Trait and factor theory, 69
Trends, occupational:
   anticipated, 175–77
   average age of workers, 173–74, 176
   by major groups, 186–94
   capitalizing patterns, 172–73
   causes, long-term, 170–74
   causes, short-term, 174–75
   changes in natural resources, 172–73
   employment of minorities, 184–86
   employment of women, 177–84
   influence of birth rate on, 171–72
   influence of technology on, 171
Two-digit occupational divisions, 203–204
Two-dimensional classification, 241–251

Unemployment, 317–18

automation and, 166–70
CETA and, 303–304
U.S. Department of Health, Education, and Welfare, Office of Education, 14, 16, 27
U.S. Employment Service, 203, 316–18
Universities. *See also* College.
   information on, 258–78
   programs in, 259–60

Values, 89–91
Veterans:
   career planning and, 513–14
   placement of, 316–17
Vertical mobility, 145–46
Vocational choice, theories of, 481. *See also* Career development, theories of.
Vocational counselor. *See* Counseling; Counselor.
Vocational education, 14–15, 104
Vocational Exploration Group, 473
Vocational guidance, defined, 22, 499
Vocational Guidance Quarterly, 336, 342–43, 347, 349, 359, 365
Vocational rehabilitation, 510–11
Vocational school, 278, 280
   visits to, 414–15
Vocational training:
   computers and, 399–400
   in high school, 290–94
Volunteer work, 6

Wages, 148, 151–52
Welfare recipients, career planning and, 511–12
Women:
   as housewives, 6
   attitudes toward, 5, 441, 443, 494
   career information for, 334, 346
   career planning and, 511, 514–16
   CETA and, 304
   delayed careers and, 504
   double-track career pattern of, 504
   education and, 169
   legislation and, 161, 183–84, 514
   marriage and, 504
   military training and, 307
   misinformation on, 12
   needs of, 515–16
   occupational chores of, 42, 47–48
   occupations ranked by, 143
   relationship of to work, 54–55
   status and, 10
   testing scales for, 84
   tests on, 80
   trends in employment of, 177, 179–84
Work:
   defined, 5–7
   function of, 7–11
   history of, 3–5, 29
   relationship between people and, 4–5, 7–11, 15, 18
   relationship with education, 30
   satisfaction with, 36, 54
   society and, 4–5
   status and, 8, 10, 136–37
Work environments:
   simulated, 408–10, 416
   synthetic, 408, 410–11, 416

Work ethic, 4, 9
Work experience programs, 290–94, 320, 415–16
Work in America, 122–23, 155
Work Incentive Programs, 306–307
Work of the Counselor, 478
Work-study programs, college, 271
Work Values Inventory, 90–91
Worker:
  functions of, 339
  traits of, 340

Worker functions arrangement, 204–205, 214, 218–21, 225
Worker traits arrangement, 69, 85, 207–208, 214, 219–21, 266–68
Working conditions, 110–11
Workshops, sheltered, 517–18
World of Work Map for Job Families, 248–50

Zero population growth, 172

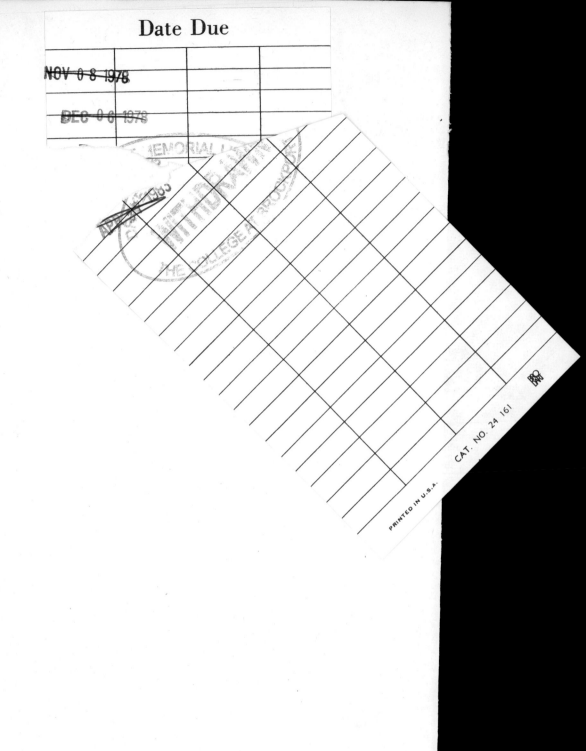